CONTENTS

Acknowledgements | v
Foreword | vi
Introduction | 1
Contribute to the control of resources | 4
Health, hygiene, safety and security of the working environment | 9
Establish and develop positive working relationships in hospitality | 13
Contribute to the development of recipes and menus | 18
Healthy eating and menu development | 29
Food safety | 37
Assessing the taste and quality of dishes | 46

1 HORS D'OEUVRE AND BUFFET ITEMS | 49
Cold preparations | 49
Gels and setting agents | 52
Sauces, chutneys and dressings | 55
Compound salads | 59
Miscellaneous | 61
Cold fish preparations | 64
Buffet items | 68
Cold meat preparations | 74
Terrines, pies, ballotines and galantines | 75
Crostinis and nibbles | 86
Canapés – hot and cold | 90

2 HOT SAUCES AND STOCKS | 97
Stocks | 98
Nages | 101
Glazes | 103
Egg-based sauces | 104
Creamed thickened sauces | 106
Soubises, and vegetable and fruit purées | 108
Oil-based sauces | 112

3 SOUPS | 115
Principles of soup making | 115
Consommés | 117
Broths | 120
Purée soups | 123
Chilled soups | 130

4 EGG DISHES | 133

5 FISH DISHES | 143
Fish | 151
Shellfish | 180

6 MEAT DISHES | 199
Lamb | 209
Beef | 220
Veal | 229
Pork | 234

7 POULTRY AND GAME | 241
Poultry | 247
Game | 267

8 INTERNATIONAL CUISINE | 283
Caribbean | 285
China | 286
India | 289
Indonesia | 294
Malaysia | 296
Mexico | 298
Middle East | 299
Spain | 301
Thailand | 303
Vietnam | 304

9 VEGETABLE, POTATO, PASTA AND VEGETARIAN DISHES 307

Potato dishes 311
Vegetable dishes 320
Vegetarian dishes 337
Pasta dishes 356

10 PASTRY 363

Preparation and materials 363
Use of modern techniques and equipment 363
The basic building blocks 366
Pastes and doughs 380
Creams 383
Sponges 384
Yeast products 389
Mousses 398

Ice cream, sorbets and frozen desserts 400
Sauces 403
Meringues and soufflés 405
E'spumas 408
Tarts, slices and gâteaux 411
Puddings 419
Biscuits and cakes 420
Chocolate goods and petits fours 423
Miscellaneous 427
Sugar 430
Marzipan 435
Chocolate 437
Pastillage 440

Glossary 441
Index 444

ADVANCED PRACTICAL COOKERY

fourth edition

a textbook for education & industry

John Campbell

Professor David Foskett
Victor Ceserani

Hodder Arnold

A MEMBER OF THE HODDER HEADLINE GROUP

Orders: please contact Bookpoint Ltd, 130 Milton Park, Abingdon, Oxon OX14 4SB. Telephone: (44) 01235 827720. Fax: (44) 01235 400454. Lines are open from 9.00 – 6.00, Monday to Saturday, with a 24 hour message answering service. You can also order through our website www.hodderheadline.co.uk.

British Library Cataloguing in Publication Data
A catalogue record for this title is available from the British Library

ISBN-10: 0340912359
ISBN-13: 9780340912355

First published 1995
Second edition published 1997
Third edition published 2002
Fourth edition published 2006

Impression number   10 9 8 7 6 5 4 3 2 1
Year   2012 2011 2010 2009 2008 2007 2006

Cover photo © Sam Bailey.
Original photography by Sam Bailey
Typeset by Fakenham Photosetting Ltd, Fakenham, Norfolk
Illustrations by Barking Dog Art
Printed in Great Britain for Hodder Arnold, an imprint of Hodder Education, a division of Hodder Headline Plc, 338 Euston Road, London NW1 3BH by The Bath Press

ACKNOWLEDGEMENTS

We gratefully acknowledge the following chefs who have contributed recipes to the book:

Anthony Marshall; Ron Maxfield; Stephen Goodlad; Mark McCann; John Williams; René Rauvert; Mehernosh Mody; and Atul Kochhar.

Additional acknowledgements to Dr Jenny Poulter, Jane Cliff and Pat Bacon for their contribution to the nutritional analysis.

We are most grateful to the following for preparing foods for the photo shoots:

Yolande Stanley MCA, Senior Lecturer, from the London School of Tourism, Hospitality and Leisure at Thames Valley University; Roger Serjent, formerly of the Conrad Hotel, Chelsea Harbour; John Campbell BSc, The Vineyard at Stockcross; Peter Eaton; and Natalie Mitchell.

We would also like to thank the British Pig Executive and the English Beef and Lamb Executive for their generous contribution to the costs of the colour photography, and finally the photographer, Sam Bailey, who did such an exemplary job.

FOREWORD

Forte plc was the original sponsor of *Advanced Practical Cookery*. As its then Chairman I was happy to write the Foreword. Forte no longer exists and I have developed a new company, Rocco Forte Hotels.

In recent years there has been a huge growth in interest in food and cooking. There is an increased awareness of what constitutes 'good food' and a much greater propensity to experience a wide range of ethnic foods. The explosion of successful restaurants, not just in London but throughout the UK, offering a variety of dishes is witness to this.

The excesses of nouvelle cuisine have been left behind, with a return to a more classical approach but still retaining the attractive presentation format of the former. People are also conscious of the health and nutritional aspects of food and are now demanding simpler food that is still well presented.

My hotel restaurants are an important part of the product I offer to my customers. They must feel like independent restaurants and attract outside customers. The restaurant must offer glamorous surroundings and value for money. It must offer dishes with which our customers are familiar and feel comfortable, as well as more original ideas. The secret is to keep it simple: too many chefs try to over-elaborate, but the delivery must be to a high quality standard.

Advanced Practical Cookery will provide an invaluable source of information for catering students and help them towards a successful career in an industry where there is a huge demand for their skills.

The Right Honourable Sir Rocco Forte

INTRODUCTION

The content of this book encompasses the requirements of those taking Food Preparation and Cooking, Kitchen and Larder, and Pâtisserie and Confectionery units at NVQ/SVQ Levels 3 and 4. The Advanced Craft qualification awarded by City & Guilds, Edexcel BTEC Level 3 Advanced Certificate and Diploma in International Cuisine, and Centra ABC Levels 2 and 3 Pâtisserie Confectionery are intended for those already working in industry, as well as those taking full- and part-time courses. This book will be useful for those engaged in supported self-study and open learning programmes, and for those wanting to increase their qualifications in the workplace. If reference to any basic knowledge is required, *Practical Cookery* should be found helpful, and *The Theory of Catering* can assist with any further information.

However, having acquired the basic culinary knowledge and skills, all students taking courses that include practical cookery or gastronomy will find this book helpful. The content will also be useful for those taking Higher National Diplomas and Degrees in Culinary Arts.

The aim is to extend the repertoire of catering students and professionals. To gain an advanced craft qualification, the chef should be able to adapt and extend existing recipes, to develop their own variations, and have a broad awareness of a wide variety of ingredients and cuisines. Where appropriate, we suggest variations for recipes, with the intention of stimulating further ways of adapting and creating different dishes. Adaptability is essential when producing dishes that, at first glance, appear impractical and expensive. By using common sense, and

with practical application, almost all recipes can be adapted to meet budgetary or any other restrictions.

In this edition of the book, John Campbell, one of Britain's top chefs, has made a major contribution, introducing modern techniques, practices and recipes. Many of the dishes can be adapted to a range of industrial sectors. The key to successful combinations is simplicity using a range of high quality fresh ingredients.

John Campbell has included recipes from his own establishment, The Vineyard at Stockcross, where he has a number of accolades including two Rising Michelin stars. In the kitchens of the Vineyard he carefully develops dishes using his knowledge of science and technology. This is evident throughout this book. However, before one is able to develop recipes using a scientific approach, a good grounding in classical cuisine is essential, so that the systems, processes and procedures which underpin professional cookery are learnt and mastered.

The dishes in this book all follow a classical approach but have been adapted for a modern industry which demonstrates flair and creativity.

Emphasis has also been placed on presentation and healthy, nutritionally balanced alternatives. This has become very important with the demand from customers for more nutritional labelling.

In this book, metric measurements are used for two main reasons: younger British students do not understand Imperial measurements and metric is the international standard. Metric also makes batching up and down, and analysis, easier. For those who prefer Imperial, approximate conversion charts are provided on the book flaps, for easy reference.

USE AND EASE OF REFERENCE

Most recipes give quantities for four and ten portions, the most useful combinations for those working in an operating kitchen, or realistic working environment.

A selection of recipes have been analysed for nutritional value, giving the student the essential underpinning knowledge now required in this area.

CURRENT TRENDS AND HEALTHY EATING

We have included separate chapters for international and vegetarian recipes, since there is a great and growing emphasis on these sorts of cuisine. Some recipes are suitable for vegans, and these have been highlighted in the text using the symbol **v**.

For those wishing to reduce fat and cholesterol levels in the diet, the following suggestions may be useful.

Consideration where suitable can be given to using:

- oils and fats high in monosaturates and polyunsaturates in place of hard fats
- the minimum of salt or low-sodium salt
- wholemeal flour in place of, or partly in place of, white flour
- natural yoghurt, quark or fromage frais (all lower in fat) in place of cream

- skimmed milk, or semi-skimmed, instead of full-cream milk
- minimum use of sugar or, in some cases, reduced-calorie sweeteners
- low-fat cheese instead of full-fat cheese.

Many of the recipes in this book have been adjusted, incorporating some of these principles as alternatives to be used as and when required. Where we state oil, sunflower oil is recommended other than for fierce heat, when pomace olive oil is more suitable. When yoghurt is stated, we mean natural yoghurt with a low fat content.

The following table offers an example of how traditional recipe ingredients may be replaced by healthier ones.

Instead of	Choose
Whole milk	Skimmed milk (or semi-skimmed)
Butter or hard margarine	Polyunsaturated margarine
Lard, hard vegetable fats	Pure vegetable oils, e.g. corn oil, sunflower oil
Full-fat cheeses, e.g. Cheddar	Low-fat cheeses, e.g. low-fat Cheddar has half the fat
Fatty meats	Lean meats (smaller portion), or chicken or fish
Cream	Plain yoghurt, quark, smetana, fromage frais

A number of non-dairy creamers are available now. Some are produced specifically for pastry work and, being sweetened, are unsuitable for savoury recipes. However, there are also various unsweetened products that may be used in place of fresh cream for soups, sauces, etc. It is important to determine the heat stability of these products before use, i.e. by testing whether they will withstand boiling without detriment to the product.

The following chart indicates which cooking oils, fats and margarines are healthiest, i.e. those with the smallest percentage of saturated fats.

Oil/fat	Saturated %	Monounsaturated %	Polyunsaturated %
Coconut oil	85	7	2
Butter	60	32	3
Palm oil	45	42	8
Lard	43	42	9
Beef dripping	40	49	4
Margarine, hard (vegetable oil only)	37	47	12
Margarine, hard (mixed oils)	37	43	17
Margarine, soft	32	42	22
Margarine, soft (mixed oils)	30	45	19
Low-fat spread	27	38	30
Margarine, polyunsaturated	24	22	54
Ground nut oil	19	48	28
Maize oil	16	29	49
Wheatgerm oil	14	11	45
Soya bean oil	14	24	57
Olive oil	14	70	11
Sunflower seed oil	13	32	50
Safflower seed oil	10	13	72
Rapeseed oil	7	64	32

The healthy eating and nutrition information in this book has been provided by Dr Jenny Poulter and Jane Cliff. Both are public health nutritionists with a proven track record in chef education, catering training, research and evaluation. It is because of national concern with the alarming increase in cases of obesity, particularly in the young, that we invited Jenny and Jane to develop the nutritional analysis for the recipes and provide healthy eating tips where appropriate.

Vegetable oil was used as the first choice of oil for the nutritional analysis, unless specified otherwise, and butter was used as the first choice over margarine. Semi-skimmed milk was used as the first choice unless otherwise stated.

We are most grateful to Jenny and Jane for their contribution and our special thanks go to Pat Bacon SRD, who undertook the recipe analysis with efficiency and patience.

CONTRIBUTE TO THE CONTROL OF RESOURCES

Units covered: HS3

ORGANISATION OF CONTROL

Control is crucial in every catering organisation: in small restaurants and tea shops, in hospital kitchens and large hotels, in contract and airline catering, in school meals ... in fact, in every establishment.

The role of the manager, and potential manager, whether he/she is called food and beverage manager or assistant food and beverage manager, executive chef, chef de cuisine, sous chef, head chef, chef de partie, or whatever, is to organise:

- themselves
- other people
- their time
- physical resources.

An essential factor of good organisation is effective control of oneself, of those responsible to you, and of physical resources, which often includes financial control. The amount of control and how it is administered will vary from establishment to establishment. However, successful control applies to all aspects of catering, namely:

- purchasing of food, etc.
- storage of food, etc.
- preparation of food
- production of food
- presentation of food
- hygiene
- safety

- security
- waste
- energy
- first-aid
- equipment
- maintenance
- legal aspects.

Control of resources

The effective and efficient management of resources requires knowledge and, if possible, experience. In addition, it is necessary to keep up to date. This may require attending courses on management, computing, hygiene, legislation, and so on. Membership of appropriate organisations, such as HCIMA, or former student associations, can also be valuable, as is attending exhibitions and trade fairs.

How the controlling of resources is administered will depend partly on the systems of the organisation but also on the way the person in control operates. Apart from knowledge and experience, respect from those for whom one is responsible is earned, not given, by the way staff are handled in the situation of the job. Having earned the respect and cooperation of staff a system of controls and checks needs to be operated that is smooth-running and not disruptive. Training and delegation may be required to ensure effective control and, periodically, it is essential to evaluate the system to see that the recording and monitoring are being effective.

The purpose of control is to make certain:

- that supplies of what is required are available

- that the supplies are of the right quality and quantity
- that they are available on time
- there is the minimum of wastage

- there is no overstocking
- there is no pilfering
- that legal requirements are complied with.

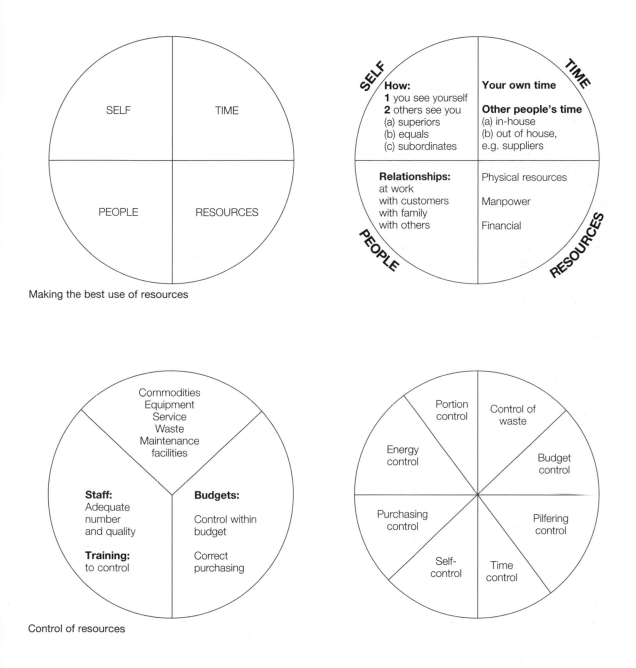

Making the best use of resources

Control of resources

MONITOR AND CONTROL RECEIPT OF GOODS

Staff responsible for receiving goods should be trained to recognise the items being delivered and to know if the quality, quantity and specific sizes, etc., are those ordered. This skill is acquired by experience and by guidance from the departmental head, e.g. head chef, who will use the items.

Purchasing specifications detailing the standards of the goods to be delivered assist in this matter. However, the chef, supervisor, storekeeper, food and beverage manager, or whoever is responsible for controlling receipt of goods, needs to check that the specification is adhered to. If the system of the establishment does not have specifications, the expected standards of goods delivered must still be checked. In the event of goods being unsatisfactory, they should not be accepted.

Receipt of goods

Receipt of deliveries must be monitored to ensure that goods delivered correspond with the delivery note and there are no discrepancies. It is essential that items are of the stipulated size or weight since this could affect portion control and costing – for example, 100 g fillets of plaice will need to be that weight, melons to be used for four portions should be of the appropriate size.

It is necessary to ensure that effective control can be practised. This means that delivery access and adequate checking and storage space are available, that these areas are clean, tidy and free from obstruction, and that staff are available to receive goods. It is important that the standard of cleanliness and temperature of the delivery vehicles is also satisfactory. If this is not up to the required

standard, the supplier must be informed at once.

Temperatures

Vehicles over 7.5 tonnes must have a temperature of 5°C or below when delivering food outside their locality. Vehicles under 7.5 tonnes making local deliveries of food should be 8°C or under.

On receipt of goods they should be transferred as soon as possible to the correct storage area. Frozen items should be stored at the following optimum temperatures:

Meat	−20°C
Vegetable	−15°C
Ice cream	−18°C to −20°C

Refrigerator temperatures should be 3–4°C and larders provided for cooling of food should have a temperature of no higher than 8°C.

It is essential that a system of reporting non-compliance with the procedures of the establishment are known. Every place of work will have a security procedure to ensure that goods are stored safely. It is important that staff are aware of the system and to whom they should report any deviation.

CONTROL THE STORAGE OF GOODS

If control of stock is to be effective, ample storage space with adequate shelving bins, etc., must be available to enable the correct storage of goods. The premises must be clean and easy to keep clean, well lit and well ventilated, dry, secure and safe. Space should be available for easy access to all items, which should not be too high. Heavy items should be stored low down.

Stock rotation is essential so as to reduce waste – the last items in are the last items to be issued. Any deterioration of stock should be identified, action taken and reported. To keep a check on stock a system of documentation is necessary, which states the amount in the stores, the amounts issued, to whom and when, and the amounts below which stock should not fall.

Shelf life and justification on 'use by' date information should be complied with. As a guide to storage, consider these points.

Canned goods	Store up to 9 months. Discard damaged, rusted, blown tins.
Bottles and jars	Store at room temperature. Store in refrigerator once opened.
Dry foods	Dry room temperature. Humid atmosphere causes deterioration.
Milk and cream	Refrigerate and use within 3 days.
Butter	Up to one month, refrigerated.
Cheese	According to the manufacturer's instruction. Soft cheese should be used as soon as possible.
Salads	Keep longer if refrigerated or in a dark, well-ventilated area.
Meat and poultry	Up to one week in refrigerator.
Meat products	For example, sausages and pies, refrigerated up to 3 days.
Fish	Use on day of purchase ideally or up to 12 hours if refrigerated.
Ice cream	Deep frozen for a week.
Frozen foods	Six months: meat $-18°C$; fruit and vegetables $-12°C$.

Persons responsible for controlling the storage of stock, in addition to checking the personnel using the stores and working as storekeepers, must also check the correct storage temperatures of storerooms, refrigerators, deep freezes, etc. The policy of the establishment may expect records of temperature checks to be recorded.

Storage temperatures

Temperature	Food item
8°C or below	Soft cheese, whole
5°C or below	Cut cheese
5°C	Cooked foods Smoked and cured fish Smoked and cured meat Sandwiches and rolls containing meat, fish, eggs (or substitutes), soft cheeses or vegetables
8°C or below	Desserts containing milk or milk substitutes (with pH value of 4.5 or more) Vegetables and fruit salads Pies and pastries containing meat, fish or substitute, or vegetables into which nothing has been added after cooking Cooked sausage rolls Uncooked or partly cooked pastries and dough products containing meat or fish or substitutes Cream cakes

Checking stock

An essential aspect of the supervisory role is the full stock audit and spot-check of goods in the stores, to assess deterioration and losses from other causes. Spot-checks by their very nature are random; stock audits will occur at specified times during the year. Some establishments have a system of daily records of stock-in-hand. This procedure assists in security since there is no time lapse between checks. This is particularly important when dealing with expensive items.

Particular attention must be paid to items of a hazardous nature, e.g. bleach and other cleaning items. They should be stored away from foods. All items used for cleaning should have a record or bin card stating amount in stock and to whom issues are made.

CONTROL THE ISSUE OF STOCK AND GOODS

To supervise the issuing of stock a system of control is needed so that a record of each item – how much, to whom and when – is kept. This enables a check to be made so that only authorised persons can obtain goods, the amount of items issued can be controlled, and it is known how much of each item is used over a period of time.

This should help avoid over-ordering and thus having too much stock on the premises. It should also diminish the risk of pilfering.

Having documentation enables accurate records to be available so that action can be taken to control the issue of goods.

To be effective the requisition document should include the date, the amount of the item or items required, and the department, section or person to whom they are to be issued. Usually a signature of the superior, e.g. chef, chef de partie or supervisor, is required. It may be desirable to draw a line under the last listed item so that unauthorised items are not then added.

IMPLEMENT THE PHYSICAL STOCK-TAKE

The purpose of a physical stock-taking procedure is to check that the documentation of existing stock tallies with the actual stock held on the premises. The reason for this exercise is to prevent capital being tied up by having too much stock in hand. It also provides information regarding the accuracy of the system and thus indicates where modifications could be made.

At the same time as the physical stock-take, details of discrepancies may become apparent that would then be investigated. Items such as returned empties, damaged stock, credit claims, etc., will be reconciled so that an accurate record is made for use by appropriate staff. This may mean that both the storekeeper and the manager responsible will take action on the stock-take details. It is for this reason that records must be accurate, legible and carefully maintained in order to achieve the aim of the exercise.

To be effective, every item should be recorded, indicating the appropriate detail such as weight, size, etc., and the number of items in stock.

HEALTH, HYGIENE, SAFETY AND SECURITY OF THE WORKING ENVIRONMENT

Units covered: HS4

MAINTAIN SECURITY AND SAFETY PROCEDURES IN OWN AREAS OF RESPONSIBILITY

To ensure that legislation regarding safety and security is implemented, it is necessary:

1 for the legislation to be known
2 that the requirements are carried out
3 that a system of checks makes certain that the legislation is complied with.

First, all people involved in an establishment must be made aware of the need for safety and security, and their legal responsibilities towards themselves, their colleagues, their employers and other members of the public.

A system of checks, both spot-checks and regular inspections at frequent intervals, needs to be set up, and the observations and recommendations resulting from these inspections should be recorded and passed to superiors for action. The details would include time and date of inspection, exact site and a clear description of the breach of security or fault of safety equipment. This information would be acted upon promptly according to the policy of the organisation.

It is the responsibility of everyone at the workplace to be conscious of safety and security, and to pass on to the appropriate people recommendations for improving the procedures for maintaining safety and security.

The types of equipment that need to be inspected to make certain that they are available and ready for use include security equipment, first-aid and fire-fighting equipment. The supervisor or person responsible for these items needs to regularly check and record that they are in working condition and that, if they have been used, they are restored ready for further use. Security systems and fire-fighting equipment are usually checked by the makers. It is the responsibility of the management of the establishment to ensure that this equipment is maintained correctly. First-aid equipment is usually the responsibility of the designated first-aider, whose functions include replenishing first-aid boxes. However, a chef de partie or supervisor will be aware that if fire extinguishers and first-aid equipment are used, he/she has a responsibility to take action to maintain the equipment by reporting to the appropriate person. It is advisable that all staff are trained in the use of fire extinguishers.

Routine checks or inspections need to be carried out in any establishment to see that standards of hygiene and safety are maintained for the benefit of workers, customers and other members of the public. Visitors, suppliers and contractors are also entitled to expect the premises to be safe when they enter. Particular attention needs to be paid to exits and entrances, passageways and the provision of adequate lighting. Floors need to be sound, uncluttered and well lit. Disposal of rubbish and bin areas need particular care regarding cleanliness and safety. Toilets, staff rooms and changing rooms need to be checked regularly. All staff must adopt hygienic and safe work practices – they should be conscious at all times, and in all places of work, of the health and safety of the premises. Failure to do so may result in accidents and the spread of infections. Any discrepancies and damage should be reported, as should any unsafe or unhealthy features.

Checks or inspections would usually be carried out by a person responsible for health and safety within the organisation, with authority to take action to remedy faults and discrepancies, and to implement improvements.

Monitoring of inspections and the recording of evidence is an important aspect of the supervisor's role. Even more important is that any shortcomings are remedied at once. Inspections should be regular, and particular attention should be paid to hazards, security, safety equipment and cleanliness.

Records, which should be accurate and legible, should include date and time of inspection, by whom and what has been checked. Any hazards, faults, lack of cleanliness, damage or discrepancies should be recorded.

Unhygienic and unsafe practices observed can best be remedied by training and giving constructive explanations as to why they are unhygienic and unsafe. Persons with infections or notifiable diseases must be made aware of their responsibility to inform their employer.

MAINTAIN A HEALTHY AND SAFE WORKING ENVIRONMENT

It is necessary to be aware of the policy and procedures of the organisation in relation to health and safety legislation. Every individual at work anywhere on the premises needs to develop an attitude towards possible hazardous situations so as to prevent accidents to themselves or others. Training is also essential to develop good practice and should include information on what hazards to look for, hygienic methods of working and the procedures to follow in the event of an incident. Records of staff training in these areas should be kept.

Checks are essential to maintain high standards of health and safety at work and to comply with the law so that employees, employers and members of the public remain safe and healthy.

Every organisation will have procedures to follow in the event of a fire, accident, flood or bomb alert; every employee needs to be acquainted with these procedures.

Every establishment must have a book to record accidents. It is also desirable to have a book to record items in need of maintenance due to wear and tear or damage so that these faults can be remedied. Details of incidents, such as power failure, flooding, infestation, contamination, etc., which do not result in an accident, should be recorded in an incident book.

Items lost, damaged or discarded should be recorded, giving details of why and how it happened and what subsequent steps have been taken.

The responsibility of chefs, supervisors and others concerned with health and safety is to ensure that training and instruction is given so as to prevent accidents and to help staff work efficiently and safely. Problems with any staff failing to comply with health and safety standards should be identified and appropriate action taken.

RISK ASSESSMENT AND REDUCTION

The prevention of both accidents and food poisoning in catering establishments is essential. It is necessary to assess each situation on its own terms and decide what action is to be taken.

In most catering establishments that are professionally operated the hazards are few and easy to check, and much of what is called for is a matter of common sense.

Accidents do occur in kitchens but rarely lead to serious injury. However, all accident situations are undesirable, and minimising their numbers depends on the development and maintenance of a safety culture. The first step in accident control is the ability to identify potential hazards.

Injuries can result from slips, trips, falls and knife cuts, and scalds and burns from hot liquids, hot surfaces and steam. Despite the existence of these hazards, experienced and knowledgeable chefs tend to foresee and avoid them.

An awareness of how to work in a kitchen and avoid these hazards develops through experience, but can be facilitated with thorough induction and training.

It is important to understand the meaning of the following three terms, which are in regular use:

1 *hazard* – the potential to cause harm
2 *risk* – the likelihood that harm will result from a particular hazard (the catering environment may have many hazards, but the aim is to have few risks)
3 *accident* – an unplanned or uncontrolled event that leads to, or could have led to, an injury, damage to plant or other loss.

Carrying out a risk assessment

A risk assessment can be divided into four areas:

1 *minimal risk* – safe conditions with safety measures in place
2 *some risk* – acceptable risk; however, attention must be paid to ensure that safety measures operate
3 *significant risk* – where safety measures are not fully in operation (also includes food most likely to cause food poisoning); requires immediate action
4 *dangerous risk* – operation of process or equipment to stop immediately; the system or equipment to be completely checked and operation recommenced after clearance.

In carrying out a risk assessment the following points should be covered:

■ assess the risks
■ determine preventative measures
■ decide who carries out safety inspections
■ determine methods of reporting back, and to whom
■ detail how to ensure inspections are effective
■ carry out safety training related to job.

The purpose of the exercise of assessing the possibility of risks and hazards is to prevent accidents.

Under the Control of Substances Hazardous to Health Regulations (COSHH) 1999, risk assessments of all hazardous chemicals and substances that employees may be exposed to at work are needed. When carrying out the legal obligations under the COSHH regulations all areas should be surveyed in order to ascertain the chemicals and substances in use.

Some examples of chemical substances found in kitchens are:

- cleaning chemicals – alkalis and acids
- detergents, sanitisers, descalers
- chemicals associated with burnishing
- pest control chemicals, insecticides and rodenticides.

Chefs and kitchen workers must also be aware of the correct handling methods required.

Further information

To find out more you may wish to refer to the following sources:

- *The Theory of Catering* (Hodder Arnold)
- The Health & Safety Executive
- www.hse.gov.uk

ESTABLISH AND DEVELOP POSITIVE WORKING RELATIONSHIPS IN HOSPITALITY

Units covered: HS2

As individuals working within an organisation we can achieve very little, but working within a group we are able to achieve a great deal more. Teamwork is essential when working in a commercial kitchen. Good, effective teamwork is an important feature of human behaviour and organisational performance. Those managing the kitchen must develop effective groups in order to achieve the high standard of work that is required to satisfy both the organisation's and the consumer's needs.

Each member of a group must regard themselves as being part of that group. They must interact with one another, perceive themselves as part of the group. Each must share the purpose of the group; this will help build trust and support and will, in turn, result in an effective performance. Cooperation is therefore important in order for the work to be carried out.

People in groups will influence one another – within the group there may be a leader and/or a hierarchical system. The pressures within the group may have a major influence on the behaviour of individual members and their performance. The style of leadership within the group has an influence on the behaviour of members within the group.

Groups help to shape the work pattern of organisations, as well as group members' behaviour and attitudes to their jobs.

THE IMPORTANCE OF TEAMWORK

Two types of team can be identified within an organisation:

1 the 'formal' team is the department or section created within a reorganised structure to pursue specified goals
2 the 'informal' team is created to deal with a particular situation; members within this team have fewer fixed organisational relationships; these teams are disbanded once they have performed their function.

Both formal and informal teams have to be developed and led. Thought has to be given to relationships, and the tasks and duties the team has to carry out.

Selecting and shaping teams to work within the kitchen is very important. This is the job of the head chef. It requires management skills. Matching each individual's talent to the task or job is an important consideration.

A good, well-developed team will be able to do the following:

- create useful ideas
- analyse problems effectively
- get things done
- communicate with each other
- respond to good leadership
- evaluate logically
- perform skilled operations with technical precision and ability
- understand and manage the control system.

Maintaining the health of the team and developing it further demands constant attention. The individual members of a group will never become a team unless effort is made to ensure that the differing personalities are able to relate to one another, communicate with each other, and value the contribution each employee or team member makes.

The chef, as a team leader, has a strong influence on his/her team or brigade. The chef in this position is expected to set examples that have to be followed. She/he has to work with the brigade, often under pressure, and sometimes dealing with conflict, personality clashes, change and stress. The chef has to adopt a range of strategies and styles of working in order to build loyalty, drive, innovation, commitment and trust in team members.

The team needs to identify its strengths and weaknesses, and develop ways to help those team members affected to overcome any weaknesses they may have.

SUCCESSFUL TEAM MANAGEMENT

Changing situations, variable resources and constant compromise are the realities of working in busy commercial kitchens. Systems and methods of managing teams and solving daily problems provide the chef with a framework in which to operate. The team has to produce meals with the people and resources at its disposal. The chef in charge of a brigade has to know how to handle the staff and make the best use of their abilities. This is one of the most difficult aspects of the chef's job, as people's behaviour is affected by many factors, including their:

- individual characteristics
- cultural attributes
- social skills.

All these have an important bearing on the complex web of relationships within the team.

The team members must be supportive of each other. Effective relationships are developed by understanding and listening to individuals. It is important that team members respect and listen to each other, cooperate and value confidentiality. The chef must be able to give honest feedback to the team.

The chef must lead rather than drive, and encourage the team to practise reasonable and supportive behaviour so that any problems are dealt with in an objective way and the team's personal skills are harnessed to achieve their full potential.

Every team has to deal with:

- the egos, and the weaknesses and/or strengths of its individual members
- the self-appointed experts within the group
- constantly changing relationships/circumstances.

The chef is able to manage the team successfully only by pulling back from the task in hand, however appealing he/she may find it. The chef must examine the processes that create efficient teamwork, finding out what it is that makes the team as a whole greater than the sum of its parts. To assist in this process, the chef must:

- have a consistent approach to solving problems
- take into account people's characters as well as their technical skills
- encourage supportive behaviour in the team
- create an open, healthy climate
- make time for the team to appraise its progress.

MOTIVATING A TEAM

A chef must motivate his/her team, by striving to make their work interesting, challenging and demanding. People must know what is expected of them, what the standards are.

Rewards are linked to effort and results. Any such factors must also work towards fulfilling (a) the needs of the organisation and (b) the expectations of team members. Improved performance should be recognised by consideration of pay and performance.

The chef in charge should attempt to intercede on behalf of his/her staff; this in turn will help to increase staff members' motivation and their commitment to the team. For the chef to manage his/her staff effectively, it is important for them to get to know them well, understand their needs and aspirations, and attempt to help them achieve their personal aims.

If a chef is able to manage the team by coordinating its members' aims with the corporate objectives – by reconciling their personal aspirations with the organisation's need to operate profitably – she/he will manage a successful team and, in addition, will enhance his/her own reputation.

COMMUNICATION

Because communication pervades nearly everything we do, even small improvements in the effectiveness of our communicating are likely to have disproportionately large benefits. In the kitchen, most jobs have some communication component. Successful communication is vital when working to build working relationships. Training and developing the team is about communicating. In work, the quality of our personal relationships depends on the quality of the communication system.

Breakdowns in communication can be identified by looking at the 'intent' and the 'effect' as two separate entities. It is when the

intent is not translated into the effect that communication can break down. Such breakdowns affect staff and team relationships, and individuals' attitudes towards and views of each other. Good relationships depend on good communication, and awareness of the potential gap between intent and effect can help clarify and prevent any misunderstanding within the group.

By bridging the gap between the intent and the effect you can begin to change the culture of the working environment: the processes become self-reinforcing in a positive direction; the staff begin to respect each other in a positive framework; they listen more carefully to each other, with positive expectations, hearing the constructive intent and responding to it.

As a chef/manager, the art is in achieving results through the team, communication being the key to the exercise. A great deal of the chef's time will be taken up with communicating in one way or another.

Communication, therefore, plays a major part in the chef/manager's role. Communication at work needs to be orientated towards action – getting something done.

DIVERSITY IN THE HOSPITALITY INDUSTRY

The hospitality industry is becoming more diverse and, for this reason, the team must celebrate and welcome diversity and embrace equal opportunities.

Diversity in the kitchen can contribute positively to the development of the team, bringing to it a range of skills and ideas from different cultures. The free movement of labour within the European Union has meant that large numbers of people from different cultures now work together in the hospitality industry.

Diversity recognises that people are different. It includes not only cultural and ethnic differences but differences in gender, age, disability and sexual orientation, background, personality and work style.

Developing effective working relationships recognises, values and celebrates these differences. Working relationships should be able to harness such differences to improve creativity and innovation, and be based on the belief that groups of people who bring different perspectives will find better solutions to problems than groups of people who are the same.

MINIMISING CONFLICT IN RELATIONSHIPS

A conflict with the manager or with colleagues can easily get entangled with issues about work and status, both of which can make it difficult to approach the problem in a rational and professional way. One of the skills of the chef/manager is the need to identify conflict, so that plans can be put in place to minimise it. The following are just some of the points that should be borne in mind.

- Conflict arises where there are already strained relationships and personality clashes between members of the team.
- Conflict often occurs in a professional kitchen when the brigade is understaffed and under pressure, especially over a long period. Pressure can also come from, say, restaurant reviews and guides, when a chef is seeking a Michelin star or other special accolade.
- Conflicts damage working relationships

and upset the team, and this will eventually show up in the finished product.

The chef and manager must also be aware of any insidious conflict that may be going on around them, in less obvious places. Covert conflicts are those that take place in secret; they can be very harmful. Although this type of conflict is often difficult to detect, it will undermine the team's performance. Many conflicts start with misunderstandings or a small upset that grows and develops out of all proportion.

It is important to reflect on and analyse the nature of conflict and individual attitudes to it. Conflicts can be very damaging and upsetting, but there can also be some positive outcomes. A conflict can be a learning curve that a chef has to enter into; it has to be handled properly and focused on in order to achieve the desired outcome.

PRIORITISING THE CUSTOMER

Developing relationships within the team means that every member understands the goals and objectives of the team. One of the main goals is to satisfy the customer's demands and expectations. Good communication within the organisation assists in the development of customer care. The kitchen must communicate effectively with the restaurant staff so that they, in turn, can communicate with the customer. Any customer complaints must be handled positively: treat customers who complain well, show them empathy. Use customer feedback – good or bad – positively. This may further develop the team and help solve any problems within the team.

Further information
To find out more, you may wish to refer to:

- *The Theory of Catering* (Hodder Arnold)

CONTRIBUTE TO THE DEVELOPMENT OF RECIPES AND MENUS

Units covered: HS9 and 2FPC13

INTRODUCTION

Why produce new recipes and new menus? In order to create or to develop customer or consumer satisfaction it is essential to prevent menu apathy and to produce interest, and thus enable the discovery of new flavours and combinations. Producing new menus and dishes with the selection of foodstuffs available from all over the world is a stimulating and exciting task. So much so that it is easy to overlook or dismiss traditional and classical dishes as being old-fashioned and out of date.

There are, however, customers who welcome the opportunity of being able to choose a traditional/classical dish occasionally. Consideration can be therefore given to including a small number of such dishes on almost any type of menu. While the creator of new recipes may enjoy the experience, it must be clear that the exercise is twofold: to satisfy (a) the customer and (b) management. For this reason, the prime considerations are the cost of the development and the selling price. It is also essential to consider the style or type of establishment and the kind of clientele for whom the changes are intended, as well as regional variations and food fashions.

The reasons for change could include:

- menu fatigue
- changes in clientele
- food fashion changes
- availability of supplies
- need to stimulate business
- new chef and staff

- the opening of a similar local establishment.

Whatever the cause, it is necessary to introduce new recipes and menus in accord with the organisation's objectives. It follows that, in every sphere of catering, recipe and menu changes may need to occur – whether this involves school meals, hospital food, speciality outlets, exclusive restaurants, or wherever. If new developments are intended, it is essential to evaluate:

- the cost of development
- the effect the change or changes will have on the existing situation
- the ability of the staff to cope
- whether adequate equipment is present and suitable suppliers available
- the presentation of the dishes
- the format of the menu.

Depending on the quality and expertise of staff it can be an interesting and possibly useful exercise to offer them the opportunity of contributing to recipe development and/or suggesting new dishes or variations to existing ones. If successful, this can boost and contribute to staff morale and assist in developing team spirit.

RECIPE DEVELOPMENT: PREPARATION

Preparation prior to the practical aspect of producing new recipes involves the need to construct a method of recording to include accurate details of ingredients, their cost, quality and availability (e.g. draw up a chart). Time needed for preparation, production and yield must also be recorded. Space should be available on the chart to specify several attempts so that comparisons can be made, and there should be adequate space for making notes.

An evaluation sheet is required so that a record can be made of the opinions of the tasting panel or persons consulted. This sheet will, as appropriate, be constructed so as to include space for details of flavours, colour, texture, presentation, and so on.

DEVELOPING NEW IDEAS

Before proceeding to develop new ideas it is essential to have a basic foundation on which to build.

The developing of new recipes is challenging, stimulating and creates new interest, but where do original ideas come from? Many are triggered by the creations of others. It is particularly worthwhile to keep abreast of what is happening in the industry, perhaps by some of the means listed below.

- Publishing:
  - trade magazines such as *Caterer and Hotelkeeper*
  - books produced by leading chefs
  - consumer magazines, food journals
  - newspaper articles
  - the library
  - the Internet.
- TV and radio:
  - *Masterchef*
  - *Junior Master Cook*
  - *Ready Steady Cook*
  - other food programmes.
- Contacts:
  - visiting other establishments
  - visiting catering exhibitions
  - lectures, demonstrations
  - competitors
  - catering organisations, etc.

Extra care needs to be taken when introducing new recipes to patients in hospitals and nursing homes, and in the provision of meals in schools and residential establishments, so as to ensure the nutritional content is suitable. Dietitians can provide advice on the dietary requirements of these persons.

Communication and information

Information sources for recipes are available everywhere to the open and enquiring mind. Every kind of establishment, from the local Chinese restaurant to the five-star hotel, can present innovative ideas. It is of particular value if it is possible to travel abroad as well as being alert to new dishes in the UK. Visits to department stores, exhibition centres, outdoor events and the like may well stimulate ideas. The range of ingredients available from catering suppliers is immense, but local markets and supermarkets should not be ignored as sources of supply.

If you have new developments in mind, it is necessary to pass on your proposals to both senior management (who will be responsible for their implementation) and fellow members of the kitchen brigade, for their constructive comments. If possible, put your ideas to the test with respected members of the catering profession with whom you are acquainted. Your proposals should include estimated food costings, time taken to produce, labour costs, equipment and facilities needed, and details of staff training if required. Knowledge of the establishment's organisation is important so that the right person or persons are involved.

Quality of materials

The highest possible standards of ingredients should be used so that a true and valid result is available for assessment of the recipe.

Staff abilities

Before implementing new recipes and menus, the standard of staff members' craft skills should be appraised in order to assess their capacity to cope with innovation. Failure to do so could jeopardise the whole project. Not only should their craft skills be assessed but their cooperation in putting new ideas into practice should be sought, and encouragement given when the outcome is successful.

Equipment and facilities

New recipes can affect the utilisation of existing equipment by overloading at peak times. The capacity of items such as pastry ovens, deep-fat fryers, salamanders, and so on, may already be fully used. New items can affect the production of the current menu; this fact should be borne in mind so that service is not impaired.

IMPLEMENTATION

Having tested and arrived at the finished recipe, staff may need to practise production and presentation of the dish. This may include both small and large quantities, depending on the establishment. In all cases, careful recording of all aspects of the operation can help in the smooth running of the exercise – in particular, basic work study should be observed. Constructive comments should be sought from staff and, in particular, any problems should be discussed.

The results of such trials runs should be conveyed to senior personnel and any problems that have been identified should be resolved.

Having validated the recipe, checked on a reliable supplier and ensured the capability of the staff, it is important that all concerned know when the dishes will be included on the menu. Storekeepers, kitchen staff and serving staff need to be briefed, as do any other departments involved, as to the time and date of implementation.

PRESENTATION OF DISHES

Of particular importance is how the customer sees the dish; when it is received it needs to appeal to the senses of sight and smell even before taste. For this reason, consideration needs to be given to presentation early in the development of the idea: what dish will be used, what will accompany it, are any particular skills needed to serve it? Foods in some establishments are prepared and cooked in front of the customer; some require the dish to be cooked fresh while the customer waits; therefore details of presentation must be recorded and, where possible, a test carried out in the actual situation.

Should the new recipe be for a food service operation that involves preparation, cooking and presentation before the customer, so that all or part of the process is seen by the potential consumer, then attention needs to be paid to the skills of the chef. Extra training – not only culinary skills, but customer-handling skills – may be needed, and particular attention should be paid to hygiene. These factors need to be observed at the development stage so that customer satisfaction is guaranteed as soon as the new recipe is implemented.

ORGANISATION

Adequate time needs to be allowed to test and develop any new recipe, to train staff, to appraise comments and modify the recipe if necessary. Staff (particularly serving staff) must be briefed on the composition of the dish, as well as being told when it will be included on the menu. They need to be asked if there are any problems; if required, this could be in a written form. Senior personnel need to be apprised orally or in writing of the implementation of the new items.

Should the new dish or dishes require skills that are unfamiliar to some staff, then the workload of individuals may need to be changed while the relevant staff are trained in the appropriate skill. In estimating how long it will take to implement the new dish factors to take account of are:

■ the skills of the staff
■ that suitable equipment is available
■ that suppliers can produce the required ingredients in the right quantity, at the desired quality and at a suitable price.

Clear written instructions may need to be provided; this means the sequence in which the ingredients are to be used, with the appropriate amount (e.g. for 10 portions or 50 portions). This to be followed by the instructions in the order that the recipe is to be followed, so that it is logical.

The introduction of new dishes will perhaps affect the existing style of operations. If dishes are prepared in front of the customer – for example, in a department store – the new dish may require more time in preparation than others on the menu, which may cause a bottleneck. The introduction of a salad bar or sweet trolley to include new dishes can affect the service of the usual dishes. If the clientele require, say, vegetarian dishes, or people of certain cultural or religious groups have special needs, then adaptations may be necessary to accommodate this in the existing set-up.

In addition to obtaining feedback (that is to say information) from staff, it is just as

important, if not more so, to obtain comments from the customer or consumer.

Finally, consider the following points:

■ the elimination of waste
■ the control of materials and ingredients
■ the careful use of energy
■ the wise use of time.

Ensure that a record is kept so that no resources are misused. Failure to control and monitor resources can be expensive in terms of time, materials and effort, and can be very wasteful.

MENU DESIGN

The function of a menu is to inform potential customers what dishes are available and, as appropriate, the number of courses, the choice on the courses and the price. The wording should make clear to the kind of customer using the establishment what to expect. The menu may be used to promote specific items such as when an ingredient is in season, children's menus, reductions for senior citizens or what is served at particular times, etc.

If printed, the type should be clear and of readable size; if handwritten, the script should be of good quality so as to create a good impression. Menus are expensive to produce but when they are attractive and fulfil the function of informing the customer, they may enhance the reputation of the establishment and increase custom.

SPECIFIC CONSIDERATIONS

When considering any development, it is necessary to take into account any current problems and issues that may affect the outcome, and also those of historic origin based on culture and religion.

It is essential to keep up to date on factors such as, for example, BSE and the effect on consumers' choice or rejection of beef. The increasing use of 'organic' foods may encourage customer demand for such foods to be used; all foods are organic, but the term has become restricted to mean those grown without the use of pesticides or processed without the use of additives. There is little difference nutritionally between organic and non-organic foods. The *Manual of Nutrition* published by HMSO is a most useful reference book for those seeking information on nutrition.

Certain groups of people have restrictions on their eating habits (religious or cultural) that must be observed when producing new recipes for them. The following list offers some examples.

- *Hindus* – no beef, mainly vegetables, no alcohol.
- *Muslims* – no pork, no alcohol, no shellfish, halal meat (requires a Muslim to be present at the killing).
- *Sikhs* – no beef, no alcohol, only meat killed with one blow to the head.
- *Jews* – no pork, meat must be kosher, only fish with fins and scales, meat and dairy produce not to be eaten together.
- *Rastafarians* – no animal products except milk, no canned or processed foods, no salt added, foods should be organic.

DEVELOPMENT OF RECIPES AND MENUS FOR SPECIAL DIETS

A balanced diet is important for health, providing the right amount and type of nutrients required to maintain a healthy lifestyle. However, some customers require special diets for health reasons. Others choose special diets for ethical, cultural and/or religious reasons.

Examples of special diets

The chef may be required, on occasion, to provide menus for individuals on special diets, such as those described below.

Low-salt diet
A high-salt diet increases the risk of high blood pressure, which in turn increases the risk of stroke and heart attack.

Milk-free diet
Soya or rice milk can be used as an alternative to cows' milk for customers who have a milk allergy or lactose intolerance.

Low-cholesterol diet
People on a low-cholesterol diet avoid high-cholesterol foods such as liver, kidney, egg yolks, fatty meats, fried foods, full-cream milk, cream, cheeses, biscuits and cakes. The chef should use lean meat or fish (grilled or poached), and low-fat milk and cheeses.

Diabetic
When someone is suffering from diabetes, their body is unable to control the level of glucose in the blood. This can lead to comas, and long-term problems such as increased risk of blindness, and cardiovascular and kidney disease. Avoid serving high-sugar dishes, fatty meats, eggs, full-cream milk, cream cakes, biscuits, and so on.

Coeliac
Someone suffering from coeliac disease has an allergy to gluten, exposure to which results in severe inflammation of the gastro-intestinal tract, pain and diarrhoea, and malnutrition due to the inability to absorb nutrients. Avoid serving all products made using wheat, barley or rye.

Vegetarianism

A vegetarian is someone who lives on a diet of grains, pulses, nuts, seeds, vegetables and fruits, with or without the use of dairy products and eggs (preferably free range). A vegetarian does not eat any meat, poultry, game, fish, shellfish or crustacea, or slaughter by-products such as gelatine or animal fats.

Strict vegetarians will not wish the utensils with which their food is prepared or served to be contaminated with any animal products. For this reason, chefs have to take special care in the preparation of vegetarian foods in a kitchen that also caters for meat and fish eaters.

Types of vegetarian

- *Lacto-ovo-vegetarian:* eats both dairy products and eggs.
- *Lacto-vegetarian:* eats dairy products but not eggs.
- *Ovo-vegetarian:* will include eggs but not dairy products.
- *Vegan:* does not eat dairy products, eggs or any other animal product (e.g. honey).
- *Fruitarian:* a type of vegan who eats very few processed or cooked foods; the fruitarian's diet consists mainly of raw fruit, grains and nuts; fruitarians believe that only plant foods that can be harvested without killing the plant should be eaten.
- *Macrobiotic:* requires a diet that follows spiritual and philosophical codes; it aims to maintain a balance between foods seen as yin (positive) and yang (negative); the diet progresses through ten levels, becoming increasingly restrictive – not all levels are vegetarian, although each level gradually eliminates animal products.
- *Demi-vegetarian:* eats little or no meat and may eat fish.
- Those who eat fish but not meat are sometimes called *pescetarians*.

Issues the chef has to consider

- Many ingredients are derived from the slaughter of animals (e.g. gelatine, which is used in confectionery, ice cream and other dairy products).
- The term 'animal fats' refers to carcass fats and may be present in a wide range of foods (e.g. biscuits and cakes); suet and lard are also types of animal fats.
- Cheese is made with rennet, which is a substance extracted from the stomach lining of slaughtered calves. Vegetarian cheese is made with rennet from a microbial source.
- Many vegetarians who eat eggs will eat only free-range eggs. This is usually due to moral objections to the battery farming of hens.

Vegetarian foods

The main vegetarian food groups are:
- cereals and grains (e.g. wheat, including bread and pasta, oats, maize, barley, rye and rice)
- potatoes
- pulses (beans, lentils, peas), nuts and seeds
- fruit and vegetables
- dairy products, or soya products (tofu, tempeh, soya protein)
- vegetable oils and fats.

Animal-derived products to be excluded from vegetarian diets, recipes and menus

- Non-vegetarian alcohol – some wines or beers may be refined using isinglass (a fish product) or dried blood.
- Animal-fat ice cream – replace with vegetable fat ice cream.
- Animal fats (suet, lard, dripping) – replace with vegetable fats/oils.
- Oils containing fish oil – replace with 100 per cent vegetable oil.
- Gelatine – replace with agar-agar.
- Meat stock – replace with vegetable stock.
- Rennet or pepsin – replace with vegetarian cheeses (i.e. made with vegetarian rennet)

or non-rennet cheeses such as cottage and cream cheese (these should not be used for vegans, unless made with soya milk).

GUIDELINES ON SERVING HEALTHY FOOD

It is recommended that everyone should follow a diet that is rich in fresh fruit and vegetables, fish, wholegrain breads, pulses, rice and pasta, and that is low in fats of all types, especially animal fats. Recommended cooking methods are grilling, poaching, steaming and 'en papillote' (cooking in an envelope/parcel), and reducing the amount of shallow-fried and deep-fried food.

The following sections offer some guidance on how to 'think healthy' when preparing food.

Meat, fish and alternatives

- Always use lean cuts of meat, trim off any excess fat, and remove the skin from chicken or chicken portions.
- Bake, grill or roast meats and fish, and do not baste with additional fats. Fish may be steamed. If frying is unavoidable, ensure that the fat is at the correct temperature and drain the food well on absorbent paper before serving. As mentioned above, cooking 'en papillote' is a healthy alternative as there is no need to use additional fats and all flavours (e.g. of the herbs, spices, vegetables used) are retained.
- Alternatives to meat, fish and eggs, are pulses, nuts, tofu, Quorn, and so on (see also the section on 'Vegetarianism', above). Dishes can also be prepared using a combination of meats and pulses, to cut down on the amount of meat used.

Fats and oils

- If there is a need to use fat, consider which type and how much.
- Use olive oil for flavour, and rapeseed oil where any flavour will be masked.
- Low-fat margarines or spreads cannot be used for baking as they contain a large amount of water, which evaporates.
- Full-fat polyunsaturated margarines contain as many calories as butter.
- Margarines contain flavourings, colours and other additives to provide that 'buttery' taste.
- Thicken sauces and gravies with cornflour, arrowroot, fecule (potato starch/flour), rice flour or barley flour rather than a fatty 'roux'.
- Always offer polyunsaturated or low-fat spreads as an alternative to butter.
- Offer low-fat sauces, salad dressings and mayonnaises separately.

Sugar

- Avoid adding sugar to savoury dishes.
- Consider the possibility of reducing the amount of sugar in any dish.
- Consider lower-fat, lower-sugar, fruit-based desserts.

Salt

- Reduce salt in recipes and leave it to customers to add more if they wish. Many people have reduced their salt consumption so that highly salted foods will be unpalatable.
- Most stock cubes and stock powders are high in salt.
- Explore the use of fresh herbs to add flavour to dishes.

Fibre

■ Where possible, increase the fibre content of dishes by using pulses, vegetables, fruit, wholemeal bread, wholemeal pasta, and so on.

Breads, cereals and potatoes

■ Offer a wide variety of interesting bread products, including teabreads, and serve with a choice of spreads.
■ Provide a wide range of breakfast cereals, particularly low-sugar, high-fibre products, and ensure that customers can choose low-fat milk, yoghurts, fresh and dried fruit, and artificial sweeteners if desired.
■ Make pasta an inviting choice, offering good portions of the fresh varieties and serving with low-fat sauces.
■ Providing generous portions of starchy foods incurs little additional cost.

Fruit and vegetables

■ Offer a range of interesting salads. Dressings should be offered separately, including a low-fat alternative.
■ Bake or steam vegetables to retain their colour, flavour and texture, and use only small quantities of fat when stir- or shallow-frying.
■ Make vegetables appealing by exploring the range and variety available.
■ Use a wide variety of fresh fruits, low-fat cream, ice cream, fromage frais and yoghurts.

Milk and dairy

■ Reduce the amount of fresh cream used in recipes.
■ Substitute cream with crème fraîche or fromage frais.

■ Where possible, use skimmed milk.
■ If possible, use low-fat cheeses such as Edam and Gouda.

FOOD ALLERGIES

Some customers have a very serious adverse reaction to certain foods. A reaction can occur within a few minutes of exposure to the allergen – typically the lips and tongue tingle and swell. There may be abdominal cramps and diarrhoea, and sometimes the person vomits. There may also be wheezing and shortness of breath followed, in rare cases, by cardiovascular failure and collapse, leading to death if very prompt action is not taken.

It is important to be aware that almost any substance can trigger an allergic reaction in someone. Although peanuts are the most common food to trigger such a reaction, other common potential 'problem foods' are:

■ beef and pork
■ cashew, pecan and brazil nuts, and walnuts
■ eggs
■ milk
■ mushrooms
■ sesame seeds
■ shellfish
■ wheat.

Other foods that, less commonly, may trigger an allergic reaction are:

■ chocolate
■ coffee
■ oranges
■ soya
■ strawberries
■ sugar
■ tomatoes
■ yeast.

Foods containing sugar			
all types of sugar	malt	maple syrup	biscuits
honey	jam	peanut butter	pudding
golden syrup	marmalade	dried fruits	sweeteners
treacle	chutney	foods labelled dextrose,	
molasses	cakes	fructose, maltose or	
		sucrose	

Foods containing yeast			
bread (not matzo or chapatis)	dried fruit	vinegar	malt
buns	unpeeled fruit	Quorn, mycoprotein	cheese – Brie and
yeast extract (Marmite/Vegemite)	yoghurt	(meat substitute)	Camembert
stock cubes	synthetic cream	edible fungi	
Bovril, Oxo	soy sauce		

It is important that chefs train their staff in product knowledge. They should know what ingredients are in the dishes.

While food allergies are mainly a medical issue, it is necessary for those concerned with providing meals to be aware of the situation. Therefore, in any catering establishment, should a customer enquire if a substance or food to which they are allergic is included in the recipe ingredients, an accurate and clear answer must be given. Failure to provide the correct information could have dire consequences; for example, a person allergic to nuts would need to know if there were walnuts in the Waldorf salad, almonds garnishing the trout, marzipan on the gateau or nuts in the ice cream. If a person inadvertently consumes a food item to which they are allergic, medical assistance will be urgently needed.

A person intolerant to milk would need to know if cheese was included in a dish, and a person allergic to nuts must know if, say, peanut butter has been used. Therefore persons *serving* the food as well as those *preparing* it, must be knowledgeable regarding its composition so as to give accurate information to potential consumers.

The following is an example of a checklist that can be used to make staff aware of the breadth of restricted items.

Because a person is allergic to one item in a family of foods, there is a possibility of their being allergic to other items in the family (as in the checklists of plant and animal families, below).

Plant families

Fungi or moulds	Grains or grasses	Onion or lily
baker's yeast	wheat	onion
brewer's yeast	corn	asparagus
mushroom	barley	chive
truffle	oats	leek
chanterelle	cane sugar	garlic
cheese	bamboo shoots	shallot
vinegar	rice	

Mustard	Rose	Pulses
broccoli	apple	peas
cabbage	pears	lentils
cauliflower	quince	soya beans
brussels sprouts	apricot	peanuts
horseradish	cherry	haricot beans
radish	raspberry	chickpeas
swede	strawberry	runner beans
turnip	loganberry	mangetout
watercress	blackberry	kidney beans

Citrus	Grape	Parsley
orange	wine	parsley
lemon	brandy	carrot
grapefruit	sherry	dill
lime	raisins	celery
tangerine	currants	fennel
ugli	sultanas	parsnip

Potato	Gourd	Mint
potato	melon	mint
tomato	cucumber	basil
aubergine	squashes	marjoram
chilli	gherkin	oregano
paprika	courgette	sage
	pumpkin	rosemary
	marrow	thyme

Animal food families

Bovines	beef, dairy products, mutton, lamb, goat
Poultry	chicken, eggs, duck, goose
Grouse	grouse, guinea fowl
Pig	pork, bacon, ham, sausage
Fish	all types of fish
Shellfish (crustaceans)	lobster, prawns, shrimps, crab, crayfish
Molluscs	snail, clam, mussel, oyster, scallop

Unfortunately some staff employed in the catering industry are themselves allergic to handling certain items of food. In the event of an employee becoming aware of this (for example, coming out in a rash), medical advice must be obtained. In certain cases, if the person cannot be cured, they may be advised to transfer to other work. Examples of foods that may cause this problem include flour, tomatoes and fish.

Further information

Specialised cookery books are available to assist those who have an allergy, or those who need to develop recipes for them. For example:

- *The Allergy Cookbook*, by Stephanie Lashford (Ashgrove Press, 1983)
- *The New Allergy Diet*, by J. Hunter, E. Workman and J. Woolner (Vermilion, 2000).

To find out more you may wish to refer to the following sources:

- *The Allergy Handbook*, by Keith Mumby (Thorsons, 1988)
- *Food Allergy and Intolerance*, by Jonathan Brostoff and Linda Gamlin (Bloomsbury, 1998)
- *HCIMA Technical Brief* No. 43
- http://www.niaid.gov/factsheets/food.htm

HEALTHY EATING AND MENU DEVELOPMENT

A RECAP ON NUTRITION

Foods contain nutrients, water and fibre. In the right quantities, all of these food components do some sort of job to help people live. The nuts and bolts of what you need to know about nutrition in order to make sense of the rest of this chapter are summarised in the table below.

Nutrition basics

Nutrient	Comment	Function
Carbohydrate	Two main types are starch and sugars	Energy provider (3.75 kcals/g)
Protein	Animal (e.g. meat, milk, eggs) or vegetable (e.g. beans) sources	Body builder (4 kcals/g)
Fat	Two main types are unsaturated (liquid, e.g. vegetable oils) or saturated (hard, e.g. butter)	Provide energy (9 kcals/g) – fat is twice as calorie dense as carbohydrate (e.g. small (30 g) cube cheese = 124 kcals compared to one (100 g) jacket potato = 136 kcals)
Vitamins and minerals	Needed in minute quantities	Regulate body processes (e.g. growth, immune and nervous functions); some act as antioxidants
Other food constituents		
Fluid	Need 1.2 litres fluid/day = 6–8 mugs of drinks daily	Essential for helping the body to function properly (e.g. kidneys, regulating body temperature, lubricant)
Fibre	Not digested/absorbed; found in wholegrain cereals, pulses, vegetables and fruit	Essential for gut health and prevents constipation

NUTRITION AND HEALTH

Over the decades our eating habits have changed. This dietary evolution, together with other shifts in lifestyle, has brought massive health problems. In particular, obesity is now hitting the headlines and the statistics for the UK are sobering:

- two-thirds of men and over half of women are now overweight or obese
- over one in five boys and over one in four girls are now overweight or obese
- on the basis of recent trends, it is predicted that by 2010 three-quarters of men in the UK will be overweight or obese.

Connected to this growing epidemic are the escalating rates of diabetes and our high rates of coronary heart disease. In addition, many cancers are related to the food we eat.

To tackle these health problems all of us need to change our patterns of eating. The messages are simple:

- base meals on starchy foods such as rice, bread, pasta (ideally whole grain varieties) and potatoes
- eat lots of fruit and vegetables (at least five portions a day)
- eat moderate amounts of meat, fish and alternatives (including a portion of oily fish each week)
- cut down on saturated fat, sugar and salt.

There are clear quantitative nutritional targets for the UK population and these have been translated into the daily guidance reproduced in the table below.

Nutritional targets for adults
■ Reduce total fat intake (the target is to keep below 95 g/day for men and 70 g/day for women)
■ Reduce saturated fat (the target is to keep below 30 g/day for men and 20 g/day for women)
■ Reduce sugars not found naturally in foods or milk (around 60 g/day max.)
■ Reduce salt intake (no more than 6 g/day)
■ Increase intakes of starchy carbohydrate (around 37 per cent of total energy intake should be starchy foods)
■ Increase fibre intake (around 18 g/day)
■ At least five portions of a variety of fruit and vegetables per day
■ Two portions of fish per week (at least one should be oily fish like salmon)

Source: Department of Health (1991) *Dietary Reference Values for Food Energy and Nutrients for the United Kingdom*. London: HMSO; Scientific Advisory Committee on Nutrition (2003) *Salt and Health*. London: The Stationery Office.

Translating these nutritional targets into food on the plate is where chefs are vitally important. They have the skills and knowledge to make healthy eating a positive experience. Some of the best cuisines of the world are based on the sort of guidelines summarised above. Dishes and meals can be built around lots of starchy foods with generous helpings of a wide range of vegetables, salad and fruit, and adding relatively small amounts of lower-fat meats plus an abundance of fish dishes, all made with unsaturated oils like sunflower, olive or sesame. Many recipes from Italy, the eastern Mediterranean, China, India and Thailand echo these principles.

THE CONCEPT OF BALANCE

Healthy eating is about balance. Chefs can help people achieve this balance by threading the principles listed above through their practice. This section illustrates how chefs can do this.

Energy balance

One of the keys to healthy eating is balancing energy input (through food) with output (through physical activity). Put simply, too much energy consumed leads to obesity. Energy is measured in calories (or joules in metric language). A 24-year-old chef needs about 2550 kcals/day to keep his body ticking over and fuel any additional physical activity like preparing food, walking round the kitchen or going to the gym. Rates of calorie expenditure vary between activities. The table below lists a range of activities together with their expenditure rates. As a rule, the harder the body works, the higher the rate of energy expenditure.

Energy expenditure for selected activities	
Running	6–20 kcals/min
Swimming	5–15 kcals/min
Cycling	4–20 kcals/min
Cooking/preparing food	2–3 kcals/min
Fitness training	4–12 kcals/min
Walking	3–6 kcals/min

For customers who want to control their weight, chefs can make significant calorie reductions simply by making a few small changes that concentrate on driving down fat levels. For example, large calorie savings can be made by:

- trimming the fat from meat
- reducing the amount of cream, butter or oils in sauces
- swapping whole milk for semi-skimmed in béchamel sauces
- dry-frying meat to seal before braising.

Balancing recipes

There are countless small steps chefs can take to drive down levels of fat, salt and sugar and,

at the same time, also bump up the starch, fibre, fruit and vegetable content of their recipes. This balancing process may involve:

- changing ingredients (e.g. swapping full-fat crème fraîche for the half-fat version)
- manipulating proportions within recipes (e.g. using relatively larger quantities of rice and white fish to meat in paella, or serving more tortillas and vegetables in relation to meat in a fajita recipe)
- switching cooking methods (e.g. oven-baking samosas instead of deep-frying, oven-roasting aubergine slices for moussaka instead of frying them in olive oil).

The example below shows how a traditional recipe for sole mornay can been modified to make it healthier. The modified version ends up much lower in fat (particularly saturated fat) and calories because the sauce is made with semi-skimmed milk and unsaturated margarine. The sauce is then finished with fromage frais and flavoured with smaller amounts of Parmesan instead of large quantities of high-fat Gruyère cheese.

Traditional sole mornay	Modified sole mornay
- Béchamel sauce made with butter, flour, whole milk - Egg yolks and cream used to finish sauce - Large quantities of Gruyère cheese used to flavour dish	- Béchamel sauce made with polyunsaturated margarine, flour and semi-skimmed milk - Fromage frais and small quantities of Parmesan used to add flavour and texture
Per portion: 28.0 g fat 15.7 g saturated fat 420 kcals	*Per portion:* 11.8 g fat 3.5 g saturated fat 272 kcals

Balancing plates

The next level of balance comes within individual courses. The idea is to:

- boost amounts of starchy foods, which can be done in lots of different ways (e.g. adding bread rolls, increasing portion sizes of potatoes, rice or pasta, using thicker dough for pizza)
- increasing the content of vegetables by, for example
  - serving more vegetables (variety and amount) with the main course
  - adding side salads
  - garnishing dishes with bunches of watercress or rocket
  - serving cucumber or fresh tomato relishes with curries
  - offering more dishes where vegetables are integral (e.g. moussaka, boeuf bourguignon)
- maximising the fruit content of puddings (e.g. using fruit coulis instead of cream, increasing the proportion of fruit in classic dishes like apple charlotte and tarte tatin, decorating classic cold desserts with combinations of fresh fruit).

The example below indicates how the balance of an individual course can change depending on the recipes used and accompaniments chosen from a menu.

Higher-fat main course	Lower-fat main course
■ Traditional sole mornay recipe using béchamel sauce made with whole milk and flavoured with cream and Gruyère cheese ■ Sauté potatoes ■ Grilled mushrooms	■ Modified sole mornay recipe using béchamel sauce made with semi-skimmed milk and flavoured with fromage frais and Parmesan ■ New potatoes ■ Broccoli and carrots
Per course: 45.3 g fat 18.0 g saturated fat 688 kcals	*Per course:* 12.3 g fat 3.5 g saturated fat 380 kcals

Balancing complete meals

Chefs can help customers balance individual courses so meals consumed are healthier. For example, higher-fat first courses (like deep-fried Camembert, or avocado stuffed with cream cheese and walnuts) can be balanced with lower-fat main courses (e.g. steamed sole with garlic, spring onion and ginger) and again with lower-fat desserts (e.g. fruit sorbets or strawberry pavlova). The example below shows how consistently lower-fat choices across a menu, together with small changes to a traditional recipe, can improve the 'health profile' of a complete meal.

Higher-fat meal (recipes from *Practical Cookery*)	Lower-fat meal (recipes from *Practical Cookery*)
■ Duck and chicken terrine (page 103) ■ Sole mornay (traditional recipe) with sauté potatoes and grilled mushrooms ■ Sticky toffee pudding with butterscotch sauce (page 516)	■ Terrine of chicken and vegetables (page 101) ■ Sole mornay (modified recipe) with new potatoes, broccoli and carrots ■ Pears in red wine (page 533)
Per meal: 128.g fat 64.2 g saturated fat 1995 kcals	*Per meal:* 29.8 g fat 12.9 g saturated fat 769 kcals

Balancing menus

In terms of healthy eating, chefs have a delicate pathway to tread. Some customers will want to indulge themselves and forget about fat and calories, while others will be consistently looking for healthier choices and ways to control calories. The demand for healthier choices will be particularly high in 'everyday eating environments' like workplace restaurants or venues that serve business lunches. In addition, the food culture in the UK has undergone a revolution over the last decade. There is now a much stronger emphasis on the highest-quality fresh ingredients put together to craft dishes that reflect many of the principles of healthy eating. Following these rules, creative chefs can help people understand that healthy eating does not necessarily have to be brown and boring.

Never before has the demand for healthier options been higher. For these reasons chefs need to consider including:

■ a variety of fish dishes (white fish is lower in fat than meat, and oily fish like salmon, fresh tuna or trout contains beneficial omega-3 fats)
■ a wide range of exciting vegetable dishes (if people are going to reach their five a day goal, they need to learn to love vegetables, and chefs can play a vital role in helping

people try something different – for example, roasted butternut squash, steamed asparagus, mashed celeriac or stir-fried pak choi)
■ pasta dishes, which inherently contain proportionately more starch than other types of dish, or adding bread to meals or using thicker dough in pizza dishes
■ desserts based on, or including, fruit (e.g. pears in red wine, blackcurrant sorbet, apple crumble, vacherin with strawberries and half-fat crème fraîche).

In this way chefs can help people achieve the sort of dietary balance required over time, as depicted below. This illustration shows the proportions of different food groups that make up a healthy eating pattern.

The Balance of Good Health

Fruit and vegetables

Bread, other cereals and potatoes

Meat, fish and alternatives

Foods containing fat
Foods and drinks containing sugar

Milk and dairy foods

There are five main groups of valuable foods

Source: reproduced by kind permission of the Food Standards Agency.

FAT FACTS

This chapter has talked a lot about fat. One of the key drivers in healthy catering is to reduce fat in recipes; the other is to change the type of fat used from saturated to unsaturated (including monounsaturated and polyunsaturated fats). Foods contain different types of fats in varying amounts. Generally, foods of animal origin contain predominantly saturated fats (which are solid at room temperature) and foods from vegetable sources tend to contain much more of the healthier unsaturated fats (which are liquid at room temperature). Many commercial spreads and margarines contain a mixture of saturated and unsaturated fats. Softer spreads tend to contain more unsaturated fats (e.g. sunflower spreads) and harder 'block' margarines are usually predominantly saturated.

Saturated fat	Unsaturated fat
Lard, suet, hard margarine Butter Fat in meat Dairy products like cheese Hidden in cakes, pastries, biscuits Egg yolk	**Monounsaturated** Olive, rapeseed, groundnut oils **Polyunsaturated** Sunflower spread and oil, corn and soya oils **Beneficial omega-3 fats** Oily fish like salmon, trout, fresh tuna

The concept of reducing fat in products, but at the same time moving towards unsaturated fats, is often difficult for people to translate into practice. An example of the direction of required change is given below.

Traditional sandwich	Healthier sandwich
■ Two slices of well-buttered white bread ■ Filled with large portion of Cheddar cheese (60 g)	■ Two thick slices of wholegrain bread spread thinly with low-fat polyunsaturated spread ■ Filling of cold chicken, teaspoon of low-calorie mayonnaise ■ Salad vegetables additionally packed into sandwich
Per sandwich: 41.4 g fat 25.9 g saturated fat 558 kcals	*Per sandwich:* 7.6 g fat 1.9 g saturated fat 289 kcals

A WORD ABOUT SALT

There is now strong evidence that points to the need to cut back on salt for our health. Currently, average daily intakes are around 9 g and we all need to get down to eating no more than 6 g/day (even less for children). Up to 80 per cent of this is hidden in everyday foods (like bread, breakfast cereals, baked beans and meat products) bought from the supermarket and some manufacturers are gradually reducing levels of salt in their products. In addition, food eaten away from home can also contain significant amounts of salt.

Chefs can help customers drive down their salt intakes by being very careful about:

- the products they use in the kitchen – for example, many commercial bouillons, soups and sauce preparations have high levels of salt
- the amount of salt they add to recipes – a heaped teaspoon holds about 8 g salt, so adding one of these to a four-portion recipe will bump up someone's salt intake by around 2 g, which is a considerable part of the 6 g maximum daily allowance.

Salt or sodium? Checking the label

- Most food labels show the amount of sodium per 100 g rather than salt per serving.
- To convert sodium to salt you need to multiply the amount of sodium by 2.5 as 1 g sodium = 2.5 g salt.
- An adult should have less than 6 g salt/day = 2.4 g sodium.

A quick guide

- A *lot of salt* in food is more than 0.5 g sodium/portion (or per 100 g for main meals).
- A *little salt* in food is less than 0.1 g sodium/portion (or per 100 g for main meals).

NUTRITIONAL EVALUATION OF THE RECIPES IN THIS BOOK

The recipes in this book have been analysed by a dietitian using a specialised computer software program (CompEat Pro, Version 5.8.0, released in 2002). This program converts foods into nutrients by drawing on a massive compositional database derived from the laboratory analysis of representative foods. The most recent version of this database, from the Food Standards Agency, has been used, alongside additional compositional data from manufacturers and approved texts.

Every effort has been made to ensure that the figures are as accurate as possible – however they must be treated as estimates only, for a number of reasons:

- the nutrient composition of individual foods can vary and an average value has been used (McCance and Widdowson (2002) *The Composition of Foods* (6th edn), Cambridge: Royal Society of Chemistry/Food Standards Agency)
- where it is more appropriate, analysis is based on the cooked weights (assumed edible portions) of a recipe item
- estimates of average weights have been made for ingredients where no weight was given (e.g. 3 eggs, 12 king-sized prawns)
- where compositional data is not available for a specific 'less common' ingredient (e.g. capers, foie gras, wild mushrooms) then the nearest best equivalent food has been used to provide the nutritional data.

In order to help you interpret this nutritional information, a system has been developed that bands recipes by virtue of their saturated fat and calorie content (see the diagram below).

In terms of health these are perhaps two of the most important parameters to look at, because:

- saturated fat content gives some indication of heart health value
- calories give an indication of fat content (usually the higher the fat content the higher the calorie content) and portion size; this is where people need to exert more control in order to tackle obesity in the UK.

The calorie content is signposted by the counter in the nutritional information box by the recipe.

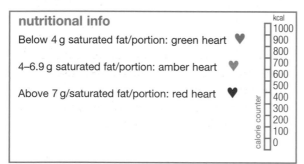

nutritional info

Below 4 g saturated fat/portion: green heart ♥

4–6.9 g saturated fat/portion: amber heart ♥

Above 7 g/saturated fat/portion: red heart ♥

calorie counter

kcal
1000
900
800
700
600
500
400
300
200
100
0

Lots of the recipes in this book are high in saturated fat (red heart), total fat and calories. This is illustrated well in the fish section, where many recipes are 'red' (i.e. contain more than 7 g saturated fat/portion) and have high calorie values even though white fish is inherently low in fat (both saturated and unsaturated). The main
reasons for this are that many of these recipes:

- rely on butter and cream to add flavour and texture
- often add large quantities of oil – to fry, seal or as a dressing
- provide very large portion sizes.

Creative chefs can use their expertise to modify these dishes sensitively, to make healthier changes in a way that does not compromise flavour, texture or appearance. This is the challenge for the next decade.

Further information

To find out more, you may wish to refer to:

- *Dietary Reference Values for Food Energy and Nutrients for the United Kingdom* (Department of Health, 1991) Sets the current main benchmarks for nutrient intakes in the UK. Available from the Stationery Office.

- *Catering For Health* (Department of Health/Food Standards Agency, 2001) Provides further detail on nutrition, plus practical advice on how to integrate healthy eating principles into catering practice. Available from the Stationery Office.

- *Catering For Health: The Recipe File* (The Stationery Office, 1988) Provides healthier recipe ideas for caterers. Available from the Stationery Office.

- *Tipping The Balance* (1999) A 23-minute video on practical tips aimed at encouraging healthier catering practice in the workplace. Available from the Food Standards Agency.

- *The Balance of Good Health* (1996) A pictorial model for food selection. Available in A4 leaflet or A3 poster format. Available from the Food Standards Agency (see www.food.gov.uk). The FSA's website is a useful source of valuable information on healthy eating relevant to caterers.

FOOD SAFETY

This section summarises the underpinning knowledge in the following NVQ units:

- 2GEN3 Maintain food safety when storing, preparing and cooking food
- 3GEN1 Ensure appropriate food safety practices are followed whilst food is prepared, cooked and served

as well as the Food Hygiene (England) Regulations 2005, which have applied to all food businesses since 1 January 2006.

FOOD HYGIENE

Food hygiene is the science and practice of maintaining health and preventing disease. Food must be handled, stored, prepared and served in such a way, and under such conditions, as to prevent as far as possible its contamination. Contamination of food may create a hazard that has the potential to cause harm to a consumer. Hazards may be biological, chemical, physical or allergenic.

Biological hazards

Bacteria are by far the most common cause of food poisoning in the UK. Some bacteria are beneficial to man, such as those in our intestines, and others are needed to manufacture products such as cheese and yoghurt. Other bacteria (also moulds and yeasts) cause food to spoil – discolour, smell unpleasant and/or become sticky or slimy, but are not harmful to health. Pathogenic bacteria (such as salmonella, staphylococcus aureus, clostridium perfringens and bacillus cereus) are the main causes of food poisoning. Low doses of campylobacter jejuni and escherichia coli can also cause illness, especially in vulnerable groups such as young children and

elderly people. These bacteria do not cause any change to the appearance, taste or smell of food, so our senses cannot tell us if the food is contaminated.

Viruses cannot grow in food and are unlikely to be involved in food poisoning; however, they have been implicated in other food-related illnesses, such as hepatitis A.

Chemical hazards

Chemical poisons such as insecticides and pesticides may enter food during growing, and metals during processing. Certain plants, such as rhubarb leaves, poisonous fungi and toxins produced by moulds, also cause chemical food poisoning. It is essential that cleaning materials, rodent poison and the like are stored safely and away from food.

Physical hazards

Contamination of food by foreign bodies such as pieces of glass is dangerous to the consumer. Other undesirable substances may appear in food, such as dead rodents, insects, sticking plasters and jewellery.

Allergenic hazards

Allergic reactions are most commonly caused by the following foods:

- peanuts (also called groundnuts)
- nuts such as almonds, hazelnuts, walnuts, brazil nuts, cashews, pecans, pistachios and macadamia nuts (unrefined nut or seed oils also contain traces of the allergen)
- fish
- shellfish
- sesame seeds
- eggs

- milk
- soya.

Even a very small amount of a food containing an allergen can cause a very severe reaction called anaphylaxis. (See also the section on food allergies, on pages 25–26.)

Some people need to avoid certain foods because of a food intolerance. Examples of foodstuffs like this are gluten, which is the protein found in wheat, rye and barley, and lactose, which is the carbohydrate in milk.

THE FACTS ON BACTERIA

Growth of bacteria

Bacteria multiply, in favourable conditions, by splitting in half. If the temperature is favourable, bacteria will divide every 10–20 minutes. Many thousands will be produced from one bacterium in only four or five hours.

In practice contaminated food will carry many hundreds or thousands of bacteria at the outset.

Favourable conditions for growth are:

- food
- moisture
- warmth
- time.

Bacteria will grow rapidly in foods that have a high protein content and contain moisture, if kept in warm conditions. Foods that need extra care are:

- stocks and sauces, gravy and soup
- meat and meat products
- milk and milk products
- eggs and egg products
- all foods that are handled and reheated
- cooked rice
- shellfish.

Bacteria need moisture to grow and do not survive in dried food such as powdered milk. Spores, however, do survive in dried products, and bacteria will begin to multiply once fluid is added.

Salt and sugar also discourage the growth of bacteria as they deny the bacteria access to the moisture in the food. Today, salt is added to food as a flavour and very high concentrations are needed to discourage bacterial growth. Similarly, only high-sugar products such as jam and crystallised fruits are preserved.

The bacteria responsible for causing food poisoning will grow at temperatures between 5°C and 63°C; this range of temperatures is known as the 'temperature danger zone'. Here are some important guidelines on cooking temperatures and bacteria.

- Most bacteria are killed by a temperature of 70°C, providing the food is held at that point for a sufficient length of time and the centre of the food reaches 70°C.
- Food that has been cooked and is being held prior to service must be kept at 63°C or above.
- Food that has been cooked and is to be chilled and reheated at a later date must be chilled to below 8°C within 90 minutes and reheated to at least 75°C in the centre of the food.
- Bacterial spores are not killed by normal cooking and require temperatures of over 120°C to destroy them.
- Ready-to-eat foods that are served cold must be held at below 5°C prior to service.
- Foods containing vinegar (e.g. pickles) discourage the growth of bacteria.
- Bacterial growth may also be affected by the presence or absence of oxygen.

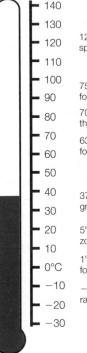

121°C: temperature that is needed to kill spores

75°C: recommended temperature for reheated foods

70°C: temperature required to ensure thorough cooking of food

63°C: minimum temperature at which cooked foods must be kept hot until serving

37°C: temperature at which most bacteria can grow very quickly

5°C to 63°C: range of the 'temperature danger zone'

1°C to 4°C: recommended temperature range for a refrigerator

−18°C to −25°C: recommended temperature range for a freezer

Control of bacteria

It is vital for food handlers to follow good personal hygiene practices to help prevent bacteria from spreading to food. Staphylococcus aureus – found in the nose, throat and wounds – can produce a toxin in food if allowed time to grow in warm conditions. Salmonella and campylobacter jejuni are found in the gut of man and animals, and can contaminate food due to poor personal hygiene.

To avoid the contamination of food with harmful bacteria, follow the guidelines listed below.

Personal hygiene

■ Hands must be washed before preparing food, after handling raw meat, poultry, shellfish, eggs or vegetables, after using the lavatory, after touching your face, hair or nose, after cleaning and removing rubbish.

■ Clean clothes must be worn and these clothes should not be worn outside food preparation areas. Outdoor clothes should be stored away from food preparation areas.

■ Hair should be tied back and a hat and/or hairnet worn when preparing food.

■ Watches or jewellery should not be worn. They can collect and spread dirt and bacteria, or fall in the food.

■ Bacteria can be spread from the skin, hair, nose or mouth, so no smoking or touching the face or hair while preparing food.

■ Food handlers should be 'fit for work' at all times. Anyone who has diarrhoea and/or vomiting should report to their manager, not handle food and, if visiting a doctor, inform him/her that they are a food handler.

■ Cuts and sores must be completely covered with a brightly coloured waterproof dressing.

Separating foods and prevention of cross-contamination

■ Plan deliveries so that, if possible, raw meat and poultry arrive at different times to other foods. Check date marks and temperatures.

■ Defrost foods in a fridge in a covered container *below* ready-to-eat foods.

■ Store ready-to-eat foods separately if possible. If they are kept in the same fridge as other foods, store *above* raw meat and poultry.

■ Prepare raw meat and poultry and other foods in different areas if possible, and clean the areas thoroughly between tasks.

■ Never use the same chopping boards or knives for raw meat/poultry and ready-to-eat foods (use colour coding).

Pest control

■ Check premises and deliveries for signs of pests:
  – rodents leave footprints in dust,

droppings, holes in walls and doors, gnawed goods or packaging, grease or smear marks

- flies – bodies of insects, excreta, maggots and pupae
- cockroaches – eggs and egg cases, actual insects, droppings, smell
- ants – small piles of sand/soil, insects, flying ants
- birds – feathers, droppings, nests, noise, birds themselves.

■ Call a pest control contractor immediately if there are signs of a pest infestation. Throw away any food that may have been contaminated. Clean and disinfect any equipment, surfaces or utensils that may have been touched by pests.
■ Use fine screens on windows, and electronic insect killers.
■ Keep external areas tidy and make sure bins have close-fitting lids.
■ Ensure that any poisons or chemicals used to control pests do not come into contact with food.

Maintenance

■ Repair structural damage as soon as it happens, e.g. damp/chipped plaster, broken tiles, holes in walls or windows.
■ Check extractor fans and filters regularly.
■ Replace chopping boards that are scratched, pitted or scored.
■ Repair or replace any equipment that is damaged and throw away cracked or chipped dishes and tableware.
■ Check that cooking, hot holding, chilling equipment and temperature probes are maintained and working properly. Check the temperature of the equipment and the food, and keep a record of these temperatures.

Cleaning

■ 'Clean as you go' and ensure that you do so very quickly to prevent cross-

contamination and keep working areas clean and tidy.
■ 'Scheduled cleaning' refers to cleaning tasks carried out at regular intervals. All areas and equipment must be included. How often? Who is responsible? What cleaning equipment and chemicals are to be used? How can the cleaning be done safely? Staff must be trained and supervised.
■ Use single-use cloths wherever possible and throw them away after each task. If cloths are reused, they must be thoroughly washed, disinfected and dried between tasks.
■ Use dishwashers to clean and disinfect equipment and utensils as the rinse temperature will kill bacteria and utensils will self-dry. (Chemical disinfectants are not required.)
■ High-priority cleaning includes items that come into contact with food and frequently touched items. Other cleaning includes floors, walls, ceilings, storage areas and display cabinets.
■ Store cleaning materials away from food.
■ Only use chemicals designed for use in food areas, and never mix chemicals.

Chilling down hot food

■ Divide food into smaller portions.
■ Use a blast chiller if possible.
■ If there is not a blast chiller, place covered pans of hot food in cold water, in a cool area of the kitchen and stir the food while it chills.
■ Place in the fridge as soon as the food is sufficiently chilled; do not leave out overnight.

Chilled storage and displaying chilled food

■ Chilled food must be kept below 8°C; fridges and chilled display equipment should be set at 5°C or below.

- The temperature of any equipment must be checked at least once a day and recorded. Use a temperature probe to check food to prove that it is at a 'safe' temperature.
- Foods that need to be kept chilled are those with a 'use by' date, food that says 'keep refrigerated' on the label, food that has been cooked and is not to be served immediately, and ready-to-eat food such as salads, cold meat and desserts.
- Food must not be used after its 'use by' date.
- Label food that has been prepared or cooked as it will have a limited shelf life.
- Do not overload chilled display units, and display food for the shortest time possible.

Cooking safely

- Where appropriate, follow the manufacturer's cooking instructions.
- Pre-heat ovens and grills.
- Do not let raw food touch or drip on to cooked food.
- Seal the surface of whole cuts and whole joints of meat such as beef, lamb and pork to kill harmful bacteria on the surface of the meat.
- Simmer soups and sauces to ensure they are hot enough to kill bacteria, and stir to get rid of cold spots.
- Check that birds are cooked properly in the thickest part of the leg. The meat should not be pink or red, and the juices should be clear. Use a temperature probe to 'spot check' that a temperature of 70°C or above has been reached.
- All processed meat products (sausages, burgers) and combination dishes must be piping hot all the way through.

Reheating

- Pre-heat equipment such as ovens or grills.
- Reheat until piping hot all the way through (do not just 'warm up' food).
- Reheat only small amounts at a time.

- Check the centre of the food with a temperature probe – it should be 75°C for at least 30 seconds in the centre.
- Serve immediately.
- Do not reheat more than once.
- Train and supervise staff.

Hot holding

- Pre-heat hot holding equipment and put only hot food into it.
- Do not use hot holding equipment to cook or reheat food.
- Food in hot holding must be kept at above 63°C as harmful bacteria can grow if the food is not kept hot enough.
- Use a temperature probe for reassurance that the holding temperature is hot enough.

Extra care

- Eggs can contain harmful bacteria and must be cooked thoroughly.
- Use pasteurised egg in any food that will not be cooked or only lightly cooked, e.g. mayonnaise and mousse.
- Use a reputable shellfish supplier. Raw prawns and scallops will change colour and texture when they are cooked, which kills live bacteria. Reheat ready-cooked prawns so that they are piping hot all the way through. Throw away any mussels and clams that do not open during cooking.
- Rice can contain spores of bacillus cereus, which are not killed by boiling the rice. If left in a warm kitchen, the spores germinate, bacteria multiply and food poisoning might occur. Keep the rice hot (above 63°C) prior to service. If you chill down rice, this must be done quickly and the rice must be reheated thoroughly.
- Pulses such as red kidney beans can contain natural toxins that might cause illness. Proper soaking and cooking will destroy these toxins. Tinned pulses have been soaked and cooked already.

FOOD SAFETY LEGISLATION

The Food Hygiene (England) Regulations 2005 will give effect to the EU Regulations and came into force on 1 January 2006. Article 5 of the Regulations states that:

> Food business operators shall put into place, implement and maintain a permanent procedure based on the principles of hazard analysis critical control points (HACCP).
>
> Food handlers must receive adequate instruction and/or training in food hygiene to enable them to handle food safely.
>
> Those responsible for the HACCP-based procedures in the business must have enough relevant knowledge and understanding to ensure the procedures are operated effectively.

The procedures will need to show the environmental health officer that there is effective food safety management in place. This includes the following elements.

- Identifying risks to food safety that might be present or occur within your business. (What can go wrong and where?)
- Controls have been put in place that deal with these risks. (What can I do about it?)
- Controls are carried out. If something goes wrong everyone is clear what to do about it and does it. (What is acceptable? How can I check? What can I do about it?)
- The procedures are kept up to date. (How do I confirm this is still working?)
- Documents and records are kept that show the procedure is working and reviewed. (What documents and records do I need?)
- One of the benefits of having a HACCP system is that it is useful in demonstrating 'due diligence'.

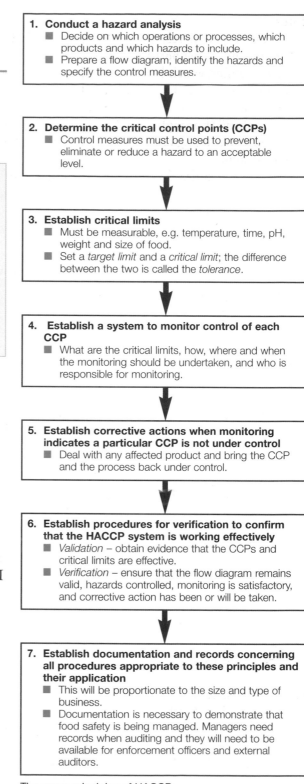

1. **Conduct a hazard analysis**
   - Decide on which operations or processes, which products and which hazards to include.
   - Prepare a flow diagram, identify the hazards and specify the control measures.

2. **Determine the critical control points (CCPs)**
   - Control measures must be used to prevent, eliminate or reduce a hazard to an acceptable level.

3. **Establish critical limits**
   - Must be measurable, e.g. temperature, time, pH, weight and size of food.
   - Set a *target limit* and a *critical limit*; the difference between the two is called the *tolerance*.

4. **Establish a system to monitor control of each CCP**
   - What are the critical limits, how, where and when the monitoring should be undertaken, and who is responsible for monitoring.

5. **Establish corrective actions when monitoring indicates a particular CCP is not under control**
   - Deal with any affected product and bring the CCP and the process back under control.

6. **Establish procedures for verification to confirm that the HACCP system is working effectively**
   - *Validation* – obtain evidence that the CCPs and critical limits are effective.
   - *Verification* – ensure that the flow diagram remains valid, hazards controlled, monitoring is satisfactory, and corrective action has been or will be taken.

7. **Establish documentation and records concerning all procedures appropriate to these principles and their application**
   - This will be proportionate to the size and type of business.
   - Documentation is necessary to demonstrate that food safety is being managed. Managers need records when auditing and they will need to be available for enforcement officers and external auditors.

The seven principles of HACCP

Notes

1 A 'team' of people responsible for the HACCP system must be identified and trained. In a small business, one person may be responsible.

2 When deciding which hazards are significant, their reduction to acceptable levels must be essential to the production of 'safe food' (e.g. poor temperature control or prolonged holding in the danger zone could result in food poisoning bacteria multiplying to large numbers). Not cooking food thoroughly could result in the survival of food poisoning bacteria.

3 Food safety training and effective supervision must take place, and staff training records must be kept.

4 Physical or chemical hazards could occur at any stage in the process.

An example of an HACCP control chart

Process steps	Hazards	Controls	Critical limit	Monitoring	Corrective action
Purchase	Contamination, pathogens, mould or foreign bodies present	Approved supplier			Change supplier
Transport and delivery	Multiplication of harmful bacteria	Refrigerated vehicles		Check delivery vehicles, date marks, temperatures	Reject if >8°C or out of date
Refrigerate	Bacterial growth; further contamination – bacteria, chemicals, etc.	Store below 5°C, separate raw and cooked foods; stock rotation	Food below 5°C	Check and record temperature twice a day; check date marks	Discard if signs of spoilage or past date mark
Prepare	Bacterial growth; further contamination	No more than 30 minutes in 'danger zone'; good personal hygiene; clean equipment and hygienic premises		Supervisor to audit at regular intervals; visual checks; cleaning schedules	Discard if >8°C for 6 hours
Cook	Survival of harmful bacteria	Thorough cooking	75°C	Check and record temperature/time	Continue cooking to 75°C
Prepare for service	Multiplication; contamination	No more than 20 minutes in 'danger zone'	2 hours	Supervisor to audit at regular intervals	Discard if >8°C for 2 hours
Chill	Multiplication; contamination	Blast chiller	90 minutes to below 10°C	Supervisor to audit at regular intervals	Discard if >20°C for 2 hours
Refrigerate	Multiplication; contamination	Store below 5°C; separate raw and ready-to-eat foods	8°C for 4 hours	Check and record temperature twice a day	Discard if >8°C for 4 hours
Reheat	Survival	Reheat to 75°C in centre	75°C (82°C in Scotland)	Check and record temperature of each batch	Continue reheating to 75°C

A practical example

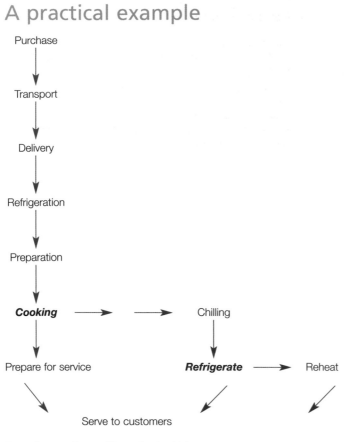

Purchase

Transport

Delivery

Refrigeration

Preparation

Cooking ⟶ ⟶ Chilling

Prepare for service   **Refrigerate** ⟶ Reheat

Serve to customers

Flow diagram for cooking a fresh chicken

Cooking

The *cooking* of the fresh chicken, which can then be held hot prior to service or chilled and refrigerated:

- hazard – pathogenic bacteria present in raw poultry
- control – the chicken must be cooked thoroughly to 75°C to kill all pathogens
- monitor – check the temperature in the thickest parts (thigh and leg joint) using visual check that the juices run clear, and/or a temperature probe
- hot holding – chicken must be kept above 63°C (use temperature probe to check)
- chill and refrigerate – chill to below 10°C within 90 minutes and place in refrigerator
- documentation – temperatures measured and recorded; hot holding equipment checked and maintained; must be hot when food placed in it; record details of any corrective action.

Cold storage

The *cold storage* of the cooked chicken in the refrigerator after cooking and chilling:

- hazard – multiplication of salmonella or campylobacter in the cooked chicken
- control – store below 5°C in refrigerator
- monitor – check temperature of the food (not fridge temperature) is below 5°C
- corrective action – if food has been above 8°C for more than four hours, it should be thrown away; the reason should be investigated and the problem put right
- documentation – temperatures measured and recorded twice a day; record details of any corrective action.

Reasons for HACCP	Adverse consequences
■ Necessary to comply with EU legislation ■ Helps demonstrate due diligence ■ Action is taken before serious problems occur ■ Food safety is integrated into recipe development and menu planning ■ All staff involved in carrying out controls ■ Generates a food safety culture ■ Risks are reduced ■ Internationally recognised	■ More likely to infringe food safety legislation ■ Reduced confidence in management from outside bodies (more frequent inspections) ■ More likely to produce unsafe food ■ Risk of civil action ■ More food is wasted ■ Food handlers do not recognise their involvement and responsibilities

References

The following sources were used as the basis for this section.

■ Food Standards Agency publications:
  – *Safer Food Better Business* (England)
  – *Safe Catering* (Northern Ireland)
  – *CookSafe* (Scotland).
■ www.food.gov.uk for advice and information.

ASSESSING THE TASTE AND QUALITY OF DISHES

It is important for chefs to assess the quality of dishes by tasting. In this way they learn about flavour and are able to become skilled in blending and mixing different flavour components.

Organoleptic assessment simply means using our senses to evaluate food. We detect the flavour of food through the senses of taste and smell. The overall taste of food is made up of one or more primary tastes of which there are five. These are:

■ sweet
■ sour
■ salt
■ bitter
■ umami.

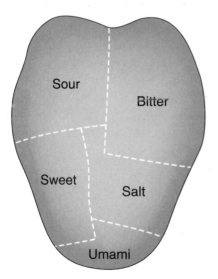

Primary tastes

The sensation of taste is detected by taste buds in the mouth, mostly on the upper surface of the tongue. Different parts of the tongue are particularly sensitive to different primary tastes.

Our sensitivity to different primary tastes varies greatly.

The colour of food is extremely important to our enjoyment of it. People are sensitive to the colour of the food they eat and will reject food that is not considered to have the accepted colour. Colouring matter is sometimes added to food to enhance its attractiveness. There is a strong link between the colour and the flavour of food. Our ability to detect the flavour of food is very much connected with its colour, for if the colour is unusual our sense of taste is confused. For example, if a fruit jelly is red it is likely that the flavour detected will be that of a red-coloured fruit, such as raspberry or strawberry, even if the flavour is lemon or banana.

The depth of colour in food also affects our sense of taste. We associate strong colours with strong flavours. For example, if a series of jellies all contain the same amount of a given flavour, but are of different shades of the same colour, then those having a stronger colour will appear also to have a stronger flavour.

Because the nose shares an airway, the pharynx, with the mouth, we smell and taste our food simultaneously, and what we call the flavour or the 'taste' of the food is really a combination of these two sensations. To quote Brillat-Savarin:

> Smell and taste form a single sense, of which the mouth is the laboratory the nose is the chimney, or to speak more exactly, of which one serves for the tasting of actual bodies and the other for the savouring of their gases.

With taste and smell, then, we first decide whether a particular food is edible and then go on to sample its chemistry simply to enjoy it.

Foods are chemical mixtures, so that we seldom encounter any of the basic taste sensations in isolation. The temperature of food also affects our sensitivity to its taste. Low temperatures decrease the rate of detection. Maximum taste sensitivity ranges from 22 to 44°C (72–105°F). Sweet and sour are enhanced at the upper end, salt and bitter at the lower end. At any given temperature, however, we are much more sensitive to bitter substances than we are to sweet, sour or salty ones, by a factor of about 10,000. Synthetic sweeteners are effective at concentrations nearer to bitter substances than to table sugar.

Our sensitivity to the flavour of food in our mouth is greatest when we breathe out with the mouth closed; air from the lungs passes along the back of the mouth on its way to the nose and brings some food vapours with it.

It is important when assessing food to remember that taste, smell and colour are closely linked and contribute to the overall assessment of the dish. Training and knowledge are therefore essential if one is to develop a discriminating palate and to acquire the ability to identify individual flavours.

Food must be presented in such a way that it can be fully appreciated by the customer. This will vary according to the culture and customs of the various groups in society. It may vary in the different sectors of the industry. For example, airline catering will be different in presentation from a Michelin Star restaurant; school meals will differ from staff feeding. In all cases, the food should look appetising, colourful and easily identifiable. Particular attention must be paid to colour, presentation, size, nutritional balance, texture, flavour and consistency of the various components that make up the dish. The garnish must also be in harmony with the dish.

In the West salt, sweet, sour and bitter were the known basic tastes. In Japan, they talk of the fifth taste called 'umami', or 'xian' as it is known in China. Asian cuisine is based on umami-rich ingredients.

The Chinese have been referring to umami for more than 1200 years. In his book *The Physiology of Taste*, published 1825, Brillat-Savarin makes reference to osmosone, generally considered a forerunner to the concept of umami.

Umami is found naturally in many foods, both animal and vegetable. It is a combination of proteins, amino acids and nucleotides, which include not only glutamates, but also inosinates and ganylates. When the proteins break down through cooking, fermenting, ageing or ripening, the umami flavours intensify.

To find out more, visit the Umami Information Centre website at www.umaminfo.com.

HORS D'OEUVRE & BUFFET ITEMS

COLD PREPARATIONS

The preparation of hors d'oeuvre and salads offers wide scope for ingenuity and creativity.

Almost all foods can be used, raw or cooked, and if carefully selected and blended, and mixed where necessary with suitable dressings can produce attractively appetising and highly popular dishes.

Ingredients

The following are just some of the ingredients that can be used.

Leaves
- round lettuce
- cos (romaine) lettuce
- iceberg lettuce
- oak leaf lettuce
- radicchio
- curly endive
- chicory
- cress
- watercress
- rocket
- corn salad (lamb's lettuce)
- sorrel
- dandelion
- escarole (broad-leafed endive, Batavian lettuce)
- nasturtium
- red cabbage
- white cabbage
- spinach
- Chinese leaves

Vegetables (raw)
- celery
- carrots
- onions
- spring onions
- pimentos (peppers)
- radishes
- tomatoes
- mushrooms
- cucumber
- celeriac
- sorrel
- spinach

Units covered
3FPC10, 3FPC9, 3FP1, 3FP3, 3FP4, 3FP5, 3FC1, 3FC2, 3FC3, 3FC4, 3FC6, 3FC11

LIST OF RECIPES

Recipe no	page no
Gels and setting agents	
2 Cep and truffle jelly dice	53
1 Crab and ginger jelly discs	53
Sauces, chutneys and dressings	
15 Bacon and hazelnut vinaigrette	57
14 Balsamic dressing	57
11 Basic vinaigrette	56
4 Cumberland sauce	55
17 Fig and apple chutney	58
18 Fig and port reduction	58
5 Fresh tomato sauce (raw) or coulis	55
6 Garlic-flavoured mayonnaise	55
3 Green or herb sauce	55
16 Herb oil	58
8 Mustard and dill sauce	56
9 Red onion confit/marmalade	56
13 Smoked oil	57
7 Tofu salad dressing	56
12 Truffle dressing	57
10 Yoghurt and cucumber dressing	56
Compound salads	
23 Beetroot and orange	60
25 Carrot, coriander and almond	61
22 Celeriac remoulade	60
21 French beans, bacon and hazelnut	60
26 New potato, mustard and mint	61
24 Penne with mozzarella and olive	60

Recipe no	page no
19 Smoked salmon, avocado and walnut salad	59
20 Tropical salad	59
Miscellaneous	
30 Avocado mousse	63
28 Cold mousses	62
31 Salmon marinated in dill (gravlax)	63
32 Stuffed round fish	64
27 Tian of green and white asparagus	61
29 Tomato mousse	63
Cold fish preparations	
42 Beetroot and treacle cured salmon	68
34 Cornish crab salad	65
39 Fish mousse	67
35 Herring, apple and potato salad	66
41 Hot smoked mackerel	67
38 Red mullet with tomatoes, garlic and saffron	66
33 Salmon and asparagus salad with a rose petal dressing and shiso	64
40 Salmon mousse	67
37 Shellfish platter	66
36 Smoked fish platter	66
Buffet items	
47 Aspic jelly 1	73
48 Aspic jelly 2	73
46 Aspic jelly flavoured with wine	73
44 Bouchées	72

Vegetables (cooked)

- sweetcorn
- baby sweetcorn
- beetroot
- potatoes
- carrots
- turnips
- peas
- beans – French, broad, runner
- artichokes
- Jerusalem artichokes
- asparagus
- broccoli

Herbs

- chives
- parsley
- flat parsley
- basil
- mint
- coriander leaves
- fennel leaves
- dill
- thyme
- lovage
- sweet cicely
- marjoram
- tarragon
- bay leaves
- chervil

Pulses

- black-eyed beans
- flageolets
- borlotti beans
- haricot beans
- chickpeas
- mung beans
- red kidney beans

Pasta

- macaroni, spaghetti, etc.
- rice – long grain, wild
- noodles

Fruits

- grapefruit
- orange
- apples
- grapes
- guava
- kiwi
- bananas
- melon

Recipe no		page no
43	Light buffet items	72
45	Savouries using barquettes and tartlets	73

Cold meat preparations

54	Cured belly of pork	75
53	Serving of cold cooked meats	74
50	Serving of cold duck	74
51	Serving of cold game	74
49	Serving of cold roast chicken	74
52	Serving of cold turkey or goose	74

Terrines, pies, ballotines and galantines

56	Ballotines	78
57	Chicken galantine	78
58	Game pies	79
59	Pâtés and terrines	80
60	Pie pastry	82
61	Raised pork pie	82
62	Scotch salmon terrine with scallops	83
55	Terrines	76
63	Terrine of free-range chicken and foie gras	84
64	Veal and ham pie	85

Crostinis and nibbles

65	Anchovy sticks	86
66	Brioches	86
71	Char-siu	88
72	Crostini	88
67	Dartois	86

Recipe no		page no
75	Goats' cheese crostini	89
68	Lamb, peach and cashew bitoks	87
69	Spinach and cheese sticks	87
70	Spring rolls	87
73	Tomato and aubergine crostini	88
74	Vegetable samosas	89

Canapés – hot and cold

76	Courgette blossoms in tempura batter	90
86	Cream cheese and smoked eel	94
83	Cucumber raita	93
79	Eastern spiced salmon tartare served on a silver spoon	91
90	Foie gras kromesky	95
78	Lightly jellied tomato and tea consommé	91
84	Mini baked potatoes – crème fraîche	93
81	Mirin-glazed tuna and pickled ginger	92
87	Parma ham and tarragon tart	94
88	Parmesan tuiles	94
92	Plum tomato and goats' cheese	95
89	Salmon tartare	95
85	Smoked salmon with blinis and caviar	93
77	Snapper and mango salad	90
80	Soba noodle norimaki	92
82	Sweet potato kofta	93
91	Wild mushroom risotto balls	95

- dates
- mango
- avocado
- pineapples
- cherries
- figs

Nuts

- walnuts
- hazelnuts
- almonds
- peanuts
- Brazil nuts
- cashew nuts
- pecans
- pine kernels

Miscellaneous

- hard-boiled eggs
- cheese
- rice
- poppyseeds
- sunflower seeds
- sesame seeds
- olives
- gherkins
- capers
- mung bean sprouts
- bamboo shoots
- water chestnuts

Meats

- cooked meats – beef/lamb/pork
- sausages, salamis
- chicken
- turkey
- duck
- ham
- bacon
- tongue

Fish

- anchovy
- tuna
- salmon
- sardine
- white fish
- mackerel
- herring
- crab
- lobster
- shrimp
- prawn
- mussel
- cockle
- squid

Cold dressings and sauces

Vinaigrette and mayonnaise are used extensively for salads, but sour cream, tofu and yoghurt may also be used.

Oils

- olive
- corn
- sunflower
- peanut
- sesame
- safflower
- walnut
- soya

Vinegars

- cider
- red wine
- white wine
- malt
- herb
- lemon
- raspberry
- balsamic

Vinaigrettes

with the addition of:

- garlic
- capers
- curry paste
- eggs
- blue cheese
- herbs

Seasonings

- English mustard
- French mustard
- Dijon mustard
- German mustard
- salt
- pepper
- spices
- herb salt

Herbs

- chervil
- tarragon
- thyme
- mint
- basil
- marjoram
- coriander
- fennel
- dill

Mayonnaise

with the addition of:

- tomato ketchup
- horseradish
- lemon juice
- herbs
- capers
- gherkins
- curry powder
- herbs

Also

- soured cream
- tofu
- yoghurt
- smetana
- crème fraîche
- quark

Fruit or vegetable sauces

see pages 110–111

GELS AND SETTING AGENTS

Agar-agar

Agar powder:

- is prepared from red seaweed
- is stabilised in the presence of water
- is insoluble in cold water, but dissolves to give random coils in boiling water (gels)
- must be added to a cold solution, and boiled
- is used in the food industry in icings, glazes, processed cheese, jelly sweets and marshmallow
- is used as an alternative to gelatine for vegetarians.

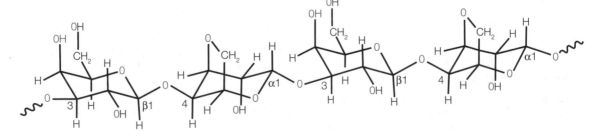

Composition of agar-agar

Here is some more useful information about agar-agar.

- A total of 99.5 per cent of an agar jelly will remain solid up to 85°C.
- Agar jellies will become liquid again at 95°C (thermoreversible).
- Agar jellies will begin to solidify after boiling at 35°C–43°C.
- Upon mechanical action (high sheer stresses such as weight and vigorous stirring) agar jellies will break down in a 'crumble' effect.
- Agar jellies are best made from solutions that are neutral.

- In a neutral solution, 99.5 per cent of the liquid will solidify; lowering the pH (getting more acidic) will lower the solution's retention properties. Increasing the quantity of agar can help with this, but a harder 'mouth-feel' is the end result.
- Enzymes from kiwi fruit, papayas, pineapple, peaches, mangos, guavas and figs will break down agar if uncooked.
- Use 0.9 g agar for 100 g of a neutral liquid.
- Use 1.1–1.3 g of agar for 100 g of an acidic liquid.

1 Crab and ginger jelly discs

	4 portions	10 portions
ginger root, peeled and sliced	50 g	125 g
water	250 ml	500 ml
sugar	20 g	50 g
cold ginger liquid	200 ml	500 ml
agar	1.8 g	4.5 g
white crab meat	30 g	60 g

1 Bring the ginger root, water and sugar to the boil, cover with clingfilm and leave to cool.

2 Strain this ginger liquid through a muslin cloth and add the agar.

3 Bring to boil again, pour onto moulds (plates can be used) so liquid height is 3-5 mm.

4 Sprinkle the crab meat on top of the liquid. Leave to cool.

5 Cut out using a round cutter.

2 Cep and truffle jelly dice

	10 portions
onion, thinly sliced	100 g
flat mushrooms, thinly sliced	250 g
clove garlic, chopped	1
sprig of thyme	1
dried ceps	100 g
Noilly Prat vermouth	100 ml

1 Sweat the onions in a little oil. Caramelise until very dark.

2 Add the flat mushrooms, cook until dry and deeply caramelised.

3 Add the garlic, thyme and dried ceps, sweat for 2 minutes and add the Noilly Prat. Cook for a further 10 minutes on a low heat until the mixture is really dark.

4 Add 600 g cold water, bring to boil and simmer, reducing liquid by half.

5 Cover with clingfilm and leave to cool.

6 Once cold, strain through a muslin cloth, and weigh:
   - 200 g mushroom stock
   - 1.8 g agar
   - 7 g chopped black truffle.

7 Add the agar to the stock and bring to boil.

8 Pour into moulds so height of liquid is approx. 6–8 mm.

9 Sprinkle truffle into liquid and leave to cool.

10 When set, cut jelly into even-sized dice.

Gelatine

What is gelatine?

Gelatine is a pure protein obtained from animal raw materials containing collagen. This natural and healthy food has excellent gelling strength – but gelatine can do a lot more. Because of its broad spectrum of capabilities it is used in the most varied industries for a large number of products.

A high-quality protein for humans

Without protein there would be no human life. Other nutrients, such as fats and carbohydrates, can replace each other in the human metabolism over long periods, but people need protein every day. The natural foodstuff gelatine is therefore of inestimable value to the human organism.

Amino acids are the building blocks of proteins. The human body is capable of making all the proteins it needs from amino acids. However, there are ten amino acids that the body cannot produce itself and that therefore have to be consumed regularly in the diet. They are called essential amino acids. Gelatine contains a total of 18 amino acids, including nine of the ten essential amino acids.

Gelatine contains:

- 84–90 per cent protein
- 1–2 per cent mineral salts
- the rest is water.

Gelatine does not contain any preservatives or other additives. It is free of cholesterol and purines (uric acid compounds).

A multi-faceted product

The most common form of gelatine is edible gelatine. This is used as an ingredient in yoghurts, deliciously light creamy foods and jelly. It gives wine gums their unique shape. Edible gelatine is a natural foodstuff and is therefore – like any other foodstuff – subject to stringent purity regulations.

An important criterion for determining the quality of gelatine is known as the 'Bloom value', which is generally between 50 and 300. This is used to determine the firmness and jelly strength of gelatine. The higher the Bloom value, the higher the jelly strength of the gelatine. Gelatine is unique in its reliable stabilisation, gelling and handling.

Leaf gelatine

One form of gelatine is leaf gelatine. Cut into rectangles with a pattern resulting from the manufacturing process, and elastic in its movements, at first glance it looks more like a work of art. Leaf gelatine can easily be portioned and is used mostly in the household, in catering, and by bakers, confectioners and butchers.

Hydrolysates

Like all gelatines, gelatine hydrolysates are pure collagen proteins, but do not have any gelling strength. They act as a source of protein, a carrier, a means of reducing common salt and enhancing flavour, and a means of clarifying drinks as well as collagen protein in dietetic nutrition. Drinkable gelatine is available in pharmacies and health food stores.

Instant gelatine

Instant gelatines are also soluble in cold water. They were specially developed to prevent the need to heat gelatine in order to dissolve it. Instant gelatines are often used to stabilise foodstuffs such as gâteaux, desserts, and other sweet and cold dishes.

SAUCES, CHUTNEYS AND DRESSINGS

3 Green or herb sauce

	4 portions	10 portions
spinach, tarragon, chervil, chives, watercress	50 g	125 g
mayonnaise	250 ml	625 ml

1 Pick, wash, blanch and refresh the green leaves.

2 Squeeze dry.

3 Pass through a very fine sieve.

4 Mix with the mayonnaise.

May be served with cold salmon or salmon trout.

4 Cumberland sauce

	4 portions	10 portions
redcurrant jelly	100 ml	250 ml
chopped shallots	5 g	12 g
lemon juice	¼	½
port	2 tbsp	5 tbsp
juice and zest of orange	1	2
English mustard	¼ level tsp	½ tsp

1 Warm and melt the jelly.

2 Blanch the shallots well and refresh.

3 Add the shallots to the jelly with the remainder of the ingredients, except the orange zest.

4 Cut a little find julienne of orange zest, blanch, refresh and add to the sauce.

May be served with cold ham.

nutritional info

This recipe provides:
336 kcals/1410 kJ
0.3 g fat
(of which 0.0 g saturated)
78.8 g carbohydrate
(of which 78.6 g sugars)
1.1 g protein
1.2 g fibre

♥

calorie counter

kcal
1000
900
800
700
600
500
400
300
200
100
0

5 Fresh tomato sauce (raw) or coulis v

	4 portions	10 portions
tomatoes, skinned and pips removed	400 g	1¼ kg
vinegar	½ tbsp	1½ tbsp
oil	3 tbsp	8 tbsp
salt and mill pepper		
chopped parsley and tarragon	1 tbsp	3 tbsp

1 Squeeze the tomatoes to remove excess juice then liquidise the flesh.

2 Place in a bowl and gradually whisk in the vinegar and oil.

3 Season and mix in the herbs.

Note: Other herbs (e.g. basil, oregano) may be used in place of tarragon.

6 Garlic-flavoured mayonnaise

	4 portions	10 portions
egg yolks	2	5
vinegar or lemon or lime juice	2 tsp	5 tsp
salt, ground white pepper		
mustard	⅛ tsp	⅜ tsp
cloves of garlic (juice or chopped)	2	5
olive oil or vegetable oil	250 ml	625 ml
boiling water	1 tsp	2 tsp

1 Place the yolks, vinegar or juice, seasoning and garlic in a bowl and mix well.

2 Gradually pour on the oil very slowly, whisking continuously.

3 Add the boiling water, whisking well.

4 Correct the seasoning.

Other suggested additions:
(a) tomato ketchup
(b) anchovy essence
(c) tomato and anchovy essence
(d) horseradish, finely grated.

7 Tofu salad dressing ▮v▮

This soya bean curd can be used as a salad dressing. As tofu is tasteless it can be flavoured with garlic, lemon, mint, etc. Tofu has to be mixed to a creamy consistency before use with skimmed milk, lemon juice, etc.

Quark, créme fraîche, fromage frais and yoghurt may also be used.

8 Mustard and dill sauce

	4 portions	10 portions
mayonnaise	125 ml	300 ml
white wine	60 ml	150 ml
caster sugar	12 g	60 g
coarse mustard	1 dsp	2½ dsp
fresh chopped dill	½ tsp	1 tsp
salt and pepper		

Mix into the mayonnaise the rest of the ingredients. Correct the seasoning with salt and pepper.

Note: There are many variations to this recipe: 60 ml double cream (150 ml for 10 portions) or natural yoghurt may be added; alternatively a French dressing base may be used in place of mayonnaise.

Can be served with gravlax (see page 63).

9 Red onion confit/marmalade

red onions, sliced	1 kg
butter	50 g
soft brown sugar	50 g
red wine vinegar	250 ml
blackcurrant cordial or red wine (optional)	60 ml

1 Slowly sauté the onions in the butter in a thick-bottomed pan.

2 Cook thoroughly but with little or no colour.

3 Add the other ingredients and reduce slowly until slightly thick.

4 Season lightly with salt and mill pepper.

5 When cold, store in covered jars or basins in the refrigerator.

Note: Can be served as a garnish/accompaniment to many dishes hot or cold.

10 Yoghurt and cucumber dressing

	4 portions	10 portions
cucumber	100 g	250 g
natural yoghurt	125 ml	300 ml
salt and pepper		
chopped mint	¼ tsp	¾ tsp

1 Peel the cucumber, blanch in boiling water for 5 minutes, refresh and drain.

2 Purée the cucumber in a food processor.

3 Add the cucumber to the natural yoghurt, season and finish with freshly chopped mint.

11 Basic vinaigrette

Makes approx. ¼ litre

wholegrain mustard	1 tsp
sherry vinegar	25 ml
grapeseed/corn oil	50 ml
light olive oil	125 ml
seasoning	

1 Place the mustard, vinegar and corn/grapeseed oil into a large bowl and whisk to an emulsion.

2 Slowly add the olive oil, about 50 ml at a time, bringing to an emulsion at each stage. Add seasoning.

3 Pour into a jar or bottle and store in the fridge until ready to use. If the mix separates during storage, simply shake the bottle or jar to re-emulsify.

12 Truffle dressing

Makes 200 ml

egg yolk	1
balsamic vinegar	1 tsp
sherry vinegar	1 tsp
chopped truffle (optional)	½ tsp
olive oil	50 ml
corn or grapeseed oil	50 ml
truffle oil	20 ml
seasoning	

1 Place the egg yolk in a mixing bowl with both the vinegars and chopped truffle if using, and whisk until a whitish foam appears.

2 Then slowly add the oils, check the seasoning and store in a plastic airtight container for up to 2 days.

13 Smoked oil v

Makes 200 ml

wood chippings	200 g
vegetable oil	200 ml

1 Place the wood chippings in a pan and start to smoke. Remove from the heat.

2 Place the oil in a bowl and put the bowl into the pan. Cover with a damp cloth and allow to smoke for 1 hour and 30 minutes.

3 When ready allow the oil to cool. Store in an airtight container.

Seasonal salad dressed with smoked oil and beetroot dressing

14 Balsamic dressing v

Makes approx. 250 ml

balsamic vinegar	50 ml
grapeseed/corn oil	50 ml
light olive oil	125 ml
seasoning	

1 Place the vinegar and corn/grapeseed oil in a large bowl and whisk to an emulsion.

2 Slowly add the olive oil, about 50 ml at a time, bringing to an emulsion at each stage. Season.

3 Pour into a jar or bottle and store in the fridge until ready to use. If the mix separates during storage, simply shake the bottle or jar to re-emulsify.

15 Bacon and hazelnut vinaigrette

	10 portions
oil	200 ml
vinegar	50 ml
toasted hazelnuts, lightly chopped	100 g
crisp bacon, cut into fine strips	100 g
seasoning	
chopped parsley to order	

1 Make a dressing with the oil and vinegar.

2 Add the hazelnuts and bacon, and season.

3 Add the chopped parsley to order.

16 Herb oil v

Makes 200 ml

flat leaf parsley, fresh picked	25 g
chives	10 g
basil leaves, fresh picked	10 g
spinach, fresh picked	100 g
corn oil	250 ml

1 Blanch all the herbs and the spinach for 1½ minutes, drain well.

2 Place with the oil in a liquidiser and blitz for 2½ minutes.

3 Pour into a clear container and allow to settle.

4 Decant when rested.

17 Fig and apple chutney

	6 portions
cooking apple, peeled and cut into 2.5 cm dice	1
onion, diced	25 g
dried fig, chopped	50 g
white wine vinegar	25 ml
English mustard	⅛ tbsp
cayenne pepper	pinch
clove garlic	½
sultanas	50 g
sugar	10 g

1 Combine all the ingredients in a heavy saucepan.

2 Bring to the boil then lower the heat and simmer for 2 hours until thick.

3 Add a splash of water if the mixture dries out before the 2 hours are up. Leave to cool, then briefly liquidise the mixture until it is the consistency of jam. Store in the refrigerator.

Terrine of ham hock and foie gras served with fig and apple chutney

18 Fig and port reduction

Makes 400 ml

port	500 ml
sugar	50 g
fresh figs	3
dried figs	60 g
vanilla pods	2

1 Boil the ingredients for 3-4 minutes, liquidise, reduce and pass to a wet jam consistency.

Note: Use to accompany terrines (recipes 55 and 63).

COMPOUND SALADS

19 Smoked salmon, avocado and walnut salad

	4 portions	10 portions
smoked salmon	100 g	250 g
avocado pears	2	5
walnuts	50 g	125 g
fennel or parsley	1 tsp	1 tbsp
vinaigrette	1 tbsp	2 tbsp
radicchio		
curly endive		

1 Cut the smoked salmon in strips and neatly slice the peeled avocado.

2 Carefully mix together with the walnuts, chopped fennel or parsley and vinaigrette.

3 Neatly pile on a base of radicchio and curly endive leaves.

Note: Flaked cooked fresh salmon or flaked smoked mackerel can be used to create a variation of this salad.

nutritional info

1 portion provides:
341 kcals/1413 kJ
32 g fat
(of which 4.8 g saturated)
2.7 g carbohydrate
(of which 1.4 g sugars)
10.7 g protein
4.2 g fibre

Calculated with 2 tbsp vinaigrette

kcal
1000
900
800
700
600
500
400
300
200
100
0

calorie counter

20 Tropical salad v

	4 portions	10 portions
melon	½*	1–2*
avocado, skinned, stoned and diced	1	2–3
kiwi fruit, peeled and sliced	1	2–3
lemon, juice of	1	2–3
olive or vegetable oil	2 tbsp	5 tbsp
salt and pepper		
mint, chopped		
Chinese leaves		

* Depending on type used/size.

1 Remove the skin and seeds from the melon, and dice.

2 Place with the avocado and kiwi fruit.

3 Add the lemon juice and carefully mix with the oil, seasoning and chopped mint.

4 Dress on a bed of Chinese leaves.

Note: Other fruits, such as fresh figs and paw paw, can also be used. In place of oil, bind with softened, creamed tofu, natural yoghurt or mayonnaise. If tofu is used it must be mixed to a creamy consistency with skimmed milk or lemon juice.

21 French beans, bacon and hazelnut

	20 portions
haricots verts	500 g
bacon rashers (back, unsmoked)	6
vinaigrette	50 ml
chives, chopped	1 tsp
roasted hazelnuts, chopped	75 g
salt and pepper	

1 Blanch the haricots verts in boiling water for 3 minutes. Refresh in ice cold water and drain.

2 Grill the bacon, remove the fat and slice into thin strips.

3 In a large mixing bowl mix together the haricots verts, bacon, vinaigrette, chives and hazelnuts.

4 Taste and season.

22 Celeriac remoulade

	25 portions
large celeriac, cut into in fine julienne	2 (400 g)
horseradish relish and mayonnaise, in equal quantities to bind	
lemon, juice of	1
seasoning	

1 Mix all ingredients together and correct the seasoning.

23 Beetroot and orange

	15 portions
large beetroot, raw	200 g
Valencia oranges	2
vinaigrette	30 ml

1 Wash and steam the beetroot for approximately 1 hour. Check to see if they are cooked by using the tip of a small knife to effortlessly pierce their flesh.

2 Allow to cool and peel.

3 Cut the beetroot into 1 cm dice.

4 Peel and segment the oranges.

5 Just prior to serving, mix all the ingredients and season well.

24 Penne with mozzarella and olive

	6 portions
cooked penne pasta, cold	500 g
extra virgin olive oil	75 g
salt and pepper	
black pitted olives	100 g
buffala mozzarella	1 ball

1 In a bowl, mix the pasta, olive oil and salt and pepper.

2 Slice the olives in half and dice the mozzarella into even chunks.

3 Add to the pasta and mix together.

25 Carrot, coriander and almond

	6 portions
flaked almonds	20 g
coriander	20 leaves
carrots, large	500 g
sea salt and black pepper	
vinaigrette	20 ml

1 Place the almonds on a tray and toast under a hot salamander for approximately 2 minutes.

2 Wash the picked coriander. Dry and cut into julienne with a sharp knife.

3 Peel the carrots on a slight angle and slice very thin.

4 Season lightly with coarse sea salt and black pepper.

5 Mix in the other ingredients.

26 New potato, mustard and mint

	8 portions
new or ratte potatoes (washed)	1 kg
mint	bunch
shallots	2
mayonnaise	100 ml
wholegrain mustard	1 tsp
seasoning	

1 Place the potatoes in salted boiling water.

2 Boil for 12 minutes then place the mint in the water and boil for 1 minute.

3 Remove the pan from the heat and allow the residual heat to finish the cooking and the mint to infuse.

4 Meanwhile, slice the shallots, and add to the mayonnaise and mustard.

5 Once the potatoes have cooled completely, cut into 1 cm dice (uneven is fine) and mix with the mayonnaise mixture.

6 Adjust seasoning and serve.

MISCELLANEOUS

27 Tian of green and white asparagus
Anthony Marshall

garlic	50 g
thyme	1 bunch
black pepper	10 g
gelatine sheets	6
green asparagus (medium)	2 kg
white asparagus (medium)	2 kg
salt	10 g
shallots	500 g
chives	1 bunch
extra virgin olive oil	100 ml
sundried tomatoes in oil	100 g

To make the jelly:

1 Bring to the boil in a pan 500 ml of water. Add a touch of garlic, thyme and black pepper.

2 Melt 6 sheets of gelatine in warm water and add to the bouillon.

3 Pass through a fine sieve and leave to cool.

To make the tian:

4 Trim and peel the asparagus.

5 Cook the colours separately in salted water infused with thyme for approx. 4–5 mins. Cool down immediately in iced water.

6 Trim each length of asparagus to exactly 8 cm long. (Keep the trimmings.)

7 Slice the trimmings of asparagus and sauté with the shallots and remaining garlic, leave to cool.

8 Using a metal ring (approx. 7 cm in diameter) place the spears of asparagus around the inside of the ring in alternate colours. Use the sautéed mixture to fill the centre of the ring and pack tightly.

9 Pour the jelly over the top of the mixture inside the metal ring and place in the refrigerator to set.

To make the sauce:

10 Finely chop the chives and add to the olive oil. Cut the tomatoes into a find julienne and add to the mixture. Season well.

To plate:

11 Heat the metal ring of asparagus very quickly with a flame torch to loosen the edges. Place in the centre of a plate and carefully spoon the dressing in a circle around the edge.

28 Cold mousses

A mousse is basically a purée of the bulk ingredient from which it takes its name, with the addition of a suitable non-dairy or cream sauce, cream and aspic jelly. The result should be a light creamy mixture, just sufficiently set to stand when removed from a mould.

Care must be taken when mixing not to curdle the mixture as this will produce a 'bitty' appearance with small white grains of cream showing. The cream should only be half whipped as a rubbery texture will otherwise be obtained; also, if fresh cream is over-whipped the mixture will curdle.

Various types of mousse are used as part of other dishes as well as dishes on their own. A mould of a particular substance may be filled with a mousse of the same basic ingredient. Whole decorated chickens may have the breast reformed with a mousse such as ham, tomato or foie gras. Mousse may be piped to fill cornets of ham, borders for chicken suprêmes or cold egg dishes.

Although most recipes quote a lined mould for the mousse to be placed in when being served as an individual dish, mousses may often be poured into a glass bowl (or even smaller dishes for individual portions) to be decorated on top when set, then glazed. Although truffle is frequently quoted, garnishing paste or other materials are now used for decoration.

Note: Convenience aspic jelly granules may be used for all mousse recipes.

29 Tomato mousse

	4 portions	10 portions
onion, finely chopped	50 g	125 g
butter or margarine	50 g	125 g
white stock or consommé	500 ml	2½ litre
tomatoes, skinned, deseeded and diced	250 g	600 g
tomato purée	25 g	60 g
salt and pepper		
pinch of paprika		
velouté	125 ml	600 ml
aspic jelly	125 ml	600 ml
whipping cream, half whipped	125 ml	600 ml

1 Sweat the onion in the butter or margarine without colour.

2 Moisten with the stock or consommé, and reduce by half.

3 Add the tomatoes and tomato purée. Simmer for approximately 20 minutes, season and add paprika.

4 Add the velouté and aspic, simmer for 2 minutes, then liquidise.

5 Place in a basin on ice, stir until setting point, and fold in the half-whipped cream.

6 Use as required: either place in individual moulds, allow to set, turn out on to individual plates, decorate and serve as a first course, or use as part of a cold dish.

30 Avocado mousse

	4 portions	10 portions
large avocado	1	2–3
lemon, juice of	1	2–3
salt and pepper		
mayonnaise	60 ml	150 ml
aspic jelly	60 ml	150 ml
or sheets gelatine	1–2	2–3
double cream or unsweetened vegetable creamer	60 ml	150 ml
salad vegetables for garnish		

1 Cut the avocado in half, remove the stone and peel.

2 Pass through a sieve or liquidise in a food processor.

3 Add the lemon juice and seasoning and place in a bowl.

4 Stir in the mayonnaise and aspic jelly or the soaked, melted gelatine.

5 Place on ice and stir until setting point, then carefully fold in the beaten cream.

6 Pour into individual china dishes or dariole moulds.

7 When set, unmould the darioles on to plates and decorate with lettuce, tomatoes, radish and cucumber.

31 Salmon marinated in dill (gravlax)

	4 portions	10 portions
middle-cut, fresh, descaled raw salmon	¾ kg	1¾ kg
bunch dill, washed and chopped	1	2
caster sugar	25 g	60 g
salt	25 g	60 g
peppercorns, crushed	1 tbsp	2 tbsp

1 Cut the salmon lengthwise and remove all the bones.

2 Place one half, skin-side down, in a deep dish.

3 Add the dill, sugar, salt and peppercorns.

4 Cover with the other piece of salmon, skin-side up.

5 Cover with foil, lay a tray or dish on top, and evenly distribute weights on the foil.

6 Refrigerate for 48 hours, turning the fish every 12 hours and basting with the liquid produced by the ingredients. Separate the halves of salmon and baste between them.

7 Replace the foil, tray and weights between basting.

8 Lift the fish from the marinade, remove the dill and seasoning, wash, dry and top with chopped dill.

9 Place the halves of salmon on a board, skin-side down.

10 Slice thinly, detaching the slice from the skin.

11 Garnish gravlax with lemon and serve with mustard and dill sauce (see page 56).

32 Stuffed round fish

Trout, red mullet and sea bass should have the back bone removed, leaving the head and tail intact on the skin. The cavity can then be filled with a suitable stuffing:

- trout with a salmon or lobster forcemeat with diced mushrooms

- red mullet with a white fish forcemeat with chopped fennel

- sea bass with a crayfish forcemeat with diced crayfish.

The fish is then reshaped (held in shape with greased greaseproof paper if necessary) and gently poached in a little stock or stock and wine in the oven.

When cooled the fish may be served:

- plain with a suitable accompanying cold sauce

- the skin removed, the fish cleaned, garnished with salad

- decorated and coated with a fish aspic or fish wine aspic.

COLD FISH PREPARATIONS

33 Salmon and asparagus salad with a rose petal dressing and shiso Anthony Marshall

	4 portions	10 portions
asparagus spears	20	50
thyme	20 g	50 g
Scotch smoked salmon	200 g	500 g
shiso	100 g	250 g
curly endive (spider lettuce)	100 g	250 g
oakleaf	40 g	100 g
lollo rosso	2	5
rose head	4	10
yellow tomatoes (skinned)	4	10
red tomatoes (skinned)	4	10

1 Peel and clean the asparagus and place into boiled salted water with thyme to add some flavour. Leave until the tips are cooked.

2 Remove and place into a bowl of iced water to refresh.

3 Cut the smoked salmon into fine slivers.

4 Wash and mix the salads together and cut the rose petals into fine strips (ready to add to the dressing).

5 Place the salmon neatly on the plate with five tips of asparagus in the centre, with yellow and red tomato quarters in between.

6 Add the dressing (see below) to the salad, drain and place salad in the middle of the salmon and sprinkle with shiso.

Note: Shiso is a small-leafed purple-coloured herb similar to mustard and cress with a basil-like flavour. The dish may also be finished with fine slices of radish and herb mayonnaise.

Rose petal dressing

	4 portions	10 portions
rose petal vinegar	1 tsp	2½ tsp
virgin oil	1 tsp	2½ tsp
shallot, finely cut	30 g	75 g

Mix the oil and vinegar together, then add the shallots and finely cut rose petals (preferably yellow and red ones).

34 Cornish crab salad with lime and pimentos, grilled scallops, and a warm potato and chive salad on a red pepper coulis
Ron Maxfield

	4 portions	10 portions
small new potatoes	200 g	500 g
white crab meat	200 g	500 g
mixed lettuce – oakleaf, lollo rosso, radicchio, frisée		
sprigs of dill	5	12
mayonnaise	100 ml	250 ml
chopped chives	2 tbsp	5 tbsp
pepper coulis	12 tbsp	30 tbsp
scallops	12	30
sprigs of chervil	12	30
sprig of thyme		
Coulis		
red peppers	2	5
shallots	2	5
fish stock	250 ml	600 ml
salt and pepper		
Salad dressing		
finely diced pimento (red, yellow, green)	2 tbsp	5 tbsp
walnut oil	100 ml	250 ml
white wine vinegar	2 tsp	5 tsp
Dijon mustard	1 tsp	2–3 tsp
lime, juice of	1	2–3
salt and pepper		
honey	1 tsp	2 tsp

1 To make the coulis: remove seeds from red peppers and chop roughly.

2 Sweat off pepper with finely sliced shallots, add small sprig of thyme.

3 Add fish stock and reduce stock by three-quarters.

4 Put the contents into a liquidiser and blitz until smooth in consistency.

5 Season with salt and pepper.

6 To make the salad dressing: whisk together the vinegar, honey and mustard.

7 Slowly whisk in the oil.

8 Season with salt and pepper.

9 Add the finely diced pimento and the lime juice.

10 Cook the potatoes and slice into 6 mm discs.

11 Take the crab meat and add some of the dressing with plenty of diced pimento and check seasoning.

12 Place the salad into a 7.5 cm pastry ring in the middle of your plate. Place the crab meat on top of the salad and remove pastry ring.

13 Place the dill around the top of the salad.

14 Take the warm potatoes and place in the mayonnaise with the chives, and season.

15 Place the warm coulis at three intervals on the plate and place the cooked scallops on to the coulis.

16 Place the warm potato salad in between the scallops and garnish with the sprigs of chervil and thyme.

35 Herring, apple and potato salad

	4 portions	10 portions
smoked herrings	2	5
cooked potato	100 g	250 g
eating apple	100 g	250 g
chopped parsley, chervil and fennel	1 tsp	1 tbsp
vinaigrette		

1 Fillet and skin the herrings and cut the flesh into dice.

2 Mix with the diced potato and diced apple.

3 Add the herbs and vinaigrette. Correct seasoning.

Note: As a variation smoked mackerel, eel or trout could be used.

36 Smoked fish platter

	4 portions	10 portions
fillets of smoked mackerel	2	5
fillet(s) of smoked trout	1	2–3
smoked eel or halibut	200 g	500 g
smoked salmon	100 g	250 g
lemon	1	2
mayonnaise with horseradish	60 ml	150 ml

1 Carefully remove the skin from the mackerel, trout and eel or halibut fillets, and divide into four pieces.

2 Arrange with a cornet of salmon on each plate.

3 Garnish with a quarter of lemon.

4 Serve separately, mayonnaise sauce containing finely grated horseradish.

37 Shellfish platter

A selection of shellfish (e.g. lobster, crab, prawns and shrimps) neatly arranged and served with quarters of lemon and mayonnaise sauce separately.

38 Red mullet with tomatoes, garlic and saffron

	4 portions	10 portions
red mullet	4 × 150 g	10 × 150 g
salt and pepper		
dry white wine	125 ml	300 ml
vegetable oil	60 ml	150 ml
tomatoes, skinned, deseeded and diced	150 g	375 g
clove of garlic (crushed)	1	2–3
sprig of thyme, bay leaf		
pinch of saffron		
peeled lemon	4 slices	10 slices

1 Clean, prepare and dry the fish.

2 Place in a suitable oiled dish. Season with salt and pepper.

3 Add the white wine, oil, tomatoes, garlic, herbs and saffron.

4 Cover with aluminium foil and bake in the oven at 220°C for approximately 7 minutes. Allow to cool in dish.

5 Serve on individual plates with a little of the cooking liquor, garnished with a slice of peeled lemon.

nutritional info

1 portion provides:
298 kcals/1228 kJ
18.7 g fat
(of which 2 g saturated)
1.4 g carbohydrate
(of which 1.4 g sugars)
26.8 g protein
0.4 g fibre

♥

kcal
1000
900
800
700
600
500
400
300
200
100
0

calorie counter

39 Fish mousse

Fish mousse will inevitably vary according to the fish used to make the mousse. The recipe below is for the base. The table that follows it gives the whipping cream addition quantities.

fish trimmed of bone, skin and scales, cut into 2½ cm dice	150 g
salt	1 tsp
ground pepper	pinch

fish type	*quantity of whipping cream*
monkfish	500 ml
salmon	375 ml
scallops	450 ml
sea bass	500 ml
turbot	300 ml

1 Place the fish in a cold food processor bowl with the blade attachment; blend to a fine mince, stopping twice to ensure that the excess is scraped from the sides of the bowl.

2 Add the salt and pepper, ensuring even distribution. The salt will firm up the mousse, swelling the protein and allowing the cream to be incorporated more easily. Chill the mousse in the refrigerator for 10–15 minutes.

3 Place back in the processor then add the cream in a steady stream, taking about 40 seconds in all – too fast and the cream will whip, too slow and the fat in the cream will be over-worked and split the mousse.

4 Test poach: place a small amount of the mousse in a piece of clingfilm and seal; poach in simmering water for 1–2 minutes until firm and check for seasoning – add if necessary. Store in the fridge, well covered, for up to 2 days.

40 Salmon mousse

	4 portions	10 portions
cooked salmon, free from skin and bone	400 g	1¼ kg
velouté	125 ml	300 ml
fish aspic jelly	125 ml	300 ml
a little sweated paprika if desired		
salt and pepper		
whipping cream, half whipped	250 ml	600 ml

1 Purée the salmon, place in a saucepan with the velouté and aspic, and boil for 2 minutes.

2 Pass through a sieve, add the sweated paprika, and mix well. Season.

3 Place in a basin over a bowl of ice, stir until setting point, then fold in the half-whipped cream.

4 Pour into a glass bowl or individual moulds. Decorate and use as required.

41 Hot smoked mackerel

Makes 4 portions

hardwood chips	400 g
coarse salt	60 g
sugar	60 g
mackerel fillets, skin on but boned	4 (500–600 g)
freshly ground black pepper	2 tbsp
Dijon mustard	1 tbsp
fresh lemon juice	2 tbsp

1 Cover the wood chips with water and soak for at least 1 hour and up to 24 hours. Mix together the salt and sugar, and sprinkle over the fish on both sides. Let sit for 30 to 40 minutes, refrigerated if the room is especially warm. Mix together the pepper, mustard and lemon juice, and rub into the fillets; marinate for another 30 minutes.

2 Drain the fish of its accumulated liquid, brush off any of the rub that has not dissolved. Wash off the fillets and pat dry. Place the fish on a perforated steaming tray. Place a deep stainless container under the mackerel tray and add the soaked smoking chips.

3 Gently heat and keep a constant temperature (not too high as this will burn the chips, or so low as not to cook the fish). Check if the fish is cooked after 15 minutes.

4 It can then be served immediately or chilled and served cold with a horseradish sauce (the traditional accompaniment for smoked fish).

42 Beetroot and treacle cured salmon

	10 portions
fresh salmon fillet, skin on	1 × 800g
beetroots, medium-sized, raw	100 g
Maldon salt	100 g
caster sugar	100 g
freshly ground black pepper	2 tsp
fresh dill, chopped	75 g
treacle	4 tbsp

1 Trim the salmon into a neat shape and, feeling with your fingertips and using tweezers, pull out any bones. Place the fillet in a shallow dish, skin side down.

2 Peel and coarsely grate the beetroots (wear rubber gloves to keep your fingers from staining). Mix together the salt, sugar, pepper and half the chopped dill, and place to one side

3 Pour the treacle over the salmon and spread evenly.

4 Press the salt and sugar mixture evenly all over the salmon, cover with clingfilm and lay a board or another tray on top that fits just inside the first to weigh the cure mixture down on the flesh.

5 Chill for 24 hours. The cure will cause liquid to seep out of the salmon – this is quite normal. Don't drain it away; it will help cure the underneath of the flesh as well.

6 After 24 hours, uncover, scrape away and discard the beetroot mixture and wash the fish under cold water. Pat dry, sprinkle with the rest of the dill and wrap firmly in clingfilm. Leave for another 4 to 8 hours then uncover and, using a sharp, long knife, carve thinly at an angle into D-shaped slices. Serve with buttered rye bread and thick crème fraîche seasoned with black pepper, horseradish and chopped chives.

BUFFET ITEMS

The preparation and presentation of attractive, inviting cold buffets should give pleasure to customers and help stimulate their appetites. When preparing and decorating dishes it must always be borne in mind that they are to be presented and served in front of customers; therefore, *ease* of service is important and should be considered when choosing the method of decoration. A cold buffet should not look a wreck after a handful of customers or one or two portions have been served.

Sound standards of personal, kitchen and food hygiene are essential as cold foods, if not hygienically prepared, cooked, handled, stored and displayed, can easily be infected and lead to food poisoning.

Preparing a cold buffet

Here is an example of the sequence of events prior to preparation of a cold buffet.

1 Agree the required dishes for the buffet and the amount of each.
2 Compile lists of ingredients.
3 Order food sufficiently in advance to allow time for preparation, cooking, cooling and decorating.

There are numerous variations to a cold buffet, depending on:

1 the time of year, which can affect choice of seasonal foods
2 the time of day – breakfast, lunch, dinner, supper

Hot buffet

Cold meats and salads

Sushi

Cold sweets

Smoked fish and shellfish

3 the occasion and number of guests – for example,
- 8.30 am meeting of EEC Ministers in March, 50 guests
- 1 o'clock wedding reception in June, 250 guests
- gathering of 1000 international lawyers in October at 8 pm
- midnight supper in February for 500 following gala performance of an opera

4 any special requests by the host/hostess.

Once all requirements are known, then a sensibly varied, colourful and appetising range of dishes can be prepared. It is not necessarily the number of dishes that give a cold buffet customer appeal, but rather the choice of foods, their quality and the way that they are displayed – for example:

- smoked salmon
- tomato and cucumber
- roast beef
- potato salad
- York ham
- potted shrimps
- vegetable salad
- green salad

On the other hand, for a large special occasion the following may be prepared:

- fresh prawns
- chicken
- stuffed eggs
- duck
- stuffed tomatoes
- York ham
- chicken pie
- dressed crawfish
- eel terrine
- game pie
- minted carrot salad
- roast turkey
- roast venison
- lobster
- dressed crab
- green salad
- pheasant
- roast saddle of lamb
- potato salad
- vegetable salad
- ox tongue
- dressed salmon

As the chef has prepared all these dishes, he/she should be involved in their display and the following points borne in mind.

1 Display food under refrigeration if possible. If not, then keep in cool/cold storage until the last possible moment, bearing in mind that cold buffet food is a favourite target for bacteria. (Refer to *Guidelines for the Catering Industry on the Food Hygiene Regulations Amendments 1990, 1991 and 1995*, HMSO.)

2 Select the most outstanding dish as the centrepiece.

Roger Serjent

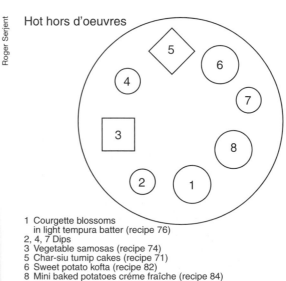

Hot hors d'oeuvres

1 Courgette blossoms in light tempura batter (recipe 76)
2, 4, 7 Dips
3 Vegetable samosas (recipe 74)
5 Char-siu turnip cakes (recipe 71)
6 Sweet potato kofta (recipe 82)
8 Mini baked potatoes crème fraîche (recipe 84)

Smoked salmon

Asparagus and dressed crab

Sushi

Smoked fish

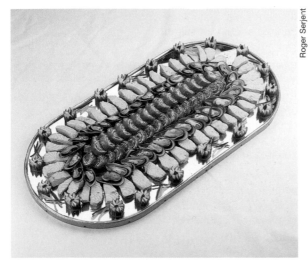

Salmon, smoked salmon, mussels

Cured meats

3 Consider carefully how the food is to be served or even self-served by the customers when placing all dishes in position. The satisfactory service of many excellent cold buffets is often spoiled because insufficient thought has been given to the *way* in which they are to be served.

4 If the customers are to help themselves then see that all dishes are within reach.

5 Ensure that the various complementing dressings and salads are by the appropriate dishes, otherwise customers will be moving backwards and forwards unnecessarily and causing hold-ups.

6 On self-service buffets, dishes quickly become untidy. Have staff on hand to remove and replace or tidy up dishes as required.

Hot buffet procedure
Self-Service for Heated Foods

Many establishments provide a range of heated foods for buffet-style self-service, particularly for tourists abroad. This food is frequently presented in containers with a lift-up cover and is provided with a small amount of heat under the container.

The advantage of this is that food is available over a period of time and there is a minimum need for service staff.

However, to ensure a satisfactory standard of food hygiene it is essential that *all* the food is hot, not just that by the heat source. The amount of food in the container should not exceed that which can be kept hot, therefore the amount in the container should be replenished a small amount at a time with very hot food.

In hot climates this is particularly important, even where there is air conditioning.

43 Light buffet items

These are small items of food, hot or cold, that are served at cocktail parties, buffet receptions and may be offered as an accompaniment to drinks before any meal (luncheon, dinner or supper). The following are typical items for cocktail parties and light buffets.

1 Hot savoury pastry patties of lobster, chicken, crab, salmon, mushroom, ham, etc., small pizzas, quiches, brochettes, hamburgers.

2 Hot sausages (chipolatas), various fillings, such as chicken livers, prunes, mushrooms, tomatoes, gherkins, etc., wrapped in bacon and skewered and cooked under the salamander. Fried goujons of fish.

3 Savoury finger toasts to include any of the cold canapés. These may also be prepared on biscuits or shaped pieces of pastry. On the bases the following may be used: salami, ham, tongue, thinly sliced cooked meats, smoked salmon, caviar, mock caviar, sardine, eggs, etc.

4 Game chips, gaufrette potatoes, fried fish balls, celery sticks spread with cheese.

5 Sandwiches, bridge rolls – open or closed but always small.

6 Sweets such as trifles, charlottes, jellies, bavarois, fruit salad, gateaux, strawberries and raspberries with fresh cream, ice creams, pastries.

7 Beverages, coffee, tea, fruit cup, punch bowl, iced coffee.

Canapés may be served on neat pieces of buttered toast or puff or short pastry or blinis, rye bread, etc. A variety of foods may be used – slices of hard-boiled egg, thin slices of cooked meats, smoked sausages, fish, anchovies, prawns, etc. The size of a canapé should be suitable for a mouthful.

44 Bouchées

Bouchée fillings are numerous as bouchées are served both hot and cold. They may be served as cocktail savouries, or as a first course, a fish course or as a savoury. All fillings should be bound with a suitable sauce, for example:

- mushroom – chicken velouté or béchamel
- shrimp – fish velouté or béchamel or curry
- prawn – fish velouté or béchamel or curry
- chicken – chicken velouté

- ham – chicken velouté or béchamel or curry
- lobster – fish velouté or béchamel or mayonnaise
- vegetable – mayonnaise, natural yoghurt, fromage frais, quark or béchamel.

45 Savouries using barquettes and tartlets

A variety of savouries may be served either as hot appetisers (at a cocktail reception) or as the last course of an evening meal. The tartlet or barquette may be made from thinly rolled short paste and cooked blind.

Examples of fillings

- Shrimps in curry sauce.
- Chicken livers in a light juice or devilled sauce.
- Mushrooms in béchamel, suprême or aurora sauce.
- Poached soft roes with devilled sauce.
- Poached soft roes covered with cheese soufflé mixture and baked.

The cooked tartlets or barquettes should be warmed through before service, the filling prepared separately and placed neatly in them. They may then be garnished with a sprig of parsley.

46 Aspic jelly flavoured with wine

When an aspic is flavoured with wine the following quantities may be used, but the wine must be added only when the aspic is almost cold. If wine is added earlier it can spoil the clarification process, giving a cloudy rather than a sparkling clear aspic.

- White or red wines: 125 ml to 1 litre
- Sherry or port: 60 ml to 1 litre

In all cases the liquid quantity of stock should be reduced by the quantity of wine to be added *or* extra gelatine used.

47 Aspic jelly 1

Aspic is a savoury jelly that may be used on cold egg, fish, meat, poultry, game and vegetable dishes that are prepared for cold buffets so as to give them an attractive appearance. For meat dishes a beef or veal stock is made; for fowl, chicken stock; and for fish, fish stock.

Aspic jelly is produced from fish, poultry, game or meat stock with the addition of gelatine. Vegetarian aspic jelly is produced from vegetable stock with the addition of agar-agar as a setting agent.

Great care must be taken when using aspic jelly as it is an ideal medium for the growth of micro-organisms. Therefore the following procedures should be observed.

1 Always use fresh aspic and bring to a simmer: temperature must be 82°C for 15 seconds. Cool quickly and use sparingly.

2 Avoid using warm aspic, especially over long periods.

3 Do not store aspic for long periods at room temperature.

4 If required for further use, chill rapidly and store in the refrigerator.

5 If stored in refrigerator, simmer for 10 minutes before further use. Discard after 24 hours' storage.

6 Once a dish has been glazed with aspic it may be kept refrigerated for up to 8 hours.

7 Once removed from the refrigerator it must be consumed within 2 hours and then, if uneaten, discarded.

8 It is advisable, if possible, to make only the quantity required for use and so avoid storage. Where possible, display in refrigerated units.

Uses

- As a glaze for cold preparations.
- To prevent food from losing moisture.
- As a garnish for certain dishes, chopped or cut into shapes.
- To aid presentation and appearance.

48 Aspic jelly 2

	4 portions	10 portions
whites of egg	2–3	5
strong, fat-free seasoned stock (as required poultry, meat, game or fish)	1 litre	2½ litre
vinegar	1 tbsp	2½ tbsp
sprigs tarragon	2	5
leaf gelatine	75 g	190 g

1 Whisk the egg whites in a thick-bottomed pan with ¼ litre of the cold stock and the vinegar and tarragon.

2 Heat the rest of the stock, add the gelatine (previously soaked for 10 minutes in cold water) and whisk until dissolved.

3 Add the stock and dissolved gelatine into the thick-bottomed pan. Whisk well.

4 Place on the stove and allow to come gently to the boil until clarified.

5 Strain through muslin.

6 If the jelly is not clear, repeat the whole procedure using egg whites only.

nutritional info

This recipe provides:
397 kcals/1668 kJ
0.0 g fat
(of which 0.0 g saturated)
7.4 g carbohydrate
(of which 0.1 g sugars)
91.3 g protein
0.0 g fibre

kcal
1000
900
800
700
600
500
400
300
200
100
0

calorie counter

COLD MEAT PREPARATIONS

49 The serving of cold roast chicken

If the chicken is to be displayed whole at a buffet it may be brushed with aspic or oil. It is then dressed on a suitably sized oval dish with watercress and a little diced aspic jelly.

To keep roast suckling pig and roast chicken or duck moist and succulent, roast 2–3 hours before it is required and **do not refrigerate**.

When serving individual portions it is usual to serve either a whole wing of chicken neatly trimmed, or a half chicken. If a half is served, the leg is removed, the wing trimmed, and the surplus bone removed from the leg, which is then placed in the wing (1½ kg chickens). Larger chickens may be cut into four portions, the wings in two lengthwise and the legs in two joints. Sometimes the chicken may be requested sliced; it is usual to slice the breast only and then reform it on the dish in its original shape.

50 The serving of cold duck

Use the same methods as for chicken. Serve with sage and onion dressing and apple sauce.

51 The serving of cold game

Larger birds, such as pheasant, may be sliced or served in halves or quarters; small birds, whole or in halves. The birds are served with watercress and game chips. Most of the smaller birds are served on a fried bread croûte spread with a little of the corresponding pâté, farce au gratin, or pâté maison.

52 The serving of cold turkey or goose

For display, cold turkey or goose may be brushed with jelly or oil, but otherwise it is normally served sliced, with the dark meat under the white, chopped jelly and watercress. Serve turkey with a dressing and cranberry sauce. Serve goose as for duck.

53 The serving of cold cooked meats

Roast meats may also be served on a buffet by allowing them to cool quickly, directly from the oven either at ambient temperature or by blast chilling. In this way the meat is cool and succulent for eating. In this case the meats are garnished with salad, vegetables and fresh herbs.

Cold cooked meat should be sliced as near to serving time as possible, and arranged neatly on a dish. Finely diced or chopped aspic may be placed around the edge. It may be decorated with a bunch of picked watercress or presented in the piece with 3 or 4 slices cut.

Whole joints, particularly ribs of beef, are often placed on a buffet table. They should either be boned or have any bones that may hinder carving removed before being cooked. They should be trimmed if necessary, strings removed and, after glazing with aspic jelly or brushing with oil, dressed on a dish garnished with watercress; lettuce leaves and fancy-cut pieces of tomato may also be used to garnish the dish.

Fillet of beef Wellington and roast suckling pig are popular cold buffet dishes.

54 Cured belly of pork

	15 portions*
salt	150 g
sugar	50 g
Spanish smoked paprika	20 g
pork belly, trimmed of skin and fat scored	1 (1.2–1.5 kg)
confit oil	2 litres
thyme	1 sprig
bay leaves	3
garlic	3 cloves

* Depending on size of cut

1 Mix the salt, sugar and paprika together, and rub into the pork belly meat side.

2 Wrap in clingfilm and allow to cure for 1½ hours. Rinse quickly under running water, but don't try to wash out all the salt, just pat dry.

3 Roll the belly into a cylindrical shape and tie in even sections.

4 Pre-heat oven to 87°C. Meanwhile, heat the confit oil on the stove, adding the thyme, bay leaves and garlic. In a thick-bottomed pan, seal the pork all over until golden brown then immerse in the confit oil. Place in the oven for 3 hours.

5 Test if cooked by squeezing with your forefinger and thumb – the meat should just give. Remove carefully and allow to cool at room temperature. Once at room temperature, wrap tightly in clingfilm and refrigerate.

6 This can be served cold with an acidic chutney or pan-fried and served with a sauerkraut.

TERRINES, PIES, BALLOTINES AND GALANTINES

Pâtés and terrines are standard features in any French charcuterie, and provide the basis of many a lunch for those travelling in that country.

It is difficult to make a firm distinction between a pâté and a terrine. A fine-textured liver pâté is almost always called a pâté, yet a coarse, meaty product might be called either a *pâté de campagne* or a *terrine maison*.

Originally, a pâté was always enclosed in pastry (dough) and was made with almost any sort of meat or fish. Later it came to be baked in an earthenware dish (a terrine), which was lined with thinly sliced pork fat to keep the mixture moist.

Most pâtés and terrines contain a good proportion of pork, especially fat belly pork (fresh pork sides). When making a pâté or terrine, if possible choose a particular cut of meat and either mince (grind) it yourself or have it minced (ground) by the butcher, rather than buying ready-minced (ground) meat. Fat is essential to the texture of the pâté or terrine, and enables it to be sliced without crumbling. It also means that a pâté or terrine is served without butter and with just crusty French bread or a good wholewheat bread, plus some gherkins or olives, or a crisp salad.

A pâté or terrine is sometimes served as a first course; in this case it is usually accompanied by thin, crisp melba toast, or warm, freshly made white or brown toast, or a selection of savoury crackers.

The modern-day method of making terrines affords more poetic licence than purists would allow. However, things move on and if we can use modern techniques and ingredient combinations, that should only be better for us and the customers alike.

Listed below are the basic principles of making terrines – adopt these and you can be more confident of a consistent result.

Step-by-step guide to making a terrine

1 Have a picture of how the terrine should look when sliced and be mindful that you will cut laterally through your layers, revealing a mosaic finish. Therefore, layering is essential to the visual presentation.

2 A binding agent is needed if making a pressed terrine (i.e. cooking all components separately, adding them together warm and pressing overnight).

3 Always use strict levels of hygiene. Wear hygienic latex gloves if putting together a pressed terrine due to the fact that the terrine will not be heated again, so any bacterial transfer from hands to food will only multiply and not be destroyed.

4 When seasoning a pressed terrine, over-season slightly because your tastebuds are more active for savoury notes when the temperature range is between 38°C and 47°C. Because the terrine is served cold, the savoury notes are less susceptible to being picked up by the tastebuds, so slightly over-seasoned ingredients when warm will decant into a flavoursome and moderately seasoned product.

5 Use of ingredients is also important – for example, the use of fresh herbs and half-cooked onions will send the terrine sour very quickly, and under-cooked foie gras will make the terrine bitter.

6 If making a pressed terrine with chicken, cooking the chicken through is essential – if you have a 10 cm strip cut laterally that is just undercooked, you will lose up to eight portions of terrine.

7 For storage, it is essential that the terrine is wrapped tightly with clingfilm to prevent oxidisation and, when slicing, slice through the clingfilm to prevent crumbling and cross-contamination from hand-to-terrine contact. If you are right handed, the left part of the terrine will be touched up to 25 times before being served – this will increase the bacterial count for the last remaining terrines.

55 Terrines

These are cooked in ovenproof dishes fitted with a lid. Once the mixture is in the dish the lid may be replaced and sealed with a plain flour and water paste to prevent the steam escaping. Terrines can be made from chicken, duck, veal, hare, rabbit, turkey and chicken livers, etc.

1 The forcemeat is made in the same way as for a pâté, as is the filling, which is marinaded in the liquor and spices.

2 Line the bottom and sides of the terrine with thin slices of larding bacon.

3 Add half the forcemeat (if this is too dry, moisten with a little good stock).

4 Neatly lay in the marinated garnish.

5 Add the remainder of the forcemeat and spread it evenly.

6 Cover the top with larding bacon and add a bay leaf and a sprig of thyme.

7 Put a thin layer of flour and water paste around the rim of the terrine and press the lid down firmly to seal it.

8 Place the terrine in a bain-marie and cook it in a moderate oven, 190°C, for approximately 1¼ hours.

9 If the fat that rises to the top of the terrine is perfectly clear (shows no signs of blood) when lightly pressed with the fingers, this indicates that it is cooked.

10 When cooked, remove from the bain-marie,

Boning a chicken through the back

remove the lid and add a piece of clean wood that will fit inside the dish; place a weight of 1–1½ kg to press the meat down evenly. Allow to cool.

11 When cool, remove the weight and board, and all the fat from the surface.

12 To remove the terrine from the dish, place it in boiling water for a few seconds.

13 Turn the terrine out, trim and clean it, and cut it into slices as required.

Note: If the terrine is to be served in its cooking dish then wash and thoroughly dry the dish before returning the terrine to it.

If the terrine is then to be covered with a layer of aspic jelly, all fat must be removed from the top beforehand.

56 Ballotines

Ballotines are boned-out stuffed legs of poultry, usually chicken, duck or turkey, which can be prepared, stuffed with a variety of forcemeat stuffings, cooked, cooled and prepared for service cold.

They can be served:

■ simply, garnished with a suitable salad

■ decorated and coated with aspic
■ coated with a white or brown chaud-froid and decorated.

Note: When preparing ballotines, keep the skin long as this will help to form a good shape; which can be long, round or like a small ham.

57 Chicken galantine

	8 portions
chicken meat free from all sinew	200 g
lean veal	100 g
belly of pork	100 g
bread soaked in 125 ml milk	75 g
thin slices of fat bacon or lardons	
ham	25 g
tongue — cut into ½ cm batons	25 g
bacon	25 g
blanched and skinned pistachio nuts	12 g
egg	1
salt, pepper and nutmeg to season	
double cream	250 ml
chicken stock	

1 Clean and carefully skin a chicken, place the skin in cold water to remove blood spots.

2 Bone the chicken and save one suprême for garnish.

3 Pass the rest through a fine mincer with the veal, pork and squeezed, soaked breadcrumbs.

4 Remove into a basin, mix in the egg and seasoning and pass through a sieve.

5 If using a food processor, add the egg while the mixture is in the processor and continue to chop until very fine.

6 Place into a basin over a bowl of ice, add the cream slowly, mixing well between each addition.

7 Place a clean damp cloth on the table, arrange the chicken skin on the cloth. Cover with slices of fat bacon, to about 5 cm from the edge.

8 Spread on one-third of the mixture.

9 Garnish with alternate strips of ham, tongue, bacon, pistachio nuts and the chicken suprême also cut into ½ cm batons.

10 Place another layer of mixture on top and repeat the process.

11 Finish with a one-third layer of the mixture.

12 Roll the galantine up carefully. Tie both ends tightly.

13 Poach in chicken stock for approximately 1½ hours.

14 When thoroughly cold remove cloth.

15 Cut into slices, serve garnished with salad.

Galantine may be served as a starter with an appropriate garnish such as a small tossed salad.

Note: To enhance the flavour of the mixture, some fresh chopped herbs, such as tarragon and chervil, may be added.

Making a chicken galantine

Boned out chicken through the back

Adding prepared mixture

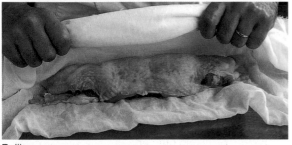

Rolling

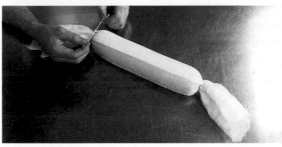

Tying in cloth

58 Game pies

These can be made from hare, rabbit or any of the game birds. The filling should be marinated in the liquor, salt and spices for 1–2 hours.

Forcemeat	4 portions	10 portions
game flesh	200 g	500 g
fat bacon	200 g	500 g
beaten egg	1	2–3
salt	10 g	25 g
spices		

Filling		
game fillets	300 g	750 g
larding bacon	200 g	500 g
brandy or Madeira	60 ml	150 ml
salt	15 g	35 g
spices		

Prepare, cook and finish as for pâté en croûte (see pages 80–81).

59 Pâtés and terrines

The composition of these two preparations is similar, the difference being the actual cooking and the receptacle in which they are cooked.

The filling consists of a forcemeat, prepared from the required meat, poultry or game well seasoned with herbs, spices and any other garnish that may be relevant to the particular pâté or terrine.

To make a pâté a raised pie mould is lined with pie pastry, then with thin slices of larding bacon. The forcemeat is then added with the garnish in between layers until the mould is full, the last layer being forcemeat. The top is covered with larding bacon and pie pastry, neatly decorated, and then one or more holes 1 cm are made in the top into which are inserted short, oiled, stiff-paper funnels to enable steam to escape during cooking. The top is then egg washed 2–3 times and baked for 1¼–1½ hours at 190°C. When cold, the pie is filled through the holes in the top with a well-flavoured aspic jelly or a flavour to suit the pie.

Making a pâté en croûte

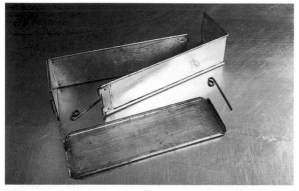

Collapsible mould so that pâté can be removed without damage

Rolling pastry

Shaping pastry

Folding pastry

Lining mould

Adding filling

Crimping edges

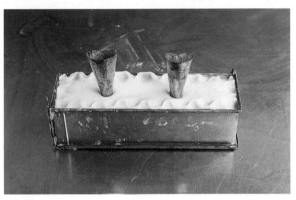

Inserting funnels

Adding aspic jelly after cooking and cooling of the pâté

Slicing

60 Pie pastry

	4 portions	10 portions
flour	400 g	1¼ kg
salt		
butter or margarine	100 g	250 g
lard	100 g	250 g
egg	1	2–3
water	125 ml	300 ml

1 Sieve the flour and salt.

2 Rub in the fat.

3 Add beaten egg and water.

4 Mix well and allow to rest before using.

61 Raised pork pie

Certain pies are not cooked in moulds but are hand raised using a hot water pastry.

Hot water paste	4 portions	10 portions
strong plain flour	250 g	625 g
salt		
lard or margarine (alternatively use 4 parts lard and 1 part butter or margarine)	125 g	300 g
water	125 ml	312 ml

	4 portions	10 portions
Filling		
shoulder of pork (without bone)	300 g	750 g
bacon	100 g	250 g
allspice, or mixed spice, and chopped sage	½ tsp	1¼ tsp
salt and pepper		
bread soaked in milk	50 g	125 g
stock or water	2 tbsp	5 tbsp

nutritional info

1 portion provides:
683 kcals/2867 kJ
41.8 fat
(of which 17.1 saturated)
54.1 g carbohydrate
(of which 1.5 g sugars)
26.1 g protein
3.2 g fibre

♥ kcal
1000
900
800
700
600
500
400
300
200
100
0
calorie counter

1 Sift the flour and salt into a basin.

2 Make a well in the centre.

3 Boil the fat with the water and pour immediately into the flour.

4 Mix with a wooden spoon until cool.

5 Mix to a smooth paste and use while still warm.

Chicken pie – cook and finish as for pâté en croûte (see page 81). Chicken pies prepared and cooked for serving hot can also be used for serving cold. It is advisable to put one leaf of gelatine (soaked) on the chicken before covering with pastry. The recipe can be found in *Practical Cookery*.

1 Cut the pork and bacon into small, even pieces and combine with the rest of the ingredients.

2 Keep one-quarter of the paste warm and covered.

3 Roll out the remaining three-quarters and carefully line a well-greased raised pie mould.

4 Add the filling and press down firmly.

5 Roll out the remaining pastry for the lid.

6 Eggwash the edges of the pie.

7 Add the lid, seal firmly, neaten the edges, cut off any surplus paste.

8 Decorate if desired.

9 Make a hole 1 cm in diameter in the centre of the pie.

10 Brush all over with eggwash.

11 Bake in a hot oven, 230–250°C, for approximately 20 minutes.

12 Reduce the heat to moderate 150–200°C and cook for 1½–2 hours in all.

13 If the pie colours too quickly, cover with greaseproof paper. Remove from the oven and carefully remove tin. Eggwash the pie all over and return to the oven for a few minutes.

14 Remove from the oven and fill with approximately 125 ml of good hot stock in which 5 g of gelatine has been dissolved.

15 Serve when cold, garnished with picked watercress and offer a suitable salad.

62 Scotch salmon terrine layered with scallops, served on a lime yoghurt dressing
Stephen Goodlad

	4 portions	10 portions
scallops, cleaned out of shell	400 g	1 kg
sole flesh	80 g	200 g
egg whites	1	3
double cream	250 ml	625 ml
brunoise vegetables (carrot, leek, celery)	40 g	100 g
soft butter	20 g	50 g
fine herbs	1 tsp	1 tbsp
dry sherry	10 ml	25 ml
side fresh salmon (from 4 kg wild salmon)*	½	1
leaf spinach, cooked	160 g	400 g
single cream	40 ml	100 ml
lime, juice of	½	1
natural yoghurt	50 ml	125 ml
sprigs of picked chervil	1	3

* A 1½ kg side yields 1 kg salmon to line terrine after trimming.

1 Purée 200 g scallops and the sole flesh in a food processor, add the egg whites and seasoning, then slowly blend in 125 ml double cream.

2 Remove the purée and push it through a fine drum sieve.

3 Beat the remaining double cream into the purée, and leave the bowl to rest on ice for 30 minutes.

4 Add the brunoise of vegetables, which have been sweated down in the butter and herbs and deglazed with the dry sherry. Cool and add to the purée.

5 Fillet the salmon, remove the skin, bones and the brown pieces of flesh. Cut into the same size as the terrine and butterfly.

6 Place the salmon between a piece of lightly greased clingfilm (with oil) and gently tap it out using a cutlet bat. This will lubricate the salmon and make flattening it easier.

7 Grease the terrine with clarified butter and silicone paper, then line the salmon into the mould.

8 Cover with spinach, lay the spinach out flat and place fresh scallops down the middle. Spread a thin layer of mousse over the scallops to hold them in place.

9 Roll the spinach into a sausage shape the same length as the terrine.

10 Place a layer of mousse halfway up the lined terrine, lay the spinach sausage into the mousse, cover with the remaining mousse, then fold the overlapping salmon.

11 Cover with greaseproof paper, place the lid on and poach in a bain-marie for 1 hour in a low oven, 160°C.

12 Remove from the oven and allow to cool. Leave overnight in the terrine to set.

13 Stir the single cream and lime juice into the yoghurt. Use to sauce medium-sized plates.

14 Remove the terrine from the mould. Slice with a warm, thin-bladed knife and lay on top of the sauce on a 30 cm plate. Place a sprig of chervil at the top of the plate and serve.

Note: It is advisable to use wild salmon when available and in season at its cheapest, but farmed salmon or salmon trout can also be used. It is a good idea to lay the salmon on to greased silicone paper. This will make it easier to line the terrine and to turn it out when set.

63 Terrine of free-range chicken and foie gras

The terrine indicates the true essence of a kitchen and some say a good kitchen can be marked on its terrine as there are so many different cooking techniques involved. Years of development went into this recipe to get the taste and presentation just right. I have served this version with dried fig and parsnip purée, which offsets the bitter undertones of the terrine caused by the foie gras and mushrooms.

Terrine	25 portions
lobe of foie gras	700 g
free-range chickens, legs removed	3 × 1.2 kg
savoy cabbage	2
dried haricot beans (soaked)	100 g
lamb jus	250 mls
corn oil	250 mls
shitake mushrooms, medium	20
garlic cloves	3
sprigs of thyme	4
white wine	125 mls
black trompette, or other wild mushrooms	200 g
globe artichoke bottoms, cooked	4
semi-dried grapes	200 g
duck or goose fat	125 mls
seasoning	
parsnip purée	1 kg
butter	50 g
Parma ham	12 slices
Dried figs	
Ripe figs	3
Icing sugar for dusting	
Garnish – sprigs of chervil	
Truffle oil	

1 Place the foie gras in an upturned bowl covered with a damp tea towel. Leave at room temperature for 2 hours to bring the foie gras to a workable temperature.

2 The liver should open under its own weight to give two sides to the lobe, revealing some blood vessels, fat and sinew.

3 Season the chicken crowns; lightly fry in 60 ml of corn oil until sealed.

4 Transfer to a roasting tray and roast in the oven at 180°C for approximately 18–20 minutes until cooked.

5 Remove from the oven and leave to cool breast side down. This is to ensure the juices run into the breast and not through the carcass.

6 Take the cabbage and remove any withered leaves. Remove approximately two layers of the remaining outer leaves. Trim off the central branch of each leaf, leaving two tender sides. Wash well.

7 Blanch in boiling, salted water for 2 mins. Refresh well under running cold water. Drain well on a cloth.

8 Cook the haricot beans until tender, then refresh and drain.

9 Heat the lamb jus.

10 In a frying pan, add 125 ml of corn oil. Heat and gently fry the shitake mushroom tops. Add the garlic and thyme. Cook for 1–2 minutes, add white wine and lamb jus, and rest of prepared mushrooms.

11 Bring to the boil, remove from heat and allow mushrooms to cool in the sauce.

12 Lay a sheet of plastic wrap on a work surface and place the soft and open foie gras onto it carefully. With a small, sharp knife remove the main artery that divides the two halves of the lobe.

13 Carefully ease out the rest of the veins that run through the foie gras. Cut the foie gras carefully into 5 cm strips. Wrap and return to fridge until firm.

14 Build the terrine. Cover a work surface with a double layer of plastic wrap measuring 30 cm × 45 cm. Use to line the terrine mould, expelling all the air.

15 Make sure all the ingredients are just above room temperature so that they can be pressed effectively and absorb some of the other flavours in the terrine.

16 Remove the chicken breasts from the bone and trim off any fat, sinew and skin.

17 Cut in three lengthways and place in the tray.

18 Strain off the mushrooms, discarding the garlic and thyme but retaining the cooking liquor.

19 Place the mushrooms, artichoke bottoms, haricot beans, cabbage leaves, and semi dried grapes in the tray with the chicken breasts.

20 Melt the duck or goose fat and pour over the ingredients on the tray.

21 Season well.

22 Lay the foie gras in a baking tray. Place in a low oven for approximately 8 minutes.

23 Place strips of cabbage leaves the exact width of your terrine in the bottom.

24 Arrange the ingredients on the tray neatly in the terrine with the foie gras. Brush each layer with lamb jus.

25 Cover with cabbage leaves; press down well. Cover with cling film to make a tight-fitting seal.

26 Wrap the whole terrine in cling film.

27 Pierce small holes in the plastic, approximately 1 cm apart. This will allow the excess juices to escape while the terrine is pressing. Place a

weight covered with foil on top of the terrine to press it down.

28 Place in the fridge. Ensure the weight is level and that it will not move.

29 Leave for 4 hours.

30 To serve, carefully unwrap the terrine. Trim the sides if needed.

31 On a work surface, lay 6 slices of Parma ham on a sheet of cling film. Place the terrine on this.

32 Lay the other 6 slices of ham on top of the terrine. Press the ham against the terrine and wrap tightly with the cling film. Store in fridge for a further 24 hours.

33 For the dried figs, remove the two ends of the figs and cut each one into 2 thick slices. Place on a try with silicone dust and icing sugar. Dry for 24 hours. These may be stored in an airtight container until needed.

34 Make a purée of parsnips, then add the butter and place over heat until the purée is thick. Season well. Allow to cool.

35 To serve, slice the terrine, place on plates and remove the clingfilm.

36 Place a quennelle of cold parsnip purée on the plate, and decorate with a dried fig. Garnish with truffle oil and chervil.

64 Veal and ham pie

Forcemeat	4 portions	10 portions
lean veal	100 g	250 g
lean pork	100 g	250 g
fat bacon	200 g	500 g
egg (beaten)	1	2–3
salt	10 g	25 g
Spice, seasoning, e.g. nutmeg, mace, allspice, or freshly chopped herbs, e.g. basil, thyme and sage		

Pass the meats through a fine mincer then mix with the egg, salt and spice or herbs.

Filling	4 portions	10 portions
veal fillet	300 g	750 g
pork fillet	300 g	750 g
lean ham or gammon	200 g	500 g
larding bacon	200 g	500 g
brandy, sherry or Madeira (optional)	60 ml	150 ml
spices, e.g. nutmeg, cinnamon, allspice, or freshly chopped herbs		
salt	15 g	35 g

Marinade the meats in the brandy, spices and salt for 1–2 hours. Then prepare, cook and finish as for pâté en croûte or/and raise using hot water pastry (see recipe 61).

CROSTINIS AND NIBBLES

Customers may request snacks and hors d'oeuvre at almost any time of the day or night. An interesting variety should be offered and in order to give an appetising presentation, they should be prepared as near to service time as possible, in which case they need not be refrigerated. Items to be baked should be served warm but not too hot, as guests may have to eat them with their fingers. Because, at most receptions, the guests remain standing, items should not be larger than a comfortable mouthful.

Although an attractive display should always be provided, in the interests of hygiene cold snacks, canapés, etc., should not be allowed to go into the reception until the last possible moment.

Hot snacks are normally offered after the guests have arrived, during the reception, and sent out from the kitchen in small quantities.

When to be served as reception snacks all the following items should be made to a size suitable for one bite.

65 Anchovy sticks

	4 portions	10 portions
puff pastry	150 g	375 g
anchovy fillets	100 g	250 g
eggwash		

1 Roll out half the puff pastry in a rectangle 7 cm × 12 cm.

2 Place on a lightly greased baking sheet.

3 Lay on the anchovy fillets; eggwash the edges.

4 Roll out remaining puff pastry slightly larger than the first half.

5 Cover the anchovies with this pastry, seal down the edges well.

6 Eggwash all over, mark edges with the back of a small knife. Cut into sticks ½ cm wide.

7 Bake in a moderate oven, 220°C, for approximately 10 minutes until golden brown.

8 May be served hot or cold.

66 Brioches

Small bite-sized brioches may be made for appetisers using recipe 502. The centre is scooped out and various fillings may be used. Here are some examples.

Fish
■ creamed smoked haddock
■ lobster in lobster sauce
■ prawns in curry sauce
■ mussels in cream or curry sauce, etc.

Meat
■ diced cooked beef or lamb in red wine or tomato sauce
■ diced cooked chicken, veal or rabbit in cream or white wine sauce

Vegetables
■ finely diced ratatouille
■ mushrooms in cream sauce
■ courgettes in tomato sauce

67 Dartois

These savoury puff pastry slices are made and cooked in a long strip, then cut after cooking.

Fillings include:
■ smoked haddock
■ chicken and mushroom
■ chicken
■ sardines
■ tuna
■ anchovies
■ ratatouille
■ mushroom.

68 Lamb, peach and cashew bitoks

	4 portions	10 portions
dried peaches	100 g	250 g
minced lamb	450 g	1¼ kg
clove of garlic, crushed and chopped	1	2–3
salt and pepper		
egg	1	2–3
breadcrumbs	50 g	125 g
cashew nuts	50 g	125 g

1 Reconstitute the peaches in boiling water for 5 minutes; drain well. Chop finely and add to the lamb.

2 Add the garlic and season. Bind with the egg and breadcrumbs.

3 Form into small cocktail pieces, insert a cashew nut into each and mould into balls. Flatten slightly.

4 Fry the bitoks in a shallow pan in vegetable oil; drain.

5 Place on a dish with a cocktail stick in each. Serve a yoghurt and cucumber dressing separately.

Note: Pine kernels may be used in place of cashew nuts, and beef or chicken used in place of lamb.

69 Spinach and cheese sticks

As for anchovy sticks; in place of anchovies use chopped, cooked spinach bound with béchamel and sprinkled with grated Parmesan cheese.

70 Spring rolls

	4 portions	10 portions
Batter		
eggs	2	5
milk	125 ml	312 ml
flour	50 g	125 g
salt		
Filling		
sesame oil	50 g	125 g
finely chopped onion	25 g	60 g
sliced bamboo shoots	50 g	125 g
cooked, diced pork	50 g	125 g
finely diced celery	25 g	60 g
groundnut oil	1 tbsp	2½ tbsp
ve-tsin*	½ tbsp	1¼ tbsp
peeled shrimps	100 g	250 g

1 Make the batter by, first, beating the eggs and milk together.

2 Gradually add the flour, season and strain.

3 Lightly oil a small shallow pan, diameter approximately 8 cm. Heat over a fierce heat.

4 Gently pour in a thin layer of the batter. Cook for 1 minute on one side only. Turn out and allow to cool.

5 Prepare the filling: heat the sesame oil in a suitable pan, add the finely chopped onion and sweat without colour for 2 minutes.

6 Add all other ingredients except the shrimps, mix well. Simmer for 3 minutes.

7 Turn out into a clean basin and leave to cool. Add the shrimps.

8 Put a small spoonful of filling on to the cooked side of each pancake, roll up, tucking in and sealing the edges with eggwash. Place on a tray and chill well for approximately 20 minutes.

9 Deep-fry in hot oil, approximately 190°C, until golden brown; drain well and serve immediately on a dish on dish paper.

*Ve-tsin is a flavour enhancer, similar to monosodium glutamate.

71　Char-siu: radish/turnip cake in spring roll pastry or bean-curd skin

Yields 30

mooli, diced	375 g
rice flour	100 g approx.
salt	1 tsp
sugar	1 tsp
spring onions, chopped	1 bunch
spring roll wrappers	
Char-siu sauce	
light soy sauce	100 ml
hoi sin sauce	100 ml
oyster sauce	50 ml
honey	50 ml
five spice powder	4 tsp
whisky	30 ml
For sauce, mix all ingredients together	

1　Steam the mooli until tender.

2　Purée in a food processor.

3　Add the rice four, salt, sugar and onions. Note that the texture should be slightly thicker than choux pastry. If too slack add a little more rice flour.

4　Lay sheets of clingfilm on a flat surface, then pipe the mixture onto the clingfilm approximately 2 cm diameter.

5　Roll up like a sausage, and tie each end.

6　Steam for approximately 45–50 minutes.

7　Allow to cool before unwrapping.

8　Cut into 4 cm lengths.

9　Dip in char-siu sauce for flavour and colour.

10　Wrap in spring roll pastry and lightly deep-fry in oil, 180°C.

11　Serve with a dipping sauce, e.g. soy sauce.

Alternatively, the radish/turnip cakes may be wrapped in sheets of bean-curd skin.

72　Crostini **v**

	12 portions
French baguette, thinly sliced	1
olive oil	
cloves garlic, thinly sliced	3
thyme, chopped	
salt and pepper	

1　Lay out the baguette slices on a tray.

2　Drizzle olive oil over the slices.

3　Place garlic and thyme on each slice and season.

4　Place in a hot oven, 180°C, for 4 minutes until golden brown and crispy.

73　Tomato and aubergine crostini **v**

Makes 24 crostinis

crostini (see recipe 72)	24
Italian round aubergines	2
shallots, finely diced	2
cloves garlic, chopped	3
olive oil	100 ml
plum tomatoes, skinned, deseeded, petals, chopped	8
basil, chopped	
salt and pepper	

1　Peel the aubergines, dice, salt and leave to one side for 2 hours.

2　Drain excess water from the aubergines and squeeze out.

3　Sweat the shallots and garlic for 2 minutes in olive oil.

4　Add the chopped tomatoes for 2 minutes.

5　In a separate pan, fry the aubergines, add the tomato mix and cook out for 35 minutes until the aubergines are soft.

6　Drain off the excess olive oil. Cool.

7　When cool, adjust the seasoning and mix in the basil.

8　Place a small spoonful of mix on top of each crostini and serve.

74 Vegetable samosas v

Makes 18 pieces

Filling

oil	1 tbsp
carrots, peeled and julienned	2
mooli, peeled and julienned	50 g
savoy cabbage julienned	50 g
spring onions, julienned	4
beansprouts	50 g
sultanas	10 g
ginger root, finely diced	3 g
toasted sesame seeds	3 g
dark soy sauce	50 ml

Pastry

sheets standard spring roll pastry	6

For the filling

1 Heat the oil a large saucepan.

2 Sweat the carrots and mooli for 2 minutes.

3 Add the cabbage, spring onions, beansprouts and sultanas.

4 Sweat on a high heat until dry (approximately 4 minutes).

5 Add the ginger, sesame seeds and soy sauce. Season.

6 Reduce liquid by half and chill.

For the pastry

1 Toss all the filling ingredients together in a bowl until well mixed.

2 Adjust the seasoning with salt, pepper and lemon juice.

3 Using one sheet of spring roll pastry at a time, cut into thirds, giving you three equal strips.

4 Place 1 tbsp of filling at one end of the strip and diagonally fold the pastry to form a triangle.

5 Stick the edges with a little water and flour mix.

6 Fill the other strips in the same way and then repeat with the other sheet of pastry.

7 Deep-fry until golden brown and crisp.

Goats' cheese crostini with bite-sized others (pork belly with mustard jelly; smoked salmon with créme fraîche caviar; confit foie gras with fig and apple)

75 Goats' cheese crostini

Makes 15 crostinis

goats' cheese (Crottin is preferable)	200 g
red onions, cut into quarters and finely sliced	100 g
thin baguette bread, toasted	12 slices

1 Place the goats' cheese in the freezer for 30 minutes. When very cold, peel off the rind using a sharp knife.

2 Gently crumble the cheese with the fingers.

3 Spread the finely sliced onions onto the toasted bread.

4 Cover liberally with the cheese. Grill lightly until melted and golden.

5 Serve warm.

CANAPÉS – HOT AND COLD

76 Courgette blossoms in tempura batter — Roger Serjent

Lightly flour the courgette blossoms, dip into tempura batter, and deep-fry in hot oil, 175°C, until crisp and lightly coloured. Drain well, then serve immediately.

77 Snapper and mango salad served on an oriental spoon

Poaching liquid	
coconut milk	1 litre
ginger, sliced	1 whole
palm sugar	4 tbsp
thai fish sauce	30 ml
red snapper	1 kg
Salad	
coconut shavings	3 tbsp
spring onions, sliced	6
red chillies, small sliced rounds	3
pickled ginger cut into julienne	1 tbsp
cucumber, deseeded cut into julienne	½
mint leaves, torn	1 tbsp
coriander leaves	1 tbsp
spearmint leaves, torn	2 tbsp
shallots, finely sliced rounds	3 tsp
lime leaves in fine julienne	6
Shallot rings	
shallots	3 finely sliced
rice flour	
Coconut dressing for the salad	
kaffir lime juice, strained	500 ml
coconut vinegar	500 ml
thai fish sauce	125 ml
Thai sugar syrup	125 ml
olive oil	125 ml
sesame oil	30 ml
seasoning	

Whisk all the dressing ingredients together.

1 Prepare poaching liquor; bring milk, ginger, sugar and fish sauce to simmering point. Do not allow to boil rapidly.

2 Place the fish into the liquor and poach until just cooked.

3 Allow to cool in milk.

4 Prepare the salad, by gently mixing the ingredients together, add flaked fish and mix in coconut dressing.

5 Dust the shallots with rice flour and deep-fry until crisp.

6 Sprinkle the shallots on the salad.

7 Serve the salad on an oriental spoon as a canapé, then decorate with coriander.

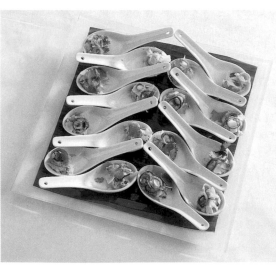

Roger Serjent

78 Lightly jellied tomato and tea consommé

Serve in liqueur glasses; yields 100 glasses

Tomatoes, chopped	50
sundried tomatoes (no oil)	30
chervil	1 bunch
water	3 litres
jasmine tea	1 tbsp or 3 jasmine tea bags
gelatine	6 leaves
spring onions, finely sliced and black fungus for garnish	

1 Mix tomatoes, dried tomatoes, chervil and water in a pan.

2 Bring to a gentle simmer but do not boil.

3 Gently simmer for 10 minutes, then remove from heat.

4 Add the jasmine tea and allow to infuse for 20 minutes. Season.

5 Strain through a fine sieve and then through a coffee filter.

6 Skim and allow sediment to settle.

7 Remove the consommé leaving the sediment (similar to clarifying butter).

8 Reheat the oiled, soaked leaf gelatine, garnish with finely sliced spring onions and chopped black fungus.

9 Allow to set, place into glasses and finish each glass with tomato concassée.

Roger Serjent

79 Eastern spiced salmon tartare served on a silver spoon

Yields approx. 40

salmon, finely diced	180 g
garlic clove, chopped	1
shallot, finely chopped	1
leek cut into brunoise	1 tbsp
ginger, fresh, finely chopped	½ tsp
coriander, chopped	1 tbsp
curry powder	½ tsp
ground cumin	½ tsp
chives, chopped	1 tbsp
tamari soy sauce	to taste
hazelnut oil	
seasoning	

1 Bind all ingredients together in a bowl, with enough oil to moisten but not to excess.

2 Mould onto silver spoons. Decorate with crème fraîche and chervil.

Roger Serjent

80 Soba noodle norimaki

Yields approx. 50

soba noddles	225 g
coriander, chopped	4 tbsp
spring onions, chopped	40 g
soy sauce	2 tbsp
fresh ginger, chopped	1 tbsp
red wine vinegar	2 tbsp
pickled ginger, chopped	2 tbsp
norimaki sheets	
cucumber, peeled, seeded and cut into julienne	1
red pepper, seeded and cut into julienne	1

1 Cook the soba noodles in boiling water and then cool.

2 Mix the coriander, spring onions, soy sauce, ginger, vinegar and pickled ginger together.

3 Add the drained noodles, then mix well.

4 Lay out a sheet of norimaki and lay the noodles into it, approx. 0.5 cm thick and running lengthways.

5 Lay some cucumber and red peppers on top, then roll neatly and tightly as for sushi rolls.

6 Chill well in refrigerator, and when ready to serve cut into 1 cm-thick rounds on the slant.

7 It may be easier to lay the norimaki sheets on clingfilm first, and then roll with the clingfilm. This will help achieve a tighter roll and assist in shaping. Remove the clingfilm after cutting.

Roger Serjent

81 Mirin-glazed tuna and pickled ginger

Yields approx. 40

tuna	1½ kg
Teriyaki marinade	
tamari soy sauce	225 ml
lime juice and zest, chopped	2
brown sugar	3 tbsp
garlic cloves, chopped	4
fresh ginger, chopped	1 tbsp

Mix all ingredients together in a pan, bring to the boil, reduce to a syrupy consistency, allow to cool.

Garnish

Wasabi (Japanese horseradish paste)
Pickled ginger

1 Cut the tuna into bite-size pieces, 1 cm–2 cm square, place in a tray, marinate in the teriyaki marinade for at least 1 hour.

2 Remove from the marinade, drain quickly, seal and char the tuna on a grill pan leaving the centre raw.

3 Allow to cool, place into open chopsticks, decorate with a little wasabi and a slice of pickled ginger.

82 Sweet potato kofta

Yields 100

cumin seeds	4 tsp
coriander seeds	4 tsp
sweet potato	1 kg
potatoes	400 g
chickpeas, cooked	300 g
chickpea flour	400 g
ginger, finely chopped	80 g
red chilli brunoise	8
coriander	2 bunches
seasoning	

1 Roast the cumin and coriander seeds then crush.

2 Steam the potatoes until just cooked then cool and peel.

3 Grate the potatoes into a bowl.

4 Purée the chickpeas in a food processor, and then place into a bowl.

5 Add the chickpea flour to the chickpeas and mix well.

6 Add remaining ingredients; mix well.

7 Using two teaspoons and hot water, quenelle the mixture.

8 Place onto a tray with chickpea flour.

9 When needed for service, deep-fry in hot oil at 180°C, until golden brown, drain, serve as required with cucumber raita (see below).

83 Cucumber raita

green yoghurt	400 g
cucumber, peeled, seeded and finely diced	1
mint, chopped	1 bunch

Mix all ingredients together. Serve in dipping bowls.

84 Mini baked potatoes – crème fraîche

Small new potatoes, baked. Cut cross on top, fill with crème fraîche containing chopped olives.

Other fillings may also be used:

- purée of avocado with lime
- thick tomato coulis with chopped basil
- caviar/lumpfish roe
- chopped prawns in mayonnaise
- flaked haddock braised with curry sauce
- creamed chicken with a slice of mango.

85 Smoked salmon with blinis and caviar

smoked salmon, thinly sliced	400 g
blinis (see below)	
sour cream	¼ pint
caviar	10 g
herbs to garnish	

Blinis

yeast	15 g
egg yolks	6
buckwheat	120 g
milk	
egg whites	6

1 To make the blinis, disperse yeast in a small amount of warm milk.

2 Mix in egg yolks and then buckwheat flour.

3 Adjust texture with milk until smooth.

4 Whip egg whites into meringue and then fold into base.

5 Allow to rest for 20 minutes and then cook in small rounds in a non-stick pan with a little oil.

6 Turn over when first side is golden (30–40 seconds) and then cook the other side to the same colour.

7 Allow to cool before use.

Place the salmon neatly onto the blinis, top with sour cream and caviar, and garnish with herbs.

86 Cream cheese and smoked eel

cucumber, peeled	½
cream cheese	250 g
chives, chopped	1 tsp
smoked eel	100 g
seasoning	

1 Slice the cucumber approx. 0.5 cm thick.

2 Mix all the other ingredients together and check the seasoning.

3 Place a quenelle on to each cucumber slice and serve.

87 Parma ham and tarragon tart

egg custard (see below)	
thinly sliced Parma ham	100 g
chopped tarragon	1 tsp
small shortcrust pastry tartlets	20
seasoning	
Egg custard	
milk	100 ml
single cream	40 ml
whole egg	1
yolk	1
seasoning	

Combine all the ingredients for the egg custard and pass through a fine sieve (care should be taken not to over-season with salt as the ham will be salty).

1 Cut the ham into julienne, mix with the tarragon and place in the bottom of each of the tartlets.

2 Fill the tartlets up with the custard mixture and place in the oven on a 180°C setting for 6–8 minutes until the custard just sets.

3 Remove and serve warm.

88 Parmesan tuiles

Makes 30 medium-sized tuiles

Parmesan Reggiano	250 g

Finely grate the Parmesan and sprinkle into cutters on baking paper to form rounds 4 cm wide by 0.5 cm thick. Bake at 180°C until golden brown. Remove immediately and shape into tile-like pieces, then allow to cool and serve.

Note: Reggiano must be used as Padano, the other cheese type, will not set hard due to its fat content.

89 Salmon tartare

	20 portions
organic salmon, fresh and free from bone, skin and blood line	300 g
chives, chopped	1 tsp
crème fraîche	50 g
seasoning	
thin croûtes (see recipe 72)	30
chervil	
caviar (optional)	

1 Chop the salmon into 3 mm cubes.

2 Mix in the chives and crème fraîche.

3 Check seasoning.

4 Spoon a small mound of salmon mix onto each croûte and garnish with chervil.

5 If using caviar, place a small amount on each croûte and serve immediately.

90 Foie gras kromesky

	30 portions
chicken and foie gras parfait	500 g
pané anglaise (flour, beaten egg and fresh white breadcrumbs)	
fig and port reduction (optional)	

1 Cut the parfait into 1½ cm cubes.

2 Allow to chill for 10 minutes in the freezer.

3 Pass twice through the pané.

4 Chill and deep fry.

5 Serve immediately with the fig and port reduction (see page 58).

91 Wild mushroom risotto balls

	40 portions
mixed wild mushrooms (washed and trimmed)	300 g
oil	50 ml
shallots, diced	2
garlic clove, chopped	1
cooked and cooled risotto	300 g
pané anglaise (flour, beaten egg and fresh white breadcrumbs)	
seasoning	

1 Cut the wild mushrooms into ½ cm dice.

2 Heat the oil and sweat off the shallots and garlic.

3 Add the mushrooms and cook slowly until soft. Once cooked allow to cool.

4 Mix the risotto and mushrooms together.

5 Check seasoning and mould into 1½ cm spheres. Allow to set in the fridge for 30 minutes.

6 Pass twice through the pané.

7 Chill, deep-fry, drain well and serve.

92 Plum tomato and goats' cheese

	24 portions
small plum tomatoes	12
shallots	2
garlic clove, chopped	1
olive oil	
goats' cheese	250 g
double cream	50 ml
salt and pepper	

1 Cut the tomatoes in half and scoop out the seeds with a spoon.

2 Sweat the shallots and garlic in olive oil for 2 minutes and cool.

3 Put the goats' cheese and double cream in a bowl, and mix together until smooth.

4 Place some of the shallot mix in the bottom of each tomato.

5 On top, place one quenelle of goats' cheese mix.

6 Put a cocktail stick in each tomato and serve.

HOT SAUCES & STOCKS

chapter 2

HOT SAUCES & STOCKS

Units covered
3FPC1

LIST OF RECIPES

Recipe no	page no	Recipe no	page no
Stocks		110 Suprêmes of chicken in cream sauce	107
94 Fish stock	99	109 Suprême sauce	106
96 Lamb jus (meat base)	100	111 Veal escalopes with cream sauce	107
95 Shellfish stock	99	113 Yoghurt/fromage frais thickened sauces	108
97 Stock-reduced base sauce	100	**Soubises, and vegetable and fruit purées**	
93 White chicken stock	98	119 Avocado sauce	110
Nages		121 Avocado and celery sauce	110
101 Crayfish coulis sauce	102	120 Avocado and fennel sauce	110
102 Lobster sauce	103	122 Beetroot sauce	110
98 Mushroom nage	101	123 Broccoli sauce	111
100 Shellfish nage	102	115 Cauliflower soubise	109
99 Vegetable nage	101	118 Celeriac purée	110
Glazes		124 Fresh tomato sauce (cooked)	111
103 Butter sauce (beurre blanc)	104	116 Garlic soubise	109
104 Butter thickened (monter au beurre)	104	125 Gooseberry sauce	111
Egg-based sauces		114 Onion soubise	108
106 Béarnaise sauce	105	117 Parsnip purée	109
105 Hollandaise sauce	105	126 Pesto sauce	111
107 Sabayon sauce	106	**Oil-based sauces**	
108 Sabayon with olive oil	106	127 Garlic, red onion and ginger oil	113
Creamed thickened sauces		128 Roasted pepper oil	113
112 Smitaine sauce	107		

STOCKS

As stocks are the foundation of many kitchen preparations, great care must be taken in their preparation. The function of stock is to add flavour and give body.

93 White chicken stock

Makes 2 litres

chicken carcass/wings	20 kg
onions, peeled	6
carrots, peeled	8
bulb of garlic	1
leeks, washed and blemishes removed	4
celery sticks	8
bay leaves	2
sprigs of thyme	6
whole white peppercorns	30 g

1 Remove any excess fat from the chicken carcasses and wash off under cold water.

2 Place all the bones into a pot that will hold all the ingredients, leaving 5 cm at the top to skim.

3 Add all the other ingredients and cold water, and bring to a simmer; immediately skim all the fat that rises to the surface.

4 Turn the heat off and allow the bones and vegetables to sink. Once this has happened turn the heat back on, skim and bring to just under a simmer, making as little movement as possible to create more of an infusion than a stock. Skim continuously.

5 Leave to simmer (infuse) for 10 hours then pass through a fine sieve into a clean pan; reduce down rapidly, until you have about 2 litres remaining.

94 Fish stock

Makes 2 litres

fish bones, no heads, gills or roe (turbot, sole and brill bones are best)	5 kg
olive oil	100 ml
onions, finely chopped	3
leeks, finely chopped	3
celery sticks, finely chopped	3
fennel bulb, finely chopped	1
dry white wine	350 ml
parsley stalks	10
sprigs of thyme	3
white peppercorns	15
lemons, finely sliced	2

1 Wash off the bones in cold water for 1 hour. Heat the olive oil in a pan that will hold all the ingredients, leaving a 1 cm gap at the top for skimming.

2 Add all the vegetables and sweat off without colour for 3 minutes.

3 Add the fish bones and sweat for a further 3 minutes.

4 Next add the white wine and water to cover. Bring to a simmer, skim off the impurities, and add the herbs, peppercorns and lemon. Turn off the heat.

5 Infuse for 25 minutes, then pass into another pan and reduce by half. The stock is now ready for use.

95 Shellfish stock

Makes 2 litres

olive oil	50 ml
unshelled prawns	500 g
crab bodies (gills removed), roughly smashed	1 kg
carrots, chopped	2
onion, chopped	1
celery stick, chopped	1
fennel, chopped	½ bulb
garlic cloves	2
tomato paste	3 tbsp
white wine	200 ml
cold water	2 litres
fish stock	500 ml
parsley, thyme and bay leaf	
star anise	2

1 Place the stock pot on a medium heat and add the oil, whole prawns and crab bodies.

2 Sweat for 8 minutes until slightly golden. Add the chopped vegetables, garlic and tomato paste, and continue sweating for a further 8 minutes.

3 Pour in the wine, bring to the boil and reduce by half.

4 Add the water, stock, herbs and star anise; cook for 30 minutes, skimming frequently.

5 Strain the liquid through a fine sieve and leave to cool. Store in the refrigerator for up to 3 days.

96 Lamb jus (meat base)

Makes 2 litres

thyme	bunch
bay leaves, fresh	4
garlic	2 bulbs
red wine	1 litre
lamb bones	20 kg
veal bones	10 kg
white onions, peeled	6
large carrots, peeled	8
celery sticks	7
leeks	4
tomato purée	6 tbsp

1 Pre-heat the oven to 175°C. Place the herbs, garlic and the wine in a large, deep container. Place all the bones on to a roasting rack on top of the container of herbs and wine, and roast in the oven for 50–60 minutes. When the bones are completely roasted and have taken on a dark golden-brown appearance, remove from oven.

2 Place all the ingredients in a large pot and cover with cold water. Put the pot onto the heat and bring to the simmer; immediately skim all fat that rises to the surface.

3 Turn the heat off and allow the bones and vegetables to sink. Once this has happened, turn the heat back on and bring to just under a simmer, making as little movement as possible to create more of an infusion than a stock.

4 Skim continuously. Leave to simmer (infuse) for 12 hours then pass through a fine sieve into a clean pan and reduce down rapidly, until you have about 1.5 litres remaining.

97 Stock-reduced base sauce

Makes 4 litres

Most establishments have discontinued using traditional espagnole and demi-glace as the basis for brown sauces and use instead rich, well-flavoured brown stocks of veal, chicken, etc., reduced until the lightest form of natural thickening from the ingredients is achieved.

No flour is used in the thickening process and consequently a lighter-textured sauce is produced. Care needs to be taken when reducing this type of sauce so that the end product is not too strong or bitter. The following recipe is for reduced veal stock.

veal bones, chopped	4 kg
calves' feet, split lengthways	2
carrots	400 g
onions	200 g
celery	100 g
tomatoes, quartered	1 kg
mushrooms, chopped	200 g
large bouquet garni	1
unpeeled cloves of garlic (optional)	4

1 Brown the bones and calves' feet in a roasting tray in the oven.

2 Place the browned bones in a stock pot, cover with cold water and bring to simmering point.

3 Using the same roasting tray and the fat from the bones, brown off the carrots, onions and celery.

4 Drain off the fat, add the vegetables to the stock and deglaze the tray.

5 Add the remainder of the ingredients, simmer gently for 4–5 hours. Skim frequently.

6 Strain the stock into a clean pan and reduce until a light consistency is achieved.

NAGES

Nages are a lighter form of the traditional stocks we have come to know throughout the classic kitchen foundation. Nages, if cooked properly, offer a great range of subtle flavours that can be moved around on the palate, therefore they can be used to cook, add to or enhance various ingredients without over-dominating the core flavour of the dish – a real 'must' in any kitchen armoury.

98 Mushroom nage

Makes 2 litres

field mushrooms	2 kg
onion, sliced	350 g
garlic cloves	2
thyme	2 sprigs
butter	200 g
water	3 litres
dried ceps	150 g

1 Sauté off the mushrooms, onion, garlic and thyme in a little oil and the butter until nut brown in colour.

2 Add the water and simmer for 20–25 minutes.

3 Remove from the heat and add the dried ceps. Cover with clingfilm until cold.

4 Leave overnight and pass through a fine chinois.

Uses

Mushroom nage has a number of uses, including soups, sauces, risotto and consommé, and is an interesting variation or alternative to vegetable stock, especially with vegetarian dishes.

Flavour

The aroma is the first sensation you will notice: one of a forest on a damp morning. The flavour is similarly very earthy, nutty and fragrant.

Storage

Store in a refrigerator for up to one week and freeze for up to one month.

99 Vegetable nage

Makes 2 litres

onions, chopped	3
celery sticks, chopped	2
leeks, chopped	2
carrots, chopped	4
dry white wine	200 ml
garlic bulb, cut across middle	1
white peppercorns	10
pink peppercorns	10
star anise	3
sprigs thyme	2
sprigs parsley	2
sprigs chervil	2
sprigs tarragon	2
cold water	2 litres

1 Place all the vegetables in a pan. Cover with water and bring to the boil.

2 When boiling, add white wine and return to the boil.

3 Turn down to a simmer for 10 minutes.

4 Remove from the heat, add all the aromats and cover with clingfilm. Cool thoroughly.

5 Place in refrigerator and leave for at least 12 hours before using, or overnight.

Uses

Vegetable nage is very useful for soups and sauces.

Flavour

The flavour you capture in this recipe comes primarily from the 12-hour infusion that takes place after cooking the stock. Once left to infuse the nage will have a clean and distinct vegetable flavour with undertones of herbs and spices.

Storage

Store in a refrigerator for up to one week and freeze for up to one month.

100 Shellfish nage

Makes 2 litres

olive oil	50 ml
unshelled prawns	500 g
cock crab body, no claws, gills removed (roughly smashed)	1 kg
carrots, chopped	2
onion, chopped	1
celery stick, chopped	1
fennel, chopped	½ bulb
garlic cloves	2
tomato purée	3 tbsp
dry white wine	200 ml
cold water	2 litres
fish stock	500 ml
star anise	2
bay leaf	1
sprigs parsley	5
sprigs thyme	5

1 Take a pan big enough to hold all the ingredients and put on a medium heat.

2 Heat the oil, then add the prawns and crab body.

3 Sweat off for 8 minutes. Add the vegetables and tomato purée, and continue to sweat for a further 8 minutes then add the wine, water, stock and herbs.

4 Bring to a simmer and skim off any impurities. Continue to cook for 30 minutes, skimming when a scum develops on the top of the nage.

5 When ready, pass the nage into a container through a fine sieve; do not force. Refrigerate and use as required.

Uses

Shellfish nage can be used in soups, sauces and risottos, and can be reduced to a glaze. With a small amount of milk added, it can be 'cappuccinoed' using a hand blender.

Flavour

Light and fragrant, with a hint of aromatic spices and herbs. It gives an excellent flavour to all types of fish dishes and sauces.

Storage

Store for up to three days in an airtight container in the refrigerator, or freeze for up to one month.

101 Crayfish coulis sauce

Makes 1 litre

live freshwater crayfish or Dublin Bay prawns	2 kg
butter or oil	75 g
onion — finely cut	100 g
carrot — finely cut	100 g
celery — finely cut	50 g
brandy	30 ml
tomato purée	100 g
dry white wine	250 ml
bouquet garni	
double cream	500 ml
salt and cayenne pepper	

1 Heat the butter or oil in a thick-bottomed pan.

2 Add the crayfish, cover with a lid and cook for 5–6 minutes.

3 Remove the pan from heat, remove the crayfish, detach and shell the tails, and reserve.

4 Pound or crush all the shells.

5 Return pan to the heat, add a little more butter or oil if necessary.

6 Add the vegetables, cover with a lid and sweat for 2–5 minutes.

7 Add the crushed shells; sweat well, but do not allow them to brown.

8 Add brandy and ignite, mix in the tomato purée.

9 Add white wine and bouquet garni, bring to the boil, simmer for 10 minutes.

10 Add the cream and simmer for 10 minutes.

11 Correct seasoning and strain firmly to extract all juices and flavour.

Note: This sauce can also be made using the crushed soft shell of cooked crayfish, crab, crawfish, shrimps, prawns and lobster, but obviously the sauce will not have the same flavour or quality as when the whole live shellfish are used.

Lobster sauce or coulis can be made from the following recipe, omitting the flour and finishing with 250 ml double cream.

102 Lobster sauce

Makes 1 litre

live hen lobster	¾–1 kg
butter or oil	75 g
onion } **roughly cut (mirepoix)**	100 g
carrot	100 g
celery	50 g
brandy	60 ml
flour	75 g
tomato purée	100 g
fish stock	1¼ litres
dry white wine	120 ml
bouquet garni	
crushed clove garlic	½
salt	

1 Wash the lobster well.

2 Cut in half lengthwise, tail first, then the carapace.

3 Discard the dark green sac from the carapace, clean the trail from the tail, remove any spawn into a basin.

4 Wash the lobster pieces.

5 Crack the claws and the four claw joints.

6 Melt the butter or oil in a thick-bottomed pan.

7 Add the lobster pieces and the onion, carrot and celery.

8 Allow to cook steadily without colouring the butter for a few minutes, stirring continuously with a wooden spoon.

9 Add the brandy and allow it to ignite.

10 Remove from the heat, mix in the flour and tomato purée.

11 Return to a gentle heat and cook out the roux.

12 Cool slightly, gradually add the fish stock and white wine.

13 Stir to the oil.

14 Add the bouquet garni and garlic, and season lightly with salt.

15 Simmer for 15–20 minutes.

16 Remove the lobster pieces.

17 Remove the lobster meat from the pieces.

18 Crush the lobster shells, return them to the sauce and continue simmering for ¼–¾ hour.

19 Crush the lobster spawn, stir into the sauce, reboil and pass through a coarse strainer.

This sauce may be made in a less expensive way by substituting cooked lobster shell (not shell from the claws), which should be well crushed, in place of the live lobster.

GLAZES

A glaze is a stock, fond or nage that has been reduced allowing a high percentage of water to be removed through boiling, thus permitting the concentration of solids and flavour to increase. This yields an intense sauce that should be used sparingly to finish a dish; alternatively, it can be refrigerated or frozen and added to a weak stock to give it the vibrant boost it may need.

Butter as a sauce
Clarified butter
Clarified butter is butter that has been melted and skimmed. After that, the fat element of the butter is carefully poured off, leaving the milky residue behind. This gives a clear fat that can reach higher temperatures than normal butter without burning, but that can also be used to nap over steamed vegetables, or poached or grilled fish.

Beurre noisette
'Beurre noisette' basically translates to 'nut butter', and its flavour comes from the caramelisation of the milk element in the butter solids. It is achieved by placing diced hard butter into a moderately hot pan and

bringing to a foam (a good indication that it is ready). While it is foaming under heat, the milk element is cooking in the fat, which creates a popping/cracking sound. This is due to the water mixing with the fat – not too dissimilar to the deep-frying of moist products. When this cracking/popping stops, therefore, this means that there is no more liquid in the fat and all the proteins have now caramelised, yielding that nutty flavour. Like clarified butter, this can be served with poached or steamed vegetables and fish, but the classic use is with shallow-fried fish. If you take the butter a little further, however, and almost burn the sediment, then add a little vinegar, this is called black butter and is traditionally served with skate.

Beurre fondu/emulsion

This is basically an emulsion between fat and liquid – for example, melted butter emulsified with any nage described above will give you a slightly thicker sauce that can be used to coat vegetables or fish. However, to intensify the flavour, if you were to add a beurre noisette to the pan or your cooking medium was clarified butter, you could start cooking the product in the pan with the fat. Once it is half cooked, arrest the cooking by adding a nage and then bring quickly to the boil. Through this boiling process the fat and the stock will become emulsified, which gives an emulsified sauce made in the pan, but with the cooking juices also added.

103 Butter sauce (beurre blanc)

	4 portions	10 portions
water	125 ml	300 ml
wine vinegar	125 ml	300 ml
shallot, finely chopped	50 g	125 g
unsalted butter	200 g	500 g
lemon juice	1 tsp	2½ tsp
salt and pepper		

1 Reduce the water, vinegar and shallots in a thick-bottomed pan to approximately 2 tablespoons.

2 Allow to cool slightly.

3 Gradually whisk in the butter in small amounts, whisking continually until the mixture becomes creamy.

4 Whisk in the lemon juice, season lightly and keep warm in a bain-marie.

Note: The sauce may be strained if desired. It can be varied by adding, for example, freshly shredded sorrel or spinach, or blanched fine julienne of lemon or lime. It is suitable for serving with fish dishes.

104 Butter thickened (monter au beurre)

Many sauces can be given a final finish to enrich flavour and given a sheen by the thorough mixing in of small pieces of butter at the last moment before serving.

The traditional way of making à la carte classic fish sauces is to strain off the liquid in which the fish has

been poached, reduce it to a glaze and then, away from the heat, gradually and thoroughly mix in small pieces of butter. If the sauce is to be glazed then some lightly whipped double cream may be added.

EGG-BASED SAUCES

Note: To reduce the risk of salmonella infection, use pasteurised egg yolks. Once made, egg-based sauces should not be kept warm for more than 2 hours, they should then be discarded.

105 Hollandaise sauce

Makes 500 g

peppercorns, crushed	12
white wine vinegar	3 tbsp
egg yolks	6
melted butter	325 g
salt and cayenne pepper	

nutritional info ♥

1 large portion provides:
972 kJ/236.0 kcal
25.3 g fat (of which 15.0 g saturated)
0.2 g carbohydrate (of which 0.2 g sugars)
1.8 g protein
0.0 g fibre

Contains egg yolks and butter.

calorie counter
kcal
1000
900
800
700
600
500
400
300
200
100
0

1 Place the peppercorns and vinegar in a small pan and reduce to one-third.

2 Add 1 tablespoon of cold water and allow to cool. Add the egg yolks.

3 Put on a bain-marie and whisk continuously to a sabayon consistency.

4 Remove from the heat and gradually whisk in the melted butter.

5 Add seasoning. Pass through muslin or a fine chinois.

6 Store in an appropriate container at room temperature.

Note: Egg-based sauces should not be kept warm for more than 2 hours. After this time, they should be thrown away, but are best made fresh to order.

Variations

- Mousseline sauce: hollandaise base with lightly whipped cream.
- Maltaise sauce: hollandaise base with lightly grated zest and juice of one blood orange.

106 Béarnaise sauce

Makes 500 g

shallots, chopped	50 g
tarragon	10 g
peppercorns, crushed	12
white wine vinegar	3 tbsp
egg yolks	6
melted butter	325 g
salt and cayenne pepper	
chervil and tarragon to finish, chopped	

nutritional info ♥

1 large portion provides:
980 kJ/238.0 kcal
25.3 g fat (of which 15.0 g saturated)
0.6 g carbohydrate (of which 0.5 g sugars)
1.9 g protein
0.1 g fibre

Contains egg yolks and butter.

calorie counter
kcal
1000
900
800
700
600
500
400
300
200
100
0

1 Place the shallots, tarragon, peppercorns and vinegar in a small pan and reduce to one-third.

2 Add 1 tablespoon of cold water and allow to cool. Add the egg yolks.

3 Put on a bain-marie and whisk continuously to a sabayon consistency.

4 Remove from the heat and gradually whisk in the melted butter.

5 Add seasoning. Pass through muslin or a fine chinois.

6 To finish, add the chopped chervil and tarragon.

7 Store in an appropriate container at room temperature.

Note: Egg-based sauces should not be kept warm for more than 2 hours. After this time, they should be thrown away, but are best made fresh to order.

Variations

- Choron sauce: 200 g tomato concassée, well dried. Do not add the chopped tarragon and chervil to finish.
- Foyot or valois sauce: 25 g warm meat glaze.
- Paloise sauce: this sauce is made as for béarnaise using chopped mint stalks in place of the tarragon in the reduction. To finish, add chopped mint instead of the chervil and tarragon.

107 Sabayon sauce

	8 portions
egg yolks	4
caster or unrefined sugar	100 g
dry white wine	¼ litre

1 Whisk egg yolks and sugar in a 1 litre pan or basin until white.

2 Dilute with the wine.

3 Place pan or basin in a bain-marie of warm water.

4 Whisk mixture continuously until it increases to 4 times its bulk and is firm and frothy.

Sabayon sauce may be offered as an accompaniment to any suitable hot sweet, e.g. pudding soufflé.

It may also be made using milk in place of wine, which can be flavoured according to taste, e.g. with vanilla, nutmeg, cinnamon.

108 Sabayon with olive oil (may be used as an alternative to sauce hollandaise)

	4–6 portions	8–12 portions
crushed peppercorns	6	15
vinegar	1 tbsp	2½ tbsp
egg yolks	3	8
olive oil	250 ml	625 ml
salt, cayenne pepper		

1 Place the peppercorns and vinegar in a small sauteuse or stainless-steel pan and reduce to one-third.

2 Add 1 tablespoon of cold water and allow to cool.

3 Add the egg yolks and whisk over a gentle heat in a sabayon.

4 Remove from heat. Cool.

5 Gradually whisk in the tepid olive oil.

6 Correct the seasoning.

7 Pass through a muslin or fine strainer.

8 Serve warm.

Should the sauce curdle, place a teaspoon of boiling water in a clean sauteuse and gradually whisk in the curdled sauce. If this fails to reconstitute the sauce then place an egg yolk in a clean sauteuse with a dessertspoon of water. Whisk lightly over gentle heat until slightly thickened. Remove from heat and gradually add the curdled sauce whisking continuously. To stabilise the sauce during service, 60 ml thick béchamel may be added before straining.

This sauce is healthier than hollandaise because it does not contain the cholesterol of a hollandaise made with butter.

CREAMED THICKENED SAUCES

These are used mainly in poached fish, veal and chicken dishes.

109 Suprême sauce

Makes ½ litre, 8–12 portions

This sauce can be served hot with boiled chicken, vol-au-vents, etc., and can also be used for white chaud-froid sauce. It is a velouté made from chicken stock flavoured with well-washed mushroom trimmings.

chicken velouté	½ litre
mushroom trimmings (white)	25 g
cream	60 ml
egg yolk	1
lemon juice	2–3 drops

1 Allow the velouté to cook out with the mushroom trimmings.

2 Pass through a fine strainer. Reboil.

3 Mix the cream and egg yolk in a basin (liaison).

4 Add a little of the boiling sauce to the liaison.

5 Return all to the sauce – do not reboil.

6 Mix, finish with lemon juice and correct the seasoning.

110 Suprêmes of chicken in cream sauce

	4 portions	10 portions
butter or margarine	50 g	125 g
seasoned flour	25 g	60 g
suprêmes of chicken	4	10
sherry or white wine	30 ml	75 ml
double cream or non-dairy cream	125 ml	312 ml
salt, cayenne pepper		

1 Heat the butter or margarine in a sauté pan.

2 Lightly flour the suprêmes.

3 Cook the suprêmes gently on both sides (7–9 minutes) with the minimum of colour.

4 Place the suprêmes in an earthenware serving dish; cover to keep warm.

5 Drain off the fat from the pan.

6 Deglaze the pan with the sherry or white wine.

7 Add the cream, bring to the boil and season.

8 Allow to reduce to a lightly thickened consistency. Correct the seasoning.

9 Pass through a fine chinois on to the suprêmes and serve.

An alternative method of preparing the sauce is to use half the amount of cream (fresh or non-dairy) and an equal amount of chicken velouté.

111 Veal escalopes with cream sauce

	4 portions	10 portions
butter or margarine	50 g	125 g
seasoned flour	25 g	60 g
veal escalopes (slightly battened)	4	10
sherry or white wine	30 ml	75 ml
double cream	125 ml	250 ml
salt, cayenne pepper		

1 Heat the butter in a sauté pan.

2 Lightly flour the escalopes.

3 Cook the escalopes gently on both sides with the minimum of colour. They should be a delicate light brown.

4 Place the escalopes in an earthenware serving dish; cover and keep warm.

5 Drain off all fat from the pan.

6 Deglaze the pan with the sherry or white wine.

7 Add the cream, bring to the boil and season.

8 Allow to reduce to a lightly thickened consistency, correct the seasoning.

9 Pass through a fine chinois over the escalopes and serve.

112 Smitaine sauce

Makes ½ litre

butter or margarine	25 g
onion, finely chopped	50 g
white wine	60 ml
sour cream	½ litre
seasoning	
lemon, juice of	¼

1 Melt butter or margarine in a sauteuse and cook onion without colour.

2 Add the white wine and reduce by half.

3 Add sour cream and season lightly; reduce by one-third.

4 Pass through a fine strainer and finish with lemon juice.

Use with a hached beef steak or with sausages, etc.

113 Yoghurt/fromage frais thickened sauces

Natural yoghurt or fromage frais can be used in place of cream in any sauce. This considerably reduces the fat content of the sauce and is therefore a major consideration with regard to healthy eating.

Care must be taken when adding natural yoghurt; excessive heat will give a curdled appearance.

Note: An alternative method of preparing a cream sauce is to use half the amount of cream and an equal amount of chicken velouté.

Certain vegetables, e.g. carrots and broad beans, when almost cooked can have double cream added and cooking completed to form a cream sauce. Cream sauces may also be produced from a béchamel or velouté base.

SOUBISES, AND VEGETABLE AND FRUIT PURÉES

Soubise is the traditional name given to a purée or sauce made from onions. In contemporary use this has been broadened to include other examples.

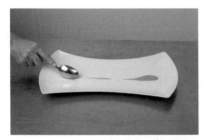

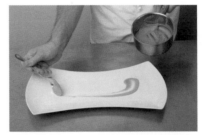

114 Onion soubise

Makes 300 g

onions, peeled	6 (750 g)
sprigs thyme	2
butter	100 g
chicken stock	250 ml
cream	125 ml

1 Slice the onions finely and pick the thyme.

2 Cook together in the butter until golden, then add the stock and reduce by half.

3 Add the cream, bring to the boil and liquidise until smooth.

nutritional info

1 large portion provides:
656 kJ/159.0 kcal
12.7 g fat (of which 7.2 g saturated)
10.2 g carbohydrate (of which 7.3 g sugars)
1.7 g protein
1.8 g fibre

Butter and double cream were used.

kcal
1000
900
800
700
600
500
400
300
200
100
0

calorie counter

115 Cauliflower soubise

Makes 300 g

onion	½
butter	50 g
cauliflower	1
chicken stock	250 ml
cream	375 ml

1 Caramelise the onions in the butter.

2 Add the cauliflower and continue to caramelise. When the colour is correct, add the stock.

3 Simmer until the cauliflower is cooked and the stock reduced by half.

4 Add the cream and reduce by half again. Blitz until smooth.

5 Pass through a fine chinois and season.

nutritional info

1 large portion provides:
817 kJ/198.4 kcal
20.5 g fat (of which 12.7 g saturated)
2.0 g carbohydrate (of which 1.7 g sugars)
1.7 g protein
0.6 g fibre

Butter and double cream were used.

♥ kcal
1000
900
800
700
600
500
400
300
200
100
0
calorie counter

116 Garlic soubise

Makes 150 g

garlic heads	5
cream	150 ml
chicken stock	150 ml

1 Peel the heads of garlic.

2 Blanch five times, each time bringing cold water to the boil.

3 On the fifth time, check the garlic is cooked. If not, continue to blanch until cooked.

4 When cooked, cover with the cream and chicken stock.

5 Bring to the boil. Infuse for 10 minutes.

6 Blitz together to the correct consistency and season.

7 Pass through a fine chinois.

nutritional info

1 large portion provides:
341 kJ/82.5 kcal
6.8 g fat (of which 4.2 g saturated)
3.6 g carbohydrate (of which 0.6 g sugars)
1.9 g protein
0.9 g fibre

Stock and double cream were used.

♥ kcal
1000
900
800
700
600
500
400
300
200
100
0
calorie counter

117 Parsnip purée

Makes 700 g

parsnips, peeled, stalks removed	1 kg
butter	50 g
vanilla pod, split	1
seasoning	
milk to aid purée	

1 Place the parsnips, butter and vanilla pod in a vac-pac and steam until soft.

2 Remove the pod and scrape out the seeds.

3 Add the rest of the ingredients and blitz with the aid of milk if necessary.

4 Pass though a fine drum sieve and season.

nutritional info

1 large portion provides:
358 kJ/85.5 kcal
4.4 g fat (of which 2.4 g saturated)
10.6 g carbohydrate (of which 4.9 g sugars)
1.6 g protein
3.8 g fibre

Whole milk and a small amount of butter were used.

♥ kcal
1000
900
800
700
600
500
400
300
200
100
0
calorie counter

118 Celeriac purée

Makes 700 g

By using the same method and ingredients as for recipe 117, above, but using celeriac instead of parsnip, adding garlic and thyme to the milk, and leaving out the vanilla, a different sauce can be achieved.

nutritional info
1 large portion provides:
193 kJ/47.2 kcal
3.8 g fat (of which 2.2 g saturated)
2.1 g carbohydrate (of which 1.6 g sugars)
1.1 g protein
3.1 g fibre
Whole milk and a small amount of butter were used.

kcal / calorie counter: 1000 900 800 700 600 500 400 300 200 100 0

1 Cut up the celeriac and cook in milk with garlic and thyme.

2 Strain off the milk and retain.

3 Add the celeriac to the blitzer and purée using the milk to bring together.

4 Check the seasoning.

Vegetable and fruit purées

Used as sauces, vegetable and fruit purées are known as a cullis or coulis.

Some vegetables and fruits are suitable for making into purées, which can then be thinned to a sauce consistency. In certain dishes where vegetables are cooked in with fish or meat, once the dish is cooked the vegetables can be puréed and thinned with the cooking liquor to make the sauce.

119 Avocado sauce [V]

Ripe, peeled, chopped avocados processed to a purée, seasoned with salt and pepper, and thinned with oil (vegan option), cream or natural yoghurt, and stirred. Use with recipes 34 or 40.

120 Avocado and fennel sauce [V]

400 g cooked fennel well processed to a purée with 2 ripe avocados.

Use with roast fish dishes.

121 Avocado and celery sauce [V]

As above, using 400 g cooked celery or celeriac.

These sauces are suitable for serving hot or cold with many vegetarian and vegan dishes.

122 Beetroot sauce

400 g cooked, peeled beetroot puréed in a food blender with sufficient red wine to give a light consistency, then strained. When heated, finish with 50 g butter, 2 teaspoons caster sugar, salt and pepper. Can be served with roast fish and cuts of venison.

123 Broccoli sauce V

Makes 250 ml

cooked broccoli	400 g
sunflower seeds	75 g
smetana *or*	250 ml
silken tofu *or*	
natural yoghurt or cream	
lemon juice	1
seasoning	

Liquidise the ingredients with ½ litre of water and strain through a coarse strainer. Use tofu to make this a vegan dish.

Use with vegetarian dishes, grilled meats or fish.

124 Fresh tomato sauce (cooked)

	4 portions
tomatoes, fully ripe	1 kg
onion, chopped	50 g
clove garlic, chopped	1
butter	25 g
salt and pepper	
pinch of sugar	

1 Skin, halve, remove the seeds and chop the tomatoes.
2 Sweat the chopped onion and garlic in the butter.
3 Add the tomatoes and season.
4 Simmer for 15 minutes.
5 Purée in a liquidiser or food processor.
6 Bring to the boil and correct the seasoning.

Note: Herbs, such as rosemary, thyme or bay leaf, may be added, and shallots used in place of onion.

Fully, ripe, well-flavoured tomatoes are needed for a good fresh tomato sauce. Italian plum tomatoes are also suitable and it is sometimes advisable to use tinned plum tomatoes if the fresh tomatoes that are available lack flavour and colour.

Asparagus, celery, fennel, mushroom, onion, salsify, spinach, tomato, watercress and yellow pepper are other vegetables that can be seasoned with herbs or spices, then processed, strained and thinned to a suitable consistency for a sauce, or enriched with butter and/or cream.

Some pulse vegetables, e.g. lentils, peas and beans, are suitable for cooking and processing into sauces.

Fruit purées, used as sauces, fall into two categories, as follows.

1 Fruits, e.g. apple, cranberry and gooseberry, that are cooked with the minimum of sugar so as to retain a degree of sharpness and are used for serving with fish, meat or poultry dishes.
2 Fruits that are puréed and used for sweet dishes, e.g. apricot, blackcurrant, blackberry, damson, plum and rhubarb, which are lightly cooked in a little water with sufficient sugar to sweeten, then liquidised and strained.

125 Gooseberry sauce V

Makes 250 ml

gooseberries, trimmed and washed	400 g
sugar	50 g
water	60–100 ml

Boil together all ingredients; liquidise and strain if required. May be served with grilled mackerel, roast goose or grilled pork chops.

126 Pesto sauce

Makes 250 ml

fresh basil leaves	100 g
pine nuts (lightly toasted)	1 tbsp
garlic (picked and crumbled)	2 cloves
Parmesan cheese (grated)	40 g
pecorino cheese (grated)	40 g
olive oil	5 tbsp
salt and pepper	

1 Place all ingredients into a food processor, and mix to a rough-textured sauce.
2 Transfer to a bowl and leave for at least 1 hour to enable the flavours to develop.

Variations: flat-leaved parsley in place of basil; walnuts in place of pine nuts.

Pesto is traditionally served with a large flat pasta called trenette.

Pesto is also used as a cordon in various fish and meat plated dishes, e.g. grilled fish, medallions of veal.

OIL-BASED SAUCES

These fall roughly into two categories, as follows.

1 Cold: mayonnaise and derivatives; vinaigrette and variations.
2 Hot: vinaigrette and variations; vinaigrettes used with some fish and vegetable dishes.

When preparing hot vinaigrettes, various flavoured oils and vinegars can be used to give a variety of tastes. Oils, such as olive, walnut, sesame seed, sunflower, grapeseed, peanut and safflower, can be flavoured by marinating herbs, e.g. basil, thyme, oregano, rosemary, garlic or onions, in them in one of two ways.

1 Place a bunch of the chosen herb/s into a bottle of oil, cork tightly and keep on a cool shelf.
2 Warm the oil with the herb/s for 15–20 minutes.

There is scope here for experimentation with various herbs, spices and vegetables, e.g. onion, garlic, shallots, so that a mise-en-place of several flavoured oils can be produced.

Red or white vinegars can be flavoured with herbs such as thyme, tarragon, dill, mint, rosemary, etc.

■ Fruit vinegars include raspberry, strawberry, blackberry, peach, plum, apple, cherry.

■ Floral vinegars, e.g. elderflower, rose.
■ Sharp vinegars, e.g. chilli, garlic, horseradish.

When making vinaigrettes for use in hot dishes, there is obviously considerable room for experimentation, and the skill lies in the blending of the ingredients and flavours of both oils and vinegars to complement the dishes with which they are to be used and ensuring that they do not dominate. For example, red mullet fillets or skate, lightly steamed, grilled or fried and lightly masked with a hot vinaigrette, is a basic recipe to which many variations can be applied, such as:

■ a lightly cooked small brunoise of vegetables added
■ finish with chopped fennel or dill.

Many vegetables simply cooked either by boiling or steaming can be given additional flavours by finishing with a light dribble of a suitably flavoured hot vinaigrette – for example:

■ sliced or diced beetroot, carrots, turnips, swedes
■ a mixture of cooked vegetables
■ crisply cooked shredded cabbage.

127   Garlic, red onion and ginger oil
Mark McCann

Makes 500 ml

olive oil	500 ml
mirepoix	200 g
onions (roast one for 10 minutes)	3 large
root ginger	150 g
garlic (one bulb roasted)	1½ bulbs
bay leaves	2
black peppercorns	8
sea salt	12 g
lemon grass (split and roasted for 5 minutes)	1 stick
cinnamon	1 stick
olive oil	1 tsp
white wine vinegar	1 tsp

1 Heat 1 teaspoon of olive oil in a pan.

2 Sweat the mirepoix, the two onions that have not been roasted, 75 g of the ginger and the ½ bulb of garlic that has not been roasted. Fry until golden brown.

3 Add one of the bay leaves, the peppercorns and sea salt, and cook for 3–4 minutes.

4 Add half the olive oil and bring up to boiling point.

5 Remove from the heat and allow to cool.

6 When completely cold, pass through a chinois into a kilner jar.

7 Add the lemon grass, cinnamon and remaining ingredients.

8 For the best flavour, leave for one month.

128   Roasted pepper oil
Mark McCann

Makes 500 ml

virgin olive oil	500 ml
mirepoix	200 g
red pepper	2
yellow pepper — cleaned and roasted	2
green pepper	2
bay leaves	2
black peppercorns	8
cloves garlic	2
sea salt	½ tsp
virgin olive oil	1 tsp
white wine vinegar	1 tsp

1 Heat 1 teaspoon of olive oil in a pan.

2 Sweat the mirepoix and one of each of the peppers until golden brown.

3 Add 1 bay leaf, the black peppercorns, one clove of garlic and the sea salt, and cook for a further 3–4 minutes.

4 Add half the olive oil and bring to the simmering point.

5 Take off the heat and allow to cool.

6 When completely cool, pass through a chinois into a clean kilner jar.

7 Add the white wine vinegar and the remaining olive oil, roasted garlic, roasted peppers and remaining bay leaf.

8 For full flavour, leave for at least one month before use.

SOUPS

PRINCIPLES OF SOUP MAKING

In keeping with healthy eating practices the following points should be considered when making soup.

1 Purée soups may be thickened using vegetables and require no flour.
2 Wholemeal flour can be used for thickened soups.
3 Cream and velouté soups may be made with skimmed milk and finished with non-dairy cream, natural yoghurt or fromage frais.
4 Velouté soups may be finished with non-dairy cream, low-fat natural yoghurt, quark or fromage frais.

Variations can be created, as in the following examples.

1 Combining finished soups, e.g. adding a watercress soup to a tomato soup.
2 Using the main ingredients together, e.g. tomatoes and watercress in the initial preparation.
3 Careful use of different herbs to introduce a subtle flavour, e.g. basil, rosemary, chervil.
4 Using a garnish that is varied, e.g. blanched watercress leaves, chopped chives and tomato concassée, and finishing with non-dairy cream or yoghurt.

The following are some examples of 'combination' soups:

- watercress with lettuce
- watercress and spinach
- watercress and courgettes
- leek and onion
- leek and broccoli
- leek and tomato
- leek and cucumber
- potato and endive
- tomato with courgette
- potato and spinach
- tomato and mushroom
- tomato and celery
- tomato and cauliflower
- tomato and cucumber
- chicken and mushroom
- chicken and leek

An essential ingredient for soup is the liquid and only the best quality stock of the appropriate flavour should be used to enhance the soup. Care should be taken, however, to preserve the flavour of the main ingredient – for example, mushroom and lettuce should not be overpowered by an over-strong stock.

Units covered
3FPC2

LIST OF RECIPES

Recipe no	page no	Recipe no	page no
Consommés		145 Cream of celery and cheese soup	127
130 Borscht	118	146 Cream of tomato and orange soup	128
131 Consommé of shellfish with crayfish and		149 Mulligatawny	129
Parmesan gnocchi	118	148 Okra or gumbo soup	129
129 Consommé of wild duck and beetroot	117	139 Pea and ham soup	124
132 Mussel soup	119	142 Potato and leek soup	126
133 Tomato and garlic consommé	120	138 Pumpkin soup with confit rabbit	123
Broths		140 Red lentil and bacon soup	124
137 Clam chowder	122	147 Roasted plum tomato and olive soup	128
136 Lentil and mushroom soup	121	141 Watercress and beetroot soup	125
135 Prawn bisque	121	**Chilled soups**	
134 Vegetable broth	120	152 Chive, potato and cucumber soup	
Purée soups		with cream	131
143 Carrot and orange soup	126	153 Fruit soups	131
144 Chicken soup with mushrooms and		151 Gazpacho	130
tongue	127	150 Vichyssoise	130

The following table indicates the variety of stocks, finishes, accompaniments and garnishes that can be used in the making and serving of soups.

by. Some hearty soups are still with us today – for example, Scotch broth, minestrone, bouillabaisse, pea and ham, chowder, and many more, some of which are described below.

Stocks	Finishes	Accompaniments	Garnishes
bacon	cream	toasted flutes	julienne or brunoise of:
ham	milk	bread sticks	beetroot — celery
chicken	yolks	Melba toast	celeriac — peppers
beef	yoghurt	toast spread with pâté	carrots — beans
veal	quark	cheese straws	turnips — leeks
game	fromage frais	grated cheese	mushrooms — game
mutton	non-dairy cream	profiteroles	poultry — meat
vegetable	port	croutons	lightly fried bacon cordons
fish	Madeira		also savoury pancakes
	white wine		meatballs, quenelles
	coconut milk or cream		chopped or leaves of:
	warm milk		parsley — mint
			sorrel — chervil, etc.
			ravioli or tortellini

Originally soup meant basic sustenance and, in most houses, it would be a one-pot meal that would consist of scrag ends of meat, vegetables, pulses and roots, and would be cooked for a while to extract lots of flavour. Soups can almost be classified as a lighter style of stew, but basically soup was originally seen as a meal in itself – served with a generous chunk of bread and a warm hearth to enjoy it

Since then, more sophisticated dining concepts have altered the role of soups and more restaurant chefs are now offering a lighter slant to the soup approach. Classically, 15 or 20 years ago, most soups were thickened by either purée or by roux, the latter method seemingly the most common. Nowadays the approach is lighter, with a reduction in flour and fat offering a most sophisticated dish.

There are many ways to classify soup: the classic velouté thickened with a liaison, purée of lentils with ham hock stock, broth with a clear liquid, or even the crystal clarity of a consommé – all still grace our modern restaurant tables. However, the fundamental foundation to today's dining is a lighter and more sophisticated approach. With this in mind, a combination of the above with a careful approach to thickening will yield a modern and up-to-date soup.

CONSOMMÉS

129 Consommé of wild duck and beetroot

	4 portions	10 portions
wild duck leg, chopped and minced with no fat	200 g	500 g
water	125 ml	300 ml
small onion, chopped finely	1	3
small carrot, chopped finely	1	3
celery, small stick, chopped finely	1	3
bouquet garni	1	3
salt	¼ tsp	½ tsp
white peppercorns	4	10
sherry vinegar	2 tbsp	5 tbsp
raw beetroot, grated	200 g	500 g
egg whites	2	5
cold game stock	1.25 litres	3 litres
To finish		
beetroot, cooked and diced	150 g	375 g
duck breast, roasted	2	5

1 Mix all the ingredients together, excluding the stock. Place into a saucepan. Add the stock and mix well.

2 Heat slowly to simmering point, whisking occasionally until the froth rises to the surface.

3 Remove the whisk, cover and simmer very gently for 45–60 minutes. Do not allow to boil or the froth will break and cloud the consommé.

4 Strain slowly through a muslin and, if necessary, strain again.

5 Re-heat and re-season if required, however salt will make the clarity of consommé slightly cloudy.

6 Serve garnished with the diced cooked beetroot and julienne of roast wild duck breast.

nutritional info

♥

1 large portion provides:
682 kJ/162.9 kcal
7.8 g fat (of which 2.5 g saturated)
3.6 g carbohydrate (of which 3.2 g sugars)
19.6 g protein
0.7 g fibre

There is a little fat from the duck breast.

kcal
1000
900
800
700
600
500
400
300
200
100
0

calorie counter

130 Borscht

This is an unclarified broth of eastern European origin, mainly from Russia and Poland.

Stock	4 portions	10 portions
duck (half-roasted)	1 × 2 kg	2 × 2 kg
boiling beef (blanched and refreshed)	200 g	500 g
beef stock	2 litres	5 litres
beetroot juice	*250 ml	600 ml
onion	50 g	125 g
carrots	50 g	125 g
celery	50 g	125 g
leek	50 g	125 g
bouquet garni		
Garnish		
carrot	50 g (2 oz)	125 g (5 oz)
leek	50 g (2 oz)	125 g (5 oz)
cabbage	50 g (2 oz)	125 g (5 oz)
beetroot	50 g (2 oz)	125 g (5 oz)
cooked duck, diced	50 g (2 oz)	125 g (5 oz)
cooked beef, diced	50 g (2 oz)	125 g (5 oz)
Accompaniments		
* beetroot juice		
sour cream		
** small duck patties		

nutritional info

1 large portion provides:
428 kJ/102 kcal
2.4 g fat (of which 0.8 g saturated)
11.1 g carbohydrate (of which 10.1 g sugars)
9.5 g protein
2.9 g fibre

There is a little fat from the duck; there will be more if sour cream is served.

1 Make a good brown stock, allow to simmer and reduce to half the amount.

2 Strain through a double muslin, skim well, correct the seasoning, add the garnish and simmer gently until cooked. (For the garnish, the vegetables are cooked in short, thick batons.)

Note: * Grate raw peeled beetroot and squeeze firmly to obtain the juice.
** Duck patties can be made as small as possible from any type of paste, e.g. short or puff, and the filling should be a well-flavoured and seasoned duck mixture with, for example, sweated chopped onion and cabbage.

131 Consommé of shellfish with crayfish and Parmesan gnocchi

	4 portions	10 portions
crushed crayfish claws and meat	200 g	500 g
cleaned and soaked scallop skirts excluding roe and sack	100 g (1)	250 g (3)
water	125 ml	300 ml
small onion, chopped finely	1	3
small carrot, chopped finely	1	3
celery, small stick, chopped finely	1	3
shellfish nage	400 ml	1 litre
bouquet garni	1	3
salt	¼ tsp	½ tsp
white peppercorns	4	10
sherry vinegar	2 tbsp	5 tbsp
egg whites	3	7

To finish		
cooked crayfish tails	12	30
pieces of gnocchi (see recipe 385)	12	30

nutritional info

1 large portion provides:
1063 kJ/254.5 kcal
14.5 g fat (of which 7.6 g saturated)
12.6 g carbohydrate (of which 0.9 g sugars)
19.2 g protein
0.5 g fibre

There is some fat from the crayfish. Half of the gnocchi recipe was used for this analysis.

1 Mix all the ingredients together, excluding the stock. Place into a saucepan. Add the stock and mix well.

2 Heat slowly to simmering point, whisking occasionally until the froth rises to the surface.

3 Remove the whisk, cover and simmer very gently for 45–60 minutes. Do not allow to boil or the froth will break and cloud the consommé.

4 Strain slowly through a muslin and, if necessary, strain again.

5 Re-heat and re-season if required, however salt will make the clarity of consommé slightly cloudy.

6 Serve garnished with crayfish tails and gnocchi.

132 Mussel soup

	4 portions	10 portions
mussels	400 g	1¼ kg
fish stock	1 litre	2½ litre
shallots or onions	50 g	125 g
celery	50 g	125 g
leek	50 g	125 g
parsley		
salt and pepper		
white wine	60 ml	150 ml
cream } liaison	125 ml	300 ml
egg yolk }	1	2–3

1 Scrape and thoroughly clean the mussels.

2 Place in a pan with the stock, chopped vegetables and herbs; season.

3 Cover with a lid and simmer for 5 minutes.

4 Extract the mussels from the shells and remove the beards. Discard any closed shells.

5 Strain the liquid through a double muslin and bring to the boil; add the wine.

6 Correct the seasoning, finish with a liaison and garnish with the mussels and more chopped parsley.

Note: Variations for this soup include using scallops in place of mussels, and fennel and dill in place of parsley. A further variation is to prepare a potato soup using fish stock, garnish with mussels and finish with cream.

nutritional info

1 large portion provides:
834 kJ/201.9 kcal
18.8 g fat (of which 10.9 g saturated)
3.2 g carbohydrate (of which 2.1 g sugars)
5.0 g protein
0.6 g fibre

Liaison of egg yolk and cream.

♥

kcal
1000
900
800
700
600
500
400
300
200
100
0

calorie counter

133 Tomato and garlic consommé v

	4 portions	10 portions
plum tomatoes	3 kg	7 kg
large onion, chopped finely	1	3
celery stick, chopped finely	1	3
garlic cloves, crushed	5	12
salt		
To finish		
tomato concassée	4 tbsp	10 tbsp
basil, julienned		

1 Chop the tomatoes roughly. Place in a food processor and, using the pulse button, pulse the tomatoes for 5–10 seconds.

2 Mix the tomatoes with the rest of the ingredients. Sprinkle with a little salt and place in a clean, damp tea towel or muslin and hang overnight.

3 This will yield a clear, intensely flavoured tomato water. This can be served chilled or heated slightly and garnished with the tomato concassée and julienne of basil.

nutritional info

1 large portion provides:
44 kJ/10.4 kcal
0.1 g fat (of which 0.0 g saturated)
2.0 g carbohydrate (of which 1.9 g sugars)
0.3 g protein
0.4 g fibre

There is no fat in the recipe.

calorie counter
kcal
1000
900
800
700
600
500
400
300
200
100
0

BROTHS

134 Vegetable broth v

	4 portions	10 portions
olive oil	1 tbsp	3 tbsp
large onion, finely chopped	1	3
large garlic clove, chopped	1	3
large courgette, skin on, chopped	1	3
raw peas	100 g	250 g
green beans, raw, topped and tailed	100 g	250 g
cumin seeds	½ tsp	1 tsp
red chilli, chopped and seeds removed	½ tsp	1 tsp
bay leaf	1 tsp	2 tsp
tomato purée	1 tbsp	2 tbsp
vegetable nage	400 ml	1 litre
salt and pepper		
plum tomatoes, cut for concassée	3	7

1 Heat the olive oil in a pan over a medium flame. Stir in the chopped onion and garlic and sauté for 5–8 minutes. The onion should be just turning soft.

2 Add the rest of the vegetables, excluding the tomatoes. Stir, reduce the heat to low and cook for a further 5 minutes.

3 Stir in the cumin seeds, chilli and bay leaf, and cook for a further 1 minute.

4 Add the tomato paste and cook for a further minute. Add the nage.

5 Bring to the boil and simmer for 15 minutes until the vegetables are tender.

6 Adjust the seasoning and add the tomato concassée. Serve with crusty homemade bread.

nutritional info

1 large portion provides:
415 kJ/99.9 kcal
3.8 g fat (of which 0.6 g saturated)
12.6 g carbohydrate (of which 8.4 g sugars)
4.7 g protein
3.9 g fibre

A little olive oil was used to sauté the onion.

calorie counter
kcal
1000
900
800
700
600
500
400
300
200
100
0

135 Prawn bisque

	4 portions	10 portions
oil	50 ml	125 ml
butter	30 g	75 g
unshelled prawns	250 g	625 g
flour	20 g	50 g
tomato purée	1 tbsp	2 tbsp
shellfish nage	1 litre	2½ litres
fish stock	150 ml	375 ml
whipping cream	120 ml	300 ml
dry sherry	75 ml	180 ml
paprika, pinch		
seasoning		
chopped chives		

1 Heat the oil and the butter. Add the prawns and cook for 3–4 minutes on a moderately high heat.

2 Sprinkle in the flour and cook for a further 2–3 minutes.

3 Add the tomato purée and cook for a further 2 minutes.

4 Meanwhile, bring the nage up to a simmer and, once the tomato purée has been cooked in, slowly add to the prawn mix, being mindful that you have formed a roux; stir in the fish stock to prevent lumping.

5 Once all the stock has been added, bring to the boil and simmer for 3–4 minutes.

6 Pass through a fine sieve, return the shells to the pan and pound to extract more flavour and more colour.

7 Pour over the fish stock, bring to the boil, then pass this back onto the already passed soup.

8 Bring to the boil, add the cream and sherry, correct the seasoning and served with chopped chives.

nutritional info

1 large portion provides:
1404 kJ/340.4 kcal
33.9 g fat (of which 14.9 g saturated)
6.2 g carbohydrate (of which 2.3 g sugars)
2.9 g protein
0.3 g fibre

The prawns were cooked in oil and butter; cream was added to serve.

kcal
calorie counter
1000
900
800
700
600
500
400
300
200
100
0

136 Lentil and mushroom soup

	4 portions	10 portions
butter	50 g	125 g
large onions, chopped	2	5
carrots, peeled and finely chopped	3	7
garlic cloves, finely chopped	2	5
piece of smoked bacon or pancetta	100 g	250 g
soaked puy lentils	200 g	500 g
white wine	150 ml	375 ml
mushroom nage	300 ml	750 ml
vegetable nage	300 ml	750 ml
salt and pepper to taste		
To finish		
cooked wild mushrooms	250 g	625 g

1 Add the butter to the pan and sauté the vegetables, bacon and lentils for 5 minutes.

2 Add the wine and nages, and cook for approximately 50 minutes on a low heat.

3 Remove the piece of bacon and retain for garnish.

4 Purée in a food processor, adding more stock if necessary, if the soup becomes too thick.

5 To finish, add the cooked wild mushrooms and cooked bacon, diced.

6 Serve immediately.

nutritional info

1 large portion provides:
1258 kJ/301.1 kcal
13.0 g fat (of which 7.3 g saturated)
34.4 g carbohydrate (of which 11.4 g sugars)
13.8 g protein
5.2 g fibre

Butter was used to sauté the vegetables, bacon and lentils. There is fat from the bacon.

kcal
calorie counter
1000
900
800
700
600
500
400
300
200
100
0

137 Clam chowder

	4 portions	10 portions
Clams		
medium shallots, finely diced	3	7
butter	50 g	125 g
Venus clams, shells tightly closed	1 kg	2½ kg
white wine or vermouth	200 ml	500 ml
Chowder		
corn oil	50 ml	125 ml
smoked bacon, cut into 1 cm dice	50 g	125 g
medium onion, cut into 1 cm dice	1	2
medium carrot, cut into 1 cm dice	1	2
medium potato, peeled and cut into 1 cm dice	1	2
cloves garlic, finely chopped	2	5
stick celery, cut into 1 cm dice	1	2
medium yellow bell pepper, cut into 1 cm dice	1	2
chicken stock	1 litre	2½ litres
whipping cream	100 ml	250 ml
salt and pepper		
butter	50 g	125 g
Garnish		
chervil, chopped		

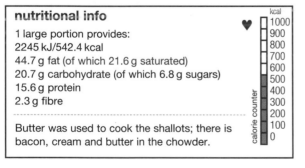

nutritional info

1 large portion provides:
2245 kJ/542.4 kcal
44.7 g fat (of which 21.6 g saturated)
20.7 g carbohydrate (of which 6.8 g sugars)
15.6 g protein
2.3 g fibre

Butter was used to cook the shallots; there is bacon, cream and butter in the chowder.

For the clams

1 Take a large saucepan with a tight-fitting lid and place over a medium heat with the shallots and butter. Cook for 1 minute without letting the shallots colour.

2 Add the washed clams, shake the pan, then add the wine or vermouth, and place the lid on the pan immediately.

3 Leave the clams to steam for 1–2 minutes so that they open and exude an intense liquor. Remove the lid and make sure all the clams are open; if only 95 per cent are open, remove the pan from the heat and discard any with closed shells.

4 Place a colander over a large bowl, and pour the contents of the pan into the colander, reserving the liquor for the chowder.

5 Allow the clams to cool. Pick out the meat and discard the shells. Store the clam meat in an airtight container in the fridge until you are ready to serve the chowder.

For the chowder

1 In a large saucepan, heat the oil. When hot, add the bacon and cook for about 5 minutes until crisp and brown.

2 Using a perforated spoon, transfer the bacon onto kitchen paper to drain.

3 Add the onion, carrot, potato, garlic and celery to the saucepan, reduce the heat to medium-low and cook the vegetables without colouring.

4 Add the bell peppers and cook for 5 minutes.

5 Pour in the reserved liquor from the clams and the chicken stock. Bring to the boil and simmer for 10 minutes or until the volume of liquid has reduced by about half.

6 Add the cooked bacon and cream, then bring to the boil and reduce for a further 2 minutes until the soup thickens slightly. Season.

7 At this point the soup can be cooled and stored for 2 days in the refrigerator, but is best made on the day of serving.

7 Just before serving, whisk in the butter.

To finish

1 Add the clams to the hot chowder and stir for 30 seconds until they are reheated.

2 Place in serving bowls, garnish with chopped chervil and serve.

PURÉE SOUPS

138 Pumpkin soup with confit rabbit

	4 portions	10 portions
Pumpkin soup		
butter	150 g	375 g
pumpkin, peeled and chopped	600 g	1½ kg
salt and pepper		
chicken stock	400 ml	1 litre
Parmesan	100 g	250 g
Confit rabbit		
rabbit legs	4	10
Maldon salt	100 g	250 g
sprigs thyme	2	5
garlic cloves, sliced	1	2
confit oil	1 litre	2½ litres

For the pumpkin soup

1 Melt the butter in a pan and add the chopped pumpkin and seasoning. Cook slowly until the pumpkin is soft.

2 Add chicken stock and bring to the boil. Cook for 6 minutes.

3 Remove from the heat and add the Parmesan.

4 Blitz and pass through a fine chinois.

5 Adjust the seasoning.

For the confit rabbit

1 Place the rabbit legs on a stainless-steel tray. Sprinkle with salt, thyme and garlic.

2 Marinate for 6 hours, then wash off the marinade.

3 Put the rabbit legs in a pan with the confit oil (the legs must be covered by the oil).

4 Confit for 3 hours at 90°C or until cooked.

5 Once cooked, strain the oil from the legs.

6 Flake the meat from the legs and serve as a garnish for the soup.

Note: The confit rabbit can be used as it is, or with a mousse and herbs to form a ravioli mix (see photo).

---

nutritional info ♥

1 large portion provides:
2148 kJ/584.0 kcal
53.8 g fat (of which 27.0 g saturated)
4.0 g carbohydrate (of which 3.0 g sugars)
21.4 g protein
1.6 g fibre

Butter and parmesan were used in the soup and confit oil to cook the rabbit.

kcal
1000
900
800
700
600
500
400
300
200
100
0

calorie counter

139   Pea and ham soup

	4 portions	10 portions
Ham stock		
ham hock	1	2
cold water	1 litre	2½ litres
onion, peeled	25 g	50 g
whole carrot, peeled	1	2
Soup		
frozen peas	1 kg	2½ kg
vegetable oil	10 ml	25 ml
butter	100 g	250 g
shallots, chopped	2	5
milk	250 ml	625 ml
ham stock	250 ml	625 ml
double cream	100 ml	250 ml

Note: The ham stock will take approx. 6 hours to make, therefore a good idea would be to make it the day before and keep it chilled in the refrigerator.

For the ham stock

1 Place the ham hock in a pan and cover with cold water. Place in the onion and carrot.

2 Bring to the boil and then turn down to a slow simmer.

3 When the hock is cooked, the centre bone will slide out in one smooth motion.

For the pea soup

1 Blanch the peas in a small pan of boiling water for 1 minute, then drain.

2 Heat the oil and butter in a large saucepan and cook the shallots without letting them colour.

3 Add the peas and cook for a further 2–3 minutes, again without colouring. Add the milk and ham stock, bring to a simmer for 2 minutes.

4 Cool the mixture slightly, then transfer to a food processor and liquidise until very smooth – this may take a while. After liquidising, stir in the cream.

5 At this point, the soup can be cooled completely and stored in an airtight container in the fridge until ready to serve.

nutritional info

1 large portion provides:
2276 kJ/548.4 kcal
41.2 g fat (of which 23.7 g saturated)
28.8 g carbohydrate (of which 11.4 g sugars)
17.2 g protein
13.1 g fibre

The saturated fat comes from the ham, cream and butter. Whole milk was used for this analysis.

♥ calorie counter: kcal 1000 900 800 700 600 500 400 300 200 100 0

140   Red lentil and bacon soup

	4 portions	10 portions
baby shallots	3	8
leeks	100 g	250 g
celery sticks	50 g	125 g
oil	100 ml	250 ml
pancetta bacon, chopped into small pieces	200 g	500 g
red lentils	400 g	1 kg
chicken stock	1.2 litres	3 litres

1 Slice the shallots, leek and celery into 1 cm dice.

2 Heat about 100 ml of oil in a pan. Add the vegetables and bacon, and cook until they are slightly coloured.

3 Add the lentils and cover them with the chicken stock. Bring to the boil and turn the heat down to a very slow simmer.

4 Cook this until all the lentils have broken down.

5 Allow to cool for 10 minutes and then purée until smooth.

nutritional info

1 large portion provides:
1620 kJ/390.1 kcal
28.8 g fat (of which 4.2 g saturated)
17.9 g carbohydrate (of which 3.4 g sugars)
15.9 g protein
2.0 g fibre

There is some saturated fat from the bacon.

♥ calorie counter: kcal 1000 900 800 700 600 500 400 300 200 100 0

141 Watercress and beetroot soup

	4 portions	10 portions
Beetroot		
large beetroots	2	5
water for cooking		
white wine vinegar	150 ml	375 ml
water	100 ml	250 ml
sugar	150 ml	375 ml
bay leaf	1	2
Watercress soup		
onions	160 g	400 g
leeks	175 g	430 g
butter (for the onions and leeks)	125 g	300 g
potatoes, diced small	750 g	1.8 kg
water	1.8 litres	4.5 litres
salt	15 g	30 g
pepper to taste		
spinach	125 g	300 g
watercress	600 g	1½ kg
butter (for the spinach and watercress)	125 g	300 g

Note: The beetroot for this dish is best left overnight to develop the flavour.

For the beetroot

1 Place the beetroot in a pan and cover with the water. Bring to the boil.

2 Turn down to a simmer until cooked (about 1½ hours).

3 While the beetroot is cooking, place the vinegar, water and sugar in a separate pan and bring to the boil.

4 Boil this for 5 minutes, then take off the heat.

5 Once the beetroot is cooked, drain the liquid and peel the beetroot while it is still warm, then cut into dice.

6 Add the bay leaf to the vinegar/water/sugar mixture, and pour over the diced beetroot. Reserve for at least 2 hours before using.

For the watercress soup

1 Sweat the onion and leek without colour in the butter. Cook until very tender.

2 Add the potatoes and bring quickly to the boil with the water. Season with salt and pepper and allow to cool (blast chill).

3 Separately sweat the spinach and watercress in the butter until wilted. Transfer to a suitable container and add ice (to help preserve the colour).

4 When both are cool, liquidise each mix separately and pass through a chinois.

5 Add the potato purée to the watercress purée until the correct consistency and flavour has been achieved.

6 Correct seasoning.

7 Meanwhile place a small amount of the drained beetroot in each serving bowl and top with the hot soup.

nutritional info

1 large portion provides:
2822 kJ/681.2 kcal
53.4 g fat (of which 32.8 g saturated)
42.3 g carbohydrate (of which 9.8 g sugars)
10.3 g protein
8.0 g fibre

There is a large amount of butter in the watercress soup.

♥

| kcal |
| 1000 |
| 900 |
| 800 |
| 700 |
| 600 |
| 500 |
| 400 |
| 300 |
| 200 |
| 100 |
| 0 |

calorie counter

142 Potato and leek soup

	4 portions	10 portions
onions, finely sliced	160 g	400 g
leeks, cut in ½ cm dice	175 g	430 g
butter	125 g	300 g
potatoes, cut into ½ cm dice	750 g	1.8 kg
water	1.8 litres	4.5 litres
salt	15 g	30 g
pepper to taste		
cream	125 ml	300 ml

1 Sweat the onion and leek without colour in the butter. Cook until very tender.

2 Add the potatoes and bring quickly to the boil with the water.

3 Season with salt and pepper and allow to cool (blast chill).

4 When re-heating, whisk and add a little cream.

5 Check seasoning again and serve.

nutritional info

1 large portion provides:
1694 kJ/411.5 kcal
42.8 g fat (of which 26.8 g saturated)
5.2 g carbohydrate (of which 3.9 g sugars)
1.9 g protein
1.5 g fibre

The onion and leek were sweated in butter, and cream added. Whole milk was used for this analysis.

143 Carrot and orange soup

	4 portions	10 portions
carrots, sliced	400 g	1¼ kg
white of leek, sliced	50 g	125 g
onion, sliced	50 g	125 g
butter or margarine	25 g	60 g
flour	25 g	60 g
tomato purée	1 tsp	2–3 tsp
white stock	1 litre	2½ litres
oranges, zest and juice of	2	5
bouquet garni		
salt and pepper		
natural yoghurt	125 ml	300 ml

1 Gently sweat the sliced vegetables in the butter or margarine without colour, until soft. Mix in the flour.

2 Cook over a gentle heat without colouring.

3 Mix in the tomato purée.

4 Gradually add the boiling stock. Stir well.

5 Prepare a fine julienne from the zest of the oranges, blanch and refresh.

6 Add the orange juice to the soup.

7 Add bouquet garni, salt and pepper.

8 Simmer gently for approximately 45 minutes.

9 Remove bouquet garni, liquidise and pass through a coarse strainer.

10 Return to a clean pan, reboil, correct the seasoning and consistency, finish with yoghurt. Garnish with the blanched julienne of orange zest.

Note: Alternatively, the soup may be finished with cream or fromage frais.

nutritional info

1 portion provides:
579 kJ/138 kcals
5.8 g fat
(of which 3.6 g saturated)
19.1 g carbohydrate
(of which 13.4 g sugars)
3.5 g protein
2.9 g fibre

144 Chicken soup with mushrooms and tongue

		4 portions	10 portions
chicken velouté		1 litre	2½ litres
mushroom trimmings		200 g	500 g
yolk of egg	liaison	2	5
cream		125 ml	312 ml
salt and pepper			
mushrooms		25 g	60 g
chicken	julienne garnish	25 g	60 g
tongue		25 g	60 g

nutritional info

1 portion provides:
calculated with double cream
1948 kJ/469 kcals
40 g fat
(of which 10.7 g saturated)
20.7 g carbohydrate
(of which sugars 1.6 g)
7.8 g protein
1.4 g fibre

♥ calorie counter kcal 1000 900 800 700 600 500 400 300 200 100 0

1 Prepare a chicken velouté, adding the chopped mushroom trimmings at the initial stage.

2 Liquidise and add the liaison by adding some soup to the liaison of yolks and cream and returning all to the pan.

3 Bring almost to the boil, stirring continuously and being careful not to boil, then strain into a clean pan.

4 Correct the seasoning and consistency, add the garnish and serve.

Note: 100 g raw minced chicken may be cooked in the velouté then liquidised with the soup to give a stronger chicken flavour (for 10 portions, increase the proportion 2½ times).

145 Cream of celery and cheese soup

		4 portions	10 portions
celery		200 g	500 g
onions	choppped	50 g	125 g
leeks		50 g	125 g
butter or margarine		50 g	125 g
flour		50 g	125 g
white stock		750 ml	2¼ litres
bouquet garni			
salt and pepper			
cheese (Stilton or strong Cheddar), grated		100 g	250 g
milk *or*		250 ml	600 ml
cream		125 ml	300 ml

1 Sweat the vegetables in the fat without colour.

2 Mix in the flour, cook for a few minutes and cool.

3 Gradually add the hot stock, stir to the boil.

4 Add the bouquet garni, season and simmer for approximately 45 minutes.

5 Skim, remove the bouquet garni and pass or liquidise.

6 Return to a clean pan, bring to the boil, add the cheese and stir until incorporated into the soup.

7 Correct the seasoning and consistency, add the milk or cream and serve.

nutritional info

Using 125 ml single cream
1 portion provides:
1293 kJ/311 kcals
25.1 g fat
(of which 15.9 g saturated)
12.9 g carbohydrate
(of which 2.9 g sugars)
9.2 g protein
1 g fibre

♥ calorie counter kcal 1000 900 800 700 600 500 400 300 200 100 0

146 Cream of tomato and orange soup

Prepare a cream of tomato soup. Prior to straining, add thinly peeled strips of orange zest and simmer for a few minutes. The juice of one orange may be added and a blanched julienne of orange zest used for garnish to every 500 ml of soup. Serve hot.

nutritional info

1 large portion provides:
1017 kJ/243.7 kcal
13.2 g fat (of which 8.1 g saturated)
26.4 g carbohydrate (of which 16.1 g sugars)
6.4 g protein
2.8 g fibre

Includes butter and bacon.

147 Roasted plum tomato and olive soup

	4 portions	10 portions
plum tomatoes	400 g	1½ kg
small onions	1	2
cloves of garlic	1	2
sprigs of basil	2	4
tomato purée	2 tbsp	4 tbsp
olive oil	25 g	50 g
black and green olives	50 g	100 g
balsamic vinegar	1 tsp	3 tsp
water	500 ml	1½ litres
salt and pepper		
sugar	10 g	25 g
croutes (see recipe 72)	2	3
sundried tomato paste	1 tbsp	3 tbsp
Parmesan	25 g	75 g
black olives	2	5
chopped parsley	25 g	50 g

1 Roughly chop the plum tomatoes, onion, garlic and basil.

2 Place into a roasting tray with tomato purée and a few drops of olive oil. Roast at 204°C for 10 minutes.

3 Remove from the oven and put into a saucepan. Add water.

4 Simmer for 20 minutes, stirring occasionally.

5 Liquidise for 2–3 minutes with olives. Pass through a conical sieve.

6 Check the consistency of the soup, add seasoning, a pinch of sugar and a few drops of balsamic vinegar.

7 Slice the dinner rolls into rounds and lightly toast both sides.

8 Spread with sundried tomato paste and Parmesan.

9 When the soup is required, bring to the boil. Put into soup cups and top with croutes and a slice of black olive and chopped parsley.

nutritional info

1 large portion provides:
873 kJ/208.0 kcal
10.7 g fat (of which 2.6 g saturated)
22.9 g carbohydrate (of which 9.4 g sugars)
6.6 g protein
2.9 g fibre

A small amount of olive oil was used to roast the vegetables; a little parmesan was also added.

148 Okra or gumbo soup

	4 portions	10 portions
butter, oil or margarine	50 g	125 g
okra	200 g	500 g
leek, in brunoise	100 g	250 g
chicken stock	750 ml	2¼ litres
lean ham, diced	25 g	60 g
cooked chicken	25 g	60 g
salt and pepper		
cooked rice	25 g	60 g
tomato, peeled, deseeded and diced	50 g	125 g

nutritional info

Using butter
1 portion provides:
581 kJ/140 kcals
11.5 g fat
(of which 7.1 g saturated)
4.5 g carbohydrate
(of which 2.2 g sugars)
4.9 g protein
2.7 g fibre

1 Heat the fat or oil and sweat the sliced okra in a thick-bottomed pan, covered with a lid, until nearly cooked.

2 Add the leeks and cook until soft.

3 Add the stock, diced ham and chicken, and simmer for 5 minutes.

4 Correct the seasoning, add the rice and tomato, bring to the boil and serve.

149 Mulligatawny (traditional)

	4 portions	10 portions
chopped onion	100 g	250 g
clove of garlic (chopped)	½	1–2
butter, margarine or oil	50 g	125 g
flour, white or wholemeal	50 g	125 g
curry powder	1 dsp	2½ dsp
tomato purée	1 dsp	2½ dsp
brown stock	1 litre	2½ litres
chopped apple	25 g	60 g
ground ginger	6 g	15 g
chopped chutney	1 dsp	2½ dsp
desiccated coconut	25 g	60 g
salt		
cooked rice, white or wholegrain	10 g	25 g

nutritional info

Using sunflower oil
1 portion provides:
952 kJ/227 kcals
17.1 g fat
(of which 5.0 g saturated)
16.3 g carbohydrate
(of which 4.1 g sugars)
3.3 g protein
2.6 g fibre

1 Lightly brown the onion and garlic in the fat or oil.

2 Mix in the flour and curry powder, cook out for a few minutes, browning slightly.

3 Mix in the tomato purée. Cool slightly.

4 Gradually mix in the brown stock. Stir to the boil.

5 Add the remainder of the ingredients (except the rice) and season with salt.

6 Simmer for 30–45 minutes.

7 Pass firmly through a medium strainer or liquidise.

8 Return to a clean pan and reboil.

9 Correct the seasoning and consistency.

10 Place the rice in a warm soup tureen and pour in the soup.

CHILLED SOUPS

150 Vichyssoise

	4 portions	10 portions
onions, finely sliced	160 g	400 g
leeks, finely sliced	175 g	430 g
butter	125 g	300 g
potatoes, diced small	750 g	1.8 kg
water/vegetable nage	1.8 ml	4½ litres
salt	15 g	30 g
pepper to taste		
Garnish		
whipped cream		
chives, chopped		

1 Sweat the sliced onion and leek without colour in the butter. Cook until very tender.

2 Add the potatoes and bring quickly to the boil with the water or vegetable nage.

3 Liquidise in food processor and allow to cool, check seasoning. Note that seasoning needs to reflect the serving temperature.

4 Serve cold with whipped cream and chopped chives.

Vichyssoise with Parmesan gnocchi (see recipe 181)

nutritional info

1 large portion provides:
1653 kJ/397.2 kcal
26.4 g fat (of which 16.3 g saturated)
36.9 g carbohydrate (of which 4.5 g sugars)
5.3 g protein
4.0 g fibre

The onion and leek were sweated in butter, and cream added.

151 Gazpacho

	4 portions	10 portions
plum tomatoes, ripe	2½ kg	6.25 kg
white onion, roughly chopped	1	2
cucumber, peeled and roughly chopped	1	2
garlic clove, crushed	½	1
red peppers, peeled and deseeded	550 g	1.3 kg
salt	40 g	80 g
cayenne pepper	2 g	5 g
Chardonnay vinegar or white wine vinegar	6 g	15 g
sugar (to taste, depending on season)	30 g	75 g

1 Mix all the ingredients together and leave to marinate overnight in the fridge.

2 Next day, blitz the ingredients in a food processor and strain through a chinois.

nutritional info

1 large portion provides:
940 kJ/222.1 kcal
2.8 g fat (of which 0.8 g saturated)
43.8 g carbohydrate (of which 41.6 g sugars)
7.8 g protein
10.4 g fibre

There is no fat or oil in the recipe.

3 Discard the remaining pulp into a colander lined with muslin (this is to catch the extra juices that will come from the pulp).

4 The juices from the pulp can be used to thin out the gazpacho until it reaches the correct consistency.

5 Check seasoning. Store in the refrigerator.

152 Chive, potato and cucumber soup with cream

		4 portions	10 portions
onions		50 g	125 g
spring onions	chopped	50 g	125 g
celery		50 g	125 g
butter		50 g	125 g
chicken stock		375 ml	1 litre
potatoes, diced		400 g	1 kg
cucumber, diced		1	2–3
salt and pepper			
cream		125 ml	300 ml
chopped parsley			
chopped chives			

nutritional info

chive poato & cucumber soup
1 large portion provides:
1413 kJ/341.3 kcal
27.5 g fat (of which 17.0 g saturated)
20.8 g carbohydrate (of which 3.8 g sugars)
3.8 g protein
2.4 g fibre

Butter was used to sweat the onions and celery, and the dish was finished with cream.

1 Sweat the onions and celery without colour in the butter.

2 Add the stock, potatoes and cucumber; season and simmer until soft.

3 Liquidise and cool. Correct the seasoning and consistency.

4 Finish with cream, parsley and chives.

5 Chill and serve.

Note: This soup is usually served chilled but may be served hot.

153 Fruit soups V

	4 portions	10 portions
raisins, seedless	50 g	125 g
currants	50 g	125 g
dried apples, diced	50 g	125 g
dried apricots, diced	50 g	125 g
prunes (stoned), diced	50 g	125 g
water	500 ml	1¼ litres
orange, in segments	1	2–3
lemon, in segments	1	2–3
pineapple juice	500 ml	1¼ litres

nutritional info

1 large portion provides:
781 kJ/182.4 kcal
0.4 g fat (of which 0.0 g saturated)
45.8 g carbohydrate (of which 45.8 g sugars)
2.0 g protein
3.1 g fibre

No fat is used in the recipe.

Soups with a fruit base are usually served cold and may be offered for breakfast as well as lunch or dinner.

1 Soak the dried fruit overnight in the water or a mixture of water and wine.

2 Drain, cover the dried fruit with water and cook for 10 mins.

3 Add the diced orange and lemon segments, free from pith, and the pineapple juice, and simmer for a few minutes. Serve hot or cold.

Note: This soup may also be finished with 125 ml Madeira, port or dry sherry.

Many other fruit soups can be made using, for example, pineapple, apple, strawberries, raspberries, cherries, redcurrants, melon and peach. The fruits that require cooking, such as pineapple, apple and cherry, are prepared, cut up, cooked in sugar syrup and puréed. They are then mixed with white or red wine or garnished as follows.

Pineapple

Small dice of pineapple macerated in syrup and lemon juice.

Apple

Diced apple and sultanas cooked in sugar syrup with cinnamon or clove flavouring.

Cherry

This soup may require light thickening with diluted arrowroot or cornflour. Garnish with chopped, stoned, cooked cherries.

Fruits that do not require cooking must be fully ripe. They are puréed and mixed with a combination of sugar syrups and red or white wine.

EGG DISHES

PRODUCTION

The science of an egg

Egg proteins change when you heat them, beat them or mix them with other ingredients. Understanding these changes can help you understand the roles that eggs play in cooking.

Proteins are made of long chains of amino acids. The proteins in an egg white are globular proteins, which means that the long protein molecule is twisted and folded, and curled up into a more or less spherical shape. A variety of weak chemical bonds keep the protein curled up tight as it drifts placidly in the water that surrounds it.

When you apply heat, you agitate those placidly drifting egg white proteins, bouncing them around. They slam into the surrounding water molecules and bash into each other. All this bashing about breaks the weak bonds that keep the protein curled up. The egg proteins uncurl and bump into other proteins that have also uncurled. New chemical bonds form, but rather than binding the protein to itself, these bonds connect one protein to another.

After enough of this bashing and bonding, the solitary egg proteins are solitary no longer: they've formed a network of interconnected proteins. The water in which the proteins once floated is captured and held in the protein web. If you leave the eggs at a high temperature for too long, too many bonds form and the egg white becomes rubbery.

LIST OF RECIPES

Recipe no	page no	Recipe no	page no
167 Egg Fabergé	142	157 Omelette with mushrooms and chicken livers	137
161 Egg on the dish with sliced onion, bacon and potato	139	158 Omelette with potatoes and Gruyère cheese	138
154 Eggs Benedict	135	166 Poached eggs with chicken and tomato and cream sauces	141
160 Eggs in cocotte with shrimps, cream and cheese	138	165 Poached eggs with prawns, sherry and French mustard	141
162 Eggs on the dish with chicken livers and mushrooms in Madeira sauce	139	164 Soft-boiled eggs with mushroom duxelle and cheese sauce	140
163 Eggs on the dish with grilled lamb's kidney and Madeira sauce	140	155 Tortilla (Spanish omelette)	136
159 Light fluffy omelette	138		
156 Omelette with creamed smoked haddock and cheese (Arnold Bennett)	137		

INTRODUCTION

EGGS

The term egg applies not only to those of the hen, but also to the edible eggs of other birds, such as turkeys, geese, ducks, guinea fowl, quails and gulls. Around 28 million hens eggs are consumed each day in the UK and approximately 95% of these are produced in the UK.

The British Egg Products Association (BEPA) introduced a strict Code of Practice in 1993 which covers all stages of production, from sourcing of raw materials to packaging and finished production standards. Members of BEPA can qualify to show a Date Stamp on their products which signifies that the products have been produced to standards higher than those demanded by UK and European law. The aim of the Date Stamp is to reduce the risk of infection in hens, to monitor and take remedial action where necessary and to ensure that eggs are held and distributed under the best conditions.

Food value

Eggs contain most nutrients and are low in calories: two eggs contain 180 calories. Egg protein is complete and easily digestible, therefore it is useful for balancing meals. Eggs may also be used as the main dish; they are a protective food and provide energy and material for growth and repair of the body.

Production

Hens' eggs are graded in four sizes:

- small 48 g
- medium 58 g
- large 68 g
- very large 76 g

The size of an egg does not affect the quality but does affect the price. The eggs are tested for quality, then weighed and graded under European law.

- Grade A – naturally clean, fresh eggs, internally perfect with intact shells and an air cell not exceeding 6 mm in depth.
- Grade B – eggs which have been down-graded because they have been cleaned or preserved, or because they are internally imperfect, cracked or have an air cell exceeding 6mm but not more than 9 mm in depth.
- Grade C – are eggs which are fit for breaking for manufacturing purposes but cannot be sold in their shells to the public.

They are then packed into boxes containing 360 (or 180). The wholesale price of eggs is quoted per long hundred (120). All egg-boxes leaving the packing station are dated.

The lion quality mark on eggs and egg boxes

means that the eggs have been produced to the highest standards of food safety in the world.

Hens' eggs

1 Eggshells should be clean, well shaped, strong and slightly rough.
2 When broken there should be a high proportion of thick white to thin white.
3 The yolk should be firm, round and of a good even colour. As eggs are kept, the thick white gradually changes into thin white and water passes from the whites to the yolks. The yolks lose their strength and shape and begin to flatten; water evaporates from the eggs and is replaced by air and, as water is heavier than air, fresh eggs weigh more than stale ones.

Storage and use

1 Store in a cool place, under refrigeration 0–5°C (eggshells are porous and should not be stored near strong-smelling foods, such as cheese, onion, fish and raw meat, because the odours will be absorbed).
2 Rotate the stocks – first in first out.
3 Wash your hands before and after handling eggs.
4 Do not use cracked eggs.

It is important to understand that food-poisoning *Salmonella* bacteria can be passed into eggs from hens. Department of Health advice to food manufacturers and caterers is that for all recipes using raw eggs that involve no cooking, pasteurised eggs (frozen, liquid or dried) should be used instead.

Turkeys' and guinea fowls' eggs may be used in place of hens' eggs. Goose or duck eggs should always be cooked thoroughly.

Quails' eggs are popular and may be used in many ways: for serving as a first course, as a light course or with salads, and as a garnish to many other dishes.

154 Eggs Benedict

Note: The cooking bath must be deep and must have a minimum of 20 per cent distilled or white wine vinegar added.

	4 portions	10 portions
cooking medium (see note)		
large eggs	8	20
unsalted butter	2 tbsp	5 tbsp
plain English muffins, split and toasted	4	10
slices smoked bacon or sweet cure bacon, cooked	12	30
Hollandaise sauce (see recipe 105)	200 g	500 g

nutritional info

1 large portion provides:
3501 kJ/840.5 kcal
61.9 g fat (of which 28.8 g saturated)
34.0 g carbohydrate (of which 2.0 g sugars)
39.0 g protein
1.4 g fibre

The saturated fat comes from the egg yolk, butter, bacon and hollandaise.

1 Bring the cooking medium to a slight simmer.

2 Crack an egg into a cup and carefully slide it into the hot poaching liquid. Quickly repeat with all the eggs.

3 Poach the eggs for 3 minutes, turning them occasionally with a spoon, until the whites are firm.

4 Using a slotted spoon, remove the eggs and transfer to a kitchen towel. Lightly dab the eggs with the towel to remove any excess water.

5 While the eggs are poaching, butter the muffins and place 2 halves on each plate.

6 Re-heat the bacon and place on top of the muffins, then top with the drained eggs.

7 To finish, lightly spoon over a generous helping of hollandaise sauce and serve immediately, or serve the hollandaise separately.

155 Tortilla (Spanish omelette)

Makes 10–12 servings for tapas or 4–6 servings for a light starter

olive oil	150 ml
russet potatoes	1 kg (approx. 4 medium or 2 large)
large onion (red or white), chopped	1
garlic cloves, chopped	4
coarse salt	
large eggs, lightly beaten	6
coarse salt and black pepper to taste	
chopped fresh flat-leaf parsley or chives for garnish	

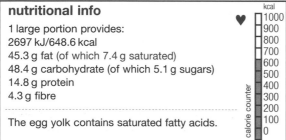

nutritional info

1 large portion provides:
2697 kJ/648.6 kcal
45.3 g fat (of which 7.4 g saturated)
48.4 g carbohydrate (of which 5.1 g sugars)
14.8 g protein
4.3 g fibre

The egg yolk contains saturated fatty acids.

1 Peel the potatoes and slice them into 3 mm slices. (*Tip:* do not put the potatoes in water.)

2 Layer the potatoes, one at a time (so that they don't stick together), on the bottom of the skillet. Add a layer of onions and garlic, and then continue adding potatoes and onions in alternate layers. Lightly salt each layer of potatoes. Reduce the heat to moderately low, and cook for approximately 10 to 12 minutes, lifting and turning the potatoes occasionally, until they are tender but not brown, and the potatoes are cooked through (they should remain separate and not in a cake). (*Tip:* the secret is to 'cook' the sliced potatoes in the oil slowly, in a frying pan without really frying or browning them.)

3 Remove the potatoes and onion with a slotted spoon to a baking sheet lined with paper towels, and let them drain. Pour the oil out of the skillet into a cup; wipe out the non-stick pan and remove any pieces of onions or potatoes stuck to it (it will be used again to set the omelette and must be completely clean to avoid sticking).

4 In a large bowl, beat eggs until they are light and slightly foamy; season to taste with salt and lots of black pepper. Carefully add the potatoes and onions, gently pressing them down so that they are completely covered by the eggs. Let the mixture stand for 10 to 15 minutes.

5 Add 3 tbsp of the reserved oil back to the non-stick pan. Heat the oil skillet over moderately high heat until very hot but not smoking (it must be hot or the eggs will stick); add the potato and egg mixture, spreading the potatoes evenly around the pan. Reduce the heat to low, shake the pan often and run a spatula around the side and bottom to make sure the omelette is not sticking. After approximately 8–10 minutes, when the omelette is cooked three-quarters of the way through (the top is no longer liquid) and the bottom is beginning to brown, place a large plate over the pan and invert the omelette onto the plate.

6 Add 2 additional tbsp of the reserved oil to the hot pan. Increase heat to get the oil hot; immediately reduce heat to low. Gently slide the omelette (cooked side up) back into the skillet, and cook for approximately 5 minutes or until cooked through and the underside is moderately browned. Remove from heat, transfer omelette to a large plate (omelette will slide out of the skillet onto the plate); let it come to room temperature and sprinkle with the chopped herbs.

7 The omelette can be served warm, or allow it to go cold and serve with a crisp green salad.

156 Omelette with creamed smoked haddock and cheese (Arnold Bennett)

	4 portions	10 portions
butter or margarine	12 g	30 g
cooked, flaked, smoked haddock	50 g	125 g
mornay sauce	90 ml	225 ml
egg flat omelette	4 × 3	10 × 3
Parmesan cheese	10 g	25 g

1 Melt the butter or margarine in a suitable pan, reheat the smoked haddock. Bind with a little of the mornay sauce.

2 Prepare a flat omelette and place on to a plate.

3 Arrange the fish on top of the omelette, coat with the remainder of the sauce, sprinkle with Parmesan cheese and glaze under the salamander. Serve immediately.

nutritional info

1 large portion provides:
1944 kJ/468.1 kcal
37.2 g fat (of which 16.2 g saturated)
3.3 g carbohydrate (of which 1.4 g sugars)
30.4 g protein
0.1 g fibre

Contains butter, mornay sauce and additional parmesan.

157 Omelette with mushrooms and chicken livers

	4 portions	10 portions
chicken livers	100 g	250 g
butter or margarine	50 g	125 g
sliced mushrooms	50 g	125 g
jus-lié	60 ml	150 ml
salt and pepper		
egg omelettes	4 × 2	10 × 2
chopped tarragon		

1 Trim the livers, cut into quarters, sauté quickly in half the butter or margarine, keeping slightly undercooked.

2 Sauté the mushrooms in the remaining butter or margarine.

3 Add the mushrooms to the chicken livers, bind with jus-lié and season with salt and pepper.

4 Make the omelettes and fold.

5 Serve the omelettes on individual plates. Cut an incision in the tops, fill with mushrooms and chicken livers, and sprinkle with chopped tarragon. Serve a little sauce around the omelettes.

nutritional info

1 large portion provides:
1613 kJ/389.3 kcal
33.5 g fat (of which 16.1 g saturated)
0.3 g carbohydrate (of which 0.2 g sugars)
21.8 g protein
0.1 g fibre

Butter was used to sauté the mushrooms. There is fat in the egg yolk.

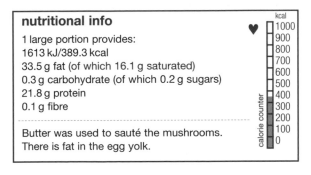

158 Omelette with potatoes and Gruyère cheese

	4 portions	10 portions
potatoes	100 g	250 g
oil	60 ml	150 ml
salt and pepper		
eggs	8	20
Gruyère cheese	100 g	250 g
butter or margarine	100 g	250 g

1 Cut the potatoes into ¼ cm dice, fry in the oil until lightly brown, drain and season with salt.

2 Beat the eggs well, season, add the potatoes.

3 Cut the cheese into ¼ cm dice and add to the mixture.

4 Use the butter or margarine to make 4 or 10 flat omelettes.

5 Serve on individual plates at once.

nutritional info

1 large portion provides:
2642 kJ/638.8 kcal
58.3 g fat (of which 24.1 g saturated)
4.5 g carbohydrate (of which 0.3 g sugars)
24.5 g protein
0.3 g fibre

The fat comes from the egg yolk, cheese and butter.

kcal
1000
900
800
700
600
500
400
300
200
100
0

calorie counter

159 Light fluffy omelette

For each omelette

2–3 egg yolks

salt and pepper

2–3 egg whites

25 g butter or margarine

1 Beat the yolks with salt and pepper.

2 Half beat the whites, fold the yolks into the whites.

3 Heat the butter or margarine in the omelette pan and pour in the mixture; cook, stirring with a fork, until nearly set.

4 Fold the omelette in half, finish cooking in the oven until set.

5 Serve on individual plates immediately.

160 Eggs in cocotte with shrimps, cream and cheese

	4 portions	10 portions
butter or margarine	50 g	125 g
peeled shrimps (potted or fresh)	100 g	250 g
eggs	4	10
cream	4 tbsp	10 tbsp
grated Parmesan cheese	20 g	50 g

1 Butter the cocottes.

2 Add the shrimps.

3 Break the eggs on top.

4 Place in a shallow tray containing 1 cm water.

5 Cook in a steamer or moderate oven until the eggs are lightly set.

6 Pour on the cream, sprinkle with cheese and lightly brown under the salamander.

nutritional info

1 large portion provides:
997 kJ/239.9 kcal
19.0 g fat (of which 9.5 g saturated)
8.3 g carbohydrate (of which 8.2 g sugars)
9.5 g protein
1.4 g fibre

Butter was used in the dishes.

kcal
1000
900
800
700
600
500
400
300
200
100
0

calorie counter

161 Eggs on the dish (sur le plat) with sliced onion, bacon and potato

	4 portions	10 portions
onion, shredded	50 g	125 g
oil	60 ml	150 ml
small potatoes	2	5
lardons of bacon	100 g	250 g
butter	50 g	125 g
eggs	4	10
salt and pepper		
cream	4 tbsp	10 tbsp
chopped parsley		

1 Sauté the onions in oil until they are lightly coloured.

2 Peel and slice the potatoes then fry them separately in oil until cooked and golden brown; drain.

3 Add the onions to the potatoes.

4 Blanch the lardons; quickly fry in the butter, do not drain.

5 Divide the potatoes, onions and lardons into individual egg dishes.

6 Break in the eggs, season with salt and pepper and mask with cream. Cook in a moderate oven until the eggs are set.

7 Sprinkle with chopped parsley and serve immediately

nutritional info

1 large portion provides:
2053 kJ/496.5 kcal
44.7 g fat (of which 16.9 g saturated)
9.9 g carbohydrate (of which 1.3 g sugars)
14.2 g protein
0.8 g fibre

Contains egg yolk, cream and bacon.

162 Eggs on the dish (sur le plat) with chicken livers and mushroom in Madeira sauce

	4 portions	10 portions
butter or margarine	75 g	180 g
eggs	4	10
salt and pepper		
chicken livers	50 g	125 g
oil	1 tbsp	2–3 tbsp
sliced button mushrooms	50 g	125 g
demi-glace or jus-lié	125 ml	300 ml
Madeira wine	2 tbsp	5 tbsp
parsley or chervil		

1 Divide two-thirds of the butter between egg dishes and allow to melt.

2 Break in the eggs, season with salt and pepper, place on a baking sheet. Cook in a moderate oven until set.

3 Clean the chicken livers, slice neatly.

4 Sauté the chicken livers in the oil, keeping them undercooked. Drain and season with salt and pepper.

5 Sauté the sliced mushrooms in the remaining butter or margarine.

6 Boil the demi-glace or jus-lié with the Madeira wine, strain and add the mushrooms.

7 Arrange a cordon of Madeira sauce and mushrooms around the eggs, garnish with chicken livers and a sprig of parsley or chervil and serve.

nutritional info

1 large portion provides:
1143 kJ/276.5 kcal
25.7 g fat (of which 12.4 g saturated)
0.3 g carbohydrate (of which 0.3 g sugars)
11.1 g protein
0.1 g fibre

Butter was used in the dishes and to sauté the mushrooms.

163 Eggs on the dish (sur le plat) with grilled lamb's kidney and Madeira sauce

	4 portions	10 portions
lamb's kidneys	2	5
salt and pepper		
oil	2 tbsp	5 tbsp
butter or margarine	50 g	125 g
eggs	4	10
demi-glace or jus-lié	125 ml	300 ml
Madeira wine	2 tbsp	5 tbsp
parsley or chervil		

1 Remove the membrane from the kidneys, cut in half and remove centre core.

2 Place on a suitable tray. Season and brush with oil; grill under salamander, leaving them slightly undercooked.

3 Divide the butter between the egg dishes, melt, break in the eggs and season with salt and pepper.

4 Place on a baking sheet and cook in a moderate oven until set.

5 Boil the demi-glace or jus-lié, add the Madeira wine and strain.

6 Serve the eggs with a cordon of Madeira sauce, garnished with half a grilled kidney and a sprig of parsley or chervil.

nutritional info

1 large portion provides:
1172 kJ/282.7 kcal
23.9 g fat (of which 9.6 g saturated)
0.7 g carbohydrate (of which 0.6 g sugars)
15.0 g protein
0.0 g fibre

Butter was used in the dishes.

kcal: 1000 900 800 700 600 500 400 300 200 100 0 — calorie counter

164 Soft-boiled eggs with mushroom duxelle and cheese sauce

	4 portions	10 portions
eggs	4	10
short pastry	100 g	250 g
Duxelle		
shallots	25 g	60 g
mushrooms, chopped	100 g	250 g
butter or margarine	50 g	125 g
salt and pepper		
mornay sauce (cheese sauce)	125 ml	600 ml
grated Parmesan cheese	25 g	60 g

1 Soft boil the eggs for 5–6 minutes then remove and place in a basin of cold water to cool. Shell. Retain in cold water.

2 Line individual tartlet moulds with short pastry and bake blind.

3 Prepare the mushroom duxelle and season.

4 Place tartlet cases in individual serving dishes and fill with the duxelle.

5 Reheat the eggs in simmering salted water, drain. Place the reheated eggs in the tartlet cases.

6 Mask with mornay sauce, sprinkle with grated Parmesan cheese and gratinate. Serve immediately.

nutritional info

1 large portion provides:
1629 kJ/392.2 kcal
30.6 g fat (of which 14.7 g saturated)
16.2 g carbohydrate (of which 2.2 g sugars)
14.0 g protein
0.7 g fibre

The egg yolk contains saturated fatty acids.

kcal: 1000 900 800 700 600 500 400 300 200 100 0 — calorie counter

165 Poached eggs with prawns, sherry and French mustard

	4 portions	10 portions
eggs	4	10
tomatoes, medium-sized, peeled and sliced	4	10
prawns	100 g	250 g
butter or margarine	25 g	60 g
sherry	2 tbsp	5 tbsp
mornay sauce	250 ml	600 ml
French mustard	½ tsp	1¼ tsp
grated Parmesan cheese	50 g	125 g

1 Poach the eggs and reserve in a basin of cold water.

2 Divide the tomatoes into individual dishes (e.g. egg dishes) season lightly with salt and pepper. Place on a baking sheet in a moderate oven for approximately 5 minutes.

3 Warm the prawns in the butter and sherry.

4 Reheat the mornay sauce and flavour with the French mustard.

5 Reheat the eggs, drain well. Place on top of the slices of cooked tomato.

6 Sprinkle the prawns over the eggs.

7 Coat with mornay sauce and sprinkle with Parmesan cheese.

8 Glaze under the salamander. Serve immediately.

nutritional info

1 large portion provides:
1271 kJ/305.4 kcal
20.1 g fat (of which 10.0 g saturated)
10.9 g carbohydrate (of which 6.1 g sugars)
19.1 g protein
1.0 g fibre

Contains butter, mornay sauce and extra parmesan cheese.

♥ calorie counter: kcal 1000 900 800 700 600 500 400 300 200 100 0

166 Poached eggs with chicken and tomato and cream sauces

	4 portions	10 portions
eggs	4	10
short pastry	100 g	250 g
cooked chicken, diced	50 g	125 g
tomatoes, peeled, deseeded and diced	50 g	125 g
butter or margarine	50 g	125 g
chicken velouté	125 ml	300 ml
double cream	1 tbsp	2–3 tbsp
tomato sauce	125 ml	300 ml
meat glaze		

1 Poach the eggs and retain in cold water.

2 Line tartlet moulds with short pastry, bake blind.

3 Reheat the diced chicken and tomatoes in the butter or margarine.

4 Place the chicken and tomato in the bottom of the tartlet cases.

5 Reheat the eggs in simmering salted water; drain well. Arrange the eggs on top of the chicken and tomato.

6 Boil the chicken velouté, add the cream and strain.

7 Mask each egg with the two sauces: tomato sauce on one half and supreme sauce on the other.

8 Separate the two sauces with a thin line of warm meat glaze and serve.

nutritional info

1 large portion provides:
1624 kJ/390.8 kcal
30.4 g fat (of which 13.9 g saturated)
15.8 g carbohydrate (of which 1.9 g sugars)
14.5 g protein
1.0 g fibre

The fat comes from the pastry, eggs and double cream.

♥ calorie counter: kcal 1000 900 800 700 600 500 400 300 200 100 0

167 Egg Fabergé
John Williams

	10 portions
egg shells	10
truffle	100 g
long macaroni tubes	20
lobster mousse (must be light)	750 g
soft boiled quails' eggs	10
cucumber spaghetti	100 g
langoustines	30
double cream	150 ml
chives, chopped	5 g

1 Clean the egg shells and allow to dry.

2 Take truffle, cut into lengths the size of the cooked macaroni tubes.

3 Round the lengths of truffle down to fit neatly into the macaroni tubes.

4 Cut into roundels 2 mm thick. Eight roundels are required for each egg.

5 Place shell in egg cup, this will make it easier to work with.

6 Grease the inside of the shell.

7 Place one of the roundels in the centre of the shell.

8 Place the other seven roundels tightly together around the centre roundel.

9 Half fill with lobster mousse.

10 Place soft-boiled quails' egg with point facing down into the shell.

11 Add lobster mousse to the top of the shell.

12 Wrap in clingfilm.

13 Cook in steamer at 80°C for 12–15 mins.

14 When cooked allow to rest for 5 mins.

15 Warm the cucumber spaghetti, langoustines and chive cream.

16 Arrange cucumber in a nest on the centre of the plate.

17 Arrange the langoustines around the cucumber.

18 Peel the shell from the mousse, taking care with the macaroni.

19 Sit this in nest of cucumber with the truffle and macaroni facing upwards.

20 Finish with langoustine and chive cream around the outside of the cucumber.

John Williams

FISH DISHES

FISH

Origins

Fish are vertebrates (animals with a back bone) and are split into two primary groups: flat and round. From this they can be split again, into sub- or secondary groups such as pelagic (oil-rich fish that swim midwater, such as mackerel and herring) and demersal (white fish that live at or near the bottom of the sea, such as cod, haddock, whiting and plaice).

Marine and fresh water fish were a crucial part of man's diet long before prehistoric societies learnt how to cultivate vegetables and domesticate livestock. Fish provided essential proteins and vitamins; they were easy to catch and eat, and predominantly eaten raw.

There are more than 20,000 species of fish in the seas of the world, yet we use only a fraction of the resources available. Undoubtedly certain types are neither edible nor ethical – however, the European market has a dozen types of fish that make up a large percentage of our consumption. The Japanese and, closer to home, the Portuguese are the exceptions to the rule when it comes to utilisation of a high proportion of fish species.

More people are eating fish in preference to meat these days and customers should always be offered a reasonable choice. The dishes available should include simply prepared and cooked items. It is a mistake to include on the menu all rich and elaborate dishes as good fresh fish is often at its best when simply cooked, e.g. grilled sea bass with fennel.

Units covered
3FCPC1, 3FP1,
3FC2, 3FP2

LIST OF RECIPES

Recipe no	page no
Basic fish stock	
168 Fish stock	151
En papillote	
169 Fish en papillote	151
Tuna	
171 Braised tuna, Italian style	152
170 Seared tuna niçoise	151
Red snapper	
172 Baked red snapper, tomato and garlic fondue	153
Salmon	
175 Crispy seared salmon with horseradish foam and caviar	156
174 Grilled salmon, pea soup and quails' eggs	155
173 Organic salmon 'mi cuit' with buttered greens	154
176 Ravioli of salmon and girolles with a shellfish sauce	156
Sardines	
177 Baked stuffed sardines	157
Sole	
179 Pan-fried fillets of sole with rocket and broad beans	158
178 Whole sole grilled with traditional accompaniments	157
Turbot/brill	
182 Pan-fried turbot with Alsace cabbage	161
180 Pan-fried turbot with braised oxtail and lemon oil	158
181 Poached brill with wild crayfish gnocchi	160

Recipe no	page no
Red mullet	
185 Nage of red mullet with baby leeks	163
183 Pan-fried red mullet with artichokes and Swiss chard	162
184 Red mullet ceviche with organic leaves	162
Monkfish	
186 Monkfish	164
187 Roast monkfish with smoked bacon and white bean cassoulet	164
Halibut	
188 Malt-poached halibut with chicken hearts and skin	165
Hake	
189 Poached hake with cockles and prawns	166
Cod	
191 Oven-baked marinated cod with bok choi	168
190 Roast salt cod and clam chowder	166
Sea bass	
194 Baked stuffed sea bass	171
192 Roast fillet of sea bass with vanilla and fennel	169
193 Steamed sea bass with asparagus and capers	170
Eel	
195 Eels	171
196 Eel with white wine, horseradish and parsley	172
197 Fried eels with spring onion and mustard sauce	172
Squid	
198 Squid	173

The contemporary trend is for hot fish sauces to be lightly thickened, preferably without the use of a roux-based sauce. However, in large-scale cookery, when considerable quantities of fish sauces may be required, the use of fish velouté may be necessary.

Any fish or shellfish cooked by poaching can alternatively be cooked by steaming. Combination steam/convection ovens are

Recipe no	page no		Recipe no	page no
199 Squid with white wine, garlic and chilli	173		Shrimps	
200 Stuffed squid	174		221 Potted shrimps	188
Skate			Langoustines	
201 Pan-fried skate with capers and beurre noisette	174		224 Dublin Bay Prawns	190
			222 Langoustine and mussel soup	188
202 Skate with mustard and lemon on spinach	174		223 Poached langoustines with aioli dip	189
			Lobster	
Miscellaneous fish recipes			226 Lobster beignets with tomato chutney	191
203 Bouillabaisse	175		227 Lobster mornay	192
212 Fish and shellfish soufflé	179		229 Lobster Newburg	193
208 Fish forcemeat or farce	177		225 Lobster tail gratin	190
209 Fish sausages	178		228 Lobster thermidor	192
211 Fish soufflés	179		Crawfish	
207 Mousse, mousseline, quenelle	177		230 Crawfish	193
204 Rouille (red chilli pepper mayonnaise)	175		Mussels	
210 Russian fish pie (Coulibiac)	178		231 Mussels	193
206 Shallow-fried fish with artichokes and potatoes (Murat)	176		233 Mussels gratin with white wine	194
			232 Mussels in white wine sauce	194
205 Stir-fried fish	176		Cockles	
Basic shellfish stock			235 Cockle chowder	195
213 Shellfish stock	182		234 Cockles	194
Oysters			Clams	
216 Oyster fricassée	185		236 Clams	196
214 Oysters	184		Scallops	
215 Oysters in their own shells	184		239 Scallop ceviche with organic leaves	198
Crab			237 Scallops with caramelised cauliflower	196
217 Crab	185		238 Seared scallop salad with honey-lime dressing	197
220 Crab cakes with rocket salad and lemon dressing	187			
219 Crab salad with pink grapefruit	186			
218 Dressed crab	186			

commonly used in many kitchens; fish cooked in a controlled moist atmosphere at temperatures below 99°C benefits as shrinkage is kept to the minimum, overcooking is easier to control and the texture of the fish is moist and succulent.

The following checklist summarises the main points to look for when choosing and buying fish.

Boning and stuffing a whole round fish (see recipes 177 and 194)

Checklist for choosing and buying fish

WHOLE FISH	FILLETS	SMOKED FISH	FROZEN FISH
<ul><li>clear, bright eyes, not sunken</li><li>bright red gills</li><li>scales should not be missing and they should be firmly attached to the skin</li><li>moist skin (fresh fish feels slightly slippery)</li><li>shiny skin with bright natural colouring</li><li>tail should be stiff and the flesh should feel firm</li><li>should have a fresh sea smell and no trace of ammonia</li></ul>	<ul><li>neat, trim fillets with firm flesh</li><li>fillets should be firm and closely packed together, not ragged or gaping</li><li>white fish should have a white translucent colour with no discolouration</li></ul>	<ul><li>glossy appearance</li><li>flesh should feel firm and not sticky</li><li>pleasant, smoky smell</li></ul>	<ul><li>frozen hard with no signs of thawing</li><li>the packaging should not be damaged</li><li>no evidence of freezer burn (i.e. dull, white, dry patches)</li></ul>

Cooking

Fish is a very economical to prepare as it cooks quickly and thus can actually represent a fuel saving. When cooked, fish loses its translucent look and in most cases takes on an opaque white colour. It will also flake easily and has to be considered as a delicate product after preparation.

Fish easily becomes dry and loses its flavour if overcooked; for this reason, carefully considered methods of cookery need to be applied as certain fish will dry out too quickly before benefiting from the chosen cooking approach. Overcooked and dry fish is to be avoided as it will reduce the eating quality.

Storage

Spoilage is mainly caused by the actions of enzymes and bacteria. Enzymes are present in the gut of the living fish and help convert its food to tissue and energy. When the fish dies, these enzymes carry on working and help the bacteria in the digestive system to penetrate the belly wall and start breaking down the flesh itself. Bacteria exist on the skin and in the fish intestine. While the fish is alive, the normal defence mechanisms of the body prevent the bacteria from invading the flesh. Once the fish dies, however, the bacteria invade the flesh and start to break it down – the higher the temperature the faster the deterioration. Note that although these bacteria are harmless to humans, eating quality is reduced and the smell will deteriorate dramatically.

Fish, once caught, has a shelf life of 6 to 8 days if kept properly in a refrigerator at a temperature of between 0°C and 5°C. If the fish is delivered whole with the innards still in the fish, then gut and wash the cavity well before storage.

Fresh fish

Fresh fish should be used as soon as possible, but it can be stored overnight. Rinse, pat dry, cover with clingfilm and store towards the bottom of the refrigerator.

Ready-to-eat cooked fish, such as 'hot' smoked mackerel, prawns and crab, should be stored on shelves above other raw foodstuffs to avoid cross-contamination.

Smoked fish

Smoked fish should be well wrapped up and kept separate from other fish to prevent the smell and dye penetrating other foods.

The smoking of fish
Fish can be either cold smoked or hot smoked. In either case if the fish are not to be consumed immediately they are salted before smoking. This can be done either by soaking them in a brine solution (strong enough to keep a potato afloat) or rubbing in dry salt. This is to improve flavour and help the keeping quality.

Cold smoking
This takes place at a temperature of approximately 24°C, which smokes but does not cook the fish. Smoke boxes can be bought or improvised. Sawdust is used and different woods can impart different flavours. Herbs, e.g. thyme and rosemary, can also be incorporated. Fish can either be left whole or filleted. Smoked salmon is prepared by cold smoking usually over a fire of oak chips and peat. Kippers, haddock and young halibut are also cold smoked, as are bloaters – these are lightly salted herring smoked without the gut being removed, which is what gives them their more pronounced gamey flavour.

Hot smoking
This takes place at approximately 82°C. Eel, trout, buckling, bloater (ungutted herring), sprats and mackerel are smoked and lightly cooked at one and the same time.

Frozen fish

Frozen fish should be stored at −18°C to −20°C. and thawed out overnight in a refrigerator. It should *not* be thawed out in water as this spoils the taste and texture of the fish, and valuable water-soluble nutrients are lost. Fish should not be re-frozen as this will impair its taste and texture.

Seasonality

Key: ● = At best, ○ = Available, blank = not available, * = spawning and roeing

	JAN	FEB	MAR	APR	MAY	JUN	JUL	AUG	SEP	OCT	NOV	DEC
Bream	○	○	○	○	○*	○*	○*	○	○	○	○	○
Brill	●	●	○*	○*	○*	●	●	●	●	●	●	●
Cod	●	●	○*	○*	○	○	○	○	○	●	●	●
Eel						○	●	●	●	●	○	
Mullet (grey)	○	○	○*	○*	○	○	○	○	○	○	○	○
Gurnard	○	○	○	○	○	○	○	○	○	○	○	○
Haddock	●	●	○	○	○	○	○	○	●	●	●	●
Hake	●	●	○*	○*	○*	●	●	●	○	○	○	○
Halibut	●	●	●	○*	○*	○	○	○	●	●	●	●
Herring	●	●	○	●	○	○	○	○	●	●	●	●
John Dory	○	○	○	○	●	●	●	●	○	○	○	○
Mackerel	○	○	○	○	○	●	●	●	●	●	●	○
Monkfish	○	○	○	○	○	○	○	○	○	○	○	○
Plaice	○	○	○*	○*	○	○	○	○	○	○	○	○
Red mullet					●	●	●	●	○			
Salmon (farmed)	○	○	○	○	○	○	○	○	○	○	○	○
Salmon (wild)				○	●	●	●					
Sardines	●	●	●	●					○	●	●	●
Sea bass	○	○	○	○*	○*	●	●	●	●	●	●	○
Sea trout					●	●	●	●*	○*	○*	○*	
Skate	●	●			○	○	●	●	●	●	●	●
Squid	○							○	●	●	●	○
Sole (Dover)	○*					○	○	○	○	●	●	●
Sole (lemon)	●	●	●	●	●	●						
Trout	○	○	○	○	○	○	●	●	●	●		
Tuna	○	○	○	○	○	○	○	○	○	○	○	○
Turbot	●	●	○	○*	○*	○*	○	○	●	●	●	●
Whiting	●	○									●	●

Code:

Available ○

At best ●

* Spawning and roeing – this can deprive the flesh of nutrients and will decrease the yield.

Gutting and scaling

Scaling a red mullet

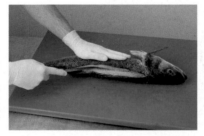

Gutting a red mullet

Filleting

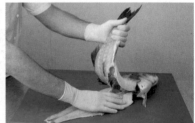

Filleting a sea bass

Filleting a turbot

Filleting a salmon

Boning and trimming

Pin boning a red mullet

Trimming a portion of red mullet

Trimming a sea bass

Methods of cookery

Method of cookery applied	Recipe covering method
Bake	169, 172, 177, 191, 194, 200, 210, 211, 212, 225, 233
Boil	230, 235
Braise	171, 194, 200
Compound	217, 218, 219, 221, 235, 236
Cure	173, 184, 239
Deep-fry	197, 226
En papillote	169
Grill by overhead heat (salamander)	174, 178, 220, 227, 228
Pan-fry, stir-fry	179, 180, 182, 183, 201, 205, 206, 237
Poach	176, 181, 185, 188, 189, 196, 202, 203, 209, 216, 222, 223, 224
Raw	214, 215
Roast	187, 190, 192
Sauté	199, 206
Sear	170, 175, 229, 237, 238
Steam	192, 193, 202, 232

FISH

168 Fish stock

The quality of fish stock must be of the highest level if good-quality fish dishes are to be produced. Care must be taken at all times to use only fresh, clean, selected fish bones, then to sweat them in butter with onion, season lightly with herbs and, where possible, moisten with white wine. Never allow fish stock to infuse for more than 20 minutes otherwise the flavour will be impaired.

169 Fish en papillote

The fish should be portioned, free from bones and may or may not be skinned. The garnish can be a fine selection of vegetables chosen from carrots, leeks, celery, white mushrooms and wild mushrooms, a small amount of freshly chopped herbs may be added as desired.

Moisten with a little dry white wine, then seal the foil parcel and bake for 15–20 minutes (size and fish dependent). Serve with an appropriate sauce (e.g. white wine).

Note: This method of cookery is fresh-tasting and lends itself to most fish or shellfish preparations.

Salmon en papilotte

170 Seared tuna niçoise

Salad	4 portions	10 portions
vegetable oil	100 ml	250 ml
tuna loin with no bloodline or skin	500 g	1250 g
chervil and chives, chopped	3 tbsp	7 tbsp
new potatoes, cooked and peeled	12	30
vinaigrette	50 ml	125 ml
extra fine beans, topped/ tailed and blanched	225 g	550 g
plum tomatoes, blanched, peeled, cut into quarters, seeds removed	8	20
baby gem lettuce, cored and washed	3	7
kalamata olives, stoned	16	40
pickled anchovy fillet (not the brown salted version)	12	30
lightly boiled and shelled quails' eggs	12	30

Dressing		
garlic cloves, well crushed	1	3
tablespoon chopped flat leaf parsley	1	3
egg yolk	1	3
vegetable oil	200 ml	500 ml
olive oil	50 ml	125 ml
seasoning		

nutritional info

1 large portion provides:
5269 kJ/1272 kcal
112.9 g fat (of which 16.5 g saturated)
19.7 g carbohydrate (of which 7.7 g sugars)
45.8 g protein
4.4 g fibre

Contains vegetable oil, eggs, olive oil and vegetable oil in the dressing.

kcal
1000
900
800
700
600
500
400
300
200
100
0

calorie counter

1 Heat the oil in a non-stick frying pan, place the tuna in the pan, searing and browning the outside of the loin.

2 Sprinkle the herbs on a layer of clingfilm, place on the warm tuna, wrap immediately and place in the fridge to absorb the herb flavours.

3 Colour the new potatoes in a little hot oil; once coloured add the vinaigrette, remove the pan from the heat and allow to infuse. Reserve to one side.

4 Place the beans, tomatoes, baby gem, olives and anchovies in a bowl with the dressing and coat well.

5 Arrange the potatoes and quails' eggs on the plate top with the salad tomato mix.

6 Slice the tuna through the clingfilm, retaining the shape; remove the clingfilm and place the tuna on top of the salad.

7 Finish the dish by drizzling the dressing left in the bowl from the salad. Mix and serve.

Note: A true classic. This variation only sears the tuna, allowing a fresher tuna flavour as opposed to the drier fully cooked version.

171 Braised tuna Italian style

	4 portions	10 portions
piece of tuna	1 × 600 g	3 × 600 g
shallots, chopped	100 g	250 g
mushrooms, chopped	200 g	500 g
white wine	125 ml	300 ml
fish stock	125 ml	300 ml
Marinade		
lemon, juice of	1	2–3
olive oil	60 ml	150 ml
onion, sliced	100 g	250 g
carrot, sliced	100 g	250 g
bay leaf	½	1
thyme, salt and pepper		

nutritional info

1 large portion provides:
1557.25 kJ/373.11 kcal
22.3 g fat (of which 4.02 g saturated)
6.36 g carbohydrate (of which 4.97 g sugars)
37.2 g protein
1.86 g fibre

There is a small amount of saturated fatty acids from the tuna and olive oil.

1 Mix together the ingredients for the marinade and marinate the pieces of fish for 1 hour.

2 Remove, dry well and colour in hot oil.

3 Place in braising pan, add shallots and mushrooms.

4 Cover with a lid, cook gently in oven for 15–20 minutes.

5 Add white wine and fish stock, cover, return to oven.

6 Braise gently for approximately 45 minutes until cooked.

7 Carefully remove the fish, correct the seasoning of the liquid (which may be lightly thickened with beurre manié, if required) and serve.

Notes:

■ Other ingredients that may be used when braising tuna include tomatoes, garlic, basil, vinegar.

■ Slices of tuna can also be shallow-fried or cooked meunière with or without the meunière variations.

172 Baked red snapper, tomato and garlic fondue

	4 portions	10 portions
Snapper		
whole snapper, scaled and gutted	4 × 350 g	10 × 350 g
garlic cloves, split	8	20
lemon cut into 8	1	3
fennel, roughly chopped	200 g	500 g
sprigs of thyme	4	10
seasoning		
Fondue		
ripe plum tomatoes	12	30
olive oil	100 ml	250 ml
large shallots, finely chopped	2	5
clove garlic, crushed	1	3
coriander, chopped	1 tsp	3 tsp
Basil pesto		
small bunch fresh basil leaves	1	3
olive oil	100 g	250 g
pine nuts	3 tbsp	7 tbsp
garlic cloves, finely chopped	3	7
Parmesan cheese, grated	100 g	250 g

nutritional info

1 large portion provides:

5124 kJ/1240 kcal

117.3 g fat (of which 19.5 g saturated)
9.0 g carbohydrate (of which 7.1 g sugars)
37.6 g protein
3.5 g fibre

Oil used to cook fish; oil, cheese and pine nuts in the pesto.

♥ kcal
1000
900
800
700
600
500
400
300
200
100
0

calorie counter

For the snapper

1 Ensure the cavity is clean and place the garlic, lemon, fennel and thyme evenly between the fish.

2 Score (ciselé) the thickest part of the fish 3 mm deep to ensure even cooking.

3 With cocktail sticks, secure the aromats in the fish cavity.

For the tomato fondue

1 Peel, deseed and cut the tomatoes concassée.

2 Heat the olive oil in a saucepan, add the shallots and crushed garlic, and cook for 2–3 minutes without letting them colour.

3 Add the tomato concassée to the shallots and cook for a further 1–2 minutes until the tomato starts to soften. Adjust the seasoning to taste, add the coriander, then remove from the pan and set aside in a covered container until ready to serve.

For the basil pesto

1 Place all the ingredients, excluding the Parmesan, in a food processor and blitz until semi-smooth.

2 Add about a third of the Parmesan cheese at a time, each time slowing down the processor; blend slowly until it forms a thick, smooth paste.

To finish

1 Pre-heat the oven to 180°C.

2 Place the snapper on a baking tray and drizzle with the vegetable oil. Season and cook for 10–12 minutes.

3 Remove and cover with foil allowing the residual heat to penetrate to the bone and keeping the fish moist.

4 Meanwhile, warm the fondue and place in the centre of a serving dish or plates.

5 Remove the snapper from the tray and empty the cavity of the aromats.

6 Drain and place on the fondue.

7 Finish the dish with the pesto dressing.

Note: Snapper is a meaty fish and benefits well from this method, however other species of fish will also benefit from baking: sea bass, red mullet and even a small salmon.

173 Organic salmon 'mi cuit' with buttered greens

	4 portions	10 portions
Salmon		
pieces salmon fillet (about 120 g), trimmed of skin and grey fat	4	10
Cooking oil		
corn oil	1 litre	3 litres
star anise	2	5
bay leaves	2	5
used vanilla pods	3	7
peppercorns	20	50
Horseradish sauce		
mashed potato (dry)	200 g	500 g
horseradish cream	1 tbsp	3 tbsp
double cream	60 ml	150 ml
butter	60 ml	150 ml
salt and pepper		
Greens		
green cabbage, blanched	100 g	250 g
baby bok choi, blanched	4	9
spinach, washed and picked	200 g	500 g
butter	50 g	125 g

nutritional info

1 large portion provides:
3279 kJ/792 kcal
70.0 g fat (of which 24.6 g saturated)
13.0 g carbohydrate (of which 4.1 g sugars)
28.4 g protein
3.5 g fibre

Contains horseradish cream, double cream and butter in the sauce; butter is used to cook the greens.

For the cooking oil

1 Place all the ingredients in pan and heat slowly to about 80°C. Leave to infuse for 1 hour.

2 Remove from the heat and leave at room temperature for at least 24 hours to take on more of the flavour.

For the horseradish and potato sauce

1 Place the potato (retaining 10 per cent), horseradish and other ingredients in a saucepan over a low heat until the consistency resembles a thick, puréed soup. If not, adjust by adding more cream or potato.

2 Adjust the seasoning to taste and keep warm.

To complete

1 Heat the infused cooking oil to 40–43°C using a digital probe to maintain the temperature, and moving the pan on and off the stove.

2 When the oil is at the required temperature, place the salmon pieces in it and cook for 40 minutes. When done, the flesh will still be pinky-orange inside, but do not let this put you off as this means it is cooked perfectly.

3 Remove and drain.

4 In the meantime, reheat the greens in the butter and place in the centre of the plate.

5 Spoon the sauce around and serve immediately.

Note: The term 'mi cuit' is directly translated as 'just cooked' and that is what this salmon is, due to the temperature of the oil and setting temperature of the fish proteins in the salmon. The cooking medium must not go too far above the protein setting temperature if the flesh is to remain soft as the proteins will harden, making the fish tough. This process works best with organic salmon as the environment it swims in is less claustrophobic, and free from pesticides and bacteria – due to the low cooking temperature of the fish this is important. The process of supply, handling and serving are all crucial to the safe production of this dish: adopt a safe critical path and the dish will be safe.

174 Grilled salmon, pea soup and quails' eggs

	4 portions	10 portions
Soup		
vegetable oil	50 ml	125 ml
shallots, peeled and sliced	2	5
garlic cloves, crushed	1	3
raw potato, chopped	200 g	500 g
peas	600 g	1½ kg
milk	500 ml	1¼ litres
stem of mint	1	3
Salmon		
salmon fillet	4 × 150 g	10 × 150 g
plain flour	25 g	60 g
olive oil	4 tbsp	9 tbsp
To finish		
spinach, washed	200 g	500 g
peas, cooked and crushed	600 g	1½ kg
butter	50 g	125 g
seasoning		
quails' eggs, lightly poached	8	20
first press olive oil		
fresh herbs		

For the soup

1 Heat the oil and add the shallots and garlic, cook without colour for 2 minutes.

2 Then add the potato and cook for a further 2 minutes.

3 Add the peas and milk, bring to the boil and remove from the heat.

4 Add the mint sprig and allow to infuse for 3-4 minutes. Remove and then blitz the soup in a processor.

5 Pass through a strainer and retain.

For the salmon

1 Heat a lower-heat grill ensuring the bars are clean.

2 Lightly oil the bars and then dust the salmon fillet in the flour.

3 Carefully place the salmon fillet on the grill and score.

4 Once sealed rotate the fish 45 degrees and mark, creating a diamond shape.

5 After 2–3 minutes turn the salmon over taking care not to break the flesh.

6 After 2 minutes cooking on the other side check if cooked by gently pushing your index finger into the centre – the fish should still have a little structure.

To finish

1 Wilt the spinach in a hot pan, add the peas and butter and season.

2 Place the poached eggs in the soup and quickly re-heat.

3 Place a mound of spinach and peas in the centre of a bowl with the salmon on top and 2 quails' eggs per bowl.

4 Finish the dish with a drizzle of fine olive oil and fresh herbs.

Note: This is a suitable summer dish, light and very seasonal. As an alternative replace the salmon with the salt cod from recipe 190.

---

nutritional info

1 large portion provides:
5032 kJ/1213 kcal
83.7 g fat (of which 29.3 g saturated)
53.4 g carbohydrate (of which 13.2 g sugars)
64.9 g protein
15.9 g fibre

Butter is used for the salmon and spinach.

♥

calorie counter

kcal
1000
900
800
700
600
500
400
300
200
100
0

175 Crispy seared salmon with horseradish foam and caviar

	4 portions	10 portions
salmon fillet steaks, skin on, scaled	4 × 140 g	10 × 140 g
vegetable oil		
baby spinach, washed	400 g	1 kg
butter		
spears of asparagus, blanched	12	30
garlic cloves, chopped	1	3
caviar (optional)	50 g	125 g
chervil		
Foam		
shallots, sliced	2	5
sprig of thyme	1	3
butter	80 g	200 g
white wine	60 ml	150 ml
double cream	60 ml	150 ml
horseradish, grated	20 g	50 g
lemons, juice of	1	3

1 Place salmon skin-side down in a hot pan with a little vegetable oil and cook on a medium heat until two-thirds of the salmon is cooked.

2 For the foam, sweat the shallots and thyme in half the butter, adding white wine after 2 minutes and reduce by half.

3 Add the cream and horseradish, bring to the boil and infuse for 15 minutes off the heat.

4 Pass through a fine chinois and work in the other half of the butter and the lemon juice while the mix is hot (this will stop it from splitting).

5 Wilt the spinach in a little butter, add the asparagus to re-heat and arrange neatly in the centre of each serving dish.

6 Place the seared salmon skin-side up on the asparagus and spinach, and finish with a quenelle of caviar. Garnish with chervil.

Note: This dish can be adapted in many ways by substituting the caviar with avruga caviar to save the expense. Alternatively, if cost is not an issue, why not use smoked salmon (a smaller portion to replace the caviar) and sear that in the same way. The horseradish will be a great foil for this.

nutritional info

1 large portion provides:
2209 kJ/533.4 kcal
41.7 g fat (of which 18.3 g saturated)
4.8 g carbohydrate (of which 4.1 g sugars)
34.7 g protein
3.5 g fibre

Contains butter and double cream in the foam.

♥ kcal 1000 900 800 700 600 500 400 300 200 100 0 — calorie counter

176 Ravioli of salmon and girolles with a shellfish sauce — Steve Munkley

Serves 4

Pasta	
pasta flour	250 g
whole eggs	2
egg yolks	3
olive oil	5 ml
Filling and sauce	
cubes of clean salmon	4 × 75 g
cooked girolles	80 g
blanched pak choi leaves	8
fish cream sauce	200 ml
cockles	24
mussels	16
tomato cut into concassée	1
chopped chives	1 tsp

nutritional info

1 large portion provides:
2449.02 kJ/583.78 kcal
26.77 g fat (of which 9.75 g saturated)
53.80 g carbohydrate (of which 2.28 g sugars)
35.2 g protein
2.73 g fibre

There is egg in the pasta and cream in the sauce.

♥ kcal 1000 900 800 700 600 500 400 300 200 100 0 — calorie counter

1 Make the pasta by blending all the ingredients in a food processor, then leave to rest for 30 minutes.

2 Season the pieces of salmon then top each with 20 g of mushrooms. Wrap in pak choi leaf.

3 Roll out the pasta very thin, cut into two equal-sized sheets, place the salmon on, brush around each piece with water and then cover with the second sheet of pasta and form your raviolis.

4 Place a large pan of salted boiling water on the stove. When simmering cook raviolis for approximately 8–10 minutes, drain well.

5 Reheat the fish cream sauce adding the cockles and mussels, then just before serving add the concassée and chives.

6 When plating, spoon the sauce into the centre of the plate and put the ravioli on top.

Steve Munkley

177 Baked stuffed sardines

1 Slit the stomach openings of the sardines and gut.

2 From the same opening carefully cut along each side of the back bones and remove by cutting through the end with fish scissors.

3 Scale, wash, dry and season the fish.

4 A variety of stuffings can be used – for example:
   (a) cooked chopped spinach with cooked chopped onion, garlic, nutmeg, salt, pepper
   (b) fish forcemeat
   (c) thick duxelle.

5 Place the stuffed sardines in a greased ovenproof dish.

6 Sprinkle with breadcrumbs and oil.

7 Bake in hot oven, 200°C, for approximately 10 minutes and serve.

Notes: Herring, mackerel, sea bass and trout can also be prepared and cooked in this way (see photos on page 146), and there is considerable scope for flair and imagination in the different stuffings and methods of cooking the fish.

Fresh sardines are also popular when plainly grilled and served with quarters of lemon.

178 Whole sole grilled with traditional accompaniments

	4 portions	10 portions
whole sole, white and black skin removed	4	10
butter for grilling	200 g	500 g
seasoning		
parsley butter	100 g	250 g
lemons, peeled and cut into rondels	1	3

nutritional info

1 large portion provides:
3320 kJ/798 kcal
57.4 g fat (of which 33.4 g saturated)
0.6 g carbohydrate (of which 0.6 g sugars)
70.0 g protein
0.0 g fibre

Butter is used to cook the sole and parsley butter is served.

kcal
1000
900
800
700
600
500
400
300
200
100
0

calorie counter

1 Ensure the fish is clean of roe, scales and skin.

2 Place on a buttered grilling tray and rub soft butter in to the flesh.

3 Season and place under the grill.

4 When the butter starts to brown slightly, remove from the grill and turn the fish over carefully using a roasting fork or a long palette knife.

5 With a spoon, baste the flesh of the uncooked side and continue cooking. Extra care should be taken as the tail end will cook faster than the head end, therefore the gradual reduction in heat towards the front of the grill is where the tail should be cooked.

6 To check whether the fish is done, place your thumb just behind the gill area and you should feel the flesh ease away from the bone.

7 Finish with parsley butter and a wedge of lemon.

Note: This is a classic recipe using slip, Dover or lemon sole. There is no need to modernise it.

179 Pan-fried fillets of sole with rocket and broad beans

	4 portions	10 portions
trimmed sole fillets	16	40
seasoning		
butter	200 g	500 g
cooked and shelled broad beans	250 g	625 g
picked and washed rocket	300 g	750 g
vinaigrette	50 ml	125 ml

nutritional info

1 large portion provides:
3025 kJ/727 kcal
52.9 g fat (of which 27.8 g saturated)
45.6 g carbohydrate (of which 2.6 g sugars)
57.8 g protein
5.0 g fibre

Noisette butter is used.

1 Heat a little oil in a non-stick pan.

2 Place the fillets of sole on a tray and season on both sides.

3 Place the fish in the pan carefully (presentation side down).

4 Cook for 1 minute on a medium/high heat, and then carefully turn the fish, remove the pan from the heat and allow the residual heat to finish the cooking.

5 Place the sole fillets (4 per portion) on serving plates and keep warm.

6 Place the butter in the cooking pan, heat to the noisette stage, add the broad beans and cook for 30 seconds to 1 minute just to re-heat the beans.

7 Nap the beans, add a little noisette butter over the fish and top with a dressed rocket salad.

Note: This is a very simple and quick dish. Any salad or greens, if they are quickly cooked or lightly dressed, can go with this dish.

180 Pan-fried turbot with braised oxtail and lemon oil

	4 portions	10 portions
Lemon oil		
vegetable oil	200 ml	500 ml
sticks of lemon grass, crushed	3	7
lemons in rind	2	5
Baby gems		
vegetable oil	25 ml	60 ml
heads baby gem lettuce, halved lengthways	2	5
butter	75 g	175 g
orange juice	50 ml	125 ml
fish stock	50 ml	125 ml
To finish		
cooked oxtail meat, free from bone and gristle (see recipe 257)	200 g	500 g
meat glaze	100 ml	250 ml
sherry vinegar	4 tsp	5 tsp
vegetable oil	2 tbsp	5 tbsp
mixed wild or cultivated mushrooms	120 g	300 g
button onions, cooked	12	30
vegetable oil	50 ml	125 ml

	4 portions	10 portions
pieces turbot fillet, about 120 g each	4	10
salt and pepper		
herb mash (mashed potato with 2 tbsp/5 tbsp chopped herbs added)	200 g	500 g
lemon oil (see above)	50 ml	125 ml
chive tips and chervil sprigs, to garnish		

nutritional info

1 large portion provides:
2388 kJ/576 kcal
46.2 g fat (of which 11.3 g saturated)
12.3 g carbohydrate (of which 4.3 g sugars)
28.2 g protein
1.8 g fibre

Butter is used to cook the lettuce and oxtail added to the dish.

For the lemon oil

1 Combine all the ingredients for the lemon oil and leave at room temperature for 1 day.

2 Decant and store in the refrigerator.

For the baby lettuce

1 Take a frying pan large enough to fit the halves of baby gem comfortably. Place the empty pan over a medium heat, add the oil, then the baby gems and cook until slightly browned, taking care not to scorch the leaves.

2 Add a third of the butter to the pan and cook until it foams and turns a nutty-brown colour.

3 Pour in the orange juice and fish stock to deglaze the pan, then cover loosely with foil and cook at a simmer for 4–5 minutes or until the core of the lettuce starts to soften. Remove the lettuce from the pan and keep warm until serving.

To complete

1 Place the oxtail in the meat glaze to reheat just before serving, add a little sherry vinegar – just enough so that you can taste a little acid in the sauce but can't quite work out what it is, allowing the true flavours of the dish to come through.

2 In a small frying pan, add the vegetable oil, then the mushrooms. Sauté until slightly coloured, then add the rest of the butter and bring to a foam.

3 Remove from the heat, drain and keep warm. Heat the onions and keep warm with the mushrooms. Bring the baby gem and herb mash up to serving temperature if they have been allowed to cool.

4 Place a frying pan that will accommodate the turbot fillets over a medium heat and add the vegetable oil.

5 Season the fish lightly with salt and ground white pepper, place in the pan and cook until golden brown on one side. Turn, then reduce the heat and cook for a further 2 minutes or so – the exact time will depend on the thickness of fillet.

6 To test if cooked, press the fish – the flesh should just give a little. Alternatively, if you prefer your fish to be cooked through, keep cooking until the flesh is firm.

7 Place a spoonful of herb mash potato in the centre of the serving plate and cover with the baby gem.

8 Surround with the warm mushrooms and onions. Spoon over a little of the oxtail and sauce, then place the cooked fish on top and drizzle more sauce around plate.

9 Finish by dripping on the lemon oil, then garnish with herbs as required.

Note: This combination works incredibly well, the two bold flavours of each part acting harmoniously together. Brill, monkfish or cod can be used instead of the turbot.

181 Poached brill with wild crayfish gnocchi

	4 portions	10 portions
brill fillet pieces, skin removed (approx. 150 g each)	4	10
butter	100 g	250 g
freshwater crayfish	20	50
fish stock/bouillon for poaching	2 litres	5 litres
chives, chopped	2 tbsp	5 tbsp
Gnocchi		
dry mash potato (baked)	350 g	875 g
grade 'OO' flour	125 g	300 g
grated Parmesan	75 g	180 g
butter	15 g	40 g
egg yolks	2	5
Crayfish reduction		
crayfish tail shells and claws, once meat removed		
carrots	1	3
celery sticks	1	3
garlic cloves	2	5
shallots	1	3
leeks	75 g	180 g
red wine	250 ml	635 ml
white wine	125 ml	300 ml
brandy	100 ml	250 ml
star anise	1	3
white peppercorns	10	25
sticks of lemon grass	½	1
bay leaf	1	3
basil and coriander sprigs	1	3
chicken stock	500 ml	1¼ litres
fish stock	500 ml	1¼ litres
water	2 litres	5 litres

nutritional info

1 large portion provides:
2439 kJ/579 kcal
17.7 g fat (of which 7.7 g saturated)
44.0 g carbohydrate (of which 5.0 g sugars)
63.5 g protein
3.5 g fibre

Contains butter, egg yolk and parmesan in the gnocchi.

For the gnocchi

1 Add the dry mash, flour and Parmesan to a bowl and mix in the melted butter.

2 Add the eggs and mix lightly as for pastry (bring to a crumb and then mould together).

3 Rest for 1 hour then roll out to desired shape and cut.

4 Blanch in boiling water for 30 seconds and store on a dry cloth.

For the crayfish reduction

1 Remove the meat from the crayfish and reserve, then seal off the tail shells and claws in a little oil quickly for one minute. Drain and remove the shells and place in a colander.

2 In the same pan add a little oil, then add the carrot, celery, garlic, shallots and leeks. Colour until a golden brown, return the shells to the pan and cook for a further 2 minutes.

3 Add the red and white wine and brandy. Flame and reduce by half.

4 At this point put in the star anise, lemon grass, peppercorns and herbs.

5 Add the chicken and fish stock, and the water, bring to the boil, then simmer and cook for 40 minutes.

6 Pass, reduce to a glaze and it is then ready for use.

To finish

1 Bring the poaching liquor up to a simmer, add the brill, return to the boil and remove from the heat immediately, allowing the fish to cook for 3-4 minutes in the residual heat.

2 Add the butter to a pan and, when it starts to foam, add the gnocchi and cook for 1–2 minutes until golden. Remove and put into a clean pan with the shellfish reduction, chives and crayfish meat.

3 Warm slightly and retain.

4 Remove the fish carefully from the poaching liquor and allow to drain. Meanwhile, place the crayfish gnocchi and tails in the centre of a bowl, placing the brill carefully on top.

5 This dish can be served with a rocket salad with a lemon dressing.

Note: Turbot can be used instead of brill and lobster or langoustine instead of crayfish.

182 Pan-fried turbot with Alsace cabbage

	4 portions	10 portions
vegetable oil	50 ml	125 ml
seasoning		
turbot fillets (approx. 180 g pieces)	4	10
butter	50 g	125 g
lemons for juicing	1	3
Cabbage		
vegetable oil	50 ml	125 ml
butter	50 g	125 g
large (or double the amount small) shallots, finely diced	2	5
cloves garlic, chopped and sprout removed	2	5
large carrot, peeled and thinly sliced	1	3
sprigs thyme	2	5
bay leaf	1	3
savoy cabbage, finely sliced and stalks removed	1	3
water	50 ml	125 ml
fish stock	50 ml	125 ml

nutritional info

1 large portion provides:

2638 kJ/636 kcal

51.1 g fat (of which 17.4 g saturated)
9.5 g carbohydrate (of which 8.4 g sugars)
35.2 g protein
4.9 g fibre

Butter is used to cook the cabbage and the turbot.

For the cabbage

1 Place a large pan with a tight-fitting lid over a medium heat. Add the oil and butter, heat gently, then add the shallots, garlic and carrot, and cook for 2 minutes without letting them colour.

2 Add the thyme, bay leaf and cabbage to the pan and cook for a further 3 minutes, again without colouring.

3 Pour in the water and fish stock, cover and steam for 3 minutes. If serving immediately, drain, then adjust the seasoning to taste and serve. Otherwise spread the cabbage out thinly on a tray and store covered in the fridge for up to 24 hours.

To finish

1 Heat the oil in a non-stick pan, season the turbot fillets and place in the hot oil presentation side down.

2 When the turbot is golden brown turn in the pan and add the butter.

3 Bring to a light foam, but not noisette.

4 To finish add a squeeze of lemon.

5 Place a mound of cabbage in the centre of the serving plate and top with the turbot.

183 Pan-fried red mullet with artichokes and Swiss chard

	4 portions	10 portions
vegetable oil	100 ml	250 ml
seasoning		
red mullet fillets (approx. 120 g each), pinned and scaled	4	10
shitake mushrooms, sliced	8	20
Swiss chard, picked and washed (use spinach if chard unavailable)	200 g	500 g
green beans, trimmed and blanched	200 g	500 g
baby artichokes, cooked and trimmed	8	20
fish stock	80 ml	200 ml
crayfish reduction (see recipe 181)	80 ml	200 ml
soft herbs (chervil, chives, dill), washed and picked	50 g	125 g
lemon oil (see recipe 180)	50 ml	125 ml

1 Heat the oil in a non-stick pan, season the red mullet and place skin-side down.

2 Seal the skin side for 1 minute only with good colour, remove from the pan and reserve.

3 Add the mushrooms to the pan and hard cook until they become crisp.

4 Add the Swiss chard, green beans and artichokes, and cook for a further minute.

5 Add the fish stock and the reduction. Bring to the boil.

6 Add the fish skin-side up and cook for a further minute.

7 Divide the contents of the pan evenly over the serving plate, garnish with the soft herbs and drizzle with lemon oil.

Note: Red mullet has a distinctive and strong fish flavour. Pairing it with Swiss chard, artichokes and shitake mushrooms more than compensates for its bold approach.

nutritional info

1 large portion provides:
2246 kJ/542 kcal
42.8 g fat (of which 4.6 g saturated)
12.6 g carbohydrate (of which 3.2 g sugars)
28.5 g protein
1.5 g fibre

There is some saturated fat from the oil used

calorie counter
kcal
1000
900
800
700
600
500
400
300
200
100
0

184 Red mullet ceviche with organic leaves

	4 portions	10 portions
shallots, finely diced	2	5
olive oil	1 tbsp	3 tbsp
white wine vinegar	50 ml	125 ml
fish stock	1 litre	2½ litres
lemons, juice of	1	3
cucumber, diced	2 tbsp	5 tbsp
red mullet fillets (approx. 120 g each), pinned and scaled	4	10
organic salad leaf (5 varieties)	300 g	750 g
vinaigrette	50 ml	125 ml
caviar (optional)	50 g	125 g
Saffron dressing		
water	10 ml	25 ml
saffron		
vegetable oil	50 ml	125 ml
vinegar	10 ml	25 ml

nutritional info

1 large portion provides:
1487 kJ/358 kcal
27.1 g fat (of which 3.0 g saturated)
3.4 g carbohydrate (of which 3.1 g sugars)
24.8 g protein
0.9 g fibre

Olive oil was used.

calorie counter
kcal
1000
900
800
700
600
500
400
300
200
100
0

1 Bring the shallots, olive oil, white wine vinegar and fish stock to the boil. Add the lemon and cucumber, and allow to cool at room temperature.

2 Place the red mullet in a container and cover with the liquid. Top with clingfilm to ensure all the air is kept out, capitalising on maximum curing. This will need to remain in the fridge for a minimum of 6 hours.

For the dressing

1 Add water and a pinch of saffron to a pan and bring to the boil.

2 Whisk in the vegetable oil and vinegar.

3 Season.

To finish

1 Mix the dressed leaves lightly in vinaigrette.

2 Place the red mullet carefully on a plate with a little of the curing liquor, shallots and cucumber.

3 Top with the organic salad and finish with the saffron dressing and caviar (if using).

Note: A cured dish always tastes of the true ingredients. Using red mullet, as here, the flavours are bold and earthy, and paired with the saffron it makes a perfect summer starter.

185 Nage of red mullet with baby leeks

	4 portions	10 portions
mussels, cooked and out of shell	16	40
lemons, juice of	2	5
baby spinach	200 g	500 g
baby leeks	12	30
spears of baby asparagus	12	30
pieces of green beans	24	60
red mullet fillets (approx. 120 g each), pinned and scaled	4	10
Nage		
large onion	1	3
carrots, peeled	2	5
celery sticks	2	5
leeks	2	5
garlic cloves	1	3
half white and half pink peppercorns	12	30
star anise	1	3
white wine	375 ml	950 ml
Noilly Prat vermouth	375 ml	950 ml
chervil	10 g	25 g
parsley	10 g	25 g
tarragon	10 g	25 g
chives, chopped	1 tbsp	3 tbsp

1 In a large pan place the onions, carrots, celery and leeks, which have been cut into 2 cm pieces.

2 Just cover the vegetables with water. Bring to the boil. Simmer for 4–5 minutes. Remove from the heat and add the rest of the ingredients.

3 Cover with clingfilm and allow to cool to room temperature. Place into a plastic container and store in the fridge overnight to develop flavour.

4 Pass through a fine sieve. The resulting nage can be bottled for later use.

5 To finish, place 500 ml of the vegetable nage in a pan, add the mussels, a squeeze of lemon, spinach, baby leeks, asparagus and green beans.

6 Bring to the boil, check the seasoning and retain.

7 Heat a non-stick pan with a little vegetable oil. Season the mullet fillets and cook for one minute on each side (thickness dependent).

8 Divide the vegetable garnish between the bowls. Place the red mullet on top of the vegetable garnish and, returning the pan the mullet was cooked in to the stove, pour in the nage.

9 When the nage has returned to the boil, spoon over the fish and garnish. Serve immediately.

Note: This dish is open to many substitutions of fish and shellfish but one key point to remember is that the nage should not be allowed to overpower the main ingredients.

nutritional info

♥

1 large portion provides:
1183 kJ/282 kcal
7.7 g fat (of which 0.6 g saturated)
14.5 g carbohydrate (of which 7.7 g sugars)
36.0 g protein
10.6 g fibre

No oil was used in the cooking.

kcal
1000
900
800
700
600
500
400
300
200
100
0

calorie counter

186 Monkfish

Also known as angler fish, monkfish has firm, white flesh and is prepared by skinning, removing any dark patches, filleting and removing any gristle before cooking. It is suitable for adding to bouillabaisse and fish soups, and can be prepared and cooked in a variety of ways, e.g. as for any of the cod or hake recipes.

187 Roast monkfish with smoked bacon and white bean cassoulet

	4 portions	10 portions
paprika	10 g	25 g
flour	40 g	100 g
monkfish tail, boned, skinned and trimmed	1 large (1½ kg)	3 large (1½ kg)
lemons, juice of	1	3
Cassoulet		
vegetable oil	60 ml	150 ml
carrot, onion and celery brunoise	100 g	250 g
pancetta, skinned and cut into lardons	200 g	500 g
fish stock	20 ml	50 ml
white beans, cooked	200 g	250 g
cream	100 ml	250 ml
wholegrain mustard	1 tsp	3 tsp
chives, chopped	1 tbsp	3 tbsp
Pickled-braised fennel		
medium fennel bulbs	2	5
vegetable oil	4 tsp	10 tsp
carrots, peeled	50 g	125 g
onions, peeled	50 g	125 g
garlic clove, split	1	3
white wine vinegar	75 ml	200 ml
chicken stock	200 ml	500 ml
butter	50 g	125 g

For the pickled-braised fennel

1 Remove the tops and root of the fennel, halve and shred the bulb finely.

2 Heat the oil in a saucepan and add all the vegetables. Cook for 5–6 minutes without letting them colour.

3 Add the vinegar and cook for a further 2 minutes, then add the chicken stock and simmer until half the liquid is evaporated and the fennel is tender.

4 Remove and discard the carrot and shallot, and keep the fennel mix warm.

For the white beans

1 Heat the vegetable oil in a thick-bottomed pan, add the brunoise and cook without colour for 2 minutes.

2 Add the pancetta and cook for a further 2 minutes, and then add the fish stock and the cooked beans.

3 Bring to the boil and reduce to a simmer for 5 minutes, ensuring the bacon flavour penetrates the beans.

4 Add the cream, reduce to a semi-thick sauce and keep warm.

To complete

1 Pre-heat the oven to 180°C.

2 Mix the paprika and flour together, and roll the monkfish well in the mix.

3 Heat the oil in a thick-bottomed pan that can go into an oven comfortably.

4 Place the monkfish in the pan and brown well on all sides, place in the oven for 12 minutes, turning and basting every 2–3 minutes.

5 Once cooked, allow to rest for a further 3 minutes.

6 Meanwhile bring the beans and fennel up to a simmer, adding the mustard and chives to the beans and the butter to the fennel.

7 With the beans at this point the mix cannot be reboiled, as the mustard will split the mix and the butter will need to be emulsified into the stock of the fennel mix.

8 Place the fennel mix in the centre of the plates and the bean mix around.

9 Carve the monkfish, divide evenly between the plates, drizzle with the lemon juice and serve immediately.

Note: Monkfish has a tendency to squeeze out moisture when cooked, even if it is cooked perfectly. Be mindful of this: allow the fish to rest before serving and drain well on kitchen paper before placing on the dish.

188 Malt-poached halibut with chicken hearts and skin

	4 portions	10 portions
Poaching liquor		
skinless halibut steaks (approx. 180 g each)	4	10
malt extract	75 g	200 g
milk	400 ml	1 litre
bay leaf	1	3
garlic clove, split	1	3
Hearts		
chicken hearts, washed and split	8	20
shallots, finely chopped	1	3
meat glaze	100 ml	250 ml
sherry vinegar	20 ml	50 ml
chives, chopped	1 tsp	3 tsp
Skin		
pieces of skin from the breast area of a chicken	4	10
sea salt flakes	10 g	25 g
To finish		
baby leeks	8	20
wild mushrooms	100 g	250 g
mashed potato	200 g	500 g
Malt foam		
malt extract	30 g	75 g
milk	200 ml	500 ml
soy lecithin	10 g	25 g

nutritional info

1 large portion provides:
1838 kJ/437 kcal
11.6 g fat (of which 5.1 g saturated)
33.7 g carbohydrate (of which 6.9 g sugars)
50.3 g protein
21.4 g fibre

Contains some milk and small piece of chicken skin.

calorie counter

kcal
1000
900
800
700
600
500
400
300
200
100
0

1 Blanch the chicken skin in boiling water for 30 seconds, dry well and place between 2 pieces of greaseproof paper with a little oil and sea salt. Bake in the oven on 180°C for 10–12 minutes until crisp and golden.

2 For the poaching liquor mix all the ingredients (except the fish) together, bring to the boil and leave to infuse for 1 hour.

3 For the malt foam, mix the malt and milk together then, with a hand blender, create a vortex in the mix and slowly add the soy lecithin until it is fully dispersed.

4 Bring the mix to the boil then aerate, knock back the foam and aerate again (the first foam will not hold but the second will; if, however it does not, add a little more soy).

5 Place to one side until ready to use (do not allow to re-boil once the soy has been added).

6 Bring the poaching liquor to the boil again and place in the fish, remove from the heat and allow the residual heat to cook the fish through.

7 Reheat the vegetable garnish in a little butter or use boiling water and heat the mash with a little milk.

8 Put a small pan on the stove with a little oil and then quickly cook the chicken hearts with the chopped shallot.

9 When cooked add the meat glaze, the sherry vinegar and the chopped chives, keep warm.

10 Arrange the garnish on the plate as desired, remove and drain the fish, place on the garnish.

11 Foam the malt foam with a hand blender, removing only the foam from the surface, nap over the fish. Finish the dish with a piece of chicken skin and arrange the chicken hearts around the fish and drizzle any excess sauce from the pan around the plate to finish.

Note: We all like that crisp, roast, salted chicken skin! Why save it only for chicken? This recipe offers the skin with the crunchy texture and the flavour we have come to recognise. The poaching liquid is flavoured with malt, which adds an extra dimension to the dish and, together with the acidity of the chicken hearts, gives a great combination of flavours.

189 Poached hake with cockles and prawns

	4 portions	10 portions
onion, finely chopped	100 g	250 g
oil	1 tbsp	2½ tbsp
fish stock	250 ml	600 ml
parsley, chopped	1 tbsp	2½ tbsp
hake steaks or fillets	4 × 150 g	10 × 150 g
shelled cockles	8–12	20–30
shelled prawns	8–12	20–30
salt and pepper		
hard-boiled eggs, coarsely chopped	2	5
chopped parsley (for garnish)		

1 Lightly colour the onion in the oil, add the fish stock and parsley and simmer for 10–15 minutes.

2 Place the fish in a shallow ovenproof dish, and add cockles and prawns.

3 Pour on the fish stock and onion, season lightly.

4 Poach gently, remove any bones and skin from the fish.

5 If there is an excess of liquid, strain and reduce.

6 Serve coated with the unthickened cooking liquor, sprinkled with the egg and parsley.

nutritional info

1 large portion provides:
974.6 kJ/232.71 kcal
9.5 g fat (of which 1.76 g saturated)
2.14 g carbohydrate (of which 1.54 g sugars)
34.7 g protein
0.39 g fibre

The fish is poached, but a small amount of egg was used as garnish.

190 Roast salt cod and clam chowder

	4 portions	10 portions
Salt cod		
cod fillet, skinned and trimmed	500 g	1¼ kg
ground cumin	2 tbsp	5 tbsp
five-spice powder	1 tbsp	3 tbsp
sea salt	200 g	500 g
Clams		
shallots, finely diced	2 medium	5 medium
butter	50 g	125 g
clams, shells tightly closed	500 g	1¼ kg
white wine or dry vermouth	20 ml	50 ml
Chowder		
vegetable oil	50 ml	125 ml
smoked bacon, cut into 1 cm dice	50 g	125 g
medium onion, cut into 1 cm dice	1	3
medium carrot, cut into 1 cm dice	1	3
garlic cloves, finely chopped	2	5
celery sticks, cut into 1 cm dice	1	3
medium potato, peeled and cut into 1 cm dice	1	3
medium yellow pepper, cut into 1 cm dice	1	3
chicken stock	1 litre	2½ litres
whipping cream	100 ml	250 ml
butter	50 g	125 g
salt and pepper		
To finish		
heads escarole leaves, picked and stalks removed *or*	1	3
spinach	200 g	500 g
chopped chervil		

nutritional info

1 large portion provides:
2759 kJ/664 kcal
46.5 g fat (of which 21.5 g saturated)
18.8 g carbohydrate (of which 7.1 g sugars)
48.3 g protein
2.2 g fibre

Includes bacon, whipping cream and butter in the chowder.

For the salt cod

1 Place the skinned and trimmed cod fillet on a tray. Rub it all over with the spices and sprinkle evenly with the salt (note: if the fish tapers at one end, reduce the amount of salt placed on this area).

2 Wrap in clingfilm and place in the fridge. After 2 hours, turn the cod fillet over and return to the fridge for 1 hour.

3 Fill a clean sink half full with cold water. Unwrap the cod, rinse off the salt in the sink and leave the cod to soak for 30 minutes.

4 Remove from the water and dry well.

For the clams

1 Take a large saucepan with a tight-fitting lid and place over a medium heat with the shallots and butter, cook for 1 minute without letting the shallots colour.

2 Add the washed clams, shake the pan, then add the wine and place the lid on the pan immediately. Leave the clams to steam for 1–2 minutes so that they open and exude an intense liquor.

3 Remove the lid and make sure all the clams are open. Remove the pan from the heat and discard any with closed shells.

4 Place a colander over a large bowl, and pour the contents of the pan into the colander, reserving the liquor for the chowder.

5 Allow the clams to cool. Pick out the meat and discard the shells. Store the clam meat in an airtight container in the fridge until you are ready to serve the chowder.

For the chowder

1 In a large saucepan, heat the oil. When hot, add the bacon and cook for about 5 minutes until crisp and brown.

2 Using a perforated spoon, transfer the bacon onto kitchen paper to drain. Add the onion, carrot, garlic, celery and potato to the saucepan, reduce the heat to medium-low and cook the vegetables for 3–4 minutes without colouring.

3 Add the peppers and cook for 5 minutes. Pour in the reserved liquor from the clams and the chicken stock.

4 Bring to the boil and simmer for 10 minutes or until the volume of liquid has reduced by about half.

5 Add the cooked bacon and cream, then bring to the boil and reduce for a further 2 minutes until the soup thickens slightly.

6 Just before serving, whisk in the butter.

To complete

1 Remove the cod fillet from the fridge and cut into equal portions.

2 Wilt the escarole/spinach in a large pan, drain and set aside, keeping warm.

3 Heat a non-stick pan on the stove with 50 ml vegetable oil, place in the cod portions and cook for 2 minutes until golden brown on one side, turn and remove the pan from the heat, allowing the cod to finish cooking off on the stove in the residual heat of the pan.

4 Add the clams to the hot chowder and stir for 30 seconds until they are reheated.

5 Place the escarole/spinach in a small ball in the centre of the serving bowls, lay the cod on top of this and then add the chowder. Garnish with the chervil.

Note: For this recipe the cod should be salted in advance – salting the day before use and storing in the refrigerator will yield a better result.

191 Oven-baked marinated cod with bok choi

	4 portions	10 portions
cod fillet (approx. 175 g each) with skin off	4	10
baby bok choi	4	10
red pepper, cut into julienne	1	3
yellow pepper, cut into julienne	1	3
red onion, thinly sliced	1	3
bean sprouts	100 g	250 g
sesame oil	1 tbsp	3 tbsp
vegetable oil	2 tbsp	5 tbsp
soy sauce	1 tbsp	3 tbsp
coriander, chopped	1 tbsp	3 tbsp
Marinade		
soy sauce	100 ml	250 ml
sesame oil	50 ml	125 ml
rice wine	100 ml	250 ml
black bean paste	100 g	250 g

nutritional info

1 large portion provides:
1676 kJ/402 kcal
22.9 g fat (of which 3.1 g saturated)
12.6 g carbohydrate (of which 10.9 g sugars)
36.9 g protein
2.8 g fibre

Oils were used for the marinade only.

For the marinade

1 Mix all the ingredients together to a smooth consistency.

2 Place the cod fillets in the marinade for 12 hours.

3 After that, remove the fillets and wash off the excess marinade (it is not essential to get it all off).

For the cod

1 Pre-heat the oven to 180°C.

2 Put the cod on a lightly oiled baking tray and place in the oven.

3 Meanwhile heat the oil in a wok (if not available, use a heavy cast pan to retain the heat).

4 Place all the ingredients in the wok/pan excluding the soy and coriander.

5 Cook for 2–3 minutes until cooked but with a bite. Retain and keep warm.

6 Check the cod; it should take between 5 and 6 minutes according to thickness and, if timed well, will be ready when the vegetables are cooked.

7 Place the vegetables in the centre of the serving plate/dish and top with the cod. Any excess juices from the baking tray or the wok/pan may be poured around the fish, then serve.

Note: There is an eastern influence here, which can be adapted to suit a more European palate by changing the marinade to one using lemon and garlic, and using spinach, green beans and even olives to accompany the fish.

192 Roast fillet of sea bass with vanilla and fennel

	4 portions	10 portions
sea bass fillets (approx. 160 g each, cut from a 2–3 kg fish) skin on, scaled and pin-boned	4	10
seasoning		
vegetable oil	50 ml	125 ml
Fennel		
bulbs of baby fennel	8	20
vegetable oil	50 ml	125 ml
fish stock	500 ml	1¼ litres
clove of garlic	1	3
Vanilla sauce		
shallots, peeled and sliced	1	3
fish stock	500 ml	1¼ litres
white wine	200 ml	500 ml
vanilla pods	2	5
butter	50 g	125 g
chives, chopped	1 tsp	3 tsp
tomato concassée	100 g	250 g

nutritional info

1 large portion provides:
2057 kJ/496 kcal
39.5 g fat (of which 10.1 g saturated)
3.5 g carbohydrate (of which 2.9 g sugars)
31.9 g protein
1.7 g fibre

Butter is used in the sauce.

♥

kcal
1000
900
800
700
600
500
400
300
200
100
0

calorie counter

For the fennel

1 Trim the fennel bulbs well, ensuring they are free from blemishes and root.

2 Heat the oil in a pan, place in the fennel and slightly brown.

3 Add the stock and garlic, bring to the boil and cook until tender.

For the sauce

1 Heat a small amount of vegetable oil in a pan.

2 Place in the shallot and cook without colour, add the stock, white wine and split vanilla, and reduce by two-thirds.

3 Pass through a chinois and reserve for serving.

4 Add the butter and chopped chives.

To finish

1 Pre-heat the oven to 180°C.

2 Heat the oil in a non-stick pan and place the seasoned sea bass fillets in skin-side down.

3 Cook for 2 minutes on the stove and then place in the oven for 3 minutes (depending on thickness) still with the skin-side down.

4 Meanwhile, reheat the fennel and add the tomato concassée to the sauce.

5 Remove the sea bass from the oven and turn in the pan, finishing the flesh side for 30 seconds to 1 minute.

6 Lay the fennel in the centre of the plate and place the sea bass on top.

7 Finish the dish with the sauce over the bass and around, serve immediately.

Note: A marriage of flavour: vanilla, bass and fennel are made for each other. This fish can also be steamed.

193 Steamed sea bass with asparagus and capers

	4 portions	10 portions
Sea bass		
sea bass fillets (approx. 160 g each, cut from a 2–3 kg fish) skin on, scaled and pin-boned	4	10
court bouillon	1½ l	3¾ l
salt and pepper		
Caper dressing		
fine capers	1 tbsp	3 tbsp
aged balsamic vinegar	5 tbsp	12 tbsp
lemon oil (see recipe 180)	5 tbsp	12 tbsp
Fennel cream		
fennel bulbs	1	3
garlic clove	1	3
vegetable oil	50 ml	125 ml
fish stock	100 ml	250 ml
whipping cream	100 ml	250 ml
butter	50 g	125 g
Garnish		
asparagus spears	8	20
extra fine green beans, blanched	100 g	250 g

nutritional info

1 large portion provides:
3356 kJ/812 kcal
73.7 g fat (of which 24.6 g saturated)
3.0 g carbohydrate (of which 2.6 g sugars)
33.4 g protein
1.7 g fibre

Butter was used to cook the fish and cream in the fennel cream.

For the caper dressing

1 In a small bowl, combine all the dressing ingredients, adjust the seasoning to taste and set aside until serving.

For the fennel cream

1 Remove the root and stalks from the fennel bulbs and trim off any blemishes on the outer leaves.

2 Finely chop the fennel and crush the garlic. Heat the oil in a saucepan, add the fennel and garlic and cook slowly over a moderate heat for 6–7 minutes without letting them colour.

3 Add the fish stock, raise the heat under the pan and boil until reduced by half.

4 Pour in the cream, return to the boil and simmer until reduced by half.

5 Remove the pan from the heat and allow to cool slightly.

6 Transfer the mixture to a food processor and purée until fine. Return the sauce to a clean pan and set aside in a warm place – you need to whisk in the butter just before serving.

To complete

1 Ensure the sea bass is free of bones and scales.

2 Bring the court bouillon to a simmer and place the bass fillets in the bouillon.

3 Place the pan to one side, away from the heat, and allow to cook through with residual heat.

4 Meanwhile, reheat the asparagus and beans in a little butter.

5 Drain the fish, place it on the beans and asparagus on suitable plates.

6 Whisk the butter into the fennel cream, pour over the fish, and garnish the dish with the caper dressing.

194 Baked stuffed sea bass

	4 portions	10 portions
shallot, finely chopped	50 g	125 g
butter	150 g	375 g
mushrooms, chopped	150 g	375 g
salt and pepper		
tomato, skinned, deseeded, diced	100 g	250 g
pinch of chopped marjoram		
egg, beaten	1	2–3
few drops of lemon juice		
fresh breadcrumbs		
sea bass, scaled and gutted	1 kg	2½ kg
white wine	60 ml	150 ml

1 Cook the shallots in the butter without colour.

2 Add mushrooms, season and cook until dry.

3 Add tomato and marjoram, remove from heat, mix in the egg and lemon juice.

4 Bring to suitable consistency by adding breadcrumbs.

5 Clean, wash and stuff the fish. Place in buttered ovenproof dish and season.

6 Pour on the wine, sprinkle with breadcrumbs and remainder of butter in small thin pieces.

7 Bake at 200°C, basting frequently until cooked and lightly browned, approximately 15–25 minutes depending on size, and serve.

Note: The photos on page 146 show the techniques involved in preparing a stuffed fish.

nutritional info

♥

1 large portion provides:
1824 kJ/440.04 kcal
35.9 g fat (of which 20.6 g saturated)
2.1 g carbohydrate (of which 1.8 g sugars)
27.3 g protein
0.8 g fibre

There is butter and egg in the stuffing, and butter was used with the wine to bake the fish.

kcal
1000
900
800
700
600
500
400
300
200
100
0

calorie counter

195 Eels

These must be bought live and kept alive until required because once killed they toughen and deteriorate quickly. A sharp blow to the head will kill them. To remove the skins, make an incision skin deep around the neck, ease the skin back and using a cloth with a firm grip tear off the skin in one move. Slit the bellies, gut them and remove the coagulated blood from the back bones. Cut off the fins and wash well in running water. They can then be cut into pieces (6 cm) or filleted according to dish requirements.

Note: Eels can be prepared and cooked in a variety of ways: stewed, poached, braised, shallow- or deep-fried. They can also be made into pâtés, pies and terrines.

196 Eel with white wine, horseradish and parsley

	4 portions	10 portions
onion, chopped	50 g	125 g
butter	100 g	250 g
prepared eels	600 g	1½ kg
white wine	125 ml	300 ml
bouquet garni	1	2
potatoes, diced	200 g	500 g
whipping cream	100 ml	250 ml
fresh grated horseradish	1 tsp	3 tsp
parsley, chopped		
oil for frying		

nutritional info

1 large portion provides:
2770 kJ/669 kcal
58.0 g fat (of which 30.2 g saturated)
10.6 g carbohydrate (of which 2.0 g sugars)
26.9 g protein
0.9 g fibre

Butter was used to sweat the onions and cook the eel, and there is cream in the sauce.

1 Sweat the onions in the butter for 4–5 minutes without colour.

2 Add the eel to the pan and seal well.

3 Add the white wine, bring to the boil adding the bouquet garni and simmer for 15 minutes.

4 Add the potato and cook for a further 20 minutes until the eel is tender.

5 Remove the eel and potatoes and keep warm, pass the stock off into a clean pan and reduce to sauce consistency.

6 Add the cream, horseradish and chopped parsley, and bring to the boil.

7 Check the consistency and seasoning, correct if necessary.

8 Add the cooked eels to the pan of sauce, coat well and place in a serving dish.

Note: This is a traditional dish but still a classic. An eel is made up of lateral muscle groups either side of the back bone that work to move the fish around. Eels need a longer cooking time than other fish and shellfish species.

197 Fried eels with spring onion and mustard sauce

	4 portions	10 portions
prepared eels cut into 8 cm pieces	600 g	2¼ kg
onion, sliced	100 g	250 g
carrot, sliced	100 g	250 g
white wine	250 ml	600 ml
bouquet garni		
salt and pepper		
Sauce		
hard-boiled egg yolks	3	8
Dijon mustard	1 tbsp	2½ tbsp
olive oil	125 ml	300 ml
spring onions, chopped	4	10
salt and pepper		
flour, egg, breadcrumbs (pané)		

nutritional info

1 large portion provides:
1988 kJ/478.0 kcal
34.1 g fat (of which 7.3 g saturated)
12.6 g carbohydrate (of which 2.3 g sugars)
31.0 g protein
0.9 g fibre

There is egg yolk in the sauce.

1 Simmer the eels, onions, carrots, wine, bouquet garni and seasoning until tender.

2 Remove the eels, drain and dry well.

3 Prepare the sauce by mashing the egg yolks and mixing in the mustard and oil, finally add the spring onions and salt and pepper.

4 Pané the eel pieces and deep-fry at 195°C.

5 Serve accompanied with the sauce.

Note: This dish can also be prepared with boned-out eel pieces.

198 Squid

Squid should either be cooked very quickly or braised for an hour or so. Only fresh squid is suitable for stir-frying, shallow-frying or grilling.

1 Pull the head away from the body together with the innards.

2 Cut off the tentacles just below the eye, remove the small round cartilage at the base of the tentacles.

3 Discard the head, innards and pieces of cartilage.

4 Taking care not to break the ink bag remove the long transparent blade of cartilage (the back bone or quill).

5 Scrape or peel off the reddish membrane that covers the pouch, rub with salt and wash under cold water.

199 Squid with white wine, garlic and chilli

	4 portions	10 portions
squid, cleaned	600 g	1½ kg
vegetable oil	60 ml	150 ml
garlic cloves, crushed	2	5
sprigs of parsley, chopped	3–4	7–8
red chilli pepper, seeds removed, finely chopped	1	3
white wine	60 ml	150 ml
fish stock	60 ml	150 ml

nutritional info

1 large portion provides:
1084 kJ/260 kcal
17.6 g fat (of which 2.4 g saturated)
2.3 g carbohydrate (of which 0.3 g sugars)
23.4 g protein
0.2 g fibre

Oil was used to fry the squid.

♥ kcal
1000
900
800
700
600
500
400
300
200
100
0

calorie counter

1 Cut the squid in to halves and then into thick strips.

2 Place a pan containing the vegetable oil on the hottest point on the stove.

3 Place the squid in the pan and sauté quickly (this will not take long – the squid will toughen if cooked for too long).

4 Add the garlic, chopped parsley and the chilli. Toss the squid around the pan, working in all the flavours.

5 Add the wine and stock, quickly bring to the boil, check the seasoning and serve.

Note: The texture of squid is unlike that of other species. The flesh is very high in protein and dense, giving it that 'rubbery' texture when overcooked. Cook quickly and over a high heat.

200 Stuffed squid

The pocket of the cleaned squid is suitable for stuffing, and a variety of ingredients and flavourings can be used – for example:

- anchovy, garlic, chilli, parsley
- rice, onions, spinach, dill

- oil, garlic, parsley, white wine, white breadcrumbs.

After stuffing, the openings must be secured with string and the squid can then either be baked or braised.

201 Pan-fried skate with capers and beurre noisette

	4 portions	10 portions
vegetable oil	50 ml	125 ml
seasoning		
skate, skinless fillets (approx. 160 g each)	4	10
butter	175 g	450 g
lemons, juice of	2	5
flat parsley, chopped	2 tbsp	5 tbsp
small capers	100 g	250 g

nutritional info

1 large portion provides:
2366 kJ/572 kcal
51.9 g fat (of which 24.7 g saturated)
1.4 g carbohydrate (of which 1.3 g sugars)
25.0 g protein
1.1 g fibre

Beurre noisette was used.

1 Place a skillet on the hottest part of the stove and an empty sauté pan to the side of the stove, achieving a moderate heat (this is for the beurre noisette).

2 Ensure the skate wings are fresh, and free from ammonia aromas and skin.

3 Add the vegetable oil to the skillet and place in the seasoned skate wings, cook with colour for 1–2 minutes and then carefully turn; at this point ease the skillet to a cooler point of the stove while the beurre noisette cooks.

4 Place the butter in the pan and allow to foam (at this point remove the skate and place in the serving dish).

5 Add the lemon, parsley and capers to the beurre noisette, stir well.

6 To finish, nap the beurre noisette over the skate wing and serve.

Note: Because skate pass urine through their wings, if they are not super-fresh they will start to smell of ammonia after 3–4 days; this is a key indicator of their freshness.

202 Skate with mustard and lemon on spinach

	4 portions	10 portions
skate	4 × 150–200 g	10 × 150–200 g
spinach, cooked	1 kg	2½ kg
butter	200 g	500 g
nutmeg		
salt and pepper		
lemon, juice of	1	2
French mustard (according to taste)	2–3 tsp	5–6 tsp

nutritional info

1 large portion provides:
2229 kJ/537.8 kcal
44.1 g fat (of which 26.3 g saturated)
2.9 g carbohydrate (of which 2.8 g sugars)
32.5 g protein
5.3 g fibre

The fish is poached, but there is butter in the sauce.

1 Poach or steam the fish, drain well.

2 Reheat spinach in half the butter, add a rub of nutmeg and season.

3 Boil the lemon juice and an equal amount of water and reduce.

4 Remove from heat, incorporate the remaining butter, then the mustard and correct seasoning.

5 Place the spinach on serving dish, add the skate.

6 Coat with sauce and serve.

Note: The skate flesh may be removed from the bones if desired.

203 Bouillabaisse

	4 portions	10 portions
assorted prepared fish, e.g. red mullet, whiting, sole, gurnard, small conger eel, John Dory, crawfish tail	1½ kg	3¾ kg
mussels (optional)	500 ml	1¼ kg
chopped onion or white of leek	75 g	180 g
garlic, crushed	10 g	25 g
white wine	125 ml	300 ml
water	500 ml	1¼ litres
tomatoes, skinned, deseeded, diced *or*	100 g	250 g
tomato purée	25 g	60 g
pinch of saffron		
bouquet garni (fennel, aniseed, parsley, celery)		
olive oil	125 ml	300 ml
chopped parsley	5 g	12 g
salt and pepper		
butter ⎫ beurre manié	25 g	60 g
flour ⎭	10 g	25 g
French bread		

nutritional info

1 portion provides:
689 kcals/2881 kJ
42.3 g fat
(of which 8.5 g saturated)
4.8 g carbohydrate
(of which 2.1 g sugars)
protein 67.6 g
0.5 g fibre

♥ kcal
1000
900
800
700
600
500
400
300
200
100
0

calorie counter

This is a thick, full-bodied fish stew – sometimes served as a soup – for which there are many variations. When made in the south of France, a selection of Mediterranean fish is used. If made in the north of France the following recipe could be typical.

1 Clean, descale and wash the fish. Cut into 2 cm pieces on the bone; the heads may be removed. Clean the mussels if using, and leave in their shells.

2 Place the cut fish, with the mussels and crawfish on top, in a clean pan.

3 Simmer the onion, garlic, wine, water, tomato, saffron and bouquet garni for 20 minutes.

4 Pour on to the fish, add the oil and parsley, bring to the boil and simmer for approximately 15 minutes.

5 Correct the seasoning and thicken with the beurre manié.

6 The liquor may be served first as a soup, followed by the fish accompanied by French bread that has been toasted, left plain or rubbed with garlic.

Note: If using soft fish, e.g. whiting, add it 10 minutes after the other fish.

204 Rouille (red chilli pepper mayonnaise) served with bouillabaisse and some other fish soups

½ dried or fresh red chilli pepper or 2 tsp cayenne pepper	
garlic	4–5 cloves
egg yolks	2
salt	
olive oil	125 ml
tomato paste (optional)	2–3 tsp

1 Cut peppers in pieces.

2 Add garlic, egg yolks and a little salt.

3 Pound in a mortar with a pestle until smooth.

4 Gradually work in the olive oil until thick and creamy.

5 Add tomato paste and season, it should be hot in taste.

Note: Rouille can also be made in a blender.

205 Stir-fried fish

Any firmly textured fish is suitable for stir-frying, e.g. sole, turbot, brill and perch. The cleaned, filleted and skinned fish should be cut into pieces 2 × 4 cm which may then be used fresh or marinated for 15 minutes. Shrimp, prawn and squid are also used. Prawns should be shelled and deveined by holding the tail firmly and making a small cut along the centre of the back. The black vein can be pulled out and thrown away. Squid should be cleaned and scored lightly in two directions. This is so that it can be cooked quickly, in about 30 seconds, and remain tender, delicate and juicy.

Stir-fry dishes originate mainly from Chinese cookery and are traditionally prepared in a wok. The whole essence of stir-fry cookery is that the food is only cooked to order and is cooked quickly over fierce heat. Because of this all ingredients to be used in the dish must be prepared and ready at hand before cooking begins. The following table lists some suggestions for stir-fried fish dishes.

FISH	ADDITIONAL INGREDIENTS	MARINADE INGREDIENTS	SAUCE INGREDIENTS
shrimp prawn lobster scallops	spring onion, shallots, cucumber, courgette, mushrooms, chicken, ginger, wine	oil, garlic, ginger, wine, salt, pepper,	soy sauce oyster sauce wine bean paste (yellow or black)

206 Shallow-fried fish with artichokes and potatoes (Murat)

	4 portions	10 portions
fish fillets	400–600 g	1½ kg
potatoes, peeled	300 g	750 g
artichoke bottoms, cooked in a blanc	2	5
oil	60 ml	125 ml
butter	100 g	250 g
juice of lemon	1	2
parsley, chopped		

nutritional info

1 large portion provides:
2002.8 kJ/482.65 kcal
36.6 g fat (of which 14.9 g saturated)
14.0 g carbohydrate (of which 1.2 g sugars)
25.4 g protein
1.0 g fibre

The vegetables and fish are fried, and a noisette butter was included.

1 Cut the fish into goujons.

2 Cut the potatoes into short batons – 1½ × ½ × ½ cm – shallow-fry in butter and oil, and drain in a colander.

3 Cut the artichokes into quarters or eighths, shallow-fry and drain on top of the potatoes.

4 Flour the fish, shake off the surplus, and shallow-fry quickly in oil and butter until golden brown. Place the fish on a serving dish.

5 Prepare 50 g beurre noisette in a clean pan, add the potatoes, artichokes and seasoning, toss carefully to mix.

6 Sprinkle with lemon juice, mask over the fish, finish with chopped parsley to serve.

Note: If artichokes are unavailable, mushrooms (button or wild) can be used.

207 Mousse, mousseline, quenelle

These are all made from the same basic mixture known as forcemeat. Salmon, sole, trout, brill, turbot, halibut, whiting, pike and lobster can all be used for fish forcemeat in the preparation of, for example, mousse of sole, mousselines of salmon, quenelles of turbot, all of which would be served with a suitable sauce (white wine, butter sauce, lobster, shrimp, saffron and mushroom).

208 Fish forcemeat or farce

	4 portions	10 portions
fish, free from skin and bone	300 g	1 kg
salt, white pepper		
egg whites	1–2	4–5
double cream, ice cold	250–500 ml	600 ml–1¼ litres

1 Process the fish and seasoning to a fine purée.

2 Continue processing, slowly adding the egg whites until thoroughly absorbed.

3 Pass the mixture through a fine sieve and place into a shallow pan or bowl.

4 Leave on ice or in refrigerator until very cold.

5 Beating the mixture continuously, slowly incorporate the cream.

Notes: When half the cream is incorporated, test the consistency and seasoning by cooking a teaspoonful in a small pan of simmering water. If the mixture is very firm, a little more cream may be added, then test the mixture again and continue until the mixture is of a mousse consistency.

As mousses are cooked in buttered moulds in a bain-marie in the oven and turned out for service, the mixture should not be made too soft otherwise they will break up.

Mousses are made in buttered moulds, usually one per portion but larger moulds for two to four can be made if required. It is sounder practice to use individual moulds because for large moulds the mousse needs to be of a firmer consistency to prevent it collapsing. They are cooked in a bain-marie in a moderate oven or in a low-pressure steamer.

Mousselines are moulded using two tablespoons, dipping the spoons frequently into boiling water to prevent the mixture sticking. They are normally moulded into shallow buttered trays, covered with salted water or fish stock, covered with buttered greaseproof paper and gently poached in the oven or steamed.

Quenelles are made in various shapes and sizes as required:

- moulded with dessert or teaspoons
- piped with a small plain tube.

They are cooked in the same way as mousselines. When making lobster mousse, use raw lobster meat and ideally some raw lobster roe as this gives authentic colour to the mousse when cooked. For scallop mousse use cooked scallops. In order to achieve sufficient bulk it is sometimes necessary to add a little other fish, e.g. whiting, sole, pike. Shellfish mousselines are best cooked in shallow individual moulds because of their looser texture.

209 Fish sausages (cervelas de poisson)

As with meat sausages, the variations of fish sausages that can be produced are virtually endless. Almost any type of fish or shellfish can be used, either chopped or minced. The filling can also be a combination of two or more fish, and additional ingredients can be added (e.g. dry duxelle, brunoise of skinned red peppers, a suitable chopped herb such as dill, chervil, parsley and/or a touch of spice).

The selected fish can also be made into a firm mousseline mixture as in the following recipe for pike sausages (cervelas de brochet).

pike meat	200 g
egg white	1
double cream	½ litre
salt, white pepper	
sausage skins	100 g

Note: The number of sausages produced will vary according to the size required.

1 Prepare mousseline mixture as above.

2 Place sausage skins in water; then hang up, knot one end.

3 Using a forcing bag, stuff the skins with mousse, being careful not to force it, then knot the other end with a piece of string.

4 Divide sausage into sections by loosely tying with string.

5 Gently poach the sausages in water at 82°C for 15 minutes.

6 Once cooked, carefully remove the sausages and allow to drain for 1–2 minutes.

7 With a sharp knife, remove the sausage skins carefully so as not to spoil the shape, drain well on a clean serviette and serve with a suitable sauce and garnish.

210 Russian fish pie (Coulibiac)

This dish can be made using brioche or puff paste.

	4 portions	10 portions
brioche or puff paste	200 g	500 g
coarse semolina or rice, cooked in good stock as for pilaff	100 g	250 g
salmon, cut in small thick slices and fried very lightly in butter	400 g	1¼ kg
onion, finely chopped	50 g	125 g
mushrooms, chopped	100 g	250 g
parsley, chopped	1 tbsp	2½ tbsp
hard-boiled egg, chopped	1	2½
fresh vesiga, cooked and roughly chopped	50 g	125 g
melted butter	200 g	500 g

nutritional info

1 large portion provides:
3461 kJ/833.63 kcal
66.5 g fat (of which 28.5 g saturated)
35.3 g carbohydrate (of which 1.7 g sugars)
26.8 g protein
0.5 g fibre

The salmon was fried in butter. The analysis did not include the vesiga.

1 Roll out the paste thinly into a rectangle approximately 30 × 18 cm.

2 Place the ingredients in layers one on top of the other along the centre, alternating the layers, and starting and finishing with the semolina or rice.

3 Eggwash the edges of the paste and fold over to enclose the filling completely.

4 Seal the ends and turn over on to a lightly greased baking sheet so that the sealed edges are underneath.

5 Allow to prove in a warm place for approximately 30 minutes.

6 Brush all over with melted butter and cut two small holes neatly in the top to allow steam to escape.

7 Bake at 190°C for approximately 40 minutes.

8 When removed from the oven, pour some melted butter into the two holes.

9 To serve, cut into thick slices and offer a butter-type sauce, e.g. hollandaise, separately.

Notes:

1 If using puff pastry, eggwash the completed dish before baking instead of brushing with butter.

2 Individual coulibiacs can be made using a 20 cm pastry cutter.

3 Vesiga is the spinal cord of the sturgeon obtained commercially in the shape of white, semi-transparent dry gelatinous ribbon. It must be soaked in cold water for 4–5 hours when it will swell to 4–5 times the size and the weight will increase six-fold. It is then gently simmered in white stock for 3½–4½ hours. If it is not possible to obtain vesiga, a layer of fish forcemeat may be substituted.

4 Coulibiac has for many years been a popular dish in high-class restaurants around the world. If the ingredients in this recipe are not available or are too expensive then other fish may be used to replace salmon, e.g. haddock. If vesiga is unobtainable then use more of all the other ingredients. With imagination many variations of this dish can be conceived.

211 Fish soufflés

	4 portions
raw fish, free from skin and bone	300 g
butter	50 g
thick béchamel	250 ml
salt and cayenne pepper	
eggs, separated	3

Haddock, sole, salmon, turbot, lobster, crab, etc., can all be used for soufflés.

1 Cook the fish in the butter and process to a purée.

2 Mix with the béchamel, pass through a fine sieve and season well.

3 Warm the mixture and beat in the egg yolks.

4 Carefully fold in the stiffly beaten egg whites.

5 Place into individual buttered and floured soufflé moulds.

6 Bake at 220°C for approximately 14 minutes; serve immediately.

Notes: If individual moulds are used, less cooking time is required. A suitable sauce may be offered, e.g. white wine, mushroom, shrimp, saffron, lobster.

The use of an extra beaten egg white will increase the lightness of the soufflé. A pinch of egg white powder added before whipping will strengthen the foam.

Lobster soufflés can be cooked and served in the cleaned half shells of the lobsters.

212 Fish and shellfish soufflé   René Pauvert

	4 portions	10 portions
Fish mousseline preparation		
sole fillet	50 g	125 g
scallop (white only)	50 g	125 g
egg white	1	2½
unsalted soft butter	5 g	12½ g
salt and cayenne to taste		
single cream	80 g	200 g
Soufflé		
egg white	7	17½
salt and cayenne to taste		

1 Lightly salt the flesh of the fish (sole and scallop) and place to rest for 10 minutes in the fridge until really cold.

2 Purée the flesh with the egg whites and the soft butter and cayenne.

3 Pass the flesh through a fine sieve and place into a stainless-steel bowl over ice.

4 Carefully incorporate the cream little by little.

5 Season to taste and keep cool.

6 For the souffle, take individual soufflé moulds, grease them with soft unsalted butter and coat with fresh breadcrumbs.

7 Whisk the egg whites with a touch of salt, until stiff.

8 Add a small amount of egg white into the mousseline, incorporate well, then gently fold in the rest of the egg. Season to taste.

9 Pour the mixture into the moulds up to the rim.

10 Cook for about 14 minutes at 200°C.

You could serve this soufflé with a sauce Americaine with small dice of poached scallop. Or you could incorporate in the middle of the soufflé the same sauce Americaine reduced to a glaze with dice of sole fillet and scallop, and tarragon.

SHELLFISH

Origins

Shellfish, such as lobsters and crabs, are all invertebrates (i.e. they do not possess an internal skeleton) and are split into two main groups: *molluscs* have either an external hinged double shell (e.g. scallops, mussels) or a single spiral shell (e.g. winkles, whelks), or have soft bodies with an internal shell (e.g. squid, octopus); *crustaceans* have tough outer shells that act like armour, and also have flexible joints to allow quick movement (e.g. crab, lobster).

Choosing and buying

Shellfish are prized for their tender, fine-textured flesh, which can be prepared in a variety of ways, but are prone to rapid spoilage. The reason for this is that they contain quantities of certain proteins, amino acids, which encourage bacterial growth.

To ensure freshness and best flavour it is preferable to choose live specimens and cook them yourself. This is often possible with the expansion of globalisation, air freight and such like, creating a healthy trade in live shellfish.

Bear in mind the following points when choosing shellfish:

- shells should not be cracked or broken
- shells of mussels and oysters should be tightly shut; open shells that do not close when tapped sharply should be discarded
- lobsters, crabs and prawns should have a good colour and be heavy for their size
- lobsters and crabs should have all their limbs.

Cooking

The flesh of fish and shellfish is different to meat and, as a consequence, their muscle make-up is very different too, making their connective tissue very fragile, the muscle fibres shorter and the fat content relatively low. Generally, care should be taken when cooking and shellfish should be cooked as little as possible, to the point that the protein in the muscle groups just coagulate. Beyond this point the flesh tends to dry out, leading to toughening and a dry texture. Shellfish are known for their dramatic colour changing: from blue/grey to a vibrant orange colour. This is because they contain red and yellow pigments called carotenoids, bound to molecules of protein. The protein bonds obscure the yellow/red pigment and, once heat is applied, the bonds are broken and the vibrant pigmentation revealed.

Storage

All shellfish will start to spoil as soon as they have been removed from their natural environment, therefore the longer shellfish are stored the more they will deteriorate due to the bacteria present (see the guidelines on choosing and buying, above). Best practice would be to cook immediately and store as for cooked fish. Shellfish can be blanched quickly to remove the shell and membrane (especially in lobsters), but they will still need to be stored as for a raw product as they will require further cooking.

Types or varieties of shellfish

Cockles

These are enclosed in pretty cream-coloured shells of 2–3 cm. Cockles are soaked in salt water to purge and then steamed. They may be used in soups, salads and fish dishes, or served as a dish by themselves.

Shrimps

Shrimps are used for garnishes, decorating fish dishes, cocktails, sauces, salads, hors d'oeuvres, potted shrimps, omelettes and savouries.

Prawns

Prawns are larger than shrimps; they may be used for garnishing and decorating fish dishes, for cocktails, canapés, salad, hors d'oeuvres, and for hot dishes such as curried prawns.

Scampi, Dublin Bay prawns

Scampi are found in the Mediterranean. The Dublin Bay prawn, which is of the same family, is caught around the Scottish coast. These shellfish resemble small lobsters, about 20 cm long, and only the tail flesh is used.

Crayfish

Crayfish are a type of small freshwater lobster used for garnishing cold buffet dishes and for recipes using lobster. They are dark brown or grey, turning pink when cooked. Average size is 8 cm.

Lobster

Lobsters are served cold in cocktails, hors d'oeuvres, salads, sandwiches and on buffets. When hot they are used for soup, and grilled and served in numerous dishes with various sauces. They are also used as a garnish to fish dishes.

Crawfish (rock lobster)

Crawfish are like large lobsters without claws, but with long antennae. They are brick red in colour when raw and cooked. Owing to their size and appearance they are used mostly on cold buffets but they can be served hot. The best size is 1½–2 kg.

Crab

Crabs are used for hors d'oeuvres, cocktails, salads, dressed crab, sandwiches and bouchées. Soft-shelled crabs are eaten in their entirety. They are considered to have an excellent flavour and may be deep- or shallow-fried, or grilled.

Oysters

Whitstable and Colchester are the chief English centres for oysters; they occur here naturally and are also farmed. Since the majority of oysters are eaten raw it is essential that they are thoroughly cleansed before hotels and restaurants receive them.

The popular way of eating oysters is in the raw state. They may also be served in soups, hot cocktail savouries, fish garnishes, as a fish dish, and in meat puddings and savouries.

Quality and purchasing points

1 Oysters must be alive; this is indicated by the firmly closed shells.
2 They are graded in terms of size, and the price varies accordingly.
3 Oysters should smell fresh.
4 They should be purchased daily.
5 English oysters are in season from September to April (when there is an 'R' in the month).
6 During the summer months oysters are imported from France, Holland and Portugal.

Storage

Oysters are stored in barrels or boxes, covered with damp sacks and kept in a cold room to keep them moist and alive. The shells should be tightly closed; if they are open, tap them sharply – if they do not shut at once, discard them.

213 Shellfish stock

Makes 1¼ litres

This can be made from the well-crushed soft shells of some shellfish, e.g. shrimp, prawn, crayfish, lobster, crawfish and crab. This stock is used for soups and sauces.

butter or oil	75 g
shell and trimmings	1 kg
onion ⎫	100 g
carrot ⎬ roughly cut	100 g
celery ⎭	50 g
tomato purée	100 g
fish stock or water	1¼ litres
bouquet garni	

1 Melt butter or oil in a thick-bottomed pan.

2 Add the well-pounded or crushed shells and sweat steadily for 5 minutes, stirring frequently.

3 Add the vegetables, sweat for a further 5 minutes.

4 Mix in the tomato purée and add the stock or water.

5 Bring to the boil, add bouquet garni, simmer for 45 minutes and strain.

Note: Added optional ingredients: 60 ml brandy added after the sweating process, then ignite; 125–250 ml white wine; ½ garlic clove, crushed.

Seasonality

	JAN	FEB	MAR	APR	MAY	JUN	JUL	AUG	SEP	OCT	NOV	DEC
Crab (brown cock)	At best	At best	At best	At best	Available	Available	Available	Available	Available	Available	Available	Available
Crab (spider)	Available	Available	Available	Available	At best	At best	At best	At best	At best	At best	Available	Available
Crab (brown hen)	At best	At best	Available	Available	Available	Available	At best	At best	At best	At best	At best	At best
Clams	At best	At best	At best	Available	Available	Available	Available	Available	Available	Available		
Cockles	At best	Available	At best	Available	At best	Available	Available	Available	Available	Available	Available	Available
Crayfish (signal)					At best	At best	Available	Available	Available	Available		
Lobster	Available	Available	Available	Available	Available	Available	At best	At best	Available	Available	At best	Available
Langoustines			At best	At best	At best	Available	Available	Available	Available			
Mussels	Available	Available	Available	Available	Available	Available	Available	Available	At best	At best	At best	At best
Oysters (rock)	At best	At best	At best	At best	At best	Available	Available	Available	At best	At best	At best	At best
Oysters (native)	At best	At best	At best	At best					At best	At best	At best	At best
Prawns						Available	Available	Available	Available	Available	Available	
Scallops	Available	Available	Available	Available	Available	Available	At best	At best	Available	Available	Available	At best

Code:

Available

At best

Preparing shellfish

Mussels: removing the beard

Opening and cleaning a scallop

Removing shell from lobster

Removing an oyster from the shell

214 Oysters

Oysters are most popular when freshly opened and eaten raw, together with their own natural juice, which should be retained carefully in the deep shell.

The shells should be tightly shut to indicate freshness. The oysters should be opened carefully with a special oyster knife so as to avoid scratching the inside shell, then turned and arranged neatly in the deep shell and served on a bed of crushed ice on a plate. They should not be washed unless gritty and the natural juices should always be left in the deep shell.

Accompaniments: brown bread and butter and lemon. It is usual to serve six oysters as a portion.

Oysters can also be cooked in a variety of ways. In all the following recipes they may be initially gently poached for a short time (10–15 seconds) in their own juice and the beards removed (overcooking will toughen them).

Examples

■ Warm the shells, add a little cheese sauce, place two oysters in each shell, coat with sauce and grated cheese, glaze and serve.

■ As previous recipe, dressing the oysters on a bed of leaf spinach.

■ Place two oysters in each shell, coat with white wine sauce, glaze and serve.

■ As previous recipe, using champagne in place of white wine.

■ Place one oyster on each shell, add a few drops of lemon, barely cover with breadcrumbs lightly fried in butter and gratinate under the salamander or in a very hot oven.

■ Pass the well-dried oysters through a light batter, or flour, egg and crumb, deep-fry and serve with quarters of lemon or lime.

Note: Oysters can also be mixed with any of the poached fish sauces together with other ingredients if required, e.g. a few lightly poached bean sprouts, button or wild mushrooms, and served in a bouchée, vol-au-vent, or any other shape of puff paste case – square, rectangular or diamond. They may then be served as a first course, fish course or main course, as required.

215 Oysters in their own shells

	4 portions	10 portions
rock or native oysters	24	40
lemons	1	3
To accompany		
brown bread and butter		
tabasco or chilli sauce		

nutritional info

1 large portion provides:
99.64 kJ/23.56 kcal
0.5 g fat (of which 0.0 g saturated)
1.2 g carbohydrate (of which 0.2 g sugars)
3.8 g protein
0.0 g fibre

No oil or fat is used.

♥

kcal
1000
900
800
700
600
500
400
300
200
100
0

calorie counter

1 Select only oysters that are tightly shut and have a fresh smell (category A oysters are best; this indicates that the waters they have grown in are clean).

2 To open an oyster, only the point of the oyster knife is used. Hold the oyster with a thick oven cloth to protect your hand.

3 With the oyster in the palm of your hand, push the point of the knife about 1 cm deep into the 'hinge' between the 'lid' and the body of the oyster.

4 Once the lid has been penetrated, push down. The lid should pop open. Lift up the top shell, cutting the muscle attached to it.

5 Remove any splintered shell from the flesh and solid shell.

6 Return the oysters back to the shell and serve on a bed of crushed ice with chilli sauce, brown bread and lemon.

Note: Make sure the oysters have been grown or fished from clean waters and remember the famous rule: only serve oysters when there is an 'R' in the month.

216 Oyster fricassée

	4 portions	10 portions
oysters, shelled and juice retained	24	40
cream	200 ml	500 ml
butter	30 g	75 g
wholegrain mustard	30 g	75 g
parsley, finely chopped	1 tsp	3 tsp
seasoning		
pinch cayenne		

nutritional info

1 large portion provides:
1389 kJ/337 kcal
34.3 g fat (of which 20.7 g saturated)
2.2 g carbohydrate (of which 1.2 g sugars)
5.2 g protein
0.4 g fibre

Contains butter and cream in the sauce.

♥

calorie counter

kcal
1000
900
800
700
600
500
400
300
200
100
0

1 Clean the oysters and retain on a clean tray in the refrigerator.

2 Heat the oyster liquor to boiling point, and strain through a double thickness of cheesecloth/muslin.

3 Add oysters to liquor and cook until plump, 1–2 minutes.

4 Remove oysters with slotted/perforated spoon and place on a clean plate, cover with clingfilm.

5 Add the cream and butter to liquor and reduce to form a sauce consistency.

6 Add the wholegrain mustard (do not re-boil), seasoning and parsley.

7 Return the oysters to the sauce, gently heat through and serve immediately.

217 Crab

Crab meat can be used in a variety of recipes – for example:

- first courses – on halves of mango or papaya or avocado coated with a mayonnaise or natural yoghurt-based sauce lightly flavoured with tomato ketchup, lemon juice, Worcester sauce, etc.
- crab tartlets or barquettes – made with short puff or filo pastry cooked blind and filled with a crab mixture like that in the recipe below, made by combining all the ingredients.

- Sprinkle with fresh white breadcrumbs and melted butter and lightly brown.
- Soup, au gratin, mornay, devilled, curried, soufflé, pancakes, crab cakes or rissoles etc., are obvious other ways of preparing and serving crab.
- However, crabs are at their best during the summer – simple crab salads will always be popular.

	4 portions	10 portions
shallot, finely chopped, cooked in oil or butter	100 g	250 g
raw mushroom, finely chopped	200 g	500 g
white wine	30 ml	125 ml
crab meat	200 g	500 g
salt and cayenne pepper		

218 Dressed crab

Serves 2

crab, cooked and cooled	1 kg
lemon, grated rind and juice	1
fresh parsley, chopped	2 tbsp
mayonnaise	4 tbsp
soft brown breadcrumbs	4 tsp
Dijon mustard	2 tsp
hard-boiled egg, finely chopped	1

nutritional info

1 large portion provides:
2044 kJ/492 kcal
35 g fat (of which 5.2 g saturated)
8.1 g carbohydrate (of which 1.9 g sugars)
36.2 g protein
0.9 g fibre

Includes mayonnaise and egg.

1 Crack open the crab claws and remove the white meat, keeping it as intact as possible, and place into a bowl.

2 Put rest of white meat from claw arms, legs and body into bowl.

3 Add grated lemon rind, half juice, 1 tablespoon of chopped parsley and 3 tablespoons of mayonnaise to the white meat and mix lightly.

4 In a separate bowl, place the breadcrumbs, remaining mayonnaise and lemon juice and the mustard.

5 Scoop out brown meat from shell (discarding the gills and the sac behind the eyes), put into bowl and mix lightly.

6 Wash shell and dry.

7 Use brown meat mixture to fill the two sides of shell and pack the white meat into centre.

8 Sprinkle finely chopped hard-boiled egg and rest of parsley over top for decoration.

9 Serve with lots of brown bread and butter, and a green salad to follow.

Note: To ensure freshness, purchase the crab live. When cleaning the cooked crab, ensure that the dead mens' fingers (feathery gills) are removed.

219 Crab salad with pink grapefruit

	4 portions	10 portions
Crab		
cooked and picked white crab meat	500 g	1¼ kg
coriander, chopped	1 tsp	3 tsp
mayonnaise	50 ml	125 ml
plum tomato concassée	100 g	250 g
grated fresh root ginger	½ tsp	1 tsp
seasoning		
chervil		
Salad		
pink grapefruit in segments	1	3
cooked green beans	100 g	250 g
organic salad leaves	200 g	500 g
honey-lime dressing (see receipe 238)		
cooked baby artichokes cut into 4	4	10

nutritional info

1 large portion provides:
1316 kJ/315 kcal
16.9 g fat (of which 2.4 g saturated)
14.3 g carbohydrate (of which 12.8 g sugars)
27.7 g protein
2.7 g fibre

Includes a little mayonnaise in the quenelles.

For the crab

1 Combine all the ingredients, check and adjust the seasoning.

2 Place in a clean bowl and retain in the refrigerator.

For the salad

1 Combine all the ingredients and mix with the dressing.

2 Place in the centre of the serving plate.

3 Top this with 3 quenelles of the crab mix.

4 Finish with the chervil and serve with brown bread and butter, or traditional sour dough bread.

Note: Crab and citrus are always a great contrast for each other; with this recipe pink grapefruit cuts through the richness of the crab well, without being too acidic.

220 Crab cakes with rocket salad and lemon dressing

	4 portions	10 portions
Crab cakes		
shallots, finely chopped	25 g	60 g
spring onions, finely chopped	4	10
fish/shellfish glaze	75 ml	185 ml
crab meat	400 g	1 kg
mayonnaise	75 g	185 g
lemons, juice of	1	3
plum tomatoes skinned, cut into concassée	2	5
wholegrain mustard	1 tsp	3 tsp
seasoning		
fresh white breadcrumbs	200 g	500 g
eggs, beaten with 100 ml of milk	2	5
flour for rolling		
Salad and dressing		
vegetable oil	170 ml	425 ml
white wine vinegar	25 ml	60 ml
lemons, juice of	1	3
seasoning		
washed and picked rocket	250 g	625 g
shaved Reggiano Parmesan	100 g	250 g

nutritional info

1 large portion provides:
3928 kJ/946 kcal
74.4 g fat (of which 13.9 g saturated)
32.4 g carbohydrate (of which 5.0 g sugars)
38.4 g protein
2.1 g fibre

Includes mayonnaise in the crab cakes and parmesan in the salad; egg and milk are used.

kcal
1000
900
800
700
600
500
400
300
200
100
0

calorie counter

To make the crab cakes

1 Mix the shallots, spring onion and the fish glaze with the hand-picked crab meat.

2 Add the mayonnaise, lemon juice, tomato concassée and mustard, check and adjust the seasoning.

3 Allow to rest for 30 minutes in the refrigerator.

4 Scale into 80–90 g balls and shape into discs 1½ cm high, place in the freezer for 30 minutes to harden.

5 When firm to the touch, coat in breadcrumbs using the flour, egg and breadcrumbs.

6 Allow to rest for a further 30 minutes.

7 Heat a little oil in a non-stick pan, carefully place the cakes in and cook on each side until golden brown.

For the salad and dressing

1 Combine the oil, vinegar and lemon juice together, check the seasoning.

2 Place the rocket and Parmesan in a large bowl and add a little dressing, just to coat.

3 Place this in the centre of each plate, top with the crab cakes and serve.

Note: Any excess crab meat can be used up in this recipe – a quick, classic dish. The crab can be exchanged for salmon or most fresh fish trimmings.

221   Potted shrimps

	4 portions	10 portions
butter	100 g	250 g
chives, chopped	2 tbsp	5 tbsp
cayenne pepper to taste		
peeled brown shrimps	600 g	1½ kg
clarified butter	6 tbsp	15 tbsp

nutritional info   ♥

1 large portion provides:
2194 kJ/529 kcal
42.7 g fat (of which 25.3 g saturated)
0.3 g carbohydrate (of which 0.3 g sugars)
36.0 g protein
0.0 g fibre

Butter is used.

kcal
1000
900
800
700
600
500
400
300
200
100
0

calorie counter

1 Put the butter, chives and cayenne pepper in a medium-sized pan and leave to melt over a gentle heat.

2 Add the peeled shrimps and stir over the heat for a couple of minutes until they have heated through, but don't let the mixture boil.

3 Divide the shrimps and butter between 4 small ramekins. Level the tops and then leave them to set in the refrigerator.

4 Spoon over a thin layer of clarified butter and leave to set once more. Serve with plenty of brown toast or crusty brown bread.

Note: A real seaside dish, full of flavour and eaten with plenty of brown bread and butter. Lobster or langoustine can be used – although timings will need to be adapted accordingly. The traditional seasoning for potted shrimps is ground mace.

222   Langoustine and mussel soup

	4 portions	10 portions
raw langoustine tails (large), bodies and claws retained for the stock	20	50
mussels, cleaned	400 g	1 kg
fish stock	300 ml	750 ml
butter	80 g	200 g
fresh bay leaves	2	5
dry white wine	50 ml	125 ml
shallots, chopped	1	3
celery sticks, cut into small dice	1	3
rindless dry-cured unsmoked bacon, cut across into short, fat strips	50 g	125 g
potatoes, peeled and cut into small dice	225 g	560 g
plain flour	20 g	50 g
full-cream milk	300 ml	750 ml
whipping cream	120 ml	300 ml
salt		
freshly ground black pepper		

nutritional info   ♥

1 large portion provides:
2355 kJ/566 kcal
36.3 g fat (of which 20.8 g saturated)
21.6 g carbohydrate (of which 5.7 g sugars)
39.3 g protein
1.2 g fibre

There is butter, cream and bacon in the recipe.

kcal
1000
900
800
700
600
500
400
300
200
100
0

calorie counter

1 If using raw langoustines, put them into the freezer for 30 minutes to kill them painlessly. Then put the langoustines and mussels into a pan and add the stock.

2 Cover, bring to the boil and steam for 2 minutes.

3 Remove from the heat and tip the contents into a colander set over a clean bowl to retain the cooking liquid.

4 Check that all the mussels have opened and discard any that remain closed.

5 Melt about one-third of the butter in a large pan, add the langoustine shells and the bay leaves, cook hard for 1 minute.

6 Add the wine and the reserved cooking liquor and while it is bubbling away, crush the shells to release all their flavour into the cooking liquid.

7 Cook for 10–12 minutes.

8 Meanwhile heat the rest of the butter in a pan, add the shallots, celery and bacon, cook gently until the shallots are soft but not coloured.

9 Add the diced potatoes and cook for 1–2 minutes, stir in the flour, then add the milk and cream.

10 Pass the cooking liquor into a clean pan and add to the roux base, stirring continuously to prevent lumps.

11 When all the stock has been added, cook out until the potatoes are soft.

12 Stir in the langoustines and mussels, and adjust the seasoning if necessary.

13 Ladle into warmed soup plates and serve with traditional sour bread.

Note: Proceed with caution when using both mussels and langoustines as they overcook quickly and this will spoil the eating quality.

223 Poached langoustines with aioli dip

	4 portions	10 portions
raw langoustine tails, large	36	90
Court bouillon		
Carrots	2	5
fennel bulbs	1	3
garlic cloves	2	5
water	1400 ml	3½ litres
white wine	290 ml	725 ml
a few fresh parsley and chervil stalks		
white peppercorns, crushed	3	7
Aioli		
sweet potato (about 250 g each), orange flesh	1	2½
mayonnaise	3 tbsp	7½ tbsp
pinches saffron strands, soaked in a little water	2	5
eggs, boiled and yolks removed and reserved	3	7
crushed garlic	½ tsp	1½ tsp
a little olive oil		
salt and pepper		
lemon, juice of	½	1

nutritional info

1 large portion provides:
1663 kJ/399 kcal
19.3 g fat (of which 3.4 g saturated)
15.5 g carbohydrate (of which 7.2 g sugars)
41.6 g protein
2.9 g fibre

No fat was used to cook the langoustines; there is mayonnaise and egg in the aioli.

kcal
1000
900
800
700
600
500
400
300
200
100
0

calorie counter

For the bouillon

1 Place vegetables in pan and cover with water.

2 Gently bring to the boil and simmer for 5–10 minutes.

3 Add the white wine, parsley, chervil stalks and crushed peppercorns.

4 Cook for a further 10 minutes then leave to stand until cool.

5 Strain out the vegetables and chill the liquid.

For the aioli

1 Pre-heat the oven to 200°C. Bake the sweet potato for about 35–45 minutes or until tender. Peel off the skin and gently crush the flesh.

2 Place sweet potato flesh in a liquidiser, add the mayonnaise, saffron, egg yolks and garlic and blend.

3 Add olive oil to moisten, season and finish with a squeeze of lemon juice.

224 Dublin Bay prawns

Langoustines, also known as scampi, freshwater crayfish, ecrevises and prawns, are used in a wide variety of dishes, hot and cold, and also as garnishes for many other dishes. Where possible they are best bought live and cooked in a court bouillon for 5–10 minutes.

If they have to be kept then this should be in a cool, moist place covered with damp sacking or seaweed.

Cleaning

The intestines can be removed either before or after cooking by grasping the middle tail fin, twisting once each way right and left, then giving a sharp pull away from the tail.

4 Remove entrails from langoustines by taking the middle segment or tail shell between thumb and forefinger, then twist it and pull.

5 Plunge the langoustines into the simmering court bouillon for 30–40 seconds. Remove and leave to cool naturally. Serve with the aioli.

Note: King or tiger prawns may be used as an alternative.

Salads

After removing the fish from the shells they can be mixed with one or two of a variety of ingredients – for example:

1 sliced cooked artichoke hearts

2 finely sliced raw button mushrooms

3 sliced roast or smoked duck or chicken, salmon (fresh or smoked)

4 chopped parsley, chive, chervil, tarragon, basil, lamb's lettuce, spinach or any other salad leaves with a suitable gentle salad dressing.

Dublin Bay prawns, crayfish and prawns can also be prepared as for any lobster recipe hot or cold.

225 Lobster tail gratin

	4 portions	10 portions
Lobster		
lobster tails (each from a 500–600 g live lobster)	4	10
butter	80 g	200 g
dry sherry	20 ml	50 ml
flour	20 g	50 g
paprika	½ tsp	1 tsp
cream	120 ml	300 ml
seasoning		
Crumb topping		
slices white bread	3	7
cup butter	40 g	100 g
chives, chopped	1 tbsp	2 tbsp
seasoning		

nutritional info

1 large portion provides:
1751 kJ/421 kcal
31.9 g fat (of which 19.5 g saturated)
18.1 g carbohydrate (of which 1.6 g sugars)
16.6 g protein
0.6 g fibre

Contains butter and cream in the sauce, and butter in the crumb topping.

kcal
1000
900
800
700
600
500
400
300
200
100
0

calorie counter

For the crumb topping

1 Remove crust from bread and place in food processor or grate fine.

2 Melt butter in a pan, add the breadcrumbs and cook until brown.

3 Add the chives and salt and pepper. When the lobster meat is returned to the shell sprinkle over.

For the lobster

1 Pre-heat the oven to 190°C.

2 Gently blanch the lobster tails until they are half done, then drain and cool.

3 Remove meat from shells and cut into small pieces, clean and save the shells.

4 Melt butter in a thick-bottomed pan. Stir in sherry and lobster, simmer for 2 minutes.

5 Stir in flour, paprika and cream until thickened, adjust the seasoning then return mixture to shells.

6 Place the filled and topped shells on a baking tray and bake in the oven for 10 minutes.

7 Serve immediately with a green salad or wilted greens.

Note: Cornish or Scottish (native) lobsters are best for this recipe; their Canadian counterparts may be used but the native varieties will yield a better result.

226 Lobster beignets with tomato chutney

	4 portions	10 portions
onion, peeled and chopped	1	2
tomatoes, peeled, seeded and diced as for concassée	1 kg	2½ kg
red wine vinegar	70 g	175 g
caster sugar	50 g	125 g
coriander powder	1 tbsp	2 tbsp
paprika	1 tbsp	2 tbsp
cooked lobster tails	4	10
plain flour	145 g	360 g
fecule (potato starch)	120 g	300 g
active dry yeast	1 tbsp	2½ tbsp
real ale or beer	300 ml	750 ml

For the chutney

1 In a large pot over medium-low heat, warm 1 tablespoon oil.

2 Add onion and cook, stirring occasionally, until tender, 5–10 minutes.

3 Add tomatoes, vinegar, sugar, coriander and paprika; bring to a simmer, stirring occasionally, until thickened, 45–55 minutes.

4 Remove from heat and let cool.

5 Slice lobster meat crosswise into 0.5 cm-thick medallions; keep chilled.

6 In a deep-fry pan, heat oil to 180°C.

For the batter

1 In a bowl, combine the flour, starch, yeast and ½ teaspoon salt; stir to mix. Add beer and stir.

2 Drop a lobster medallion into the batter, coat well and deep-fry until crispy and golden, 2–3 minutes.

3 Fry 3–4 at a time (do not crowd the fryer). Sprinkle beignets lightly with salt and serve hot with chutney.

Note: A quick, hot and spicy bar or terrace dish.

nutritional info

1 large portion provides:
2137 kJ/506 kcal
12.6 g fat (of which 1.5 g saturated)
81.0 g carbohydrate (of which 29.9 g sugars)
22.7 g protein
3.4 g fibre

No fat or oil was used to cook the lobster.

kcal
1000
900
800
700
600
500
400
300
200
100
0

calorie counter

227 Lobster mornay

	4 portions	10 portions
cooked lobsters (approx. 400 g each)	2	5
butter	25 g	60 g
salt, cayenne		
mornay sauce	250 ml	625 ml
grated cheese (Parmesan)		
parsley (to garnish)		

nutritional info

1 large portion provides:
1170 kJ/280.6 kcal
18.0 g fat (of which 10.7 g saturated)
7.8 g carbohydrate (of which 3.0 g sugars)
22.3 g protein
0.2 g fibre

There is butter and cheese in the sauce.

kcal
1000
900
800
700
600
500
400
300
200
100
0

calorie counter

1 Remove the lobsters' claws and legs.
2 Cut lobsters carefully in half lengthwise.
3 Remove all meat. Discard the sac and remove the trail from the tail.
4 Wash shell and drain on a baking sheet upside down.
5 Cut the lobster meat into escalopes.
6 Heat the butter in a thick-bottomed pan, add the lobster and season.
7 Turn two or three times; overcooking will toughen the meat.
8 Meanwhile, finish the mornay sauce.
9 Place a little sauce in the bottom of each shell.
10 Add the lobster, press down to make a flat surface.
11 Mask completely with sauce, sprinkle with grated cheese, and brown under the salamander. Serve garnished with picked parsley.

228 Lobster thermidor

	4 portions	10 portions
cooked lobsters	2	5
butter	25 g	60 g
shallot, finely chopped	12 g	30 g
dry white wine	60 ml	150 ml
English mustard, diluted	½ tsp	1 tsp
parsley, chopped		
mornay sauce	¼ litre	⅝ litre
grated Parmesan cheese	25 g	60 g

nutritional info

1 large portion provides:
1199 kJ/287.5 kcal
18.5 g fat (of which 11.0 g saturated)
8.1 g carbohydrate (of which 3.3 g sugars)
22.9 g protein
0.2 g fibre

There is butter and cheese in the sauce.

kcal
1000
900
800
700
600
500
400
300
200
100
0

calorie counter

1 Remove the lobsters' claws and legs.
2 Cut lobsters carefully in halves lengthwise. Remove the meat.
3 Discard the sac and remove the trail from the tail.
4 Wash the halves of shell and drain on a baking sheet.
5 Cut the lobster meat into thick escalopes.
6 Melt the butter in a sauteuse, add the chopped shallot and cook until tender without colour.
7 Add the white wine to the shallot and allow to reduce to a quarter of its original volume.
8 Mix in the mustard and chopped parsley.
9 Add the lobster slices, season lightly with salt, mix carefully and allow to heat slowly for 2–3 minutes. If this part of the process is overdone the lobster will become tough and chewy.
10 Meanwhile spoon a little of the warm mornay sauce into the bottom of each lobster half shell.
11 Neatly add the warmed lobster pieces and the juice in which they were reheated. If there is an excess of liquid it should be reduced and incorporated into the mornay sauce.
12 Coat the half lobsters with the remaining mornay sauce, sprinkle with Parmesan cheese and place under a salamander until a golden brown. Serve garnished with picked parsley.

229 Lobster Newburg

cooked lobster meat cut into thickish pieces		4 portions	10 portions
cooked lobster meat cut into thickish pieces		400 g	1¼ kg
butter		50 g	125 g
Madeira		60 ml	150 ml
cream	liaison	120 ml	150 ml
egg yolks		2	5

1 Gently reheat the lobster pieces in the butter.

2 Add Madeira and allow to gently almost completely reduce.

3 With the pan over gentle heat, pour in the liaison and allow to thicken by gentle continuous shaking; do not allow to boil. Correct seasoning, using a touch of cayenne if required.

4 Serve with pilaff rice separately.

Note: A lobster butter made from the crushed soft lobster shells will improve the colour of the sauce.

1 Sweat the crushed lobster shells in 25–50 g butter over a fierce heat, stirring well.

2 Moisten with stock or water, boil for 10 minutes, strain.

3 Clarify the butter by simmering to evaporate the liquid.

nutritional info

1 large portion provides:

1556 kJ/375.3 kcal

30.7 g fat (of which 17.5 g saturated)

0.6 g carbohydrate (of which 0.6 g sugars)

24.1 g protein

0.0 g fibre

Liaison of egg yolk and cream.

kcal
1000
900
800
700
600
500
400
300
200
100
0

calorie counter

230 Crawfish, also known as rock lobster

Both the body and the flesh of the crawfish are similar to the lobster, the main difference being that the crawfish does not have main claws. All the flesh is contained in the tail.

Crawfish are boiled in the same way as lobsters and the meat can be used for any of the lobster recipes. Because of its spectacular image the crawfish cooked, dressed and presented whole is a popular addition to cold buffets.

231 Mussels

When mussels are fresh the shells should be tightly closed. If the shells are open there is the possibility of danger from food poisoning therefore the mussels should be discarded.

Preparation for cooking

1 Scrape the shells to remove any barnacles, etc.

2 Wash well and drain in a colander.

To cook

1 Take a thick-bottomed pan with a tight-fitting lid.

2 For 1 litre mussels, place in the pan 25 g chopped shallot or onion.

3 Add the mussels, cover with a lid and cook on a fierce heat for 4–5 minutes until the shells open completely.

Preparation for use

1 Remove mussels from shells, checking carefully for sand, weed and beard.

2 Retain the liquid.

232 Mussels in white wine sauce

	4 portions	10 portions
shallots, chopped	50 g	125 g
parsley, chopped	1 tbsp	2 tbsp
white wine	60 ml	150 ml
strong fish stock	200 ml	500 ml
mussels	2 kg	5 kg
butter	25 g	60 ml
flour	25 g	60 ml
seasoning		

nutritional info

1 large portion provides:
750 kJ/178 kcal
7.9 g fat (of which 3.6 g saturated)
9.4 g carbohydrate (of which 0.9 g sugars)
17.7 g protein
0.4 g fibre

A little butter was used for the roux.

calorie counter

kcal
1000
900
800
700
600
500
400
300
200
100
0

1 Take a thick-bottomed pan and add the shallots, parsley, wine, fish stock and the cleaned mussels.

2 Cover with a tight-fitting lid and cook over a high heat until the shells open.

3 Drain off all the cooking liquor in a colander set over a clean bowl to retain the cooking juices.

4 Carefully check the mussels and discard any that have not opened.

5 Place in a dish and cover to keep warm.

6 Make a roux from the flour and butter; pour over the cooking liquor, ensuring it is free from sand and stirring continuously to avoid lumps.

7 Correct the seasoning and garnish with more chopped parsley.

8 Pour over the mussels and serve.

233 Mussels gratin with white wine

Using the recipe above, mix equal quantities of grated Gruyère and fresh breadcrumbs, sprinkle over the dish and gratinate until golden brown under the salamander; alternatively, bake in a moderate to high oven until golden brown on the top.

234 Cockles

Cockles live in sand, therefore it is essential to wash them well under running cold water and then leave them in cold salted water, changed frequently until no traces of sand remain.

Cockles are cooked:
■ In unsalted water until the shells open
■ On a preheated griddle
■ As for any of the mussel recipes.

They can be used for soup, sauces, salads and as garnishes for fish dishes.

235 Cockle chowder

	4 portions	10 portions
Cockles		
medium shallots, finely diced	2	5
butter	50 g	125 g
cockles, shells tightly closed	2 kg	5 kg
white wine or vermouth	200 ml	500 ml
Chowder		
vegetable oil	50 ml	125 ml
smoked bacon, cut into 1 cm dice	50 g	125 g
medium onion, cut into 1 cm dice	1	3
medium carrot, cut into 1 cm dice	1	3
garlic cloves, finely chopped	2	5
celery sticks, cut into 1 cm dice	1	3
medium potato, peeled and cut into 1 cm dice	1	3
medium yellow pepper, cut into 1 cm dice	1	3
chicken stock	1 litre	2½ litres
whipping cream	100 ml	500 ml
butter	50 g	125 g
salt and pepper		

nutritional info

1 large portion provides:

2223 kJ/536 kcal
45.0 g fat (of which 21.4 g saturated)
13.9 g carbohydrate (of which 7.3 g sugars)
19.9 g protein
2.4 g fibre

Butter was used to cook the shallots; there are butter, cream and bacon in the chowder.

For the cockles

1 Take a large saucepan with a tight-fitting lid and place over a medium heat, add the shallots and butter and cook for 1 minute without letting the shallots colour.

2 Add the washed cockles, shake the pan, then add the wine and place the lid on the pan immediately. Leave the cockles to steam for 1–2 minutes so that they open and exude an intense liquor.

3 Remove the lid and make sure all the cockles are open. Remove the pan from the heat and discard any with closed shells.

4 Place a colander over a large bowl, and pour the contents of the pan into the colander, reserving the liquor for the chowder.

5 Allow the cockles to cool. Pick out the meat, check carefully for sand and discard the shells. Store the cockle meat in an airtight container in the fridge until you are ready to serve the chowder.

For the chowder

1 In a large saucepan, heat the oil. When hot, add the bacon and cook for about 5 minutes until crisp and brown.

2 Using a perforated spoon, transfer the bacon onto kitchen paper to drain. Add the onion, carrot, garlic, celery and potato to the saucepan, reduce the heat to medium-low and cook the vegetables for 3–4 minutes without colouring.

3 Add the peppers and cook for 5 minutes. Pour in the reserved liquor from the cockles and the chicken stock.

4 Bring to the boil and simmer for 10 minutes or until the volume of liquid has reduced by about half.

5 Add the cooked bacon and cream, then bring to the boil and reduce for a further 2 minutes until the soup thickens slightly.

6 Just before serving, whisk in the butter.

To finish

1 While the chowder is cooking, carefully remove the meat from the shell, checking for sand, and place in a clean pan.

2 Combine the chowder base and the cockle meat together, reheat carefully and serve.

236 Clams

To ensure freshness, the shells of clams should be tightly shut. They can be steamed or poached like mussels and certain types are eaten raw.

Clams should be soaked in salt water for a few hours so that the sand in which they exist can be ejected.

Clams can be prepared and served raw (certain types only) or cooked with lemon juice, au gratin (fresh breadcrumbs, chopped garlic, parsley, melted butter), in pasta, stir-fry and fish dishes as garnishes or/and a component of a sea food mixture, and as a soup (clam chowder).

The history behind scallops

The word scallop comes from the old French *escalope* meaning 'shell', referring to the shell that houses the scallop. Scallops are mentioned in print as far back as 1280, when Marco Polo referred to them as one of the seafoods sold in the marketplace in Hangchow, China. Paris restaurateur Gustave Chatagnier featured a special scallops dish on his menu in 1936.

With the advent of new equipment in 1965, able to process deepwater molluscs, calico scallops became a major harvest off the shores of North Carolina and Florida, with catches averaging 12 million kilos a year between 1984 and 1994.

Probably the most famous scallop dish is Coquille St-Jacques. The word *coquille* means shell in French. This dish has some religious history, but only related to the shell itself. The scallop shell was used as a badge of reverence and identification by pilgrims visiting the Spanish shrine of St James (St Jacques in French). The famous basic dish is made of a blend of scallops in a cream and butter sauce, and is traditionally served in the beautiful shell of the scallop.

Note: When selecting scallops, always make hand-dived scallops your first choice as dredged ones are sometimes unethical. You pay a bit more for the hand-dived but the difference in quality is certainly worth it. For opening and cleaning scallops, see page 183.

237 Scallops with caramelised cauliflower

	4 portions	10 portions
raisins	100 g	250 g
capers	100 g	250 g
water	180 ml	450 ml
sherry vinegar	1 tbsp	2 tbsp
grated nutmeg		
salt and cayenne pepper		
butter	30 g	75 g
head of cauliflower, sliced into ½ cm-thick pieces	½	1
large hand-dived scallops (roe removed)	12	30

nutritional info

1 large portion provides:
923 kJ/220 kcal
7.8 g fat (of which 4.3 g saturated)
22.0 g carbohydrate (of which 19.7 g sugars)
16.6 g protein
2.1 g fibre

Butter was used to cook the cauliflower.

kcal
1000
900
800
700
600
500
400
300
200
100
0

calorie counter

1 In a small saucepan, cook the raisins and capers in the water until the raisins are plump, about 5 minutes.

2 Pour mixture into blender and add the vinegar, nutmeg, salt and pepper, blend just until smooth.

3 Set sauce aside.

4 In a sauté pan, heat butter and cook the cauliflower until golden on both sides. To prevent cauliflower from burning, if necessary, add about 1 tablespoon of water to pan during cooking. Set cauliflower aside.

5 In a separate pan, sauté the scallops in a little butter, about 1½ minutes on each side. To serve, place 3 scallops on each plate, top with cauliflower and finish with the caper-raisin emulsion.

238 Seared scallop salad with honey-lime dressing

	4 portions	10 portions
Honey-lime dressing		
limes, juice of	⅔	⅚
honey, or to taste	25 g	60 g
white wine or rice vinegar	1 tbsp	2 tbsp
seasoning		
Seared scallops		
grapeseed or peanut oil	50 ml	125 ml
chopped mangetout, red pepper and courgette cut into thin strips	500 g	1250 g
mixed greens (such as pea shoots, watercress, baby spinach or escarole)	400 g	1 kg
large scallops (roe removed)	12	30

For the dressing

1 In a non-reactive bowl whisk together the lime juice, honey, vinegar and salt until the honey is completely incorporated. Taste and adjust accordingly. Set aside.

For the seared scallops

1 Heat oil in a large cast-iron or non-stick pan over medium-high heat.

2 Place the vegetable strips into pan and quickly sauté

3 Arrange on the plate and top with the salad leaves.

4 Clean the pan and add a little more butter, sear the scallops very quickly until golden.

Note: The lime is a great foil here, with the acidity cutting effectively through the sweetness of the scallops.

nutritional info

1 large portion provides:
829 kJ/198 kcal
13.3 g fat (of which 2.7 g saturated)
7.0 g carbohydrate (of which 5.0 g sugars)
13.2 g protein
0.0 g fibre

A small amount of oil was used for cooking.

calorie counter

kcal
♥ 1000
900
800
700
600
500
400
300
200
100
0

239 Scallop ceviche with organic leaves

Note: This recipe should be made one day prior to serving.

	4 portions	10 portions
large scallops (roe removed)	12	30
limes, juice of	2	5
oranges, juice of	1	3
lemons, grated rind	1	3
limes, grated rind	1	3
orange	1	1
salt and freshly cracked pepper to taste		
orange liqueur	2 tbsp	5 tbsp
vinaigrette	50 ml	125 ml
organic leaves (5 varieties)	500 g	1¼ kg

1 Slice the raw scallops thinly (laterally into 3) and lay on a clean non-reactive tray.

2 Mix all the other ingredients (except the organic leaves) and pour evenly over the scallops.

3 Leave covered in the refrigerator overnight. (The acid in the citrus juice will cook/cure the scallops.)

4 To serve, arrange the scallops in a circle form (9 slices), dress the leaves and arrange in the centre of the scallops.

5 Drizzle any excess cure/dressing around the scallops and serve.

Note: Only the freshest scallops can be used for this recipe as the slightest taint of age will dominate and spoil the dish.

nutritional info

1 large portion provides:
616 kJ/147 kcal
7.6 g fat (of which 1.4 g saturated)
5.9 g carbohydrate (of which 4.0 g sugars)
14.2 g protein
1.2 g fibre

Contains oil in the vinaigrette only.

♥ kcal
1000
900
800
700
600
500
400
300
200
100
0

calorie counter

MEAT DISHES

MEAT

Origins

From the earliest times, man has been a carnivorous animal. Because meat provides so much protein and essential vitamins, early people could spend less of their time eating and could successfully turn their energies to activities that, in time, placed them above their peers. Meat was from the first equated with life and early hunting was designed to supply a plentiful amount of animals. Although today there has been a reappraisal of the importance of meat in the diet – whether its drawbacks, like cholesterol and high price, outweigh its value as a protein provider or, in the case of vegetarians, ethical considerations – meat is still the most expensive item on the budget and a great deal of thought should be put into choosing and using it wisely.

Butcher's meat today is largely a product of selective breeding and feeding techniques, whereby animals are reared carefully to reach high standards and meet specific needs: the present-day demand is for lean and tender meat – modern cattle, sheep and pigs are well fleshed yet compact creatures compared to their forebears of a century ago.

Choosing and buying

Meat from specific parts of an animal may be cut and cooked according to local custom and, more strictly, by religious observance – especially in Jewish kosher and Mohammedan halal butchery, which stipulates the killing of the animal by an authorised person of the religion, total voiding of the blood by draining, soaking and salting, and the consumption of the meat within 72 hours. Kosher dietary laws further demand that only the forequarters of permitted animals – goats, sheep, deer and cattle – may be used.

Meat is a natural and therefore not a uniform product, varying in quality from carcass to carcass, while flavour, texture and appearance are determined by the type of animal and the way it has been fed. There is no reason to think that flavour is obtained only in meat that possesses a proportion of fat, although fat does give a characteristic

Units covered
3FP3, 3FC3

LIST OF RECIPES

Recipe no	page no	Recipe no	page no
Lamb		250 Slow-cooked beef fillet with onion ravioli	220
247 Braised-roast belly of lamb with cauliflower risotto and balsamic jelly	217	253 Slow-cooked sirloin with lyonnaise onions and carrot purée	223
248 Lambs' kidneys with juniper and wild mushrooms	218	251 Tournedos Rossini (classical)	221
249 Lambs' liver flavoured with lavender and sage, served with avocado and sherry sauce	219	252 Tournedos Rossini (modern)	222
243 Pot roast chump of lamb with root vegetables	213	257 Traditional braised oxtail with garlic mash	227
244 Roast leg of lamb with minted couscous and buttered peas	214	**Veal**	
242 Roast rump of lamb, flageolets purée and balsamic dressing	212	265 Calves' liver with raspberry vinegar	234
245 Roast shoulder of lamb with potatoes boulangère	215	262 Hay-baked sweetbreads with braised cabbage	232
246 Slow-cooked best end of lamb with lentils	216	261 Osso bucco	231
240 Slow-cooked saddle of lamb, braised cabbage and chocolate	210	260 Sautéed veal kidneys with shallot sauce	230
241 Stuffed saddle of lamb with apricot farce	211	263 Veal chops with cream and mustard sauce	233
Beef		264 Veal kidneys with mustard and cream sauce	233
254 Boeuf bourguignonne	224	**Pork**	
255 Braised short rib with horseradish couscous	225	268 Cured-confited belly with sauerkraut and sherry jus	237
256 Bresaola (cured silverside)	226	269 Homemade black pudding with apple and onion salad	238
259 Pickled ox tongue	229	267 Roast shoulder of pork with crackling and apple	236
258 Roast wing rib with Yorkshire pudding	228	270 Roast stuffed suckling pig	239
		266 Slow-cooked pork loin with white beans and grain mustard	234

flavour to meat and helps to keep it moist during roasting. Neither is the colour of meat any guide to quality. Consumers are inclined to choose light-coloured meat – bright red beef, for example – because they think that it will be fresher than an alternative dark-red piece. Freshly butchered beef is bright red because the pigment in the tissues, myoglobin, has been chemically affected by the oxygen in the air. After several hours, the colour changes to dark red or brown as the pigment is further oxidised to become metamyoglobin. The colour of fat can vary from almost pure white in lamb, to bright yellow in beef. Colour depends on the feed,

on the breed and, to a certain extent, on the time of year.

The most useful guide to tenderness and quality is a knowledge of the cuts of meat and their location on the carcass. The various cuts are described under their respective headings, but in principle the leanest and tenderest cuts – the 'prime' cuts – come from the hindquarters. The 'coarse' cuts, or meat from the neck, legs and forequarters, those parts of the animal that have had plenty of muscular exercise and where fibres have become hardened, provide meat for braising and stewing. Many consider these cuts to have more flavour, although they require slow cooking to make them tender. The meat from young animals is generally more tender and since tenderness is a prime factor, animals may be injected before slaughter with an enzyme, such as papin, which softens the fibres and muscles. This merely speeds up a natural and more satisfactory process: meat contains its own proteolytic enzymes, which gradually break down the protein cell walls as the carcass ages; that is why meat is hung for from 10 to 20 days in controlled conditions of temperature and humidity before being offered for sale. Meat that is aged longer becomes more expensive as the cost of refrigeration is high and the meat itself shrinks because of evaporation and the trimming of the outside hardened edges.

Cooking

Meat is an extremely versatile product that can be cooked in a multitude of ways, and matched with practically any vegetable, fruit and herb. The cut (shin, steak, brisket), the method of heating (roasting, braising, grilling), and the time and temperature all affect the way the meat will taste. Raw meat is difficult to chew because the muscle fibre contains an elastic protein (collagen), which is softened only by mincing – as in steak tartare – or by cooking. When you cook meat, the protein gradually coagulates as the internal temperature increases. At 69°C coagulation is complete, the protein begins to harden and further cooking makes the meat tougher.

Since tenderness combined with flavour is the aim in meat cookery, much depends on the ratio of time and temperature. In principle, slow cooking retains the juices and produces a more tender result than does fast cooking at high temperatures. There are, of course, occasions when high temperatures are essential: for instance, you need to grill a steak under a hot flame for a very limited time in order to obtain a crisp, brown surface and a pink, juicy interior – using a low temperature would not give you the desired result. But in potentially tough cuts such as breast or where there is a quantity of connective tissue (neck of lamb), a slow rate of cooking converts the tissues to gelatine and helps to make the meat more tender. Meat containing bone will take longer to cook because bone is a poor conductor of heat. Tough or coarse cuts of meat should be cooked by braising, pot roasting or stewing. Marinating in a suitable marinade, such as wine and wine vinegar, helps to tenderise the meat and imparts an additional flavour. Searing meat in hot fat or in a hot oven before roasting or stewing helps to produce a crisp exterior by coagulating the protein but does not, as is widely supposed, seal in the juices. However, if the external temperature is too high and cooking prolonged, rapid evaporation and contraction of the meat will cause considerable loss of juices and fat. Salt sprinkled on meat before cooking will also hasten loss of moisture since salt is hygroscopic and absorbs water.

Meat bones are useful for giving flavour to soups and stocks, especially beef ones with plenty of marrow. Veal bones are gelatinous and help to enrich and thicken soups and sauces. Fat can be rendered down for frying, or used as an ingredient when suet or lard is called for.

The cooking of meat

To take this one step further, when fibrous proteins are heated they contract and squeeze out the associated water. For example, when a steak is cooked the proteins contract, therefore squeezing out all the water/juices. If the heat is increased or continues, the steak will then become dry and, consequently, the eating quality will be impaired. Cuts of meat also contain elastin and collagen: elastin (the muscle group associated with tendons and arteries) is extremely stretchy and further cooking adds to its strength; collagen (the main muscle proteins, which amount to the highest proportion of mass in the muscle) is rather tough and chewy. Meat that has a higher proportion of both, usually from the major and highly worked muscle groups, would not be suitable for prime cooking. However these cuts of meat may be cooked for longer at the correct temperature (braising), dissolving the collagen as it is water soluble, forming gelatine and offering a tasty joint of meat.

Prime cuts, such as beef fillets, have little collagen in their make-up (approximately 3 per cent) and do not require long cooking to tenderise the joint. Although most chefs would adopt a high temperature for a short period on the prime cuts, this does not always yield a perfect result. Due to the lack of fat and collagen in such cuts of meat, high heat will render the muscle fibres dry and, consequently, the eating quality is impaired. A lower temperature and longer in the oven will produce a gradual heat, therefore there is less extreme coagulation in the tissues and less fluid will have been squeezed out in the process.

To put this theory into simple terms – traditionally, when cooking meat, a fillet steak (for example) would be sealed in hot oil (180°C–200°C or even hotter) and then the heat would be reduced slightly to finish the cooking. The process that takes place is one of (to put it scientifically) 'thermal energy' or molecular conduction: the first layer of molecules heating the next, and so on, until the desired degree of cooking is achieved at the core (rare, medium, etc.). To achieve a core temperature of 55°C–60°C, 25 per cent

of the meat would be overcooked. Therefore if the temperature was to be reduced to a constant 59°C (just before the protein collapses) and the meat cooked for longer, adopting the molecular conduction theory, more than 95 per cent of the meat would be perfectly cooked.

When cooking meats at low temperatures there is one obvious flaw: the meat will not be exposed to the high cooking temperatures that develop that beautiful roasted flavour. This chemical reaction of browning is called the Maillard reaction and is an extremely complicated chain of reactions that involves carbons, proteins, sulphurs, etc. One thing we do know about this reaction is that at 140°C and above, you will start to release the wonderful roasted meat flavours. Therefore, when slow-cooking meats they will need to be started very quickly on a hot pan on the stove to initiate this Maillard reaction in the meat and give the meat a roasted flavour. In some cases you will need to quickly return the meat to the pan to re-caramelise the outside; alternatively, if the joint is dense and large, remove from the low oven and increase the temperature to 190–200°C. When the oven is up to temperature, return the joint to it for a short while to crisp up the outside. The density of the meat and size of the joint will ensure that there will be very little secondary cooking or residual heat left to cook through to the core.

The collagen that makes up connective tissue requires long cooking at moderate temperature to render it supple in the mouth and to be converted into gelatine (a form of secondary/internal basting). When basting, care should be taken not to destroy the secondary basting properties of the collagen as at temperatures above 88°C the collagen will dissolve rapidly into the braising medium, impairing the eating quality. As cooking methods and understanding of meats develop, we now know more about the effect that heat has on the make-up of meat. Therefore, the traditional braising method of bringing the casserole to a simmer and placing it in the oven at 140°C could, in theory, render the structure of the meat dry due to the fact that at 88°C collagen rapidly dissolves into the cooking medium, yielding a beautifully gelatinous and well-flavoured sauce, and making the eating quality of the meat dry and tough.

To modernise the braising approach the cooking medium would need to be at between 80°C and 85°C; this is best controlled on the top of the stove. Alternatively, set your oven at 90°C (approximately) checking the cooking medium once in a while.

All the techniques above, which are used to slow-cook prime, secondary and highly worked muscle groups, are very controlled and accurate, and rely on constant attention to ensure that they are not rapidly cooking, and that they are in fact actually cooking, if cooking at low temperatures. The general rule of thumb is: the more collagen, the higher the temperature needed to enable the collagen to dissolve, forming gelatine that will then in turn baste the meat and offer a perfectly braised and moist piece of meat.

When slow-cooking prime joints, the rule of thumb is to reduce the temperature of cooking as, in some cases, shrinkage can occur from 59°C ranging up to 65°C for sirloin of beef.

Sirloin of beef obviously has more collagen than fillet (it is essentially a worked muscle group) and is generally cooked on a high heat, either roasted or pan-fried. To adopt the above method, you can render the sirloin extremely tender, full of moisture, with a roasted outer and the flavoursome roasted meat taste that is craved. An average sirloin joint for roasting can weigh from 2–5 kg whole off the bone. The method is to seal the meat on the outside, as you would normally, place into a pre-heated oven at 180°C, cook at 180°C for 10 minutes, then reduce the temperature to 64°C (the oven door will need to be open at this stage). Once the oven has come down to 64°C, close the door and cook for a further 1 hour 50 minutes. This will give you an extremely tender piece of sirloin.

Degree of cooking

This is not a sure-fire rule but it can certainly help those who do not experience the cooking of meat on a regular basis. First, open the hand you do not write with palm facing towards you, then touch your thumb with your little finger with little pressure, then with the first finger of your strongest hand touch the muscle under the thumb – this is the feeling you should look for when you require well-done meat. Follow this technique through the fingers, as follows, according to the degree of cooking you require:

- little finger – well done – 72°C
- next finger – medium to well – 64°C
- middle finger – medium – 60°C
- forefinger – rare to medium – 58°C.

Use of a heat probe will ensure greater accuracy.

Seasonality

Beef, veal and pork are predominantly available all year round. Price may fluctuate on the global market due to countries or unions with internal difficulties – for example, BSE, holiday periods. In some cases, the weather may influence the price of meat and what joints are readily bought – for example, in the colder months, more robust dishes or

Pork

The first people to taste roast pork were probably the Chinese, and Neolithic sites excavated in China show that pigs, used as food, were the only domestic animals present.

In the eighteenth century an Asian variety, *Sus scrofa vittatus*, was introduced. It was found easier to handle and confine, and had potentially good prospects for cross-breeding. Many of our modern pig strains are descended from this Asian stock.

One of the most controversial aspects of pork is the fact that it is taboo in certain religions. It has been variously proposed that pork is basically unhygienic and in hot climates presents a health hazard, or that the pig was once a tribal emblem (a totem) and thus sacrosanct. One theory suggests that pork has similarities to human flesh; it is also thought to be the cause of some diseases. It is possible that religion grew from these theories and primeval rites. The pig then became associated with primitive, human sacrifice and was condemned as a food. In ancient Turkey pigs were associated with death. Be that as it may, pork is greatly esteemed by many nations as a prime and tender meat.

Pigs, as everyone knows, will eat almost anything – they are nature's vacuum cleaners, omnivorous and greedy, but pig farmers have to control their diet to produce the right combination of fatness, weight and carcass quality. Pigs cannot eat grass alone and are fed cereals, proteins, minerals and compound vitamins; diet influences the flavour of the meat, and it is likely that the free-ranging, ancestral pigs, though probably tougher and fattier than today's breeds, had a more natural flavour.

Fillet

A boneless cut of lean meat from the hindquarters. It is suitable for grilling or frying.

Loin

A lean joint that sometimes includes the kidney. It is suitable for roasting.

Loin chop

Taken from the hind loin, it is suitable for grilling or frying.

Chump

Available on or off the bone from the hind loin, it is suitable for roasting.

Leg

The hind leg, usually roasted.

Shoulder

A tender fore end cut that is available boned or on the bone. It is used for casseroles and kebabs.

Spare rib

Taken from the fore end of the animal, it is sold whole or as spare rib chops. It is suitable for roasting, grilling or frying.

Belly

This generally yields bacon, but is sometimes sold fresh and used in sausage-making; otherwise it is grilled or baked.

Hock

A small bony cut from the hindquarters. It is stewed or used for soups.

Ribs

Rib bones taken from the underside; they are used for barbecuing.

Veal

Veal is the meat from dairy calves, usually slaughtered at three months of age. Today this meat is in short supply – due to more efficient dairy production from fewer animals – and expensive, with ethical values now playing a part in the buying market.

In countries where livestock, and especially cattle, were considered a valuable commodity, veal was usually the outcome of calf mortality. Nevertheless, in France and Italy it was a highly prized meat; King François I was said to have demanded veal for the table daily. It is likely that the popularity of French veal was partly due to the influence of Italian cooking introduced to the court by Catherine de Medici, wife of Henri II.

One particular cut of veal, the scallop, has had a curious military history. It probably originated in Spain, and was introduced to the city of Milan when Milan was part of the Spanish empire in the sixteenth century. The *scallopine Milanese* may have been named after the scallop shell – the emblem of Spain's patron saint, St James – and featured in Milanese homes as a delicacy brought to Italy by the scallop-bearers, the troops of Charles V.

Unlike beef, veal can be judged by the colour of the meat. The whiter it is, the greater proportion of the calf's diet has been milk and the more likely the meat is to be tender with a delicate flavour.

Fillet
A boneless cut from the hindquarters. Sometimes sold for roasting but more often sliced into escalopes.

Loin
A cut from the back of the animal that is available on the bone or boned and rolled. It can be roasted.

Veal chops
These are taken from the loin and have the bone in them. They may be grilled or fried.

Best end
A cut that is suitable for roasting, braising or stewing.

Leg
A prime cut that is usually roasted.

Knuckle
This is the end of the leg. It is a bony cut and is used for boiling and stewing (e.g. osso bucco).

Shoulder
This can be boned and rolled for roasting, but is usually cut up for stews and pies.

Methods of preparation
Tying

Tying and rolling of a sirloin

Boning and trimming

Tunnel boning a leg of lamb

Methods of cookery

Method of cookery applied	Recipe covering method
Braise	247, 254, 255, 257, 259
Confit	268
Cure	256, 259, 268
Pan-fry	251, 252, 269
Poach	269
Pot roast	243, 262
Roast	240, 241, 242, 244, 245, 246, 250, 253, 258, 266, 267, 270
Sauté	248, 249, 251, 252, 260, 263, 264, 265
Stew	254, 261
Stuff	241, 270

LAMB

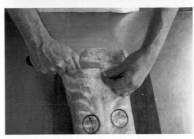

Boning and tying a saddle of lamb

The saddle may be divided as follows.

Remove skin, starting from head to tail and from breast to back, split down the centre of the back bone to produce two loins. Each loin can be roasted whole, boned and stuffed, or cut into loin and chump chops.

Saddle for roasting (see page 211)

1 Skin and remove the kidney.

2 Trim the excess fat and sinew.
3 Cut off the flaps leaving about 15 cm each side so as to meet in the middle under the saddle.
4 Remove the aitch, or pelvic bone.
5 Score neatly and tie with string.
6 For presentation the tail may be left on, protected with paper and tied back.
7 The saddle can also be completely boned, stuffed and tied.

Preparing stuffed saddle of lamb (recipe 241)

240 Slow-cooked saddle of lamb, braised cabbage and chocolate

	4 portions	10 portions
Lamb		
garlic cloves	2	5
oil	50 ml	125 ml
sprig of thyme		
long saddle (boned, sinew and fat removed – eye of loin)	1	2
Cabbage		
red onions	2	5
head of red cabbage	½	1
red wine	500 ml	1¼ litres
stick cinnamon	½	1
cassis	150 ml	375 ml
brown sugar	50 g	125 g
redcurrant jelly	1 tbsp	2 tbsp
Sauce		
lamb jus	200 ml	500 ml
sherry vinegar	5 ml	12 ml
cooked peas	200 g	500 g
To finish		
good-quality dark chocolate, chopped into small pieces	75 g	200 g
cooked green beans	200 g	500 g
portion of sautéed potatoes		

nutritional info

♥

1 large portion provides:
2677 kJ/641 kcal
33.6 g fat (of which 4.7 g saturated)
40.9 g carbohydrate (of which 35.5 g sugars)
45.8 g protein
6.3 g fibre

There is fat in the lamb meat.

calorie counter

kcal
1000
900
800
700
600
500
400
300
200
100
0

For the lamb

1 Crush the garlic and mix with the oil and thyme. Place the trimmed lamb loin in the oil and allow to infuse overnight.

2 Pre-heat the oven to 59°C. When ready to cook, drain off the oil and seal in a hot pan until all sides are golden (this should take no more than 1½ minutes). Then wrap in clingfilm and place in the pre-heated oven for a minimum of 35 minutes (the lamb will start to overcook after 60 minutes, so be mindful of this).

For the cabbage

1 Slice and sweat the red onions in a pan and put to one side.

2 Slice the red cabbage and add to the red onions in a pan along with the red wine, cinnamon, cassis and brown sugar.

3 Cover with tin foil and put in oven at 150°C; check after 1 hour.

4 When cooked, strain off the liquor, reduce to a glaze and finish with the redcurrant jelly.

5 Mix the glaze into the cabbage and chill.

For the sauce

1 Remove the lamb from the oven and take off the clingfilm.

2 Heat a little oil in a non-stick pan and place the lamb saddles in for a short period, just to re-seal. This should take no more than 1 minute. Allow to rest for 2 minutes.

3 Meanwhile, reheat the lamb jus, and add the sherry vinegar (to taste) and the peas.

To finish

1 Place a mound of cabbage in the centre of the plate and top with buttered green beans.

2 Carve the lamb into equal portions and divide between the plates.

3 Pour over the sauce and finish with a sprinkling of chocolate around the plate and side orders or sautéed potatoes.

Note: The method of cookery here – slow cooking at low temperature – permits you to use saddle of lamb instead of best end, giving you the same results in terms of tenderness and a deeper flavour from the lamb.

241 Stuffed saddle of lamb with apricot farce

		4 portions	10 portions
Lamb			
saddle, boned		1	2
best lamb mince		250 g	625 g
dried apricots, chopped	farce	100 g	250 g
chives, chopped		1 tsp	2 tsp
seasoning			
pig's caul/crepinette		200 g	500 g
oil		50 ml	125 g
lamb jus		200 ml	500 ml
Fondant potato			
medium potatoes, preferably Maris Pipers		4	10
vegetable oil		50 ml	125 ml
garlic cloves, split		2	5
butter		150 g	375 g
water or white stock		100 ml	250 ml
seasoning			
Roast vegetables			
Butter		50 g	125 g
Oil		50 ml	125 ml
medium carrots, peeled and cut into 4		2	5
medium parsnips, peeled and cut into 4		2	5
leeks, trimmed of green and root, cut into 10 cm lengths		2	5

nutritional info

♥

1 large portion provides:
4086 kJ/983 kcal
70.2 g fat (of which 27.8 g saturated)
40.8 g carbohydrate (of which 19.6 g sugars)
49.2 g protein
8.0 g fibre

Tripe was used for pig's caul, for this analysis.
Includes lamb plus lamb mince for stuffing,
and oil to cook.

calorie counter

kcal
1000
900
800
700
600
500
400
300
200
100
0

For the lamb

1 Pre-heat the oven to 180°C.

2 With the lamb on the chopping board, fat side down, bat out the fat flanks either side.

3 Mix all the farce ingredients and place in the lamb's centre cavity. Wrap over the fat flanks, encasing the farce and creating a tight cylinder shape.

4 Open up the crepinette onto the board and lay the lamb inside. Tightly double-wrap the lamb with crepinette and tie in four equal sections (tie tightly, but not overtight, as during cooking the lamb will expand and either burst from the wrap or split the string).

5 Heat the oil in a thick-bottomed pan and seal the lamb saddle all over until golden. Place in the oven for 20 minutes on 180°C, then reduce the temperature to 65°C for a further 45 minutes.

6 Check if cooked by inserting a probe in the centre, which should read 55–59°C.

For the fondant potato

1 Pre-heat the oven to 170°C.

2 Peel the potatoes and cut into slabs approximately 4 cm thick.

3 Using a round pastry cutter, cut the slabs of potato into 5 cm rounds and trim off the sharp edges.

4 In an ovenproof saucepan, heat the vegetable oil over a medium-high heat.

5 Add the potatoes and garlic, brown the potatoes on one side, taking care not to scorch them. Turn the potatoes over when golden brown and add the butter, water and seasoning.

6 Bring to a simmer, then transfer to the oven for 12–15 minutes or until the centre of the potatoes is soft. Remove from the oven and leave to soak up the butter for about 1 hour.

7 If the liquid in the pan has evaporated and only butter is left as the cooking medium, top up the pan with hot liquid and bring back to an emulsion.

To finish

1 Start to cook the fondant potatoes (see above).

2 Start to cook the lamb (see above).

3 Meanwhile, place the butter and oil for the vegetables in a thick pan, and heat and cook the vegetables until golden on the stove.

4 Drain into colander and keep warm.

5 Remove the lamb from the oven when ready and allow to rest for 10 minutes.

6 Remove the string and place on a carving board.

7 Meanwhile, arrange the fondants and roast vegetables on the plate. Slice the lamb into four equal pieces and place neatly over the vegetables.

8 Finish the dish by coating the lamb and around with lamb jus.

Note: For a variation, omit the dried apricots for mint and peas, then substitute the cabbage and potato for a light couscous salad and wilted greens.

242 Roast rump of lamb, flageolets purée and balsamic dressing

	4 portions	10 portions
Lamb		
lamb rumps off the bone (150–160 g each), trimmed	4	10
salt and pepper		
Flageolets purée		
dried flageolet beans	225 g	560 g
chicken stock	1 litre	2½ litres
smoked back bacon or pancetta trimmings	100 g	250 g
carrots	50 g	125 g
shallots	1	3
garlic cloves	2	5
sprig thyme	1	3
salt	10 g	25 g
Fondant potato		
medium potatoes, preferably Maris Pipers	4	10
vegetable oil	50 ml	125 ml
garlic cloves, split	2	5
butter	150 g	375 g
water	100 ml	250 ml
seasoning		
Balsamic dressing		
garlic clove	1	3
redcurrant jelly	2 tsp	5 tsp
lemon oil (see recipe 180)	1 tsp	3 tsp
good-quality balsamic vinegar	2 tsp	5 tsp
thyme leaves	1 tsp	3 tsp
dried tomato fillets, diced	6	15
lamb jus	300 ml	750 ml
To finish		
spinach, washed and picked	200 g	500 g

nutritional info

1 large portion provides:
3870 kJ/930 kcal
61.4 g fat (of which 22.9 g saturated)
43.3 g carbohydrate (of which 10.6 g sugars)
53.2 g protein
18.7 g fibre

Broad beans were used instead of flageolot beans. High fibre content due to the beans; fat from the lamb and bacon; oil in the fondant potato.

calorie counter — kcal: 1000, 900, 800, 700, 600, 500, 400, 300, 200, 100, 0

For the flageolet purée

1 Soak the beans overnight. Next day, rinse in cold water and place in a saucepan over medium heat with the stock, bacon, carrot, shallot, garlic and thyme.

2 Simmer for 20 minutes, then add the salt and cook the flageolets for a further 30 minutes until tender.

3 If the liquid starts to reduce too much top up with some filtered water.

4 Leave the beans to cool in the cooking liquid. When cold, strain off and reserve the liquid. Remove and discard the garlic. Place the beans and other ingredients in a food processor and liquidise until very smooth, adding the retained cooking liquor if the consistency appears to be too thick.

5 When the beans are the consistency of soft mashed potato, keep warm until ready to serve.

For the fondant potato

1 Pre-heat the oven to 170°C.

2 Peel the potatoes and cut into slabs approximately 4 cm thick.

3 Using a round pastry cutter, cut the slabs of potato into 5 cm rounds and trim off the sharp edges.

4 In an ovenproof saucepan, heat the vegetable oil over a medium-high heat.

5 Add the potatoes and garlic, brown the potatoes on one side, taking care not to scorch them. Turn the potatoes over when golden brown and add the butter, water and seasoning.

6 Bring to a simmer, then transfer to the oven for 12–15 minutes or until the centre of the potatoes is soft. Remove from the oven and leave to soak up the butter for about 1 hour.

7 If the water in the pan has evaporated and only butter is left as the cooking medium, top up the pan with hot water and bring back to an emulsion.

For the balsamic dressing

1 In a small saucepan, combine all the ingredients for the dressing and bring to a simmer.

2 Leave to simmer for 1–2 minutes until the flavour has infused fully.

3 Cover with clingfilm and retain for serving.

To complete

1 Pre-heat the oven to 180°C.

2 Place a large frying pan on the stove over a medium-high heat and add the oil.

3 Season the lamb with salt and pepper and place in the pan, fat-side down.

4 Cook until golden brown on the fatty side, then turn over and seal the lean side.

5 When all the lamb is sealed, place it on a wire rack over a baking sheet and cook in the oven for 12–13 minutes, turning occasionally.

6 Test the lamb is cooked by using the 'finger and thumb technique' (see page 203).

7 Meanwhile, drain the potatoes and reheat in the oven until warm.

8 Reheat the flageolets and, when the lamb is cooked, remove it from the oven and leave to rest in a warm place for 7–10 minutes.

9 In a saucepan, wilt the spinach in a little butter, then drain and place on the serving plates. Top with the fondant.

10 Warm the dressing through.

11 Spoon on the flageolet purée.

12 Carve the lamb and arrange on the fondant potato.

13 Pour the sauce over, ensuring each plate has an equal serving.

Note: Roast lamb and flageolet purée are synonymous with each other in classic French recipes. You may need to soak the beans overnight. The fondants need to be made 1 hour before serving to ensure maximum flavour.

243 Pot roast chump of lamb with root vegetables

	4 portions	10 portions
beef dripping	100 g	250 g
lamb chump, trimmed and boned	400 g	1 kg
small whole onions, peeled	400 g	1 kg
small carrots, peeled	400 g	1 kg
celery sticks, cut in three	400 g	1 kg
swede, peeled and cut into chunks	200 g	500 g
field mushrooms	100 g	250 g
hot stock	275 ml	700 ml
clarified butter	200 ml	500 ml
bay leaves	1	3
sprig of thyme		
butter	25 g	60 g
flour	25 g	60 g
seasoning		

nutritional info

1 large portion provides:
3231 kJ/781 kcal
66.1 g fat (of which 37.7 g saturated)
24.4 g carbohydrate (of which 16.7 g sugars)
23.7 g protein
6.3 g fibre

Contains beef dripping, butter and clarified butter.

1 Pre-heat the oven to 140°C.

2 Melt the dripping in a thick cooking pot and when, it's hot, put in the lamb and sear and brown it all over, then transfer it to a plate. Next lightly brown the onions, carrots, celery and swede, and remove them temporarily to the plate.

3 Empty all the fat from the pot, then replace the lamb chump and arrange the vegetables and mushrooms around the meat. Add the hot stock, clarified butter, bay leaves and thyme, and a little salt and pepper. Cover with foil and a tightly fitting lid and, as soon as you hear simmering, place in the centre of the oven and leave for about 15 minutes.

4 When ready, place the meat and vegetables on a warmed serving dish, then skim off the fat. Bring the liquid to the boil and boil briskly until reduced slightly. Mix the butter and flour to a paste, then add this to the liquid and whisk until the sauce thickens. Serve with the meat and some sharp English mustard.

Note: This method of cookery traps in flavour, keeps the meat moist and makes a sauce while doing so. The root vegetables in this will give the meat flavour, which makes them a suitable garnish with the lamb.

244 Roast leg of lamb with minted couscous and buttered peas

	4 portions	10 portions
Leg of lamb		
leg of lamb (1.8–2 kg)	1	2
olive oil	3 tbsp	5 tbsp
seasoning		
garlic cloves	4	10
sprigs of rosemary	2	5
butter	40 g	100 g
brown stock	300 ml	750 ml
white wine	200 ml	500 ml
Couscous		
light chicken stock	400 ml	1 litre
olive oil	50 ml	125 ml
salt and cayenne pepper		
couscous	200 g	500 g
mint leaves, cut into julienne	3	7
lemon, juice of	½	1
Garnish		
fresh peas	400 g	1 kg
seasoning		
butter	50 g	125 g

nutritional info ♥

1 large portion provides:
3531 kJ/852 kcal
56.2 g fat (of which 15.0 g saturated)
38.1 g carbohydrate (of which 2.9 g sugars)
50.1 g protein
4.8 g fibre

Butter was used to cook the lamb; the oil adds calories.

kcal
1000
900
800
700
600
500
400
300
200
100
0
calorie counter

For the lamb

1 Pre-heat the oven to 200°C. Rub the leg of lamb with a little oil, salt and pepper.

2 Peel three-quarters of the cloves of garlic and cut in half lengthways. Make six incisions in each leg of lamb and insert a piece of garlic and a small piece of rosemary into each. Break up the rest of the garlic without peeling.

3 Place the lamb in a hot roasting tray with the rest of the oil and sear over a medium heat until golden on all sides. Add the butter and remaining garlic and continue to heat until foaming.

4 Turn the oven down to 190°C and continue to cook for 45–60 minutes.

5 Remove the lamb, allow to rest and keep warm.

6 Meanwhile, return the roasting tray to the stove and scrape it with a spatula to lift the roasting sugars.

7 Add the stock and wine, bring to the boil, skim and reduce by half. Any juices that have run from the leg of lamb can be added to the roasting tray. Then pass the sauce through a fine sieve and retain for serving.

For the couscous

1 Bring the stock, oil, salt and cayenne pepper to the boil.

2 Place the couscous in a bowl and pour on the liquid. Place clingfilm tightly over the top and leave for 5 minutes.

3 Remove the clingfilm and add a little more oil to help free the grains.

4 Add the mint to the mix and allow to infuse.

5 Finish with lemon juice and check the seasoning.

To serve

1 Place a pan of water on the stove and bring to the boil. Add the peas and cook for 3 minutes until they are just cooked, but retain their vibrant green colour.

2 Drain, season, add a knob of butter and toss well.

3 Place in a hot serving dish – these can be served separately.

4 Carve the lamb, place on the plate with a mound of couscous and a sauce boat of the fine roast gravy.

Note: This dish can be used with shoulder of lamb, adjusting the cooking time. Couscous can also be replaced by a potato (e.g. boulangère, fondant or roast) to offer a more traditional accompaniment.

245 Roast shoulder of lamb with potatoes boulangère

	4 portions	10 portions
Shoulder of lamb		
shoulder of lamb (1.8–2 kg)	1	2
olive oil	3 tbsp	7 tbsp
seasoning		
garlic cloves	4	10
sprigs of rosemary	2	5
butter	40 g	100 g
Boulangère potatoes		
butter	180 g	450 g
onions, sliced	200 g	500 g
bay leaves (optional)	2	5
paprika	1 tsp	3 tsp
russet or Maris Piper potatoes, peeled	1½ kg	3¾ kg
lamb or chicken stock (container size dependent)	400 ml	1 litre
seasoning and ground black pepper		

nutritional info	kcal
1 large portion provides: 4516 kJ/1085 kcal 69.4 g fat (of which 29.9 g saturated) 69.8 g carbohydrate (of which 5.6 g sugars) 49.2 g protein 5.7 g fibre Butter is used for cooking and in the potatoes.	1000 900 800 700 600 500 400 300 200 100 0

For the shoulder of lamb

1 Pre-heat the oven to 200°C. Rub the shoulder of lamb with a little oil, salt and pepper.

2 Peel the cloves of garlic and cut in half lengthways. Make eight incisions in each shoulder of lamb and insert a piece of garlic and a small piece of rosemary into each one.

3 Place the lamb in a hot roasting tray with the rest of the oil and sear over a medium heat until golden on all sides. Add the butter and continue to heat until foaming.

4 Continue to boil and add any juices that have run from the leg of lamb. When reduced by half, whisk in a knob of butter, then pass the sauce through a fine sieve. Serve with the lamb and vegetables.

For the boulangère potatoes

1 Pre-heat the oven to 180°C. Melt 60 g butter in a sauté pan over medium heat.

2 Add the onions, bay leaves and paprika, and sauté until translucent. Season lightly with salt and pepper. Remove the onions and cool.

3 Slice potatoes and place flat-side down in a buttered and seasoned baking dish. Top this with a thin layer of the onions, repeating this process

until the potato and onion are depleted. Pour in enough stock to cover the potatoes and onions two-thirds of the way up the dish.

4 Top the layer of potatoes with the remaining butter and mill some freshly ground pepper over the top.

To cook and finish

1 Place the golden shoulder of lamb on a cooling wire suitable for the oven and place on top of the boulangère potatoes

2 Place in the oven and cook for 30 minutes, at which point turn the oven down to 140°C.

3 Baste every 20 minutes from the juices that drip into the potatoes. After 1 hour 30 minutes, check

the shoulder is cooked by inserting a trussing needle or probe (the core temperature should be 58°C).

4 Remove the lamb and allow to rest.

5 Turn the oven up to 200°C allowing the potatoes to develop a golden top. Meanwhile, when the lamb is well rested, carve, lay it on the plates and serve with roast root vegetables, with the boulangère in the centre of the table.

Note: This is a real classic with the boulangère being cooked under the lamb, allowing all the roasting juices to be caught by the potatoes, adding extra flavour and basting at the same time.

246 Slow-cooked best end of lamb with lentils

	4 portions	10 portions
lamb stock	300 ml	750 ml
baby onions, cooked	200 g	500 g
tomato concassée	100 g	250 g
puy lentils, soaked overnight	50 g	125 g
bouquet garni	150 g	375 g
small onion(s), peeled and halved	150 g	375 g
small carrot(s), peeled	150 g	375 g
sherry vinegar	30 ml	75 ml
butter	40 g	100 g
savoy cabbage, cut into fine strips	100 g	250 g
lemon thyme and parsley, chopped	2 tbsp	5 tbsp
whole best ends of lamb (8 bones each)	2	5
olive oil	50 ml	125 ml
garlic mashed potato	350 g	875 g
seasoning		

nutritional info

1 large portion provides:
3059 kJ/736 kcal
50.4 g fat (of which 17.3 g saturated)
31.0 g carbohydrate (of which 9.2 g sugars)
41.1 g protein
3.7 g fibre

Red lentils used instead of puy for this analysis. Butter is used for the cabbage and lentils.

For the lamb

1 Have the lamb stock, cooked baby onions and tomato concassée ready. Boil the lamb stock until reduced by two-thirds. Set aside.

2 Drain the lentils, then place in a saucepan with the bouquet garni, onion and carrot. Cover with fresh water, bring to the boil, then turn down to a simmer and cook for about 15–20 minutes until just tender.

3 Drain, remove the bouquet garni, onion and carrot, then set aside. At this point, sprinkle the lentils with a little sherry vinegar while warm, allowing the flavour to go into the lentils.

4 In a small pan, melt half the butter and sweat the cabbage for 2 minutes or until just wilted, stirring occasionally. Mix with the lentils and set aside.

5 Pre-heat the oven to 70°C. Mix together the herbs and roll the best end in the herbs on the meat side.

6 Heat the oil in an ovenproof pan and brown on all sides. Slow roast in the oven for 35–40 minutes. Meanwhile, add the baby onions and tomato concassée to the sauce. Reheat the garlic mash. With a little butter, reheat the lentils and cabbage and keep warm.

7 Once the lamb is cooked, place the cabbage and lentils in the centre of the plate. Carve the lamb

(4 cutlets each) and arrange over the cabbage mixture.

8 Bring the sauce to the boil, correct the seasoning and pour over the lamb dish. Serve.

Note: If you wanted to offer the lamb off the bone this can be taken off when cooked and then carved as for a loin.

247 Braised-roast belly of lamb with cauliflower risotto and balsamic jelly

	4 portions	10 portions
Lamb		
lamb bellies (weighing 250–300 g each)	4	10
vegetable oil	50 ml	125 ml
large-cut mirepoix	500 g	1¼ kg
braising stock	1 litre	3 litres
garlic cloves	3	7
sprig of thyme	1	2
bay leaf	1	2
Jelly		
balsamic vinegar (not aged)	250 ml	625 ml
mombazilliac wine	125 ml	300 ml
apple juice	125 g	300 g
agar-agar (powdered)	2.4 g	6 g
Risotto		
chicken stock	1 litre	2½ litres
vegetable oil	50 ml	125 ml
shallots, finely chopped	2	5
garlic clove, split	½	1
carnaroli rice	250 g	725 g
white wine	4 tbsp	10 tbsp
butter	75 g	180 g
Parmesan cheese, grated	50 g	125 g
cauliflower florets, roasted	400 g	1 kg
chives, chopped	2 tsp	5 tsp
seasoning		
To finish		
spinach, washed	200 g	500 g
baby carrots, peeled and cooked	12	30
lamb jus (see page 100)	200 ml	500 ml

nutritional info

1 large portion provides:
4298 kJ/1031 kcal
61.1 g fat (of which 15.4 g saturated)
67.6 g carbohydrate (of which 11.6 g sugars)
53.7 g protein
4.6 g fibre

The belly is fatty and there is parmesan in the risotto.

calorie counter

kcal
1000
900
800
700
600
500
400
300
200
100
0

For the lamb

1 Trim the excess fat from the belly.

2 Seal quickly in hot oil.

3 Roast the large-cut mirepoix in a pan with hot oil until golden brown.

4 Place the braising liquid, garlic, thyme and bay leaves in a pan. Bring to the boil.

5 Place the bellies and roasted mirepoix into the liquid and cook for 1½ hours (depending on the size and thickness).

6 When cooked, drain off liquid and retain. Place between two trays and add a little weight on top to assist pressing.

7 When cold, place on a board and cut into portion size required.

For the jelly

1 Reduce the vinegar by half.

2 Reduce the mombazilliac and apple juice together by half.

3 Mix them both together and allow to cool.

4 Add the agar-agar to the mix, mixing thoroughly.

5 Return to the boil, whisking for 1 minute.

6 Pour into a shallow container and allow to set at room temperature.

7 Store in the refrigerator until ready.

For the risotto

1 In a saucepan, bring the chicken stock to a simmer.

2 In a separate, heavy pan, heat the vegetable oil over a medium heat and sweat the shallots and garlic for 3 minutes without letting them colour. Add the rice and sweat for a further 2 minutes, again without colouring. Pour in the wine and simmer until it has reduced to a glaze. Begin adding the stock in small stages – about 50–75 ml at a time.

3 Bring the risotto to the boil each time, allowing the stock to evaporate while stirring continuously. Each process of adding and simmering will take approximately 3 minutes. Repeat several times until the rice is cooked but not chalky to the bite – in total it should take about 20–22 minutes from the first addition of chicken stock.

4 Add the butter, Parmesan and cauliflower florets and work to an emulsion, add the chives, correct the seasoning and consistency (if too thick add more stock, if too wet (soft) reduce the liquid a little) and serve.

To complete

1 Start the risotto and, at the halfway point of the cooking, heat the retained cooking liquor from the lamb bellies and place them in it carefully.

2 Bring to a simmer, take off the heat and allow them to slowly heat through.

3 Meanwhile, finish the risotto and heat the vegetable garnish in a little butter.

4 Cut the jelly into even dice and place in the lamb jus and gently heat through (the jelly will not melt until 83°C, therefore be careful not to simmer or boil the jus).

5 Arrange the vegetables on the plate, remove the lamb and drain.

6 Place the risotto on the plate with the vegetables, top with the drained lamb and jus, and serve.

Note: When boning all the saddles and using the eye, the excess is belly flank that, if cooked well, is a great preparation. Slow cooking is required. The cauliflower risotto can be changed for pea, leaving in the balsamic jelly, which will work equally well.

248 Lambs' kidneys with juniper and wild mushrooms

	4 portions	10 portions
English lambs' kidneys	12	30
shallots, chopped	25 g	60 g
juniper berries, crushed	12	30
gin, marinated with the berries for one day	60 ml	150 ml
English white wine	125 ml	300 ml
strong lamb stock	½ litre	1¼ litre
selected wild mushrooms	50 g	125 g
oil and butter, to sauté large potatoes	2	5

nutritional info

1 large portion provides:
821 kJ/193.9 kcal
3.5 g fat (of which 1.1 g saturated)
18.0 g carbohydrate (of which 1.2 g sugars)
23.7 g protein
0.4 g fibre

The fat content will be higher if butter is added to the mushrooms

kcal
1000
900
800
700
600
500
400
300
200
100
0

calorie counter

1 Remove the fat and thin film of tissue covering the kidneys.

2 Season well and sauté in a hot pan, keeping them pink. Remove and keep warm.

3 Add the shallots and some crushed juniper berries to the pan, flambé with a little gin, pour in the white wine and reduce well. Add the lamb stock and reduce by half. Pass and finish with butter.

4 Prepare the mushrooms and sauté in hot oil, adding butter to maintain their earthy flavour, then keep warm.

5 Finely shred the potatoes into matchsticks on a mandolin, dry in a clean cloth, season and cook in butter as a fine potato cake.

6 To serve, place the potato cake in the centre of a serving dish, slice the kidneys and arrange attractively in a circle on the potato. Garnish the kidneys with the wild mushrooms, cordon the dish with the sauce and serve immediately.

249 Lambs' liver flavoured with lavender and sage, served with avocado and sherry sauce

	4 portions	10 portions
lamb's liver	400 g	1 kg
milk	250 ml	625 ml
honey	50 g	125 g
sage (chopped) bunch	1	2
lavender, bunch	1	2
garlic cloves	2	4
avocado	1	2–3
sesame oil	25 ml	50 ml
Sauce		
baby onions	200 g	500 g
garlic clove, crushed	1	1
sesame oil	25 ml	50 ml
sherry	50 ml	125 ml
veal stock	250 ml	625 ml
unsalted butter	50 g	125 g

nutritional info

1 large portion provides:
2123 kJ/509 kcal
38.62 g fat (of which 13.3 g saturated)
17.6 g carbohydrate (of which 15.6 g sugars)
24.0 g protein
2.0 g fibre

Contains sesame oil, avocado and butter

♥ calorie counter
kcal
1000
900
800
700
600
500
400
300
200
100
0

1 Remove skin and arteries from the liver, and place on one side.

2 Mix the milk, honey and half chopped sage, with the lavender and uncrushed garlic cloves.

3 Place the liver in the milk mixture and leave for 24 hours.

4 For the sauce, peel the baby onions, blanch them, then refresh.

5 Sauté the crushed garlic in sesame oil with the baby onions. Add the sherry and reduce by half.

6 Add the veal stock and reduce this by two-thirds. Take off heat and cool slightly.

7 Whisk in the unsalted butter and season.

8 Peel the avocado, stone it and cut into chunks. Reserve.

9 Heat sesame oil for the liver, remove the liver from the marinade and drain. Season liver with salt, pepper, sage and any remaining lavender.

10 Sauté liver lightly until pink.

11 Sauté the avocado in the butter until soft, season with salt.

12 To serve, pour the sauce on to the plate, place the liver on top. Garnish with the avocado and the onions from the sauce. If you have any remaining sage or lavender use this too.

BEEF

Larding a fillet of beef: method 1   Method 2

250 Slow-cooked beef fillet with onion ravioli

	4 portions	10 portions
Beef		
corn oil		
centre cut fillet	1 × 600 g	2 × 750 g
strands of thyme	3	7
garlic clove, thinly sliced	1	2
Ravioli pasta		
Flour	550 g	1400 g
egg yolks	5	12
eggs	4	10
Chicken mousse		
breast of chicken	300 g	1 kg
salt to taste		
cream	200 ml	500 ml
Ravioli mix		
chicken mousse (see above)	300 g	750 g
lyonnaise onions	100 g	250 g
parsley	25 g	60 g
sherry vinegar	50 ml	125 ml
seasoning		
To finish		
haricot verts, cooked	200 g	500 g
button onions, cooked	12 (100 g)	30 (250 g)
sherry jus	200 ml	500 ml
picked lemon thyme	1 tsp	2 tsp

nutritional info

1 large portion provides:
5119 kJ/1221 kcal
52.5 g fat (of which 25.3 g saturated)
116.4 g carbohydrate (of which 9.1 g sugars)
77.2 g protein
6.9 g fibre

♥ kcal
1000
900
800
700
600
500
400
300
200
100
0

calorie counter

Contains cream in the mousse and egg yolk in the ravioli.

For the beef

1 Pre-heat the oven to 59°C.

2 Heat a pan with a little corn oil and carefully put the beef fillet in it, browning on all sides. Add thyme and garlic at the end (this operation should take no more than 2 minutes).

3 Remove from the pan and allow to cool.

4 Wrap the fillet in clingfilm and place in an oven already pre-set at between 55 and 60°C (the theory behind this cooking is that, for a medium rare 'doneness', the core temperature will be between 57 and 59°C; therefore, to achieve this preferred cooking degree throughout the fillet, the oven should be set at between 55 and 60°C).

5 It will take approximately 50–60 minutes for the temperature to penetrate to the core of the fillet. This will then last for an extra 1–1½ hours after this time (obviously the longer in the oven, the more it will dry out).

6 When ready to serve, remove from the oven and re-seal the fillet in a hot pan – this should take no more than 30 seconds. There is no need to rest the meat as the proteins will not have shrunk to a degree that require it to be rested.

For the mousse

1 Blitz the chicken for 1 minute with the salt.

2 After standing for 30 seconds, add the cream.

3 Pass through a fine sieve and reserve.

For the ravioli pasta

1 Place the flour in a food processor.

2 Whisk the eggs together and pass through chinois to get rid of any membrane.

3 Slowly incorporate the egg mix into the flour.

4 When all the liquid is used, take out of the food processor.

5 Work together on the bench, as though working bread dough, for 5 minutes.

6 Rest for 1 hour before rolling out to your required thickness.

For the ravioli mix

1 Place the chicken mousse, lyonnaise onions and parsley in a bowl. Mix well.

2 Add the sherry vinegar and check the seasoning.

3 Weigh out into 25 g balls and reserve until you need to make the raviolis.

To make the raviolis

1 Roll the pasta very thinly and cut into discs approx. 12 cm in diameter.

2 Cover the 8 discs in clingfilm to prevent them drying out.

3 Lay a disc on the workbench and dab with a little water.

4 Place in the centre a ball of mousse and top with another disc ensuring that all the air is removed and an even shape is formed.

5 When all raviolis are complete, blanch in boiling water for 2 minutes then arrest the cooking with iced water.

6 Drain, store and cover in clingfilm to prevent drying.

To finish

1 Reheat the haricots verts, button onions and sauce, keeping them all warm. Meanwhile, reheat the raviolis in boiling water for 2 minutes. Remove and allow to drain. Carve the beef into equal slices (two per portion).

2 Place the button onions and haricots verts in the centre of the plate, top with the beef, then the ravioli on top of the beef. Finish with the sauce and serve garnished with lemon thyme.

Note: A modern cooking method is adopted here. The risk involved in cooking at high heat for a short period of time and getting the cooking degree correct has always been an issue, however with this method the beef can stay in the oven for up to 2 hours and still be able to be served due to the protein shrink temperature (see page 202).

251 Tournedos Rossini (classical)

	4 portions	10 portions
Tournedos		
butter	50 g	125 g
olive oil	1 tsp	2 tsp
beef tournedos, 7–8 cm across and 4 cm deep (approx. 150 g each), at room temperature	4	10
seasoning	4	10
thick slices of foie gras	4	10
thick slices of good white bread, each slice cut into a circle the size of the steak	4	10
field mushrooms, slightly larger than the steaks	4 × 50 g	10 × 50 g
To serve		
chervil sprigs		
watercress sprigs		
red wine jus		

nutritional info

1 large portion provides:
2591 kJ/619 kcal
36.4 g fat (of which 14.7 g saturated)
30.3 g carbohydrate (of which 1.9 g sugars)
44.7 g protein
1.5 g fibre

Contains butter and olive oil.

1 Heat the butter and olive oil in a large, heavy-based frying pan. Add the beef tournedos and fry, without moving them, for 3 minutes.

2 Turn the tournedos over and cook for a further 3 minutes, until the steaks are crusted on the outside but rare inside. Season with salt and freshly ground pepper, and set aside to rest.

3 Heat the frying pan the tournedos were cooked in. Add the foie gras and fry until just caramelised.

4 Remove the foie gras and keep warm.

5 Add the bread slices to the pan and fry until crisp.

6 Meanwhile, grill the field mushrooms until tender.

7 Place the fried bread slices in the centre of two

plates; top each serving with the steak, then the foie gras, then the mushroom.

8 To finish, garnish with the chervil, and watercress, and pour over the jus.

252 Tournedos Rossini (modern)

Tournedos	4 portions	10 portions
Oil	50 ml	125 ml
tournedos of beef (approx. 200 g each)	4	10
girolles, washed and prepared	500 g	1¼ kg
butter	50 g	125 g
slices white bread, without crusts and trimmed to the size of the beef	2	5
garlic cloves, thinly sliced	1½	3
slices foie gras (approx. 30 g each)	4	10
shallot sauce	200 ml	500 ml
truffle, sliced	1	2
Madeira jelly (see below) cut into 1 cm dice	100 g	250 g
thin slices Parma ham (baked in an oven until crisp)	4	10
chervil		
seasoning		
Jelly		
Madeira	125 ml	300 ml
port	100 ml	250 ml
brandy	50 ml	125 ml
agar-agar (powdered)	2.1 g	5.25 g

nutritional info

1 large portion provides:
3532 kJ/848 kcal
59.4 g fat (of which 21.5 g saturated)
17.9 g carbohydrate (of which 3.2 g sugars)
57.3 g protein
2.2 g fibre

Liver pate was used instead of foie gras and mushrooms instead of truffles for this analysis. Contains oil, butter and parma ham.

kcal
1000
900
800
700
600
500
400
300
200
100
0

calorie counter

For the jelly

1 Mix all the ingredients together.

2 Place in a pan and bring to the boil, whisking for 1 minute.

3 Pour into a shallow container and allow to set at room temperature.

4 Store in the refrigerator until ready.

For the tournedos

1 In a small frying pan, add the oil and heat it, lightly season the tournedos and seal well in the pan. Cook until desired cuission is achieved. Remove from the pan and rest on a wire rack somewhere warm.

2 In the same pan, add the girolles and butter and bring to a foam. Carefully remove the girolles from the butter using a slotted/perforated spoon. Keep warm.

3 In the same pan add the bread slices and cook until golden and crisp. Remove and put them on the draining tray next to the beef.

4 Remove the butter from the pan, leaving a small amount of residue in the bottom. Heat up and then place in the garlic slices. Cook gently for 1–2 minutes.

5 Add the foie gras slices and cook gently.

6 Meanwhile, reheat the sauce and slice the truffle.

To finish

1 Place the tournedos on top of the bread croute, then the crisp ham slice on top of the beef with the foie gras topping the Parma ham.

2 Finally, arrange the girolles and jelly around the plate with the beef stack in the centre. Drizzle the sauce over and around, and finish with freshly sliced truffle and chervil.

Note: The modernisation comes from the use of wild mushrooms instead of field, and Madeira jelly instead of Madeira jus. Why not try a pork variation and use fillet, with a roast apple croute, and top with black pudding instead of foie gras: 'pork Rossini'?

253 Slow-cooked sirloin with Lyonnaise onions and carrot purée

	4 portions	10 portions
Beef		
sirloin, denuded with fat tied back on	1.2 kg	3 kg
seasoning		
oil	50 ml	125 ml
garlic clove, sliced	1	2
sprigs thyme	1	2
bay leaves	1	2
Lyonnaise onions		
Onions	200 g	500 g
seasoning		
Carrot purée		
medium-sized carrots	600 g	1½ kg
star anise	1	2
To serve		
jus de viande (meat juice)	150 ml	375 ml
sprigs of chervil		

nutritional info
1 large portion provides:
1949 kJ/467 kcal
25.3 g fat (of which 6.9 g saturated)
16.0 g carbohydrate (of which 14.0 g sugars)
44.8 g protein
4.3 g fibre
A small amount of butter was used in the onions and oil was used to cook the beef.

kcal
♥ 1000
900
800
700
600
500
400
300
200
100
0
calorie counter

For the beef

1 Pre-heat the oven to 180°C. Season the beef and heat the oil in the pan. Add the garlic, thyme, bay leaves and the beef.

2 Place the beef in the oven for 15 minutes. Remove, and turn the oven down to 69°C. When the oven has reached this new temperature, return the beef to it for a further 1 hour 10 minutes.

3 While the beef is cooking make the carrot purée and the Lyonnaise onions (see below) and keep warm.

For the onions

1 Finely slice the onions and put them into a large induction pan while cold.

2 Put on medium heat and season.

3 When the onions are starting to colour, turn down and cook slowly for approximately 2 hours.

4 Cool and refrigerate.

For the carrot purée

1 Peel the carrots and juice just over half of them into a small pan.

2 Cut the remaining carrots into equal slices of about 1 cm and place into the carrot juice.

3 Boil the carrots, ensuring that you scrape down the sides of the pan.

4 For the last 8 minutes of cooking, before all the liquid has completely evaporated, drop in the star anise. Pass, retaining the juice.

5 Remove the star anise pod(s) and blitz the purée for 7 minutes, adding the retained juice.

To finish

1 When the beef is cooked, remove from the oven and carve evenly. Place a portion of carrot purée and Lyonnaise onions on each plate. Top with the beef and pour over the jus de viande (meat juice), garnish with sprigs of chervil and serve.

Note: Although adopting the same slow cooking method as for the beef fillet (recipe 250), in this case we are using a slightly higher temperature as the collagen content in the sirloin is a little higher than it is the fillet.

254 Boeuf bourguignonne

	4 portions	10 portions
Beef		
beef shin pre-soaked in red wine (see below) for 12 hours	600 g	1½ kg
olive oil	50 ml	125 ml
bottle of inexpensive red Bordeaux wine	1	2
onion	100 g	250 g
carrot	100 g	250 g
celery sticks	75 g	180 g
leek	100 g	250 g
cloves of garlic	2	5
sprig fresh thyme	1	2
bay leaf	1	2
seasoning		
veal/brown stock to cover		
Garnish		
button onions, cooked	12 (150 g)	30 (300 g)
cooked bacon lardons	150 g	300 g
button mushrooms, cooked	12 (150 g)	30 (300 g)
parsley, chopped	2 tsp	5 tsp
To finish		
mashed potato	300 g	750 g
washed, picked spinach	300 g	750 g
cooked green beans	250 g	625 g

1 Pre-heat the oven to 180°C.

2 Trim the beef shin of all fat and sinew, and cut into 2½ cm-thick rondelles.

3 Heat a little oil in a thick-bottomed pan and seal/brown the shin. Place in a large ovenproof dish.

4 Meanwhile, reduce the red wine by half.

5 Peel and trim the vegetables as appropriate, then add them to the pan that the beef has just come out of and gently brown the edges. Then place this, along with the garlic and herbs, in the ovenproof dish with the meat.

6 Add the reduced red wine to the casserole, then pour in enough stock to cover the meat and vegetables. Bring to the boil, then cook in the oven pre-heated to 180°C for 40 minutes; after that, turn the oven down to 90–95°C and cook for a further 4 hours until tender.

7 Remove from the oven and allow the meat to cool in the liquor. When cold, remove any fat. Reheat gently at the same temperature to serve.

8 Heat the garnish elements separately and sprinkle over each portion. Serve with a mound of mashed potato, wilted spinach and buttered haricots verts. Finish the whole dish with chopped parsley.

Note: Another classic. Other joints of beef can be used here: beef or veal cheek can be used, reducing the time for the veal, or modernise the dish by using the slow-cooked fillet preparation and serving the same garnish.

nutritional info

1 large portion provides:
2144 kJ/513 kcal
27.3 g fat (of which 8.1 g saturated)
22.0 g carbohydrate (of which 8.8 g sugars)
46.1 g protein
6.3 g fibre

Olive oil is used to seal the beef, and lardons for garnish.

calorie counter

kcal
1000
900
800
700
600
500
400
300
200
100
0

255 Braised short rib with horseradish couscous

	4 portions	10 portions
Rib meat		
rib meat off the bone	400 g	1 kg
vegetable oil	50 ml	125 ml
onion ⎱ mirepoix, medium cut	125 g	300 g
carrot ⎰	125 g	300 g
garlic clove	1	2
sprigs of thyme	1	2
red wine	400 ml	1 litre
brown stock	300 ml	750 ml
sherry vinegar	25 ml	60 ml
Couscous		
water	300 ml	750 ml
olive oil	50 ml	125 ml
salt and cayenne pepper		
couscous	150 g	375 g
fresh horseradish, grated	20 g	50 g
lemon, juice of	½	1
To finish		
salad rocket	260 g	625 g
shaved Parmesan	100 g	250 g
vinaigrette	50 ml	125 ml

nutritional info

1 large portion provides:
3019 kJ/726 kcal
44.91 g fat (of which 11.2 g saturated)
46.2 g carbohydrate (of which 6.6 g sugars)
36.3 g protein
2.1 g fibre

Oil is used to brown the meat and vegetables, and in the cous cous; parmesan is added at the end.

♥

kcal
1000
900
800
700
600
500
400
300
200
100
0

calorie counter

For the rib meat

1 Pre-heat the oven to 130°C. Trim any excess fat from the meat.

2 Heat the oil in a heavy casserole and add the rib meat, mirepoix, garlic and thyme. Cook for 5–6 minutes until brown.

3 Add the wine, bring to the boil and simmer until reduced by half. Add the stock, then cover with foil and cook in the oven for 2 hours.

4 Remove from the oven and leave the meat to cool in the liquor. Remove the ribs and set aside. Strain the sauce into a clean pan and bring to the boil.

5 Simmer until it has reduced to a thick sauce, but be careful not to over-reduce.

6 Meanwhile, trim any elastin or connective tissue from the rib meat, being careful to leave it whole and keep warm.

7 The sauce may need to be adjusted with the vinegar to cut through the richness – be careful not to add too much as you want only an undertone of vinegar.

For the couscous

1 Bring the water, oil, salt and cayenne pepper to the boil.

2 Place the couscous in a bowl with the finely grated horseradish and pour on the liquid. Place clingfilm tightly over the top and leave for 5 minutes.

3 Remove the clingfilm and add a little more oil to help free the grains.

4 Allow to infuse.

5 Finish with lemon juice and check the seasoning.

To finish

1 Mix the rocket, Parmesan and vinaigrette together and check the seasoning.

2 Place a mould of couscous on the plate and divide the rib meat equally between the plates.

3 Pour over the sauce, top the ribs with the salad and serve.

Note: Ribs are full of flavour due to the amount of collagen in them – the animal breathes continuously, working the muscle group a great deal, hence the amount of flavour. This is a very versatile piece of meat.

256 Bresaola (cured silverside)

	10 portions
beef silverside, trimmed of all fat	3 kg
red wine, inexpensive Burgundy	2 litres
coarse salt	500 g
branches rosemary (each about 15–23 cm)	6
sprig of thyme	1
bay leaves	5
carrots, quartered	2
onions, white	2
garlic cloves, crushed	2
black peppercorns	12
juniper berries, crushed	8
orange's worth of orange peel	1

nutritional info

♥

1 large portion provides:
1395 kJ/332 kcal
10.2 g fat (of which 4.0 g saturated)
0.2 g carbohydrate (of which 0.2 g sugars)
43.3 g protein
0.0 g fibre

The raw beef is salted and aged; there is no added fat.

calorie counter

kcal
1000
900
800
700
600
500
400
300
200
100
0

For the marinade

1 Put all the ingredients, except the meat, into a tub (plastic or otherwise) large enough to hold the marinade and the meat. Mix well for a minute or two.

For the bresaola

1 Place the meat in the marinade. All the meat should be covered. Cover the container and place at the back of the refrigerator.

2 Leave for a week, or until the meat feels quite firm. Turn the beef over once at the mid-cycle of the process. At the end of the marinating period, remove from the marinade, dry and wrap in two layers of cheesecloth. Hang in a cool place to dry. Place paper on the floor as the meat drips a bit during the first few days of drying.

3 The meat should be hanged for at least a 3 weeks. At the end of this time the meat should feel firm, with no give when you press it with your fingers. For a 5 kg piece of silverside, three weeks should be sufficient. The firmness test is the best method to judge readiness. Mould may form during the drying process.

4 When drying is complete, remove any white mould with a brush and scraper. Wash the bresaola with vinegar. Pat dry and rub the entire bresaola with olive oil. Wrap in greaseproof paper and keep in the refrigerator.

5 Serve sliced very thinly with rocket salad and shaved Parmesan.

Note: Bresaola della Valtellina takes its name from the famous geographical district in which it was first produced. Since ancient times, techniques for preserving meat by salting and drying have been known. The use of such techniques in the Valtellina district of Italy is noted in writings dating back as far as 1400. Bresaola is made from raw beef that has been salted and naturally aged. The meat, which is eaten raw, has a delicate flavour and a capacity to melt in the mouth that is highly appreciated by consumers.

257 Traditional braised oxtail with garlic mash

	4 portions	10 portions
Oxtail		
oxtails, trimmed of fat	4	10
seasoning		
beef dripping	100 g	250 g
carrots, chopped	225 g	550 g
onions, chopped	225 g	550 g
celery sticks, chopped	225 g	550 g
leeks, chopped	225 g	550 g
tomatoes, chopped	450 g	1 kg
sprig of thyme	1	2
bay leaf	1	2
garlic clove, crushed	1	3
red wine	570 ml	1½ litres
veal/brown stock	2¼ litres	6 litres
Garnish		
carrot, finely diced	100 g	250 g
onion, finely diced	100 g	250 g
celery sticks, finely diced	75 g	185 g
small leeks, finely diced	75 g	185 g
tomatoes, skinned, deseeded and diced	4	10
cooked mashed potato with garlic	500 g	1¼ kg
fresh parsley, chopped	1 heaped tbsp	3 tbsp

1. Pre-heat the oven to 200°C.

2. Separate the trimmed tails between the joints and season with salt and pepper.

3. In a large pan, fry the tails in the dripping until brown on all sides, then drain in a colander.

4. Fry the chopped carrots, onions, celery and leeks in the same pan, collecting all the residue from the tails.

5. Add the chopped tomatoes, thyme, bay leaf and garlic, and continue to cook for a few minutes.

6. Place the tails in a large braising pan with the vegetables.

7. Pour the red wine into the first pan and boil to reduce until almost dry.

8. Add some of the stock then pour onto the meat in the braising pan and cover with the remaining stock.

9. Bring the tails to a simmer and braise in the pre-heated oven for 1½–2 hours until the meat is tender.

10. Lift the pieces of meat from the sauce and keep to one side.

11. Push the sauce through a sieve into a pan, then boil to reduce it, skimming off all impurities, to a good sauce consistency.

12. While the sauce is reducing, quickly cook the diced garnish carrot, onion, celery and leek in 1 tbsp water and a little butter for 1 to 2 minutes.

13. When the sauce is ready, add the tails and vegetable garnish, and simmer until the tails are warmed through.

14. Add the diced tomato, and spoon into hot bowls allowing 3 or 4 oxtail pieces per portion.

15. Serve a large bowl of garlic mash in the centre of the table and a large sourdough loaf.

16. Sprinkle the oxtail with chopped parsley and serve.

17. Serve with the garlic mash.

Note: Choose oxtails that clearly have plenty of flesh around the bone: one complete oxtail will serve two people. It is particularly good with haricot or cannellini beans, which seem to absorb a great deal of the flavour.

nutritional info

1 large portion provides:

2457 kJ/587 kcal

27.0 g fat (of which 12.2 g saturated)
41.7 g carbohydrate (of which 20.4 g sugars)
46.5 g protein
8.68 g fibre

Dripping is used to brown.

calorie counter
kcal
1000
900
800
700
600
500
400
300
200
100
0

258 Roast wing rib with Yorkshire pudding

	10 portions
Beef	
piece wing rib of beef	1 × 2 kg
beef dripping	25 g
Yorkshire pudding	
eggs	2
milk	200 ml
ice cold water	100 ml
plain flour	110 g
Gravy	
carrots ⎫ mirepoix	50 g
onion ⎬	50 g
red wine	200 ml
plain flour	30 g
beef stock	300 ml
prepared English mustard or horseradish sauce, to serve	

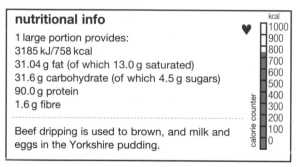

nutritional info

1 large portion provides:
3185 kJ/758 kcal
31.04 g fat (of which 13.0 g saturated)
31.6 g carbohydrate (of which 4.5 g sugars)
90.0 g protein
1.6 g fibre

Beef dripping is used to brown, and milk and eggs in the Yorkshire pudding.

calorie counter: kcal 1000 900 800 700 600 500 400 300 200 100 0

For the Yorkshire pudding

1 Place the eggs, milk and water in a bowl and combine well with a whisk.

2 Gradually add the flour to avoids lumps, and whisk to a smooth batter consistency.

3 Place in the refrigerator over night to rest (this will give you a better lift in the oven).

4 Pre-heat the oven to 180°C.

5 Heat oil in a Yorkshire pudding tray by placing a small amount in the bottom of each well, and place the tray in the oven for 5 minutes.

6 Carefully fill the wells on the tray to two-thirds full and return to the oven.

7 When the puddings have risen, and are golden brown, remove from the oven and keep warm.

For the beef

1 Pre-heat the oven to 195°C.

2 Place the dripping in a heavy roasting tray and heat on the stove top.

3 Place the beef in the tray and brown well on all sides.

4 Place in the oven on 195°C for 15 minutes then turn down to 75°C for 2 hours.

5 Remove and allow to rest before carving.

For the gravy

1 Remove the beef. Place the tray with the fat, sediment and the juice back on the stove.

2 Add the mirepoix and brown well.

3 Add the red wine and reduce by two-thirds.

4 Mix the flour and a little stock together to form a viscous batter-like mix.

5 Add the stock to the roasting tray and bring to the boil.

6 Pour in the flour mix and whisk in to the liquid in the tray.

7 Bring to the boil, simmer and correct the seasoning.

8 Pass through a sieve and retain for service.

To complete

1 Slice the beef and warm the Yorkshire puddings, serve with the gravy, horseradish and mustard.

Note: This dish would work well with most vegetables or potatoes. As an alternative why not add slightly blanched root vegetables to the roasting tray at the start of the beef cooking, remove and reheat for service? They will get maximum flavour from the beef and juices.

259 Pickled ox tongue

	4 portions	10 portions
ox tongues	1 kg	2½ kg
pink salt	380 g	950 g
star anise	2	3
Mirepoix:		
carrot	250 g	625 g
onions	250 g	625 g
leeks	250 g	625 g
celery	250 g	625 g
red wine vinegar	500 ml	1¼ ml
chicken stock	1 litre	2½ litres
red wine	500 ml	1¼ ml

1 Wash the ox tongues and place in 2 litres of water with the pink salt and star anise for 3 hours.

2 Roast the mirepoix in a heavy-duty pan until golden brown.

3 Add the red wine vinegar and bring to the boil.

4 Add the chicken stock and red wine.

5 Pour onto the ox tongues and cook for 3 hours.

6 Remove the tongues from the liquid and pass the liquor.

7 Peel off the skin and store in retained liquor until cold. Remove from the liquid and wrap tightly in clingfilm.

nutritional info

1 large portion provides:
2128 kJ/513 kcal
41.8 g fat (of which 16.9 g saturated)
0.0 g carbohydrate (of which 0.0 g sugars)
34.1 g protein
0.0 g fibre

Data on saturated fats was estimated based on other data about ox tongue.

kcal
1000
900
800
700
600
500
400
300
200
100
0

calorie counter

Uses

Ox tongue can be sliced thinly when cold and served with pickled beetroot salad or, alternatively, diced and put through a meat sauce for either fish or meat preparations. The texture of ox tongue is quite spongy, so when using warm in certain dishes something with a crisp, crunchy texture should be added to the dish to balance out the plate.

Note: Tongue has been cooked, pressed, pickled and canned since before the Second World War and remains an under-utilised product.

VEAL

Preparation of veal escalopes

Boning a loin of veal

260 Sautéed veal kidneys with shallot sauce

	4 portions	10 portions
veal kidneys, free from fat and cut into individual nodules	250 g	625 g
shallots, sliced	50 g	125 g
butter	75 g	180 g
white wine vinegar	50 ml	125 ml
cream	250 g	625 g
tarragon, chopped	1 tsp	2 tsp
vegetable oil	1 tbsp	3 tbsp
brandy	75 ml	180 ml

nutritional info

1 large portion provides:
2212 kJ/536 kcal
53.1 g fat (of which 31.5 g saturated)
2.2 g carbohydrate (of which 2.0 g sugars)
12.1 g protein
0.2 g fibre

Ox kidneys were used instead of veal for this analysis. Contains butter and cream in the sauce, and oil is used to cook the kidneys.

♥

kcal
1000
900
800
700
600
500
400
300
200
100
0

calorie counter

For the sauce

1 Place a hot pan in the middle of the stove for the kidneys.

2 Sweat the shallots in butter in a pan and add the white wine vinegar. Reduce by half.

3 Add cream and bring to the boil. Reserve to finish.

To sauté the kidneys

1 Place the vegetable oil and the kidneys in the hot pan.

2 Caramelise to a golden-brown colour.

3 Turn over and remove the pan from the stove.

4 Let the residual heat carry on cooking for 3–4 minutes.

To finish

1 Remove the kidneys from the pan, drain off the liquid, return the pan to the stove and deglaze with the brandy.

2 Reduce slightly and add the shallot sauce.

3 Bring to the boil, add the tarragon, return the kidneys to the pan and serve.

Uses

This dish would traditionally be served with sautéed potatoes and haricots verts, but due to the versatility of the kidneys, pretty much most things will suit (excluding salad).

Note: The offal in veal has a subtle flavour due to the age of the animal and pairing it with the shallots here offers an undertone of sweetness to the slightly bitter note of the kidney.

261 Osso bucco

	4 portions	10 portions
salt and ground pepper		
plain flour	45 g	112 g
thick slices of veal shin on the bone, the size of the steak	4 × 200 g	10 × 200 g
butter	50 g	125 g
oil	2 tbsp	5 tbsp
white wine	150 ml	375 ml
plum tomatoes	450 g	1⅛ kg
light veal or chicken stock	300 ml	750 ml
sprigs of parsley and thyme, and one bay leaf		

1 Pre-heat the oven to 180°C.

2 Season the flour and use to coat the meat well on both sides.

3 Heat the butter and oil in a casserole, add the veal and fry, turning once, until browned on both sides. Add the wine and cook, uncovered, for 10 minutes. Blanch, peel and chop the tomatoes, and add along with the stock and herbs.

4 Cover and cook in the centre of the oven until the meat is very tender and falls away from the marrow bone in the middle.

Uses

Delicious served with sauté potatoes or with a risotto alla Milanese.

Note: Part of the attraction of this dish is the marrow found in the bones. Although very rich, it is a special treat. Traditionally, osso bucco is served with a gremolata, which is a combination of chopped parsley, garlic and lemon zest that is added to the dish at the very end. It has been omitted from this recipe, offering you a simple base.

nutritional info

1 large portion provides:

1732 kJ/413 kcal
19.7 g fat (of which 8.5 g saturated)
12.5 g carbohydrate (of which 3.9 g sugars)
47.3 g protein
1.5 g fibre

Butter and oil are used to brown.

kcal
1000
900
800
700
600
500
400
300
200
100
0

calorie counter

262 Hay-baked sweetbreads with braised cabbage

	4 portions	10 portions
Sweetbreads		
a good handful of clean hay		
sprig of thyme	1	2
sprig of rosemary	1	2
vegetable oil	50 ml	125 ml
veal sweetbreads, trimmed, blanched, membrane removed	1 kg	2½ kg
light stock	500 ml	1¼ litres
garlic cloves	1	3
bay leaf	1	2
Cabbage		
vegetable oil	50 ml	125 ml
butter	50 g	125 g
shallots, finely diced	100 g	250 g
cloves garlic, chopped and sprouts removed	2	5
carrot, peeled and thinly sliced	100 g	250 g
sprigs thyme	2	3
bay leaf	1	3
savoy cabbage, finely sliced, stalks removed	1	2
water	50 ml	125 ml
fish stock	50 ml	125 ml
To serve		
veal jus	200 ml	500 ml

nutritional info

1 large portion provides:
3963 kJ/949 kcal
63.2 g fat (of which 23.3 g saturated)
14.5 g carbohydrate (of which 13.1 g sugars)
82.5 g protein
8.8 g fibre

Lamb sweet breads were used instead of veal for this analysis. Oil and butter are used to cook the cabbage.

For the sweetbreads

1 Pre-heat the oven to 80°C.

2 Mix the hay, thyme and rosemary together, ensuring the herbs are woven well into the hay.

3 Place the oil in a thick-bottomed pan, ensuring the sweetbreads are dry, and seal all over until lightly golden.

4 Remove from the pan and wrap each sweetbread in the hay.

5 Pour the light stock into the pan from the sweetbreads. Deglaze and pour into a large casserole container suitable to take the sweetbreads comfortably.

6 Pour the stock into the container with the garlic and bay leaf, and place in the sweetbreads. Note that the hay needs to act as a trivet, enabling the sweetbreads to bake as opposed to half-poach.

7 Return to the stove and bring to the boil. Cover with foil, place in the pre-heated oven and cook for 1 hour, checking every 20 minutes until cooked.

8 Meanwhile, start the cabbage.

For the cabbage

1 Place a large pan with a tight-fitting lid over a medium heat. Add the oil and butter, heat gently, then add the shallots, garlic and carrot and cook for 2 minutes without letting them colour.

2 Add the thyme, bay leaf and cabbage to the pan and cook for a further 3 minutes, again without colouring.

3 Pour in the water and fish stock, cover and steam for 3 minutes. Drain, then adjust the seasoning to taste and serve, or reserve to finish.

To finish

1 Assuming the cabbage has been retained warm, remove the sweetbreads from the hay and remove any loose strands of hay.

2 Place the cabbage in the centre of serving plates. Carve the sweetbreads into equal portions and rest over the cabbage.

3 To finish, pour the veal jus over and around and serve immediately.

4 Serve with potatoes with a crunch or bite as the texture of the cabbage and sweetbreads is soft.

Note: This method of cookery keeps the moisture in and adds a fresh herbaceous tone to the sweetbreads from the hay. You can weave in most hard herbs to the hay before cooking to add more flavour.

263 Veal chops with cream and mustard sauce

	4 portions	10 portions
veal chops	4	10
butter or oil	50 g	125 g
dry white wine	125 ml	300 ml
veal stock	125 ml	300 ml
bouquet garni		
slat and pepper		
double cream	60 ml	150 ml
French mustard, to taste		
parsley, chopped		

1 Shallow-fry the chops on both sides in hot butter or oil, pour off the fat.

2 Add white wine, stock, bouquet garni and season lightly; cover and simmer gently until cooked.

3 Remove chops and bouquet garni, reduce liquid by two-thirds, then add cream, the juice from the chops and bring to boil.

4 Strain the sauce, mix in the mustard and parsley, correct seasoning, pour over chops and serve.

nutritional info

1 large portion provides:
1390 kJ/331 kcal
12.74 g fat (of which 7.3 g saturated)
29.2 g carbohydrate (of which 4.5 g sugars)
26.7 g protein
2.6 g fibre

The chops are fried in butter, and there is double cream in the sauce.

264 Veal kidneys with mustard and cream sauce

	4 portions	10 portions
kidneys, skinned and trimmed, cut into walnut-sized pieces	400 g	1¼ kg
butter	100 g	250 g
double cream	250 ml	600 ml
lemon, grated zest of	1	2–3
French mustard, according to taste	1–2 tbsp	3–5 tbsp
salt and pepper		

1 Sauté the kidneys in a little hot butter for 3–4 mins, drain in a colander.

2 Boil the cream, lemon zest, mustard, salt and pepper for 2–3 mins.

3 Strain into a clean pan and incorporate the remaining butter. Add kidneys, do not reboil, correct seasoning and serve.

Note: Variations can include: brandy, chopped shallots, a chopped herb (e.g. tarragon, chervil or chives), and cultivated or wild mushrooms, either singly or in combination.

nutritional info

1 large portion provides:
2439 kJ/591 kcal
56.6 g fat (of which 34.7 g saturated)
1.7 g carbohydrate (of which 1.6 g sugars)
18.7 g protein
0.0 g fibre

The kidneys are sauted in butter, and there is double cream in the sauce.

265 Calves' liver with raspberry vinegar

	4 portions	10 portions
calves' liver, sliced	400 g	1¼ kg
butter	100 g	250 g
shallots, finely chopped	50 g	125 g
raspberry vinegar	60 ml	150 ml
veal stock	90 ml	300 ml
salt, mill pepper		

nutritional info

1 large portion provides:
1235 kJ/298 kcal
23.98 g fat (of which 14.0 g saturated)
1.3 g carbohydrate (of which 1.0 g sugars)
18.7 g protein
0.2 g fibre

The liver is fried in butter, and butter poured over when served.

1 Shallow-fry the liver on both sides in half the butter and remove from the pan.

2 Cook the shallots in the same pan.

3 Add the raspberry vinegar and stock, reduce slightly and strain.

4 Mix in the remaining butter, correct seasoning and pour over the liver.

Note: This recipe can also be prepared using any other fruit or wine vinegar.

PORK

266 Slow-cooked pork loin with white beans and grain mustard

	4 portions	10 portions
White beans		
dried cannellini beans, soaked overnight	150 g	375 g
onion, halved	1	3
clove garlic, split	1	3
sprigs thyme	2	5
salt, to taste		
double cream	50 ml	125 ml
chives, chopped	10 g	20 g
wholegrain mustard	2 tsp	5 tsp
Pork		
short loin pork, eye meat only	½ (1 kg)	1 (2 kg)
vegetable oil	100 ml	250 ml
seasoning		
Braised-pickled fennel		
medium fennel bulbs	2 (200 g)	5 (500 g)
vegetable oil	4 tsp	10 tsp
carrot, peeled	½	1
shallot, peeled	½ (25 g)	1 (50 g)
clove garlic, split	1	2
white wine vinegar	75 ml	180 ml
chicken stock	200 ml	500 ml
butter	50 g	125 g
To finish		
Butter	50 g	125 g
fresh ceps	12	30
reduced chicken stock	150 ml	375 ml
small escarole	1	2
a few sprigs of soft herbs	1	2

nutritional info

1 large portion provides:
2404 kJ/574 kcal
29.4 g fat (of which 14.1 g saturated)
25.1 g carbohydrate (of which 5.6 g sugars)
53.0 g protein
8.6 g fibre

Butter beans were used instead of cannellini beans, and lettuce instead of escarole for this analysis. The pork is sealed with oil, double cream is used with the beans, and oil used to cook the fennel.

For the braised-pickled fennel

1 Remove the tops and root of the fennel, halve and shred the bulb finely.

2 Heat the oil in a saucepan and add all the whole vegetables.

3 Cook for 5–6 minutes without letting them colour.

4 Add the vinegar and cook for a further 2 minutes, then add the chicken stock and simmer until half the liquid is evaporated and the fennel is tender.

5 Remove and discard the carrot and shallot.

6 If making in advance, transfer the mixture to an airtight container and store in the fridge overnight.

For the loin of pork

1 Pre-heat the oven to 90°C.

2 Tie the pork up to ensure that it keeps its shape during and after cooking.

3 Place a large, heavy frying pan over a medium-hot heat and add the vegetable oil.

4 Season the pork with salt and pepper, add the pork to the pan and seal to give a light-brown colour all over

5 Remove the pork from the pan and allow to cool slightly. Wrap in a double layer of clingfilm. (Alternatively, place it in a roasting bag.)

6 Lay the pork on a roasting tray and place in the oven for 1½–2 hours until the pork is slightly firm and has a core temperature of 64°C when measured with a core probe thermometer.

7 Once cooked, remove from the oven but leave the pork wrapped in the plastic until ready for serving – it will remain warm and moist for 20 minutes in a warm kitchen.

For the white beans

1 Drain the soaked beans, place in a saucepan with the onion, garlic and thyme, and add enough cold soft or bottled water to cover the beans by 5 cm. Bring to the boil over a high heat.

2 Reduce the heat to a slight simmer and cook for 20 minutes, add the salt and continue simmering for a further 15 minutes until the beans are cooked through, topping up with extra water as necessary.

3 Drain the beans, reserving half the cooking liquid and passing the cooking liquid through a fine strainer into a clean pan.

4 Add the cream and bring to a simmer over a medium heat, cooking for about 5 minutes or until the cream thickens slightly.

5 Adjust the salt and pepper to taste, cover with plastic wrap and set aside in a warm place for up to 30 minutes – do not allow the sauce to go cold as it may split when reheated. The chives and mustard need to be added at the last moment before serving.

To complete

1 Have the beans and fennel warm and ready to finish.

2 When the pork is cooked and has been resting for at least 15 minutes, whisk the butter into the fennel and adjust the seasoning to taste.

3 Heat 50 g of butter in a frying pan over a moderate heat and cook the cleaned ceps for 3–4 minutes. Add the chicken stock and escarole, and cook until the leaves have wilted.

4 Remove the mixture from the pan and drain.

5 Adjust the seasoning to taste and place in the centre of the warmed serving plates.

6 Finish the fennel with the butter and add this to the plates.

7 Slice the pork loins into 12 x 1 cm slices and lay them on top of the escarole, mushrooms and fennel. Warm the beans and add the mustard and chives. Surround the pork with the white beans.

8 Garnish with the herbs and serve.

Note: All the flavours used in this dish are commonly associated with pork but the various cooking methods and the manner in which the components are finished makes it something special and the flavour extraction is outstanding. The pork loin is initially sealed in hot oil, allowed to cool, then wrapped in plastic and cooked slowly at a very low temperature for 2 hours, ensuring that all the flavours and juices are kept in the meat.

267 Roast shoulder of pork with crackling and apple

	10 portions
Pork	
pork shoulder joint	1–1½ kg
olive oil to rub on joint	
fine sea salt and freshly ground black pepper	
Bramley apple sauce	
Bramley cooking apples	500 g
butter	25 g
caster sugar	3 tbsp
Gravy	
plain flour	2 tsp
meat or vegetable stock	450 ml

nutritional info

♥

1 large portion provides:
1711 kJ/410 kcal
28.6 g fat (of which 9.6 g saturated)
29.1 g carbohydrate (of which 11.7 g sugars)
10.9 g protein
0.8 g fibre

calorie counter

kcal
1000
900
800
700
600
500
400
300
200
100
0

Separate figures were used for the pork crackling and the meat, based on estimated serving sizes. Olive oil is rubbed on the meat and there is butter in the apple sauce.

1 Pre-heat the oven to 180°C.

2 Rub the pork skin all over with kitchen paper. Leave for half an hour for the skin to dry (if the skin is moist it will not make crackling). Check the skin is evenly scored. If it is not, make further cuts in the flesh with a large, very sharp knife.

3 Brush the skin very lightly with oil. Sprinkle the skin with a thin, even layer of salt and a little pepper. Set the joint in a roasting tin and place in a pre-heated oven for 30 minutes, then reduce the temperature to 160°C for a further 1 hour 20 minutes.

4 Meanwhile, make the Bramley apple sauce. Cut the apples into quarters using a small, sharp knife.

Peel, core and slice the quarters then place in a pan with 3 tbsp cold water and bring to the boil. Reduce the heat to medium, cover the pan with a lid and cook for 6–8 minutes, until the apples are soft and pulpy.

5 Remove the apples from the heat and beat with a wooden spoon until smooth, then beat in the butter and sugar. If the sauce is too thin, return it to the heat and cook gently, stirring until it thickens slightly. Transfer to a serving bowl.

6 When the pork is cooked, remove from the oven and rest. Cover loosely with foil and leave for 15 minutes while you make the gravy. Using a large spoon, remove as much surface fat from the pan juices as you can. Place the roasting tin on the hob and reheat the juices. Remove from the heat and stir in the flour. Return to the hob and cook gently for 2 minutes. Gradually add the stock, stirring all the time until the gravy is slightly thickened. Simmer for 5 minutes. Pass and check seasoning.

7 Using a sharp carving knife and a fork to steady the meat, remove the crackling from the joint and place on a board. Cut the crackling into pieces (you can do this with kitchen scissors). Carve the pork into thick slices and serve each portion with some crackling, gravy and a generous spoonful of apple sauce.

Note: As this is a traditional roast, most seasonal vegetables will go with it. This is a pure autumnal dish in every way – rich, flavoursome and, above all, what most would consider a traditional Sunday lunch.

How to get the best crackling on roast pork is the subject of much debate in the kitchen. The secret of success is a good layer of fat beneath the rind. Also, the rind should be scored evenly all over. It helps if you choose a larger joint like this shoulder so there is more time in the oven to develop crisp crackling.

268 Cured-confited belly with sauerkraut and sherry jus

Pork	10 portions
salt	150 g
sugar	50 g
Spanish smoked paprika	20 g
belly trimmed of skin and fat scored (weighing 1.2–1.5 kg)	1
confit oil	2 litres
sprig of thyme	1
bay leaves	3
garlic cloves	3
Sauerkraut	
white cabbage (250 g)	¼ head
lamb jus	500 ml
sherry vinegar	75 ml
Madeira	300 ml
Sherry jus	
oil	100 ml
shallots, finely sliced	3
button mushrooms, finely sliced	400 g
dry sherry	150 ml
Madeira	150 ml
chicken stock	400 ml
lamb jus	100 ml

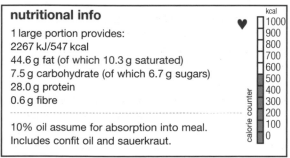

nutritional info

1 large portion provides:
2267 kJ/547 kcal
44.6 g fat (of which 10.3 g saturated)
7.5 g carbohydrate (of which 6.7 g sugars)
28.0 g protein
0.6 g fibre

10% oil assume for absorption into meal.
Includes confit oil and sauerkraut.

kcal
1000
900
800
700
600
500
400
300
200
100
0

calorie counter

For the pork

1 Mix the salt, sugar and paprika together and rub into the pork belly meat side.

2 Wrap in clingfilm and allow to cure for 1½ hours. Rinse quickly under running water, but don't try to wash out all the salt, just pat dry.

3 Roll the belly into a cylindrical shape and tie in even sections.

4 Pre-heat the oven to 87°C. Meanwhile, heat the confit oil on the stove, adding the thyme, bay leaves and garlic. In a thick-bottomed pan, seal the pork all over until golden brown then immerse in the confit oil. Place in the oven for 3 hours.

5 Test if cooked by squeezing with your forefinger and thumb – the meat should just give. Remove carefully and allow to cool at room temperature.

For the sauerkraut

1 Thinly slice the cabbage, removing any stalk.

2 Sweat the cabbage in a pan until it softens.

3 On the side, reduce the lamb jus to 400 ml.

4 Add the sherry vinegar to the Madeira and reduce to 150 ml.

5 When both the jus and Madeira are reduced, add them to the cabbage and continue to reduce until the lamb jus turns into a glace and covers the cabbage.

6 Keep warm.

For the sherry jus

1 Heat the oil in a pan to a high heat, add the shallots and button mushrooms, and pan-fry hard until golden and crisp (this is to enable the flavour from the mushrooms and shallots to be released into the pan, the sherry and Madeira added after this is then absorbed by the mushrooms and more flavour is extracted).

2 Add the Madeira and sherry and reduce by half.

3 Add the chicken stock and lamb jus, and reduce this by half. Reduce to a simmer until a viscous consistency is achieved. Pass and reserve.

To finish

1 Reheat the sauerkraut if cold and place in the centre of the serving dish.

2 Carve the pork carefully into 12 pieces and lay it over the sauerkraut.

3 Pour over the sherry jus and serve.

Note: This is a true Alsace/Germanic dish, which can either be served with freshly boiled potatoes sprinkled with chopped parsley or served with knak, sour bread or even pumpernickel.

Belly of pork is very flavoursome due to its fat content, and salt and pork are a great foil for each other. The curing here offers a deep but subtle salt note – due to the fact that the salt has been added as a cure and not as a seasoning the flavour tends to be deeper and less salty to the taste.

269 Homemade black pudding with apple and onion salad

Preparation of a black pudding

	4 portions	10 portions
Black pudding		
good-quality black pudding	750 g	2 kg
dry black pudding mix	150 g	375 g
water	250 ml	625 ml
fresh pigs' blood	70 ml	175 ml
run of hog skin soaked in water overnight	1	3
Salad		
red onion	1	2
vegetable oil	50 ml	125 ml
garlic clove, crushed	1	2
sprig of thyme	1	2
bay leaf	½	2
To finish		
butter	50 g	125 g
russet apples	2	5
washed and picked organic leaves	250 g	625 g
vinaigrette	50 ml	125 ml

nutritional info

♥

1 large portion provides:
3963 kJ/653 kcal
73.2 g fat (of which 22.7 g saturated)
51.9 g carbohydrate (of which 13.0 g sugars)
25.0 g protein
2.4 g fibre

These estimations are based on fresh black pudding, not dry mix, and hog skin was not included. There is fat in the black pudding and oil is used to roast the onion.

kcal
1000
900
800
700
600
500
400
300
200
100
0
calorie counter

For the black pudding

1 Blitz the fresh black pudding and the dry mix together in a food processor until well mixed and soft to handle.

2 Mix the water and fresh blood together and mix into the dried black pudding mix in a bowl.

3 When incorporated, put the mix in a piping bag and pipe the mix into the hog skin ensuring no air bubbles form in the skin.

4 When piped, tie both ends of the sausage and allow to rest overnight.

5 The following day, place sausage in a pan of warm water and cover with a kitchen cloth.

6 Bring the water up to 80°C and leave for 1 hour at a constant heat.

7 Refresh after 1 hour in cold water and allow to set.

For the salad

1 Pre-heat the oven to 180°C.

2 Peel the red onion whole, retaining the root intact.

3 Cut into 8 equal pieces through the root and mix with the oil, garlic, thyme and bay leaf.

4 Place the mix onto a baking sheet and place in the oven for 5–6 minutes until the onion starts to char.

5 Remove, drain and allow to cool to room temperature.

To finish

1 Cut the black pudding into 5 inch pieces and remove the skin.

2 Heat a little oil in a pan and place in the black pudding pieces (be mindful that there is enough room for the pudding to pan-fry as opposed to steam).

3 Once the black pudding is starting to crisp up add 50 g butter and allow to foam.

4 Meanwhile cut the apple into batons, free from skin and core.

5 Remove the black pudding from the pan, season and place and allow to cool slightly.

6 Lay the onion and apple batons on a plate and top with the vinaigrette-dressed salad.

7 Next to the salad place each portion of 2 pieces of black pudding and serve.

270 Roast stuffed suckling pig

Makes 10–20 portions

A suckling pig is a young milk-fed pig, 8–10 weeks old, weighing 3–5 kg, which takes approximately 2–2½ hours to roast. If the stuffing is cooked separately allow about half an hour less.

A golden-brown, crisp skin is essential, therefore the cooking must always be timed so that the pig does not have to stand for too long before serving. Brush the skin with oil frequently during cooking to ensure its crispness.

Basic stuffing

finely chopped onion, cooked without colour in pork fat or butter	1 kg
fresh bread cubes, soaked in milk and squeezed dry, or fresh breadcrumbs	400 g
butter	100 g
freshly chopped sage *or*	50 g
dried sage	25 g
parsley	50 g
grated nutmeg	
salt and pepper	
eggs	2

nutritional info

1 large portion provides:
1885 kJ/449 kcal
20.6 g fat (of which 10.6 g saturated)
29.1 g carbohydrate (of which 7.3 g sugars)
38.8 g protein
2.3 g fibre

These estimations are based on the amount of meat served per portion. Contains butter and eggs in the stuffing, and is roasted with the skin on.

Thoroughly mix all the ingredients for the stuffing.

Variations can include the addition of any of the following: 200 g chopped chestnuts; 200 g chopped dessert apple or stoned cherries or cranberries; 100 g chopped mushrooms; 100 g chopped bacon, ham or pork sausage meat; juice of 2 crushed cloves of garlic; rosemary or basil in place of sage, or a combination of all three; 60 ml brandy.

1 Stuff the pig loosely with the stuffing mixture and sew up the opening securely with string.

2 Truss the forelegs and hindlegs so that the pig lies flat on its belly during cooking.

3 Place a block of wood in its mouth to keep it open, and cover the ears and tail with foil to prevent burning.

4 Score the pig's back to allow fat to escape.

5 Brush with oil or melted butter and roast at 200°C, basting frequently. Allow 25 minutes for every ½ kg.

6 A few minutes before the pig is cooked, remove the foil from ears and tail.

7 When cooked, transfer the pig to a wooden board, deglaze the pan and make roast gravy. Apple sauce should also be served.

8 Place a red apple in the mouth, and cherries or cranberries in the eye sockets, and serve.

POULTRY & GAME

POULTRY

Origins

The word poultry is used to describe all domestic birds that are bred especially for the table; it covers chickens, turkeys, ducks, geese, guinea fowl and squab (pigeon). Over the years poultry farming has developed enormously and today poultry is the most popular meat from any animal or bird. In Britain alone some 800,000 tons of poultry are eaten each year – this includes free-range, organic and battery-reared chickens.

Choosing and buying

Nowadays poultry is readily available both fresh and frozen, and suppliers sell birds either oven-ready or fresh (with the entrails still in). Generally a large bird gives better value because the meat-to-bone proportion is higher. As well as being available whole, poultry can be bought in individual portions: breasts, drumsticks, thighs, halves, quarters, and so on. Chicken and turkey are also frequently available smoked, as gourmet items.

Cooking

Chicken is a delicate meat and needs considerable cooking due to its high protein content (especially the breast). A high heat would render the fibres tough and dry; therefore consideration needs to be applied in order to deliver the desired result. Much depends on the age of the bird: tender, young poultry can be grilled, roasted or fried; older birds or poultry that has special high-worked muscle groups (for example, guinea fowl, poulet noir) would need slower cooking. For example, the French dish *coq au vin* would tend to be made from older birds – not necessarily cockerels, but birds of 3 kg-plus. Therefore, the age and type of the poultry determines the method and recipe.

Units covered
3FP4, 3FP5,
3FC4, 3FC5

LIST OF RECIPES

Recipe no	page no
Generic recipes	
271 Chestnut and apple forcemeat	247
274 Chicken forcemeat or farce	248
276 Chicken mousse	248
275 Chicken mousse, mousselines and quenelles	248
277 Chicken soufflé	249
278 Chicken soufflé with creamed mushrooms	249
273 Pork, sage and onion forcemeat	247
272 Prune and foie gras stuffing	247
Chicken/guinea fowl	
292 Ballotine of chicken leg with lentils and tarragon	255
279 Breast and wing of chicken (suprême)	250
290 Chicken escalopes	254
291 Chicken escalope with lemon, capers and wilted greens	255
289 Chicken Kiev	254
281 Chicken sauté	250
293 Confit chicken leg with leeks and artichokes	256
282 Cutting for sauté, fricassée, pies, etc.	250
288 Fricassée of guinea fowl with wild mushrooms	253
285 Grilled chicken escalopes with asparagus and balsamic vinegar	252

Recipe no	page no
287 Guinea fowl	253
295 Guinea fowl en papillote with aromatic vegetables and herbs	257
294 Poached guinea fowl with muscat grapes and salsify	256
280 Preparation for suprêmes	250
283 Sauté of chicken chasseur	251
284 Sauté of chicken with mushrooms	251
286 Traditional roast chicken	252
Duck	
300 Ballotine of duck leg with black pudding and apple	261
301 Confit duck leg rillette	261
297 Confit duck leg with red cabbage and green beans	258
298 Garbure of duck	259
299 Pan-fried breast of duck with vanilla and lime	259
296 Roast Gressingham duck with jasmine tea and fruit sauce	257
Goose	
302 Goose	262
303 Roast goose with citrus fruits	262
Turkey	
308 Pan-fried turkey escalopes with prunes and smoked bacon	264
305 Stuffed leg of turkey	263

Storage

Fresh, uncooked poultry should be used within two to three days of purchase, provided it has been kept in a refrigerator. Poultry must be covered at all times and kept below all other food items, mainly on the bottom shelf; to ensure that no cross-contamination occurs. If the poultry has been purchased frozen, it should be removed from the freezer, placed directly into the fridge on a drip tray, covered and allowed to defrost thoroughly in the fridge. Cooked poultry too should be used within two to three days and kept separately from all other raw products.

GAME

Origins

The word game is used, for culinary purposes, to describe animals or birds that are hunted for food, although many types of categorised game are now being bred domestically – squab (pigeon), ducks, venison, etc. Wild animals, because of their diet and general lifestyle, have select enzymes in their tissues, which are more abundant in game than in poultry. These tissues break down or metabolise meat proteins; they become active about 24 hours after the animal has been killed, softening the meat and making it gelatinous and more palatable, as well as giving the characteristic

Recipe no	page no	Recipe no	page no
307 Traditional roast turkey	263	322 Roast partridge	272
304 Turkey	263	Grouse	
306 Turkey escalopes	263	324 Traditional roast grouse	273
Pigeon		Quail	
310 Pot au feu of pigeon	266	327 Pot-roasted quail with roast carrots and	
309 Roast pigeon with red chard, celeriac		mashed potato	275
and treacle	265	325 Quails	274
311 Sauté of pigeon salad with rocket,		326 Quail with pomegranate and blood	
Parmesan and beetroot	266	orange	275
Feathered game		Rabbit	
312 Game farce	268	330 Braised baron of rabbit with olives and	
319 Grouse	269	tomatoes	277
314 Partridge	269	331 Casserole of tame rabbit forestière	278
313 Pheasant	269	328 Rabbits	276
316 Snipe	269	329 Rabbit saddle stuffed with its own livers	276
318 Teal	269	Hare	
317 Wild duck	269	332 Hare	279
315 Woodcock	269	333 Jugged hare	279
Pheasant		Venison	
320 Poached pheasant crown with chestnuts		337 Medallions of venison with red wine,	
and cabbage	270	walnuts and chocolate	282
321 Roast breast of pheasant with vanilla		336 Pot roast rack of venison with	
and pear	271	buttered greens and Merlot sauce	280
Partridge		334 Venison	280
323 Braised partridge with cabbage	273	335 Venison cutlets, chops and steaks	280

'gamey' flavour. They also contain micro-organisms (anaerobes), which also help to break down the proteins.

Choosing and buying

The most important factor when buying game is to know its life age and its hanging age since this will determine the method of cookery. Indications of age are by no means infallible, but there are some general guidelines when buying young birds – soft-textured feet, pliable breastbones – and young partridges have pointed flight feathers (the first large feather of the wing), while in older birds, the feathers are more rounded. There are many other distinctive guidelines you can use when selecting game, however the grading of game is a specialised subject and best left to the experts.

Hanging of game

Game bought from a main dealer will probably have been hung correctly. If, however, you require your game (or any other meat that benefits from hanging) to be hung specifically for you, speak to your butcher or game dealer. The general rules are to hang in a cool, dry, airy place, protected from flies to prevent maggot infestation. However, there is no real need to hang game, due to the metabolic enzymes present, so if you object to the strong flavour hanging promotes, a short hanging period, or no hanging at all, may be preferable. As a general rule you should hang the carcass until you detect the first whiff of tainting. In Britain, birds are usually hung from their heads, feet down, and rabbits and other game hung with their heads down.

Cooking of game

Game meat responds best to roasting. Young game birds in particular should be roasted and it is traditional to leave them unstuffed. Due to the low fat content of game, especially wild non-domestic varieties, added fat in the form of sliced streaky bacon, lardons and the like can be wrapped around the bird to help baste while cooking, retaining moisture. Older, tougher game or high-worked muscle groups, such as a haunch of venison, should be casseroled or made into pies or terrines. Marinating in oil, vinegar or wine with herbs and spices helps make tough meat more tender; it may also enhance the taste and it speeds up the action of the metabolic enzyme that breaks the game down.

Storage of game

It would be wise to allow game to be hung at specific game dealers as current legislation does not allow a normal kitchen environment to hang or pluck game. Game should be wrapped well and careful consideration given to its age; strict labelling is essential because, when in prime condition, the meat may have a slightly tainted smell, which may be difficult to discern from the smell that denotes the meat is past its best.

Seasonality of game

	JAN	FEB	MAR	APR	MAY	JUN	JUL	AUG	SEP	OCT	NOV	DEC
Furred												
Hare												
Rabbit												
Venison												
Feathered												
Goose (wild)												
Goose (farmed)												
Grouse								12th				
Mallard												
Moorhen												
Partridge (English grey leg)												
Partridge (French red leg)												
Pheasant												
Pigeon (farmed)												
Pigeon (English wood)												

	JAN	FEB	MAR	APR	MAY	JUN	JUL	AUG	SEP	OCT	NOV	DEC
Quail												
Snipe								12th				
Teal												
Woodcock												

Code:

Available

At best

PREPARATION

Drawing and washing

This is the process that is carried out when the bird is sold with all its entrails still inside. To remove, make a small lateral incision into the backside of the bird, then insert your forefinger and middle finger, and roll them around the inner cavity of the bird, thus loosening the membrane that holds the innards in. When loose, remove from the wider backside and discard. Ensure that all the innards are removed, wash and dry well.

Leg removal and crowning

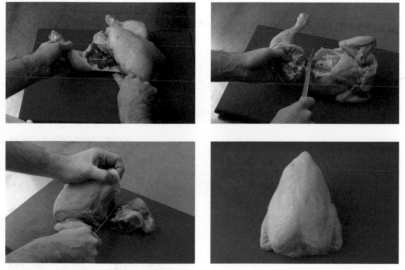

Leg removal and preparing the crown

Preparation of ballotines

Boning (for tunnel boning, see Chapter 6, page 208)

Preparation of ballotines

Stuffing

In the interests of food safety, stuffing should be used only in small birds (e.g. poussins or ballotines), where a savoury stuffing is required. For larger birds (e.g. turkeys, chickens, geese, ducks) it is safer to cook the stuffing separately and the term 'forcemeat' can be used in place of stuffing.

Methods of cookery

Method of cookery applied	Recipe covering method
Bake	277, 278
Braise	323, 330
Casserole	310, 331
Confit	293, 297, 301
Deep-fry	289
En papillote	295
Grill	285
Jugged	333
Pan-fry	291, 299, 308, 337
Poach	276, 294, 320
Pot roast	327, 336
Roast	286, 292, 296, 300, 303, 307, 309, 310, 321, 322, 324, 326, 329
Sauté	283, 284, 311

POULTRY
Generic recipes

271 Chestnut and apple forcemeat

For turkey – enough for an 8 kg bird

eating apples, peeled and cored	450 g
tinned whole unsweetened chestnuts, roughly mashed	900 g
salted or fresh belly of pork, cut into small dice	175 g
shallots, finely chopped (approx. 50 g)	2
garlic cloves, crushed	2
parsley, finely chopped	3 tbsp
egg	1

1 Gently stew the apples, covered, in 1 tbsp water until reduced to a pulp.

2 Add to the roughly mashed chestnuts, pork, shallots, garlic and parsley, and bind with the egg.

272 Prune and foie gras stuffing

For goose – enough for a 6 kg bird

prunes, stoned and soft	49–50
white wine *or*	300 ml
dry white vermouth	150 ml
beef stock	425 ml
goose liver, finely chopped (approx. 200 g)	1
shallots, finely chopped	2 tbsp
butter	10 g
port	150 ml
foie gras, chopped	110 g
breadcrumbs	2–3 tbsp
allspice	pinch
thyme	pinch
salt and pepper, to taste	

1 Simmer the prunes with the wine and stock in a covered pan for about 10 minutes, until tender. Drain them, reserving the cooking liquid.

2 Sauté the goose liver and shallots in butter in a small sauté pan for 2 minutes. Scrape into a mixing bowl.

3 Boil the port in the sauté pan until reduced to 2 tbsp. Add to the mixing bowl.

4 Add the foie gras to the bowl and mix well until everything is incorporated. If the mixture is too wet for easy stuffing, beat in the breadcrumbs.

5 Season to taste with the allspice, thyme, salt and pepper. Fill each prune with 1 tsp stuffing, then stuff them into the cavity, and skewer or tie closed.

273 Pork, sage and onion forcemeat

For turkey – enough for an 8 kg bird

large onion, finely chopped (approx. 100 g)	1
dried sage	1 heaped tsp
white breadcrumbs	4 heaped tbsp
boiling water	2–3 tbsp
sausage meat	900 g
salt and freshly ground black pepper	

1 Mix the onion, sage and breadcrumbs in a large bowl, then add the boiling water and cool thoroughly.

2 Work the sausage meat into it and season.

274 Chicken forcemeat or farce

	4 portions
prepared chicken (without skin or bone)	400 g
salt and pepper	
nutmeg	
whites of egg	3
double cream, very cold	375–500 ml

1. Remove all the sinew from the flesh of the chicken.

2. Lightly season and process to a purée.

3. Gradually add the egg whites, mixing thoroughly, then pass through a sieve.

4. Place mixture in a bowl on ice until very cold.

5. While on ice gradually combine cream, mixing thoroughly. Test a little of the mixture by gently cooking in simmering water. If the mixture is too light add a little more white of egg; if too stiff, add a little more cream. Check seasoning.

nutritional info

1 large portion provides:
2407 kJ/581.6 kcal
52.4 g fat (of which 31.9 g saturated)
1.6 g carbohydrate (of which 1.6 g sugars)
26.0 g protein
0.0 g fibre

Contains double cream.

kcal: 1000 900 800 700 600 500 400 300 200 100 0 (calorie counter)

275 Chicken mousse, mousselines and quenelles

These chicken dishes are smooth and light in texture and easy to digest. They are made from a mixture known as chicken forcemeat or farce (see recipe 274).

Mousses are cooked in buttered moulds in a bain-marie in a moderate oven, then turned out of the mould for service. Therefore the basic mixture must be fairly firm so that the mousse does not break up. They can be cooked in individual, or 2- or 4-portion moulds.

Mousselines are moulded using two tablespoons, which are dipped into hot water to prevent the mixture sticking to them. The mousselines are then placed into a buttered shallow dish and carefully covered with chicken stock. They are then covered with buttered paper and cooked gently in the oven. Usually two mousselines are served to a portion.

Quenelles are shaped with two spoons as for mousselines but the sizes can be varied by using different-sized spoons, according to requirements, e.g. using teaspoons if the quenelles are required for vol-au-vent. The mixture can also be piped into pea-sized shapes and used to garnish soups.

Note: Mousse, mousseline and quenelles may also be made from other foods, e.g. ham, hare, partridge, pheasant, quail. They can be prepared in different sizes according to the dish requirement and can be used as a light first course (e.g. mousselines of quail, fresh herb sauce), as a main course (e.g. mousselines of ham with spinach and cheese sauce), or as a garnish to other dishes.

276 Chicken mousse

chicken breast	350 ml
whipping cream	250 ml
salt and pepper to season	

1. Roughly dice the chicken and place in the freezer for 10 minutes to chill.

2. When the chicken is cold, place in a food processor and blend slightly, then season with a little salt.

3. Pour in the cold cream gradually until all of it has emulsified with the chicken.

4. Remove and test poach in a little simmering water, adjust the seasoning and store well clingfilmed in the refrigerator.

277 Chicken soufflé

	4 portions	10 portions
raw chicken, without skin or sinew	250 g	600 g
butter	50 g	125 g
thick velouté	250 ml	600 ml
salt and pepper		
egg, separated	3	8

nutritional info

1 large portion provides:
397 kJ/94.6 kcal
5.1 g fat (of which 3.2 g saturated)
0.4 g carbohydrate (of which 0.4 g sugars)
11.7 g protein
0.0 g fibre

Eggs and butter are used to make the souffle.

kcal
1000
900
800
700
600
500
400
300
200
100
0

calorie counter

1 Finely dice the chicken and cook in the butter.

2 Add to the velouté and purée in a food processor.

3 Pass through a fine sieve and season.

4 Beat the yolks into the warm mixture.

5 Fold in the stiffly beaten whites carefully.

6 Place into individual buttered moulds or one mould.

7 Bake at 220–230°C for approximately 15 minutes and serve.

8 Serve a suitable sauce separately, for example mushroom or suprême sauce.

Note: for a lighter soufflé use 3 egg yolks and 4 egg whites.

It is advisable to add a little egg white powder to the fresh egg whites to strengthen them, which will develop a better foam and improve the rise.

278 Chicken soufflé with creamed mushrooms
René Pauvert

	4 portions	10 portions
chicken breast	100 g	250 g
soft unsalted butter	5 g	12 g
single cream	80 g	200 g
salt and cayenne, to taste		
white breadcrumbs, to coat		
egg whites	7	18

1 Lightly season the chicken, purée with the butter and place in refrigerator for 10–15 minutes until cold.

2 Pass the mixture through a fine sieve and place in a stainless-steel bowl on ice.

3 Carefully incorporate the cream little by little.

4 Check seasoning and keep it cool.

5 Lightly butter individual soufflé moulds and coat with fresh white breadcrumbs.

6 Whisk the egg whites with a pinch of salt until stiff.

7 Add a small amount of egg white to the mousseline, incorporate well, then gently fold in the remainder, season to taste.

8 Pour half the mixture into the moulds, add a

spoonful of the ragôut, then the remainder of the mixture.

9 Bake at 200°C for about 14 minutes.

10 Serve with a morille cream sauce.

Ragôut of mushrooms with cream

	4 portions	10 portions
diced raw chicken breast or thigh	25 g	60 g
butter	5 g	12 g
mushrooms, quartered	25 g	60 g
shallots, finely chopped	5 g	12 g
white wine	2 tbsp	5 tbsp
brown chicken stock	100 ml	250 ml
double cream	50 ml	120 ml
salt and cayenne, to taste		

1 Sauté the chicken in butter. Add the mushrooms, finely chopped shallots, deglaze with white wine, reduce, add the chicken stock, reduce and then add the cream.

2 Adjust to a sauce consistency, season to taste and allow to cool.

Chicken/guinea fowl

279 Breast and wing of chicken (suprême)

The word suprême is traditionally used to describe half the white meat of a whole chicken. In contemporary menu practice the word wing or breast is often used in place of suprême.

Therefore there are two suprêmes to a chicken. Each has a fillet, which is lifted off, the sinew is removed, an incision is made along the thick side of the

suprême and the fillet inserted, then the suprême is lightly flattened.

Suprêmes can be poached or shallow-fried in butter, oil or margarine. When shallow-fried they can be garnished as for sauté of chicken. For certain dishes the breasts can be stuffed, floured or crumbed before shallow-frying.

280 Preparation for suprêmes

The suprême is the wing and half the breast of a chicken with the trimmed wing bone attached, i.e. the white meat of one chicken yields two suprêmes.

1 Use chicken weighing 1¼–1½ kg.

2 Cut off both legs from the chicken.

3 Remove the skin from the breasts.

4 Remove the wishbone.

5 Scrape the wing bone bare adjoining the breasts.

6 Cut off the winglets near the joints leaving 1½–2 cm of bare bone attached to the breasts.

7 Cut the breasts close to the breast bone and follow the bone down to the wing joint.

8 Cut through the joint.

9 Lay the chicken on its side and pull the suprêmes off, assisting with the knife.

10 Lift the fillets from the suprêmes and remove the sinew from each.

11 Make an incision lengthways, along the thick side of the suprêmes, open and place the fillets inside.

12 Close, lightly flatten with a bat moistened with water and trim if necessary.

281 Chicken sauté

Chickens 1¼–1½ kg in weight are suitable to cut into 8 pieces for 4 portions. The pieces can be prepared on the bone or skinned and boned out. Boning out slightly increases shrinkage, the portions look smaller and preparation time is increased, but it facilitates ease of eating.

Chicken is prepared in this manner for fricassée, blanquette and chicken pies; the winglets, giblets and carcass are used for chicken stock. There are many garnishes for chicken sauté and a few examples follow. Further variety can be introduced by using herbs (e.g. tarragon, basil, rosemary etc.), wines (e.g. dry white, dry sherry, vermouth) and different garnishes (e.g. wild mushrooms and ceps).

282 Cutting for sauté, fricassée, pies, etc.

1 Remove the feet at the first joint.

2 Remove the legs from the carcass.

3 Cut each leg in two at the joint.

4 Remove the wishbone. Remove winglets and trim.

5 Remove the wings carefully, leaving two equal portions on the breast.

6 Remove the breast and cut in two.

7 Trim the carcass and cut into three pieces.

283 Sauté of chicken chasseur

	4 portions	10 portions
Sautéed chicken		
See recipes 281 and 282		
Chasseur sauce		
oil	25 g	60 g
shallots, chopped	20 g	50 g
garlic cloves, chopped	1	2
button mushrooms, finely sliced	75 g	185 g
white wine	75 ml	185 ml
reduced brown stock	250 ml	625 ml
tomato concassée	100 g	250 g
parsley, chopped	1 tsp	2½ tsp
tarragon, chopped	1 tsp	2½ tsp
salt and pepper		

1 Prepare and cook the chicken for sauté (see recipes 281 and 282), dress neatly in a serving dish and keep warm.

2 Heat the oil in a thick-bottomed sauté pan and add the shallots, cooking gently for 2–3 minutes without colour.

3 Add the garlic and mushrooms. Cover and cook for a further 2–3 minutes without colour. Add the wine and reduce by half. Add the reduced brown stock and simmer for 5–10 minutes.

4 Adjust the sauce by further reduction and correct the seasoning. Just before serving, add the tomato concassée and chopped herbs.

5 Place the chicken portions either on a plate or an earthenware dish, nap the sauce and serve immediately.

Note: The tomato petals for the concassée can be prepared a day in advance and allowed to dry out on kitchen paper.

nutritional info

1 large portion (150 g of cooked chicken) provides:
959 kJ/228 kcal
9.6 g fat (of which 1.7 g saturated)
1.5 g carbohydrate (of which 1.2 g sugars)
34.1 g protein
0.6 g fibre

There is no additional fat in the sauce.

kcal: 1000 900 800 700 600 500 400 300 200 100 0 — calorie counter

284 Sauté of chicken with mushrooms

	4 portions	10 portions
Sautéed chicken		
See recipes 281 and 282		
Mushroom sauce		
oil	25 g	60 g
shallots, chopped	20 g	50 g
garlic cloves, chopped	1	2
button mushrooms, finely sliced	25 g	65 g
field mushrooms, sliced	25 g	65 g
wild mushrooms, cut into quarters	50 g	125 g
white wine	75 ml	185 ml
reduced brown stock	125 ml	310 ml
chicken stock	125 ml	310 ml
whipping cream	150 ml	375 ml
sherry vinegar	2 tbsp	5 tbsp
salt and pepper		
chives, chopped	1 tsp	2 tsp

nutritional info

1 large portion (150g cooked chicken) provides:
1531 kJ/368 kcal
24.6 g fat (of which 11.1 g saturated)
1.8 g carbohydrate (of which 1.5 g sugars)
34.6 g protein
0.2 g fibre

The sauce contains whipping cream.

kcal: 1000 900 800 700 600 500 400 300 200 100 0 — calorie counter

1 Prepare and cook the chicken for sauté (see recipes 281 and 282).

2 Heat oil in a thick-bottomed sauté pan and add the shallots, cooking gently for 2–3 minutes without colour.

3 Add the garlic and mushrooms. Cover and cook for a further 2–3 minutes without colour. Add the wine and reduce by half. Add the reduced brown stock and chicken stock, and simmer for 15 minutes.

4 Add the whipping cream, bring to the boil and turn down to a simmer.

5 Adjust the consistency of the sauce by further reduction and correct the seasoning. On tasting the sauce, to achieve a cleaner flavour of mushrooms and stock, 'season' with the sherry vinegar, which will allow the bold flavours to come through.

6 Just before serving, add the chopped chives.

7 Place the chicken portions either on a plate or an earthenware dish, nap the sauce and serve immediately.

Note: Ballotines can be cooked and served as for sauté recipes. The mushroom sauce can be made and applied to most poultry and light game birds, and even pork.

285 Grilled chicken escalopes with asparagus and balsamic vinegar

	4 portions	10 portions
asparagus pieces	20	50
banana shallots finely diced	2	5
vinaigrette	20 ml	50 ml
lemon, juice of	1	3
chicken breast escalopes (see recipe 290)	4 × 150 g	10 × 150 g
vegetable oil	50 ml	125 ml
salt and pepper		
aged balsamic vinegar	20 ml	50 ml

1 Cook the prepared asparagus in boiling salted water for approx. 4 minutes, refresh in ice water.

2 Sweat the shallots without colour until soft, drain and mix with the vinaigrette and lemon juice to form a dressing.

3 Place the escalopes on an oiled tray and season with salt and pepper.

4 Place the escalopes on a pre-heated grill and grill gently for 3–4 minutes either side, ensuring an even bar mark on the sides.

5 Warm the asparagus through in boiling water, drain and place in the shallot dressing.

6 Take the cooked chicken escalopes and place on a plate or serving dish, lay the asparagus on top, finish with the dressing and balsamic vinegar.

7 Serve immediately.

Note: If a grill is unavailable it is possible to obtain the same marking effect with the use of a bar-marking iron – this process is known as quadrillage.

nutritional info

1 large portion provides:
1329 kJ/318 kcal
17.0 g fat (of which 2.4 g saturated)
3.5 g carbohydrate (of which 2.9 g sugars)
37.8 g protein
1.2 g fibre

Little oil is used in cooking and the escalopes are grilled.

286 Traditional roast chicken

	4 portions	10 portions
chicken	1 × 1.3 kg	2 × 1.6 kg
salt		
oil	50 g	125 g
brown stock	125 ml	310 ml
game chips	25 g	60 g
bunch watercress		
bread sauce	125 ml	310 ml

nutritional info

1 large portion (including game chips and bread sauce) provides:
1931 kJ/465 kcal
35.7 g fat (of which 8.8 g saturated)
5.6 g carbohydrate (of which 2.3 g sugars)
30.7 g protein
0.3 g fibre

1 Season the chicken inside and out with salt and place on its side in a roasting tin. Cover with the oil.

2 Place in hot oven for approximately 20–25 minutes then turn on to the other leg.

3 Cook for a further 20–25 minutes approximately. Baste frequently.

4 To test if cooked, pierce with a fork between the drumstick and thigh, and hold over a plate. The juice issuing from the chicken should not show

any sign of blood. If using a temperature probe, proceed as for turkey.

5 Make roast gravy with the stock and sediment in the roasting tray.

6 Serve with game chips in front and the watercress at the back of the bird, and with bread sauce and roast gravy separately.

Note: This recipe can be applied to all poultry, with the cooking times adjusted to suit the size of the bird (e.g. poussin, capon).

287 Guinea fowl

Guinea fowl can be used in a similar manner to chicken. The flesh is of a dry nature and has little fat, therefore when roasted or pot roasted it is usual to bard (see page 268) the guinea fowl and not to overcook it.

288 Fricassée of guinea fowl with wild mushrooms

	4 portions	10 portions
guinea fowl	1 × 1.3 kg	2 × 1.6 kg
salt and pepper		
butter	50 g	125 g
flour	35 g	90 g
chicken stock	½ litre	1¼ litres
yolks of eggs	1–2	3–5
cream	4 tsp	10 tsp
wild mushrooms, cooked and chopped	200 g	500 g
parsley, chopped	2 tsp	5 tsp

nutritional info

1 large portion provides:
2537 kJ/606 kcal
28.3 g fat (of which 11.6 g saturated)
7.5 g carbohydrate (of which 0.7 g sugars)
80.7 g protein
0.9 g fibre

Butter is used to cook the fowl, and egg yolks and cream in the sauce. Partridge was used instead of guinea fowl for this analysis.

1 Cut the guinea fowl as for sauté (see recipes 281 and 282), and season with salt and pepper.

2 Place the butter in a sauté pan. Heat gently. Add pieces of bird. Cover with a lid.

3 Cook gently on both sides without colouring. Mix in the flour.

4 Cook out carefully without colouring. Gradually mix in the stock.

5 Bring to the boil and skim. Allow to simmer gently until cooked.

6 Mix the yolks and cream in a basin (liaison).

7 Pick out the guinea fowl into a clean pan.

8 Pour a little boiling sauce on to the yolks and cream, and mix well.

9 Pour all back into the sauce, combine thoroughly but do not re-boil.

10 Correct the seasoning and pass through a fine strainer.

Fricassée of guinea fowl with wild mushrooms (a) classical and (b) modern

11 Add the cooked wild mushrooms, mix and incorporate well.

12 Pour over the guinea fowl and reheat without boiling.

13 Serve sprinkled with chopped parsley. The dish may also be garnished with heart-shaped croutons, fried in butter.

Note: To reduce the cost of this recipe, button or field mushrooms can be used, although the flavour of the wild mushrooms makes an excellent base for the guinea fowl.

289 Chicken Kiev

	4 portions	10 portions
suprêmes of chicken	4 × 150 g	10 × 150 g
butter	100 g	250 g
seasoned flour	25 g	65 g
eggs	2	5
breadcrumbs	100 g	250 g

1 Make an incision along the thick sides of the suprêmes. Insert 25 g cold butter into each. Season.

2 Pass through seasoned flour, eggwash and crumbs, ensuring complete coverage. Eggwash and crumb twice if necessary.

3 Deep-fry, drain and serve.

Note: Chopped garlic and parsley can be added to the butter before insertion to add a variation, or other fine herbs can be used – for example, tarragon or chives.

nutritional info

♥

1 large portion provides:
2092 kJ/500 kcal
26.0 g fat (of which 14.4 g saturated)
24.4 g carbohydrate (of which 0.9 g sugars)
43.5 g protein
0.7 g fibre

Butter is used in the kiev and the cooking method is deep frying.

calorie counter

kcal
1000
900
800
700
600
500
400
300
200
100
0

290 Chicken escalopes

These can be prepared in a number of ways.

1 75–100 g slices of chicken breast thinly beaten out using a little water, then left plain, or flour, egg and crumbed.

2 Boned and skinned chicken thighs treated as above.

3 Minced raw breast and/or leg of chicken bound with a little egg white, shaped, flattened and either left plain, or egg and crumbed.

Chicken escalopes can then be cooked and served in a wide variety of ways using different garnishes and sauces. Any recipe using a cut of chicken can be adapted to use chicken escalopes, but often the simpler recipes are most effective, e.g. egg and crumbed chicken escalope with asparagus tips.

291 Chicken escalope with lemon, capers and wilted greens

	4 portions	10 portions
chicken breast escalopes (see recipe 290)	4 × 150 g	10 × 150 g
pané anglaise	250 g	600 g
lemons, peeled and pithed, leaving the fruit only	2	5
vegetable oil	50 ml	125 ml
prepared and blanched mixed greens, e.g. spinach, spring cabbage, pak choi	250 g	625 g
butter	50 g	125 g
salt and pepper		
baby capers	2 tbsp	5 tbsp

1 Take the escalopes, pané evenly and set aside.

2 Slice the lemon into 8 even slices, removing the seeds.

3 To a pre-heated pan, add the oil and gently place in the chicken.

4 Cook gently on an even heat for approx. 3–4 minutes both sides until the breadcrumbs are an even golden brown.

5 Reheat the greens in the melted butter and season lightly.

6 Place the greens in the centre of the plate and top with a chicken escalope.

7 Place 2 slices of lemon on the chicken and sprinkle the capers on and around to finish.

Note: This dish will work equally well with a plain escalope of turkey, veal or pork. Or why not pané using ground porridge oats for a healthier option?

nutritional info

1 large portion provides:
2393 kJ/571 kcal
28.52 g fat (of which 9.40 g saturated)
35.33 g carbohydrate (of which 2.31 g sugars)
45.3 g protein
1.92 g fibre

Oil is used to pan fry the chicken and butter to cook the pak choi. Capers were used instead of gherkins for this analysis.

292 Ballotine of chicken leg with lentils and tarragon

		4 portions	10 portions
large chicken legs		4 × 200 g	10 × 200 g
chicken mousse (see recipe 276)		300 g	750 g
oil		50 ml	125 ml
cooked lentils (dry)	filling	75 g	185 g
chives, chopped		1 tsp	3 tsp
tarragon, chopped		2 tsp	5 tsp
chicken stock		125 ml	500 ml

1 Bone out the chicken as for ballotine (see page 246).

2 Combine all the ingredients for the filling well, taking care not to overwork the mousse as splitting may occur.

3 Fill the chicken leg cavity with the mousse and carefully wrap in foil, ensuring the mousse is well encased in the chicken leg.

4 Place the leg in the pre-heated oven for 25 minutes, then remove and allow to rest for a further 5 minutes.

5 Remove from the foil, place in a hot pan with the oil and cook until golden brown, rest for a further 3 minutes.

6 While resting, deglaze the pan with the chicken stock, scraping the base of the pan for residual cooking matter, reduce by two-thirds.

7 Carve in to three pieces, serve with a seasonal garnish and pour over the roasting juices.

Note: If large legs are used for this recipe it makes a hearty winter dish that could be served with braised vegetables or a simple gratin dauphinoise drizzled with the roast pan juices from the legs.

nutritional info

1 large portion provides:
2756 kJ/654 kcal
15.13 g fat (of which 4.23 g saturated)
13.68 g carbohydrate (of which 0.85 g sugars)
116.2 g protein
1.44 g fibre

Oil is used to brown the leg.

293 Confit chicken leg with leeks and artichokes

	4 portions	10 portions
confit oil*	1 litre	2½ litres
garlic cloves	4	10
bay leaf	1	3
sprig of thyme		
chicken legs	4 × 200 g	10 × 200 g
vegetable oil	50 ml	125 ml
globe artichokes, prepared, cooked and cut into quarters	4	10
whole leeks, blanched	2	5
brown chicken stock	250 ml	625 ml
butter	50 g	125 g
chives, chopped	1 tbsp	3 tbsp
seasoning		

* Confit oil is 50/50 olive oil and vegetable oil infused with herbs, garlic, whole spice or any specific flavour you wish to impart into the oil; then, through slow cooking in the oil, the foodstuff picks up the flavour.

1 Gently heat the confit oil, add the garlic, bay and thyme.

2 Put the chicken legs in the oil and place on a medium to low heat, ensuring the legs are covered.

3 Cook gently for 3–3½ hours.

4 To test if the legs are cooked, squeeze the flesh on the thigh bone and it should just fall away.

5 When cooked, remove the legs carefully and place on a draining tray.

6 Heat the vegetable oil in a medium sauté pan, add the artichokes and leeks, colour slightly and then add the brown chicken stock.

7 Reduce the heat to a simmer and cook for 4–5 minutes; meanwhile place the confit leg on a baking tray and place in a pre-heated oven at 210°C; remove when the skin is golden brown (approx. 5 minutes), taking care as the meat is delicate.

8 Place the chicken in a serving dish or on a plate, check the leeks and artichokes are cooked through, and bring the stock to a rapid boil, working in the butter to form an emulsion.

9 Add the chopped chives to the sauce and nap over the chicken leg.

Note: This dish utilises the by-product of the chicken crown; it is not only very cost-effective but has great depth of flavour due to the work the muscle group has done.

294 Poached guinea fowl with muscat grapes and salsify

	4 portions	10 portions
chicken stock	2 litres	5 litres
guinea fowl crowns	2 (300 g)	5 (750 g)
vegetable oil	50 ml	125 ml
button onions	12	30
reduced chicken stock	250 g	625 g
natural yoghurt	100 g	250 g
juice of lemon	1	3
cooked salsify batons	200 g	500 g
salt and pepper		
peeled muscat grapes	250 g	625 g

1 Bring the stock up to a simmer; place the crowns in the stock and simmer for 11 minutes.

2 Meanwhile, place the oil in a medium pan and heat to a moderate heat. Place the onions in the pan and colour slightly. Add the reduced chicken stock and cook the onions gently.

3 When the onions are cooked put to one side and retain. Remove the guinea fowl crowns and rest for 2–3 minutes, breast-side down.

4 Remove the breasts from the crown (see page 245) and check if cooked; if not quite cooked place back in the cooking liquor for 1–2 minutes. Then place the breasts on a plate or in a serving dish and keep warm.

5 Add the yoghurt, lemon juice and salsify to the onions with the reduced stock. Warm slightly – *do not boil* – adjust the seasoning, add the peeled grapes and pour over the guinea fowl.

Note: Recipes 293 and 294 can be applied to most light poultry dishes, and the sauce may also apply to not only poached poultry but also roast. If using with a roast bird, why not emulsify some of the fat from the roasting pan to increase the flavour of the sauce? If muscat grapes are unavailable, normal green table grapes will suffice.

295 Guinea fowl en papillote with aromatic vegetables and herbs

	4 portions	10 portions
guinea fowl breasts	4 × 150 g	10 × 150 g
butter	50 g	125 g
shallots, chopped	25 g	65 g
onions, sliced	25 g	65 g
carrots, cut into julienne	25 g	65 g
leeks, cut into julienne	25 g	65 g
sticks of lemon grass	1	2½
sprigs lemon thyme	3	7
oil	25 g	65 g
dry white wine	100 ml	250 ml
seasoning		
coriander, chopped	15 g	35 g

1 In a pre-heated pan seal off the guinea fowl breasts in butter.

2 Sweat the shallots, onions, carrots, leeks and herbs in half the butter without colour. Add the wine and allow to reduce.

3 Season and add the coriander.

4 Cut greaseproof paper or aluminium foil into large heart shapes, big enough to hold one breast each. Oil the paper or foil liberally.

5 Place a small pile of the vegetable and herb mix to one side of the centre of the paper or foil. Place a breast on top and cover with a little of the wine mix. Fold or pleat the paper or foil tightly. Place on an oiled tray in a hot oven (240°C) until the bag expands. Cook for approximately 8 minutes. Serve immediately.

Note: This method of cookery is very healthy as little oil or fat is used, therefore it can be adopted for most poultry preparations. The choice of aromats or herbs used will obviously reflect the end product. One thing to bear in mind, though, is that hard herbs and big pieces of aromats will not release their flavour quickly enough to penetrate the protein.

nutritional info

1 large portion provides:
1540 kJ/370 kcal
23.82 g fat (of which 9.15 g saturated)
1.81 g carbohydrate (of which 1.43 g sugars)
37.2 g protein
0.46 g fibre

Butter is used to seal the guinea fowl and sweat off the vegetables, and the paper or foil used for the papillote is oiled. Partridge was used instead of guinea fowl for this analysis.

calorie counter: 1000 900 800 700 600 500 400 300 200 100 0 kcal

Duck

Recipes are for birds of approx. 1.6 kg

296 Roast Gressingham duck with jasmine tea and fruit sauce

	4 portions	10 portions
sultanas	100 g	250 g
hot jasmine tea	200 ml	500 ml
oven-ready Gressingham ducklings, wishbones removed, wings and neck cut short (reserve for sauce)	1 × 1.6 kg	2 × 2 kg
water	700 ml	1¾ l
unsalted butter	10 g	25 g
caster sugar	10 g	25 g
orange juice	150 ml	375 ml
soy sauce	1 tsp	3 tsp
cherry brandy	100 ml	250 ml
jasmine tea leaves	10 g	25 g
lime, juice of	¼	1
salt and pepper		
duck fat	1 tbsp	3 tbsp

nutritional info

1 large portion provides:
2045 kJ/487 kcal
18.55 g fat (of which 6.56 g saturated)
32.88 g carbohydrate (of which 18.55 g sugars)
40.5 g protein
0.56 g fibre

Butter and duck fat are used to make the sauce, and fat remains in the flesh of the duck.

calorie counter: 1000 900 800 700 600 500 400 300 200 100 0 kcal

1 Soak the sultanas in hot jasmine tea for 24 hours.

2 Chop the wings and neck into small pieces. Place in a large pan and caramelise.

3 Drain and cover with water, bring to the boil and skim.

4 Pass through a fine sieve and boil to reduce to 200 ml. Keep warm.

5 In a separate pan, melt the butter and sugar together to make a caramel. Add the orange juice, soy sauce, cherry brandy and the reduced duck stock, boil and reduce by half.

6 Bring to simmering point, add the jasmine tea leaves and leave to infuse for 1 minute.

7 Add the lime juice, taste and correct seasoning with salt and pepper.

8 Strain through a fine sieve to remove the tea leaves. Reserve.

9 With the point of a very sharp knife, score very light criss-cross lines across the breasts and legs (so the fat will run out easily).

10 Cut the legs off the ducks just above the joint.

11 Melt the fat in a large roasting tray on the top of the cooker and colour the ducklings for about 5 minutes each side and for 3 minutes on each breast.

12 Season with salt and pepper, then roast in the oven – on one breast for 10 minutes, then on the other for another 10 minutes, then a further 15 minutes on their backs (a total of 35 minutes).

13 Remove from the oven and discard the fat. Let the ducklings rest on their breasts for 5–10 minutes. Carve and serve.

14 Add the sultanas to the sauce, pour over the carved duck and serve.

Note: Steps 1–9 can be prepared 24–48 hours before the dish is to be served, and can be stored ready to use when needed.

297 Confit duck leg with red cabbage and green beans

	4 portions	10 portions
confit oil*	1 litre	2½ litres
garlic cloves	4	10
bay leaf	1	3
sprig of thyme	1	2
duck legs	4 × 200 g	10 × 200 g
butter	50 g	125 g
green beans, cooked and trimmed	300 g	750 g
braised red cabbage (recipe 403)	250 g	625 g
seasoning		

* Confit oil is 50/50 olive oil and vegetable oil infused with herbs, garlic, whole spice or any specific flavour you wish to impart into the oil; then, through slow cooking in the oil, the foodstuff picks up the flavour.

1 Gently heat the confit oil, add the garlic, bay leaf and thyme.

2 Put the duck legs in the oil and place on a medium to low heat, ensuring the legs are covered.

3 Cook gently for 4–4½ hours (if using goose, 5–6½ hours may be needed).

4 To test if the legs are cooked, squeeze the flesh on the thigh bone and it should just fall away.

5 When cooked, remove the legs carefully and place on a draining tray.

6 When drained, put the confit leg on a baking tray and place in a pre-heated oven at 210°C; remove when the skin is golden brown (approx. 9–10 minutes), taking care as the meat is delicate.

7 Heat the butter in a medium sauté pan and reheat the green beans.

8 Place the braised cabbage in a small pan and reheat slowly.

9 Place the duck leg in a serving dish or plate along with the red cabbage and green beans.

Note: Confit duck legs can be prepared up to three or four days in advance. Remove them carefully from the fat they are stored in, clean off any excess fat and place directly into the oven. This is a great time-saver in a busy service.

298 Garbure of duck

	4 portions	10 portions
duck legs confit, with skin and bone removed	4 × 150 g	10 × 150 g
small green cabbage	½	3
small onion	½	3
Napoli salami in thin batons	40 g	100 g
chicken stock	200 ml	500 ml
haricots blanc, half-cooked	25 g	65 g
flageolet, half-cooked	25 g	65 g
butter	75 g	185 g
leek, in rounds	1	3
bouquet garni	small	large
potatoes, cut into 1 cm dice	250 g	625 g
chopped parsley	2 tsp	6 tsp

1 Place all ingredients in a pan (except the potatoes and parsley) and cook slowly for 1 hour, stirring frequently.

2 After 1 hour add the potatoes and cook for a further 25 minutes.

3 Remove the bouquet garni, add the parsley and work in the butter on a high heat.

4 Serve in a bowl with traditional country French bread, toasted.

Note: This recipe can also double up as a secondary protein element on most duck dishes. It is also a cost-saving addition as you will be able to reduce the amount of prime breast meat that is needed.

299 Pan-fried breast of duck with vanilla and lime

When roasting game birds or poultry, the rule of thumb has always been that they must be cooked on the bone to retain their flavour and shape. In this, and most other duck recipes, the breast is taken off the bone first to ensure that all the fat is rendered down to give a crispy skin. This process also helps to time the cooking to perfection, which is normally difficult because the ratio of bone to meat to fat can differ from duck to duck. The inclusion of lime and vanilla in this dish works well because it cuts through the richness of the bird.

	4 portions	10 portions
Duck		
Barbary duck breasts off the bone	4 × 150 g	10 × 150 g
Vanilla sauce		
vanilla pods	3	7
oil, to brown mirepoix		
mirepoix	200 g	500 g
port wine	25 ml	60 ml
brandy	25 ml	60 ml
armagnac	10 ml	25 ml
red wine	75 ml	185 ml
brown stock reduced to glaze	250 ml	625 ml
good-quality vanilla extract	25 ml	65 ml
To finish		
spinach, picked and washed	200 g	500 g
butter	20 g	50 g
limes, cut into segments	3	8

nutritional info

♥

1 large portion provides:

1114 kJ/266 kcal
14.39 g fat (of which 5.68 g saturated)
3.16 g carbohydrate (of which 2.74 g sugars)
31.3 g protein
1.85 g fibre

Oil is used to cook the duck and butter to cook the spinach.

kcal
1000
900
800
700
600
500
400
300
200
100
0

calorie counter

For the vanilla sauce

1 Cut the vanilla pods lengthways with a sharp knife and scrape the seeds from the centre; retain seeds for later use.

2 In a saucepan, heat a little oil and cook the mirepoix until slightly golden brown. Add the vanilla pod husks and cook for 2–3 minutes to extract the flavour.

3 Add the liquor and stir to the boil. Pour in the brown stock and simmer for 45 minutes.

4 Add the vanilla extract and pour the sauce through a fine strainer into a clean pan. Remove the pod husks, wash them off and retain for another use.

5 Add the seeds from the pod to the sauce, whisking to disperse them evenly.

For the duck

1 Pat dry the duck breasts if necessary, then trim any sinew and excess fat from the meat-side of the breast.

2 Turn the breast with the flesh-side facing down and, using a sharp knife, score the fat, working up the breast, being careful not to cut too far into the breast and expose the meat.

To complete

1 Heat a heavy-based pan on the stove over a medium heat. Place the duck breasts in the pan fat-side down and allow the fat to render into the pan, creating a cooking medium for the duck.

2 Cook, turning occasionally, for 6–7 minutes and ensure that the skin achieves a golden-brown colour and that the fat is rendered from the breast.

3 When the duck is cooked pink, remove from the pan and leave to rest for 5–6 minutes in a warm place.

4 Warm the sauce, wilt the spinach in some butter and season to taste. Drain the spinach well and place a thin line of it down the centre of the plate. Cut each duck breast in two diagonally, giving two good strips.

5 Place on the spinach, garnish the dish with the lime segments, pour over the sauce and serve.

Note: The sauce in this recipe can be made in advance if needed and stored for later use. If vanilla pods are not available increase the amount of vanilla extract.

300 Ballotine of duck leg with black pudding and apple

	4 portions	10 portions
large duck legs	4 × 200 g	10 × 200 g
good-quality black pudding cut into ½ cm dice	200 g	500 g
dried apple chopped into ½ cm dice	75 g	185 g
chives, chopped	1 tsp	3 tsp
chicken mousse (see recipe 276)	300 g	750 g

1 Bone out the duck leg as for ballotine (see page 246).

2 Combine all ingredients well, taking care not to overwork the mousse as splitting may occur.

3 Fill the duck cavity with the mousse and carefully wrap in foil, ensuring the mousse is well encased in the duck leg.

4 Place the leg in the pre-heated oven for 25 minutes, remove and allow to rest for a further 5 minutes.

5 Remove from the foil and place in a hot pan with oil and cook until golden brown, rest for a further 3 minutes.

6 Carve into 3 pieces and serve (e.g. with braised red cabbage scented with orange and bay leaf, and a starch gratin using half potato and half celeriac).

Note: This recipe can be applied to chicken ballotine, however the cooking time should be reduced accordingly, by approx. 5–10 minutes.

301 Confit duck leg rillette

	4 portions	10 portions
duck confit legs, skin and bone removed	4 × 200 g	10 × 200 g
shallots, cooked and chopped	200 g	500 g
parsley, chopped	15 g	40 g
cognac	15 ml	35 ml
orange zest (optional)	1	3
freshly ground black pepper		
sea salt flakes		
fat reserved from the confit	30 g	75 g

1 Place the duck confit meat in the oven to warm through, which will allow the food processor to break down the meat more easily.

2 Combine all the ingredients, except the fat, in the bowl of an electric mixer fitted with a dough hook.

Beat at low speed for about 1 minute, or until everything is well mixed. Or use a food processor, taking care not to purée the mixture or let it turn into a paste. The texture should be like finely shredded meat.

3 Place in ramekins and press down lightly, ensuring an even top. Pour over the reserved confit fat ensuring that it covers the meat to form a seal when set.

4 Use immediately (if doing so, serve without topping off with the oil), or clingfilm well and store in the refrigerator for up to 1 week.

5 Serve with a chutney or a relish as an hors d'oeuvre (starter).

Note: This preparation can be made with either guinea fowl, pheasant or chicken, and offers a use for surplus legs.

Goose

302 Goose

Goose, average weight 5–6 kg
Gosling, average weight 2½–3½ kg

The preparation for cleaning and trussing is the same as for chicken.

Roast goose is traditionally served with sage and onion dressing and apple sauce. Other dressings include peeled apple quarters and stoned prunes, and peeled apple quarters and peeled chestnuts.

For roasting goose proceed as for roast duck using a moderate oven 200–230°C, allowing 15–20 minutes per ½ kg.

303 Roast goose with citrus fruits

	4 portions	10 portions
oven-ready goose, crowned	1 × 4 kg	2 × 5 kg
orange	1	3
lemon	1	3
lime	1	3
salt and pepper		
chicken stock	400 ml	1 litre
confit fat	1 litre	2½ litres
confit goose legs (see duck confit, recipe 301)	2	4

1 Pre-heat the oven to 210°C. Take the goose and crown (see page 245), remove all pens and down.

2 Lightly score the fat in a harlequin style 3 mm apart, being careful not to penetrate the meat into both breasts.

3 Zest and juice the citrus fruits and mix together, season, place the shells of the fruit inside the goose carcass and ensure it is tightly packed.

4 Place a cooking wire over a drip tray and place the goose on top, pour the zest and the juice mix over the breasts and rub into the fat incisions.

5 Place the tray with the goose into a hot pre-heated oven and leave for 10 minutes.

6 Meanwhile bring the stock the boil; after the first 10 minutes of cooking carefully open the oven door and pour the hot stock over the goose – this will supercharge the oven and goose, releasing more fat from the breasts. Close the oven door and drop the temperature to 175°C.

7 Leave for 1¼ hours, basting at 20-minute intervals with the fat and stock in the roasting tray.

8 For the last 30 minutes add the confit legs to the oven. Remove the legs and crown from the oven, placing the crown breast-side down to ensure maximum moisture retention.

9 Remove the breasts and carve into portions, giving each serving both leg and breast meat, and serve with roast gravy.

Note: This recipe utilises all the goose with both muscle groups afforded different methods of cooking to maximise their flavour and texture.

Turkey

304 Turkey

Turkeys can vary in weight from 3½–20 kg.

They are cleaned and trussed in the same way as chicken. The wishbone should always be removed before trussing. The sinews should be drawn out of the legs. Allow 200g per portion raw weight.

Note: When cooking a large turkey the legs may be removed, boned, rolled, tied and roasted separately from the remainder of the bird. This will reduce the cooking time and enable the legs and breast to cook more evenly.

Stuffings may be rolled in foil, steamed or baked and thickly sliced. If a firmer stuffing is required, mix in one or two raw eggs before cooking.

305 Stuffed leg of turkey

Ensure that the sinews are withdrawn from the turkey leg, remove the leg from the turkey and bone out, season and stuff, then tie with string. Roast, braise or pot roast, remove the string and allow to stand before carving in thick slices.

Suitable stuffings include chestnut, walnut, peanuts or mixed nuts in pork sausage meat or those stuffings suggested for chicken or duck ballotines.

Sauces such as jus-lié, containing cranberries, blackcurrants or redcurrants, may be served.

306 Turkey escalopes

100g slices cut from the boned out turkey breast can be beaten out using a little water, then flour, egg and crumbed. They may then be shallow-fried on both sides and served with a variety of sauces and garnishes. The escalopes can also be left in a thicker cut, stuffed and then egg and crumbed. For simpler dishes they can be lightly coated in seasoned flour and cooked gently in butter, margarine or oil on both sides with the minimum of colour.

Examples of recipes that can be adapted using turkey include:

- veal kidneys with mustard and cream sauce, recipe 264
- chicken recipes.

307 Traditional roast turkey

	4 portions	10 portions
turkey, with legs on	1 small hen	4–5 kg
sea salt and freshly ground black pepper		
unsalted butter, melted	250 g	625 g

nutritional info

1 large portion provides:
1076 kJ/257 kcal
9.75 g fat (of which 3.15 g saturated)
0.00 g carbohydrate (of which 0.00 g sugars)
42.0 g protein
0.00 g fibre

A rack is used when roasting the turkey but butter is used for basting.

kcal
1000
900
800
700
600
500
400
300
200
100
0

calorie counter

1 Adjust a rack to lowest position and remove the other racks in the oven. Pre-heat to 165°C. Remove turkey parts from neck and breast cavities and reserve for other uses, if desired. Dry bird well with paper towels, inside and out. Salt and pepper inside the breast cavity.

2 Set the bird on a roasting rack in a roasting pan, breast-side up, brush generously with half the butter and season with salt and pepper. Tent the bird with foil.

3 Roast the turkey for 2 hours. Remove the foil and baste with the remaining butter. Increase the oven temperature to 220°C and continue to roast until an instant-read thermometer registers 74°C in the thigh of the bird, about 45 minutes more.

4 Remove turkey from the oven and set aside to rest for 15 minutes before carving. Carve and serve with roast gravy, cranberry sauce, bread sauce, and either or both sausage meat and chestnut dressing and parsley and thyme dressing. Chipolata sausages and rolled rashers of grilled bacon may also be served.

Note: The secret to keeping turkey moist is to baste as much as you can and, when the turkey is cooked, place it on its breast, breast-side down, allowing all the cavity juices to penetrate the meat.

308 Pan-fried turkey escalopes with prunes and smoked bacon

100g slices cut from the boned out turkey breast can be beaten out using a little water, then flour, egg and crumbed. They may then be shallow-fried on both sides and served with a variety of sauces and garnishes. The escalopes can also be left in a thicker cut, stuffed and then egg and crumbed. For simpler dishes they can be lightly coated in seasoned flour and cooked gently in butter, margarine or oil on both sides with the minimum of colour.

	4 portions	10 portions
baby onions, peeled and blanched	16	40
chicken stock	250 ml	625 ml
butter	50 g	125 g
bay leaf	1	3
sprig thyme	1	3
turkey escalopes	4 × 150 g	10 × 150 g
salt and pepper		
smoked bacon lardons	250 g	625 g
vegetable oil	25 ml	65 ml
soaked pitted prunes	250 g	625 g
parsley, chopped	30 g	75 g

1 Cook the prepared baby onions in the chicken stock, butter, bay leaf and thyme; when ready remove the bay leaf and thyme and set aside.

2 Place the escalopes on an oiled tray and season lightly with salt and pepper.

3 Place the escalopes in a pre-heated sauté pan and gently fry for 3–4 minutes either side, ensuring a good even colour.

4 In a little oil, quickly fry off the bacon lardons and set aside to drain.

5 Place the soaked prunes in with the onions and bacon lardons, and bring gently to a simmer, then emulsify with butter to form a stew-like consistency.

6 Take the onion and bacon stew and place in a serving dish or plate. Place the cooked turkey escalope on the top and garnish with chopped parsley.

7 Serve immediately.

Note: This recipe can also apply to chicken suprême/escalope. Ensure that the time is increased for the suprême, however, as the meat will be denser.

nutritional info

1 large portion provides:
2371 kJ/568 kcal
32.83 g fat (of which 12.82 g saturated)
20.99 g carbohydrate (of which 20.78 g sugars)
48.3 g protein
3.87 g fibre

Contains a large amount of smoked bacon. More butter than oil is used. Chicken was used for the saturated fat analysis.

kcal	
1000	
900	
800	
700	
600	
500	
400	
300	
200	
100	
0	

calorie counter

Pigeon

309 Roast pigeon with red chard, celeriac and treacle

As pigeons do not have gall bladders it is not necessary to remove the livers when they are drawn and cleaned.

Tender young pigeons less than 12 months old can be roasted, pot roasted or split open and grilled, and served, for example, with a Robert, charcutière or devilled sauce.

Young pigeons can be cut in halves, flattened slightly, seasoned, shallow-fried in butter and cooked and finished as for sautés of chicken, e.g. chasseur, bordelaise.

	4 portions	10 portions
celeriac, peeled and cut into 2½ cm dice	1	2
milk and water, to cook the celeriac		
squab pigeon crowns (350–400 g each)	4	10
butter, to place in the squab cavity	50 g	125 g
parsnip batons	12	30
butter, to cook the parsnips	75 g	185 g
vegetable stock	200 ml	500 ml
reduced brown stock	100 ml	250 ml
red chard, picked and washed	200 g	500 g
black treacle	5 g	15 g

nutritional info

♥

1 large portion provides:
2735 kJ/655 kcal
40.56 g fat (of which 18.35 g saturated)
6.24 g carbohydrate (of which 3.25 g sugars)
66.9 g protein
2.08 g fibre

A large quantity of butter is used for cooking and in the sauce. Chicken was used for the saturated fat analysis.

kcal
1000
900
800
700
600
500
400
300
200
100
0

calorie counter

1 In a saucepan, cook the chopped celeriac until soft in a mixture of half milk and half water.

2 Drain off all the liquid, then purée the celeriac in a food processor.

3 When smooth, place in a clean pan and return to the stove. Cook until thick, letting as much moisture evaporate as possible.

4 Pre-heat the oven to 180°C. Adjust the seasoning to taste.

5 Roast the squab on the bone for 3 minutes on its back and 3 minutes on its breast.

6 Remove and rest with the butter evenly placed in the cavity to add extra moisture to the bird.

7 Cook the parsnips in butter and vegetable stock, place to one side and keep warm.

8 Wilt the chard, season and drain.

9 Warm the celeriac purée and place on the plate with the chard and the parsnip batons.

10 Carefully remove the two breasts from the bone, place on the chard and liberally drizzle the sauce over the breasts and the plate.

11 If red chard is unavailable you can substitute with spinach or pak choi.

12 Reduce brown stock by half again, add treacle sauce and plate.

Note: All elements of this dish can be used elsewhere – for example, the celeriac purée is a suitable component for most poultry dishes.

310 Pot au feu of pigeon

	4 portions	10 portions
squabs, legs removed	6 (approx. 2 kg)	10 (approx. 3½ kg)
carrot, peeled and cut into 4 laterally	1	3
celery stick, cut into 4	1	3
baby turnips	8	20
medium turnips, peeled and blanched	2	4
leek, washed, cut in rounds	1	3
small shallots, peeled and left whole	8	20
smoked streaky bacon, rind removed	100 g	250 g
chicken/game stock	400 ml	1 litre
bouquet garni with 4 black peppercorns and 1 clove garlic	1	3
salt		

1 Place the squab legs in a large casserole and arrange the vegetables tightly in one layer with the legs, add the bacon, then cover with the stock to about 4 cm above the ingredients (you may need to top this up with water).

2 Add the muslin-wrapped bouquet garni. Season with salt and bring to a gentle boil.

3 Skim off any impurities, cover with a lid (leaving a small gap), and simmer gently for 50 minutes.

4 Skim off any fat or impurities, then add the squab breasts and cook for a further 12 minutes.

5 Taste the broth, correct the seasoning and serve with rich mashed potato or minted new potatoes, depending on the season.

Note: This is a family or social dish, designed to be placed in the middle of the table and served with warm, crusty bread, mashed potato or buttered new potatoes, for a great accompaniment to a gathering of 'friends and conversation'.

nutritional info

1 large portion provides:
1545 kJ/367 kcal
11.29 g fat (of which 3.44 g saturated)
11.12 g carbohydrate (of which 9.98 g sugars)
56.2 g protein
4.79 g fibre

Cooked in stock with vegetables. There is a small amount of fat from the streaky bacon. Chicken was used for the saturated fat analysis

311 Sauté of pigeon salad with rocket, Parmesan and beetroot

	4 portions	10 portions
squab crowns (350–400 g each) (see page 245)	4	10
oil	50 ml	125 ml
pigeon/game glaze (reduced stock from pigeon bones)	50 ml	125 ml
salad dressing	50 ml	125 ml
salt and pepper		
cooked beetroot batons	100 g	250 g
mixed salad leaves	200 g	500 g
rocket, washed and picked	250 g	600 g
shaved Parmesan	50 g	125 g

nutritional info

1 large portion provides:
2059 kJ/492 kcal
27.69 g fat (of which 6.33 g saturated)
4.96 g carbohydrate (of which 4.79 g sugars)
56.2 g protein
1.49 g fibre

Oil is used to sauté the pigeon, and a small amount of parmesan is used. Chicken was used for the saturated fat analysis.

1 Remove the breasts from crown (see page 245) and cut each breast into three.

2 Heat the oil in a pan, place in the squab and sauté for 2–3 minutes with a little colour, leaving the meat pink.

3 Remove from the pan and place on a draining wire in a warm place. Add the squab glaze and dressing to the pan, removing all sediment.

4 Season the squab before presenting on the plate.

5 Pour into a small dish and allow to cool slightly. Arrange the squab and beetroot in the centre of a plate, dress the mixed leaves, rocket and

Parmesan and place carefully on the squab. Finish the dish with the remaining jus/dressing.

Note: This is a suitable summer dish as the squabs could even be chargrilled or cooked on a barbecue for greater depth of flavour. Alternatively, this preparation would be just as effective with partridge.

GAME

Game is the name given to certain wild birds and animals that are eaten; there are two kinds of game:

1 feathered
2 furred.

Handling and preparing game

Food value

As it is less fatty than poultry or meat, game is easily digested, with the exception of water fowl, owing to their oily flesh. Game is useful for building and repairing body tissues and for energy.

Storage

1 Hanging is essential for all game. It drains the flesh of blood and begins the process of disintegration, which is vital to make the flesh soft and edible, and also to develop flavour.

2 The hanging time is determined by the type, condition and age of the game, and the storage temperature.

3 Old birds need to hang for a longer time than young birds.

4 Game birds are not plucked or drawn before hanging.

5 Venison and hare are hung with the skin on.

6 Game must be hung in a well-ventilated, dry, cold storeroom; this need not be refrigerated.

7 Game birds should be hung by the neck with the feet down.

Quality points for buying

Venison

Joints of venison should be well fleshed and a dark brownish-red colour.

Hares and rabbits

The ears of hares and rabbits should tear easily. With old hares the lip is more pronounced than in young animals. The rabbit is distinguished from the hare by shorter ears, feet and body.

Birds

1 The beak should break easily.
2 The breast plumage ought to be soft.
3 The breast should be plump.
4 Quill feathers should be pointed, not rounded.
5 The legs should be smooth.

FEATHERED GAME

Grouse, pheasant, partridge are the most popular game birds. Woodcock, snipe, wild duck and plover are used but much less so. All these birds are protected by game laws and can only be shot in season. Quail is a game bird, but large numbers of quail are reared and are available all year round.

The term includes all edible birds that live in freedom, but only the following are generally used in catering today:

■ pheasant

- partridge
- woodcock
- snipe
- wild duck
- teal
- grouse.

The flavour of most game birds is improved by their being hung for a few days in a moderate draught before being plucked. Hanging is to some degree essential for all game. It drains the flesh of blood and begins a process of disintegration, which is essential to make the flesh tender and develop flavour – this is due to the action of enzymes. Game birds should be hung with the feet down. Care should be taken with the water birds – wild duck, teal, etc. – not to allow them to get too high, because the oiliness of their flesh will quickly turn them rancid.

When game birds are roasted they should always be served on a croûte of fried bread, garnished with thick round pieces of toasted French bread spread with game farce, game chips and picked watercress.

Barding

As game birds are deficient in fat, a thin slice of fat bacon (bard) should be tied over the breast during cooking to prevent it from drying; this is also placed on the breast when serving. Roast gravy, bread sauce and browned breadcrumbs (toasted or fried) are served separately.

Barding of a bird: modern

Barding of a bird: traditional

312 Game farce

	4 portions	10 portions
butter or margarine	50 g	125 g
game livers	100 g	250 g
onion, chopped	25 g	60 g
sprig of thyme		
bay leaf	1	2–3
salt, pepper		

1 Heat half the butter in a frying pan.

2 Quickly toss the seasoned livers, onion and herbs, browning well but keeping underdone. Pass through a sieve or mincer.

3 Mix in the remaining butter. Correct the seasoning.

313 Pheasant

Young birds have a flexible beak, pliable breast bone, grey legs and underdeveloped spurs or none at all. The last large feather in the wing is pointed.

- They may be roasted or braised or pot roasted.
- Season – 1 October to 1 February.
- They should be hung well.

314 Partridge

Young birds indicated as for pheasant, the legs should also be smooth.

- May be roasted, braised, etc.
- Season – 1 September to 1 February.
- Three to five days' hanging is ample time.

315 Woodcock

A good-quality bird should have soft supple feet, clean mouth and throat, fat and firm breast. It has a distinctive flavour that is accentuated by the entrails being left in during cooking. The vent must be checked carefully for cleanliness.

- Usually roasted.
- Season – September to April.
- Hang for three to four days.

316 Snipe

Snipe resemble woodcock but are smaller. Points of quality are the same as for woodcock. The flavour of the flesh can be accentuated in the same way as for the woodcock.

- May be roasted and are sometimes cooked in steak puddings or pies.
- Season – October to November.
- Hang for three to four days.

Snipe and woodcock are prepared with the head left on and the beak is used for trussing. The head is prepared by removing the skin and eyes.

317 Wild duck

The most common is the mallard, which is the ancestor of the domestic duck. The beak and webbed feet should be soft and pliable.

- They may be roasted, slightly underdone or braised.
- Season – August to February.

It is particularly important that water birds be eaten only in season; out of season the flesh becomes coarse and acquires a fishy flavour.

318 Teal

This is a smaller species of wild duck. Select as for wild duck.

- May be roasted or braised.
- Season – October to January.

319 Grouse

This is one of the most popular game birds.

Young birds have soft downy plumes on the breast and under the wings. They also have pointed wings and a rounded, soft spur knob; the spur becomes hard and scaly in older birds.

- Usually served roasted, left slightly underdone.
- Grouse is equally popular hot or cold.
- Season – 12 August to 10 December.

Pheasant

320 Poached pheasant crown with chestnuts and cabbage

	4 portions	10 portions
chicken stock	2 litres	5 litres
pheasant crowns (see page 245)	2	5
butter	50 g	125 g
savoy cabbages, cored, shredded and blanched	2	5
cooked bacon lardons	75 g	187 g
reduced chicken stock	250 ml	625 ml
cooked chestnuts	175 g	437 g
double cream	50 ml	125 ml
parsley, chopped	5 g	12.5 g
salt and pepper		
lemons, juice of	1	2½

nutritional info

1 large portion provides:
2417 kJ/581 kcal
37.35 g fat (of which 17.48 g saturated)
22.70 g carbohydrate (of which 9.40 g sugars)
39.7 g protein
5.74 g fibre

Butter is used for the cabbage and bacon lardons, and double cream in the sauce.

kcal
1000
900
800
700
600
500
400
300
200
100
0

calorie counter

1 Bring the stock up to a simmer and place the crowns in it; simmer for 11 minutes.

2 Meanwhile, place the butter in a medium pan on a moderate heat and melt. Add the cabbage and bacon lardons and 100 ml of reduced chicken stock.

3 When the cabbage and bacon have formed an emulsion with the butter and stock, put to one side and retain.

4 Remove the pheasant crowns and rest for 2–3 minutes breast-side down.

5 Remove the breasts from the crown (see page 245) and check if cooked; if not quite cooked place back in the cooking liquor for 1–2 minutes. Then place the cooked breasts in a serving dish and keep warm.

6 Add the cooked chestnuts to the remaining reduced chicken stock and bring to the boil, adding the cream. At this point add the chopped parsley and check the seasoning – if the sauce appears to be rich this can be modified with a little lemon juice. You should not be able to taste the lemon but using it allows the deep flavours of the sauce to come through.

7 Place the cabbage mix in the centre of the plate and top this with the pheasant; finish with the sauce over and around, ensuring an even distribution of chestnuts.

Note: With the legs from the crowns, why not make a pheasant leg garbure (see recipe 298) and serve as a secondary part of the preparation, taking the dish from four portions to eight?

321 Roast breast of pheasant with vanilla and pear

		4 portions	10 portions
cold water		250 ml	625 ml
caster sugar	* for curing the breasts	90 g	225 g
salt		90 g	225 g
large pheasant breasts, removed from the bone with skin and wing tip attached		4	10
unsalted butter		70 g	175 g
shallots, diced		4	9
large vanilla beans, scraped to gather the seeds		1	3
dry white wine, preferably Chardonnay		150 ml	375 ml
pear/apple cider		300 ml	750 ml
whipping cream		300 ml	750 ml
preserved ginger, finely chopped		15 g	35 g
freshly ground black pepper			
salt			
dry red wine		250 ml	625 ml
honey		75 g	185 g
coriander seeds, toasted and finely crushed		10 g	25 g
pears (preferably red), halved, cored and sliced into 1 cm-thick slices		2	5
sprigs of chervil			

'Cure' is used in the same way here as for curing bacon, using the salt and the sugar in the recipe.

nutritional info

1 large portion provides:
2830 kJ/680 kcal
47.09 g fat (of which 24.45 g saturated)
27.93 g carbohydrate (of which 27.22 g sugars)
39.0 g protein
2.20 g fibre

Butter is used for cooking and in the sauce, and whipping cream in the sauce, but no oil. Sugar for curing was estimated at 10%.

kcal
1000
900
800
700
600
500
400
300
200
100
0

calorie counter

To cure the pheasant

1 In a large bowl combine the water, 25 g/62.5 g each of sugar and salt, mixing to dissolve.

2 Add the pheasant breasts, cover with plastic wrap and refrigerate overnight.

To make the sauces

1 In a large sauté pan, heat 1 tbsp/2½ tbsp of the butter over medium to medium-high heat. Add the shallots, cooking until tender (about 3 minutes). Add the vanilla bean and seeds, white wine, cider and cream. Bring to a simmer, cooking until the liquids are reduced and thickened to sauce consistency (about 10 minutes). Add the ginger, season with salt and pepper, keep warm.

2 In another saucepan, combine the red wine and the honey. Bring to a simmer over high heat, cooking until reduced to coat the back of a spoon (about 15 minutes). Reserve.

To cook the pheasants

1 Pre-heat the oven to 190°C.

2 In a large sauté pan, add 2 tbsp/5 tbsp butter and melt over a high heat. Season the pheasant with salt, pepper and coriander. Add the pheasant skin-side down, cooking until browned and well seared (about 5 minutes). Turn over and transfer the pan to the lower rack of the oven. Cook until just about medium (about 6 to 8 minutes, depending on the size of the pheasant breast). Carefully remove the hot pan from the oven. Allow to rest for a couple of minutes before cutting.

3 In another large pan, heat 1 tbsp/2½ tbsp of the butter over high heat. Add the pears, cooking until they just begin to soften slightly (about 2 minutes).

Add 2 tbsp/5 tbsp of the sugar, cooking and stirring occasionally until browned on the edges (about 4 minutes). Remove the pears and keep warm.

To serve

1 Position the pear slices in the centre of the plate. Slice the pheasant on a bias to yield 4 or 6 thin broad slices. Spoon the vanilla-ginger and red wine sauce over and around the pheasant and on the plate. Garnish with the vanilla bean and sprigs of chervil over the pheasant. Serve immediately.

Note: This dish will work equally well with corn-fed chicken or guinea fowl. Again, as for recipe 299, vanilla extract can be used instead of vanilla pods.

Partridge

322 Roast partridge

	4 portions	10 portions
grey-legged partridges (approx. 400 g each), oven-ready, with livers	4	10
unsalted butter	20 g	50 g
groundnut oil	20 g	50 g
salt		
freshly ground pepper		
roasting juices from veal, pork or beef	70 ml	175 ml
water	50 ml	125 ml

nutritional info

1 large portion provides:
2118 kJ/506 kcal
23.51 g fat (of which 7.40 g saturated)
0.03 g carbohydrate (of which 0.03 g sugars)
73.4 g protein
0.00 g fibre

Butter and oil are used to sear the partridge and fry the liver.

1 Shorten the wings and sear the partridges under a flame to remove the feather stubs. Remove any trace of gall from the liver. Wash briefly, pat dry and reserve.

2 In a roasting tray sear the wing bones and the partridges in butter and oil for 2 minutes on each side and 2 minutes on the breast (6 minutes in total) until they are brown.

3 Season with salt and pepper, and roast in the pre-heated oven for 5–6 minutes, according to the size of the partridges.

4 Remove from the oven and place the partridges on a cooling wire breast-side down, cover loosely with aluminium foil and allow to rest.

5 In the same roasting tray, fry the livers in the remaining butter and oil for 1 minute, and reserve. Spoon out the excess fat and add the roasting juices and water to the winglets, bring to the boil, then simmer for 5 minutes.

6 Taste and season with salt and pepper, then strain through a fine sieve.

7 Serve with roasted seasonal vegetables (e.g. roast parsnips, carrots and braised cabbage). Suggested accompaniments: bread sauce, roast gravy, watercress and game chips.

Note: Simply roasted partridge is a great autumnal and winter base for most accompaniments: braised cabbage, roast carrots, parsnips, and so on.

323 Braised partridge with cabbage

Older or red-legged partridges are suitable for this dish.

	4 portions	10 portions
old partridges	2	5
lard, butter, margarine or oil	100 g	250 g
cabbage	400 g	1¼ kg
belly of pork or bacon (in the piece)	100 g	250 g
carrot, peeled and grooved	1	2–3
studded onion	1	2–3
bouquet garni		
white stock	1 litre	2½ litres
frankfurter sausages or pork chipolatas	8	20

nutritional info

1 portion provides:
750 kcals/3137 kJ
57.6 g fat
(of which 14 g saturated)
11.5 g carbohydrate
(of which 6.2 g sugars)
47.8 g protein

Based on 100 g cooked meat and oil

♥ kcal
1000
900
800
700
600
500
400
300
200
100
0

calorie counter

1 Season the partridges, rub with the fat, brown quickly in a hot oven and remove.

2 Trim the cabbage, remove the core, separate the leaves and wash thoroughly.

3 Blanch the cabbage leaves and the belly of pork for 5 minutes. Refresh and drain well to remove all water. Remove the rind from the pork.

4 Place half the cabbage in a deep ovenproof dish; add the pork rind, the partridges, carrot, onion, bouquet garni, the remaining fat, and stock, and season lightly.

5 Add the remaining cabbage and bring to the boil, cover with greased greaseproof paper or foil and a lid, and braise slowly until tender, approximately 1½–2 hours.

6 Add the sausages halfway through the cooking time by placing them under the cabbage.

7 Remove the bouquet garni and onion, and serve everything else, the pork and carrot being sliced.

Grouse

324 Traditional roast grouse

	4 portions	10 portions
Grouse		
young grouse (approx. 750 g each), wings removed	4	10
hearts and livers from the grouse		
sage leaves	4	10
butter	20 g	50 g
salt and pepper		
Stock		
oil	30 ml	80 ml
grouse wings		
giblets		
large onion	1	2
celery stick	1	3
carrot	1	3
red wine	250 ml	625 ml
water		
sprig of thyme		
bay leaf	1	3
Toast		
small slices of bread	16	40
duck fat		
To serve		
bread sauce		
bunches watercress	1	2
game chips		

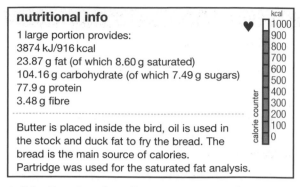

nutritional info

1 large portion provides:
3874 kJ/916 kcal
23.87 g fat (of which 8.60 g saturated)
104.16 g carbohydrate (of which 7.49 g sugars)
77.9 g protein
3.48 g fibre

Butter is placed inside the bird, oil is used in the stock and duck fat to fry the bread. The bread is the main source of calories. Partridge was used for the saturated fat analysis.

1 Trim the wings from the young grouse, draw and reserve the livers, hearts and giblets. Season birds liberally inside and out, and put the livers and hearts back in with a sage leaf and a knob of butter. Pre-heat the oven to its maximum (240°C).

2 Brown the wings and the remaining giblets with the diced onion, celery and carrot. Deglaze pan with red wine, cover with water and simmer for 30 minutes with the thyme and bay leaf. Strain and reserve.

3 Meanwhile, fry the bread in duck fat. Make bread sauce and pick through watercress.

4 To cook, place birds at top of oven and leave for 6 minutes, by which time the legs should be starting to brown.

5 Put bird back in oven for another 7 minutes until, when inserted into the deepest point above the wing, a temperature probe reads 57–60°C.

6 Remove from the pan and leave the birds to rest for 10 minutes in a warm place, on top of the toast, so that the blood drips into it.

7 Put the roasting tray over a flame, add a splash of brandy and the stock, and allow to bubble down to a thin gravy.

8 To serve, scoop out the liver, heart and foie gras, mash these up and serve on the toast. Stick a bunch of the watercress into the grouse's cavity and put the bird and toast onto a plate with some bread sauce and game chips. Pour a little of the gravy over each bird and serve remaining gravy separately.

Note: Good-quality grouse is essential for this dish – birds that have not been over-hung. The meat will already have a strong pungent flavour embedded in it from the birds' diet of heather.

Quail

325 Quails

Only plump birds with firm white fat should be selected. When prepared the entrails are drawn but the heart and liver are retained inside the birds. They may be roasted, spit-roasted, cooked 'en casserole' or poached in a rich well-flavoured chicken or veal stock (or a combination of both).

Quails may also be boned out from the back, stuffed with a forcemeat, made as follows, then cooked by any of the above mentioned methods.

	4 portions	10 portions
Forcemeat		
finely minced pork (half lean, half fat)	200 g	500 g
quail and chicken livers	400 g	900 g
shallot or onion, chopped	50 g	125 g
mushroom, chopped	25 g	60 g
pinch of thyme, half bay leaf		
salt, pepper, mixed spice		

1 Gently fry the pork to extract the fat.

2 Increase the heat, add the livers and the remainder of the ingredients.

3 Fry quickly to brown the livers but keep them pink.

4 Allow to cool and pass through a sieve or mince finely.

326 Quail with pomegranate and blood orange

	4 portions	10 portions
oil	10 ml	25 ml
butter	50 g	125 g
salt and pepper		
oven-ready quails (approx. 75 g each)	8	20
blood oranges	2	5
pomegranate	1	2
mixed leaves	200 g	650 g
split cooked green beans	100 g	250 g
vinaigrette		

nutritional info

1 large portion provides:
1118 kJ/267 kcal
13.30 g fat (of which 2.59 g saturated)
8.24 g carbohydrate (of which 8.01 g sugars)
29.2 g protein
2.49 g fibre

Some butter and oil are used to cook the quail. Partridge was used for the saturated fat analysis.

1 Pre-heat the oven to 180°C.

2 Heat a medium saucepan and add the oil and butter.

3 Season the quails and place in the pan, backs down, colour evenly all over, place in a roasting tray and cook for 6 minutes.

4 Meanwhile, segment the oranges and set aside.

5 Remove the seeds from the pomegranate and also set aside.

6 When cooked, remove the quails from the oven and rest for 2–3 minutes.

7 Remove the quail breasts from the bone and slice into 4 pieces.

8 On the centre of the plate combine the dressed leaves, beans and oranges with a dessertspoon of vinaigrette.

8 Place the quail around the leaves, finish with the pomegranate seeds and serve immediately.

Note: This recipe can also be applied to partridge and squab by adjusting the cooking times. Alternatively you can substitute the mixed leaves for a sauerkraut preparation, and removing the pomegranate will give you a hot starter to serve in the autumn/winter months.

327 Pot-roasted quail with roast carrots and mashed potato

	4 portions	10 portions
quails (approx. 75 g each)	12	30
pancetta, thinly sliced	12 (approx. 250 g)	30 (approx. 625 g)
fresh sage leaves	12	30
vegetable oil	15 ml	50 ml
salt and freshly ground pepper		
carrots, peeled and cut into quarters	3 (100 g)	8 (250 g)
dry white wine	125 ml	310 ml
red wine	125 ml	310 ml
brown stock	250 ml	625 ml
unsalted butter	50 g	125 g
portions of mashed potato	4 (200 g)	10 (500 g)

nutritional info

1 large portion provides:
2839 kJ/680 kcal
41.89 g fat (of which 16.61 g saturated)
9.99 g carbohydrate (of which 2.47 g sugars)
66.1 g protein
1.15 g fibre

Pancetta, butter and oil are used. Partridge was used for the saturated fat analysis and streaky bacon used instead of pancetta.

1 Wash the quails thoroughly inside and out, then place them in a large colander to drain for at least 20 minutes; pat the quail dry.

2 Stuff the cavity of each bird with 1 slice of pancetta and 1 sage leaf.

3 Put the oil in a large thick-bottomed roasting pan on high heat. When the fat is hot, add all the quails in a single layer and cook until browned on one side, gradually turning them, and continue cooking until they are evenly browned all over.

4 Lightly sprinkle the quails with salt and pepper, then add the carrots and cook for a couple of minutes until a slight colour appears.

5 Add the wine and brown stock then turn the birds once, let the wine bubble for about 1 minute, then lower the heat to moderate and partially cover the pan. Cook the quails until the meat feels very tender when poked with a fork and comes away from the bone (approx. 35 minutes).

6 Check from time to time that there are sufficient juices in the pan to keep the birds from sticking; if this does occur, add 1 to 2 tbsp of water at a time. When the quail are done, transfer them to a warmed tray and reserve.

7 Turn up the heat and reduce the cooking juices to a glaze – enough to coat all the birds, scraping the bottom of the pan with a wooden spoon to loosen any cooking residues.

8 Add the butter and whisk in to form an emulsion; at this point if the sauce splits or is too thick add a little water and re-boil.

9 Remove the carrots from the pan and place neatly on the plate with the potato purée.

10 Pour the juices over the quail and serve immediately.

Rabbit

328 Rabbits

Rabbits are available wild or farm reared.

Preparation

1 Carefully remove the fur.

2 Cut an incision along the belly.

3 Remove the intestines.

4 Clean out the forequarter removing all traces of blood.

Depending on the required use and size of rabbit, it can be cut as follows.

1 Legs, forelegs, forequarter (well trimmed) into two pieces each, saddle into two or three pieces.

2 Saddles can be removed and left whole for roasting, braising or pot roasting.

3 The two nuts of meat can be removed from the saddle, half cut through lengthwise and carefully beaten out using a little cold water to form escalopes.

Rabbit can be used in a wide variety of dishes, e.g. pâtés, terrines, pies, salads, roast, braised, pot roasted, white and brown stews, curries.

329 Rabbit saddle stuffed with its own livers

	4 portions	10 portions
Saddle		
long saddles rabbit (approx. 400 g each), livers retained	3	5
spinach leaves	100 g	250 g
thin slices Parma ham	9	23
Lentil sauce		
brown chicken stock	300 ml	750 ml
cold butter, diced	40 g	100 g
plum tomatoes, cut into concassée	3	8
cooked umbri or puy lentils	30 g	75 g
chives, chopped	1 tsp	4 tsp
sherry vinegar, to taste		
To serve		
spinach, picked, washed and wilted	300 g	750 g

nutritional info

1 large portion provides:
1393 kJ/333 kcal
18.21 g fat (of which 2.66 g saturated)
6.64 g carbohydrate (of which 2.47 g sugars)
36.0 g protein
2.66 g fibre

Cooked in foil, and butter is used in the lentil sauce.

♥ calorie counter

kcal
1000
900
800
700
600
500
400
300
200
100
0

For the rabbit

1 Split the two natural halves of the rabbit liver with a sharp knife.

2 Keeping them as whole as possible, remove any sinew. Wrap the livers in the spinach leaves.

3 Trim off any excess fat from the belly flaps of the rabbit.

4 Lay the spinach-wrapped livers in the cavity of the rabbit.

5 Lay 2 pieces of the Parma ham on a 30 cm-square sheet of kitchen foil and place the rabbit saddle with the livers facing upwards on the ham.

6 Roll into a sausage shape, twisting the ends of the foil to ensure a tight parcel.

7 Repeat with the remaining rabbits and place in the fridge overnight to rest.

For the lentil sauce

1 Place the chicken stock in a saucepan, bring to the boil and simmer until the volume has reduced to 150 ml.

2 Add the butter to the reduced stock and whisk to an emulsion, add the tomatoes, lentils and chives, and adjust the seasoning to taste. Finish with the sherry vinegar so you can just taste the acid in the background.

To complete

1 Pre-heat the oven to 180°C. Place the rabbit saddles on a baking tray and roast for 17 minutes, turning after 10 minutes.

2 Remove the rabbit from the oven and rest for 3–4 minutes in the foil.

3 Remove the foil from the rabbit and slice each saddle into 4 equal pieces.

4 Lay the sliced rabbit on wilted spinach and garnish the dish with the lentil sauce. Serve immediately

Note: If thinking ahead, the best approach for this dish is to prepare the rabbit saddle the day before or at least 8 hours before cooking, to allow the meat to rest and form an even cylinder – otherwise, when sliced, it will tend to spring open.

330 Braised baron of rabbit with olives and tomatoes

		4 portions	10 portions
farm-raised rabbit barons (approx. 750–800 g each), including bones and trim for gravy		2	5
carrot		1	3
onion		1	3
celery stick		1	3
olive oil		90 ml	225 ml
balsamic vinegar		15 ml	40 ml
caster sugar		10 g	25 g
bottle (750 ml) dry white wine		1	2½
butter, to brown the meat			
basil leaves		12	30
black olives	Mediterranean influence	32	80
pieces home-dried tomato		8	20
salt and pepper			

nutritional info

1 large portion provides:
2365 kJ/568 kcal
40.98 g fat (of which 8.42 g saturated)
5.47 g carbohydrate (of which 4.75 g sugars)
44.6 g protein
0.87 g fibre

♥ calorie counter

kcal
1000
900
800
700
600
500
400
300
200
100
0

1 Well ahead of time, prepare the sauce; cut the rabbits across at the point where the ribs end and chop the forequarters into small pieces.

2 Cut the vegetables into a mirepoix.

3 In a large saucepan, brown the bones and mirepoix in 2 tbsp/5 tbsp of the olive oil.

4 Add the vinegar and sugar, and toss to coat. Cook until light brown.

5 Pour over almost all the white wine, reserving about 1 glass/2½ glasses (150 ml/375 ml) for deglazing the roasting pan later. Boil hard to reduce until almost all the liquid has gone and it is syrupy.

6 Just cover with cold water, return to the boil and skim.

7 Turn down and simmer for 1½ hours.

8 Sieve the resulting stock into a bowl, wash out the saucepan and return the stock to it.

9 Bring back to the boil, skim again and, once more, return to a slow simmer until reduced by half. Reserve.

10 Cut the rabbit legs into two (thigh and drumstick), and the rack into two.

11 In a large saucepan, brown the meat cuts in foaming butter; when golden brown add the finished stock and cook for a further 1½ hours.

12 When cooked, pass the sauce through a fine strainer, bring to the boil and reduce by half.

13 While reducing, put the rabbit into a casserole/serving dish, julienne the basil and remove the stones from the olives.

14 When the sauce is reduced by half, add the tomatoes, olives and basil. Correct the seasoning, pour over the rabbit and serve.

Note: The 'Mediterranean influence' can be omitted, substituted with a British theme – woodland mushrooms, parsnips – and served with braised cabbage.

331 Casserole of tame rabbit forestière

	4 portions	10 portions
farmed rabbits (approx. 750 g each), including bones and trim for the sauce	2	5
mirepoix	300 g	750 g
oil	70 ml	175 ml
red wine	500 ml	1¼ litres
reduced brown stock	500 ml	1¼ litres
white wine	250 ml	625 ml
button onions	16	40
ceps	250 g	625 g
cream	250 ml	625 ml
chives, chopped	20 g	50 g
pre-blanched bacon lardons	500 g	1¼ litres
salt and pepper		

1 Remove the legs front and back; cut the saddle into four and the hind legs into two.

2 Take the rest of the carcass (the rib, belly flank, neck and shoulder blades) and brown with the mirepoix in half the oil.

3 Add the red wine and 300 ml/750 ml of the stock, bring to the boil and turn down to a simmer.

4 Cover and simmer for 1½ hours.

5 Meanwhile, put the remaining oil in a thick-bottomed pan or casserole and brown the pieces of rabbit.

6 Place in a clean earthenware dish and then in a pre-heated oven for 15 minutes, turning after 10 minutes.

7 Add a small ladle of the cooking stock to the roasting pan and cook for a further 10–15 minutes, basting through the cooking process.

8 While it is cooking, heat a little oil in a pan, brown the onions and ceps, and add the rest of the stock. Cook through and reserve.

9 Remove the rabbit from the oven and place in a serving dish, retain and keep warm.

10 Meanwhile, add the white wine and deglaze the roasting dish. Pass the cooked stock into the reduced wine and reduce rapidly to 200 ml.

11 Add the onions, ceps, cream, chives and cooked bacon. Adjust the seasoning and pour over the rabbit.

12 This can be served with mashed potato, gratin Dauphinoise, or anything autumnal or with a winter influence (e.g. a selection of root vegetables).

Note: This dish can be made a day in advance if needed. It uses a classic sauce forestière, which can be adapted to use button mushrooms (instead of ceps), different herbs, etc. – the choice is yours.

Hare

332 Hare

Young hare 2½–3 kg in weight should be used. To test a young hare it should be possible to take the ear between the fingers and tear it quite easily, also the hare lip, which is clearly marked in older animals, should be only faintly defined.

A hare should be hung for about a week before cleaning it out.

333 Jugged hare

Hare	4 portions	10 portions
hare (approx. 2½ kg each), skinned and cut into pieces	1	3
rendered duck fat/lard	25 g	65 g
plain flour	20 g	50 g
cold water	400 ml	1 litre
redcurrant jelly	2 tsp	5 tsp
salt and pepper		
Marinade		
red wine	750 ml	1⅞ l
mirepoix	250 g	625 g
black peppercorns	10	25
bay leaves	2	5
juniper berries, crushed	3	8

nutritional info

1 large portion provides:
1029 kJ/246 kcal
10.28 g fat (of which 5.68 g saturated)
6.24 g carbohydrate (of which 1.68 g sugars)
32.3 g protein
0.19 g fibre

Duck fat or lard is used to brown the hare.
Chicken was used for the saturated fat analysis.

kcal
1000
900
800
700
600
500
400
300
200
100
0

calorie counter

For the hare

1 Remove as much blood as possible from the cavity (the game supplier should have retained the blood once the hare had been killed and butchered). Reserve the blood in the fridge well covered.

2 Remove the legs front and back, trim off the rib cage and cut the long saddle into 4 pieces.

3 Mix all the marinade ingredients together and boil for 5 minutes. Allow to cool to room temperature.

4 Once room temperature is achieved, pour the marinade over the hare pieces and place in the fridge for 24 hours.

5 Pre-heat the oven to 125°C, drain the rabbit pieces out of the marinade and separate from the mirepoix.

6 Place a little of the rendered duck fat or lard in a thick-bottomed pan and brown the hare pieces well. Place in a casserole along with the vegetable mirepoix from the marinade and the flour and cook for 2 minutes.

7 Add the marinating liquid and the rest of the ingredients (redcurrant jelly, seasoning), mix well and bring to the boil. Place in the oven with a tight-fitting lid for 3 hours until tender.

8 When cooked remove from the oven and strain the cooking liquor, placing the cooked hare in a serving dish. Discard the vegetables and bring the liquor up to the boil, simmer and skim if necessary.

9 Take the retained blood and mix with a little red wine vinegar and water so that it is less solidified. Add to the sauce but *do not boil* as this will split the mix.

10 Pour over the hare pieces and serve with mashed potato and seasonal winter vegetables.

Note: Traditionally, fried heart-shaped croutons, with the points dipped in the sauce, and chopped parsley are used as a garnish. Once the *liaison au sang* (blood thickening) is added to the sauce, it must not be boiled as this will coagulate the blood and the sauce will appear to be split.

Venison

334 Venison

Venison is the meat of the red deer, fallow deer and roebuck. Of these three, the meat of the roebuck is considered to have the best and most delicate eating quality. The prime cuts are the legs, loins and best ends. The shoulders of young animals can be boned, rolled and roasted, but if in any doubt as to their tenderness, they should be cut up and used for stewed or braised dishes.

After slaughter, carcasses should be hung well in a cool place for several days and when cut into joints are usually marinated before being cooked.

335 Venison cutlets, chops and steaks

1 Venison cutlets, cut from the best end, and chops, cut from the loin, are usually well trimmed, and cooked by shallow-frying, provided that the meat is tender. If in doubt they should be braised.

2 After they are cooked they should be removed from the pan, the fat poured off and the pan deglazed with stock, red wine, brandy, Madeira or sherry, which is then added to the accompanying sauce.

3 A spicy, peppery sauce is usually offered, which can be varied by the addition of any one or more extra ingredients, e.g. cream, yoghurt, redcurrant jelly, choice of cooked beetroot, sliced button or wild mushrooms, cooked pieces of chestnut, etc.

4 Accompaniments can include, for example, a purée of green, brown or yellow lentils, a purée of any other dried bean, purée of braised chestnuts, braised red cabbage, or purée of a root vegetable, e.g. celeriac, turnip, swede, carrot, parsnip or any combination of these.

5 Venison steaks or escalopes are cut from the boned-out nuts of meat from the loins, well trimmed and slightly thinned with a meat bat.

6 The escalopes can be quickly shallow-fried and finished as for cutlets and chops, with a variety of accompanying sauces and garnishes.

336 Pot roast rack of venison with buttered greens and Merlot sauce

	4 portions	10 portions
Venison		
venison rack, bones cleaned and trimmed	2 kg	5 kg
vegetable oil	50 ml	125 ml
small mirepoix	250 g	625 g
clarified butter	100 g	250 g
garlic cloves	2	5
sprig of thyme	1	3
salt and pepper		
Merlot sauce		
oil	100 g	200 g
venison trimmings and bones	450 g	1 kg
cracked pepper	½ tsp	1½ tsp
bay leaf	1	3
sprig thyme	1	2
carrot, peeled and roughly chopped	1	3
onion, peeled and roughly chopped	½	2
garlic cloves, split	2	5
Merlot wine	330 ml	800 ml
chicken stock	1½ litres	2½ litres
Greens		
butter	50 g	125 g
spinach leaves	250 g	500 g
spring cabbage, cut into 1½ cm strips (blanched for 2 minutes and refreshed in an ice bath)	1	2
escarole, stalks removed	1	3

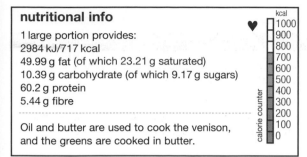

nutritional info

1 large portion provides:
2984 kJ/717 kcal
49.99 g fat (of which 23.21 g saturated)
10.39 g carbohydrate (of which 9.17 g sugars)
60.2 g protein
5.44 g fibre

Oil and butter are used to cook the venison, and the greens are cooked in butter.

For the venison

1 Pre-heat the oven to 180°C. Trim the venison so that the bones rise 5 cm above the meat. Tie the venison with kitchen string at intervals along the joint, tying 3 pieces of string between each bone.

2 Place a large pan with a tight-fitting lid over a high heat, add the oil and seal the venison, turning until it is a light golden colour all over.

3 Transfer the meat to a tray and cook the mirepoix in the same way.

4 Add the venison back to the pan, placing it on top of the mirepoix, and cover in the clarified butter. Add the garlic, thyme and seasoning. Place in the oven for 20–25 minutes until medium rare (the residual heat will cook it further).

5 Remove from the oven and set aside to rest for 10 minutes.

For the Merlot sauce

1 In a large saucepan, heat the oil over a medium heat. Working in batches to prevent steaming and give a good colour, cook the venison trimmings until brown, add the cracked pepper, bay leaf and thyme. Remove from the pan and set aside in a bowl.

2 Reduce the heat and, in the same pan, cook the carrots, onion and garlic for about 10 minutes or until brown. Return the meat to the pan and stir well.

3 Raise the heat and, when the pan is quite hot, add the wine. Bring to the boil.

4 Boil rapidly until the volume of liquid has reduced by half. Add the chicken stock, return to the boil, then lower the heat right down and cook the sauce for about 1 hour.

5 Stir every 10 minutes to prevent sticking and skim off any sediment that rises to the surface.

6 When the sauce has reduced to approx. 400 ml (for 10 portions, 1 l), pour it through a fine strainer into a clean pan.

7 Bring to the boil and simmer until the volume of liquid has reduced to 200 ml/500 ml, giving a rich plum-coloured sauce.

To complete

1 Add the butter to a pan, place in the greens and heat through, warm the sauce and then slice the venison.

2 Lay the buttered greens in the centre of the plate with the venison on top and finish with the Merlot sauce.

Note: The rich Merlot sauce can be use for other rich meat dishes; it can be made two or three days ahead and stored in an airtight container in the refrigerator.

337 Medallions of venison with red wine, walnuts and chocolate

	4 portions	10 portions
vegetable oil	50 ml	125 ml
trimmed venison loin	750 g	1800 g
salt and pepper		
Merlot sauce (see recipe 336)	200 ml	500 ml
broken walnut pieces	40 g	100 g
70 per cent bitter chocolate in small broken pieces	50 g	125 g

nutritional info

1 large portion provides:
1834 kJ/439 kcal
26.96 g fat (of which 5.62 g saturated)
8.38 g carbohydrate (of which 8.18 g sugars)
43.7 g protein
0.66 g fibre

Oil is used to seal the venison, and it is served with chocolate pieces.

kcal
1000
900
800
700
600
500
400
300
200
100
0

calorie counter

1 Pre-heat the oven to 190°C. Heat the oil in a heavy frying pan and seal the venison loin, add salt and pepper, place on a baking tray and then in the oven, and cook for 6–8 minutes medium rare or according to taste.

2 Meanwhile, warm the sauce and add the broken walnuts.

3 Slice the venison loin equally, nap over the sauce and sprinkle liberally with chocolate pieces.

Note: This method of sprinkling the chocolate on afterwards allows you to taste the sauce and the chocolate separately.

INTERNATIONAL CUISINE

INTRODUCTION

As our multi-cultural society and the popularity of overseas dishes continue to grow, it becomes increasingly important to have a basic working knowledge of international cuisine.

Many countries, such as China, Japan and India, and areas like the Middle East, have long-established culinary traditions with a wide range of dishes dating back for two to three thousand years. Now, because of customer demands and changes in society, all students of cookery need to have at least a basic but sound understanding of multi-cultural dishes. The following recipes are examples of such dishes, however these will vary according to different regions.

Contributes to units
3FP1, 3FP2,
3FP3, 3FP4,
3FC1, 3FC2,
3FC3, 3FC4,
3FPC2

LIST OF RECIPES

Recipe no	page no
Caribbean	
340 Baked christophenes with onion and cheese filling	286
338 Piononos (plantain with minced beef filling)	285
339 Salt fish and akee	285
China	
342 Beef with mango and black pepper	287
343 Chicken with peppers and black bean sauce	287
341 Lemon and ginger chicken	286
344 Peking duck	288
345 Plum sauce	289
India	
351 Alu-chloe	292
349 Baigon ka chokha	291
348 Changezie champen	290
346 Crab Malabar	289
352 Onion bhajias	292
350 Palak lamb	291
347 Policha meen	290
353 Samosas	292
Indonesia	
358 Kukus ikan sebalah madura (fillet of halibut madura)	296
355 Rendang (beef curry)	294
356 Rendang kambang kot baru (lamb in spicy coconut sauce)	295
357 Saus rendang (spicy coconut sauce)	295
354 Sop bobor (spinach and coconut soup)	294
Malaysia	
360 Ayam kicap baah asam (spiced fried chicken and plum sauce)	297
359 Daging masak meruh (beef in red sauce)	296
361 Ikan bahan dengan kunyit celi padi (stuffed red snapper)	297

Recipe no	page no
Mexico	
362 Chancho adobado (pork in orange and lemon sauce with sweet potatoes)	298
363 Huachinango veracruzano (red snapper with tomato sauce)	298
Middle East	
368 Bacalhau trás-os-montes (baked cod with ham)	300
364 Borani (spinach and yoghurt salad)	299
366 Dajaj mahshi (roast chicken with rice and pine kernel stuffing)	299
367 Lubya khadra billahma (lamb with French beans)	300
365 Mast va khiar (yoghurt, vegetable and herb salad)	299
369 Truchas a'la navarra (marinated trout with herbs)	301
Spain	
370 Canja (chicken soup with lemon and mint)	301
372 Porco con ameijuas a alentejaru (pork with clams)	302
371 Riñones al jerez (sautéed kidneys with sherry sauce)	301
Thailand	
373 Dom yam nua (beef soup with chives)	303
374 Phat priu wan (sweet and sour pork and snow peas)	303
376 Pla cian (fried fish, Thai style)	304
375 Pla nergn (steamed fish, Thai style)	303
Vietnam	
378 Bò xào magi (beef and bok choy with black bean sauce)	305
379 Cá xót ngot (fish with sweet chilli sauce)	306
377 Thit n'òng mi dâu phong (fried pork with noodles and peanuts)	304

CARIBBEAN

338 Piononos: deep-fried plantain rings with spiced minced-beef filling

	4 portions	10 portions
large ripe plantains	2	5
butter or margarine	50 g	125 g
vegetable oil	2 tsp	5 tsp
vegetable oil mixed with 1 (2½) tsp annatto	2 tbsp	5 tbsp
lean minced topside of beef	400 g	1¼ kg
onion, finely chopped	50 g	125 g
green pepper, finely chopped	50 g	125 g
red chilli, finely chopped	1	2–3
garlic clove, crushed and chopped	1	2–3
plain flour	25 g	60 g
ham, chopped	100 g	250 g
tomato concassée	100 g	250 g
seasoning		
brown stock or water	125 ml	300 ml
olives, chopped	6	15
capers, chopped	25 g	60 g
malt vinegar	1 tbsp	2–3 tbsp
eggs, beaten	4	10

1 Peel the plantains and cut each one lengthways into thick strips, approximately 6 mm.

2 Place the butter in a suitable pan and fry the plantains both sides until golden brown, drain well.

3 Heat the vegetable oil and annatto in a suitable pan, quickly fry the minced beef.

4 Add the onions, peppers, chillies and garlic, and cook for 5 minutes stirring frequently.

5 Add the flour, stir well and cook for a further 5 minutes.

6 Stir in the ham, tomatoes and seasoning.

7 Moisten with a little water or brown stock.

8 Continue to cook until the mixture resembles a paste-like consistency.

9 Add the chopped olives and capers, the vinegar and the correct seasoning.

10 To make the piononos, shape each strip of plantain into a ring about 7.5 cm in diameter, overlap by 8 mm. Secure with a cocktail stick.

11 Fill each with the beef mixture. *Do not overfill.*

12 Dip each of the piononos into seasoned flour, brush off excess flour. Dip into beaten egg.

13 Carefully deep-fry in a suitable pan at 180°C for approximately 3 minutes.

14 Serve immediately with red beans and rice.

Red beans and rice

The easiest way to serve this dish is to prepare a braised rice and garnish with cooked red beans.

339 Salt fish and akee

	4 portions	10 portions
salt cod	400 g	1¼ kg
fish stock or water		
salt pork, diced	100 g	250 g
onion, chopped	100 g	250 g
red chilli, chopped	1	2–3
canned akee	400 g	1¼ kg
thyme		
mill pepper		
tomato to garnish		

1 Soak the cod for 12 hours, change the water 3–4 times.

2 Drain the cod, rinse under cold water.

3 Poach it in boiling water or fish stock for approximately 10–15 minutes.

4 Remove it from the cooking liquor and flake it free from the skin and bone.

5 Deep-fry the diced pork in a frying pan until crisp and brown and all the fat is rendered. Discard the pork.

6 Add the onions and chillies to the pork fat, cook for approximately 5 minutes.

7 Add the flaked cod, akee, thyme and mill pepper, cook for 2 minutes.

8 Serve in a suitable dish garnished with tomato.

Note: Akee is a Caribbean fruit which may be purchased fresh or in cans.

340 Baked christophenes with onion and cheese filling

	4 portions	10 portions
large christophenes, approx. 300 g each	2	5
butter or margarine	75 g	180 g
onions, finely chopped	150 g	375 g
Parmesan cheese, finely grated	25 g	60 g
seasoning		

1 Wash and cut the christophenes in half lengthways.

2 Place in boiling salted water and gently simmer until slightly under cooked (al dente).

3 Refresh and drain.

4 Remove the seeds.

5 Cut into boat-like shells, approximately 6 mm thick.

6 Chop the scooped-out pulp coarsely.

7 In half the butter, sweat the onions without colour.

8 Add the pulp, cheese and seasoning.

9 Stir until the mixture is thick and most of the liquid has been evaporated.

10 Fill the christophene shells with the mixture.

11 Place in a suitable dish, brush with butter, sprinkle with a little more cheese.

12 Place in oven at 180°C to reheat and brown. Serve immediately.

Note: The christophenes may also be coated with a cheese sauce and glazed.

CHINA

341 Lemon and ginger chicken

	4 portions	10 portions
chicken breasts	4 × 150 g	10 × 150 g
cornflour	1½ tbsp	3¾ tbsp
egg whites	3	7
Sauce		
lemon juice	62 ml	155 ml
chicken stock	250 ml	625 ml
green ginger, grated	1 tsp	2½ tsp
honey	1 tbsp	2½ tbsp
sugar	2 tbsp	5 tbsp
cornflour	1 tbsp	2½ tbsp
piece of green ginger, sliced	2½ cm	6 cm approx.
shallot	1	3

1 Skin the chicken breasts, remove bone, cut into 5 mm strips.

2 Mix the cornflour and beaten egg whites, add chicken and mix well.

3 Heat sufficient oil in a wok to deep-fry the chicken until golden brown.

4 Remove chicken, drain well, keep warm.

5 Mix lemon juice and chicken stock, grated ginger, honey and sugar in a suitable pan, bring to boil. Mix the cornflour with a little water, add to the sauce, bring to boil, stir until it thickens.

6 Heat a little oil in the wok, add sliced ginger, fry for 1 minute, add sauce, simmer for 2 minutes, pour over chicken. Garnish with finely chopped shallots.

7 Serve with fried rice (see below).

Fried rice

egg (beaten with a pinch of salt and pepper)	
150–200 g cooked rice per person	
salt and pepper and soy sauce, to taste	
dash of sesame oil	
1 tbsp spring onion, finely chopped	

1 Heat a wok to a medium heat, add a little oil. Add the egg and scramble quickly.

2 Add the rice and stir-fry. Add seasoning. Top with the spring onion.

nutritional info	kcal
1 large portion provides: 878 kJ/207 kcal 1.0 g fat (of which 0.2 g saturated) 30.8 g carbohydrate (of which 15.4 g sugars) 20.5 g protein 0.2 g fibre The skin is removed.	♥ 1000 900 800 700 600 500 400 300 200 100 0 calorie counter

342 Beef with mango and black pepper

	4 portions	10 portions
beef topside or fillet	300 g	750 g
mango	1	2
oil	4 tbsp	10 tbsp
ginger, shredded	1 tsp	2 tsp
spring onion, finely sliced	2	5
sesame oil		
Marinade		
suet	1 tsp	2¼ tsp
sugar	½ tsp	1¼ tsp
potato starch	2 tsp	5 tsp
bicarbonate of soda	⅛ tsp	⅜ tsp
soy sauce	1 tsp	2½ tsp
ground black pepper	¼ tsp	½ tsp
rose liqueur	2 tsp	2½ tsp
water	4 tbsp	9 tbsp
oil	1 tbsp	2½ tbsp
sesame oil	½ tsp	1¼ tsp
Sauce		
oyster sauce	1 tbsp	2½ tbsp
shao xing wine	1 tbsp	2½ tbsp
dark soy sauce	½ tsp	1 tsp
water	4 tbsp	9 tbsp
sugar	⅛ tsp	¼ tsp
pepper	⅛ tsp	¼ tsp

nutritional info

1 large portion provides:
971 kJ/233 kcal
14.4 g fat (of which 3.9 g saturated)
9.3 g carbohydrate (of which 6.2 g sugars)
17.1 g protein
1.2 g fibre

Oil is used throughout. Lean beef was used for this analysis.

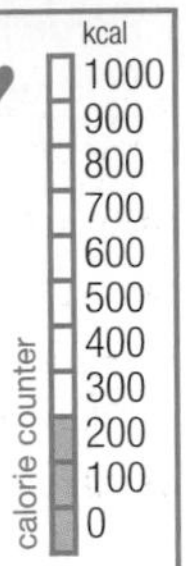

1 Cut the beef into 2 cm dice. Mix all the ingredients for the marinade and marinate the beef overnight.

2 Peel the mango, cut into strips.

3 Mix all the ingredients for the sauce together in a suitable bowl.

4 Heat the oil in a suitable wok and quickly fry the beef. Drain well.

5 Heat the second amount of oil in the wok, quickly fry the grated ginger. Add the beef. Add the sauce ingredients, reduce by half. Season.

6 Add the mango. Stir well to incorporate.

7 Add the spring onion and sesame oil.

8 Serve immediately on plates.

343 Chicken with peppers and black bean sauce

	4 portions	10 portions
Chicken with peppers		
chicken breast	4 × 150 g	10 × 150 g
red pepper	½	1½
green pepper	½	1½
yellow pepper	½	1½
onion, finely chopped	50 g	125 g
oil	1 tbsp	2½ tbsp
shao xing wine (dry white)	½ tbsp	2 tbsp
black bean sauce	1 tbsp	2 tbsp
chicken stock	2 tbsp	5 tbsp
sesame oil	½ tsp	1 tsp
Marinade		
potato starch	1 tsp	2½ tsp
salt	1 tsp	2½ tsp
sugar	½ tsp	1 tsp
pepper	¼ tsp	½ tsp
shao xing wine	2 tsp	5 tsp
water	2 tbsp	5 tbsp
oil	1 tbsp	2½ tbsp
sesame oil	1 tsp	2 tsp
Black bean sauce		
black beans	50 g	125 g
ginger finely chopped	1 tbsp	2½ tbsp
garlic cloves, finely chopped	2	5
red chilli chopped	½	1½
garlic crushed in fried flakes	1 tsp	2½ tsp
shao xing wine	1 tbsp	2½ tbsp
sugar	1½ tsp	4 tsp
light soy sauce	1 tsp	2½ tsp
ground white pepper	½ tsp	1½ tsp
sesame oil	½ tsp	1½ tsp

nutritional info

1 large portion provides:
1418 kJ/339 kcal
18.4 g fat (of which 2.5 g saturated)
6.6 g carbohydrate (of which 5.2 g sugars)
37.3 g protein
1.6 g fibre

The skin is removed, but oil used to stir fry.

♥ kcal
1000
900
800
700
600
500
400
300
200
100
0

calorie counter

For the chicken with peppers

1　Skin the chicken breasts and cut into strips.

2　Place in a bowl with the marinade except the oils. Mix thoroughly, add the oil. Leave the chicken to coat, cover and marinate overnight.

3　Deseed the peppers and cut in 1½ cm squares. Finely chop the onion.

4　Heat the oil in a wok, quickly stir-fry the chicken, add the onion and peppers, cook for a further minute. Add the wine.

5　Add the black bean sauce (see below) and cook for another minute. Adjust the consistency with a little chicken stock.

6　Add the sesame oil. Serve on plates with rice.

For the black bean sauce

1　Soak the black beans in warm water to remove excess salt and grit.

2　Drain and rinse well.

3　Heat 1 tbsp of oil in a wok and gently fry the ginger for 1 minute. Add the garlic and continue for a further minute.

4　Add the chilli and cook for a further minute. Add the black beans, stir-fry until fragrant.

5　Remove from heat, place in a bowl. Add the remaining ingredients and mix well. Cover with clingfilm and steam for 30 minutes. Cool and store in refrigerator until required.

344　Peking duck

	4 portions	10 portions
duck, cleaned and prepared	1 × 1½ kg	2 × 1½ kg
Chinese five spice powder	1 tsp	2 tsp
salt	2 tsp	4 tsp
Chinese oyster sauce	2 tbsp	4 tbsp
peanut oil, for frying		
Glaze		
golden syrup	2 tbsp	4 tbsp
distilled white malt vinegar	2 tsp	4 tsp
sake or vodka	2 tsp	4 tsp
water	125 ml	250 ml
To serve		
cooked rice *or*	1 kg	2 kg
Peking duck pancakes	16	32
cucumber, cut into 5 cm strips	200 g	400 g
spring onions	8	16
plum sauce or hoisin sauce	250 ml	500 ml

nutritional info

1 large portion provides:
3779 kJ/895 kcal
24.7 g fat (of which 6.0 g saturated)
137.9 g carbohydrate (of which 59.0 g sugars)
39.2 g protein
3.9 g fibre

Fat is used in cooking.

♥ kcal
1000
900
800
700
600
500
400
300
200
100
0

calorie counter

1　Wash the duck under running cold water, dry well on a cloth or kitchen paper.

2　In a bowl mix the Chinese five spice, salt and oyster sauce. Rub all over the inside of the bird.

3　Tie a long string around the neck of the bird so that the duck can be hung up.

4　Put the duck into a colander and pour boiling water over it 5 times, letting the bird dry off between each pouring. Pat dry again.

5　Place the ingredients for the glaze into a suitable saucepan. Bring to boil and reduce to a syrup. Brush the glaze over the duck. Hang the duck up by the string in a hot, breezy place to dry out. This can be done with an electric fan.

6　Fill a large wok one-third full with peanut oil and heat to 190°C. Deep-fry the duck for approximately 30 minutes, then turn and deep-fry for a further 30 minutes. Alternatively, roast the duck in the normal way.

7　When cooked, slice the duck and serve with rice, or slice with pancakes, cucumber, spring onions and plum or hoisin sauce.

345 Plum sauce

Makes 750 ml

plums	1 kg
brown sugar	250 g
Szechuan peppercorns, pan-roasted	1 tbsp
fennel seeds, pan-roasted	1 tbsp
whole cloves	1 tsp
whole star anise	3
cinnamon stick, crushed	1
fresh ginger, peeled and grated	12 g
white rice vinegar	375 ml

1 Cut the plums into quarters, remove the stones.

2 Place all ingredients in a saucepan and bring to the boil, stirring well. Simmer for 20 minutes.

3 Strain, pour into sterilised jars, seal and store in the refrigerator.

INDIA

346 Crab Malabar

Mehernosh Mody

Serves four

vegetable oil	2 tbsp
mustard seeds	½ tsp
poppy seeds	½ tsp
stem curry leaves	1
Spanish onion, chopped	½
cloves garlic, peeled and finely chopped	4
turmeric powder	½ tsp
yoghurt	3 tbsp
coconut milk	150 ml
fresh or frozen crab meat, flaked and with all moisture gently pressed out	200 g
sweetcorn kernels	2 tbsp
salt, to taste	
fresh chopped coriander leaves to garnish	
the crab shells to contain the mixture, if whole crabs have been used	

Mehernosh Mody

1 Heat the oil in a pan. Add the mustard seeds, wait until they splutter for a few seconds then add the poppy seeds.

2 Wait for a few seconds again before adding the curry leaves followed by the chopped onion and garlic, then sauté for a further minute.

3 Add the turmeric powder and sauté for 10 seconds before lowering the heat and adding the yoghurt.

4 Simmer for a bare minute then add the coconut milk and continue to simmer for a further 3 to 4 minutes.

5 Put in the crabmeat and the corn kernels, and mix in.

6 Return to the boil and check seasoning, adding salt to taste.

7 The dish can be served warm or cold, in the crab shells if applicable, and garnished with the chopped coriander leaves.

347 Policha meen

Mehernosh Mody

Serves four

grey mullets weighing about 500 g each, scaled and gutted (sea bass may be used as a substitute)	2
turmeric powder	½ tsp
salt	½ tsp
lemon, juice of	1
Chutney	
fresh green peppercorns, stripped from the stem	4 tbsp
fresh coriander	½ bunch
green chillies, deseeded	2
cloves garlic, peeled	5
cumin powder	½ tsp
lemon, juice of	½
salt, to taste	
banana leaf to wrap the fish in (kitchen paper or foil may be used instead)	1
sprigs of fresh green pepper and fresh red chillies cut into fine julienne to garnish	

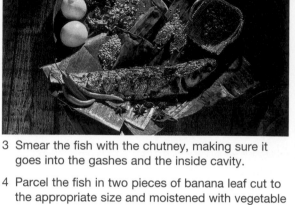

1 Cut 3 gashes on either side of the fish; rub in the turmeric powder, salt and lemon juice to coat the fish. Set aside for at least 1 hour.

2 Grind or process all the chutney ingredients (not too finely), incorporating the lemon juice and a pinch of salt.

3 Smear the fish with the chutney, making sure it goes into the gashes and the inside cavity.

4 Parcel the fish in two pieces of banana leaf cut to the appropriate size and moistened with vegetable oil. You can secure the parcels with string or with toothpicks (alternatively parcel the fish in oiled kitchen paper or foil).

5 Bake for 15 minutes in an oven heated to 180°C.

6 Serve hot in the banana leaf with tomato rougail as an accompaniment, and garnish with the green pepper and julienned red chillies.

348 Changezie champen

Atul Kochhar

Serves four

lamb chops or cutlets	8
Marinade	
garlic paste	20 g
green chilli paste	10 g
toasted fennel seeds	5 g
mace powder	¼ tsp
cardamom powder	½ tsp
double cream	250 ml
crushed black pepper	½ tsp
salt	½ tsp
roasted gram flour	30 g
vegetable oil	50 ml
sesame seeds	30 g

1 Mix all the spices and pastes in double cream to form a marinade.

2 Stir in the roasted gram flour and vegetable oil and leave the marinade for 30 minutes at room temperature.

3 Add the lamb chops to the marinade and leave it to rest at room temperature for 1½ hours.

4 Skewer the lamb chops and cook for 15 minutes in a moderately hot tandoor.

5 Remove and rest the chops for 5 minutes, baste with oil.

6 Roll the chops over sesame seeds on the edges and cook again for another 5 minutes.

7 Remove, baste with butter and sprinkle on crushed black pepper and lemon juice.

8 Serve with mint chutney and sliced onions.

Note: Alternatively, chops can also be cooked on a hot grill or in an oven, although this will sacrifice the barbeque flavour.

349 Baigan ka chokha   Atul Kochhar

Caviar of aubergine with spices and herbs

Serves four

red onion	50 g
coriander leaves	20 g
mint leaves	20 g
ginger	10 g
green chilli	2
aubergines (large)	2
toasted cumin powder	10 g
lime juice	10 ml
salt	½ tsp
olive oil	1 tbsp

1 Chop the red onion into fine dice.

2 Wash and chop the herbs.

3 Scrape, wash and chop the ginger into fine dice and slice the chilli into thin roundels.

4 Roast the aubergines in a hot tandoor until charred. Remove, cook and skin.

5 Chop the aubergine flesh coarsely and store in the refrigerator until required.

6 Place the cold aubergine pulp in a mixing bowl. Add the spices, herbs, olive oil and salt, and mix together.

7 Place back in the refrigerator for pulp to set, so it will be easy to handle with a spoon to form quenelles.

8 Use as an accompaniment to roasted lamb chops, for example.

350 Palak lamb

A medium-spiced dish from the Punjab

	4 portions	10 portions
vegetable ghee or oil	62 ml	155 ml
cumin seeds	1 tsp	2½ tsp
onion, finely chopped	50 g	125 g
fresh ginger, finely chopped	12 g	30 g
garlic clove, crushed	1	3
shoulder loin or leg of lamb, cut into 2½ cm dice	400 g	1 kg
hot curry paste	2 tsp	5 tsp
natural yoghurt	125 ml	312 ml
salt, to taste		
tomato purée	25 g	62 g
spinach, chopped	200 g	500 g
coriander lemon for garnish		

1 Heat the ghee or oil in a suitable frying pan.

2 Add the cumin seeds and fry for 1 minute.

3 Add the onion and fry until golden brown.

4 Add the ginger and garlic and stir-fry until all is brown.

5 Add the lamb and simmer for 15–20 minutes.

6 Add the curry paste, yoghurt and salt.

7 Cook for 5 minutes. Add water if necessary to prevent sticking.

8 Stir in the tomato purée and spinach. Cover and simmer for 10–15 minutes, until the lamb is tender.

9 Serve garnished with coriander leaves.

351 Alu-chloe

A vegetarian curry from north India

	4 portions	10 portions
vegetable ghee or oil	45 ml	125 ml
small cinnamon sticks	4	10
bay leaves	4	10
cumin seeds	1 tsp	2½ tsp
onion, finely chopped	100 g	250 g
garlic cloves, finely chopped	2	5
chopped plum tomatoes, canned	400 g	1 kg
hot curry paste	3 tsp	7½ tsp
salt, to taste		
potato, cut into 12 mm dice	100 g	250 g
chickpeas (canned, drained weight)	400 g	1 kg
water	125 ml	300 ml
chopped coriander leaves	50 g	125 g
tamarind sauce or lemon juice	2 tsp	5 tsp

1 Heat the ghee in a suitable pan.
2 Add the cinnamon, bay leaves and cumin seeds. Fry for approximately 1 minute.
3 Add the onion and garlic. Fry until golden brown.
4 Add the chopped tomatoes, curry paste and salt. Fry for a further 2–3 minutes.
5 Stir in the potatoes and water. Bring to the boil. Cover and simmer until the potatoes are cooked.
6 Add the chickpeas and allow to heat through.
7 Stir in the coriander and lemon juice. Serve immediately.

352 Onion bhajias v

	4 portions	10 portions
besan or gram flour	45 g (3 tsp)	112 g (7½ tsp)
hot curry powder	1 tsp	2½ tsp
salt		
water	75 ml (5 tsp)	187 ml (12½ tsp)
onion, finely shredded	100 g	250 g

1 Mix together the flour, curry powder and salt.
2 Blend in the water carefully to form a smooth, thick batter.
3 Stir in the onion.
4 Drop the mixture off a tablespoon into deep oil at 200°C. Fry for approximately 5–10 minutes until golden brown.
5 Drain well and serve as a snack or an accompaniment, with mango chutney as a dip.

353 Samosas

	4 portions	10 portions
short or filo pastry	400 g	1 kg

1 Make the pastry from ghee fat and fairly strong flour as the dough should be fairly elastic. Brush the pastry with ghee or vegetable oil after rolling into a smooth ball.
2 Take a small piece of dough and roll into a ball (approximately 25 mm diameter). Keep the rest of the dough covered with either a wet cloth, clingfilm or plastic, otherwise a skin will form on it.
3 Roll the ball into a circle approximately 90 cm in diameter on a lightly floured surface. Cut the circle in half.
4 Moisten the straight edge with eggwash or water.
5 Shape the semi-circle into a cone. Fill the cone with approximately 1½ teaspoons of filling. Moisten the top edges and press them together well.
6 The samosas may be made in advance, covered with cling film or plastic, and refrigerated before being deep-fried.
7 Deep fry at 180°C until golden brown. Remove from fryer and drain well.
8 Serve on a dish garnished with coriander leaves, with a suitable chutney served separately.

Potato filling

	4 portions	10 portions
potatoes, peeled	200 g	500 g
vegetable oil	1½ tsp	3¾ tsp
black mustard seeds	½ tsp	1¼ tsp
onions, finely chopped	50 g	125 g
fresh ginger, finely chopped	12 g	30 g
fennel seeds	1 tsp	2½ tsp
cumin seeds	¼ tsp	1 tsp
turmeric	¼ tsp	1 tsp
frozen peas	75 g	187 g
salt, to taste		
water	2½ tsp	6¼ tsp
fresh coriander, finely chopped	1 tsp	2½ tsp
garam masala	½ tsp	2½ tsp
cayenne pepper	pinch	pinch

1 Cut the potatoes into 6 mm dice. Cook in water until only just cooked.

2 Heat the oil in a suitable pan. Add the mustard seeds and cook until they burst.

3 Add the onions and ginger. Fry for 7–8 minutes, stirring continuously until golden brown.

4 Stir in the fennel, cumin and turmeric. Add the potatoes, peas, salt and water.

5 Reduce to a low heat, cover the pan and cook for 5 minutes.

6 Stir in the coriander and cook for a further 5 minutes.

7 Remove from the heat and stir in the garam masala and the cayenne seasoning.

8 Remove from pan. Place into a suitable bowl and allow the filling to cool before using.

Lamb filling

	4 portions	10 portions
saffron	½ tsp	1¼ tsp
boiling water	2½ tsp	6¼ tsp
vegetable oil	3 tsp	7½ tsp
fresh ginger, finely chopped	12 g	30 g
garlic cloves, crushed	2	5
onions, finely chopped	50 g	125 g
salt, to taste		
lean minced lamb	400 g	1 kg
cayenne pepper	pinch	pinch
garam masala	1 tsp	2½ tsp

1 Infuse the saffron in the boiling water. Allow to stand for 10 minutes.

2 Heat the vegetable oil in a suitable pan. Add the ginger, garlic, onions and salt, stirring continuously. Fry for 7–8 minutes, until the onions are soft and golden brown.

3 Stir in the lamb and add the saffron with the water. Keep stirring the lamb until it is cooked.

4 Add the cayenne and garam masala. Reduce the heat and allow to cook gently for a further 10 minutes.

5 The mixture should be fairly tight with very little moisture.

6 Transfer to a bowl and allow to cool before using.

Note: Samosas may be oven baked to reduce the fat content.

INDONESIA

354 Sop bobor (spinach and coconut soup)

	4 portions	10 portions
onions, finely chopped	25 g	60 g
vegetable oil	75 ml	150 ml
garlic, chopped	12 g	30 g
lesser galangal, peeled and finely chopped	12 g	40 g
salam leaf	1	2½–3
lemon grass stalk, crushed	1	2½–3
coriander powder	3 g (½ tsp)	10 g (1½ tsp)
brown sugar	12 g	25 g
chicken stock	500 ml	1¼ litres
coconut milk	250 ml	600 ml
spinach leaves	100 g	250 g
coconut flesh, diced	100 g	250 g
salt and pepper		
Garnish		
spinach leaves, finely chopped	50 g	125 g
coconut flesh, diced	50 g	125 g

1 Sauté the onions in the oil, add the garlic and lesser galangal. Sweat for 2–3 minutes without colour.

2 Add the salam leaf, lemon grass, coriander powder and brown sugar. Sauté for a further 2–3 minutes.

3 Cover with chicken stock, add the coconut milk, bring to the boil, stir frequently.

4 Add the chopped spinach leaves and diced coconut flesh. Season with salt and pepper. Reduce the heat, simmer for 15 minutes.

5 Remove the salam leaf and lemon grass.

6 Purée the soup in a liquidiser.

7 Serve in individual soup bowls, garnished with finely shredded spinach and diced coconut flesh.

Note: If fresh coconut flesh is not available, use dried coconut flakes soaked in water for 10 minutes.

Lesser galangal (kencur) is a rhizome that originated in India and is used sparingly. It has a hot, strong flavour. Fresh kencur can be found in Asian food stores, and can also be purchased in a powdered form (kaempferia galanga).

Wood fungus (jamur kuping) may be added to this recipe. It is also called cloud ear fungus, because it swells to a curled shape when soaked in water. Sold in dried form and greyish black in colour, it turns brown and translucent when soaked.

355 Rendang (beef curry)

	4 portions	10 portions
cooking oil	70 ml	150 ml
onion, finely chopped	100 g	250 g
garlic cloves, crushed	2	5
fresh ginger, finely chopped	12 g	30 g
hot Thai curry blend	2 tsp	5 tsp
ground lemon grass	1 tsp	2½ tsp
desiccated coconut	100 g	250 g
rump or sirloin cut into thin strips	400 g	1 kg
creamed coconut	100 g	250 g
hot water	¼ litre	¾ litre
salt, to taste		

1 Heat the oil in a suitable pan. Fry the onions, garlic and ginger until lightly coloured.

2 Add the curry blend and lemon grass. Continue to fry for a further 2 minutes.

3 Add the desiccated coconut and fry for a further 1 minute.

4 Quickly fry the beef in a separate pan. Drain off excess oil.

5 Place the beef in a clean saucepan. Season and add the coconut milk (creamed coconut and hot water blended together).

6 Add the other prepared ingredients to the beef.

7 Bring to the boil, then simmer until the beef is tender and the liquid has evaporated. Stir occasionally.

8 This curry should be served quite dry.

9 Serve with prawn crackers.

356 Rendang kambang kot baru (lamb in spicy coconut sauce)

	4 portions	10 portions
peanut oil	35 ml	125 ml
shallots	25 g	60 g
garlic clove, finely chopped	1	2½
candlenuts *or* brazils *or* macadamia nuts, ground	50 g	125 g
turmeric powder	5 g (1 tsp)	12 g (2½ tsp)
coriander powder	5 g (1 tsp)	12 g (2½ tsp)
lemon grass stalk, finely chopped	1	2–3
loin chops	4 × 150 g	10 × 150 g
white cabbage leaves, blanched	4	10
spicy coconut sauce (see recipe 357)	500 ml	1¼ litres

1 Place the peanut oil, shallots, garlic and ground nuts in a basin. Sprinkle with turmeric and coriander. Add the lemon grass and season. Mix to a thick paste. Add oil until a spreadable mixture is obtained.

2 Spread mixture on to the lamb, marinate for 2 hours in a refrigerator.

3 Quickly fry the lamb on both sides for 1 minute.

4 Wrap each chop in a blanched cabbage leaf.

5 Place the lamb in a suitable pan for braising, cover with hot spicy coconut sauce. Place a lid on the pan and braise in a moderate oven (180°C) for approximately 10 minutes.

6 Serve with stir-fry vegetables, flavoured with turmeric.

357 Saus rendang (spicy coconut sauce)

Makes 500 ml

peanut oil	35 ml
shallots, finely chopped	50 g
ginger, finely chopped	12 g
garlic clove, finely chopped	1
greater galangal, peeled and finely chopped	12 g
candlenuts, brazil nuts or macadamia nuts	25 g
lemon grass stalk, chopped	1
kaffir lime leaves	4
turmeric powder	2 g
coriander powder	2 g (½ tsp)
red chilli juice	375 ml
coconut milk	250 ml
salt	

1 In a saucepan, heat the peanut oil and sauté the shallots, ginger, garlic and greater galangal for approximately 5 minutes, until they are a light-brown colour.

2 Add the nuts, lemon grass, lime leaves, turmeric and coriander. Continue to sauté for a further 2 minutes.

3 Add the chilli juice and coconut milk and season. Bring to the boil and simmer for approximately 6–10 minutes, stirring continuously.

4 Remove the lime leaves.

5 Liquidise and pass through a strainer, use as required.

Note: Greater galangal is less aromatic and pungent than lesser galangal. It is always used fresh in Indonesia. If unavailable, use fresh ginger but double the amount.

358 Kukus ikan sebalah madura (fillet of halibut madura)

	4 portions	10 portions
pieces of halibut fillet	4 × 100 g	10 × 100 g
julienne of chillies	25 g	60 g
sweet basil leaves (kemangi)	25 g	60 g
seasoning		
fish stock	140 ml	300 ml
shallots	50 g	125 g
potatoes, small cubes or balls	50 g	125 g
carrots, small cubes or balls	50 g	125 g
green beans, small pieces	50 g	125 g
peanut oil	15 ml (3 tsp)	60 ml (7½ tsp)
garlic, peeled and chopped	6 g	15 g
banyuwangi sauce	140 ml	300 ml
sour turmeric sauce	70 ml	150 ml
whole green beans, blanched	4	10

1 Sprinkle the halibut with the chillies and chopped basil leaves and season.

2 Place in a suitable pan with enough fish stock to come halfway up the fish. Cover with greased paper, poach in a moderate oven for approximately 5–8 minutes.

3 Keep warm.

4 Blanch the finely chopped shallots, potatoes and carrots for 1 minute.

5 Blanch and refresh the green beans.

6 Heat the peanut oil in a suitable pan. Sauté the blanched vegetables and garlic for approximately 2–5 minutes until tender.

7 Remove the vegetables. Keep warm.

8 On plates, place the banyuwangi sauce with a little sour turmeric sauce on top.

9 Carefully place the halibut on top.

10 Garnish with sautéed vegetables and the blanched whole green beans, tied in a knot.

MALAYSIA

359 Daging masak meruh (beef in red sauce)

	4 portions	10 portions
shallots, sliced	200 g	500 g
sultanas	25 g	60 g
ginger, peeled and grated	½ tsp	2 tsp
red chillies, dried	20	50
lemon grass stalks	2	4
turmeric root, peeled	½ tsp	1 tsp
spring onions	4	9
coriander, chopped	1 tsp	2 tsp
coconut, fresh, grated	50 g	125 g
thin coconut milk	250 ml	625 ml
topside of beef, diced	600 g	1½ kg
thick coconut milk	125 ml	300 ml
cashew nuts, toasted	50 g	125 g
caster sugar	12 g	30 g

nutritional info

1 large portion provides:
1573 kJ/374 kcal
39.2 g fat (of which 15.1 g saturated)
21.8 g carbohydrate (of which 18.9 g sugars)
39.2 g protein
2.3 g fibre

A large amount of coconut and coconut milk is used.

♥ kcal
1000
900
800
700
600
500
400
300
200
100
0

calorie counter

1 Deep-fry the sliced shallots until golden brown, then fry the sultanas for 1–2 minutes and remove.

2 Place the ginger, deseeded chillies, lemon grass and turmeric root in a food processor and grind to a paste.

3 Slice the spring onions and chop the coriander.

4 Toast the grated coconut until golden brown.

5 Boil the thin coconut milk in a suitable pan, add the ginger paste to the beef and then place in the boiled coconut milk.

6 Add the thick coconut milk and simmer gently for approximately 1 hour, then add the cashew nuts, shallots and sultanas, mix well to fully incorporate with the beef.

7 Add the sugar and toasted coconut, and season lightly.

8 Add half the spring onions and coriander. Cook for a further 5 minutes.

9 Serve on suitable plates garnished with spring onions and coriander.

10 Serve with plain rice.

360 Ayam kicap baah asam (spiced fried chicken and plum sauce)

	4 portions	10 portions
1 whole chicken cut for sauté	1 × 1200 g	2 × 1200 g
cornflour	50 g	125 g
red chillies	2	5
green chillies	2	5
garlic	4 cloves	10
coconut oil	3 tbsp	7 tbsp
curry leaves	5 g	12 g
chicken stock	125 ml	300 ml
yellow plum sauce (recipe 345)	125 ml	300 ml

1 Cut the chicken as for sauté.

2 Pass the chicken through the cornflour and deep-fry until golden brown.

3 Remove the stalks from the chillies, cut in half lengthwise and remove the seeds. Slice thinly.

4 Thinly slice the garlic. In a wok, quickly fry the garlic in the coconut oil until golden brown, add the chicken, chillies and curry leaves, and fry for 3–4 minutes.

5 Add the chicken stock and simmer to reduce by one-third. Add the plum sauce and reduce to the required consistency.

6 Serve with plain boiled rice.

361 Ikan bahan dengan kunyit celi padi (stuffed red snapper)

	4 portions	10 portions
red snapper	4	10
red chillies	12	30
red onions	300 g	750 g
turmeric powder	12 g	25 g
salt	1 tsp	2 tsp
vegetable oil	4 tbsp	10 tbsp
red chillies	4	10
spring onions	8	20
fresh coriander sprigs	4	10

1 Prepare the red snapper by removing the scales, eyes and gills.

2 Gut the fish by making a cut from the stomach to the head, remove all the innards. Clean under running cold water to remove debris.

3 Across the back make three incisions (ciseler).

4 Remove the stalk and seeds from the first lot of chillies and chop them.

5 Finely chop the onions.

6 In a pestle place the chillies, onions, turmeric powder and salt, blend to a paste. (Alternatively use a food processor.)

7 Rub the fish with the paste inside and out.

8 Heat some oil in a suitable wok or pan, and gently fry the fish for 4–5 minutes on each side.

9 Serve on a suitable plate garnished with chilli, spring onion and coriander.

10 Serve with plain boiled rice.

Note: Other fish that may be used include mackerel, trout and red mullet.

MEXICO

362 Chancho adobado (pork in orange and lemon sauce with sweet potatoes)

	4 portions	10 portions
distilled vinegar	250 ml	625 ml
liquid annatto (colouring)	1 tsp	2½ tsp
ground cumin seeds	1½ tsp	4 tsp
garlic cloves, chopped and crushed	2	5
seasoning		
boneless pork (cut into 2½ cm cubes)	1 kg	2½ kg
olive oil	2 tbsp	5 tbsp
fresh orange juice	250 ml	625 ml
lemon, juice of	1	2
sweet potatoes boiled (peeled and sliced 6 mm thick)	4	10

1 Place the vinegar, annatto, cumin, garlic and seasoning into bowl, mix well.

2 Place in the pork, stir and marinate for 24 hours in a refrigerator.

3 Remove the pork from the marinade – *keep the marinade*.

4 Dry the pork quickly, fry in hot oil until golden brown.

5 Drain off the fat, add the marinade.

6 Bring to the boil, remove the residue, cover with the lid and simmer gently until the pork is cooked.

7 Add the orange and lemon juice, simmer for 2–3 minutes.

8 Remove the pork, keep warm.

9 Reduce the sauce by one-third, lightly thicken if required with arrowroot. Correct the seasoning.

10 Add back the pork.

11 Serve in a suitable dish, garnished with the slices of cooked sweet potato.

363 Huachinango veracruzano (red snapper with tomato sauce, olives and potatoes)

	4 portions	10 portions
medium-sized potatoes	1 kg	2½ kg
medium-sized tomatoes, skinned, seeded and coarsely chopped *or*	10	25
drained plum tomatoes	1 kg	2 kg
olive oil	3 tbsp	7 tbsp
onion, finely chopped	100 g	250 g
garlic cloves, crushed and chopped	2	5
red chilli, chopped	1	3
stuffed pimento olives	50 g	125 g
lemons or limes, juice of	2	5
salt	pinch	pinch
ground cinnamon	¼ tsp	¾ tsp
ground cloves	¼ tsp	¾ tsp
seasoning		
red snapper fillets	4	10
flour	50 g	125 g
triangles of white bread	4	10
butter or margarine	50 g	125 g
parsley, chopped		

1 Cook the potatoes plain boiled.

2 In a food processor, place the tomatoes and garlic, mix to a purée.

3 Heat half the oil in a suitable pan, add the chopped onion, cook without a cover.

4 Add the tomatoes, garlic, chopped chillies, olives, lime or lemon juice, salt, cinnamon, cloves and seasoning, and cook for 5 minutes to extract flavours.

5 Meanwhile, pass the fish fillets through the flour.

6 With the remainder of the oil, fry the fillets until golden brown on both sides.

7 Place fillets in a suitable serving dish.

8 Fry the bread triangles in the butter until crisp and brown.

9 To serve, mask the fish with the tomato sauce, garnished with the slices of boiled or steamed potatoes and triangles of bread, and sprinkle with chopped parsley.

MIDDLE EAST

364 Borani (spinach and yoghurt salad)

	4 portions	10 portions
fresh spinach	200 g	500 g
lemon, juice of	1	½
onion, finely chopped	50 g	125 g
seasoning		
plain yoghurt	250 ml	625 ml
fresh mint, finely chopped	2½ tsp	5 tsp

1 Wash the spinach well. Drain, remove stalks.

2 Blanch the spinach in boiling salted water for approximately 2 minutes, refresh and drain.

3 Chop spinach finely.

4 Place spinach in a basin, add the lemon juice and onions, mix and season.

5 Stir in yoghurt, mix thoroughly.

6 Refrigerate for 1 hour before serving. Serve sprinkled with fresh mint.

365 Mast va khiar (yoghurt, vegetable and herb salad)

	4 portions	10 portions
cucumber	1 medium	2 large
green pepper, finely chopped	½	1½
spring onions, finely chopped including part of the green	4	10
lemon, juice of	½	1½
chopped fresh tarragon	1½ tbsp	4 tbsp
chopped fresh dill	2½ tbsp	6 tbsp
seasoning		
plain yoghurt	250 ml	625 ml

1 Peel the cucumber and chop finely.

2 Place in a bowl, with the green pepper, spring onions, lemon juice and fresh herbs. Mix well and season.

3 Add the yoghurt, mix well.

4 Chill for 1 hour before serving.

366 Dajaj mahshi (roast chicken with rice and pine kernel stuffing)

	4 portions	10 portions
onions, finely chopped	50 g	125 g
butter	50 g	125 g
chicken liver and heart		
pine kernels	1½ tbsp	3 tbsp
water (to cook the rice)	375 ml	1 litre
uncooked long-grain rice	162 g	½ kg
currants	50 g	125 g
seasoning		
melted butter	50 g	125 g
chicken	1 × 1½ kg	2½ × 1½ kg
yoghurt	2½ tbsp	7 tbsp

1 Sweat the onions in butter with colour.

2 Add the finely chopped liver and heart and the pine kernels, cook for a further 2–3 minutes.

3 Add the washed rice, currants and seasoning.

4 Stir well, add the water, bring to boil, cook until the rice is cooked and all the moisture has been absorbed.

5 Remove from heat, stir in the melted butter.

6 Stuff the chicken with the rice, truss to secure the filling. Keep any remainder of rice to serve separately.

7 Place in a suitable roasting pan, season and smear with yoghurt.

8 Roast in a suitable oven in the normal way, baste constantly with yoghurt.

9 Serve the chicken whole or portioned with the rice.

367 Lubya khadra billahma (lamb with French beans)

	4 portions	10 portions
French beans, trimmed and cut into 5 cm lengths	800 g	2 kg
neck of lamb, boned, cut into 2½ cm cubes	400 g	1 kg
olive oil	2½ tbsp	6 tbsp
onion, finely chopped	100 g	250 g
tomatoes, peeled, seeded, cut into concassée	6	15
seasoning		
ground nutmeg	½ tsp	1½ tsp
ground allspice	½ tsp	1½ tsp

1 Place the beans in the bottom of a suitable pan.

2 Sauté the lamb in the olive oil until brown.

3 Place the lamb on top of the beans.

4 Fry the onions in the same pan until soft and slightly brown.

5 Place the onions over the lamb, add the tomato concassée. Add seasoning and spices.

6 Add a little water, cover with a lid, cook for approximately 1 hour until tender.

7 It is important to make sure that the casserole never boils dry, that the beans are well covered, and that the meat and other ingredients have sufficient but not excessive moisture during the cooking process.

8 Serve once the meat is tender, with steamed or boiled rice.

Note: The tomatoes may be replaced with canned plum tomatoes. It is also advisable to add a little tomato purée during the cooking process.

368 Bacalhau trás-os-montes (baked cod with ham, tomato and black olives)

	4 portions	10 portions
pieces salt cod	4 × 100 g	10 × 100 g
milk	375 ml	1 litre
olive oil	4 tbsp	6 tbsp
slices of smoked ham	12	30
slices of tomato	4	10
sieved hard-boiled eggs	2	5
black olives, stoned	50 g	125 g
parsley, chopped		

1 Soak the salt cod in water for approximately 12 hours, change the water 2 or 3 times.

2 Drain the cod, rinse under cold water.

3 Arrange the cod in a suitable dish.

4 Boil the milk, pour over the cod.

5 Allow to stand for 1 hour.

6 Drain, discard the milk.

7 Pour the olive oil over the fish, place in a moderate oven (180°C approximately), basting occasionally with the oil.

8 After 10 minutes, place on the slices of ham, and a slice of tomato on each fish portion.

9 Baste with the oil, cook for a further 5 minutes.

10 When the fish is cooked, sprinkle with boiled egg yolks, and the olives cut neatly into small pieces.

11 Serve from the baking dish sprinkled with chopped parsley.

369 Truchas a'la navarra (marinated trout baked with red wine and herbs)

	4 portions	10 portions
red wine	125 ml	375 ml
olive oil	3 tbsp	8 tbsp
onion, finely chopped	50 g	125 g
black peppercorns	15–20	35–50
mint, chopped	2 tsp	3 tsp
rosemary, chopped	½ tsp	1½ tsp
thyme, chopped	½ tsp	1½ tsp
bay leaf, chopped	½	1
seasoning		
trout, cleaned	4 × 200 g	10 × 200 g
yolks of egg, lightly beaten	3	8

1 Put the red wine, olive oil, onions, peppercorns, herbs and salt into a suitable baking dish. Stir well.

2 Place the cleaned trout into this marinade, allow to stand for 1 hour, turning once.

3 Place the dish on the stove, bring to boil, cover fish with a buttered greaseproof sheet and lid.

4 Place in a suitable oven, moderately hot, until the fish is just cooked.

5 Remove the trout and keep warm.

6 Strain the cooking liquor. Bring back to the boil.

7 Beat the egg yolks, add slowly to the cooking liquor, whisking continuously. *Do not allow to boil* otherwise it will curdle. Heat to 80°C.

8 Correct seasoning.

9 Place the trout in a suitable serving dish, mask with sauce.

10 Traditionally, the trout is accompanied by hot, fresh boiled potatoes.

SPAIN

370 Canja (chicken soup with lemon and mint)

	4 portions	10 portions
onions, finely chopped	100 g	250 g
good chicken stock	1 litre	2½ litres
short-grain rice	50 g	125 g
julienne of cooked chicken	200 g	500 g
lemon, juice of	1	3
mint, chopped	1 tbsp	2½ tbsp

1 Add the chopped onions to the boiling chicken stock.

2 Add the rice, cook until tender.

3 Add the chicken, lemon juice and mint.

4 Correct seasoning, serve immediately.

371 Riñones al jerez (sautéed kidneys with sherry sauce)

	4 portions	10 portions
olive oil	4 tbsp	10 tbsp
onion, finely chopped	75 g	200 g
garlic clove, chopped	1	2
small bay leaf	1	2
flour	12 g	30 g
beef or chicken stock	125 ml	310 ml
parsley, finely chopped	1 tbsp	2 tbsp
calves' kidneys	750 g	1.8 kg
dry sherry	62 ml	186 ml
seasoning		

1 Heat 2 tablespoons of olive oil in a suitable frying pan.

2 Add the onions, garlic and bay leaf. Gently fry to a light golden-brown colour.

3 Add the flour and mix well.

4 Pour in the stock and stir continuously until boiling.

5 Add the parsley.

6 Season the kidneys (trimmed and cut into regular dice), fry quickly in the remainder of the olive oil. Remove kidneys and keep warm.

7 Deglaze the pan with sherry. Remove from heat.

8 Return kidneys to the sherry pan. Add the onion sauce.

9 Correct seasoning and consistency.

10 Serve at once with saffron rice garnished with chopped red pimento.

Note: Lambs' or pigs' kidneys may be used in place of calves' kidneys. In the case of lambs' kidneys, cut in half and remove the inner white core.

372 Porco con ameijuas a alentejaru (marinated pork with clams, tomatoes and coriander)

	4 portions	10 portions
dry white wine	250 ml	725 ml
paprika	2 tsp	4½ tsp
seasoning		
garlic cloves, cut in half	2	5
small bay leaf	1	2½
lean boneless pork	1 kg	2½ kg
lard	75 g	187 g
onion, shredded	200 g	500 g
large red pepper, seeded and cut into 13 mm strips	1	2
cloves of garlic, chopped and crushed	2	5
medium tomatoes, peeled, deseeded and finely chopped	2	5
small clams, washed and thoroughly scrubbed	12	30
fresh coriander, finely chopped	3 tbsp	8 tbsp
lemon wedges, to garnish		

1 Mix the white wine, paprika and seasoning.

2 Add garlic cloves cut in half and the bay leaf.

3 Place the diced pork into this marinade, mix well and allow to stand for 3 hours, turning occasionally.

4 Remove the pork from the marinade. Pass the marinade through a fine strainer, reserve.

5 Melt half the lard in a suitable frying pan. Quickly fry the pork until golden brown and cooked through.

6 Remove pork, pour off excess fat, deglaze with the marinade, reduce by half.

7 Melt the remainder of the lard in a suitable casserole, gently fry the onion and red pepper, cook for 5 minutes until soft but not coloured.

8 Add the chopped and crushed garlic and the tomatoes. Correct seasoning. Cook for 5 minutes.

9 Spread the clams, hinge side down, over the sauce. Cover the casserole and cook over a high heat for abut 8–10 minutes, until the clams open. (Discard any clams that remain closed.)

10 Stir in the reserved pork and all its juices, simmer for 5 minutes. Sprinkle the top with coriander, garnish with lemon wedges. Serve at once.

Note: The number of clams may be doubled if costs allow. Oysters could also be used.

THAILAND

373 Dom yam nua (beef soup with chives)

	4 portions	10 portions
beef, cut into strips	200 g	500 g
good brown stock	1 litre	2½ litres
garlic cloves, crushed and chopped	2	5
lemon grass stalk, crushed	1	2½
lime, juice of	½ tsp	1 tsp
nam pla (fish sauce)	1 tsp	2½ tsp
chives, chopped	60 g	125 g
seasoning		

1 Place the beef, stock, garlic, lemon grass, lime juice and *nam pla* in a suitable saucepan.

2 Bring to the boil and simmer for approximately 1 hour.

3 Serve in individual bowls, garnished with chopped chives.

4 Season liberally with salt and pepper to taste.

Note: *Nam pla* is a fish sauce that is a characteristic of several Thai dishes. It is a brown salty sauce made from fermented fish. It can be purchased from specialist shops.

As an alternative, grill 1 teaspoon of dried shrimp paste for 5 minutes each side and crush with 125 ml of soy sauce.

374 Phat priu wan (sweet and sour pork and snow peas)

	4 portions	10 portions
vegetable oil	62 ml	150 ml
garlic cloves, chopped and crushed	4	10
loin of pork, free from bone and excess fat	400 g	1¼ kg
prawns	300 g	1 kg
soy sauce	62 ml	150 ml
monosodium glutamate (optional)		
mangetout	300 g	1 kg

1 Heat the oil in suitable wok and brown the garlic.

2 Add the thinly sliced pork and stir-fry until lightly browned.

3 Add the prawns and stir-fry for 1 minute.

4 Add all seasoning and stir-fry for another 2 minutes.

5 Add the mangetout, stir-fry for another 2–3 minutes.

6 Serve immediately.

375 Pla nergn (steamed fish, Thai style)

	4 portions	10 portions
dried chillies, soaked, drained and seeded	2	5
onion, chopped	100 g	250 g
garlic cloves, crushed	3	7–8
lemon grass stalk	1	2–3
salt and pepper		
nam pla (fish sauce)	2 tbsp	5 tbsp
white fish (sole, plaice, cod) cut into scallops/slices	400 g	1¼ kg
thick coconut milk	125 ml	300 ml
egg, beaten	1	2–3
large cabbage leaves	4	10
rice flour	12 g	25 g
spring onions	2	5
coriander stalk	1	2–3
chilli	1	2–3

1 Purée the chillies, onion, garlic cloves and lemon grass in a food processor. Season the purée, with salt, pepper and fish sauce.

2 Add the fish and half of the coconut milk.

3 Mix in the beaten egg.

4 Line a suitable dish with the cabbage leaves and spread the fish mixture on top.

5 Mix the rice flour with the remaining coconut milk and pour over the fish.

6 Sprinkle with finely chopped spring onions, coriander and chilli.

7 Cover with aluminium foil, lightly greased. Either steam over boiling water in a suitable steamer or in a combination oven for approximately 20–30 minutes.

8 Serve in portions with boiled white rice.

376 Pla cian (fried fish, Thai-style)

	4 portions	10 portions
oil, for frying		
whole sole, lemon sole or plaice	1 × 600 g–1 kg	2½ × 600 g–1 kg
spring onions, cut into julienne	2	5
garlic cloves, crushed	4	10
fresh ginger, shredded	50 g	125 g
red chillies, sliced	2	5
soy sauce	2 tbsp	5 tbsp
palm sugar or brown sugar	1 tbsp	2–3 tbsp
tamarind	25 g	60 g
water	62 ml	150 ml
nam pla (fish sauce)	1 tbsp	2–3 tbsp

1 Heat the oil in a suitable pan, fry the fish on both sides, until crispy and brown. Place in a suitable dish.

2 In fresh oil, fry the spring onions, garlic and ginger, until lightly brown.

3 Add the chillies and seasoning to all other ingredients.

4 There should be sufficient liquor in the pan to mask the fish, if not add a little more water or fish stock.

5 Mask over the fried fish.

6 Served with boiled white rice.

Note: Palm sugar is sugar from the sap of the coconut palm. Tamarind is a tropical fruit with an acid taste.

VIETNAM

377 Thit n'òng mi dâu phong (fried pork with noodles and peanuts)

	4 portions	10 portions
spinach	150 g	375 g
pickled mooli (Chinese white radish) and carrot	100 g	250 g
spring onions	4	10
sugar	25 g	62g
rice wine	250 ml	625 ml
bird's eye chillies, chopped	8	20
boned loin of pork	500 g	1¼ kg
vegetable oil	2 tbsp	5 tbsp
peanuts, roasted and crushed	100 g	250 g
rice noodles, cooked	200 g	500 g

1 Wash the spinach well, shred finely.

2 Prepare the garnish by cutting the mooli and carrots into batons, 4 cm × ½ cm. Prepare the spring onions and cut in half.

3 Boil the sugar and the rice wine, simmer. Add the chopped chillies, spring onions, mooli and carrots, and allow to cool.

4 Cut the pork into strips 4 cm × 6 cm. Heat the oil in the wok, stir-fry the pork, add the spinach and peanuts, cook for 1 minute.

5 Reheat the cooked noodles in boiling water, drain. Place in the centre of plates. Add the pork. Serve the garnish alongside with a little of the rice wine syrup.

nutritional info

1 large portion provides:
1267 kJ/302 kcal
13.3 g fat (of which 2.1 g saturated)
30.9 g carbohydrate (of which 11.0 g sugars)
34.1 g protein
0.1 g fibre

Oil is used to fry the chicken.

378 Bò xào magi (beef and bok choy with black bean sauce)

	4 portions	10 portions
rump steak, thinly sliced	600 g	1½ kg
sesame oil	1 tbsp	2½ tbsp
fish sauce	1 tbsp	2½ tbsp
cornflour	25 g	62g
egg, lightly beaten	1	2
asparagus	200 g	500 g
peanut oil	3 tbsp	7 tbsp
onions, sliced	200 g	500 g
garlic cloves	2	5
lemon grass, finely chopped	1 tbsp	2½ tbsp
fresh ginger, grated	1 tbsp	2½ tbsp
baby bok choy, chopped	300 g	750 g
Black bean sauce		
cornflour	2 tsp	5 tsp
water	125 ml	375 ml
black bean sauce	4 tbsp	9 tbsp
fish sauce	1 tbsp	3 tbsp
brown sugar	1 tbsp	3 tbsp

1 Place the thinly sliced rump steak into a bowl, add sesame oil and fish sauce, mix well. Marinate for 30 minutes.

2 Mix the cornflour with the beaten egg, add to the beef and mix well.

3 Prepare the asparagus spears, cut into halves.

4 Heat 1 tbsp of the peanut oil in a wok, add half the beef mixture, stir-fry until brown, drain well. Proceed to do the same with the second half of the beef.

5 Heat remaining peanut oil in a wok, add onions, garlic, lemon grass and ginger, stir-fry until the onions are soft.

6 Add bok choy and asparagus, stir-fry until bok choy is just wilted.

7 Place vegetables on plates, top with the beef, drizzle with black bean sauce (see below).

For the black bean sauce

1 Mix cornflour with the water with remaining ingredients in wok, stir over heat until mixture boils and thickens.

nutritional info

1 large portion provides:
1728 kJ/413 kcal
19.7 g fat (of which 5.1 g saturated)
20.7 g carbohydrate (of which 10.5 g sugars)
39.3 g protein
2.8 g fibre

Peanut oil is used to fry the beef, onions and garlic.

♥ kcal
1000
900
800
700
600
500
400
300
200
100
0

calorie counter

379 Cá xót ngot (fish with sweet chilli sauce)

	4 portions	10 portions
plain flour	150 g	375 g
cornflour	50 g	125 g
sugar	1 tsp	2½ tsp
ground turmeric	¼ tsp	1 tsp
green shallots, finely chopped	2	5
egg whites	2	5
water	250 ml	625 ml
fish fillets (e.g. plaice, lemon sole)	4 × 100 g	10 × 100 g
oil, for deep-frying		
Sweet chilli sauce		
soy sauce	2 tbsp	5 tbsp
mild sweet chilli sauce	125 ml	375 ml
malt vinegar	2 tbsp	5 tbsp
brown sugar	1 tbsp	2½ tbsp
chicken stock	125 ml	375 ml
fresh coriander leaves, chopped	2 tbsp	5 tbsp
cornflour	2 tsp	5 tsp
water	150 ml	625 ml

1 Sift the flour, sugar and turmeric into a bowl, stir in the shallots and combined egg whites and water. Mix into a smooth batter, adjust consistency and add water if required.

2 Dip fish fillets separately into batter to coat completely, remove excess batter.

3 Deep-fry fish in hot oil until lightly brown, drain on absorbent paper. Dress on plates with chilli sauces.

For the sweet chilli sauce

1 Combine sauces, vinegar, sugar, stock and coriander in a suitable pan. Stir in the blended cornflour and water.

2 Stir over heat until mixture boils and thickens slightly.

nutritional info

1 large portion provides:
1821 kJ/432 kcal
13.4 g fat (of which 1.6 g saturated)
57.6 g carbohydrate (of which 13.9 g sugars)
23.9 g protein
1.9 g fibre

Oil is used to fry the fish.

VEGETABLE, POTATO, PASTA & VEGETARIAN DISHES

THE CLASSIFICATION OF VEGETABLES AND POTATOES

Vegetables

Vegetables, like fruits, are the edible products of certain plants. They share several characteristics: they are savoury rather than sweet; we add salt to them; and, in most countries they are associated with poultry, meat or fish as part of a meal or as an ingredient. Some vegetables are botanically classed as fruits: tomatoes are berries, and avocados are drupes, but both are commonly used as vegetables because they are not sweet.

By the Middle Ages, extensive vegetable farming was carried out in Europe, especially in the Low Countries, and market gardeners were able to export a proportion of their harvest. Following the Spanish conquest of South America in the late fifteenth century, there was an important exchange of crops between the Old World and the New. Throughout the sixteenth and seventeenth centuries crops were gradually established in both continents. From the Americas came maize, potatoes, sweet potatoes, tomatoes, peppers, kidney beans, pumpkins, Jerusalem artichokes and French beans. Settlers from Europe introduced to America broad beans, chickpeas, black-eyed peas, radishes, carrots, cabbages, okra and yams (black-eyed peas, okra and yams being brought on the slave ships from Africa).

Units covered
3FC6, 3FPC3

LIST OF RECIPES

Recipe no	page no
Potato dishes	
392 Anna potatoes	318
394 Candied sweet potatoes	318
380 Crispy olive potatoes	311
387 Deep-fried hash browns	315
389 Fondant potatoes	316
388 Gratin Dauphinoise	316
383 Hot potato salad	313
391 Mashed potato	317
386 Maxim potatoes	315
384 Potato blinis	313
395 Potato cakes with chives	319
396 Potatoes cooked with button onions and tomatoes	319
381 Potatoes in white wine with anchovies	312
390 Potatoes Lyonnaise	317
385 Potato gnocchi	314
382 Rösti	312
393 Sweet potatoes	318
Vegetable dishes	
409 Artichokes with spinach and cheese sauce	325
400 Aubergine caviar	321
410 Aubergine soufflé	326
411 Baby sweetcorn	326
412 Bamboo shoots	326
413 Bean sprouts	327
399 Braised chicory	321
403 Braised red cabbage	323

Recipe no	page no
404 Braised red cabbage with apples, red wine and juniper	324
398 Braised-roast salsify	320
415 Broad beans with tomato and coriander	327
402 Bubble and squeak	322
418 Cardoon fritters	328
416 Cardoons	328
417 Cardoons with onions and cheese	328
419 Chinese cabbage	329
421 Christophene	329
422 Colcannon	330
405 Confit onions	324
439 Deep-fried vegetables in tempura batter	336
437 Fried yam cakes	335
438 Grilled vegetables	336
423 Kohlrabi	330
408 Leaf spinach with pine nuts and garlic	325
424 Mooli	330
425 Okra	331
427 Palm hearts	331
401 Parmesan fried courgettes with pesto	322
407 Parsnip and vanilla purée	324
431 Salsify fritters	333
430 Salsify with onion, tomato and garlic	332
429 Scorzonera	332
406 Shallot purée	325
420 Spicy stir-fry Chinese cabbage	329
432 Squash	333
426 Stewed okra	331
428 Stewed palm hearts	331

The production of vegetables for the table became a well-developed industry, especially in France, when the chemist Nicholas Appert pioneered canned foods at the end of the eighteenth century. Appert's technique was soon to revolutionise the marketing of vegetables and was not to be equalled in importance in this field until the American physicist Clarence Birdseye introduced a new process for freezing foods in 1929.

Flavour accounts for a very small percentage of a vegetable's composition. Most contain at least 80 per cent water, the remainder being carbohydrate, protein and fat. Squashes, in particular, contain a high percentage of water, while potatoes contain a great deal of starch, which is used by the vegetables as a reserve food supply. Invert sugars are also a food source, and sucrose is present in corn, carrots, parsnips, onions, and so on. When vegetables age, the woody lignin increases, water evaporates and sugars become concentrated – old raw carrots appear to be sweeter than young ones, for example. But sugars change as soon as the vegetable is separated from the plant. (A good example is corn, which is often rushed straight from the stalk to the pot in order to preserve its taste.)

When choosing vegetables you should obviously avoid those that are limp and

Recipe no		page no	Recipe no		page no
414	Stir-fried bean sprouts	327	467	Oriental vegetable kebabs with herb sauce	354
434	Stuffed vegetables	333	447	Potato and leek soup	342
433	Swiss chard	333	463	Ravioli stuffed with spinach and cumin served with lemon sauce	351
397	Vegetables à la Greque	320			
435	Wild mushrooms	334	460	Risotto with coconut milk and wilted baby spinach	350
436	Yams	335			
	Vegetarian dishes		448	Spicy squash (pumpkin) soup	343
450	Aubergine pasta bake	344	454	Spinach, ricotta and artichoke filo bake with cranberries	346
443	Aubergine raita	340			
449	Aubergine stir-fry, Japanese style	343	445	Thai-style potato curry	341
469	Baked babagnough and aubergine charlotte	356	466	Tofu and vegetable flan with walnut sauce	353
444	Barley with shitake mushrooms	341	455	Vegetable, bean and saffron risotto	347
446	Bean bourguignonne	342	468	Vegetable olives	355
441	Brown vegetable stock	340	461	Vegetable shashliks served on tabbouleh	350
457	Courgettes cooked with tomatoes	348			
451	Cracked wheat and mint salad	345	464	Vegetarian terrine	352
456	Filo pastry filled with tabbouleh and feta cheese	348	440	White vegetable stock	340
				Pasta dishes	
442	Fungi stock	340	470	Asparagus sauce	359
452	Galette of aubergine with tomatoes and mozzarella	345	472	Cep and truffle relish	360
			475	Lasagne	362
458	Goats' cheese and red pepper tart	349	471	Pea and pancetta sauce	359
465	Gratin of nuts with a tomato and red wine sauce and basil	353	473	Tagliatelle Arrabiata	360
			474	Tagliatelle with pesto and squid	361
453	Honey-roasted vegetables with cracked wheat	346			
459	Leek roulade with ricotta and sweetcorn	349			
462	Marinades	351			

wilting, discoloured or damaged by harvesting. Leaf vegetables need careful picking over to avoid serving garden pests on the plate. Vegetables should be prepared for the pot as simply as possible. Wash them just before cooking, don't soak them and, as they lose nutrients through peeling and cutting, they should be peeled only thinly (vitamins are usually found just under the skin).

On contact with air certain vegetables tend to discolour, regardless of whether they are cooked or raw. This is because certain enzymes cause oxidisation. This activity can be halted by the addition of an acid, which is why cooks plunge celeriac – and apples – into acidulated water (water with a little lemon juice added) after peeling them.

Blanching helps to preserve colour, especially in green vegetables, but some vegetables' dyes are lost in the cooking process. Purple broccoli contains both chlorophyll (green) and anthocyanin (purple), the latter being water soluble, so cooked broccoli always looks green. Red cabbage reacts like litmus paper – it turns blue in the presence of an alkali (the lime in tap water), so you need to add a dash of acid, such as vinegar, to preserve the colour.

Potatoes

Potatoes are one of the most interesting vegetables you will find and, at long last, those selling them are becoming aware that the variety matters.

The first thing you need to know about a potato is whether it is floury or waxy. This determines how you must cook it. It also helps if you have some idea of the dry matter content. High dry matter means a floury potato – good for mashing, good for frying – but if you're the sort of person who leaves potatoes boiling in the pan for 20 minutes before looking at them, you may be disappointed when you take off the lid and see that your supper has turned into potato soup.

Waxy potatoes are great for boiling – they don't fall apart if you boil for too long (within reason) and they are good cold. Examples are Pink Fir and immature Jersey Royal, and there are lots more.

Floury potatoes are the best for mashing, for baking and for eating cold – but you must cook them carefully because overcooking will cause them to disintegrate. If you steam them, the timing isn't quite so critical, but you must still not overcook them or the texture will be lost. The cut surface of a perfectly cooked floury potato will have a beautiful white floury finish if you've got it right.

Good-flavoured mid- and main-crop potatoes include Golden Wonder, Kerr's Pink, British Queen, King Edward, Red King Edward, Binji, Pink Fir and Edzell Blue. Charlotte is good when young but not so good later on. Yukon Gold is a fine-flavoured potato with yellow flesh. Desiree is another yellowish-fleshed potato – a good all-rounder but its flavour is not quite as good as that of the other varieties listed above.

Shetland Black is good if you can get it – bluish-coloured flesh and a sweet flavour.

Congo is quite like Salad Blue; it has blue flesh but tastes more buttery.

Best for chips are probably Golden Wonder and Maris Piper, with Desiree a close third.

Green potatoes: alkaloids

Alkaloids are alkaline-behaving, nitrogen-containing complexes that are poisonous at high doses. From the vast range of commonly eaten plant products we consume, the potato most seriously threatens us with alkaloid poisoning. The production of alkaloids in the potato tuber is stimulated by exposure to light and either to very cold or warm storage facilities. Fortunately there are warning signals to detect the presence of alkaloids; the first and most obvious of these is the production of chlorophyll in the tuber itself, making the potato appear green on the exposed area, this is an obvious indication of the presence of alkaloids. The other is feeling a peppery or burning sensation when the potato is placed on the tongue. These substances are not destroyed during cooking or with the application of heat and must be removed from the potato and discarded; because most alkaloids are concentrated less than 2 mm below the surface they are not too difficult to remove and just double-peeling the skin should suffice. Another part of the potato that has a high concentration of alkaloids is the sprouting shoot from the potato itself – any such potatoes should be discarded.

Plant structure and cooking vegetables

Plant texture is determined by both the cell wall structure and the inner water pressure, or turgor, of the tissue. The application of heat, whether by boiling, baking or stir-frying, tenderises the food by weakening the cell walls and extracting water. First, heat denatures the proteins that make up the cell membranes, which thereby lose the selective permeability that regulates the cells' water content. Water leaks from the cells, the tissue loses turgor, and the plant becomes wilted and flabby. Even boiled vegetables, surrounded by water as they are, lose water during cooking, as weighing before and after will demonstrate.

Then there are the changes in the cell walls. While cellulose is not affected by heat, the hemicelluloses and pectins are; some hemicelluloses dissolve. In addition, the distribution of the pectic substances is altered: the amount of soluble pectin increases at the expense of the insoluble protopectins, and the walls lose still more of their 'cement'. The result: substantially weakened cell walls and more tender tissue.

The problem in cooking vegetables, of course, is how to make the tissue tender without making it too soft. Usually we take the common-sense approach of sampling the food during cooking and stopping when it is tender but still firm. In some cases colour can be used to indicate that a vegetable is cooked. One possible generalisation is that leaf vegetables, with their relatively thin, exposed and delicate layer of tissue, need only a minute of two of heating, while stem and root vegetables may require many times that amount. Experience and personal taste remain the best guides.

POTATO DISHES

380 Crispy olive potatoes

	4 portions	10 portions
small new potatoes	16	40
butter, melted	60 g	150 g
flour	3 tbsp	7 tbsp
salt	1 tsp	2 tsp
cayenne	pinch	pinch
paprika	1 tsp	2 tsp
chopped stuffed olives	90 g	225 g

1 Cook the potatoes in boiling salted water until just tender. Drain and peel when cool enough to handle.

2 Toss in melted butter to coat evenly, then coat in flour mixed with salt, cayenne and paprika.

3 Place in a buttered, shallow casserole.

4 Sprinkle with olives and bake in a pre-heated, moderately hot oven (200°C) for 20 minutes (turn potatoes after first 10 minutes to brown evenly) until piping hot and crispy.

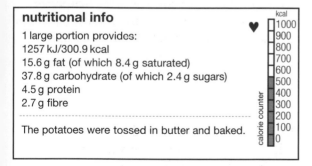

nutritional info

1 large portion provides:
1257 kJ/300.9 kcal
15.6 g fat (of which 8.4 g saturated)
37.8 g carbohydrate (of which 2.4 g sugars)
4.5 g protein
2.7 g fibre

The potatoes were tossed in butter and baked.

381 Potatoes in white wine with anchovies

	4 portions	10 portions
large waxy potatoes (approx. 200 g each)	6	14
dry white wine	4 tsp	10 tsp
wine vinegar	2 tbsp	5 tbsp
olive oil	5 tbsp	12 tbsp
freshly ground black pepper		
fresh anchovy fillets, drained	2 × 50 g	5 × 125 g
coriander leaves or flat parsley, to garnish		

nutritional info

1 large portion provides:
1616 kJ/385.6 kcal
16.2 g fat (of which 2.3 g saturated)
51.6 g carbohydrate (of which 1.8 g sugars)
11.1 g protein
3.9 g fibre

Olive oil was used.

1 Place the potatoes in a saucepan, cover with cold water and bring to the boil. Simmer until tender.

2 Drain and peel when cool enough to handle.

3 Cut into thick slices.

4 Sprinkle with wine and cool to room temperature.

5 Combine vinegar, olive oil and pepper and pour over the potatoes.

6 Scatter anchovies over the potatoes and garnish with coriander leaves.

382 Rösti

Rösti is the Swiss national potato dish, made in the shape of a thick, crispy, golden-brown cake. Sometimes the rösti is flavoured with crisp bacon and sometimes with onion. It is cut in ample wedges and served with all meat dishes or with fried eggs for breakfast.

	4 portions	10 portions
Golden Wonder or Maris Piper potatoes	1½ kg	3½ kg
Salt	1 tsp	2 tsp
speck or smoked bacon, diced	125 g	300 g
butter	30 g	75 g

nutritional info

1 large portion provides:
1599 kJ/380 kcal
9.0 g fat (of which 4.7 g saturated)
64.6 g carbohydrate (of which 2.3 g sugars)
13.8 g protein
4.9 g fibre

Includes bacon and butter.

1 Place the potatoes in a saucepan and cover with cold salted water. Bring to the boil and cook for about 10 minutes. Drain and peel when cool enough to handle.

2 Grate the potatoes.

3 Fry the speck or bacon in half the butter in a heavy frying pan.

4 Cook gently until the bacon fat is transparent.

5 Spread potatoes in frying pan to form a thick cake.

6 Cook over a low heat for about 10 minutes.

7 Slip a knife or spatula under the potato cake occasionally to ensure the underside is not becoming too brown.

8 Turn the cake out onto a large plate.

9 Add the remaining butter to the pan and, when the foam has subsided, slide the potato cake back into it.

10 Cook over a gentle heat for 8 minutes, making sure it does not become too brown.

11 Turn out onto a large heated dish and serve.

Note: The rösti can be browned quickly on both sides over a high heat and then placed in a pre-heated moderate oven (180°C) for 20 minutes to finish cooking.

383 Hot potato salad

	4 portions	10 portions
slices streaky bacon, rind removed	2 rashers (50 g)	5 (125 g)
onion, chopped	50 g	125 g
flour	15 g	35 g
white vinegar	4 tbsp	10 tbsp
water	120 ml	300 ml
salt	¼ tsp	½ tsp
sugar	1 tsp	2 tsp
freshly ground black pepper		
prepared mild mustard	2 tbsp	5 tbsp
medium potatoes, peeled, cooked and sliced	4	10

1 Fry the bacon until crisp. Remove from the pan with tongs, crumble and set aside.

2 Cook the onion in the bacon fat until soft and lightly browned.

3 Blend in flour, then stir in bacon, vinegar, water, salt, sugar, pepper and mustard.

4 Bring to the boil, stirring well.

5 Add potatoes, tossing to coat lightly and heat through.

6 Sprinkle with parsley and serve hot, or leave to cool, store in refrigerator and reheat before serving.

nutritional info

♥

1 large portion provides:
872 kJ/206 kcal
2.1 g fat (of which 0.4 g saturated)
40.9 g carbohydrate (of which 4.4 g sugars)
7.8 g protein
2.9 g fibre

Includes a small amount of bacon.

kcal
1000
900
800
700
600
500
400
300
200
100
0

calorie counter

384 Potato blinis

	4 portions	10 portions
dried mash	500 g	1¼ kg
crème fraîche	125 g	300 g
flour	25 g	60 g
whole eggs	4	10
yolks	2	5
seasoning		

nutritional info

♥

1 large portion provides:
1474 kJ/352 kcal
21.7 g fat (of which 11.1 g saturated)
28.1 g carbohydrate (of which 1.6 g sugars)
13.1 g protein
1.9 g fibre

Eggs were added to the mash and crème fraîche.

kcal
1000
900
800
700
600
500
400
300
200
100
0

calorie counter

1 Mix the mash with the crème fraîche and the flour.

2 Separate the eggs and add the yolks to the mash.

3 Whip the egg whites to a snow, carefully fold in to the mash, check for seasoning and allow to rest for 1 hour.

4 Heat a little oil in a non-stick pan and place a small amount of mix in the pan (approx. 1 tbsp), turn over when it is golden brown.

385 Potato gnocchi

This recipe yields more gnocchi than are needed for a single recipe, but their versatility makes them an ideal item to have on hand. Use them as a garnish or serve them as a meal. Part of what makes this a useful recipe is that the gnocchi freeze so well and they go directly from the freezer into boiling water so they're always at the ready.

	4 portions	10 portions
russet potatoes	1 kg	2½ kg
flour	350 g	875 g
egg yolks	4	10
Maldon salt to taste		

---

nutritional info

1 large portion provides:
2288 kJ/540 kcal
6.5 g fat (of which 1.6 g saturated)
111.0 g carbohydrate (of which 2.2 g sugars)
16.1 g protein
6.0 g fibre

Egg yolks were added to the potatoes.

calorie counter

kcal
1000
900
800
700
600
500
400
300
200
100
0

1 Pre-heat the oven to 180°C.

2 Bake the potatoes for 1 hour or until they are completely cooked.

3 Split the potatoes, scoop out the flesh and press it through a potato ricer. Place the hot potatoes on a board or counter.

4 Make a well in the centre. Place one-third of the flour in the well, add the egg yolks, then add most of the flour and the salt.

5 Use a dough scraper to 'chop' the potatoes into the flour and eggs. This process should be done quickly (15–30 seconds) as overworking the dough will make the gnocchi heavy and sticky. Add more flour as necessary.

6 The resulting dough should be homogeneous and barely sticky on the outside. Shape the dough into a ball.

7 Roll the ball of dough lightly in flour. Pull off a section of the dough and roll it by hand on a lightly floured surface into a 'snake' about 1 cm thick. Cut into 1 cm pieces and, using your hand, roll each piece into a ball.

8 Roll the balls on a gnocchi paddle or over the back of a fork to create an oval shape with indentations. Test one gnocchi by placing it in a large pot of rapidly boiling, lightly salted water. It is cooked as soon as it floats to the surface.

9 Taste for seasoning and texture and add salt to the dough if necessary, or add a bit more flour if the gnocchi seem mushy.

10 Continue forming the remaining gnocchi, placing them on a lightly floured tray until ready to cook.

11 Place the gnocchi in the boiling water. Use a slotted spoon or skimmer to remove them to a bowl of ice water as they rise to the surface.

12 Once they have cooled (about 2 minutes) drain them briefly on paper towels or a kitchen towel. Lay them in a single layer on a parchment-lined baking sheet.

13 Store on a tray in the refrigerator if they will be used that day or place them in the freezer. Once they are frozen, they can be stored in well-sealed plastic bags and kept frozen for several weeks: cook/reheat them while they are still frozen.

386 Maxim potatoes

	4 portions	10 portions
large Desiree or Yukon Gold potatoes	4 (approx. 1400 g)	10 (approx. 3½ kg)
clarified butter	600 g	1½ kg
kosher salt		

nutritional info

♥

1 large portion provides:

3456 kJ/822 kcal

62.7 g fat (of which 40.5 g saturated)

60.2 g carbohydrate (of which 2.1 g sugars)

7.7 g protein

4.6 g fibre

A large amount of clarified butter was used to coat the potatoes.

calorie counter: kcal 1000 900 800 700 600 500 400 300 200 100 0

1 Pre-heat the oven to 180–190°C.

2 Peel the potato and slice it into paper-thin rounds on a mandolin.

3 Toss the rounds with the clarified butter; they should be well coated.

4 Arrange them on a Silpat-lined baking sheet, overlapping the slices by half to form a solid sheet of potatoes, or lay them in overlapping circles in a large, heavy ovenproof skillet.

5 Sprinkle lightly with the salt.

6 Bake the potatoes for 45 to 50 minutes, or until they are crisp and golden brown. These can be made several hours ahead and left at room temperature.

387 Deep-fried hash browns

	4 portions	10 portions
butter	30 g	75 g
onions, peeled and thinly sliced	100 g	250 g
large potatoes, cooked in their skins, peeled and grated	1 kg	2½ kg
egg whites, half-beaten	1	3
dry mashed potato, no cream or butter added	200 g	500 g
potato flour	50 g	125 g
celery salt	½ tsp	1 tsp
salt and freshly ground black pepper		
good vegetable oil, for deep-frying		

nutritional info

♥

1 large portion provides:

2273 kJ/540 kcal

19.8 g fat (of which 5.8 g saturated)

82.8 g carbohydrate (of which 4.3 g sugars)

12.8 g protein

6.5 g fibre

Some butter was used to cook the onions, and oil to fry the potatoes.

calorie counter: kcal 1000 900 800 700 600 500 400 300 200 100 0

1 Heat the butter in a pan and cook the onions slowly until they are soft. Put the onions into a bowl, add the grated potato and mix them together with the egg white.

2 Stir in the mashed potato, the potato flour, celery salt and seasoning. If the mixture is a little wet, add some more potato flour.

3 Pre-heat a deep-fat fryer to 170°C with 8 cm oil. Test the mixture by rolling a couple of little balls of it in the palm of your hand and dropping them into the hot fat.

4 When they are cooked, taste them and, if necessary, adjust the seasoning.

5 Roll the rest into walnut-sized balls and cook them in batches.

Note: You can half-fry the hash browns in advance, then crisp them up in hot oil before you serve them.

388 Gratin Dauphinoise

The mountain province of Dauphine in France produces excellent potatoes, which are used in 'gratins'. The addition of cheese does not play any part in the genuine gratin Dauphinoise, but it is particularly good when the gratin is served with a baked ham. The essence of a true gratin Dauphinoise is its crisp topping, which is achieved by the glazing of the cheese.

	4 portions	10 portions
double cream	150 ml	375 ml
milk	150 ml	375 ml
garlic cloves, crushed	1–2	3–5
large floury potatoes (e.g. baking potatoes) (approx. 200 g each)	2	5
butter	25 g	60 g
salt and pepper		
Emmental cheese, grated	100 g	250 g

nutritional info

1 large portion provides:
1776 kJ/428 kcal
34.4 g fat (of which 21.4 g saturated)
19.6 g carbohydrate (of which 3.0 g sugars)
11.2 g protein
1.3 g fibre

Double cream, butter and cheese were added.

♥

calorie counter

kcal
1000
900
800
700
600
500
400
300
200
100
0

1 Place the cream, milk and garlic in a saucepan and slowly bring to the boil. Remove from the heat and allow to cool.

2 Peel and thinly slice the potatoes (about 2 mm thick).

3 Butter a small baking tray or earthenware ovenproof dish and season lightly with salt and pepper.

4 Arrange slices of potato over the bottom of the dish, overlapping as you go and lightly seasoning each layer with salt and pepper until all the potato is used.

5 Pour over the cream and milk mixture until the potatoes are just covered.

6 Press down the potatoes with something flat so that the cream covers all the potatoes.

7 Bake in a moderate oven (180°C) for about 30 minutes.

8 Turn the oven down to 150°C and sprinkle the potatoes with grated cheese.

9 Cook until tender for a further 15 minutes (approx.).

10 If the potatoes get too brown on top, cover with silver foil.

389 Fondant potatoes

	4 portions	10 portions
prepared potatoes	1 kg	2½ kg
salt to season		
white stock	600 ml	1500 ml
butter	75 g	180 kg
parsley, chopped	12 g	30 g

nutritional info

1 large portion provides:
2174 kJ/517 kcal
16.5 g fat (of which 9.8 g saturated)
86.5 g carbohydrate (of which 3.5 g sugars)
10.7 g protein
6.7 g fibre

The pototoes were brushed with melted butter.

♥

calorie counter

kcal
1000
900
800
700
600
500
400
300
200
100
0

1 Cut the peeled potatoes into even-sized pieces and trim them slightly to an even shape.

2 Place into greased baking dishes, half cover with seasoned stock and brush over with melted butter.

3 Place in a hot oven to cook, and brush over from time to time with melted butter to impart a gloss.

4 When cooked, the potatoes should be brown on top and white underneath, and all the stock should have evaporated or been absorbed by the potatoes.

5 Sprinkle with chopped parsley before serving.

390 Potatoes Lyonnaise v

	4 portions	10 portions
potatoes, sautéed	1 kg	2½ kg
onions, sautéed	275 g	650 g
parsley, chopped	12 g	30 g

1 Toss the sautéed potatoes and onions together in a frying pan.

2 Serve sprinkled with the chopped parsley.

nutritional info

1 large portion provides:
2714 kJ/648 kcal
29.0 g fat (of which 3.2 g saturated)
91.5 g carbohydrate (of which 6.9 g sugars)
11.4 g protein
7.6 g fibre

Oil was used to sauté the potatoes and onions.

kcal: 1000 900 800 700 600 500 400 300 200 100 0 — calorie counter

391 Mashed potato

	4 portions	10 portions
potatoes, peeled and cut evenly or into 8 cm blocks	2 kg	5 kg
butter	200 g	500 g
cream (whipping)	200 ml	500 ml
salt to season		

nutritional info

1 large portion provides:
3904 kJ/938 kcal
62.3 g fat (of which 38.7 g saturated)
87.7 g carbohydrate (of which 4.7 g sugars)
11.8 g protein
6.5 g fibre

Butter and cream were added.

kcal: 1000 900 800 700 600 500 400 300 200 100 0 — calorie counter

Note: For a more traditional mashed potato refer to *Practical Cookery*.

This preparation has been around for many years and is probably one of the most popular potato dishes, along with roast potatoes and chips.

When selecting potatoes to mash the following factors should be borne in mind: cooking temperature, gluten agitation, breakdown of the starch wall, and how the fat (if any) is worked in. Because so many things could affect the final result, we have provided the following checklist to guide you through what most people probably consider a relatively easy preparation.

- **Variety:** Binji, Maris Piper, Desiree or most of the 'floury' varieties.

- **Cooking speed and temperature:** If you rapidly cook floury potatoes the dry matter will eventually start to separate and allow water into the structure; the potatoes will invariably break down, allow more water in and eventually disintegrate. Place the potatoes in cold water as normal and bring to the boil. Once boiled, remove immediately and wash off in cold water – this creates a starch wall that will help prevent water penetration. Place them back in cold water and bring them up to a temperature of approx. 80–85°C and leave them to cook for 1½ hours until they are tender.

- **Pass/ricing:** Once the potatoes are cooked drain them in a colander and allow to dry slightly by evaporation, then place in a ricer or 'mouli', or push through a fine sieve (if using a fine sieve the potato should only be pushed, not scraped carefully, so as not to overwork the mix); once it has been mashed, by whatever method, place through the fine sieve.

- **Fat incorporation:** The fat and cream content that can be added is extraordinary due to the long chains of unbroken starch that wrap and trap the fat in the finished product. Up to 20 per cent of the total mass can be added fat – for example, 1 kg of mashed potato can contain 200 g of fat; this can be in the form of reduced cream and butter.

Selection of potatoes for mash: a checklist

392 Anna potatoes

oil	
peeled potatoes	600 g
salt and pepper	
butter	25 g

nutritional info

1 large portion provides:
688 kJ/159 kcal
5.4 g fat (of which 3.3 g saturated)
25.8 g carbohydrate (of which 0.9 g sugars)
3.2 g protein
2.0 g fibre

Oil was used to grease the mould, and a small amount of butter on the top.

kcal
1000
900
800
700
600
500
400
300
200
100
0

calorie counter

1 Grease an anna mould using hot oil.

2 Trim the potatoes to an even cylindrical shape.

3 Cut into slices 2 mm thick.

4 Place a layer of slices neatly overlapping in the bottom of the mould, season lightly with salt and pepper.

5 Continue arranging the slices of potato in layers, seasoning in between.

6 Add the butter to the top layer.

7 Cook in a hot oven (210–220°C) for ¾–1 hour, occasionally pressing the potatoes flat.

8 To serve, turn out of the mould and leave whole or cut into four portions.

393 Sweet potatoes v

Also known as boniato, sweet potatoes have a sticky texture; they are slightly aromatic and sweet. Small or medium-sized potatoes with firm, fresh-looking skins should be selected.

Sweet potatoes can be steamed, boiled or baked in their skins, with the centre removed and puréed or creamed. They can be made into vegetarian dishes with the addition of other ingredients, and they may also be fried or made into bread or sweet pudding.

nutritional info

1 large portion provides:
462 kJ/109 kcal
0.4 g fat (of which 0.1 g saturated)
26.5 g carbohydrate (of which 10.9 g sugars)
1.4 g protein
3.0 g fibre

The potatoes are steamed, boiled or baked with no additional fat.

kcal
1000
900
800
700
600
500
400
300
200
100
0

calorie counter

394 Candied sweet potatoes

	4 portions	10 portions
oil or butter	1 tbsp	2½ tbsp
sweet potatoes, in 1 cm dice	400 g	1¼ kg
chopped onion	100 g	250 g
honey	2 tbsp	5 tbsp
cider vinegar	2 tbsp	5 tbsp
cinnamon	¼ tsp	½ tbsp
salt		

nutritional info

1 large portion provides:
641 kJ/151 kcal
3.1 g fat (of which 0.4 g saturated)
31.0 g carbohydrate (of which 14.8 g sugars)
1.6 g protein
2.8 g fibre

A small amount of oil was used to fry the potatoes.

kcal
1000
900
800
700
600
500
400
300
200
100
0

calorie counter

1 Heat the oil in a frying pan and add the sweet potatoes.

2 Cook for 10 minutes, stirring occasionally.

3 Add the onion and cook until brown.

4 Mix the honey, cider vinegar, cinnamon and salt in a bowl. Pour the honey mixture on to the potatoes, heat through, season and serve.

395 Potato cakes with chives

	4 portions	10 portions
large potatoes	4	10
egg yolks	2	5
butter	50 g	125 g
chives, chopped	50 g	125 g
salt and pepper		

1 Bake the potatoes in their jackets.

2 Halve and remove the potato from the skins.

3 Mash with the yolks and butter.

4 Mix in the chopped chives and season.

5 Mould into round cakes, 2 cm diameter.

6 Lightly flour and shallow-fry to a golden colour on both sides.

nutritional info

1 large portion provides:
1181 kJ/282 kcal
14.2 g fat (of which 2.1 g saturated)
34.6 g carbohydrate (of which 1.4 g sugars)
6.0 g protein
2.8 g fibre

Egg yolk and butter were added.

kcal
1000
900
800
700
600
500
400
300
200
100
0

calorie counter

396 Potatoes cooked with button onions and tomatoes v

	4 portions	10 portions
potatoes, peeled	400 g	1¼ kg
button onions	100 g	250 g
garlic clove	1	2–3
vegetable stock	375 ml	1 litre
salt and pepper		
tomatoes, skinned, deseeded and diced	100 g	250 g

1 Trim and dice the potatoes into 2 cm pieces.

2 Add to the peeled onions, crushed garlic and stock.

3 Season and cook gently in a suitable pan in the oven or on the stove until the potatoes are just cooked.

4 Add the tomatoes and cook for a few more minutes, then serve.

nutritional info

1 large portion provides:
381 kJ/90 kcal
0.3 g fat (of which 0.3 g saturated)
20.3 g carbohydrate (of which 3.0 g sugars)
2.6 g protein
1.9 g fibre

There is no added fat or oil.

kcal
1000
900
800
700
600
500
400
300
200
100
0

calorie counter

VEGETABLE DISHES

397 Vegetables à la Greque v

	4 portions	10 portions
medium aubergines in caviar (approx. 150 g each) (recipe 400)	2	5
large dark-red plum tomatoes	6	15
sea salt and freshly ground black pepper		
olive oil	200 ml	500 ml
balsamic vinegar	2 tsp	5 tsp
baby carrots	8 (100 g)	20
baby fennel	4 (100 g)	10
baby leeks	8 (100 g)	20
baby courgettes	8 (100 g)	20
each of chopped basil, chervil, coriander and chives	1 tsp	3 tsp
coriander seeds, crushed	12	30
saffron strands	pinch	pinch
small servings mixed salad leaves	2	5

nutritional info

1 large portion provides:
2274 kJ/550 kcal
53.7 g fat (of which 7.7 g saturated)
15.7 g carbohydrate (of which 15.3 g sugars)
2.5 g protein
3.4 g fibre

A large amount of olive oil was used.

1 Have the aubergine caviar ready and set aside.

2 Skin the tomatoes by dipping briefly in boiling water so that the skins slip off easily. Cut each into quarters and discard the seeds.

3 Season and marinate in 3 tbsp of the oil together with 1 tsp of the balsamic vinegar and half the herbs, for about 2 hours.

4 Prepare all the vegetables by peeling or trimming. Bring the remainder of the oil and vinegar to the boil, then add all the baby vegetables, the remaining herbs, and the crushed coriander seeds and saffron strands. Remove from the heat and leave to infuse, turning once or twice, until cool. Chill for at least 30 minutes before serving.

5 Drain the tomatoes, reserving the marinade. Use the tomatoes to line the base and sides of two ramekins. Spoon in the aubergine caviar, pressing it down firmly, then chill for about 30 minutes to allow it to settle.

6 To serve, unmould a tian in to the centre of each plate and spoon over the reserved tomato marinade to glaze. Prepare the mixed salad leaves and place small mounds on top.

7 Drain the baby vegetables from their marinade, arrange them around each tian then trickle over a little of the marinade to garnish.

398 Braised-roast salsify

	4 portions	10 portions
fish or chicken stock	200 ml	500 ml
salsify	500 g	1¼ kg
cold water	700 ml	1¾ l
milk	100 ml	250 ml
lemons, juice of	1	3
rock salt	1 tbsp	3 tbsp
butter	50 g	125 g
fresh bouquet garni	1	2
sea salt and ground white pepper		

nutritional info

1 large portion provides:
598 kJ/145 kcal
11.6 g fat (of which 7.1 g saturated)
14.3 g carbohydrate (of which 3.4 g sugars)
2.6 g protein
4.0 g fibre

Butter was used for frying.

1 Have the stock ready and set aside.

2 Wash the salsify well, then peel, top and tail. Place immediately into a saucepan with the water, milk, lemon juice and rock salt.

3 Bring to the boil, then remove from the heat and leave the salsify to cool.

4 Drain, then cut into 4 cm batons or thick julienne strips. Pre-heat the oven to 180°C.

5 Heat the butter in a large, ovenproof frying pan or shallow, cast-iron casserole. Add the salsify batons and fry gently until they start to colour a little and caramelise.

6 Pour in the stock to just cover the salsify. Stir, add the bouquet garni and cook, uncovered, in the oven for 12–14 minutes until the liquid has evaporated and the salsify has become nicely glazed. Check the seasoning and serve.

399 Braised chicory

	4 portions	10 portions
fish or chicken stock	200 ml	500 ml
medium heads chicory	8	20
fresh lemon juice	3 tbsp	8 tbsp
caster sugar	3 tbsp	8 tbsp
sea salt and freshly ground black pepper		
butter	25 g	60 g

nutritional info

1 large portion provides:
476 kJ/114 kcal
6.3 g fat (of which 3.7 g saturated)
17.8 g carbohydrate (of which 13.5 g sugars)
1.1 g protein
1.8 g fibre

A small amount of butter was added.

1 Have the stock ready and set aside.

2 Trim the chicory of any bruised outside leaves, then trim the ends and use a small, sharp knife to remove the bitter core at the base of each head.

3 Bring a pan of water to the boil and add the lemon juice, 1 tbsp of the sugar and salt to taste. Blanch the chicory for 8–10 minutes and drain well.

4 Drain all the liquid from the chicory and, in a large frying pan, heat the butter and brown the chicory on all sides, deglaze with a little stock and simmer for a few minutes, basting the chicory at all times.

5 Arrange the heads in a single layer on a platter, sprinkle with the remaining sugar, and season with salt and pepper. Leave to cool for about 10 minutes.

400 Aubergine caviar **v**

	4 portions	10 portions
medium aubergines (approx. 150 g each), cut into 2 cm pieces	4	10
vegetable oil, to fry and sauté		
banana shallots, sliced	4	10
cumin	1 tbsp	3 tbsp
soaked golden raisins	100 g	250 g
tomato purée	1 tbsp	3 tbsp
basil and coriander, chopped		
seasoning		

nutritional info

1 large portion provides:
624 kJ/148 kcal
6.5 g fat (of which 0.8 g saturated)
22.3 g carbohydrate (of which 21.7 g sugars)
2.5 g protein
3.8 g fibre

A little oil was used to fry the aubergine.

1 Fry the aubergine in vegetable oil until a good golden colour, and drain.

2 Sauté the shallots in the oil and add the cumin and raisins.

3 Blend the aubergine, shallot mix and tomato purée until smooth.

4 Add the chopped herbs and adjust the seasoning.

401 Parmesan fried courgettes with pesto

	4 portions	10 portions
medium courgettes	8 (800 g)	20 (2 kg)
plain flour, seasoned	4 tbsp	10 tbsp
eggs	2	5
milk	50 ml	125 ml
Parmesan, grated	100 g	250 g
good vegetable oil for deep-frying		
salt and freshly ground black pepper		
Pesto		
basil	80 g	200 g
garlic cloves, peeled and crushed	2	5
pine nuts, lightly roasted	30 g	75 g
extra-virgin olive oil	150 ml	375 ml
Parmesan, grated	50 g	125 g

nutritional info

1 large portion provides:
2946 kJ/711 kcal
58.7 g fat (of which 14.4 g saturated)
21.6 g carbohydrate (of which 4.9 g sugars)
25.1 g protein
2.6 g fibre

Eggs and parmesan were used with the courgettes, and there is fat in the pesto.

calorie counter

kcal
1000
900
800
700
600
500
400
300
200
100
0

For the pesto

1 Put all the ingredients for the pesto in a blender and process until smooth.

For the courgettes

1 Cut each courgette in three, crossways, then each third into eight. Have ready four dishes.

2 Place the flour in the first. In the second, beat together the eggs and the milk. Place the grated Parmesan in the third. The fourth will hold the prepared courgettes.

3 Coat the courgette pieces with the flour, then the egg, and last the Parmesan. Make sure that you shake off any excess flour before dipping them in the egg or the Parmesan will not stick.

4 Heat a deep-fat fryer to 160–170°C with 10 cm of vegetable oil and cook the courgettes until they are golden. Drain them on kitchen paper and season lightly.

5 Serve them with a little pesto spooned on top.

402 Bubble and squeak v

	10 portions
swede, peeled and cut into chunks	400 g
good vegetable oil for frying	
onions, peeled and sliced	300 g
green cabbage, sliced and/or Brussels sprouts, outer leaves removed	400 g
salt and freshly ground black pepper	
firm mashed potato, no butter or cream added	350 g
plain flour for dusting	

nutritional info

1 large portion provides:
680 kJ/163 kcal
11.4 g fat (of which 1.3 g saturated)
13.9 g carbohydrate (of which 5.5 g sugars)
2.3 g protein
2.7 g fibre

Vegetable oil was used for frying, and no
butter or cream added to the potato.

	kcal
♥	1000
	900
	800
	700
	600
	500
	400
	300
	200
	100
	0

calorie counter

1 Bring a saucepan of salted water to the boil, add
the swede and cook until soft.

2 Heat 3 tbsp vegetable oil in a pan and cook the
sliced onions until they are soft. Cook the cabbage
until soft in boiling salted water. Cook the sprouts
until soft, then slice them. Put all the cooked
vegetables together in a bowl, mix well and
season.

3 Heat some more vegetable oil in a non-stick or
heavy-bottomed frying pan until it is almost
smoking and fry the mixture a little at a time until it
colours, turning with a wooden spoon. Then return
it to the bowl and leave it to cool.

4 Mix in the mashed potato, check the seasoning,
then mould the bubble and squeak mixture into
even-sized cakes.

5 Refrigerate them overnight.

6 When you are ready to serve them, lightly flour the
cakes and heat some vegetable oil in a frying pan.
Cook them on both sides until they are golden
brown.

403 Braised red cabbage

	10 portions
red onions, sliced and caramelised in duck fat	3 (approx. 450 g)
red cabbage, shredded	800 g
bouquet garni	1
red wine vinegar	40 ml
cinnamon stick	½
red wine	500 ml
cassis	150 ml
redcurrant jelly	1 tbsp
brown sugar	20 g
duck fat	40 g
salt and pepper	

nutritional info

1 large portion provides:
634 kJ/153 kcal
9.4 g fat (of which 4.6 g saturated)
15.9 g carbohydrate (of which 13.1 g sugars)
2.2 g protein
3.5 g fibre

Dripping was used instead of duck fat for
this analysis. The saturated fat comes from
the duck fat.

	kcal
♥	1000
	900
	800
	700
	600
	500
	400
	300
	200
	100
	0

calorie counter

1 Mix all ingredients and cook in the oven at 150°C
with a cartouche for 1 to 1½ hours, then remove
from oven and drain away the excess liquid (retain
the liquid).

2 To finish: place the cabbage and a little of the
cooking liquid in a pan, reheat and emulsify with
butter until it becomes thick.

Braised red cabbage with confit onions (see recipe 405)

404 Braised red cabbage with apples, red wine and juniper

	4 portions	10 portions
red cabbage, shredded	400 g	1¼ kg
vegetable oil	2 tbsp	5 tbsp
cooking apples, peeled, cored and diced	200 g	500 g
red wine	250 ml	600 ml
salt and pepper		
juniper berries	12	30

1 Blanch and refresh the cabbage.

2 Heat the oil in a casserole, add the cabbage and apples, and stir.

3 Add the wine, seasoning and juniper berries.

4 Bring to the boil, cover and braise for approximately 40–45 minutes until tender.

5 If any liquid remains when cooked, continue cooking uncovered to evaporate the liquid.

nutritional info

1 large portion provides:
368 kJ/88 kcal
5.8 g fat (of which 0.6 g saturated)
8.2 g carbohydrate (of which 7.8 g sugars)
1.3 g protein
3.3 g fibre

A small amount of oil was used.

kcal
1000
900
800
700
600
500
400
300
200
100
0
calorie counter

405 Confit onions

Makes 24 onions

duck fat or olive oil	750 g
button onions	24
fresh bay leaf	1
garlic clove, split	1
sprig of thyme	1

1 Place all the ingredients into a medium-sized saucepan, heat gently to approx. 65°C and cook for 45 minutes to 1 hour until the onions are tender.

2 Do not allow the oil to reach a high temperature as the onions will deep-fry.

406 Parsnip and vanilla purée

	10 portions
parsnips, peeled and stalks removed	1 kg
butter	75 g
vanilla pod, split	1
seasoning	
milk, to aid purée	

1 Place the parsnips, butter and vanilla in a vac pack and steam until soft. Remove the pod and scrap out the seeds, add the rest of the ingredients and blitz, adding milk if necessary.

2 Pass though a fine drum sieve and season.

nutritional info

1 large portion provides:
521 kJ/125 kcal
7.6 g fat (of which 4.3 g saturated)
12.9 g carbohydrate (of which 6.1 g sugars)
2.1 g protein
4.6 g fibre

Butter was added to the puree.

kcal
1000
900
800
700
600
500
400
300
200
100
0
calorie counter

407 Shallot purée v

	4 portions
large shallots, unpeeled	6 (400 g)
garlic clove	1
sprig thyme	1
splash of olive oil	

nutritional info

1 large portion provides:
254 kJ/61 kcal
3.0 g fat (of which 0.4 g saturated)
8.0 g carbohydrate (of which 5.6 g sugars)
1.3 g protein
1.4 g fibre

Very little olive oil was used.

kcal
1000
900
800
700
600
500
400
300
200
100
0
calorie counter

1 Pre-heat the oven to 180°C, and place the shallots, garlic, thyme and olive oil on a 30 cm-square piece of foil.

2 Fold over to make a bag and seal the edges. Put the bag on a baking tray and place in the oven for 25–30 minutes until the shallots are soft and fully cooked inside, set aside to cool.

3 Trim off the skin from the shallots, discard the rest of the ingredients, place the shallots in a food processor and purée to a smooth pulp. If the pulp is quite viscose, place it in a muslin and hang overnight.

408 Leaf spinach with pine nuts and garlic

	4 portions	10 portions
spinach	1 kg	2½ kg
pine nuts	50 g	125 g
oil or butter	1 tbsp	2–3 tbsp
garlic clove, chopped	1	2–3
salt and pepper		

1 Cook the spinach for 2–3 minutes and drain well.

2 Lightly brown the pine nuts in oil, add garlic and sweat for 2 minutes.

3 Add coarsely chopped spinach and heat through over a medium heat.

4 Correct seasoning and serve.

nutritional info

1 large portion provides:
614 kJ/149 kcal
12.5 g fat (of which 1.1 g saturated)
3.0 g carbohydrate (of which 2.8 g sugars)
6.0 g protein
3.4 g fibre

A small amount of oil was used.

kcal
1000
900
800
700
600
500
400
300
200
100
0
calorie counter

409 Artichokes with spinach and cheese sauce

Prepared and cooked artichoke bottoms are filled with leaf spinach, coated with mornay sauce, browned and served.

Variations

Other vegetables that can be substituted for spinach include asparagus points, cooked peas, and a mixture of peas and carrots; also, a duxelle-based stuffing with various additions, which may be finished either with mornay sauce or au gratin.

410 Aubergine soufflé

	4 portions	10 portions
aubergines	2	5
thick béchamel	250 ml	600 ml
grated Parmesan cheese	50 g	125 g
eggs, separated	3	7
salt and pepper		

1 Cut the aubergines in halves.

2 Slash the flesh criss-cross and deep-fry for a few minutes.

3 Drain well, scoop out the flesh and finely chop.

4 Lay the skins in a buttered gratin dish.

5 Mix the aubergine flesh with an equal quantity of béchamel.

6 Heat this mixture through, then mix in the cheese and yolks, and season.

7 Fold in the stiffly beaten whites.

8 Fill the skins with this mixture, bake at 230°C for approximately 15 minutes and serve immediately.

Note: For extra lightness use 4 egg whites to 3 yolks (10 egg whites to 7 yolks for 10 portions).

nutritional info

1 portion provides:
1160 kJ/278 kcals
18.5 g fat
(of which 9.9 g saturated)
13.9 g carbohydrate
(of which 7.7 g sugars)
15.2 g protein
4 g fibre

411 Baby sweetcorn v

These are cobs of corn that are harvested when very young. They are used widely in oriental cookery and are available from December to March.

nutritional info

1 large portion (100 g boiled or steamed) provides:
96 kJ/23 kcal
0.4 g fat (of which 0.0 g saturated)
2.0 g carbohydrate (of which 1.4 g sugars)
2.9 g protein
1.5 g fibre

There is no added fat; the fat content would increase a little if stir fried.

Always select cobs that look fresh and are undamaged. Baby corns are removed from their protective husks, cooked for a few minutes in unsalted water and may then be served whole or cut in slices and coated with butter or margarine. Unlike fully grown sweetcorn, baby corn are not removed from the cob before eating – when cooked the vegetable is tender enough to eat whole.

Baby sweetcorns are used in stir-fry dishes, e.g. with chicken, crab or prawns, and may also be served cold with vinaigrette. Baby corn looks attractive when served as one of a selection of plated vegetables.

412 Bamboo shoots v

These are the shoots of young edible bamboo, stripped of the tough outer brown skin, so that the insides are eaten. They have a texture similar to celery and a flavour rather like that of globe artichokes. They are also obtainable preserved in brine.

Methods of cooking: chopped bamboo shoots are used in a number of stir-fry dishes, meat and poultry casseroles and as a soup garnish. They can also be served hot with a hollandaise-type sauce or beurre blanc.

nutritional info

1 large portion (100 g, boiled) provides:
45 kJ/11 kcal
0.2 g fat (of which 0.1 g saturated)
0.7 g carbohydrate (of which 0.7 g sugars)
1.5 g protein
1.7 g fibre

There is no added fat; the fat content would increase a little if stir fried.

413 Bean sprouts v

These are the tender young sprouts of the germinating soya or mung bean. As they are a highly perishable vegetable, it is best to select white, plump, crisp sprouts with a fresh appearance.

Methods of cooking: first, rinse well and drain, they may be then stir-fried and served as a vegetable,

mixed in with other ingredients in stir-fry dishes, used in omelettes and also served as a crisp salad item.

Bean sprouts are available all year round. It is essential that they are very thoroughly washed before being cooked.

414 Stir-fried bean sprouts v

	4 portions	10 portions
bean sprouts	400 g	1¼ kg
vegetable oil	1 tbsp	2½ tbsp
spring onions	4–6	10–18
ginger, chopped	1 tsp	2–3 tsp
salt		
soy sauce	2 tsp	5 tsp

nutritional info

1 large portion provides:
254 kJ/61 kcal
2.8 g fat (of which 0.4 g saturated)
4.8 g carbohydrate (of which 2.8 g sugars)
3.3 g protein
1.7 g fibre

Oil was used to stir fry.

1 Wash, dry and trim the bean sprouts.

2 Heat the oil in a frying pan or wok and add the spring onions (cut into 2 cm pieces) and ginger.

3 Fry for a few seconds, then add the sprouts.

4 Stir continuously and add salt.

5 Keeping the sprouts crisp, add soy sauce and serve.

415 Broad beans with tomato and coriander v

	4 portions	10 portions
shelled broad beans	300 g	1 kg
vegetable oil	1 tbsp	2½ tbsp
tomatoes, skinned, deseeded and diced	2	5
salt and pepper		
coriander, freshly chopped	1 tbsp	2½ tbsp

nutritional info

1 large portion provides:
319 kJ/76 kcal
3.6 g fat (of which 0.4 g saturated)
6.7 g carbohydrate (of which 2.3 g sugars)
4.6 g protein
5.0 g fibre

A small amount of oil was used.

1 Cook the broad beans, keeping them slightly firm, and drain.

2 Heat the oil in a pan and add the tomatoes.

3 Add the broad beans and correct the seasoning.

4 Add the coriander and toss lightly to mix. Correct seasoning and serve.

416 Cardoons v

These are a long plant, similar to celery, with an aroma and flavour like that of the globe artichoke. Select cardoons with bright leaves, crisp stems and a fresh-looking appearance.

nutritional info

1 large portion (100 g) provides:
34 kJ/8 kcal
0.3 g fat (of which 0.1 g saturated)
0.8 g carbohydrate (of which 0.8 g sugars)
0.5 g protein
1.2 g fibre

Method of cooking: remove leaves, stalks and tough parts and cut into small pieces; cook in acidulated water for approximately 30–40 minutes.

Cardoons may be used as a plain vegetable, in other vegetable dishes or served raw as an appetiser.

417 Cardoons with onions and cheese

	4 portions	10 portions
cardoons	400 g	1¼ kg
lemons, juice of	1	2–3
onion, finely sliced	100 g	250 g
butter	25 g	60 g
salt		
grated Parmesan	50 g	125 g

1 Trim and wash the cardoons, rub with lemon juice and cut into 8 cm pieces.

2 Cook in salted lemon water for approximately 30 minutes, drain.

3 Gently cook the onion in the butter until light brown.

4 Add the cardoons and a little of the cooking liquid and simmer gently until tender.

5 Correct seasoning and serve sprinkled with cheese.

nutritional info

1 large portion provides:
479 kJ/115 kcal
9.1 g fat (of which 5.7 g saturated)
3.2 g carbohydrate (of which 2.7 g sugars)
5.4 g protein
1.5 g fibre

The onion was cooked in butter, and parmesan added.

418 Cardoon fritters

	4 portions	10 portions
cardoons	400 g	1¼ kg
Marinade		
lemons, juice of	1	2–3
onion, chopped	100 g	250 g
vegetable oil	60 ml	150 ml
parsley, chopped	1 tbsp	2–3 tbsp
salt		
frying batter		
lemon wedges, to serve		

1 Prepare and cook cardoons as in the recipe above, steps 1–2.

2 Drain well and, while hot, place in the marinade for 1 hour.

3 Drain and dry the cardoon pieces thoroughly.

4 Dip in the batter and deep-fry at 185°C until golden brown.

5 Serve with quarters of lemon.

419 Chinese cabbage v

A wide variety of Chinese cabbage – or Chinese leaves – is grown in China, but the one generally seen in Britain is similar in appearance to a large pale cos lettuce. It is crisp and delicate, with a faint cabbage flavour.

Always select fresh-looking, crisp cabbage.

Method of cooking: the hard centre stems are removed from outer leaves and they can then be stir-fried, braised, boiled or steamed like cabbage. The inner leaves can be used for salads in place of lettuce.

420 Spicy stir-fry Chinese cabbage v

	4 portions	10 portions
oil	25 g	60 g
ginger, finely chopped	25 g	60 g
cloves garlic, finely chopped	2	5
curry powder	5 g	12 g
soy sauce	25 g	60 g
sugar	10 g	60 g
stock or water	2 tbsp	5 tbsp
Chinese cabbage, chopped	600 g	2 kg

1 Heat the oil in a frying pan or wok, add the ginger, garlic and curry powder, and toss for a few seconds.

2 Add the soy sauce, sugar and stock, and bring to the boil.

3 Add the cabbage and boil for 5 minutes, stirring occasionally, and serve at once.

nutritional info

1 large portion provides:
445 kJ/107 kcal
6.9 g fat (of which 0.8 g saturated)
9.6 g carbohydrate (of which 6.5 g sugars)
2.4 g protein
2.2 g fibre

A little oil was used to stir fry.

421 Christophene v

Christophene, also known as chow-chow, chayotte or vegetable pear, looks rather like a ridged green pear and is available in several varieties including white and green, spiny and smooth-skinned, rounded and ridged, or more or less pear-shaped. Christophenes usually weigh between 150–250 g, the inside flesh is firm and white with a flavour and texture resembling a combination of marrow and cucumber.

Christophenes are peeled and the stones removed in preparation and they can be cooked in similar ways to courgettes. They are also suitable for being stuffed and braised.

nutritional info

1 large portion (150 g, boiled) provides:
111 kJ/26 kcal
0.2 g fat (of which 0.0 g saturated)
5.6 g carbohydrate (of which 4.7 g sugars)
1.1 g protein
1.7 g fibre

Contains no oil or fat.

422 Colcannon

This is an Irish dish for which there are many variations.

	4 portions	10 portions
cabbage	300 g	1 kg
peeled potatoes	200 g	500 g
leeks	100 g	250 g
milk or single cream	250 ml	600 ml
salt, pepper and nutmeg		
butter	25 g	60 g

1 Shred the cabbage, cook and drain well.

2 Cook and mash the potatoes.

3 Chop the leeks and simmer in the milk until tender.

4 Mix the leeks in with the potatoes, cabbage and seasoning.

5 Place in a serving dish, make a well in the centre, pour in the melted butter and serve.

nutritional info

1 large portion provides:
626 kJ/150 kcal
8.1 g fat (of which 4.9 g saturated)
15.3 g carbohydrate (of which 6.7 g sugars)
4.8 g protein
3.0 g fibre

Melted butter was added when served.

Using milk
1 portion provides:
625 kJ/150 kcal
8.1 g fat (of which 5 g saturated)
15.4 g carbohydrate (of which 6.9 g sugars)
4.8 g protein
3 g fibre

423 Kohlrabi v

This is a stem that swells to a turnip shape above the ground. When grown under glass it is pale green in colour, when grown outdoors it is purplish. Select kohlrabi with tops that are green, young and fresh. If the globes are too large they may be woody and tough.

Methods of cooking: trim off stems and leaves (which may be used for soups), peel thickly at the root end, thinly at top end, wash and cut into even-sized pieces. Young kohlrabi can be cooked whole. Simmer in well-flavoured stock until tender. Kohlrabi may be served with cream sauce, baked or stuffed, and added to casseroles (meat and vegetarian) and stews.

nutritional info

1 large portion (100 g, boiled) provides:
77 kJ/18 kcal
0.2 g fat (of which 0.0 g saturated)
3.1 g carbohydrate (of which 3.0 g sugars)
1.2 g protein
1.9 g fibre

Contains no oil or fat.

424 Mooli v

Mooli or white radish – or rettiche as it is sometimes known – is a parsnip-shaped member of the radish family and is available all year round. Mooli does not have a hot taste like radishes but is slightly bitter and is pleasant to eat cooked as a vegetable. Mooli should have smooth flesh, white in appearance and be a regular shape.

Mooli has a high water content, which can be reduced before cooking or serving raw by peeling and slicing, sprinkling with salt and leaving to stand for 30 minutes. Otherwise, the preparation is to wash well and grate, shred or slice before adding to salads or cooking as a vegetable.

Mooli may be used as a substitute for turnips.

nutritional info

1 large portion (25 g, grated raw) provides:
16 kJ/4 kcal
0.0 g fat (of which 0.0 g saturated)
0.7 g carbohydrate (of which 0.7 g sugars)
0.2 g protein
0.0 g fibre

425 Okra v

Okra are also known as gumbo or ladies' fingers. The flavour is slightly bitter and mild. Select pods that are firm, bright green and fresh looking.

Methods of cooking: cut off the conical cap at the stalk end, scrape the skin lightly, using a small knife, to remove any surface fuzz and the tips, then wash well. Okra can be served as a plain vegetable, tossed in butter or with tomato sauce, and may be prepared in a similar fashion to a ratatouille. Okra are also used in soups, stews, curries, pilaff rice and fried as fritters.

Okra contain a high proportion of sticky glue-like carbohydrate which, when they are used in stews, gives body to the dish.

nutritional info

1 large portion (50 g, boiled or steamed) provides:
65 kJ/16 kcal
0.5 g fat (of which 0.2 g saturated)
1.5 g carbohydrate (of which 1.3 g sugars)
1.4 g protein
2.0 g fibre

calorie counter

kcal
1000
900
800
700
600
500
400
300
200
100
0

426 Stewed okra v

	4 portions	10 portions
okra	400 g	1¼ kg
vegetable oil	25 g	60 g
onion, finely chopped	100 g	250 g
clove of garlic, finely chopped	1	2–3
tomatoes, skinned, deseeded and diced	400 g	1¼ kg
salt and mill pepper		

1 Top and tail the okra, clean, wash and drain.

2 Heat the oil in a thick-based pan, add the onions and cook gently without colour for 5 minutes.

3 Add the garlic and tomatoes, cover with a lid and simmer for 5 minutes.

4 Add the okra, season, reduce heat and cook gently on top of stove or in the oven until the okra is tender (approximately 15–20 minutes), and serve.

427 Palm hearts v

Palm hearts are the tender young shoots or buds of palm trees and are generally available tinned or bottled in brine. Fresh palm hearts have a bitter flavour and need to be blanched before being used.

Methods of cooking: palm hearts can be boiled, steamed or braised and are served hot or cold, usually cut in halves lengthwise. When hot they are accompanied by a hollandaise-type sauce or beurre blanc, when cold by mayonnaise or a herb-flavoured vinaigrette.

428 Stewed palm hearts

	4 portions	10 portions
oil	1 tbsp	2–3 tbsp
lean cooked ham	50 g	125 g
garlic, finely chopped	25 g	60 g
tomatoes, skinned, deseeded and diced	200 g	500 g
tomato purée	1 tbsp	2–3 tbsp
onion or chives, chopped	25 g	60 g
parsley, chopped	5 g	12 g
tinned palm hearts	400 g	1¼ kg

nutritional info

1 large portion provides:
305 kJ/73 kcal
3.8 g fat (of which 0.7 g saturated)
4.6 g carbohydrate (of which 3.5 g sugars)
5.4 g protein
2.8 g fibre

Bamboo shoots were used instead of palm hearts for this analysis. There is a small amount of oil and ham in the recipe.

calorie counter

kcal
1000
900
800
700
600
500
400
300
200
100
0

1 Heat the oil in a thick-bottomed pan, add the ham and garlic and cook without colour for 2–3 minutes.

2 Add the tomatoes, tomato purée, onion, parsley and seasoning.

3 Simmer gently until of a thickened consistency.

4 Add the palm hearts, mix in, simmer for 3–5 minutes and serve.

429 Scorzonera v

Scorzonera, also known as black-skinned salsify or oyster plant, has a white flesh when skinned, with a slight flavour of asparagus and oysters. Select salsify with fresh-looking leaves at the top.

Methods of cooking: wash well, boil or steam in the skin, then peel using a potato peeler and immediately place in a blanc to prevent discoloration. Cut into suitable-length pieces and serve plain, with butter, with cream or as for any cauliflower recipe. If peeling salsify raw, immediately place into cold water and lemon juice and cook in a blanc to prevent discoloration. Salsify requires approximately 20–30 minutes' cooking; test by pressing a piece between the fingers – if cooked, it will crush easily.

nutritional info

1 large portion (100 g, boiled or steamed) provides:
99 kJ/23 kcal
0.4 g fat (of which 0.0 g saturated)
8.6 g carbohydrate (of which 1.4 g sugars)
1.1 g protein
3.5 g fibre

kcal
1000 / 900 / 800 / 700 / 600 / 500 / 400 / 300 / 200 / 100 / 0
calorie counter

430 Salsify with onion, tomato and garlic

	4 portions	10 portions
salsify	400 g	1¼ kg
margarine, oil or butter	50 g	125 g
onions, chopped	50 g	125 g
clove of garlic, crushed and chopped	1	2–3
tomatoes, skinned, deseeded and diced	100 g	250 g
tomato purée	25 g	60 g
white stock	250 ml	600 ml
seasoning		
parsley, chopped		

1 Wash and peel the salsify, cut into 5 cm lengths. Place immediately into acidulated water to prevent discoloration.

2 Place salsify into a boiling blanc or acidulated water with a little oil and simmer until tender, approximately 10–40 minutes. Drain well.

3 Melt the margarine, oil or butter, add the onion and garlic. Sweat without colour.

4 Add the tomatoes, and tomato purée, cook for 5 minutes.

5 Moisten with white stock, correct seasoning.

6 Place the cooked and well-drained salsify into the tomato sauce.

7 Serve in a suitable dish, sprinkled with chopped parsley.

nutritional info

1 large portion provides:
558 kJ/135 kcal
10.7 g fat (of which 6.5 g saturated)
13.2 g carbohydrate (of which 4.1 g sugars)
2.1 g protein
3.8 g fibre

kcal
1000 / 900 / 800 / 700 / 600 / 500 / 400 / 300 / 200 / 100 / 0
calorie counter

The butter increases the saturated fat content.

With oil
1 portion provides:
636 kJ/151 kcal
12.9 g fat (of which 1.3 g saturated)
12.9 g carbohydrate (of which 3.7 g sugars)
2 g protein
3.8 g fibre

kcal
1000 / 900 / 800 / 700 / 600 / 500 / 400 / 300 / 200 / 100 / 0
calorie counter

431 Salsify fritters

Mix 400 g cooked salsify in 2 tablespoons olive oil, salt, pepper, chopped parsley and lemon juice, and leave for 30–45 minutes. Dip in a light batter, deep-fry to a golden brown and serve. (Increase the proportions 2½ times for 10 portions.)

432 Squash v

There are many different varieties of squash, which is a relative of the pumpkin. Squash should be firm with a blemish-free skin; summer squash should have a more yielding skin than winter squash, which are allowed to harden before harvesting.

The most usual variety sold is the custard squash, which is best when eaten young and can be cooked in similar ways to courgettes – sliced and lightly boiled, stewed or fried with the skins on and served with butter. Winter squash have the skin removed before cooking and can then be cooked like marrow, e.g. stuffed.

nutritional info

1 large portion (100g, boiled or steamed) provides:
155 kJ/36 kcal
0.1 g fat (of which 0.0 g saturated)
8.3 g carbohydrate (of which 4.5 g sugars)
1.1 g protein
1.6 g fibre

calorie counter: 1000 900 800 700 600 500 400 300 200 100 0 kcal

433 Swiss chard v

Swiss chard, or seakale beet, have large, ribbed, slightly curly leaves. The flavour is similar to spinach, although it is milder, and it can be prepared in the same way as any of the spinach recipes.

It can also be served *au gratin* and made into a savoury flan or quiche, using half lean cooked ham or bacon, flavoured with onion, garlic and chopped parsley.

nutritional info

1 large portion (100 g, boiled or steamed) provides:
84 kJ/20 kcal
0.1 g fat (of which 0.0 g saturated)
3.2 g carbohydrate (of which 0.4 g sugars)
1.9 g protein
0.0 g fibre

calorie counter: 1000 900 800 700 600 500 400 300 200 100 0 kcal

434 Stuffed vegetables

Certain vegetables can be stuffed and served as a first course, as a vegetable course and as an accompaniment to a main course.

The majority of vegetables used for this purpose are the bland, gourd types, such as aubergines, courgette and cucumbers, in which case the stuffing should be delicately flavoured so as not to overpower the vegetable. Below are some of the more popular types of vegetable used for this purpose and the usual type of stuffing in each case. There is, however, considerable scope for variation and experimentation in any of the stuffings.

Artichoke bottoms

Duxelle stuffing, cordon of thin demi-glace or jus-lié flavoured with tomato.

Aubergine

The cooked chopped flesh is mixed with cooked chopped onion, sliced tomatoes and chopped parsley.

The cooked chopped flesh is mixed with duxelle, sprinkled with fresh breadcrumbs, grated cheese and gratinated. Served with a cordon of light tomato sauce or tomato coulis.

The cooked chopped flesh is mixed with cooked chopped onion, garlic, tomato concassée, parsley, breadcrumbs and gratinated. Served with a cordon of light tomato sauce or coulis.

The cooked chopped flesh is mixed with diced or minced cooked mutton, cooked chopped onion, tomato concassée, cooked rice and chopped parsley. Served with a cordon of tomato sauce or coulis.

Mushrooms and ceps

Duxelle stuffing.

Stuffed ceps, forest style: equal quantities of duxelle stuffing and sausagemeat.

Stuffed cabbage

Veal stuffing and pilaff rice.

Cucumber

This can be prepared in two ways.

1 Peeled, cut into 2 cm pieces, the centres hollowed out with a parisienne spoon and then boiled, steamed or cooked in butter.

2 The peeled whole cucumber is cut in halves lengthwise, the seed pocket scooped out and the cucumber cooked by boiling, steaming or in butter.

Suitable stuffings can be made from a base of duxelle, pilaff rice or chicken forcemeat, or any combination of these.

To stuff the cucumber pieces, pipe the stuffing from a piping bag and complete the cooking in the oven. When the whole cucumber is stuffed, rejoin the two halves, wrap in pig's caul and muslin and braise.

Lettuce

Stuff with two parts chicken forcemeat, one part duxelle, and braise.

Turnips

Peel the turnips, remove the centre almost to the root and blanch the turnips. Cook and purée the scooped-out centre and mix with an equal quantity of potato purée. Refill the cavities and gently cook the turnips in butter in the oven, basting frequently. Turnips may also be stuffed with cooked spinach, chicory or rice.

Pimentos

Pilaff rice, varied if required with other ingredients, e.g. mushrooms, tomatoes or duxelle.

Duxelle stuffing with garlic and diced ham. Served with a cordon of demi-glace flavoured with tomato.

Chopped hard-boiled egg bound with thick béchamel, grated cheese and gratinated. Served with a cordon of light tomato sauce.

Scrambled egg, mushrooms and diced ham, sprinkled with breadcrumbs fried in butter.

Risotto with tomato concassée. Coat with thin tomato sauce.

Cooked tomato concassée, chopped onion, garlic and parsley, bound with fresh breadcrumbs and gratinated. May be served hot or cold.

Pilaff rice in which has been cooked dice of tomato and red pimento. Cook gently in oven and sprinkle with chopped parsley.

435 Wild mushrooms v

Ceps, morels, chanterelles and oyster mushrooms are four of the most popular of the wide variety of wild mushrooms that may be gathered.

Ceps are bun-shaped fungi with a smooth surface and a strong, distinctive flavour. Ceps are also available dried and should be soaked in warm water for approximately 30 minutes before use. The soaking liquid should be used as it contains a good flavour.

Methods of cooking: ceps hold a fair amount of water and need to be sweated gently in oil or butter and then drained, utilising the liquid. Ceps may be used in soups, egg dishes (particularly omelettes), fish, meat, game and poultry dishes. They may also be: sautéed in oil or butter with garlic and parsley and served as a vegetable; stuffed with chopped

ham, cheese, tomato and parsley; or sliced, passed through batter and deep-fried.

Morels appear in spring. They vary in colour from light to dark brown and have a meaty flavour. Morels are obtainable dried, and then require soaking for 10 minutes, are squeezed dry and used as required.

Methods of cooking: morels can be used in soups, egg dishes, meat, poultry and game dishes and as a vegetable, first course or as an accompaniment.

Chanterelles are common, trumpet-shaped and frilly. They are generally bright yellow with a delicate flavour, slightly resembling apricots, and are obtainable in summer and autumn. There are many varieties and they can be obtained dried, when they require about 25 minutes' soaking in warm water before cooking.

Methods of cooking: because of their pleated gills, chanterelles must be washed carefully under running cold water then dried well. As they have a rubbery texture they require lengthy gentle cooking in butter or oil. They can be served with egg, chicken or veal dishes.

Oyster mushrooms are ear shaped, grey or greyish brown in colour, and have an excellent flavour. They can be tough in texture and therefore need careful cooking.

Methods of cooking: cook in butter or oil with parsley and garlic, or flour, egg and breadcrumbs, then deep-fry.

436 Yams v

Yams may be white or yellow, with a texture similar to potatoes. In certain parts of the world orange-fleshed sweet potatoes are known as yams, but the true yam is sweeter and moister than the sweet potato. However, they may both be prepared and cooked in the same way.

nutritional info

1 large portion (130 g, boiled) provides:
738 kJ/173 kcal
0.4 g fat (of which 0.1 g saturated)
42.9 g carbohydrate (of which 0.9 g sugars)
2.2 g protein
1.8 g fibre

Boiled or steamed with no added fat.

437 Fried yam cakes

	4 portions	10 portions
yams	400 g	1¼ kg
butter, melted	10 g	25 g
onion	50 g	125 g
parsley, chopped	5 g	12 g
salt and pepper		
egg yolks	2	5
oil		

1 Wash, peel and finely grate the yams.

2 Add the melted butter, finely chopped onion, parsley, salt and pepper.

3 Add the egg yolks, mix well, form into a roll and cut into an even number of cakes.

4 Neaten the shapes, using a little flour only if necessary, and shallow-fry for 3–4 minutes on each side, then drain and serve.

nutritional info

1 large portion provides:
1081 kJ/258 kcal
15.1 g fat (of which 3.4 g saturated)
29.2 g carbohydrate (of which 1.4 g sugars)
3.2 g protein
1.5 g fibre

Butter and egg yolk were used to make the cakes, and they were fried in oil.

438 Grilled vegetables v

	4 portions
leeks	8
carrots	8
turnips	8
sweetcorn	8

Tender young vegetables can be cooked from raw and are best cooked on an under-fired grill or barbecue.

1 Wash, peel and trim the vegetables.

2 Dry well, brush with olive oil, season lightly.

3 Grill the vegetables with the tenderest last, e.g. turnips, carrots, leeks, sweetcorn.

4 Serve as a first course accompanied by a suitable sauce, e.g. spicy tomato sauce, or as a vegetable accompaniment to a main course.

Notes: Slices of aubergine, courgette and red and/or yellow peppers can also be used (discard the pith and seeds of the peppers).

nutritional info

1 large portion (not including sauce) provides:
308 kJ/73 kcal
1.1 g fat (of which 0.1 g saturated)
13.0 g carbohydrate (of which 11.7 g sugars)
3.8 g protein
6.4 g fibre

If vegetables other than baby ones, e.g. carrot, turnip, parsnip, are grilled, then they first need to be cut into thickish slices and par-boiled until half-cooked, drained well, dried, then brushed with oil and grilled.

They can be served plain, sprinkled with chopped mixed herbs, or with an accompanying sauce.

439 Deep-fried vegetables in tempura batter

	4 portions	10 portions
mange-tout, topped and tailed	12	30
white button mushrooms, halved	100 g	250 g
carrot, cut in matchstick pieces	100 g	250 g
sweet potato, peeled and sliced thinly	100 g	250 g
Batter		**makes 260 g**
flour		140 g
cornflour		40 g
baking powder		20 g
egg		1
water (sparkling)		

1 Flour the vegetables, then shake off excess flour.

2 Combine all the ingredients of the batter to form a smooth mixture.

3 Pass the vegetables through batter, remove excess, deep-fry in hot oil (175°C). Drain and serve immediately.

VEGETARIAN DISHES

VEGETARIAN AND VEGAN CATERING

This information has been adapted from the technical brief on vegetarian and vegan catering prepared by HCIMA (1993).

1 Introduction

1.1 People choose to eat vegetarian or vegan food for a variety of reasons.

Vegetarians
religious beliefs, ethical and ecological views against meat eating, Jews and Muslims without access to kosher or halal meat and for health reasons.

Demi-vegetarians
are people who choose to exclude red meat from their diet.

Vegans
will not eat any animal food or by-product because they consider it cruel to do so. Veganism is living entirely on the products of the plant kingdom.

1.2 Within the above groups, the foods that are avoided by each sector are as follows.

Lacto vegetarians
eat milk and cheese but not eggs, whey or *anything* that has been produced as a result of an animal being slaughtered, that is: meat, poultry, fish or any by-products such as fish oils, rennet, cochineal.

Ovo-lacto vegetarians
include eggs otherwise as for lacto vegetarians.

Demi-vegetarians
usually choose to exclude red meat, though they may eat it occasionally. White poultry and fish are generally acceptable.

Vegans
avoid *all* animals products and by-products including milk, cheese, yoghurt, eggs, fish, poultry, meat and honey. They eat only items or products from the plant kingdom.

1.3 These groups of people are generally more interested in a diet lower in fat and higher in fibre.

All vegan recipes in this book are marked with the icon: **V**

2 Special points for consideration

2.1 Protein
In a meat eater's diet, meat, poultry and fish provide a considerable amount of the daily protein intake. Protein cannot be destroyed by cooking but, more importantly, it *cannot* be stored in the body. Any vegetarian or vegan meal must therefore contain an adequate source of protein to replace meat protein.

2.2 Amino acids
Protein is made up of amino acids. Human protein tissue and animal proteins contain all the 'essential' amino acids (the body can manufacture the non-essential amino acids). Vegetable proteins, however, contain fewer of the essential amino acids. The lack of some amino acids in one plant is compensated for by another.

2.3 Protein complementing
This means combining various plant proteins in one dish or meal to provide the equivalent

amino acid profile of animal protein. Putting together 60 per cent beans (or other pulses) or nuts with 30 per cent grains or seeds and grains and 10 per cent green salad or vegetables, makes the ideal combination.

2.4 The best sources of vegetarian protein are

cheese, eggs, milk, textured vegetable protein (TVP) followed by tofu, soya beans, all other pulses and nuts. Seeds: sesame, sunflower and pumpkin. Cereals (preferably wholegrain): millet, wheat, barley and oats. Vegans exclude cheese, eggs and milk as a source of protein and substitute soya milk, soya cheese and soya yoghurt. All other items above are acceptable.

2.5 In protein equivalent terms (all cooked weights)
   50 g meat = 75 g fish
   50 g (hard) cheese
   100 g soft or cottage cheese
   2 eggs
   100 g nuts
   50 g peanut butter
   150 g pulses (lentils, peas, beans)
   75 g seeds

2.6 Pulses, nuts, seeds and to a lesser extent tubers and roots contain significant protein. Leaves, stems, buds and flowers are almost all water and have an insignificant protein content.

2.7 A dish such as ratatouille, made from 'water' vegetables is suitable only as a side dish. 'Vegetable' curries, hotpots and similar dishes should all include a recognisable and good vegetable protein source.

3 Items that must be excluded or considered in a vegetarian menu

3.1 Rennet- or pepsin-based cheeses

(rennet is an enzyme from the stomach of a newly killed calf; pepsin is from pigs' stomachs).

replace with

approved 'vegetarian' cheeses or non-rennet cheeses such as cottage and cream cheese (not suitable for vegans, unless made with soya milk). Check to ensure ready-made vegetarian dishes include vegetarian cheese.

3.2 Battery farm eggs

(hens may have been fed fish meal; also strict vegetarians consider battery rearing of hens is cruel).

replace with

free-range eggs.

Strict vegetarians will eat only free-range eggs; this is impractical for most manufacturers and caterers, so clear labelling is important so as not to mislead.

3.3 Whey
Whey is a by-product of cheese making and therefore may contain rennet. Can be found in biscuits.

Crisps may contain whey as a processing aid, this need not be stated on the label. Some museli may also contain whey.

Check all product labels of items bought in and used in the production of a vegetarian choice.

3.4 Cochineal
Cochineal, or E120, is made from the cochineal beetle.

Often present in glacé cherries and

mincemeat. Choose an alternative red colouring.

3.5 Alcohol

Alcohol – some wines or beers may be 'fined' using isinglass (a fish product) or dried blood. Some ciders contain pork to enhance their flavour.

Check with the wholesaler or manufacturer where possible if in any doubt before use in cooking or serving to a vegetarian.

3.6 Meat or bone stock for soups or sauces; animal-based flavourings for savoury dishes

replace with

stock made from vegetables or yeast extract (Tastex, Barmene, Marmite), or bought vegetable stock cubes/bouillon; soy sauce, miso, Holbrook's Worcester Sauce (which is anchovy free).

3.7 Animal fats

Animal fats (suet, lard or dripping) ordinary white cooking fats or margarine. (Some contain fish oil.) Bought-in pastry may contain lard or fish oil margarine.

replace with

Trex and Pura white vegetable fats, 100 per cent vegetable oil margarines, Suenut or Nutter (available from health food stores), White Flora.

3.8 Oils containing fish oil

replace with

100 per cent vegetable oil (sunflower, corn, soya, groundnut, walnut, sesame, olive) or mixed vegetable oil.

Note: Fish oils may well be 'hidden' in margarine and products such as biscuits, cakes and bought-in pastry items. Check suitability before using.

3.9 Setting agents

Gelatine, aspic, block or jelly crystals (for glazing, moulding, in cheesecakes and desserts). Some yoghurts are set with gelatine as are some sweets, particularly nougat and mints.

replace with

agar-agar (a fine, white odourless powder), gelozone, apple pectin.

3.10 Animal-fat ice cream

replace with

vegetable-fat ice cream.

Note: Many additives contain meat products, look for the label for: 'edible fats', 'emulsifiers', 'fatty acids' and the preservative E471. The safest course is to ask the manufacturer of any bought-in product you wish to use.

4 Claims

4.1 Never claim that a food or dish is vegetarian if you have used a non-vegetarian ingredient.

4.2 If you knowingly mislead a customer into believing you have a suitable vegetarian choice on offer, you can be prosecuted under the Trade Descriptions Act 1968 and/or the Food Safety Act 1990.

440 White vegetable stock v

		1 litre
onion		100 g
carrots	mirepoix	100 g
celery		100 g
leeks		100 g
water		1½ litre

Place all the ingredients into a saucepan, bring to the boil and allow to simmer for approximately 1 hour, skim if necessary. Strain and use.

441 Brown vegetable stock v

		1 litre
onions		100 g
carrots	mirepoix	100 g
celery		100 g
leeks		100 g
sunflower oil		60 ml
tomatoes		50 g
mushroom trimmings		50 g
peppercorns		6
water		1½ litre
yeast extract		5 g

1 Fry the mirepoix in the oil until golden brown.

2 Drain and place in a suitable saucepan. Add all the other ingredients except the yeast extract and water.

3 Cover with the water, bring to the boil.

4 Add the yeast extract, simmer gently for approximately 1 hour. Then skim if necessary and use.

442 Fungi stock v

White or brown fungi stock can be made by using the vegetable stock recipes above, adding 200–400 g white mushrooms, stalks and trimmings (all well washed), for white fungi stock.

For brown fungi stock use the brown vegetable stock recipe, adding 200–400 g open or field mushrooms, stalks and trimmings (all well washed).

443 Aubergine raita

	4 portions	10 portions
aubergines (approx. 150 g each)	1	3
yoghurt	1 litre	2½ litres
pinch of salt		
piece of ginger, finely chopped	1	2½
cumin seeds	1 tsp	2½ tsp
fenugreek	1 tsp	2½ tsp
ghee or sunflower oil	1 tbsp	2½ tbsp

1 Prick the skin of the aubergine and bake in the oven at 200°C until soft.

2 While the aubergine is cooking, whisk the yoghurt with 100 ml of water and the salt in a large salad bowl.

3 In a small saucepan or wok, fry the ginger, cumin and fenugreek for a minute in the ghee or oil and add to the raita.

4 When the aubergine is cooked, cool in water for a few minutes, then cut in half, scrape the flesh of the skin and cut it in very small pieces or, better, blend it roughly then add to the raita.

5 Cool in the refrigerator for half an hour before serving.

Note: There are many types of raita and they are a very popular side dish in India. They are made of yoghurt, water, spices and some kind of vegetable or fruit. A very refreshing dish in hot weather.

nutritional info

1 large portion provides:
1008 kJ/240 kcal
11.6 g fat (of which 6.8 g saturated)
20.8 g carbohydrate (of which 20.6 g sugars)
15.1 g protein
14.0 g fibre

Contains a large amount of ghee or oil.

kcal
1000
900
800
700
600
500
400
300
200
100
0

calorie counter

444 Barley with shitake mushrooms v

	4 portions	10 portions
barley	450 g	1125 g
dried shitake mushrooms	50 g	125 g
sunflower oil	3 tbsp	7 tbsp
bunch of spring onions, finely chopped	1	3
freshly grated ginger, to taste	½ tsp	1 tsp
organic soy sauce	80 ml	200 ml

1 Cook the barley in boiling water for 1 hour. Drain and put aside.

2 Soak the shitake mushrooms in warm water for 30 minutes, then drain (put the water aside – you'll need some later and can use the rest for a soup).

3 In a large wok, heat the sunflower oil and add the spring onions. Stir for a minute, then add the ginger, the mushrooms, 50 ml of the water from the mushrooms, and the soy sauce.

4 Cook on medium heat for 5 minutes, then add the barley, stir well and serve immediately.

nutritional info

1 large portion provides:

2080 kJ/493 kcal

13.9 g fat (of which 1.4 g saturated)

82.6 g carbohydrate (of which 4.4 g sugars)

14.3 g protein

17.1 g fibre

Sunflower oil is low in saturated fatty acids.

kcal: 1000 900 800 700 600 500 400 300 200 100 0 — calorie counter

445 Thai-style potato curry v

	4 portions	10 portions
potatoes	1 kg	2½ kg
onion	50 g	125 g
sunflower oil	50 ml	125 ml
small piece of fresh ginger root		
fresh lemon grass stick, smashed to extract flavour	1	2
fresh green chillies, chopped and seeds removed	2	5
coconut milk	210 ml	525 ml
dry mango powder (if not available, the juice of 2 limes or lemons)	1 tbsp	2½ tbsp
plum tomatoes, peeled and chopped into 1 cm dice	12	30

1 Peel and wash the potatoes and cut them into dice. Chop the onion finely and fry in sunflower oil on medium heat until golden brown.

2 Add the grated ginger, the lemon grass, chopped finely, and the chopped chillies, and fry for another 2 minutes, stirring constantly, then add the potatoes, the coconut milk, the mango powder or lemon/lime juice, the tomatoes and, if needed, water to cover.

3 Bring to the boil then lower the heat and leave to simmer for 35 minutes on a low heat, stirring occasionally. Serve with freshly cooked rice.

Note: The potatoes can be replaced with 400 g of soaked butter beans, cooked for 1 hour in water, to make a Thai-style butter bean curry. Cooked green lentils and spinach can be added at the end of the cooking process; serve immediately on a bed of brown rice.

nutritional info

1 large portion provides:

1687 kJ/401 kcal

14.2 g fat (of which 1.9 g saturated)

63.9 g carbohydrate (of which 20.7 g sugars)

8.4 g protein

7.6 g fibre

Sunflower oil was used to fry potatoes, and coconut milk in the sauce.

kcal: 1000 900 800 700 600 500 400 300 200 100 0 — calorie counter

nutritional info

1 large portion of the butter bean version of this curry provides:

1383 kJ/316 kcal

14.3 g fat (of which 2.0 g saturated)

39.3 g carbohydrate (of which 20.7 g sugars)

10.2 g protein

9.6 g fibre

Sunflower oil was used, and coconut milk added.

kcal: 1000 900 800 700 600 500 400 300 200 100 0 — calorie counter

446 Bean bourguignonne

	4 portions	10 portions
red kidney beans (dried)	300 g	750 g
sunflower oil	2 tbsp	5 tbsp
onions, finely chopped	100 g	250 g
mushrooms, washed and finely chopped	300 g	750 g
garlic cloves, chopped very finely	3	7
carrots, diced	150 g	375 g
salt, pepper and thyme to taste		
bottle red wine	½	1

nutritional info

♥

1 large portion provides:
1342 kJ/318 kcal
7.3 g fat (of which 0.9 g saturated)
46.4 g carbohydrate (of which 11.7 g sugars)
19.8 g protein
15.3 g fibre

Sunflower oil was used to fry the onions, mushrooms and garlic.

calorie counter

kcal
1000
900
800
700
600
500
400
300
200
100
0

1 Soak the beans overnight, changing the water at least once.

2 Heat the oil (ghee can also be used but this will make the dish non-vegan) in a large heavy-bottomed pot, fry the onions over a medium heat until golden brown.

3 Add the chopped mushrooms, the garlic, the carrot, and the seasoning and herbs.

4 Keep cooking, stirring constantly, until the mushrooms are soft. Add the wine, the beans and enough water to cover the beans.

5 Bring to the boil, then lower the heat to a simmer, cover and cook for 90 minutes or until the beans are soft, and serve on a bed of aromatic flavoured rice or nan bread.

447 Potato and leek soup

	4 portions	10 portions
potatoes	750 g	1875 g
leeks	200 g	500 g
onion	50 g	125 g
salt, cumin, coriander and pepper to taste		
ghee, butter or sunflower oil	2 tbsp	5 tbsp
fresh cream, to serve		
chives or parsley, to garnish		

nutritional info

♥

1 large portion provides:
902 kJ/215 kcal
6.3 g fat (of which 0.7 g saturated)
36.7 g carbohydrate (of which 4.3 g sugars)
5.3 g protein
4.1 g fibre

Sunflower oil was used: it is low in saturated fatty acids.

calorie counter

kcal
1000
900
800
700
600
500
400
300
200
100
0

1 Wash and peel the potatoes, then dice them. Cut the leeks in 4 lengthways and chop into 1 cm pieces, wash thoroughly.

2 Peel and chop the onion. Grind the spices if needed.

3 Fry the onion and leek in the ghee, butter or sunflower oil on medium heat for 5 minutes, stirring constantly, add the diced potatoes and keep stirring for another 3 minutes.

4 Add 500 ml of water, bring to the boil, add the salt, then lower the heat to a simmer.

5 Cover and cook for 20 minutes. Liquidise and serve immediately with fresh cream and chopped chive or parsley.

448 Spicy squash (pumpkin) soup v

	4 portions	10 portions
medium squash (or pumpkin) (3–3½ kg each)	1	2
onion	100 g	250 g
sunflower oil	2 tbsp	5 tbsp
turmeric powder	1 tsp	2½ tsp
coriander seeds	1 tsp	2½ tsp
pink peppercorns	1 tsp	2½ tsp
cinnamon stick	1	2½
small pinch chilli powder	1	2½
fresh coriander leaves, to serve		

nutritional info

1 large portion provides:
1147 kJ/275 kcal
4.4 g fat (of which 0.5 g saturated)
54.5 g carbohydrate (of which 7.2 g sugars)
5.1 g protein
13.8 g fibre

Sunflower oil was used: it is low in saturated fatty acids.

1 Peel the squash, spoon out the seeds and cut the flesh into small cubes. Peel and chop the onion.

2 Heat up the oil (ghee can also be used but this will make the dish non-vegan) in a heavy-bottomed pan, add the onion and the squash flesh.

3 Stir-fry for 5 minutes on medium heat, stirring occasionally.

4 Meanwhile, put all the spices in a mortar or a spice grinder and grind to a powder.

5 Add the spices to the pan and continue to stir for a minute. Add water to cover and bring to the boil, then turn the heat down to low, cover and cook until the squash is soft (about 25 minutes).

6 Blend into a smooth soup and serve with fresh coriander leaves.

449 Aubergine stir-fry, Japanese style v

	4 portions	10 portions
sunflower oil	2 tbsp	5 tbsp
piece fresh ginger root or 3 garlic cloves	1	2
spring onions, chopped	25 g	60 g
aubergines (approx. 150 g each), peeled, cut in 4 and sliced	2	5
hijiki* (soaked for 30 minutes in 80 ml of warm water; retain the water)	100 g	250 g
tamari**	2 tbsp	5 tbsp
fresh green chillies, chopped and seeds removed	1 or 2	2 or 4
sesame seeds	1 tbsp	2½ tbsp

Hijiki is a special Japanese seaweed, which tastes like fish and looks like a worm.

** *Tamari traditional soy sauce is not too salty and very mellow in flavour; it is considered to be the best type as it uses traditional methods of fermentation.*

nutritional info

1 large portion provides:
394 kJ/95 kcal
7.9 g fat (of which 1.0 g saturated)
3.4 g carbohydrate (of which 2.9 g sugars)
2.9 g protein
5.8 g fibre

Wakame seaweed was used, and sunflower oil for frying.

1 Heat the sunflower oil in a wok and then add, in this order, the grated ginger, chopped spring onions and the aubergines. Stir for a few minutes until the aubergines start to soften.

2 Add the hijiki with its soaking water, the tamari and the green chillies.

3 Cover and cook on a low heat until the aubergines are tender. Sprinkle with sesame seeds before serving if you wish. Serve with rice.

450 Aubergine pasta bake

R Priddy

	4 portions	10 portions
aubergine	1 large	3 medium
salt		
olive oil	60 ml	100 ml
garlic clove, crushed	1	2
onion, chopped	1	2–3
green or red pepper	1	3
can of tomatoes, chopped	2 × 500 g	4 × 500 g
red wine	75 ml	200 ml
tomato purée	2 tsp	5 tsp
sugar	½ tsp	1½ tsp
finely chopped basil or dried basil	1 tbsp	3 tbsp
freshly ground black pepper		
dried tagliatelle	175 g	400 g
processed cheese or vegetarian Cheddar	10 slices	25 slices
Parmesan cheese (grated)	25 g	50 g
coriander sprigs to garnish		

nutritional info

1 large portion provides:
2260 kJ/540 kcal
29.9 g fat (of which 10.6 g saturated)
50.5 g carbohydrate (of which 17.7 g sugars)
20.4 g protein
5.4 g fibre

Olive oil was used to fry the onions and aubergine, and there is added fat from the cheese.

kcal
1000
900
800
700
600
500
400
300
200
100
0

calorie counter

1 Wash and trim off the stalk of the aubergine. Slice the aubergine into ½ cm-thick slices and put them in a colander in layers, sprinkling salt between each layer. Cover with a plate and place a heavy weight on top. Leave for 1 hour to draw out the bitter juice, then rinse the slices and leave to dry on absorbent paper.

2 Heat the oven to 180°C.

3 Heat 1 tablespoon (2½ tablespoons for 10 portions) of the oil in a saucepan, add the garlic, onion, finely chopped pepper and fry gently for about 5 minutes until the onion is soft and light coloured. Stir in tomatoes with juice, wine and tomato purée. Bring to boil. Stir in the sugar, basil, and season with salt and pepper. Let the sauce boil gently to reduce and thicken.

4 Meanwhile, bring a pan of salted water to the boil and add 1 teaspoon (2½ teaspoons for 10 portions) of oil. Cook the tagliatelle for 6–7 minutes, until tender yet firm to the bite, then drain thoroughly.

5 Heat the remaining oil in a frying pan, add the aubergine slices and fry gently until they are lightly coloured on both sides. Remove with a slotted spoon and drain well on absorbent paper.

6 Spread a third of the tomato sauce over the bottom of a lightly oiled ovenproof dish. Place half the pasta on top, followed by half the aubergine slices and half the processed cheese. Cover with another third of the tomato sauce and then the remaining pasta, aubergine slices and cheese. Spread the remaining tomato sauce over the cheese and sprinkle the Parmesan cheese on top.

7 Cook the pasta bake in the oven for about 20 minutes, until heated through.

8 Garnish with coriander sprigs, if liked, and serve immediately straight from the dish.

451 Cracked wheat and mint salad v

	4 portions	10 portions
cracked wheat	250 g	625 g
tomatoes, skinned, deseeded, diced	4	10
courgettes, unpeeled, finely diced	4	10
spring onions, finely sliced	4	10
dried apricots (ready to eat), diced	8	20
raisins	50 g	125 g
vegetable oil	2 tbsp	5 tbsp
lemons, juice of	1	3
clove of garlic, crushed and chopped	1	2½
fresh mint, chopped	3 tbsp	8 tbsp
seasoning		
fresh mint for garnish		

1 Place the cracked wheat in a large bowl.

2 Scald the wheat with boiling water, and soak for 30 minutes.

3 Drain well, then squeeze out excess water, using a clean cloth.

4 Add the tomato concassée, diced courgettes, sliced spring onions, diced apricots and raisins.

5 Prepare the dressing in a suitable bowl: whisk the oil, lemon juice, garlic, mint and seasoning. Add to the cracked wheat, and mix well.

6 Chill for 1 hour.

7 Serve in a suitable bowl garnished with fresh mint.

Note: The vegetable oil may be substituted with tomato juice.

nutritional info

1 large portion provides:
1856 kJ/442 kcal
7.8 g fat (of which 0.9 g saturated)
83.7 g carbohydrate (of which 35.6 g sugars)
12.3 g protein
6.2 g fibre

Vegetable oil was used in the dressing.

kcal
1000
900
800
700
600
500
400
300
200
100
0

calorie counter

452 Galette of aubergines with tomatoes and mozzarella

	4 portions	10 portions
aubergines	400 g	1 kg
onions, finely chopped	100 g	250 g
garlic, crushed and chopped	2	5
vegetable oil		
low-fat yoghurt	500 ml	1¼ ltr
cornflour	2 tsp	5 tsp
coriander, finely chopped	1 tsp	2½ tsp
sugar	1 tsp	2½ tsp
plum tomatoes	400 g	1 kg
buffala mozzarella	150 g	375 g
seasoning		
coriander, to garnish		

nutritional info

1 large portion provides:
940 kJ/224 kcal
9.6 g fat (of which 6.2 g saturated)
20.7 g carbohydrate (of which 17.0 g sugars)
15.0 g protein
3.4 g fibre

Oil was used to fry the aubergines and onion. The mozzarella adds fat.

kcal
1000
900
800
700
600
500
400
300
200
100
0

calorie counter

1 Slice the aubergines thinly. Place on a tray and sprinkle with salt. Leave for 1 hour.

2 Dry the aubergines in a cloth. Quickly fry in oil until golden brown on both sides. Remove from pan, drain well.

3 Sweat the finely chopped onion and garlic in oil without colour.

4 Mix together the yoghurt, cornflour, coriander and sugar, add to the onion and garlic. Bring to the boil and season lightly. Remove from heat.

5 Blanch and peel the tomatoes, chop into ½ cm slices.

6 Arrange 4 large slices of aubergine on a greased baking sheet. Spread the yoghurt mixture on each slice, and top with tomato and mozzarella. Continue to build layers of aubergine, tomato and mozzarella. Finish with a layer of yoghurt mixture.

7 Bake in a hot oven (220°C) for 20 minutes until golden brown. Serve immediately, garnish with coriander.

453 Honey-roasted vegetables with cracked wheat

	4 portions	10 portions
sweet potatoes, peeled	2	5
onions, red	2	5
red peppers	1	3
yellow peppers	1	3
courgettes	2	5
olive oil	2 tbsp	5 tbsp
clear honey	2 tbsp	5 tbsp
salt and black pepper		
cinnamon stick	1	3
Cracked wheat		
cracked bulgar wheat	250 g	625 g
olive oil	2 tbsp	5 tbsp
lemon zest, grated	1	3
ground cumin	3 tsp	8 tsp
garlic, crushed and chopped	2	5

1 Prepare the vegetables. Cut the sweet potatoes into 2 cm dice and cut the red onions into wedges to match the sweet potato size. Deseed the peppers and cut into 2 cm squares. Cut the courgettes into 1 cm slices.

2 Place the vegetables in a roasting tin. Sprinkle with oil and add 1 tablespoon of honey.

3 Season with salt and black pepper and add the cinnamon stick. Roast in oven at 200°C for approximately 12–15 minutes. The vegetables should not be over-cooked, they should remain crisp.

4 Drizzle with the remaining honey, then place back in the oven for a few minutes.

5 Soak the cracked wheat in boiling water for a few minutes, then drain.

6 In a suitable pan, heat the oil, add the grated lemon zest, sweat for 2 minutes. Add the cumin and garlic and fry for 30 seconds.

7 Stir in the cracked wheat and fry for 1–2 minutes. Season.

8 Place the cracked wheat on plates, and arrange the roasted vegetables neatly around it.

nutritional info

1 large portion provides:
2166 kJ/517 kcal
13.4 g fat (of which 1.8 g saturated)
92.4 g carbohydrate (of which 25.8 g sugars)
11.4 g protein
6.1 g fibre

Olive oil is used to roast the vegetables and added to the cracked wheat.

454 Spinach, ricotta and artichoke filo bake with cranberries   Gary Thompson

	4 portions	10 portions
spinach	400 g	1 kg
ricotta	500 g	1¼ kg
tinned artichokes, drained	200 g	500 g
filo pastry	275 g	700 g
frozen cranberries	500 g	1¼ kg
butter	25 g	60 g
olive oil	1 tbsp	2–3 tbsp
onion, sliced	100 g	250 g
salt, freshly ground black pepper		
chopped fresh parsley to taste		

1 Cook, refresh and drain the spinach, then chop finely.

2 Break down the ricotta and mix with the spinach.

3 Sauté the onion in the olive oil without colour. Add to the ricotta and spinach with the chopped parsley. Season to taste.

4 Line a lightly buttered flan dish with 3 layers of filo pastry, leaving overhang.

5 Fill with spinach mixture and press drained artichokes evenly around the dish.

6 Top with cranberries.

7 Gather in the overhanging filo pastry, adding more layers to cover centre.

8 Russe up pastry, brush with butter and bake at 180°C for 35 minutes approximately.

nutritional info

1 large portion provides:
2191 kJ/523 kcal
25.2 g fat (of which 12.9 g saturated)
51.2 g carbohydrate (of which 14.7 g sugars)
24.3 g protein
7.5 g fibre

A little butter and a large amount of ricotta cheese are used.

455 Vegetable, bean and saffron risotto

	4 portions	10 portions
vegetable stock	185 ml	1 litre
saffron	5 g	12 g
sunflower margarine	50 g	125 g
onion, chopped	25 g	60 g
celery	50 g	125 g
short-grain rice	100 g	250 g
small cauliflower	1	2–3
sunflower oil	4 tbsp	10 tbsp
large aubergine	1	2–3
cooked haricot beans	100 g	250 g
cooked peas	50 g	125 g
cooked French beans	50 g	125 g
tomato sauce made with sunflower margarine and vegetable stock	250 ml	600 ml
grated Parmesan cheese	25 g	60 g

1 Infuse the vegetable stock with the saffron for approximately 5 minutes by simmering gently, while maintaining the quality of stock.

2 Melt the margarine, add the onion and celery and cook without colour for 2–3 minutes. Add the rice.

3 Cook for a further 2–3 minutes. Add the infused stock and season lightly. Cover with a lid and simmer on the side of the stove.

4 While rice is cooking prepare the rest of the vegetables. Cut the cauliflower into small florets, wash, blanch and refresh, quickly fry in the sunflower oil in a sauté pan. Add the aubergines cut into ½ cm dice and fry with the cauliflower. Add the cooked haricot beans, peas and French beans.

5 Stir all the vegetables together and bind with tomato sauce.

6 When the risotto is cooked, serve in a suitable dish, make a well in the centre. Fill the centre with the vegetables and haricot beans in tomato sauce.

7 Sprinkle the edge of the risotto with grated Parmesan cheese to serve.

Note: This dish is suitable for vegans if the Parmesan cheese is omitted.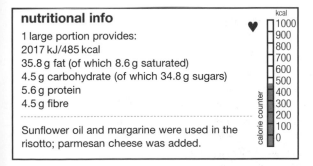

nutritional info

1 large portion provides:
2017 kJ/485 kcal
35.8 g fat (of which 8.6 g saturated)
4.5 g carbohydrate (of which 34.8 g sugars)
5.6 g protein
4.5 g fibre

Sunflower oil and margarine were used in the risotto; parmesan cheese was added.

456 Filo pastry filled with tabbouleh and feta cheese

	4 portions	10 portions
cracked bulgar wheat (tabbouleh)	150 g	375 g
cumin seeds	1 tbsp	2½ tbsp
feta cheese	200 g	500 g
tomatoes, skinned, deseeded (cut into ½ cm dice)	100 g	250 g
black olives, stoned	75 g	200 g
onion, finely chopped	50 g	125 g
parsley, chopped		
lemon juice	1	3
olive oil	3 tbsp	7 tbsp
seasoning/black pepper		
filo pastry	125 g	300 g

1 Soak the cracked wheat in cold water for approximately 20 minutes.

2 Dry roast the cumin seeds. Cut the feta cheese into 1 cm dice.

3 In a suitable bowl, combine the cumin seeds, feta cheese, tomato dice, stoned olives, chopped onion and chopped parsley.

4 Drain the cracked wheat, and add to the mixture.

5 Add the lemon juice and 2 tablespoons of olive oil. Season.

6 Choose a suitable pie dish for either 4 portions or 10 portions.

7 Lightly oil the pie dish. Brush the first sheet of filo pastry with oil. Place in the bottom of the pie dish so that it overlays the edge. Lay on the remaining sheets of filo pastry, brushed with oil in a similar fashion.

8 Fill the pie dish with the cracked wheat mixture. Form a lid by folding over the filo pastry.

9 Bake in a pre-heated oven (220°C) for approximately 40 minutes until the pastry is crisp and golden brown.

10 To serve, turn out onto a suitable dish and cut into portions.

11 Alternatively individual moulds may be used, in which case cut down the baking time to approximately 15–20 minutes.

12 Turn out onto suitable plates, serve with a coulis of sauce, e.g. a purée of yellow peppers and basil oil.

457 Courgettes cooked with tomatoes (tian)

	4 portions	10 portions
onions, peeled	200 g	450 g
olive oil	60 ml	150 ml
courgettes	300 g	750 g
garlic (optional)	1 clove	2 cloves
ripe tomatoes, sliced	400 g	1 kg
salt and pepper		
thyme	¼ tsp	½ tsp

1 Finely slice the onions and soften in half the olive oil in a thick-bottomed pan.

2 Peel alternate 1 cm strips from the courgettes to give a striped effect and cut into 5 mm thick slices.

3 Rub the oven dish vigorously with the garlic cloves.

4 Spread the onions in the dish.

5 Add alternating rows of courgette, onion and tomato.

6 Season, then sprinkle with thyme and the remaining oil.

7 Cook in a hot oven 200°C for approximately 30 minutes, pressing the mixture down from time to time.

Variation

Add a sprinkling of grated cheese; add 2(4) beaten eggs halfway though the cooking time.

Note: May be served as a first course, or as an accompanying vegetable to a main course.

Tian

This is a type of gratin dish that also gives its name to the food cooked in it. For example, an assortment of vegetables such as courgettes, onions, lightly sautéed garlic in oil, placed in the tian with perhaps cooked rice, grated cheese, chopped parsley, beaten eggs, sprinkled with olive oil and baked.

The name is also given to round moulded preparations, usually of vegetables, served hot or cold.

458 Goats' cheese and red pepper tart

	4 portions	10 portions
shortcrust pastry	200 g	450 g
red peppers	2	5
olive oil		
onions, shredded	100 g	250 g
clove of garlic, crushed and chopped	1	3
fresh basil	4 leaves	10 leaves
goats cheese	50 g	125 g
seasoning		

1 With the shortcrust pastry line individual tartlet tins.

2 Cook blind in a moderate oven (180°C) for approximately 20 minutes.

3 Skin the red pepper by quickly frying in hot oil or brushing with oil and quickly grilling until blistered.

4 Lightly sweat the onions and garlic in oil until golden brown.

5 Line the tartlets with the onions.

6 Cut the peppers in half, remove the seeds, and cut into julienne.

7 Place the peppers on top of the onions.

8 Arrange a basil leaf on top followed by slices of goats' cheese. Brush with olive oil.

9 Bake in a moderate oven (180°C) for approximately 15 minutes until the cheese has melted and is lightly coloured. Serve warm.

459 Leek roulade with ricotta and sweetcorn

	4 portions	10 portions
butter or margarine	100 g	250 g
leeks, finely shredded	1 large	2
garlic	1 clove	3
flour	75 g	200 g
milk	250 ml	625 ml
eggs, separated	4	10
seasoning		
Parmesan cheese	50 g	125 g
Ricotta filling		
ricotta cheese	100 g	250 g
sweetcorn	200 g	500 g
fresh chives	50 g	125 g
seasoning		

1 Take a swiss roll tin 25 cm × 30 cm, and grease well.

2 Line with silicone paper.

3 Melt about a third of the butter in a medium-sized saucepan. Add leeks and crushed chopped garlic, sweat until the leek is soft.

4 Melt remaining butter in a suitable pan, stir in the flour to make a white roux.

5 Add the milk gradually until the mixture boils and thickens.

6 Stir in the egg yolk and leek mixture.

7 Transfer to a mixing bowl, season with salt and pepper.

8 Carefully beat the egg whites to soft peaks, fold into leek mixture.

3 Add the broccoli, cover and cook gently until just crisp, stirring frequently and adding a little water if the mixture begins to dry.

4 Sprinkle over the herbs. Cook for 1 minute. Drain vegetables and allow to cool.

5 Warm the milk to blood heat. Whisk the egg and tofu in a basin, add seasoning then gradually incorporate milk. Whisk well.

6 Fill the flan case with the drained vegetables and add the tofu and milk mixture.

7 Bake for 20 minutes approximately at 180°C. Serve with walnut sauce (see below).

Walnut sauce

	4 portions	10 portions
onion, finely chopped	100 g	250 g
garlic clove, chopped	1	2–3
walnut oil	50 g	125 g
brown sugar	10 g	25 g
curry powder	25 g	60 g
lemon, grated zest and juice	1	2–3
peanut butter	25 g	60 g
soy sauce	1 tsp	2–3 tsp
tomato purée	25 g	60 g
vegetable stock	375 ml	900 ml
seasoning		
walnuts, very finely chopped	100 g	250 g
arrowroot	10 g	25 g

1 Fry the onion and garlic in the walnut oil, add the sugar and cook to a golden-brown colour.

2 Add the curry powder, cook for 2 minutes.

3 Add zest and juice of lemon, peanut butter, soy sauce and tomato purée. Mix well.

4 Add vegetable stock, bring to boil, simmer for 2 minutes, season.

5 Add chopped walnuts.

6 Dilute the arrowroot with a little water and gradually stir into sauce. Bring back to the boil stirring continuously. Simmer for 5 minutes.

7 Correct seasoning and consistency.

467 Oriental vegetable kebabs with herb sauce

	4 portions	10 portions
small cauliflower	1	2–3
red pepper	1	2–3
green pepper	1	2–3
button mushrooms	100 g	250 g
small courgettes	4	10
small tomatoes (very firm)	4	10
celery sticks	2	5
large aubergine	1	2–3
large leek	1	2–3
Marinade		
sunflower oil	125 ml	300 ml
red wine	250 ml	600 ml
dried mixed herbs	5 g	12 g
seasoning		
bay leaves	4–8	10–16

1 Prepare the vegetables as follows: cut cauliflower into small florets; wash peppers, remove seeds and cut into 1½–2 cm dice; wash button mushrooms, trim stalks; wash courgettes and cut into 1½–2 cm sections; blanch and peel tomatoes, cut into quarters; trim and wash celery, cut into 1½–2 cm lengths; wash aubergine, cut in half then into 2 × 1 cm batons; split leeks, wash, cut into 2 cm lengths.

2 Marinade the vegetables in the sunflower oil, red wine and dried herbs, seasoning and bay leaves for approximately 2 hours. Turn occasionally.

3 Neatly arrange vegetables on skewers.

4 Place on a greased tray, brush with oil and grill under salamander for approximately 10–15 minutes, turning occasionally.

5 The vegetables will have different textures – they should, however, be slightly firm. The cauliflower, courgettes and leek may also be blanched and refreshed before marinading to achieve different textures.

6 Serve kebabs on a bed of pilaff rice garnished with cooked peas.

7 Separately, serve a sauceboat of herb sauce made from the marinade.

Herb sauce

	4 portions	10 portions
marinade (from kebabs)	375 ml	1 litre
vegetable stock	125 ml	500 ml
yeast extract	10 g	25 g
tomato purée	50 g	125 g
onion, finely chopped	50 g	125 g
garlic cloves, chopped	1	2–3
sunflower margarine	10 g	25 g
arrowroot	10 g	25 g
seasoning		

1 Place marinade, vegetable stock, yeast extract and tomato purée into a suitable saucepan and bring to boil.

2 Sweat the onion and garlic in the margarine for 2–3 minutes without colour.

3 Add the marinade and stock liquid from step 1. Bring to boil.

4 Dilute the arrowroot in a little cold water.

5 Stir the arrowroot into the liquid and bring back to boil, stirring continuously. Simmer for 2 minutes, correct consistency. Season, strain and use as required.

468 Vegetable olives

Gary Thompson, Neil Yule

	4 portions	10 portions
mushrooms	100 g	250 g
carrots	100 g	250 g
onions	100 g	250 g
leeks	100 g	250 g
capsicums	100 g	250 g
aubergine	100 g	250 g
basil leaves, bunch		
crêpes	8 × 15 cm	20 × 15 cm
tomato sauce	1.2 litre	3 litre
béchamel	250 ml	600 g
mozzarella cheese	150 g	375 g
seasoning		

1 Cut the vegetables into a paysanne and sweat.

2 Place a basil leaf on a crêpe, add the vegetable mixture and roll up.

3 Place in an earthenware dish on a little tomato sauce.

4 Cover completely with the remaining tomato sauce, cover with foil and bake to heat thoroughly at 150°C for approximately 15 minutes.

5 Remove from the oven, remove the foil, coat the centre with a little béchamel, top with cheese and grill.

6 Sprinkle with chopped basil and serve with Italian garlic bread or French bread.

nutritional info

1 portion provides:
2321 kJ/554 kcals
29.5 g fat
(of which 10.2 g saturated)
48.4 g carbohydrate
(of which 24.3 g sugars)
26.7 g protein
6.7 g fibre

♥

kcal
1000
900
800
700
600
500
400
300
200
100
0

calorie counter

469 Baked babagnough and aubergine charlotte — Mark McCann

	4 portions	10 portions
medium aubergines	2	5
chillies	2	5
onion, halved and peeled	1	2 large
garlic cloves	6	15
sea salt	½ tsp	1¼ tsp
olive oil	2 tsp	5 tsp
lime, juice and zest	1	2
coriander, chopped	¼ bunch	1½ bunches
ground black pepper	1 pinch	2 pinch
butter	12 g	30 g

1 Remove skin from aubergine lengthways, leaving ½ cm of flesh on the skin.

2 Boil in boiling salt water until soft and then refresh in cold water.

3 Place the aubergine on a baking tray with the chillies, onion and garlic.

4 Season well with salt and spoon over the olive oil.

5 Bake in a hot oven at 160°C for approximately 15 minutes, or until a deep golden brown.

6 Remove from the oven and allow to cool.

7 When cold, finely dice the aubergine, garlic, onion and chilli.

8 Add the zest and juice of the lime and chopped coriander.

9 Correct the seasoning to taste.

10 Grease 4 ramekin moulds with melted butter and line the moulds with the aubergine skins ensuring that you overlap the edges.

11 Fill the ramekins with the aubergine mix and fold over the overlapping skins to the centre.

12 Bake in a moderate oven at 140°C for 8–10 minutes.

13 Take the dish out of the oven, turn out on to a plate and serve.

Suggested sauces

Serve a fresh tomato coulis or make a sauce from a purée of cooked lentils, thinned with a little roasted pepper oil and vegetable stock and garnished with a fine dice of sautéed red peppers.

PASTA DISHES

A short history of pasta

The history of pasta is linked with the history of wheat farming. Wheat has been farmed for at least the last 10,000 years, and there is a good chance that a form of pasta was consumed somewhere in the Middle East in that period.

The popular 'history' of pasta suggests that it was brought back from China by Marco Polo. This is factually incorrect. The real history of pasta records that the Ancient Romans were eating pasta a good thousand years before Marco Polo was born. The famous Roman chef, Apicius, makes reference to a form of pasta ribbons in his first-century cookbook.

Other historical records show that pasta-making equipment was probably used by the Etruscans, and that pasta itself may have come to Italy from Ancient Greece.

We have to wait until the twelfth century for the next specific mention of pasta, when Guglielmo di Malavalle makes reference to macaroni being served at a banquet.

The history of dried pasta probably starts with the Sicilians, and was rapidly adopted by other Italian states as the perfect food for taking on the long naval voyages that merchants and traders depended on.

The history of lasagne starts with a book by Fr Bartolomeo Secchi, which makes reference to long pasta, hollow pasta and pasta soup noodles.

During the sixteenth century pasta was still very much a luxury food. Although it was now being produced commercially, the durum wheat required was expensive, and as result pasta tended to be eaten only by the wealthy.

Pasta finally became a regular part of the national Italian diet in the seventeenth century. The ready availability of simple pasta home-manufacturing machines, coupled with the mass farming of durum wheat, meant that home-made pasta was both practical and economical.

The first large-scale pasta manufacturer was Buitoni, established in 1827. Buitoni still exists today, but is no longer an independent company being part of the Nestlé group.

Mass-produced pasta is now available all over the world, but any respectable Italian chef will still prefer to make his own, or buy from a reputable smaller company.

About dried pasta

There are an almost infinite number of types of pasta asciutta, especially if you include all the regional variations. Almost 90 per cent of the pasta eaten in Italy is dried, the remainder being home-made. A rule of thumb for cooking dried pasta and portion weights is 80–100 g per portion as a starter course and, if larger portions are required, increase accordingly; traditionally pasta is eaten predominantly as a starter

Most types of dried pasta will cook perfectly well in under 10 minutes. The cooking times on British packaging are often grossly overstated. Spaghetti that has been stored too long and is over-dry may take longer and you might not want to eat the result.

Allow between 500 ml and 1 litre of water per person – the more the better. The reason for this is that the water should always be at a fiercely rolling boil. The more water you have in proportion to pasta the quicker it will return to the boil after the pasta is added. This means fast cooking and better-textured pasta.

Some recipe books suggest you add a little oil to the water when cooking pasta. This has no benefit except when freshly made; it was a method of storage in restaurants when the pasta (predominantly spaghetti) was pre-cooked and a little oil was added to the reheating water to prevent sticking due to the exposure of starch on the spaghetti.

Tortellini and its history

Tortellini literally means 'navel of Venus' (the Roman goddess of love, the Greek equivalent of Aphrodite) and derives from its shape. As legend would have it, Venus and Jupiter were planning to get together one night. When Venus checked into an inn, the chef found out. He went to her room, peeped through the keyhole and saw Venus laying there, half-naked in bed on her back. When the chef saw her navel, he was inspired to rush to the kitchen to create a stuffed pasta that looked like it, and thus arose the legend of the famous tortellina (tortellini is plural). About the size of a 10 pence piece, this is a round, wrinkled pasta filled with cheese most of the time and, of course, other variant ingredients like meat.

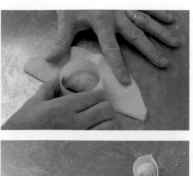

How tortellini are made

How ravioli is made

How tagliatelle is made

Pasta sauces

470 Asparagus sauce

	4 portions	10 portions
asparagus spears	300 g	750 g
vegetable broth	250–500 ml	625–1250 ml
salt		
butter	90 g	225 g
onion, peeled and very finely diced	25 g	60 g
Parmesan, freshly grated	60g	150 g

nutritional info

1 large portion provides:
1073 kJ/260 kcal
23.5 g fat (of which 14.7 g saturated)
4.3 g carbohydrate (of which 3.5 g sugars)
8.1 g protein
1.7 g fibre

Butter and parmesan cheese were used.

1 Peel and trim the asparagus, getting rid of the woody bits, then wash it thoroughly to get rid of any sand. If using sprue (i.e. very thin asparagus) just trim the woody white ends; this asparagus probably has the best flavour for this dish. Keep the peelings and trimmings.

2 Chop the asparagus into 2 cm lengths (5 cm for the sprue).

3 Boil the vegetable broth with the asparagus peelings and trimmings and salt, to taste, for 15–20 minutes to infuse, then sieve. Keep the broth hot and discard the solids.

4 Melt half the butter in a wide pan over a medium heat. Add the onion and asparagus and sweat for 3–4 minutes.

5 Add the broth and turn up the heat to a boil. Cook for 10 minutes until the asparagus is very tender and the broth has nearly evaporated.

6 Meanwhile cook the pasta (ideally garganelle), drain and add to the asparagus sauce. Add the remaining butter and the Parmesan, then toss again over a medium heat.

7 Serve immediately.

471 Pea and pancetta sauce

	4 portions	10 portions
peas in pod	1 kg	2½ kg
vegetable broth	500 ml	1250 ml
butter	75 g	180 g
onion, peeled and very finely diced	25 g	60 g
pancetta, cut into 5 mm dice	120 g	300 g
Parmesan, finely grated	60 g	60 g
salt and pepper		

nutritional info

1 large portion provides:
1582 kJ/379 kcal
23.9 g fat (of which 13.9 g saturated)
15.6 g carbohydrate (of which 11.6 g sugars)
26.4 g protein
4.2 g fibre

Lean bacon was used instead of pancetta for this analysis. The saturated fat comes from the pancetta, butter and parmesan.

1 Pod the peas. String and chop the pods, then boil in the vegetable broth for 20 minutes. Sieve and keep warm.

2 Discard the solids.

3 Melt 60 g of the butter in a saucepan, add the onion and pancetta, and sweat for 10 minutes. The pancetta should be translucent.

4 Add the peas and sweat for a further 10 minutes. Add a little of the broth and simmer over a medium heat for a minimum of 20 minutes, by which time the liquid should have reduced considerably. The pancetta should be very tender. Big peas will take up to 40 minutes. The sauce can be made in advance.

5 Cook the pasta and drain. Return to the pan, add the hot sauce, the remaining butter and the grated Parmesan. Season with freshly grated black pepper, and possibly a little salt.

472 Cep and truffle relish v

	4 portions	10 portions
onion, peeled and very finely diced	50 g	125 g
good olive oil	200 ml	500 ml
dried funghi porcini, soaked in 300 ml warm water	100 g	250 g
summer truffles (frozen are good)	100 g	250 g
salt and pepper		
truffle oil	20 ml	50 ml

nutritional info

1 large portion provides:
2434 kJ/590 kcal
55.6 g fat (of which 7.9 g saturated)
19.8 g carbohydrate (of which 3.4 g sugars)
3.7 g protein
1.1 g fibre

Mushrooms were used, and olive oil instead of truffle oil, for this analysis. The recipe calls for olive oil, to cook the onion, and truffle oil, for the relish.

kcal: 1000 900 800 700 600 500 400 300 200 100 0 (calorie counter)

1 In a wide saucepan over a low heat sweat the diced onion in the olive oil. It must cook slowly and not brown (approximately 10–15 minutes).

2 While this is cooking, carefully lift the ceps from their water – use your fingers or a spider. This ensures that the inevitable grit remains behind in the water.

3 Pat dry and dice, then add to the onions and continue to sweat together for 10 minutes further. During this time carefully strain the cep soaking water through a coffee filter or fine tea strainer.

4 When the cep and onion mix has had the 10 minutes, add the cep liquor and turn the heat up to medium.

5 Cook until the cep water is nearly completely evaporated. Set aside to cool.

6 Clean and sterilise a 450 g jar (dishwashers are good for this).

7 Grate the truffles (straight from the freezer if frozen) through the same aperture of the grater as you would Parmesan, directly over the cooked cep and onion mix.

8 Stir, taste and season, then add half the truffle oil.

9 Using a rubber spatula, transfer this mixture to the jar. Pat down in the jar, wiping the edges inside the glass with a clean cloth. Top up the jar with the remaining truffle oil – the layer of truffle oil should cover the relish completely.

10 Keep in the refrigerator; if unopened, it will keep almost indefinitely.

11 To use the relish, stir some more truffle oil into it.

473 Tagliatelle Arrabiata

	4 portions	10 portions
dried tagliatelle	200 g	500 g
olive oil	1 tbsp	2½ tbsp
onion, peeled and finely chopped	25 g	60 g
garlic cloves, peeled and finely chopped	2	4
red chilli, finely chopped	1	2
white wine	100 ml	250 ml
tomato purée	30 g	75 g
pomodorino cherry tomatoes	400 g	1 kg
salt and freshly ground black pepper		

nutritional info

1 large portion provides:
988 kJ/233 kcal
4.0 g fat (of which 0.4 g saturated)
44.3 g carbohydrate (of which 7.4 g sugars)
7.9 g protein
2.9 g fibre

A small amount of olive oil was used to sauté the onions.

kcal: 1000 900 800 700 600 500 400 300 200 100 0 (calorie counter)

1 Half fill a large saucepan with water. Season with salt and bring to the boil.

2 Cook the tagliatelle in the salted water as per the packet instructions.

3 In a medium saucepan, heat the oil.

4 Sauté the onion for 2 minutes, to soften. Stir in the garlic and chilli.

5 Pour in the wine, bring to the boil and cook off for 2 minutes.

6 Stir in the tomato purée and tomatoes, and bring the mixture to simmering point.

7 Simmer for 8–10 minutes. Season.

8 Drain the pasta and stir it into the sauce.

474 Tagliatelle with pesto and squid

	4 portions	10 portions
Pesto		
sea salt	1 tsp	2½ tsp
pine nuts, plus extra for garnish	25 g	60 g
garlic cloves, chopped	2	5
basil plant (large), leaves only	1	2
freshly grated Parmesan cheese	75 g	180 g
freshly grated pecorino cheese	25 g	60 g
extra-virgin olive oil	100–200 ml	250–500 ml
Tagliatelle		
fresh tagliatelle	200 g	500 g
Squid		
olive oil	2 tbsp	5 tbsp
squid, cleaned and scored	4	10
lemon, juice of	½	1

1 Using a mortar and pestle, prepare the pesto by pounding together the salt, pine nuts and garlic. Work in the basil leaves, pounding until you have a smooth paste. Add the cheeses, then beat in the olive oil until you have a thick, dense sauce. Adjust the amount of oil depending on the texture of pesto you prefer. Set aside.

2 Bring a large pan of salted water to the boil. Drop in the tagliatelle and boil for 4–5 minutes, or as per the packet instructions.

3 For the squid, heat the oil in a medium frying pan. Add the squid and fry for 2–3 minutes. Squeeze in half the lemon juice.

4 Drain the tagliatelle and tip into the pan with the squid. Mix in the pesto and divide the pasta between four (or ten) bowls. Scatter over the pine nuts to finish.

5 Store the remaining pesto in a jar in the refrigerator.

---

nutritional info

1 large portion provides:
3523 kJ/845 kcal
58.5 g fat (of which 11.9 g saturated)
41.9 g carbohydrate (of which 2.2 g sugars)
40.3 g protein
1.7 g fibre

Parmesan was used instead of pecorino cheese for this analysis. There are pine nuts, oil and parmesan in the pesto, and the squid is fried in olive oil.

♥

kcal
1000
900
800
700
600
500
400
300
200
100
0

calorie counter

475 Lasagne

	4 portions	10 portions
Sauce		
olive oil	3 tbsp	7 tbsp
onion, finely chopped	50 g	125 g
garlic cloves, chopped	2	5
plum tomatoes, peeled and roughly chopped	2 kg	5 kg
Meatballs		
lean ground beef	250 g	625 g
lean ground pork	250 g	625 g
fennel seeds	2 tsp	5 tsp
large egg	1	3
salt and black pepper to taste		
Pasta assembly		
dried lasagne sheets	300 g	750 g
fresh ricotta	450 g	1125 g
balls hand-rolled mozzarella, sliced	4	10
grated Parmesan	150 g	375 g

---

nutritional info

1 large portion provides:
2138 kJ/510 kcal
26.8 g fat (of which 14.2 g saturated)
34.1 g carbohydrate (of which 12.2 g sugars)
35.5 g protein
4.2 g fibre

Olive oil was used in the sauce, and fatty meat and cheese added.

♥ kcal 1000 900 800 700 600 500 400 300 200 100 0 (calorie counter)

---

1 Warm the oil in a large pot and stir in onion and garlic. When the onion is softened (about 10 minutes), add the peeled tomatoes and their juice. Break up the tomatoes as the sauce cooks.

2 While the sauce is cooking, mix the beef, pork, fennel, egg, salt and pepper together and form into meatballs a little smaller than golf balls.

3 When the sauce boils, add the meat balls. Let sit before stirring to harden meatballs. Bring to a hard boil, then lower flame and cook, partially covered for 1 hour, stirring deep in the pot from time to time. When finished, remove meatballs and chop into small pieces.

4 Cook the lasagne in an abundance of boiling water. When not quite al dente, stop cooking, drain and lay each sheet on a damp towel in preparation for assembling.

5 Pre-heat oven to 185°C and, taking a baking dish about 5 cm deep, coat the bottom of the dish sparingly with tomato sauce.

6 Line with layer of lasagne. Dot with ricotta and slices of mozzarella. Sprinkle lightly with grated Parmesan, spread with sauce, then add the chopped meatballs. Repeat the layers in same order, ending the top layer with pasta. Spread this last layer with tomato sauce and grated Parmesan.

7 Cover pan with aluminium foil and bake in a pre-heated oven at 175°C for 15 minutes. Remove foil and cook for an additional 30 minutes. Cool slightly before serving.

8 Serve with a crisp green salad and home-made garlic bread.

PASTRY

PREPARATION AND MATERIALS

All baking times and temperatures stated are approximate, as a pastry cook learns through experience how raw materials bake differently in various types of oven. When using forced air convection ovens it is often necessary to reduce the stated temperatures in accordance with manufacturers' recommendations. Also, certain ovens produce severe bottom heat and to counteract this the use of double baking sheets (one sheet on top of another) is necessary.

USE OF MODERN TECHNIQUES AND EQUIPMENT

In the modern pastry department there is a variety of new techniques and equipment that can help the pastry cook to achieve better-quality products, improve presentation and reduce time. For example, there is a wide variety of commercial basic mixes, pastes and fonds, and the range of specialist small equipment increases all the time, especially the various types of moulds available, like the florentine moulds (including the comb chocolate finish, Dockers, trellis cutters) widely used in production.

Techniques are being developed all the time: the use of silicone paper has been revolutionary in baking. Many pastry chefs pin out pastry on a silicone-lined baking sheet, cutting the shape required then removing the excess paste. This gives a better shape with no chance of sticking to the sheet.

Units covered
3FPC4, 3FPC5,
3FPC6, 3FPC7,
3FPC8, 3FPC12,
3FPC13, 3FPC14

LIST OF RECIPES

Recipe no	page no	Recipe no	page no
Pastes and doughs		504 Potato and yoghurt bread	391
481 Crêpes	382	506 Pumpkin seed and onion bloomer	392
482 Quick puff pastry/flaky pastry	382	503 'The fermente'	390
479 Raspberry cream biscuits	381	**Mousses**	
477 Sablé paste	380	515 Basic fruit mousse	398
476 Savoury flan paste	380	523 Caramel mousse	400
478 Strawberry cream biscuits	381	522 Chocolate and almond mousse	399
480 Tempura	381	519 Chocolate and orange mousse	399
Creams		521 Chocolate brandy mousse	399
486 Buttercream	384	518 Chocolate mousse	399
485 Crème brûlée	383	520 Chocolate rum mousse	399
487 Crème Chantilly	384	516 Mango mousse	398
484 Lemon curd	383	517 Pear mousse	398
483 Lemon posset	383	524 Vanilla bavarois	400
Sponges		**Ice cream, sorbets and frozen desserts**	
501 Banana cake	389	534 Champagne sorbet	402
491 Basic sponge	385	526 Chocolate ice cream	401
493 Chocolate Genoese	386	530 Chocolate sorbet	401
488 Coffee jaconde sponge	384	525 Ice cream base	400
490 Flourless chocolate sponge	385	529 Lemon sorbet	401
496 Frangipane 1	387	533 Lime sherbet	402
497 Frangipane 2	387	535 Parfait	402
494 Gâteau japonaise	386	536 Raspberry parfait	403
495 Lucerne fruit and pastry cream	387	528 Sorbet syrup	401
500 Madeira cake	388	527 Vanilla ice cream	401
499 Muffins	388	531 Vanilla sorbet	402
489 Othello sponge	385	532 Yoghurt sorbet	402
492 Plain Genoese	385	**Sauces**	
498 Pound cake	388	540 Caramel sauce	404
Yeast products		541 Chocolate fudge sauce	404
510 Blinis	393	537 Chocolate sauce	403
502 Brioche	389	538 Fruit coulis	403
514 Burgomeister rolls	397	539 Rose petal syrup	404
509 Croissants	393	**Meringues and soufflés**	
512 Danish pastries with almond fruit filling	395	543 French meringue	405
513 Danish pastries with custard filling	396	547 Grand Marnier soufflé	407
511 Danish pastry dough	394	542 Italian meringue	405
508 Hot cross buns	392	548 Snow eggs	408
507 Olive sour bread	392	545 Soufflé base	406
505 Pickled walnut and raisin bread	391	544 Swiss meringue	405
		546 Vanilla soufflé	406

Recipe no	page no
E'spumas	
553 Caramel e'spuma	410
551 Chocolate e'spuma – cold	410
549 Hot chocolate e'spuma	409
552 Mandarin e'spuma	410
550 Thyme and ginger e'spuma	410
Tarts, slices and gâteaux	
560 Apple strudel	413
556 Baked chocolate tart (aero)	412
558 Biscuit Viennoise	412
559 Chocolate décor paste	413
557 Chocolate truffle torte	412
563 Fig tart	416
567 Fruit terrine	418
565 Gâteau St Honoré	416
554 Lemon tart	411
555 Marquise	411
564 Prune and almond tart	416
566 Sugar-topped choux buns with rum flavoured pastry cream (salambos)	417
562 Swiss apple tart	415
561 Tatin of apple	415
Puddings	
568 Christmas pudding	419
569 English trifle	420
Biscuits and cakes	
575 Carrot cake	422
572 Chocolate fudge cake	421
571 Cookies – chocolate chip	421
570 Gingerbread	420
573 Griottines (cherries) clafoutis	421
574 Peanut butter cookies	422
Chocolate goods and petits fours	
587 Bergamot truffles	426
585 Caramel truffles	426
578 Cassis pâté de fruit	423
579 Cherry rolls	424
580 Chocolate caramels	424

Recipe no	page no
581 Florentines	424
584 Madeleines	425
583 Passion fruit and mango jelly	425
586 Pear and caramel truffles	426
588 Praline truffles	427
577 Pumpkin pâté de fruit	423
576 Spraying chocolate	423
582 Viennese biscuits	425
Miscellaneous	
595 Brandy snaps	429
591 Chocolate fudge	428
594 Cornets	429
590 Marshmallows	427
589 Nougat Montelimar	427
593 Sponge fingers	428
592 Turkish delight	428
Sugar	
599 Blown sugar	434
596 Poured sugar	432
600 Pulled sugar	435
598 Rock sugar	433
597 Spun sugar	433
Marzipan	
602 Almond drops and fingers	436
603 English rout biscuit	436
604 Marzipan shortcake fingers	436
601 Marzipan wafers	435
Chocolate	
608 Champagne truffles	440
605 Chocolate for hand moulding	438
606 Truffles	439
607 White chocolate truffles	439
Pastillage	
609 Gum paste (pastillage)	440

THE BASIC BUILDING BLOCKS

Flour

Flour is one of the most important ingredients in patisserie, if not *the* most important.

There are a great variety of high-quality flours made from cereals, nuts or legumes, such as chestnut flour, cornflour, and so on. They have been used in patisserie, baking, dessert cuisine and savoury cuisine in all countries throughout history. The king of all of them is without doubt wheat flour.

The composition of wheat flour

Wheat flour is basically composed of starch, gluten, sugar, fats, water and minerals.

Starch is the main component of flour. Another important element is gluten, which is elastic and impermeable. Found mainly in wheat, this is what makes wheat flour the most common flour used in bread making.

The quantity of sugar in wheat is very small and it plays a very important role in fermentation. Wheat contains only a maximum of 16 per cent water, but its presence is important. The mineral matter (ash), which is found mainly in the husk of the wheat grain and not in the kernel, determines the purity and quality of the flour.

From the ear to the final product, flour, wheat goes through several distinct processes. These are carried out in modern industrial plants, where wheat is subjected to the various treatments and phases necessary for the production of different types of flour. These arrive in perfect condition to our workplaces and are made into preparations like sponge cakes, yeast dough, puff pastries, cookies, pastries …

What you need to know about flour

- Flour is a particularly delicate living material, and it must be used and stored with special care. It must always be in the best condition, which is why storing large quantities is not recommended.
- It must be kept in a good environment: a clean, organised, disinfected and aerated storeroom.
- Warm and humid places must absolutely be avoided.

Types of flour in pastry work

- **White flour** is heavily milled and sieved to remove the outer skins and germ. It will store better without the germ, which contains fat and enzymes. About 70 per cent of the wheat is extracted to produce white flour. It is usually fortified by added calcium, iron, vitamin B1 and nicotinic acid.
- **Wholemeal flour** is the whole grain crushed into flour. (The bran is not digested by humans – this acts as roughage.) Stoneground flour is ground by stones, and is said to have a superior flavour.
- **Germ flour** (Hovis-type flour) is a mixture of 75 per cent white flour plus 25 per cent cooked germ. The germ is cooked to delay the onset of rancidity in the fat. Cooking gives a malted flavour.
- **Starch-reduced flour** is prepared for commercial products. Much of the starch is washed out, leaving the gluten and other proteins.
- **Self-raising flour** is white flour, usually of medium to soft strength, with the correct proportion of raising agent to give sufficient raising action for cake making.
- **High-ratio flour** is flour that has been finely milled in order that it is able to absorb more liquid and sugar.

Flour contains two main proteins, gliadin and glutenin, which when combined with water, produce gluten, which is elastic and as a result will stretch. When cake, pastry or bread doughs are formed, the gluten is able to give the mixture its structure.

Wheat contains a large quantity of these proteins; other cereals do not contain so much, so they are not so suitable for making cakes, bread, etc. Canadian-type hard wheat contains more gluten than British and Australian wheats.

- **Strong flours** are milled from a mixture of wheat, in which spring wheat predominates, and contains 10–16 per cent strong glutens used for bread, yeast doughs and puff pastry.
- **Medium general purpose flour** contains less strong and elastic gluten; it is used for plain cakes, scones and rich-yeast mixtures.
- **Soft flour (cake flour)** contains a small percentage of gluten to give a soft structure to a cake. Uses: sponge cakes and biscuits.

Dough

Why does dough ferment?

The phenomenon of seeing dough ferment is extraordinary and very common in our profession. However, because it is so frequent, we do not pay much attention to how it happens. It is very interesting to know why doughs ferment and what the effects are on the end product. In order to understand why yeast dough rises, we must note that the main ingredients of natural leavening are water, air and, most importantly, sugar, which is transformed into carbon dioxide and causes the leavening. This carbon dioxide forms bubbles inside the dough and makes it rise. Fermentation is a transformation undergone by organic matter (sugars).

Yeast goods

Yeast is a living organism – it is a plant of the fungi group. Yeast produces the gas carbon dioxide by fermentation. This occurs when it is given food in the form of sugar, warmth (25–29°C) and moisture, water or milk.

Types of yeast

- **Compressed yeast** is the most widely used. It is a very pure form of yeast packed and sold in cakes. It crumbles easily and has a fresh smell. It will keep in a cold place for 2–3 days.
- **Dried yeast** can be stored indefinitely if kept dry and well sealed. It takes longer to cream and is more concentrated.
- **Fresh yeast** has a pleasant characteristic smell, is a putty colour, will crumble easily and will cream readily.

Conditions for the fermentation of yeast

Yeast requires food, warmth and moisture. Yeast is destroyed at temperatures higher than those given above, and its activity is retarded at lower temperatures. Yeast can be destroyed during the mixing or rising processes if it is put in a very hot place.

Fermentation is brought about by a number of enzymes present in yeast – maltase, which acts upon maltose to form glucose, and invertase, which acts upon sucrose, producing glucose and fructose – but before these can be effective a substance called diastase, present in the flour, converts some of the starch to dextrin and maltose.

The zymase group of enzymes changes simple sugars – glucose and fructose – to carbon dioxide and alcohol.

Eggs

The egg is one of the principal ingredients of the gastronomy world. Its great versatility and extraordinary properties as a thickener, emulsifier and stabiliser make its presence important in various creations in patisserie: sauces, creams, sponge cakes, custards and ice creams. Although it is not often the main ingredient, it plays specific and determining roles in terms of texture, taste and aroma, among other things. The egg is fundamental in preparations such as brioches, crèmes anglaises, sponge cakes and crèmes pâtissières. The extent to which eggs are used (or not) makes an enormous difference to the quality of the product.

A good custard cannot be made without eggs, for they cause the required coagulation and give it the desired consistency and finesse.

Eggs are also an important ingredient in ice cream, where their yolks act as an emulsifier thanks to the lecithin they contain, which aids the emulsion of fats.

What you need to know about eggs

- Eggs act as a texture agent in, for example, patisseries and ice creams.
- They intensify the aroma of pastries like brioche.
- They enhance flavours.
- They give volume to whisked sponges and batters.
- They strengthen the structure of preparations such as sponge cakes.
- They act as a thickening agent – in crème anglaise, for example.
- They act as an emulsifier in preparations such as mayonnaise and ice cream.
- They act as a stabiliser – in ice cream, for example.
- A fresh egg should have a small, shallow air pocket inside it.
- The yolks of fresh eggs should be bulbous, firm and bright.

- The fresher the egg, the more viscous the egg white.
- Eggs should be stored far from strong odours as, despite their shells, these are easily absorbed.
- In a whole 60 g egg, the yolk weighs about 20 g, the white 30 g and the shell 10 g.
- Eggs are available in four grades: small (48 g); medium (58 g); large (68 g); very large (76 g).

Eggs in pastry work

Egg albumen (protein) is soluble in cold liquid; it begins to coagulate immediately on application of heat, becoming opaque and firm. The degree of firmness depends on the degree of heat and length of cooking time. Egg yolk does not harden to the same extent or as quickly as the white, due to the high percentage of fat. If egg is overcooked or added too quickly to hot liquid, curdling will result.

- **Thickening.** The coagulation of protein on heating to 68°C is responsible for the thickening properties.
- **Lightening.** By means of whisking either egg white or whole egg, air is entangled and lightness given to a mixture. This enables eggs to:
  – act as a raising agent in cakes
  – produce light dishes, e.g. soufflés and meringues.
- **Glazing.** Beaten egg used as a glaze (eggwash).
- **Binding.** The coagulating properties of the egg will give cohesiveness to a mixture containing dry ingredients.
- **Emulsifying.** The lecithin contained in the yolk will assist in the emulsification (mixing) of products.
- **Coating.** Beaten egg forms a protective coating for foods.
- **Enriching.** The addition of whole eggs or yolks to a mixture is a means of adding protein and fat. Eggs improve nutritive value and flavour.

When beating egg whites to form a foam a little egg white powder may be added to strengthen the mixture.

Salt

Where salt is found

Salt (chemical name 'sodium chloride') is one of the most important ingredients. It is well known that salt is a necessary part of the human diet, present in small or large proportions in many natural foods. We generally associate it with seasoning of foods to improve their flavour, but it is also necessary in the making of many sweet dishes.

Characteristics and advantages of using salt in yeast dough

Salted dough is much more manageable than unsalted. Salt is usually added a few moments before the end of the kneading, since its function is to help expand the dough's volume.

Salt considerably enhances all preparations, whether they be sweet or salty.

It is a good idea to add a pinch of salt to all sweet preparations, nougats, chocolate bonbons and cakes to intensify flavours.

Salt softens sugar and butter, activates the taste buds and enhances all aromas.

What you need to know about salt

- Salt gives us the possibility of many combinations. At times, these may seem normal (like a terrine of foie gras and coarse salt), others surprising (like praline with coarse salt).
- The addition of salt enhances the flavour of foods when its quantity is well adjusted; but if we add it in greater quantity than we are used to, it produces a very interesting, completely unknown result. It certainly is not adequate in all of our preparations, so we should be careful and check the results of our combinations.
- Chefs should take extra care when using excessive amounts of salt as over-consumption is a major cause of hypertension.

Butter

An indispensable fat

Butter is the symbol of perfection in fats. It brings flowery smoothness, perfumes and aromas, and impeccable textures to our preparations. It is a point of reference for good gastronomy. Butter has a very long history, but its origin is unknown. Many books have been written about it, but we can only conclude that it was probably discovered by accident.

Butter is an emulsion – the perfect symbiosis of water and fat. It is composed of a minimum of 82 per cent fat, a maximum of 16 per cent water and 2 per cent dry extracts.

What you need to know about butter

- Butter is the most complete fat.
- It is a very delicate ingredient that can quickly spoil if a series of basic rules are not followed in its use.
- It has the property of absorbing odours very easily. It should always be stored far from anything that produces strong odours and it should be kept well covered.
- When kept at 15°C, butter is stable and retains all its properties: finesse, perfume and creaminess.
- It should not be kept too long: it is better to always work with fresh butter.
- Good butter has a stable texture, pleasing taste, fresh odour, homogeneous colour and, most important, it must melt perfectly in your mouth.
- It softens preparations like cookies and petits fours, and keeps products like sponge cakes soft.

- Butter enhances flavour – as in brioches, for example.
- The melting point of butter is between 30°C and 35°C approximately.

Fats

Fats and oils are composed of fatty acids and glycerine. Fatty acids may be saturated or unsaturated.

- **Saturated fatty acids.** A saturated fat has each carbon atom in the fatty acids combined with two hydrogen atoms, e.g. palmitic and stearic acid. Saturated fats are solid at room temperature and predominate in fats of animal origin, e.g. butter, cream, lard, hard cheese, egg yolks, lard and suet. They are also present in hard margarines.
- **Unsaturated fatty acids**
  (a) *Monounsaturated fatty acids*. These have an adjacent pair of carbon atoms, each with only one hydrogen atom attached, so they are capable of taking up more hydrogen atoms. Monounsaturated fats are soft at room temperature but will solidify when in the coolest part of the refrigerator. They are present in many animal and vegetable fats. Oleic acid, found in olive oil, is an example of a monounsaturated fatty acid.
  (b) *Polyunsaturated fatty acids*. These have two or more pairs of carbon atoms, which are capable of taking up more hydrogen atoms. Polyunsaturated fats are very soft or oily at room temperature and will not solidify even in a refrigerator. They are present in soya bean, corn and sunflower seed oils.
- **Butter** is composed of the fat of milk, traces of curd (casein) and milk sugar lactose, water and mineral matter, which includes salt added to improve flavour and help preservation. A good butter adds flavour to cakes, biscuits and pastry.
- **Lard** is derived from pig fat. Good lard is a pure white fat. It is a tough, plastic fat, with no creaming properties but excellent shortening properties. It is usually mixed with butter or margarine for cakes and pastry to add colour and flavour.
- **Suet** is obtained from around the kidneys of beef cattle. It is a hard fat and cannot be rubbed into flour or creamed. It is added by chopping or shredding finely into the mixture. Suet is used to make suet pastry, which is usually steamed. Baking gives a hard, dry result. Commercial suet is purified fat that has been shredded and mixed with wheat or rice flour to stop the pieces of fat sticking together.
- **Vegetable fats and oils.** Soya beans, sunflower seeds, cotton seeds, groundnuts, sesame seeds, coconuts, palm kernels and olives all yield oils that are used in cooking fats and oils, margarine and creams.
- **Margarine**
  (a) *Table margarine*. This is blended to give the best possible flavour.
  (b) *Cake margarine*. This is developed to have good creaming properties.
  (c) *Pastry margarine*. This is blended to produce a tough plastic margarine that has a fairly high melting point. It may contain a high percentage of stearin (a type of fat) or may be hydrogenated to harden it.
- **High-ratio fat** is hydrogenated edible oil, to which a quantity of a very pure and refined quality emulsifying agent has been added, e.g. glyceryl monostearate (GMS), although other emulsifiers may be used. By the use of such special fats, cakes can be made containing higher than normal quantities of liquid. Combining the use of this special type of emulsifying shortening with high-ratio flour, it is possible to successfully make cakes with abnormal percentages of both sugar and liquid; high-ratio cakes are so called because of their high percentages of sugar and liquid.

- **Compounds fats and oils** are practically 100 per cent salt free and have no flavour. They are made by refining extracted vegetable oils. The blend of oils is hydrogenated to produce the consistency desired, processed by creaming and chilling, and then packed.

Creaming properties

Fats for some types of pastry work must cream well. To do this they must possess a 'plastic', waxy consistency and have a good flavour. Fats may be purchased that have had their chemistry altered so that they cream well. These are known as plasticised or pre-creamed fats.

Sweeteners

Chemical properties of sucrose (common sugar)

Common sugar, or sucrose, consists of carbon (C_{12}), hydrogen (H_{22}) and oxygen (O_{11}), and is composed of two bonded molecules (in equal parts): glucose and fructose.

Inverted sugar

Inverted sugar is, after sucrose, one of the most commonly used sugars, thanks to its properties. It is a molecularly equal mix of the products obtained in the hydrolysis of sucrose (fructose and glucose) and is made from the hydrolysis of sugar in the presence of an enzyme. According to the hydrolysis and the dry material used, we end up with two types of inverted sugar: liquid inverted sugar and liquid inverted sugar syrup.

Inverted sugar syrup

This is a white, sticky paste and has no particular odour. It has no less than 62 per cent dry matter and more than 50 per cent inverted sugar. It is what we most frequently use. With equal proportions of dry matter and sucrose, its sweetening capacity is 25–30 per cent greater.

It melts at 35°C and cannot withstand more than 75°C, unless moisture (liquid) is added; otherwise, it loses its properties. It has a constant moisture percentage – that is, it has hygroscopic properties.

Liquid inverted sugar

This is a yellowish liquid with no less than 62 per cent dry matter. It contains more than 3 per cent inverted sugar, but less than 50 per cent. It is used mainly in the commercial food industry.

Applications of inverted sugar

- It improves the aroma of products.
- It improves the texture of doughs.
- It prevents the dehydration of frozen products.
- It reduces or stops crystallisation.
- It is essential in ice cream making – it greatly improves its quality and lowers its freezing point.

Glucose

Glucose takes on various forms:

- the characteristics of a viscous syrup, called crystal glucose
- its natural state, in fruit and honey
- a dehydrated white paste (used mainly in the commercial food industry, but also used in our profession)
- 'dehydrated glucose' (atomised glucose) – a glucose syrup from which its water is evaporated; this is used in patisserie, but mainly in the commercial food industry.

Characteristics and properties of glucose syrup

- It is a transparent, viscous paste.
- It prevents the crystallisation of boiled sugars, jams and preserves.
- It delays the drying of a product.
- It adds plasticity and creaminess to ice cream and the fillings of chocolate bonbons.
- It prevents the crystallisation of ice cream.

Honey

Honey, a sweet composite that bees make with the nectar extracted from flowers, is without doubt the oldest known sugar. A golden-brown thick paste, its sweetness coefficient is 130 with respect to sucrose. It has the property of lowering the freezing point of ice cream.

It can be used like inverted sugar, but it is important to take into account that honey, unlike inverted sugar, will give flavour to the preparation. Also, it is inadequate for preparations that require long storage, since honey re-crystallises after some time.

Isomalt

Isomalt sugar is a sweetener that is still little known in the patisserie world, but it has been used for some time. It has properties distinct from those of the sweeteners already mentioned. It is produced through the hydrolysis of sugar, followed by hydrogenation (the addition of hydrogen). Produced through these industrial processes, this sugar has been used for many years in large industries, in candy and chewing gum production, and is now earning a place in gastronomy.

One of its most notable characteristics is that it can melt without the addition of water or another liquid. This is a very interesting property for making artistic decorations in caramel. Its appearance is like that of confectioners' sugar: a glossy powder. Its sweetening strength is half that of sucrose and it is much less soluble than sugar, which means that it melts less easily in the mouth.

Isomalt's main claim in gastronomy over the past five or six years has been the replacement of normal sugar or sucrose when making sugar decorations, blown sugar, pulled sugar or spun sugar as the hydroscopic properties are lower than normal sugar, therefore it will be less affected by atmospheric variance.

Milk

Milk is a basic and fundamental element of our diets throughout our lives. It is composed of water, sugar and has a minimum of 3½ per cent fat. It is essential in an infinite number of preparations, from creams, ice creams, yeast doughs, mousses and custards to certain ganaches, cookies, tuiles and muffins. A yeast dough will change considerably in texture, taste and colour if made with milk instead of water.

Milk has a lightly sweet taste and little odour. Two distinct processes are used to conserve it:

1 **pasteurisation** – the milk is heated to between 73°C and 85°C for a few seconds, then cooled quickly to 4°C
2 **sterilisation (UHT)** – the milk is heated to 140–150°C for 2 seconds, then cooled quickly.

Milk is homogenised to evenly disperse the fat, since the fat has a tendency to rise to the surface (see 'Cream', below).

What you need to know about milk

- Pasteurised milk has better taste and aroma than UHT milk.
- Milk is a useful agent in the development of flavour in sauces and creams, due to its lactic fermentation.
- Milk is an agent of colour, texture and aroma in doughs.
- Because of its lactic ferments, it facilitates the maturation of doughs and creams.
- There are other types of milk, such as sheep's, that are very interesting to use in many restaurant desserts.

Cream

Cream is another of the most used materials. It is used in many recipes because of its high fat content and great versatility.

Cream is obtained from milk when it is left to sit. A film forms on the surface because of the difference in density between fat and liquid. This process is accelerated mechanically in large industries through heat and centrifuge.

There are two main methods for conserving cream:

1 **pasteurisation** – the cream is heated to 85–90°C for a few seconds and then cooled quickly; this cream retains all its flavour properties
2 **sterilisation (UHT)** – this consists of heating the cream to 140–150°C for 2 seconds; cream treated this way loses some of its flavour properties, but it keeps longer.

Always use pasteurised cream when possible – for example, in the restaurant when specialities are made for immediate consumption. Here we have the advantage and possibility of making 'ephemeral' patisserie (dessert cuisine) – for example, a chocolate bonbon that will be consumed immediately.

What you need to know about cream

- Cream whips with the addition of air, thanks to its fat content. This retains air bubbles formed during beating.
- Cream is an agent that adds texture.
- All cream, once boiled and cooled, can be whipped again with no problem.
- Also, once it is boiled and mixed or infused, with whatever we want (maintaining certain norms), it will whip again with no problem if first left to cool for 24 hours.
- To whip cream well, it must be cold (around 4°C).
- Infusions with cream can be hot or cold. If cold, this requires an infusion time of at least 12 hours.

Chocolate (see also pages 438–440)

Main characteristics of the tree and its fruit:

- The majority of the world's cacao trees are concentrated around the equator.
- The cacao tree needs a hot, humid and rainy climate – the tropics are ideal for it.
- High levels of wind and sun can be damaging to the cacao tree and it must be protected from both.
- A productive tree can measure between 5 and 10 m in height, depending on its age.
- The fruit, or 'cocoa pod', measures between 15 and 30 cm.
- Each cocoa pod holds approximately 30–40 seeds (cocoa beans).

What you need to know about cocoa

- **Cocoa bean:** Once called 'cocoa almond' or 'cocoa grain', this is the seed that is found in the pods of cacao trees. After being treated, it is packed and sent to be sold on the international market. It is from this bean that cocoa butter, chocolate liquor, cocoa powder and cocoa nibs are extracted.
- **Cocoa nibs:** These are roasted, shelled cocoa beans broken into small pieces. This is a very interesting product with an intense flavour – 100 per cent cocoa. It gives aroma, flavour and texture to many preparations, like sponge cakes, chocolate bonbons, pound cakes, muffins, ice creams, cookies and cake decorations. Care should be taken not to use excess quantities so that the balance with the other ingredients is not upset.
- **Chocolate liquor:** This is a smooth, liquid paste. In addition to being the base for other cocoa derivatives, such as cocoa butter or cocoa powder, it can be used in all types of desserts and cakes – toffee, for example. One of its main characteristics is that it contains no sugar, which gives it a slightly bitter flavour in its pure state.
- **Cocoa butter:** Once obtained, chocolate

liquor is pressed to extract the fat (cocoa butter) and separate it from the dry extract. Cocoa butter is the 'spine' of chocolate, since its proper crystallisation determines whether chocolates (couvertures) have adequate densities and melting points. We would recommend melting cocoa butter at 55°C (it begins melting at 35°C) to achieve proper de-crystallisation. Cocoa butter is used to coat with an air pistol – mixed with chocolate in greater or lesser quantity – chocolate bonbon moulds, desserts, cakes and artistic pieces, or in pure form for moulds and marzipan figurines.

- **Cocoa powder:** Two products are extracted from pressed chocolate liquor: cocoa butter in liquid form, and dry matter, which is ground and refined to make cocoa powder. The quality of cocoa powder is a function of its finesse, its fat content, the quantity of impurities it contains, its colour and its flavour. It is very important to store it in a dry place and in an airtight container.

The why and how of tempering

As already mentioned, cocoa butter is a vital component of chocolate, since the final result depends on its good crystallisation. It determines good hardness, balance, texture and shine, and it prevents excessive hardening, whitening and the formation of beads of oil on the surface.

When we melt chocolate, the cocoa butter melts and its particles separate. To achieve a perfect result we must re-bond them by cooling the chocolate, i.e. re-crystallising the cocoa butter.

Tempering allows us to manipulate chocolate and combine it with other ingredients or make artistic pieces that, when re-crystallised, regain the texture and consistency of the chocolate before it was melted.

To sum up, tempering is the de-crystallisation and subsequent crystallisation of cocoa butter.

This is done by melting dark couverture at 55°C, then cooling two-thirds of it to 27°C, adding the rest, which we have kept warm, mixing together and raising the temperature to 31–33°C.

Tempering chocolate

The tempering curve

- **Dark couverture:** melt at 55°C, cool to 27°C, maintain at 31–33°C.
- **Milk couverture:** melt at 45°C, cool to 26°C, maintain at 28–30°C.
- **White chocolate:** melt at 40°C, cool to 25°C, maintain at 28°C.

The curve temperatures can vary + or − 1°C, depending on the brand of couverture and its cocoa content. It is a good idea to read the specification in the couverture packaging, as this will usually indicate adequate temperatures for each type.

What you need to know about tempering

- Melting the couverture in the drying oven is the best way to ensure complete dissolution of the crystals, but in a restaurant this is not always possible and a microwave can be used instead.
- There are tempering machines available that facilitate this process, but as we rarely have them in our kitchens, I have chosen to describe the classic manual method.

The tempering process

1 Melt the dark couverture in a drying oven at 55°C overnight (8–12 hours).
2 Pour two-thirds of the melted chocolate onto a marble and cool, working it with a spatula until it reaches 27°C.
3 Work the chocolate with adequate utensils and with a slow, continuous motion to avoid the incorporation of air.
4 Once at 27°C, pour into the melted chocolate, which has been kept warm, and mix until it reaches 31–33°C. If it does not reach this temperature, it can be heated quickly in the microwave or more hot melted chocolate can be added. Use a thermometer to regulate temperatures.
5 From this moment on, maintain the chocolate at 31–33°C for as long as you are using it.

There is more on tempering in the chocolate recipes section, on pages 437–440.

What you need to know about chocolate

- Its main enemies are humidity, water and quick changes in temperature.
- The ideal room temperature for working with chocolate is 18°C with 60 per cent humidity.
- Chocolate products should be stored in dry places at 15–16°C and 50 per cent humidity.
- Chocolate absorbs all odours and should therefore be stored well covered.
- The higher its fat content, the faster it melts in your mouth.
- Good chocolate is characterised by its good flavour, smoothness and crunch.
- Adding specific quantities of water or liqueur will fix the chocolate at the desired texture.
- In tempering, it is essential to check temperature with a thermometer and to perform the 'paper test'. This is done by dipping a piece of paper in the tempered chocolate. The tempering is optimal if, in about 2 minutes, it has crystallised with a flawless, uniform shine and without stains or fat drops on the surface.
- A glossy surface is a sign of good tempering.

Ice cream

Regulations governing ice cream making

Any ice cream sold must comply with the following compositional standards.

- It must contain not less than 5 per cent fat and not less than 2.5 per cent milk protein (not necessary in natural proportions).
- It must conform to the Dairy Product Regulations 1995.

For further information contact the Ice cream Alliance (see www.ice-cream.org).

After heat treatment according to the Dairy Product Regulations, the mixture is reduced to 7.1°C within 1½ hours and kept at this temperature until the freezing process begins. Ice cream needs this treatment so as to kill harmful bacteria. Freezing without correct heat treatment does not kill bacteria, it allows them to remain dormant. The storage

temperature for ice cream should not exceed
$-2°C$.

The ice cream making process

1 **Weighing:** the requisite in our profession is
weighing ingredients precisely in order to
ensure optimum results and, what is more
difficult, regularity and consistency.

2 **Pasteurisation:** without a doubt this is a
vital stage in making ice cream. Its primary
function is to minimise bacterial
contamination by heating the mixture of
ingredients to 85°C, then quickly cooling it
to 4°C.

3 **Homogenisation:** high pressure is applied
to cause the explosion of fats, facilitating
their dissolution. This process makes ice
cream more homogenous, creamier,
smoother and much lighter. It is not usually
done for home-made ice cream.

4 **Ripening:** this basic but optional stage
refines flavour, further develops aromas and
improves texture. This occurs during a rest
period (4–24 hours), which gives the
stabilisers and proteins time to act,
improving the overall structure of the ice
cream. This has the same effect on a crème
anglaise, which is much better the day after
it is made than it is on the same day.

5 **Churning:** here, the mixture is frozen while
air is simultaneously incorporated. The ice
cream is removed from the machine at
about 10°C.

Functions and approximate percentages of the main components of ice cream

- Sucrose (common sugar) not only sweetens
ice cream, but its solids also give it body.
An ice cream that contains only sucrose
(not recommended) has a higher freezing
point.
- The optimum sugar percentage of ice cream
is between 15 and 20 per cent.
- Ice cream that contains dextrose has a lower
freezing point, and better taste and texture.
- As much as 50 per cent of the sucrose can
be substituted with other sweeteners, but
the recommended amount is 25 per cent.
- Glucose improves smoothness and prevents
the crystallisation of sucrose.
- The quantity of glucose used should be
between 25 and 30 per cent of the sucrose
by weight.
- Atomised glucose is more water absorbent.
- The quantity of dextrose used should be
between 6 and 25 per cent of the
substituted sucrose (by weight).
- If we use inverted sugar in ice cream, it
lowers the freezing point.
- Inverted sugar improves texture and delays
crystallisation.
- The quantity of inverted sugar used should
be a maximum of 33 per cent of the sucrose
by weight. It has a high sweetening
coefficient and gives the mix a low freezing
point.
- Honey has more or less the same properties
as inverted sugar.
- The purpose of cream in ice cream is to
improve creaminess and taste.
- Egg yolks act as stabilisers for ice cream
due to the lecithin they contain – that is,
they facilitate the emulsion of fats in water.
- Egg yolks improve the texture and viscosity
of ice cream.
- The purpose of stabilisers is to prevent
crystal formation by absorbing the water
contained in ice cream and making a stable
gel.
- The quantity of stabilisers in ice cream
should be between 3 and 5 g per kg of mix,
with a maximum of 10 g.
- Stabilisers promote air absorption.

What you need to know about ice cream

- Maintaining hygiene with respect to materials, personnel, the kitchen and the pastry shop is essential while making ice cream.
- An excess of stabilisers in ice cream will make it sticky.
- Stabilisers should always be mixed with sugar before adding, to avoid lumps.
- Stabilisers should be added at 45°C, which is when they begin to act.
- Cold stabilisers have no effect on the mix, so the temperature must be raised to 85°C.
- Ice cream should be allowed to 'ripen' for 4–24 hours. This is a vital step that helps improve its properties.
- Ice cream should be cooled quickly to 4°C, because rapid micro-organism proliferation occurs between 20°C and 55°C.

Sugar syrups

BAUMÉ	DENSITY	BAUMÉ	DENSITY	BAUMÉ	DENSITY	BAUMÉ	DENSITY
5	= 1.0359	13	= 1.0989	21	= 1.1699	29	= 1.2515
6	= 1.0434	14	= 1.1074	22	= 1.1799	30	= 1.2624
7	= 1.0509	15	= 1.1159	23	= 1.1896	31	= 1.2736
8	= 1.0587	16	= 1.1247	24	= 1.1995	32	= 1.2850
9	= 1.0665	17	= 1.1335	25	= 1.2095	33	= 1.2964
10	= 1.0745	18	= 1.1425	26	= 1.2197	34	= 1.3082
11	= 1.0825	19	= 1.1515	27	= 1.2301	35	= 1.3199
12	= 1.0907	20	= 1.1609	28	= 1.2407	36	= 1.3319

For many pastry dishes – for example, ice cream and sorbets – sugar syrups of a definite density are required. This density is measured by a hydrometer known as a saccharometer. The saccharometer may be calibrated in either brix or degrees baumé. The instrument is a hollow glass tube sealed at each end. One end is weighted with lead shot so that when it is placed in the solution it floats upright. The scale marked in either brix or baumé indicates the depth at which the tube floats. This is influenced by the density of the sugar, which in turn is controlled by the ratio of sugar to water used for the solution. The instrument thus measures the amount of sugar in the solution.

Sorbets

Sorbets belong to the ice cream family; they are a mixture of water, sucrose, atomised glucose, stabiliser, fruit juice, fruit pulp or liqueurs.

What you need to know about sorbet

- Sorbet is always more refreshing and easier to digest than ice cream.
- Fruit for sorbets must always be of a high quality and perfectly ripe.
- The percentage of fruit used in sorbet varies according to the type of fruit, its acidity and the quality desired.

- The percentage of sugar is a function of the type of fruit used.
- The minimum sugar content in sorbet is about 13 per cent.
- As far as ripening is concerned, the syrup should be left to rest for 4–24 hours and never mixed with the fruit because its acidity would damage the stabiliser. (See the section on 'Sugar syrups'.)
- Stabiliser is added in the same way as for ice cream.
- Sorbets are not to be confused with granitas, which are semi-solid.

Stabilisers

For what do we use gelling substances?

Within the realm of stabilisers are gelling substances, thickeners and emulsifiers. These are products we use regularly, each with its own specific function; but their main purpose is to retain water to make a gel. The case of ice cream is the most obvious, in which they are used to prevent ice crystal formation. They are also used to stabilise the emulsion, increase the viscosity of the mix and to give us a smoother product that is more resistant to melting. There are many stabilising substances, both natural and artificial.

Edible gelatine

Edible gelatine is extracted from animals' bones (pork and veal). Sold in sheets of 2 g, it is easy to precisely control the amount used and manipulate it. The gelatine sheets must always be washed thoroughly with abundant cold water to remove impurities and any remaining odours. They must then be drained before use.

Gelatine sheets melt at 40°C and should be melted in a little of the liquid from the recipe before adding it to the base preparation.

Pectin

Pectin is another commonly used gelling substance because of its great absorption capacity. It comes from citrus peel (orange, lemon, etc.), though all fruits contain some pectin in their peel.

It is a good idea to always mix pectin with sugar before adding it to the rest of the ingredients.

Agar-agar

Agar-agar is a gelatinous marine algae found in Asia. It is sold in whole or powdered form and has a great absorption capacity. It dissolves very easily and, in addition to gelling, adds elasticity and resists heat (a reversible property). Suitable for vegetarian diets.

Other stabilisers

- **Carob gum** comes from the seeds of the carob tree, makes sorbets creamier and improves heat resistance.
- **Guar gum** and **carrageen** are, like agar-agar, extracted from marine algae and are some of many other existing gelling substances available, but they are less often used.

Quality requirements of fruit

Fresh fruit used for desserts and in pastry work should be:

- Whole and of fresh appearance. (For maximum flavour the fruit must be ripe but not overripe.)
- Firm, according to the type and variety.
- Clean, free from traces of pesticides and fungicides.
- Free from external moisture.
- Free from any unpleasant foreign smell or taste.
- Free from pests or disease.
- Sufficiently mature. It must be capable of

being handled and travelling without damage.

- Free of any defects characteristic of the variety in shape, size and colour.
- Free of bruising or any other damage due to weather conditions.

Batters and whisked sponges

Batters and sponges allow us to make a large assortment of desserts and cakes. Basically, they are a mix of eggs, sugar, flour and the air incorporated when these are beaten. Certain other raw materials can be combined – for example, almonds, hazelnuts, walnuts, chocolate, butter, fruit, ginger, anise, coffee and vanilla.

Sponge cakes

When preparing light batters, specifically for sponge cakes, the aim is to achieve a spongy, honeycombed effect. This goal is reached when the eggs are beaten, which causes small air bubbles to form. These are held in place by the fat in the eggs while other ingredients are added.

Once in the oven, these bubbles expand and increase the volume of the batter. Then, after some time in the oven, the egg congeals because of the heat, giving the batter the desired consistency.

There are two methods for making sponge cakes: direct and indirect. In the direct process, whole eggs are beaten. In the indirect one, yolks and whites are beaten separately; this yields a lighter sponge cake but makes it less dense and elastic.

What you need to know about sponge cakes

- You should never add flour or ground dry ingredients to a batter until the end because they impede the air absorption in the first beating stage.
- When making sponge cakes, we must always sift the dry ingredients (flour, cocoa powder, ground nuts, etc.) to avoid clumping.
- Mix in the flour as quickly and delicately as possible, because a rough addition of dry ingredients acts like a weight on the primary batter and can remove part of the air already absorbed.
- Flours used in sponge cakes are low in gluten content. In certain sponge cakes, a portion of the flour can be left out and substituted with cornstarch. This yields a softer and more aerated batter.
- The eggs used in sponge cake batters should be fresh and at room temperature so that they take in air faster.
- Adding separately beaten egg whites produces a lighter and fluffier sponge cake.
- Once sponge cake batters are beaten and poured into moulds or baking trays, they should be baked as soon as possible. Otherwise, the batter loses volume.

Puff pastry

Puff pastry is one of the most interesting creations of our profession. It brings many tastes and textures to our products. It is a dough with a centuries old origin. Basically, it consists of making layers by folding a flour paste and a fat of the same texture.

Its applications are infinite, as much in patisserie as in cooking. Its exquisite texture, soft and crunchy, is a real pleasure to the palate, and it can be combined with all types of food in sweet and savoury dishes. One of the differences of making it is in the fat used. There is no comparison between the taste and texture of a puff pastry made with butter and one made with any other fat.

When the flour paste and the fat are laid in successive folds and rolled between each turn, rather than kneaded, the two elements do not bind completely. The fat forms a separating layer which, when cooked, retains the steam generated by the water in the dough and produces the layer separation effect. The flour paste, which includes part of the fat, becomes crunchy and takes on a nice golden tone rather than becoming hard and dry.

PASTES AND DOUGHS

476 Savoury flan paste

Makes 500 g, 3 x 15 cm tarts

flour	250 g
sugar	10 g
salt	5 g
water	40 ml
butter	125 g
egg	1

1 Crumb the dry ingredients together; add the rest of the ingredients to gently form a dough.

2 Clingfilm and leave to rest in the refrigerator for several hours before using.

477 Sablé paste

egg	1
caster sugar	75 g
butter or margarine	150 g
soft flour	200 g
pinch of salt	
ground almonds	75 g

1 Lightly cream the egg and sugar without over-softening.

2 Lightly mix in the butter; do not over-soften.

3 Incorporate sieved flour, salt and the ground almonds.

4 Mix lightly to a smooth paste.

5 Rest in refrigerator before use.

Note: Alternatively, 50 per cent wholemeal and 50 per cent white flour may be used, or 70 per cent wholemeal and 30 per cent white flour.

Sablé paste may be used for petits fours, pastries and as a base for other desserts.

478 Strawberry cream biscuits (strawberry sablé)

	4 portions	10 portions
sablé paste	200 g	500 g
whipped cream	125 ml	300 ml
ripe strawberries, washed and sliced	200–300 g	500–750 g
strawberry sauce	125 ml	300 ml
icing sugar		

1 Pin out the sablé paste, ¼ cm thick.

2 Cut into rounds, 8 cm diameter, and bake in a cool oven (approximately 160°C) until light golden brown.

3 When cooked, remove from baking sheet on to a cooling grid.

4 Place a layer of cream on to half the biscuits, then a layer of strawberries, a second layer of cream and top with the remaining biscuits.

5 Dust with icing sugar and serve with the strawberry sauce.

Note: The biscuits may be decorated with rosettes of whipped cream, half a strawberry and a deep-fried mint leaf.

479 Raspberry cream biscuits (raspberry sablé)

As recipe 478 but substitute raspberries for strawberries, keeping the raspberries whole.

Note: If required, the fruit may be macerated (after slicing) in a little caster sugar and a suitable liqueur, e.g. Grand Marnier, Cointreau.

These sweets can also be made up in two layers using three biscuits instead of two.

480 Tempura

Makes 260 g

Flour	140 g
Cornflour	40 g
baking powder	20 g
egg	1
water (sparkling)	

1 Combine all the ingredients to form a smooth mixture.

2 This mix will last for 6–8 hours maximum.

Uses

Deep-frying fruits and vegetables.

481 Crêpes

Makes 45 25 cm pancakes

flour	125 g
caster sugar	15 g
pinch of salt	
eggs	2
milk, boiled and cooled	325 ml
clarified butter, warm	15 g
double cream	100 ml

For the batter

1 Combine the flour, sugar and salt in a bowl, then add the eggs, mixing well with a balloon whisk.

2 Stir in 200 ml of the milk and the warmed clarified butter to make a smooth batter.

3 Add the cream and the rest of the milk, then leave the batter to rest in a cool place for at least 1 hour before using.

Cooking the pancakes

1 Stir the batter and add your chosen flavouring.

2 Ladle in a little batter and cook the pancake for about 1 minute on each side, tossing it or turning it with a palette knife.

482 Quick puff pastry/flaky pastry

Makes 2¼ kg

plain flour	1 kg
butter (at room temperature – firm but not hard)	1 kg
salt	20 g
iced water	500 ml

1 Place the flour on a work surface, mix in the salt, break the butter into small pieces and add to the flour.

2 Roughly crumb the butter into the flour but at the same time it must not be mixed to a traditional crumb – there must be some fat pieces visible as these will make the sporadic flaky layers.

3 Add the water to the centre of the mix and bring to a dough with the least amount of agitation of the mix to preserve the layering effect achieved through keeping the butter whole.

4 Roll into a rectangle, fold and proceed as for ordinary puff pastry until you have made 2 turns, and then chill for 20 minutes.

7 Then give the chilled pastry two more turns, allow to rest for a further 20 minutes and then it is ready to use.

Note: This method makes it unnecessary to use manufactured (ready prepared) puff pastry which has a waxy taste. This recipe gives a far superior taste.

CREAMS

483 Lemon posset

Makes 725 g, 6 portions

Cream	500 ml
caster sugar	225 g
lemons, juice of	2

1 Bring the cream and sugar to the boil.

2 Simmer for 3 minutes.

3 Add the lemon juice and stir.

4 Pour into moulds and allow to set.

5 May also be served in glasses.

484 Lemon curd

Makes 710 g

egg yolks	148 g
caster sugar	250 g
lemon juice	188 g
pinch of salt	
butter	114 g
lemon zest	8 g

1 Mix the yolks and the sugar together well in a bowl.

2 Add the lemon juice, salt and butter and cook over a bain-marie slowly on a medium heat, not boiling until it has thickened.

3 Remove from the bowl when thick and then allow to cool slightly, then add the lemon zest.

4 Store in an airtight container or well clingfilmed.

Variations

- **Lime curd:** replace lemons for limes. Decrease sugar to 200 g.
- **Passion fruit curd:** use 200 g coulis and seeds (optional) and decrease to 200 g sugar.

485 Crème brûlée

Makes 1530 g, 10 portions

cream	1 litre
vanilla pods (split)	2
eggs	2
egg yolks	8 (160 g)
sugar	250 g

1 Bring the cream and split vanilla pods to the boil.

2 Mix eggs, yolks and sugar together.

3 Pour boiling cream over while stirring.

4 Pass, rest and skim, cool. Pour into suitable dishes.

5 Bake in bain-marie at 150°C until firm.

6 Allow to rest and place in the fridge.

7 Sprinkle with sugar and glaze under salamander or with a blowtorch.

486 Buttercream

Makes approx. 1 kg, to line 2 × 30 cm gâteaux

water	125 ml
caster sugar	350 g
glucose	25 g
egg whites	5
butter, at room temperature	500 g

1 Make the meringue with all the ingredients except the butter, following the recipe for Italian meringue (see recipe 540).

2 When the meringue is almost cold, set the mixer on low speed and beat in the butter, a little at a time.

3 Beat for about 5 minutes, until the mixture is very smooth and homogeneous. The buttercream is now ready to use.

Uses

Filling for gâteaux and pastries.

Note: This will keep well in the fridge for up to a week stored in an airtight container. Before using the buttercream, leave at room temperature for 1 hour and then mix well until smooth.

487 Crème Chantilly

Makes 550 g

whipping cream, well chilled	500 ml
icing sugar or 50 ml sorbet syrup	50 g
vanilla powder or vanilla extract to taste	

1 Combine the well-chilled cream with the sugar or sorbet syrup and vanilla in a chilled mixer bowl and beat at medium speed for 1 or 2 minutes.

2 Increase the speed and beat for 3 or 4 minutes, until the cream begins to thicken.

3 Do not over-beat, or the cream may turn into butter. It should be a little firmer than the ribbon stage.

SPONGES

Light sponges

488 Coffee jaconde sponge

Makes 860 g = 2 sheets, 45 × 60 cm

eggs	260 g
icing sugar	150 g
ground almonds	150 g
flour	40 g
powdered coffee	8 g
melted butter	30 g
egg whites	200 g
cream of tartar	2 g
icing sugar	20 g

1 Whisk the eggs, icing sugar, ground almonds, flour and coffee powder together until light and fluffy (until the powdered coffee has completely dissolved).

2 Add the melted butter, mix in well and remove.

3 Make cold meringue with the egg whites, cream of tartar and icing sugar.

4 Fold into the base mix and spread into sheets.

5 Bake at 200°C in deck oven.

Uses

Jaconde sponge is used for gâteaux, to line mousses, charlottes, etc.

489 Othello sponge

Makes 645 g

egg yolks	6
lemon, zest of	1
caster sugar	60 g
egg whites	8
sugar	60 g
cornflour	105 g

1 Whisk up the yolks, zest and caster sugar into a cold sabayon.

2 Whisk up the whites until fully peaked, add the sugar, mix, then add the cornflour, mixing.

3 Fold into sabayon and pipe into desired shapes.

4 Bake in deck oven at 180–190°C.

490 Flourless chocolate sponge

Makes approx. 1 kg mass, for 3 × 20 cm cake tins or 2 silicone sheets, full size

egg yolks	11
caster sugar	125 g
cocoa powder	90 g
egg whites	11
sugar	175 g

1 Whisk the yolks and caster sugar until it becomes a sabayon.

2 Fold in the sieved cocoa powder.

3 Make cold meringue with the egg whites and sugar. Fold in.

4 Bake at 180–200°C in deck oven.

Uses

Gâteaux, pastries, lining sweets.

491 Basic sponge

Makes 710 g/1 × 25 cm sponge

whole eggs	6
caster sugar	175 g
flour	175 g
butter, melted	125 g

1 Whisk eggs in machine.

2 Place sugar onto tray with silicone paper, heat in the oven.

3 When warm, pour into whisked eggs.

4 When tripled in volume (nearly white), fold in sieved flour and melted butter.

5 Fill moulds ¾ full.

6 Bake at 180–200°C in deck oven.

Uses

Swiss roll, gâteaux, pastries, lining sweets.

492 Plain Genoese

Makes 995 g/1 × 30 cm sponge

eggs	8
caster sugar	225 g
flour	225 g
melted butter	65 g

1 Whisk the eggs and sugar together to make a sabayon.

2 Slowly fold in the flour then the melted butter.

3 Place in a lined mould and bake in a moderate oven for 15–20 minutes.

493 Chocolate Genoese

Makes 1045 g/1 × 30 cm sponge

eggs	8
caster sugar	225 g
dark chocolate	50 g
flour	175 g
cocoa powder	50 g
melted butter	65 g

1 Whisk the eggs and sugar together to form a sabayon, then incorporate the melted chocolate.

2 Slowly fold in the flour and cocoa powder, followed by the melted butter, place in a lined mould and bake in a moderate oven for 15–20 minutes.

Uses

Gâteaux, pastries.

494 Gâteau japonaise

	6–8 portions
egg whites	10
caster sugar	400 g
ground almonds	200 g
cornflour	25 g
praline buttercream	200 g
chocolate fondant	50 g

1 Beat the whites to full peak and whisk in 100 g of sugar.

2 Carefully fold in the almonds, sugar and cornflour, well sifted together.

3 Pipe the mixture on to baking sheets lined with rice paper or silicone paper in circles of about 20–22 cm diameter using a 1 cm plain tube.

4 Dust with icing sugar and cook in a very cool oven at approximately 140–150°C for approximately 1 hour, until a light biscuit colour and crisp.

5 Remove silicone paper or, if using rice paper, leave on the rounds but trim the edges. Allow to cool.

6 Trim all rounds to the same size with the aid of a suitable round flan ring, and pass the trimmings through a sieve.

7 Sandwich 2 or 4 rounds together with praline buttercream, the bottom layer flat surface up and the top layer also.

8 Spread the top and sides with praline buttercream.

9 Cover the top trellis fashion. Pipe a disc of chocolate fondant in the centre.

Boiled buttercream (praline flavour)

eggs	125 ml
icing sugar	50 g
granulated or cube sugar	300 g
water	100 g
glucose	50 g
unsalted butter	400 g

1 Beat eggs and icing sugar until ribbon stage (sponge).

2 Boil granulated or cube sugar with water and glucose to 118°C.

3 Gradually add the sugar at 118°C to the eggs and icing sugar at ribbon stage, whisk continuously and allow to cool to 26°C.

4 Gradually add the unsalted butter, while continuing to whisk, until a smooth cream is obtained.

5 Mix with praline to make praline buttercream as required.

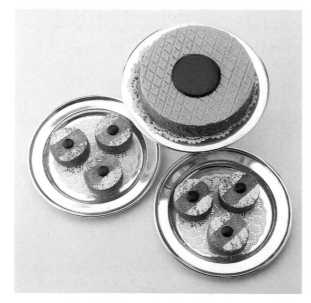

495 Lucerne fruit and pastry cream

	10 portions
Plain russe	
egg yolks	8
caster sugar	250 g
cornflour	25 g
milk	700 ml
soaked gelatine	6 g
Sponge	
soft flour	60 g
caster sugar	75 g
eggs	3
Filling	
diced, cooked apple, sprinkled with lemon juice	200 g
seedless raisins, boiled, cooled and soaked in rum	50 g
whipped cream	250 g

1 Make a plain russe: mix together the egg yolks, sugar and cornflour. Boil the milk, add to the egg yolks and continue to stir for 1 minute. Bring back to the boil.

2 Add the soaked gelatine and strain through a fine strainer.

3 Make the sponge as for recipe 567 stages 1–4. Pour into a lined swiss roll tin and bake at 230–250°C for approximately 3–4 minutes.

4 Allow the sponge to cool and use to line a half pudding sleeve.

5 Prepare the filling: add the apple and raisins to the cream, and fold in carefully 40 g of plain russe on setting point.

6 Place this mixture into the prepared pudding sleeve lined with sponge.

7 Set in the refrigerator for 3–4 hours.

8 Turn out, dust with icing sugar and mark a trellis with hot pokers to caramelise the sugar.

9 Decorate with whipped cream along the top in a rope fashion. This may be served on individual plates with a suitable sauce, e.g. raspberry or orange, or whole on a sweet trolley.

Note: Other fruits may also be used, e.g. pears, raspberries, strawberries, peaches, apricots, kiwis.

Heavy sponges

496 Frangipane 1

Makes 1175 g

caster sugar	250 g
butter	250 g
eggs	6
ground almonds	250 g
flour	65 g
lemons, zest of	2

1 Cream the sugar and butter until light and fluffy.

2 Add the eggs slowly. (If splitting/curdling occurs, add a little heat around the side of the bowl – this may be due to the temperature of the eggs being too cold and re-firming the butter, thus not allowing full homogenisation of the total mass).

3 Add the ground almonds, flour and lemon zest. Mix until combined.

4 Store in an airtight container for up to 5 days.

Uses

Flans, tartlets and tranches.

497 Frangipane 2

Makes approx. 600 g

milk	250 ml
natural vanilla essence or pod	
eggs	2
caster sugar or brown sugar	100 g
strong or wholemeal flour	25 g
butter or margarine	100 g
ground almonds	100 g
rum	1 tbsp

1 Boil the milk and vanilla in a saucepan.

2 In a basin, mix together the eggs, sugar and flour, whisk in the boiling milk, return to the boil, then allow to cool.

3 Cream the butter or margarine and mix in with the pastry cream, ground almonds and rum. Use as required – for filling gâteaux, hot sweets, etc.

498 Pound cake

Makes 1012 g/2 cakes, each 15 cm × 5 cm × 8 cm

Butter	250 g
vanilla, 1 pod, scraped	
pinch salt	
caster sugar	250 g
eggs	250 g
flour	250 g
baking powder	12 g

1 Whisk the butter, vanilla, salt and sugar until white.

2 Slowly add the eggs, fold in the sifted flour and baking powder.

3 Place in lined and greased moulds and bake at 180°C for 35 minutes.

499 Muffins

Makes 850 g/22 muffins

eggs	2
milk	230 ml
butter – melted	115 g
caster sugar	90 g
pinch of salt	
soft flour	290 g
baking powder	5 g

1 Mix the eggs, milk, butter, sugar and salt together.

2 Sift the flour and baking powder onto the wet mix and bring together gently.

3 Allow to rest in the refrigerator before adding flavours (see below).

4 Pipe into muffin trays and bake at 210°C for 25 minutes.

5 Turn out onto wire racks to cool.

Note: A variety of flavours can be incorporated into this recipe; the following are only examples and should be incorporated once the mix has rested in the fridge.

- Apricot and cinnamon: 50 g dried apricots, chopped; 5 g cinnamon.
- Banana and coconut: 100 g mashed banana; 40 g dried coconut.
- Blueberry and pecan: 50 g blueberries; 50 g pecans, chopped.
- Choc-chip and orange: 80 g chocolate chips; zest of 3 oranges.

500 Madeira cake

Makes 1730 g/3 small cake tins (15 cm × 5 cm × 8 cm)

butter	455 g
caster sugar	340 g
eggs	300 g
flour	340 g
lemon, zest of	1
milk	285 ml

1 Beat the butter, add the sugar and mix well, add the eggs one at a time with a spoonful of the flour and the lemon zest.

2 Beat well and add the remaining flour and then add the milk. Pour into lined and greased moulds and cook at 180°C for about an hour. (The mix will be quite runny.)

501 Banana cake

Makes 2 cakes (15 cm × 5 cm × 8 cm)

bananas	910 g
caster sugar	910 g
baking powder	43 g
eggs	8
vegetable oil	225 g
melted butter	285 g
flour	910 g
pinch salt	

1 Mix the bananas, sugar and baking powder to a cream.

2 Add the eggs, oil and butter.

3 Fold in the flour and salt, place in a greased tin in the oven at 170°C for 45 minutes.

YEAST PRODUCTS

Breads

502 Brioche

Makes approx. 20

milk	125 ml
yeast	25 g
strong flour	450 g
caster sugar	25 g
pinch of salt	
butter or margarine	50 g
eggs	4
malt extract	2 g
zest of lemon	
butter or margarine, softened	150 g

1 Warm the milk to 26°C, disperse the yeast in the milk, add a little flour and all the sugar. Sprinkle a little flour on the surface.

2 Stand in a basin of warm water covered with a damp cloth for 15 minutes to ferment.

3 Take the rest of the flour, salt and the butter or margarine, rub together well.

4 Make a well and add the eggs, malt, lemon zest and the ferment, when it has broken through the surface flour.

5 Mix to a smooth dough.

6 Place on a machine with a dough hook and add 150 g of the softened butter or margarine on low speed.

7 When all the butter or margarine has been incorporated, turn out of the bowl, cover with a damp cloth and allow to prove in a warm place for approximately 1 hour.

8 Knock back the dough and place it in the refrigerator until ready for use.

9 Divide into approximately 50 g pieces, mould into a brioche shape (i.e. small cottage loaf shapes) and place into deep individual fluted moulds that have been well greased.

10 Eggwash, prove and bake at approximately 230°C for around 10 minutes.

503 'The fermente'

This word can be used to describe many variations of a piece of dough that is added to the main bread as an ingredient to help add flavour, improve the crust, stabilise the growth of carbonic gas caused by the sugars and the flour, and allow the baker to reduce the yeast dramatically depending on the strength of the fermente, which will in turn reduce its staling time. The list of unique properties that this preparation offers is absolutely endless and all good bakers or chefs who are serious about making their own bread, should have a fermente. In some cases, famous bakeries (like Poulin, for example) have fermente recipes that have been passed down from generation to generation, some are many hundreds of years old.

There are various methods to achieve a fermente – for example, retaining some of the previous dough and saving it for the next day; this method tends to be somewhat diluted as you are adding only 10 per cent from the day before. The best method to use is one that is geared purposely to bread making – like the recipe below. This does, however, require some maintenance as it will need to be 'fed' every day.

strong flour	250 g
natural low-fat bio yoghurt	250 g
raisins	50 g
yeast	4 g
flour and warm water to be added as per method	

1 Mix all the ingredients together and leave in a warm place for one day.

2 Add a further 100 g flour and 100 ml warm water every day for seven days. Then strain off the raisins, remove them and discard half the mix that is left.

3 Add 100 g flour and 100 ml water again, each day for five days. At this point the mix is ready to use, however the longer it is fed (and we are talking months) the more potent, powerful and flavoursome it will be.

Notes: As the raisins are there to allow the first stages of fermentation, once this has taken place they are no longer required and that is why they are removed.

A word of caution: the mix needs to be fed every day. If you take 500 g out, you need to put 250 g of flour and 250 ml of water back in (basically, if you take 500 g out, you need to replace it with 500 g water and flour, equal quantities).

Temperature is also vital for survival of the mix, as warm temperatures above 20°C make the fermente very active and will deplete its food source (flour/gluten) within the 24-hour time span, meaning that some of the yeast culture will die. Below 11°C it will feed and develop very slowly and therefore not offer the key qualities it should. The ideal temperature is somewhere between these two zones.

Flying starter/Polish

This is a method where some of the flour from the recipe is removed (approx. 30 per cent) and mixed with the liquids from the bread recipe a couple of hours before you make the dough.

The time span of 2 hours is the absolute maximum – obviously, this is temperature dependent – but the main principle for adopting this method is that a good proportion of the flour has already been fermented and ripened, therefore a stronger flour can be used to obtain a deeper flavour.

It also prevents what bakers term 'green dough'. This is when the bread loaf or roll sits very flat and a cross-section is almost a semi-circle with a very flat edge. A good, well-fermented dough, when sliced, will yield a very thin foot that the roll loaf will sit on and offer almost a full circle when sliced laterally – the approximate percentage of loaf roll to sit on the floor of the deck oven is between 5 and 10 per cent, and not 30 per cent as in some cases when a green dough occurs.

504 Potato and yoghurt bread

Scale at 550 g, pre-bake 2 loaves

white flour strong (190 g for flying starter and 375 g for the bread)	565 g
milk	75 ml
water	175 ml
natural yoghurt	50 g
yeast	40 g
fermente (see recipe 502)	75 g
warm mashed potato (dry)	150 g
butter	20 g
Trimoline	10 g
improver	5 g
salt	10 g

To make the flying starter

1 Take 190 g of strong white flour, all the liquids, yoghurt and the yeast, mix together well and place in the prover for 30 minutes.

2 Once this is fermented add to the other ingredients (excluding the salt) and place in a mixing bowl.

3 Place on medium/low speed (3½) for 6 minutes, add the salt, mix for a further 2 minutes.

4 Bulk ferment for 30 minutes, shape into a loaf style at 350 g and place in a small tin greased with Trennwax.

5 Prove at 34°C and bake for 40–45 minutes on 240°C (top) 230°C (base) with the vent closed for the first 3 minutes.

505 Pickled walnut and raisin bread

Makes 3 loaves at 580 g per loaf

white flour strong (245 g for flying starter and 130 g for the bread)	375 g
water	450 ml
fermente	100 g
organic molasses	1 tbsp
yeast	90 g
granary flour	625 g
butter	20 g
Trimoline	15 g
improver	10 g
salt	15 g
semi-dried raisins	40 g
pickled walnuts (no juice) or 90 g drained weight	½ jar

To make the flying starter

1 Take 245 g of strong white flour, all the liquids, the fermente, molasses and the yeast, mix well together and place in the prover for 30 minutes.

2 Once this is fermented add to the other ingredients adding the salt, raisins and walnuts last.

3 Place on medium/low speed (3½) for 6 minutes.

4 Shape into a loaf style at 350 g and place in a small tin greased with Trennwax, prove at 34°C for 20 minutes, bake at 240°C (top) 230°C (base) for 40–45 minutes, with the vent closed for the first 3 minutes.

506 Pumpkin seed and onion bloomer

Makes 1.9 kg or 4 loaves at 475 g

strong white flour (245 g for starter and 130 g for the bread)	375 g
water	500 ml
fermente	100 g
yeast	80 g
malt house flour (multi-grain or granary)	625 g
butter	20 g
Trimoline	15 g
caramelised onion	100 g
cooked pumpkin	125 g
poppy seeds	5 g
pumpkin seeds	30 g
sunflower seeds	10 g
improver	10 g
salt	15 g

To make the flying starter

1 Take 245 g of strong white flour, all the liquids, fermente and the yeast, mix well together and place in the prover for 30 minutes.

2 Once this is fermented add to the other ingredients adding the salt last.

3 Place on medium/low speed (3½) for 6 minutes.

4 Bulk ferment for 30 minutes, shape into a cottage style at 475 g, prove at 34°C and bake for 40–45 minutes at 240°C (top) 230°C (base), with the vent closed for the first 3 minutes.

507 Olive sour bread

Makes 2 loaves at 425 g each

yeast	3 g
water	210 ml
salt	8 g
olive oil	37 ml
fermente	135 g
white flour (number 4)	375 g
chopped black olives	80 g

1 Mix the yeast, water, salt, oil and fermente together and fold in the flour and chopped olives.

2 Cover with a damp cloth and leave for 15 minutes at room temperature, then fold in the sides to the centre.

3 Repeat this process twice more, then divide the dough into six, shape, support and cover, and leave in the fridge overnight.

4 Prove and then bake for 30–40 minutes at 230°C (top) and 230°C (bottom), vents closed for the first 3 minutes.

5 Remove. When ready brush with olive oil and sprinkle with salt flakes.

508 Hot cross buns

Makes 1492 g, 30 buns

strong flour	750 g
yeast	50 g
caster sugar	45 g
eggs	3
butter	112 g
salt	7 g
warm water (40°C)	267 ml
mixed peel	75 g
sultanas	75 g
raisins	75 g
mixed spice	22 g
bun spice	10 g

1 Mix the flour, yeast, sugar and eggs to a dough for 10 minutes on speed no. 2.

2 Add the butter and mix until clean. Bulk ferment for 20–25 minutes. Mix in the remainder of the ingredients and scale (30 g mini/afternoon tea; 50 g normal size).

3 Allow to prove at 30°C until soft to the touch, but the outer skin springs back to reform the original shape.

4 Glaze with egg yolk and sugar syrup mix spray.

5 Pipe on crosses with a mixture made up of a thick batter of flour and water.

6 Place in the oven on 210°C for 25–30 minutes (size dependent).

7 Remove, allow to cool slightly and glaze with 50:50 sugar syrup and sprinkle with nibbed sugar.

509 Croissants

Makes approx. 20–24

bread flour	600 g
butter or margarine	100 g
milk	125 ml
water	125 ml
yeast	60 g
egg	125 ml
caster sugar	60 g
salt	10 g
butter, margarine or pastry margarine	200 g

1 Sieve the flour into a suitable basin and rub in the 100 g butter or margarine.

2 Warm the milk and water to 32°C and disperse the yeast in it. Add to the flour and fat.

3 Blend in all the rest of the ingredients except the 200g fat. Mix lightly but do not develop or toughen up the dough.

4 Rest for 10 minutes. Keep covered with a damp cloth or polythene in order to prevent skinning.

5 Roll into the dough, as in making of puff pastry, the 200 g fat and give the dough 4 single turns, resting for 15–20 minutes between turns.

6 When the fat is incorporated, roll out dough to about ½ cm thick and 22 cm wide.

7 Cut down the middle of the dough lengthways. Place one strip on another and cut into triangles approximately 10 cm wide.

8 Roll each triangle up from the widest end, pulling and stretching into a crescent.

9 Prove gently in a little steam for 45 minutes until at least double in size. Eggwash carefully. Then bake at approximately 230°C for 20–25 minutes.

Note: Double baking sheets may be required if the oven gives out a fierce bottom heat.

Making croissants

510 Blinis

Makes 535 g, 20 pieces

Leavening

lukewarm milk	250 ml
fresh yeast	15 g
plain or wholemeal flour	25 g

Batter

plain or wholemeal flour	125 g
eggs, separated	2
small pinch salt	

1 In a bowl, whisk together the lukewarm milk and yeast, then add the flour.

2 Cover the bowl with a plate and leave at room temperature (24°C) for 2 hours.

3 For the batter, using a spatula stir in the flour and egg yolks.

4 Cover with a plate and leave at room temperature for 1 hour.

5 Place the egg whites in a bowl, beat well, then add the salt and beat until stiff.

6 Fold them carefully into the batter.

7 The batter is now ready to use.

Notes: Use the batter as soon as possible, and certainly within an hour, or it will ferment and the flavour will be spoilt.

Blinis can be used in a wide variety of applications, e.g. canapés and hors d'oeuvre, as accompaniment to smoked fish and other savoury items, and are traditionally served with caviar and sour cream in Russian cuisine.

Danish pastry dough: producing the layers

Making a selection of Danish pastries

Danish pastries

511 Danish pastry dough

Makes approx. 10–12

medium-strength flour	300 g
salt	3 g
margarine	35 g
milk	100 g
yeast	30 g
egg	75 g
caster sugar	25 g
butter, margarine or pastry margarine	200 g

1 Sieve the flour and salt, rub in the margarine.

2 Warm the milk to 26°C and disperse the yeast in the milk. Add this to the flour.

3 Add the egg and sugar to make into a slack dough. Do *not* toughen by over-working.

4 Fold the fat into the dough, giving it two single turns and one double turn. Rest for 10 minutes between turns.

5 Work the pieces into the desired shapes and eggwash. Prove in a little steam and bake as indicated in the following recipes.

Note: Double baking sheets may be required if the oven gives out a fierce bottom heat.

Croissants, brioche and a selection of Danish pastries including combs, raisin wheels, apricot rounds and envelopes

512 Danish pastries with almond fruit filling

Makes approx. 10–12

Almond fruit filling

raw marzipan (commercial product)	125 g
egg	25 g
melted butter	35 g
apple, chopped	35 g
cake crumbs	50 g
water	50 g
glacé cherries	35 g
currants	35 g
sultanas	35 g
orange, zest and juice	½

1 Soften marzipan with egg and melted butter to a smooth paste.

2 Add the remaining ingredients and mix well.

Triangles

Roll out the dough ½ cm thick, cut into 8 cm squares and place a small amount of almond fruit filling into the centre. Fold over, eggwash. Prove at 29–32°C without steam. Bake at 220°C for approximately 10 minutes. Mask with hot apricot jam and lemon water icing, sprinkle with roasted flaked almonds.

Round buns

Roll out the dough into an oblong ½ cm thick. Spread the surface thinly with almond fruit filling. Roll up as for swiss roll and cut into 1 cm pieces. Place on a lightly greased baking sheet with the cut side up, prove at 20–32°C without steam. Bake at approximately 220°C. Mask with hot apricot jam and water icing, sprinkle with roasted flaked almonds.

nutritional info	kcal
Based on a yield of 12	♥ 1000
1 portion provides:	900
366 kcals/1528 kJ	800
23.3 g fat	700
(of which 12.7 g saturated)	600
35.2 g carbohydrate	500
(of which 15.1 g sugars)	400
5.9 g protein	300
	200
	100
	0

calorie counter

Crescents

Roll out dough ¼ cm thick and cut into 8 cm squares. Pipe almond fruit filling in the centre. Eggwash, fold over and press down. Cut the edge with a knife, making incisions right through, approximately 1 cm apart. Prove at 29–32°C without steam. Bake at approximately 220°C.

Combs/paws

1 Roll out dough (see recipe 510) to approx. 10 cm × 10 cm × ½ cm thick.

2 Pipe copenhagenmusse (see below) or frangipane across the centre of the dough.

3 Moisten the bottom edge with eggwash, fold over and secure.

4 Using a knife, make four cuts and fold to form an arc shape.

5 Place on a lightly greased baking sheet or directly on baking mats. Prove and bake at approximately 200–220°C for approximately 20 minutes. Brush with hot apricot glaze and sprinkle with roasted, flaked almonds.

Copenhagenmusse

granulated sugar	300 g
butter or margarine	300 g
raw marzipan	200 g
nibbed almonds	50 g

1 Mix all ingredients together.

Raisin wheels/rolls

1 Roll out the dough as for Chelsea buns and eggwash the sides (½ cm thick).

2 Lightly spread with cold custard filling and sprinkle generously with raisins.

3 Roll up and cut as for Chelsea buns. Arrange in rows on greased baking sheet or baking mat, eggwash and prove.

4 Bake at approximately 200–220°C for 15–20 minutes.

5 Brush tops with hot apricot glaze and warm white fondant.

Envelopes

1 Roll out the dough ½ cm thick, cut into 10 cm squares and eggwash lightly.

2 Bring the two opposite corners to the centre and seal.

3 Lay the pastries on a greased baking sheet or baking mat, eggwash and prove.

4 Pipe custard filling in the open ends and eggwash again. (Decorate if required with stoned cherries.)

5 Bake at approximately 200–220°C for approximately 15–20 minutes and brush with hot apricot glaze.

Imperial star

1 Roll out the dough ½ cm thick and cut into 10 cm squares.

2 Cut from each corner towards the centre.

3 Eggwash the centre. Fold alternate corners to the centre and seal to form a star.

4 Place on a greased baking sheet or baking mat.

5 Prove and bake at 200°C for 15–20 minutes.

6 Brush with hot apricot glaze and warm white fondant.

513 Danish pastries with custard filling

Makes 10–12 pastries

milk	500 ml
eggs	50 g
caster sugar	60 g
cornflour	40 g
flavour and colour as desired	

1 Boil the milk in a suitable saucepan.

2 Mix the eggs, sugar and cornflour together to a smooth paste.

3 When milk is boiling, add half to the egg paste. Mix well to a smooth consistency.

4 Return to the rest of the milk. Bring back to the boil and add flavour and colour as desired.

Apricot rounds

1 Roll out dough ½ cm thick and cut into rounds of 11 cm. Eggwash the edge.

2 Crimp the edges to form a border.

3 Fill centre with custard filling and top with half an apricot.

4 Place on a baking sheet or a baking mat. Eggwash the edges. Prove and bake at approximately 200–220° C for 15–20 minutes.

5 Brush with hot apricot glaze.

Maultaschen (lemon custard Danish)

1 Roll out the dough ½ cm thick and cut into 10 cm squares.

2 Eggwash and pipe in the centre of each a little lemon-flavoured custard filling (as per recipe above, plus zest and juice of one lemon).

3 Bring the four corners to the centre, seal lightly, eggwash and place on a greased baking sheet.

4 Roll a strip of dough ¼ cm thick and cut into 8 cm strips.

5 Press two strips on to each pastry, crosswise (these will help to retain the shape during cooking and proving).

6 Prove and cook at approximately 200–220°C for about 20 minutes.

7 Brush with hot apricot glaze and warm thin fondant.

Croquante rolls

1 Roll out the dough as for Chelsea buns and eggwash the sides.

2 Spread with cold custard filling and sprinkle generously with fine croquante.

3 Roll up and cut as for Chelsea buns. Arrange in rows in a 2 cm-deep tin. Eggwash the tops and prove.

4 Cook at approximately 200–220°C for 20 minutes.

5 Brush tops with hot apricot glaze and sprinkle with coarse croquante.

Croquante

granulated sugar	200 g
juice of lemon or pinch of cream of tartar	
nibbed almonds	150 g

1 Place sugar and lemon juice or cream of tartar in a suitable pan and stir over a gentle heat until all the sugar has melted.

2 Cook until a pale amber colour.

3 Warm the almonds, stir into the sugar and remove from the heat.

4 Turn out on to an oiled tray and allow to cool.

5 When set, crush into a fine powder with a rolling pin. Pass through a sieve to remove any large particles, and crush and sieve these.

Fruit rings

1 After giving the dough a second turn, sprinkle with washed, chopped dried fruit then give the final turn. Relax.

2 Roll out to ½ cm thick, in a strip approximately 24 cm wide.

3 Cut into 2 cm-wide pieces.

4 Twist each strip fairly tightly then form into a ring.

5 Lay on to a greased baking sheet, eggwash and prove.

6 Fill the centres with custard filling, sprinkle on a few split almonds and cook at approximately 200–220°C for about 20 minutes, then brush with hot apricot glaze.

Hazelnut custards

1 Roll out the dough to ½ cm thick and cut into 7 cm strips.

2 Lay one strip on a greased baking sheet and eggwash the edges.

3 Spread with custard filling. Cover with a strip of dough and eggwash.

4 Sprinkle well with chopped, roasted hazelnuts. Cover with a third strip of dough, seal and cut into portions. (Do not separate the pieces at this stage.)

5 Eggwash, prove and cook at approximately 200–220°C for about 20 minutes.

6 Brush with hot apricot glaze and warm thin fondant, then divide into portions.

514 Burgomeister rolls

1 Roll out the paste ½ cm thick in a large rectangle.

2 Cut out as for croissants, making the triangles longer and narrower at the bases.

3 Eggwash lightly and pipe in the centre a little burgomeistermasse.

4 Roll up the pastries from the base to the point and lay on a greased baking sheet. Do not curve them.

5 Eggwash, prove and cook at approximately 200–220°C for about 20 minutes.

6 Brush with hot apricot glaze and warm thin fondant.

Burgomeistermasse

caster sugar	150 g
butter or margarine	350 g
raw marzipan	400 g

Mix all ingredients but do not aerate.

MOUSSES

515 Basic fruit mousse

Makes 690 g, 9 portions

fruit purée	225 g
egg whites	115 g
caster sugar	100 g
gelatine sheets (bronze)	4
semi-whipped cream	225 g
desired liquor	25 g

1 Bring the fruit purée to just under boiling point.

2 Whip the egg whites to a snow, add the sugar and combine (this offers a softer, less dense meringue finish and homogenises into a mousse).

3 Slowly add the softened gelatine to the warmed fruit purée.

4 Add all the ingredients and pour into the desired moulds.

5 To serve, unmould onto suitable plates, garnish with fresh fruit and a suitable coulis.

516 Mango mousse

Makes 900 g, 15 portions

mango purée	400 g
egg whites	100 g
caster sugar	132 g
leaves of gelatine (soaked)	8
cream	260 g
fresh mango to garnish	

1 Bring the mango purée to just under boiling point.

2 Whip the egg whites to a snow, add the sugar and combine (this offers a softer, less dense meringue finish and homogenises into a mousse).

3 Add the softened gelatine to the warmed purée, slowly add all the ingredients, pour into the desired moulds and allow to set.

4 To serve, unmould onto suitable plates, garnish with fresh mango.

517 Pear mousse

Makes 760 g, 12 portions

The recipe uses powdered egg whites instead of fresh. The principle reason for this – other than hygiene, as the powdered egg white would be pasteurised – is that the less water that is added to a preparation, the more the principle ingredient can be tasted because it is not being diluted by flavourless liquid. The addition of powdered egg whites will still offer the same properties as fresh egg whites, but using the liquid in the pear purée as a re-hydrating medium. The use of powdered egg whites lends itself better to low–medium flavours like that of pear.

leaves of gelatine (soaked)	8
pear purée	500 g
powdered egg whites	25 g
double cream	200 g
Poire William	20 ml

1 Soak the gelatine in cold water.

2 Whip the purée and powdered egg white until triple in volume; semi-whip the double cream.

3 Melt the gelatine in the Poire William and incorporate with the pear meringue.

4 Fold in the whipped cream and pipe into desired moulds. Allow to set.

5 To serve, unmould on to suitable plates, and garnish with suitable fruit and a fresh fruit coulis.

518 Chocolate mousse

	4 portions	10 portions
plain chocolate	100 g	250 g
butter	25 g	60 g
eggs, separated	4	10
caster sugar	100 g	250 g
whipped cream (optional)	125 ml	300 ml

(Before using these recipes read page 135 on *Salmonella* bacteria.)

1 Break the chocolate into small pieces, place in a basin, stand in a bain-marie and allow to melt with the butter.

2 Whisk the egg yolks and sugar until almost white and thoroughly mix in the melted chocolate.

3 Carefully fold in the stiffly beaten egg whites, pour into a suitable dish or individual dishes and refrigerate until set.

4 Decorate with whipped cream if desired.

5 Finish with chocolate run-outs, shapes and a cordon of chocolate sauce.

Note: It is advisable to use pasteurised egg white and yolk.

Roger Serjent

519 Chocolate and orange mousse

Add the lightly grated zest of 2 oranges (5 for 10 portions).

520 Chocolate rum mousse

Add 1–2 tablespoons rum (2½–5 tablespoons for 10 portions).

521 Chocolate brandy mousse

Add 1–2 tablespoons brandy (2½–5 tablespoons for 10 portions).

522 Chocolate and almond mousse

Add 50 g lightly toasted sliced almonds (125 g, for 10 portions).

523 Caramel mousse

Makes 1560 g, 17 portions

leaves gelatine (soaked)	8
sugar	300 g
cream	500 ml
half-whipped cream	750 ml

1 Soften the gelatine in water.

2 Make a direct caramel with the sugar, being careful not to burn.

3 Carefully pour the cream over the caramel and simmer until the caramel has dissolved. Allow to cool, but not get completely cold.

4 Add the gelatine and then carefully fold in the whipped cream and pour into the appropriate moulds.

5 To serve, unmould on to suitable plates and garnish with fresh fruit.

524 Vanilla bavarois

	6–8 portions
gelatine	10 g
eggs, separated	2
caster sugar	50 g
milk, whole or skimmed, flavoured with vanilla	250 ml
whipping or double cream or non-dairy cream	250 ml

(Before using this recipe read page 135 on *Salmonella* bacteria.)

1 If using leaf gelatine, soak in cold water.

2 Cream the yolks and sugar in a bowl until almost white.

3 Whisk in the milk which has been brought to the boil, mix well.

4 Clean the milk saucepan (which should be a thick-bottomed one) and return the mixture to it.

5 Return to a low heat and stir continuously with a wooden spoon until the mixture coats the back of the spoon. The mixture must not boil.

6 Remove from the heat, add the gelatine, stir until dissolved.

7 Pass through a fine strainer into a clean bowl, leave in a cool place, stirring occasionally until almost at setting point.

8 Fold in the lightly beaten cream.

9 Fold in the stiffly beaten whites.

10 Pour the mixture into a mould (which may be very lightly greased with oil).

11 Allow to set in the refrigerator.

ICE CREAM, SORBETS AND FROZEN DESSERTS

525 Ice cream base

Makes 760 g, 15 portions

cream	250 ml
milk	250 ml
egg yolks	100 g
glucose	20 g
Trimoline	40 g
sugar	100 g

1 Bring the cream and milk to the boil. Mix the egg yolks, glucose, Trimoline and sugar until smooth. Pour the cream over egg mix while whisking.

2 Place back on the stove and cook until it coats the back of a spoon. Pass and chill in ice bain-marie and churn as normal.

526 Chocolate ice cream

Makes 13 × 50 g portions

ice cream base	550 ml
plain chocolate in pieces (70 per cent cocoa content)	125 g
chocolate chips, if desired	

1 While ice cream base is hot, add the chocolate pieces and mix until combined.

2 When cooled, churn.

3 When churned, fold in chocolate chips if required.

527 Vanilla ice cream

Makes 35 portions

milk	500 ml
cream	500 ml
vanilla pods (with seeds)	4
bay leaf	1
egg yolks	8
caster sugar	250 g

1 Heat the milk and cream with the vanilla and bay leaf, clingfilm and infuse for 30 minutes. Remove the bay leaf.

2 Pass, add the seeds scraped from the vanilla pods and pour this onto the whipped egg yolks and sugar.

3 Place back on the stove and cook until it coats the back of a spoon. Pass and chill in ice bain-marie and churn as normal.

528 Sorbet syrup

Makes 1650 ml

water	700 g
caster sugar	750 g
glucose	200 g

1 Bring all ingredients to the boil, but do not reduce at all.

2 Use as required at a ratio of 1 kg fruit purée to 600 g syrup

529 Lemon sorbet

Makes 1 litre, 20–25 portions

lemon juice	250 ml
water	250 ml
milk	250 ml
caster sugar	300 g

1 Bring all the ingredients together and heat to dissolve the sugar.

2 Pass, cool and churn.

530 Chocolate sorbet

Makes 450 g, 10 portions

milk	125 ml
water	125 ml
caster sugar	75 g
glucose	25 g
dark chocolate in pieces	100 g

1 Mix all the ingredients together, excluding the chocolate, and boil for 1 minute.

2 Remove from the heat and add the chocolate, emulsify, allow to cool fully then churn.

531 Vanilla sorbet v

Makes 10 portions

water	255 ml
caster sugar	110 g
glucose	25 g
vanilla pod, scraped	1

1 Mix all the ingredients together and bring to the boil. Allow to cool fully.

2 Pass and then churn.

532 Yoghurt sorbet

Makes 400 ml, 10 portions

water	110 ml
caster sugar	100 g
yoghurt	190 ml
vanilla pod, scraped	1

1 Bring the water, sugar and vanilla to the boil, cool and pass.

2 Add the yoghurt and churn.

533 Lime sherbet

Makes 475 ml, 10 portions

water	250 ml
juice and zest from one-third of the fruit	250 ml
milk	250 ml
caster sugar	185 g

1 Bring the water, lime juice and lime zest to the boil with the milk; this will make the mix separate and look like it is curdled – this is normal and should be achieved as the whole essence of a sherbet is a powdery finish on the palate and this can only be achieved by the splitting action.

2 Add the sugar, dissolve and churn.

534 Champagne sorbet

Makes 450 g, 10 portions

water	155 ml
caster sugar	75 ml
orange juice	10 ml
lemon juice	15 ml
champagne	185 ml

1 Bring the water, sugar, orange and lemon juice to the boil.

2 Allow to cool, add the champagne and churn.

535 Parfait

Makes 1750 g, 18 portions

egg yolks	16
caster sugar	300 g
water	625 ml
semi-whipped cream	1 litre

1 Whisk the egg yolks.

2 Mix the sugar and water together and cook to 121°C. Pour slowly on to the whisking yolks.

3 Finally fold in semi-whipped cream and freeze (at this point the flavouring can be added to the base mix in the quantities below).
   - Flavouring (fruit purée, etc): 400 g per 1000 ml of cream in the recipe.
   - Liquor: 100 ml per 1000 ml of cream in the recipe.

4 To serve, the parfait is cut into portions, garnished with fresh fruit and coulis, and finished with whipped cream.

536 Raspberry parfait

Makes 1105 g, 12 portions

egg yolks	10
caster sugar	200 g
raspberry purée	165 g
framboise liqueur	40 ml
semi-whipped cream	400 ml

1 Whisk the egg yolks to ribbon stage.

2 Cook sugar to 121°C and pour slowly onto the whisking yolks.

3 When cool, fold in the purée and alcohol.

4 Finally, fold in the semi-whipped cream and freeze.

5 To serve, cut into portions, garnish with suitable fruit and coulis, and whipped cream.

SAUCES

Sauces in pastry have changed dramatically over the past 15 years and have gone from the classic anglaise, Chantilly and coulis preparations to what we see in modern restaurants today.

One key factor that cements both modern and classic approaches is that both need to work with the principle ingredient. The sauce is an integral part of the dish whether it be pastry or savoury, and must be treated as such and not added to the dish for aesthetic reasons alone.

When preparing a dessert of your own, be open-minded about the sauce or dressing served and what you want this to achieve for you – whether it be the inclusion of salt, spices, vinegar, hot and cold, etc.

537 Chocolate sauce **v**

Makes 1480 g

cocoa powder	225 g
water	570 ml
caster sugar	685 g

1 Mix all the ingredients together in a pan.

2 Bring to the boil, stirring continuously to avoid burning the cocoa powder.

3 Pass, cool and store in the refrigerator.

538 Fruit coulis **v**

Makes 1500 ml

fruit purée	1 litre
caster sugar	500 g

1 Warm the purée.

2 Boil the sugar with a little water to soft-ball stage (121°C).

3 Pour the soft-ball sugar into the warm fruit purée while whisking vigorously.

4 This will then be ready to store.

Note: The reason the soft ball is achieved and mixed with the purée is that this stabilises the fruit and prevents separation once the coulis has been put onto the plate.

539 Rose petal syrup v

Makes 740 ml

water	285 ml
caster sugar	455 g
large fragrant red roses	6
lemon, juice of	1

1 Heat the water and sugar until dissolved.

2 Add the rose petals and lemon juice, boil for 5 minutes, cool, cover and leave for 24 hours at room temperature.

3 Strain and store in an airtight container.

Variation

Lavender syrup: same as above, but substituting 16 heads of lavender or 4 tablespoons of dried lavender.

Uses

These syrups are used to finish sweets.

540 Caramel sauce

Makes 740 ml

caster sugar	100 g
water	80 ml
double cream	500 ml
egg yolks, lightly beaten (optional)	2

1 In a large saucepan, dissolve the sugar with the water over a low heat and bring to boiling point.

2 Wash down the inside of the pan with a pastry brush dipped in cold water to prevent crystals from forming.

3 Cook until the sugar turns to a deep amber colour. Immediately turn off the heat and whisk in the cream.

4 Set the pan back over a high heat and stir the sauce with the whisk. Let it bubble for 2 minutes, then turn off the heat.

5 You can now strain the sauce and use it when cooled, or, for a richer, smoother sauce, pour a little caramel onto the egg yolks, then return the mixture to the pan and heat to 80°C, taking care that it does not boil.

6 Pass the sauce through a conical strainer and keep in a cool place, stirring occasionally to prevent a skin from forming.

541 Chocolate fudge sauce

Makes 16 portions

water	250 ml
golden syrup	60 ml
dark brown sugar	150 g
granulated sugar	50 g
dark cooking chocolate	200 g
condensed milk	350 g
evaporated milk	175 g
vanilla essence	

1 Place the water in a suitable saucepan, add the golden syrup, brown and white sugar, bring to boil and simmer for 3 minutes.

2 Melt the chocolate carefully in a basin over a bain-marie of hot water.

3 Add the chocolate to the sugar and water mix. *Do not boil*.

4 Heat the condensed and evaporated milk gently in a saucepan over a low heat; when warmed to simmering point add to the chocolate mixture.

5 Finish with vanilla essence.

MERINGUES AND SOUFFLÉS

Meringues

542 Italian meringue

Makes 570 g

water	80 ml
caster sugar	360 g
liquid glucose (optional)	30 g
egg whites	6

1 Pour the water into the pan and add the sugar and glucose.

2 Bring to the boil over a medium heat, stirring with a skimmer.

3 Skim the surface and wash down the inside of the pan with a pastry brush dipped in cold water.

4 Increase the heat and put in the sugar thermometer.

5 When the sugar reaches 110°C, begin beating the egg whites in an electric mixer until firm. Keep an eye on the sugar and stop cooking as soon as it reaches 121°C.

6 When the egg whites are firm, set the mixer to its lowest speed and pour in the cooked sugar in a thin, steady stream, keeping it clear of the beaters.

7 Continue to beat at low speed for about 15 minutes, until the mixture becomes tepid (about 30°C). The meringue is now ready to use.

Note: Glucose prevents the formation of sugar crystals, but is not essential.

It is not really possible to make a successful Italian meringue using smaller quantities, but the mixture will keep in an airtight container in the fridge for several days.

543 French meringue

Makes 270 g

egg whites	100 g
icing sugar, sifted	170 g

1 Using an electric mixer or a bowl and whisk, beat the egg whites with half the icing sugar until semi-firm. Add the remaining sugar and beat to obtain a firm, shiny, homogeneous mixture.

2 Pre-heat the oven to 100°C.

3 Pipe the meringue onto the paper or Silpat, using the fluted nozzle to make 18 8 cm-long meringues, or the plain nozzle to pipe 18 5 cm balls.

4 Slide the paper or Silpat onto a baking sheet and cook the meringues in the oven for 1 hour 50 minutes. Leave to cool on the paper at room temperature, then peel off the meringues, place on a wire rack and leave in a dry place.

Note: For chocolate meringues, use only 150 g icing sugar and add 30 g unsweetened cocoa powder for the last minute of whisking.

544 Swiss meringue

Makes 420 g

egg whites	4
icing sugar	300 g

1 Combine the egg whites and icing sugar in the mixing bowl.

2 Stand the bottom of the bowl in a bain-marie set over direct heat.

3 Beat the mixture continuously until it reaches a temperature of about 40°C.

4 Remove the bowl from the bain-marie and continue to beat until the mixture is completely cold.

5 Pre-heat the oven to 120°C.

6 Spoon the mixture onto baking parchment or lightly buttered and floured greaseproof paper, using 2 soup spoons, or use a piping bag fitted with different nozzles to pipe it into various shapes and sizes.

7 Lower the oven temperature to 100°C and cook the meringues for 1 hour 45 minutes.

8 They are ready when both the top and bottom are dry.

Soufflés

As long as you follow the key principles of soufflé making, you should be able to make soufflés successfully from whatever flavourings you prefer without using a recipe; however, this is not to be recommended until you have grasped the basic foundation.

When whipping the egg whites, the bowl and whisk must be free from fat or grease. Indeed, you should avoid all fats when making soufflés as they inhibit the egg proteins and burst the air bubbles. The egg whites and sugar should be whisked to a smooth, stiff peak with small air bubbles – the smaller the air bubbles, the bigger the lift. The purée used to flavour the soufflé should be reasonably thick as this will help support the soufflé while it is cooking.

The mould must be well greased to ensure that the proteins in the egg do not stick to the glaze on the porcelain. Make sure you clean off the excess soufflé mixture from around the rim of the dish as this could cause the soufflé to stick and prevent it from rising evenly. And remember always to put the unbaked soufflé into a hot oven.

545 Soufflé base

Makes 645 g, 10 portions

soft butter, to brush ramekins	
caster sugar	75 g
crème patissière	210 g
fruit purée (double strength) or other flavouring component	120 g
egg whites	240 g

1 Brush soufflé ramekins in an upward direction with soft butter. Fill with caster sugar and coat the inside of the mould evenly. Invert the ramekins and gently tap to remove excess sugar.

2 Mix the crème patissière with the fruit purée/flavour compound until smooth and elastic.

3 Whisk the egg whites until soft peaks form, then add the sugar and continue whipping until firm peaks form.

4 Working quickly, add one-third of the meringue to the crème patissière base and mix the two gently.

5 Fold the rest of the meringue into the mixture and fill the ramekins, ensuring there are no air pockets.

6 Smooth the top of the soufflé with a palette knife and place in a pre-heated oven at 185°C.

7 Bake for 8–10 minutes and serve immediately.

546 Vanilla soufflé

	4 portions	10 portions
butter and caster sugar, to coat soufflé dish		
milk	125 ml	300 ml
natural vanilla or pod		
eggs, separated	4	10
flour	10 g	25 g
caster sugar	50 g	125 g
butter	10 g	25 g

1 Coat the inside of a soufflé case/dish with fresh butter (as thinly as possible).

2 Coat the butter in the soufflé case with caster sugar, tap out surplus.

3 Boil the milk and vanilla in a thick-bottomed pan.

4 Mix half the egg yolks, the flour and sugar to a smooth consistency in a basin.

5 Add the boiling milk to the mixture, stir vigorously until completely mixed.

6 Return this mixture to a *clean* thick-bottomed pan and stir continuously with a wooden spoon over gentle heat until the mixture thickens, then remove from heat.

7 Allow to cool slightly.

8 Add the remaining egg yolks and the butter, mix thoroughly.

9 Stiffly whip the egg whites and *carefully* fold into the mixture, which should be just warm. (An extra egg white can be added for extra lightness.)

10 Place the mixture into the prepared mould and level it off with a palette knife; do not allow it to come above the level of the soufflé case.

11 Place on a baking sheet and cook in a moderately hot oven, approximately 200–230°C, until the soufflé is well risen and is firm to the touch, approximately 15–20 minutes.

12 Remove carefully from oven, dredge with icing sugar and serve at once.

Note: A little egg white powder may be added to the egg white to strengthen the mixture.

547 Grand Marnier soufflé

René Pauvert

	4 portions
egg yolk	1
whole egg	1
sugar	100 g
French flour	75 g
milk	250 ml
vanilla pod, split	¼
egg yolks	5
Soufflé	
egg whites	7
sugar	100 g
biscuit cuillère	4
Grand Marnier	100 ml

1 Whisk the single egg yolk and the egg together, add the sugar and flour.

2 Boil the milk with the vanilla pod.

3 Add the boiled milk to the mixture and return to the heat. Cook until it thickens.

4 Place in a mixer, whisk the lumps out, then add the five egg yolks.

5 Take four soufflé moulds and 'chemise' with soft butter and sugar.

6 Whisk the egg whites with a touch of salt until stiff.

7 Soak the biscuit cuillère in Grand Marnier.

8 Mix some Grand Marnier into the sweet basic.

9 Add a small amount of egg white into the basic, incorporate well, then gently fold the rest of the egg into the mixture.

10 Pour a spoonful of the mixture into the mould, then add the soaked biscuit and then the rest of the mixture up to the rim.

11 Cook for about 14 minutes at 200°C in the oven.

Note: This soufflé could be accompanied with a sauceboat of whipped cream with chocolate chips folded into it.

548 Snow eggs

	4 portions	10 portions
Poaching liquid		
milk, whole or skimmed	500 ml	1¼ litres
caster or unrefined sugar	50 g	125 g
natural vanilla essence or pod		
Meringue		
egg whites	4	10
caster sugar	50 g	125 g
Sauce anglaise		
milk from poaching		
egg yolks	4	10
caster or unrefined sugar	25 g	60 g
Caramel		
granulated or cube sugar	50 g	125 g
water	30 ml	75 ml

1 Place the milk, sugar and vanilla essence in a shallow pan and bring to boil. Draw to side of the stove and simmer.

2 Whisk the egg whites stiffly, add sugar and make meringue.

3 Using two large spoons, drop balls of the meringue into the milk, poach for 3–4 minutes, turn over and poach for another 3–4 minutes. Drain on a cloth.

4 Make the milk up to 500 ml (1¼ litre) and use to prepare a sauce anglaise with the egg yolks and the sugar. Strain and stir until cold, on ice.

5 Place a little sauce anglaise in a glass bowl, or in individual dishes, and place the snow eggs on top.

6 Mask over with sauce anglaise and decorate with a criss-cross of caramel sugar.

E'SPUMAS

The word e'spuma directly translates from Spanish into foam or bubbles, and the e'spuma is created using a classic cream whipper – a stainless steel vessel fitted with a screw top and a non-return valve which you charge with nitrogen dioxide (which constitutes 78 per cent of the air we breathe); this has minimum water solubility therefore it will not affect the product that is being charged. The principle role of this gas, then, is to force the liquid out of the canister under pressure through two nozzles, making the cream more voluminous due to mechanical agitation of the fats. Although this statement may seem quite convoluted it is necessary to explain the mechanics of this machine for the purists among us. However, the simple version is: this canister, once charged, will whip cream the same as a whisk – it is as simple as that! Below are listed the key factors that are essential to a successful preparation.

Cold fat based

- In a litre canister: 750 g is the maximum product to be placed in the canister.
- Depending on the viscosity, 1 or 2 charges can be used – low viscosity 2 charges, high viscosity 1 charge.
- Once the product has been charged, it will need to be treated like any fat-based product likely to be aerated, and not stored at room temperature because the aeration will be reduced dramatically.

Warm fat based

- In a litre canister: 600 g is the maximum product to be placed in the canister.
- Warm products tend to need 2 charges to ensure good aeration.
- 50–55°C is the optimum temperature to hold the canister charged and ready for use. Any hotter and the expansion in the canister will be too great and uncontrollable when the trigger is pressed. Too cold and

the fat molecules will tend to coat the tongue and not give optimum flavour.

Gelatine based

- In a litre canister: 750 g is the maximum product to be placed in the canister.
- Obviously the product will be liquid when it is poured into the canister. It will need to be charged immediately, placed in the fridge and agitated every 10–15 minutes to prevent total setting.
- This preparation will give you a purer flavour as there is little or no fat involved, hence the use of gelatine – as fat coats the tongue, this absence of fat will allow full penetration on the tongue.

Why use e'spumas?

The 'holy grail' boundaries of gastronomy have changed somewhat over the last 20–30 years and will no doubt continue to do so for the next 20–30, but the current approach is 'less volume, more flavour'. By offering more flavours, the dining experience will be heightened; by reducing the volume that is taken, more flavour combinations than previously can be offered – e'spumas are excellent vehicles to achieve such a result.

However, this is a marvel that should be used in slight moderation as too much on one menu will become repetitive to the palate and what was initially your motivation for using them will extinguish advantage from the outset.

549 Hot chocolate e'spuma

Makes 650 g, 20 portions

milk chocolate	300 g
dark chocolate	50 g
white chocolate	100 g
hot water	200 g

1 Melt the three types of chocolate over a bain-marie until at 45°C.

2 Add the hot water and whisk until smooth.

3 Pour mix into an e'spuma gun and charge with two gas bulbs.

4 Place in a bain-marie to keep warm.

550 Thyme and ginger e'spuma

Makes 1350 g

mirabelle plum purée	1 kg
thyme	40 g
ginger	120 g
water	500 g
icing sugar	300 g
gelatine leaves (soaked)	3

1 Bring all ingredients, except the gelatine, to the boil, allow to infuse for 5 minutes before passing.

2 Cool and store in the fridge.

3 Take 600 ml of the base and add three melted gelatine leaves.

4 Pour into an e'spuma gun and charge with two gas bulbs.

5 Chill before using in order to allow the gelatine to set.

551 Chocolate e'spuma – cold

Makes approx. 600 ml, 20 portions

dark chocolate (64 per cent cocoa solids)	150 g
cream	65 g
milk	125 g
icing sugar	30 g
yoghurt	300 g

1 Melt chocolate over a bain-marie.

2 Mix the cream, chocolate, milk and icing sugar together, then add to the melted chocolate.

3 Incorporate the yoghurt and pour into an e'spuma gun.

4 Charge with 2 gas cartridges.

5 Allow to chill before using.

552 Mandarin e'spuma

Makes 925 g, 30 portions

mandarin juice	1 litre
yoghurt	400 ml
single cream	125 ml
icing sugar	150 g

1 Reduce the mandarin juice to 250 ml and allow to cool.

2 Mix all ingredients together and pass.

3 Pour into an e'spuma gun and charge with two gas cartridges.

553 Caramel e'spuma

Makes approx. 600 ml, 20 portions

yoghurt	250 g
cream	50 g
milk	100 g
caramel sauce	166 g
icing sugar	104 g

1 Mix all ingredients together.

2 Pour into an e'spuma gun and charge with two gas cartridges.

TARTS, SLICES AND GÂTEAUX

554 Lemon tart

*Makes 1 flan half-baked blind (200 mm diameter ×
35 mm height)*

eggs	8
caster sugar	200 g
lemons, juice of (approx. 500 ml)	4
cream	265 ml
zest of lemon	1

1 Mix the eggs and sugar together.

2 Add lemon juice and cream.

3 Pass through a conical strainer.

4 Add the lemon zest.

5 Leave to rest, skim before use.

6 Pour this into a flan case.

7 Bake in deck oven at 150°C until set (approx. 1 hour).

555 Marquise

Makes 1.9 kg, 20 portions

bitter chocolate	145 g
soft butter	320 g
cocoa powder	145 g
double cream	515 ml
icing sugar	65 g
caster sugar	285 g
egg yolks	8
single espresso	1

1 Melt the chocolate in a bain-marie.

2 Melt the butter and cocoa in a bain-marie.

3 Whisk the cream and icing sugar to ribbon stage.

4 Whisk the sugar, yolks and espresso together until thick, fold in the chocolate, then the butter mix, then the cream.

5 Line the terrine with clingfilm and cut japonaise sheets (see recipe 494) to fit, then layer up the terrine with the mousse and japonaise. Jaconde sponge can be used as an alternative (see recipe 488). Chill to set.

556 Baked chocolate tart (aero)

Makes 830 g, 1 flan cooked blind (200 mm diameter × 35 mm height)

eggs	3
egg yolks	3
caster sugar	60 g
butter	200 g
chocolate pistoles	300 g

1 Whisk the eggs, yolks and sugar together.

2 Bring butter to the boil, remove and mix in chocolate pistoles until it is all melted.

3 Once sabayon is light and fluffy, fold in chocolate and butter mix.

4 Pour into cooked flan case (baked blind) and place in a deck oven at 150°C until the edge crusts (approx. 5 minutes). Chill.

5 Once set, remove from fridge.

6 Serve at room temperature.

557 Chocolate truffle torte

Makes 1575 g/2 × 30 cm gâteaux

water	150 ml
glucose	75 g
gelatine leaves (soaked)	6
chocolate pistoles	500 g
semi-whipped cream	1000 ml

1 Bring the water and glucose to the boil.

2 Add the soaked gelatine.

3 Mix until dissolved.

4 Add the chocolate pistoles and stir until dissolved.

5 Finally fold in the cream.

558 Biscuit Viennoise

This is now becoming a classical recipe developed in France for almond roulade, cold sweets and gâteaux. This recipe may also be used as a base. Spread the mixture on to small baking sheets and bake at 220°C for 4–6 minutes.

ground almonds	100 g
icing sugar	100 g
flour	80 g
whole egg	120 g
egg yolk	30 g
melted butter	30 g
egg white	180 g
caster sugar	65 g

A suitable-size baking sheet would be 60 cm × 40 cm for a base. This mixture will make two baking sheets.

1 Sieve the ground almonds, icing sugar and flour together well.

2 Add half the beaten whole egg and egg yolk; add the remainder gradually.

3 Add the melted butter.

4 Stiffly beat the egg white and the caster sugar, fold into the above mixture.

5 If required for jaconde base, the mixture will need to be knocked back.

6 Bake at 220°C for 4–6 minutes.

559 Chocolate décor paste

butter or margarine	80 g
icing sugar	80 g
egg whites	2–3
flour	60 g
cocoa powder	20 g

1 Lightly cream the butter and sugar.

2 Add the egg whites one by one, mixing well, being careful not to curdle the mixture.

3 Gently fold in the sifted flour and cocoa powder.

4 Spread on 2 Silpat trays, mark with a comb and allow to freeze.

5 When frozen, spread on the jaconde biscuit mixture and bake at 220–240°C for approximately 3–5 minutes.

Note: These mixtures allow the pastry cook to be both creative and versatile. There is also a variety of specialised equipment available for this work in the form of scrapers, combs, moulds and frames.

Cornstarch and colour may be used as a substitute for cocoa powder.

560 Apple strudel

	4–5 portions	8–10 portions
Paste		
strong flour	100 g	200 g
pinch of salt		
egg	1	1
butter, margarine or oil	12 g	25 g
hot water	40 ml	85 ml
Filling		
cooking apples	500 g	1 kg
breadcrumbs	25 g	50 g
butter, margarine or oil	12 g	25 g
brown sugar	50 g	100 g
sultanas	50 g	100 g
raisins	50 g	100 g
ground almonds	25 g	50 g
nibbed almonds	25 g	50 g
lemon grated, zest and juice of	1	2½
mixed spice	1½ g	3 g
ground cinnamon	1½ g	3 g

1 First, make the paste: sieve together flour and salt and make a well.

2 Place the egg, fat and water in the centre and work until it is a smooth dough.

3 Cover with a damp cloth and relax for 20 minutes.

4 For the filling: peel and core the apples. Cut into thin, small slices and place in a basin.

5 Fry the breadcrumbs (white or brown) in the butter, margarine or oil.

6 Add to the apples and mix well with all the other ingredients.

7 Roll out the dough into a square ¼ cm thick, place on a cloth and brush with melted fat or oil.

8 Stretch the dough on the backs of the hands until it is very thin.

9 Spread the filling on to the paste to within 1 cm from the edge.

10 With the aid of a cloth, roll up tightly and seal the ends.

11 Place on a lightly greased baking sheet and brush with melted fat or oil.

12 Bake in a moderate oven (approximately 190°C) for 35–40 minutes.

13 When baked, dust with icing sugar and serve as required.

Note: Alternatively, the strudel paste may be made with 50 per cent wholemeal and 50 per cent strong flour, or 70 per cent wholemeal and 30 per cent strong flour. With the increased proportion of wholemeal flour a little more water is required to achieve a smooth elastic dough.

Variations

(a) Proceed as for apple strudel, replacing the apples with stoned cherries – fresh, canned or frozen.

(b) Proceed as for apple strudel, but replace 50 per cent of the apples with stoned cherries (fresh, canned or frozen).

Making apple strudel

nutritional info

Using butter
1 portion provides:
1657 kJ/383 kcals
13.5 g fat (of which 4.3 g saturated)
64.1 g carbohydrate (of which 42.7 g sugars)
8 g protein
4.4 g fibre

If 50 per cent wholemeal flour is used for the
pastry, this increases fibre to 5.2 g.

	kcal
	1000
	900
	800
	700
	600
	500
calorie counter	400
	300
	200
	100
	0

561 Tatin of apple

Makes 10 portions

This is the name given to an apple tart that is cooked under a lid of pastry, but then served with the pastry underneath the fruit. This is a delicious dessert in which the taste of caramel is combined with the flavour of the fruit, finished with a crisp pastry base; it was the creation of the Tatin sisters, who ran a hotel-restaurant in Lamotte-Beuvron at the beginning of the last century. Having been made famous by the Tatin sisters the dish was first served at Maxim's in Paris, as a house speciality. It is still served there to this day.

caster sugar	100 g
glucose	10 g
water	200 ml
unsalted butter, diced	100 g
Granny Smith's apples, peeled and cored	7
lemon, juice	½
puff pastry	175 g

1 Cook the sugar, glucose and water in a thick-bottomed copper (bear in mind that the tatin will be cooked in this so it will need to be ovenproof) until it reaches a pale, amber colour, which is pre-caramel.

2 Remove from the heat and add the diced butter.

3 While the butter is melting, cut the apples into eighths, lightly sprinkle with lemon juice and place on top of the caramel/butter.

4 Place in the oven for 25 minutes until the apples are half-cooked and starting to caramelise.

5 Meanwhile, roll out the puff pastry, 3–4 mm thick, and slightly larger than the diameter of the pan.

6 Cover the apples with the pastry and bake for a further 15–20 minutes, until the pastry is golden.

7 Remove from the oven and leave to cool slightly before turning out.

8 Serve with vanilla ice cream or crème fraîche.

562 Swiss apple tart

Makes 8 portions, 1 × 25 cm tart case lined with sweet or short paste

large apples, peeled and grated	4–5
grated nutmeg	¼
cinnamon	4 g
cream	145 ml
eggs	4
sultanas	115 g
lemon, zest and juice of	1
caster sugar, to taste	

1 Mix all the ingredients together.

2 Fill the tart case carefully and bake in the oven on 170°C for 30–40 minutes, checking after 20 minutes.

3 Allow to cool naturally, before portioning and serving.

4 Serve with sauce anglaise flavoured with calvados or fresh cream.

563 Fig tart

Makes 8 portions, 1 × 25 cm tart case lined with sweet or short paste

figs	12
eggs	4
caster sugar	150 g
milk	240 ml
crème fraîche	300 g

1 Pre-heat the oven to 190°C.

2 Cut the figs into quarters down through the point to the base, without cutting right through, leaving the fig intact but opened.

3 Place the figs evenly in the flan case.

4 Mix the remaining ingredients together to form a smooth batter and pour carefully over the figs and into the tart.

5 Place in the oven for 30–35 minutes, checking every 5 minutes after 20 minutes.

6 Remove and allow to cool before serving.

7 Serve with fresh cream or sauce anglaise

564 Prune and almond tart

Makes 8 portions

pitted prunes	200 g
flaked almonds	100 g
Armagnac	100 ml
25 cm blind-baked tart case	1
frangipane (see recipe 596)	300 g

1 Pre-heat the oven to 180°C.

2 Soak the prunes and almonds in the Armagnac, overnight if possible (the longer they are left the more flavour is achieved).

3 Place the prunes and almonds into the tart case – if there is any excess Armagnac left over, pour into the frangipane and mix in.

4 Pipe in the frangipane over the prunes and place in oven for 30–35 minutes, until the top is golden and firm in the centre.

5 Allow to cool before serving.

565 Gâteau St Honoré

	6 portions
puff or short pastry	125 g
choux pastry	125 ml
cube sugar	150 g
water	60 ml
pinch of cream of tartar	
glacé cherries	50 g
crème St Honoré or chibouste	250 ml

1 Roll out the pastry ¼ cm thick and cut out a circle approximately 23 cm in diameter, place on a slightly greased baking sheet.

2 Prick with a fork and eggwash the edge and centre.

3 Pipe on a ring of choux paste, approximately ¾ cm from the edge of the pastry and pipe on a choux bun in the centre, using 1 cm plain tube.

4 On a separate baking sheet, pipe out approximately 16–20 small choux buns.

5 Eggwash the choux ring and buns and cook in a fairly hot oven (approximately 230°C) for about 20–25 minutes.

6 Place the cube sugar, water and cream of tartar into a suitable saucepan and cook to hard crack, 155°C.

7 Dip the buns in hard crack sugar. (This is the traditional finish. Decorate alternatively with half a glacé cherry on one and a diamond of angelica on the other.) As they are dipped and decorated place on the large ring. Make sure the buns match those on either side and that there is an even number.

8 Fill the finished case with rochers of crème St Honoré or chibouste, forming a dome shape in the centre. The finished item may be decorated with spun sugar (recipe 598).

Note: A rocher is a quenelle shape formed by taking a dessert or tablespoon of the mixture, dipping a second spoon in boiling water, drying it and using it while warm to remove the mixture from the first spoon. Alternatively, pipe in the filling using a St Honoré tube.

Crème St Honoré

cube sugar	200 g
eggs, separated	3
milk, whole or skimmed	125 ml
leaf gelatine, soaked and squeezed dry	6 g

1 Boil the sugar with a little water to soft ball stage, 118°C.

2 Whisk the egg whites, pour on the sugar as for Italian meringue.

3 Cook the egg yolks and milk as for sauce anglaise and add the gelatine.

4 Add to the meringue.

Crème chibouste

leaf gelatine	6 g
pastry cream	250 ml
egg whites	5
caster sugar	100 g

1 Add the soaked gelatine to the hot pastry cream.

2 Make a meringue with the egg whites and sugar.

3 Fold in the pastry cream, taking care not to over-mix, and use as required.

Note: The pastry cream may be made from skimmed milk, unrefined sugar and wholemeal flour, or in the traditional way.

566 Sugar-topped choux buns filled with rum-flavoured pastry cream on chocolate sauce (salambos)

	4 portions	10 portions
choux pastry (see below)	125 ml	300 ml
rum-flavoured pastry cream*	250 ml	600 ml
cube sugar	200 g	500 g
water	60 ml	150 ml
pinch of cream of tartar		
chocolate	250 ml	600 ml

* Pastry cream may be made in the traditional way or using skimmed milk, unrefined sugar and wholemeal flour.

1 Pipe large choux buns approximately 4 cm diameter using a 1 cm star tube on a lightly greased baking sheet.

2 Eggwash lightly and bake in a moderately hot oven (approximately 220°C) for approximately 20–25 minutes.

3 When cooked, split, allow to cool and fill with rum-flavoured pastry cream.

4 Place the cube sugar, water and cream of tartar into a suitable saucepan and cook to hard crack (155°C).

5 Dip the tops of the buns in hard crack sugar.

6 Serve individually on plates on a layer of chocolate sauce.

---

nutritional info

1 portion provides:
2776 kJ/664 kcals
21.8 g fat
(of which 12.2 g saturated)
111.9 g carbohydrate
(of which 92.5 g sugars)
12.2 g protein
0.7 g fibre

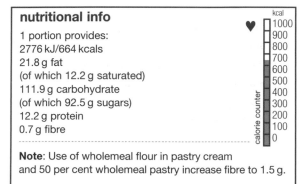

Note: Use of wholemeal flour in pastry cream and 50 per cent wholemeal pastry increase fibre to 1.5 g.

Choux paste

	4 portions	10 portions
water	250 ml	600 ml
pinch of sugar and salt		
butter, margarine or oil	100 g	250 g
flour (strong)	125 g	300 g
eggs	4	10

1 Bring the water, sugar and fat to the boil in a saucepan.

2 Remove from heat.

3 Add the sieved flour and mix in with a wooden spoon.

4 Return to a moderate heat and stir continuously until the mixture leaves the sides of the pan.

5 Remove from the heat and allow to cool.

6 Gradually add the beaten eggs, mixing well.

7 The paste should be of dropping consistency.

Note: 50 per cent, 70 per cent or 100 per cent wholemeal flour may be used.

---

567 Fruit terrine

	4 portions	10 portions
Sponge		
eggs	3	8
caster sugar	85 g	200 g
soft flour	60 g	150 g
Filling		
soft butter	100 g	250 g
icing sugar	100 g	250 g
fine-ground almonds	75 g	180 g
Cointreau	30 ml	75 ml
whipping cream	125 ml	300 ml
kiwi fruit	1	4
strawberries	75 g	180 g
peaches	50 g	125 g

1 Prepare the sponge by whisking the eggs and sugar to ribbon stage over a bain-marie of warm water.

2 Carefully fold in the sifted flour.

3 Pour into a prepared swiss roll tin lined with greasepaper paper and lightly greased.

4 Cook sponge in a hot oven (approximately 220–230°C) for approximately 4 minutes. Turn out on to a wire rack and allow to cool.

5 When cold, cut a layer of sponge to line suitable terrine(s) approximately 8 cm deep and 15–20 cm wide.

6 Place the sponge in the deep freeze to harden for easier handling.

7 Prepare the filling by creaming the butter and the icing sugar on a machine until soft, light and white.

8 Add the ground almonds and the Cointreau and mix well.

9 Carefully fold in the whipping cream, taking care *not to over-mix*.

10 Line suitable terrine(s) with greaseproof or silicone paper.

11 Arrange the layers of thin sponge in the bottom and sides.

12 Place a layer of the filling in the base, on top of the sponge, and arrange pieces of fruit over this.

13 Continue with the filling and the fruit to achieve approximately 3 layers. Finish with a thin layer of sponge.

14 Place the terrine(s) in the refrigerator to set for approximately 3–4 hours before serving.

15 Turn out, remove paper and cut into approximately 1 cm slices.

16 Serve on individual plates with a cordon of fresh raspberry sauce.

PUDDINGS

568 Christmas pudding

Makes 2285 g, 3 puddings

Dry mix	
mixed fruit	300 g
sultanas	100 g
currants	100 g
chopped mixed nuts	65 g
suet	185 g
fresh breadcrumbs	115 g
flour	115 g
brown sugar	185 g
salt	pinch
cinnamon	pinch
powdered ginger	½ tsp
mixed spice	½ tsp
Wet mix	
mixed peel	40 g
glacé cherries, chopped	60 g
orange, juice and zest of	1
lemon, juice and zest of	1
brandy	170 ml
Madeira	170 ml
Port	170 ml
Guinness	1 bottle
Eggs	3

1 Mix the dry mix and the wet mix together and leave overnight to mature. Cook at 100°C, for 5 hours.

2 Leave to cool naturally.

3 To reheat, place the wrapped pudding in the steamer for 40 minutes, allow to cool slightly and serve with brandy butter or sauce, or clotted or fresh cream, warm custard or vanilla ice cream.

4 To flame, heat the brandy in a saucepan, taking care not to heat too much, pour over the warm pudding, retaining a small ladle full; carefully light the ladle of brandy and then pour this onto the Christmas pudding.

569 English trifle

	4 portions	10 portions
milk	500 ml	1¼ litre
vanilla pod *or*	1	2–3
natural vanilla essence	2–3 drops	5–7 drops
eggs *plus* egg yolks *or*	2 (each)	5 (each)
egg yolks	8	20
caster sugar	50 g	125 g
sponge cake	200 g	500 g
raspberry or strawberry jam	150 g	375 g
medium or sweet sherry	60 ml	150 ml
double cream, whipped	250 ml	600 ml
flaked, sliced or nibbed almonds (toasted)	50 g	125 g
glacé cherries	4 or 8	10 or 20

1 Heat the milk with the vanilla pod or vanilla essence, cover with a lid, then remove from heat and stand for 15 minutes. Remove the vanilla pod.

2 Thoroughly whisk the eggs and sugar in a basin.

3 Boil the milk, add a quarter to the eggs, whisking continuously.

4 Add the remainder of the milk and clean the saucepan.

5 Return the eggs and milk to the clean pan and cook over a gentle heat, stirring continuously with a wooden spoon, until the mixture thickens.

6 Immediately remove from the heat. Strain the mixture into a clean basin and allow to cool, stirring occasionally.

7 Spread the sponge cake with jam, cut into small squares and place in a trifle bowl or individual dishes.

8 Sprinkle on the sherry, allow to soak in.

9 Pour the custard over the sponge cake and allow to set.

10 Decorate with whipped cream, almonds and halves of cherries.

Note: 100 g lightly crushed macaroon biscuits can be added with the sponge cake (250 g for 10 portions).

If whipping cream is available, use this in place of double cream as more volume can be achieved.

A layer of fresh soft fruit, e.g. raspberries or sliced strawberries, which may be macerated in a little sugar and Cointreau or Grand Marnier, can be used in place of jam.

The egg custard can be given a chocolate flavour.

The final decoration can include angelica or chocolate – grated, in curls or in piped shapes.

BISCUITS AND CAKES

570 Gingerbread

Makes 725 g/50 portions

flour	455 g
ground ginger	25 g
butter	85 g
baking powder	15 g
sugar	30 g
golden syrup	30 g
milk	85 ml

1 Pre-heat the oven to 170°C.

2 Mix the flour, ginger and butter together with the baking powder.

3 Add the sugar, syrup and the milk, work to a dough and rest in the refrigerator for 24 hours.

4 Roll out on a floured surface to the desired thickness.

5 Cut into the desired shape and bake in the oven for 15–20 minutes.

6 Remove and allow to cool before serving.

571 Cookies – chocolate chip

Makes 805 g, 30 portions

butter	110 g
sugar	100 g
soft brown sugar	90 g
baking powder	5 g
soft flour	160 g
egg	1
chocolate chips	280 g

1 Mix the butter, sugars, baking powder and flour together to form a smooth dough.

2 Add the eggs and bring to one mass.

3 Mix in the chocolate drops, being careful not to over-mix as this will make the cookies tough and hard. Allow to rest for 30 minutes.

4 Pre-heat the oven to 170°C.

5 Roll into small balls, place onto a baking sheet and put in the oven.

6 Bake for 20–25 minutes until golden on the outside but still quite soft in the centre (this is the essence of a true cookie).

7 Allow to cool naturally before serving.

572 Chocolate fudge cake

Makes 3 cakes, mould size 19 cm × 9 cm × 5 cm

chocolate	425 g
eggs	6
melted butter	300 g
golden syrup	120 g
flour	285 g
icing sugar	425 g
cocoa	65 g

1 Melt the chocolate then add the eggs, butter and golden syrup.

2 Mix all dry ingredients together, fold in the chocolate mix then pour into greased baking tray and bake for 30~45 minutes at 180°C.

573 Griottines (cherries) clafoutis

Makes 1750 g, 15 portions

griottines (cherries)	105 (approx.)
Batter 1	
eggs	4
caster sugar	80 g
milk	360 ml
kirsch, from the griottines	4 tsp
flour	80 g
Batter 2	
plain chocolate	400 g
butter	200 g
eggs	4
flour	20 g
cornflour	20 g
caster sugar	70 g

For batter 1

1 In a large bowl, beat the eggs and sugar together until well dissolved, add the milk and kirsch.

2 Sieve in the flour mix well, then strain the batter through a sieve and set aside.

For batter 2

1 Melt the chocolate and butter in a bowl placed over a pan of simmering water on a low heat. Meanwhile, place the eggs in a mixing bowl or a mixer with a whisk attachment and whisk to a thick white foam.

2 Switch the machine to the slowest speed, add both flours and mix for 30–60 seconds. Stir the chocolate and butter together, then use a hand whisk to fold this mixture into the whisked egg mixture, ensuring total incorporation.

To finish

1 Carefully fold the two batters together to make one thick batter, and store.

---

574 Peanut butter cookies

Makes 635 g, 21 cookies

butter	125 g
light-brown sugar	200 g
crunchy peanut butter	125 g
egg	1
vanilla extract	5 ml
flour	125 g

1 Cream the butter, sugar and peanut butter until light and fluffy.

2 Add the egg and vanilla extract slowly (if the mix curdles/splits add heat to recover).

3 Add flour while mixing.

4 Wrap and refrigerate for 30 minutes to rest.

5 Pre-heat the oven to 170°C.

6 Roll into small balls and bake until the edges are golden brown and the centre is still soft – the true essence of a cookie.

7 Allow to cool naturally before serving.

2 Place 110 g into each sur la plat dish with 6–7 cherries and bake for 7–8 minutes until the centre is just cooked.

---

575 Carrot cake

Makes 1485 g, 3 cakes, mould size 19 cm × 9 cm × 5 cm

butter	225 g
demerara sugar	225 g
eggs, separated	4
orange, juice and grated zest of	1
lemon juice	2 tsp
self-raising flour	170 g
baking powder	15 g
fresh ginger, grated	1 tsp
almonds, ground	55 g
walnuts, chopped	140 g
young carrots, peeled and grated	340 g
cream cheese	225 g
honey	2 tsp

1 Pre-heat the oven to 170°C.

2 Cream the butter and sugar.

3 Beat in the yolks and stir in the orange zest and juice and lemon juice.

4 Sift in the flour and baking powder, then the ginger, ground almonds and walnuts.

5 Whisk the egg whites until stiff and fold into the mix with the carrots. Pour into a tin, hollow the centre slightly.

6 Bake for 40 minutes or until the centre is firm and, when a small knife is inserted, it is removed cleanly.

7 Allow to cool naturally.

8 Beat the cheese and honey together for the topping.

9 Spread over the top and it is ready to serve.

CHOCOLATE GOODS AND PETITS FOURS

576 Spraying chocolate

cocoa butter	100 g
chocolate (60–70 per cent)	300 g

1 Melt together the cocoa butter and chocolate over a bain-marie, ensuring that there are no lumps.

2 Place in a lightly warmed chocolate machine and spray.

577 Pumpkin pâté de fruit **v**

Makes 3461g, 150 pieces, mould size 30 cm × 60 cm

pumpkin juice (passed)	1½ litre
caster sugar	1600 g
pectin, slow setting	38 g
glucose	300 g
tartaric acid	23 g

1 Mix the pumpkin the juice and 1450 g of the caster sugar. Bring to the boil.

2 Mix the pectin and the remaining 150 g of sugar together. Mix well. Sprinkle this into the boiling mix.

3 Add the glucose and bring to a constant 106°C.

4 Remove and add the tartaric acid.

5 Whisk well and pour straight into mould (30 cm x 60 cm).

6 Leave to set, then cut into 1.5 cm pieces.

578 Cassis pâté de fruit **v**

Makes 3506 g, 150 pieces, mould size 30 cm × 60 cm

cassis purée	1½ kg
caster sugar	1665 g
pectin, slow setting	30 g
glucose	300 g
tartaric acid	11 g

1 Mix the purée and 1500 g of caster sugar. Bring to the boil.

2 Thoroughly mix the pectin and the remaining 165 g of sugar together. Mix well. Sprinkle this into the boiling mix.

3 Add the glucose and bring to a constant 106°C.

4 Remove and add the tartaric acid.

5 Whisk well and pour straight into mould.

6 Leave to set, then cut into 1.5 cm pieces.

579 Cherry rolls

Makes approx. 40 pieces

soft flour	300 g
butter or margarine	200 g
icing sugar	35 g
natural vanilla essence or pod	
glacé cherries, chopped	100 g

1 Sift the flour, cream the butter and icing sugar, add the flour and vanilla and mix lightly.

2 Fraiser* the paste and add the chopped glacé cherries.

3 Roll into a sausage shape, 2 cm diameter, and place into the refrigerator to harden.

4 When firm, cut into rounds 1½ cm thick.

5 Place on to a lightly greased baking sheet and bake at approximately 200°C for 10–12 minutes.

* Fraiser means to rub or scrape down, using either a palette knife or the heel of the hand.

580 Chocolate caramels

Makes approx. 50–60 pieces

glucose	150 g
caster sugar	200 g
plain chocolate	100 g
single cream	250 ml

1 Boil together the glucose, sugar and chocolate with half the cream to 118°C.

2 Once this temperature has been reached add the remaining cream and bring back to 118°C.

3 Pour on to an oiled marble slab or on to a suitable oiled tray and cut into pieces while still warm.

4 Place into paper cases.

Florentines, cherry rolls, chocolate caramels and truffles

581 Florentines

Makes approx. 70–80 pieces

butter	200 g
caster sugar	200 g
fresh cream	50 g
cherries, chopped	50 g
cut mixed peel	100 g
sultanas	75 g
nibbed almonds	200 g
flaked almonds	200 g
soft flour	25 g
chocolate couverture or baker's chocolate	

1 Place the butter, sugar and cream in a saucepan and bring to the boil to 115°C.

2 Remove from heat and add all the remaining ingredients, except the chocolate. Allow to cool.

3 Prepare the baking sheets, lined with silicone paper.

4 Spoon the mixture on to the lined baking sheets into rounds approximately 10 g in weight, not too close together. Alternatively, use special florentine moulds.

5 Bake at 200°C for approximately 10–12 minutes.

6 When cooked, the florentines will spread over the baking sheet; bring back to form a neat round with a plain cutter as soon as they are removed from the oven.

7 Remove from baking sheets and allow to cool.

8 Coat the backs of each florentine with couverture or baker's chocolate and mark with a comb scraper.

582 Viennese biscuits

Makes approx. 40 pieces

butter or margarine	350 g
caster sugar	350 g
eggs	2
natural vanilla essence	2 drops
soft flour	450 g
melted chocolate, to finish	

1 Cream the butter and sugar in a basin until white and light.

2 Add the eggs, one at a time, and cream well.

3 Add the vanilla essence and then the flour carefully by gradually incorporating into the butter, sugar and egg mixture.

4 Pipe on to lightly greased baking sheets, using a 1 cm star tube.

5 Allow to stand for 2 hours, or longer if possible.

6 Cook at 200°C for approximately 15 minutes and allow to cool.

7 To finish, dip the points into melted chocolate.

583 Passion fruit and mango jelly v

Makes 2385 g, 100 portions, mould size 30 cm × 60 cm

passion fruit purée	800 g
mango purée	400 g
caster sugar	1140 g
pectin, slow setting	30 g
tartaric acid	15

1 Mix together the two purées and add 1080 g of the caster sugar. Bring to the boil.

2 Thoroughly mix the pectin and the remaining 60 g of sugar together. Mix well. Sprinkle this into the boiling mix. Bring to a constant 106°C.

3 Remove and add the tartaric acid.

4 Whisk well and pour straight into mould.

5 Leave to set, then cut into 1.5 cm pieces.

584 Madeleines

Makes 585 g, 45 portions

caster sugar	125 g
eggs	3
vanilla pod, seeds from	1
flour	150 g
baking powder	1 tsp
buerre noisette	125 g

1 Whisk the sugar, eggs and vanilla seeds to a hot sabayon.

2 Fold in the flour and the baking powder.

3 Fold in the buerre noisette and chill for up to 2 hours.

4 Pipe into well buttered madeline moulds and bake in a moderate oven.

5 Turn out and allow cool.

585 Caramel truffles

Makes 1585 g, 120 portions

cream	500 g
Trimoline	100 g
caster sugar	325 g
plain chocolate	575 g
milk chocolate	75 g
butter	10 g

1 Place the sugar and Trimoline together in a pan and take to a caramel, being mindful that it will turn from caramel to burnt quickly.

2 Remove from the heat and slowly add the cream. Return to the heat to dissolve the set caramel.

3 Once dissolved, add the chocolate and emulsify.

4 Add the butter.

5 Remove and allow to chill naturally.

6 Once it has reached room temperature place in a disposable piping bag.

7 Snip off the end of the bag and carefully pipe the mix into the desired chocolate spheres.

8 Allow to set and carefully close the top of each sphere with melted chocolate.

9 Once set, roll in desired chocolate, allow to set and then serve.

Note: spheres can be purchased from good provision distributors in milk, dark and white with all the major manufacturers making the product.

586 Pear and caramel truffles

Makes 1195 g, 80 portions

caster sugar	380 g
cream	300 g
glucose	65 g
milk chocolate	300 g
Poire William	150 g

1 Make a direct caramel with the sugar

2 Add the cream and glucose together and bring to the boil, ensuring that there are no lumps.

3 Allow the mixture to cool to below 50°C, then add the chocolate.

4 Emulsify in the Poire William.

5 Allow to cool naturally. It is then ready to use.

6 Follow the same procedures as for caramel truffles (recipe 584).

587 Bergamot truffles

Makes 3350 g, 200 pieces

cream	500 ml
milk chocolate, chopped	450 g
white chocolate, chopped	1550 g
plain chocolate, chopped	400 g
bergamot flavouring (1 pipette or 28 drops)	
brandy	200 ml
butter	250 g

1 Boil the cream and chopped chocolate over a bain-marie then add the bergamot and brandy.

2 Mix in the butter and stir to a smooth consistency, chill into gastro trays and freeze.

3 Cut into 1½ cm cubes, enrobe and then roll in cocoa powder.

588 Praline truffles

Makes 1 kg

milk chocolate	500 g
praline (see below)	250 g
butter	250 g

Praline

hazelnuts or almonds, blanched, peeled and roasted	200 g
sugar, caramelised	200 g

For the praline

1 Coat the nuts with the caramel, allow to set and crush to a fine powder.

For the truffles

1 Melt the chocolate over a bain-marie.

2 Once viscous, add the praline and the butter, and blend well to a homogeneous mix.

 Pipe while soft and allow to set in the refrigerator.

MISCELLANEOUS

589 Nougat Montelimar

Makes approx. 50–60 pieces

granulated sugar	350 g
water	100 g
honey	100 g
glucose	100 g
egg white	35 g
glacé cherries	50 g
pistachio nuts	50 g
nibbed almonds	25 g
flaked almonds or flaked hazelnuts	25 g

1 Place the sugar and water into a suitable pan, bring to the boil and cook to 107°C.

2 When the temperature has been reached, add the honey and glucose and cook to 137°C.

3 Meanwhile whisk the egg whites to full peak in a machine, then add the syrup at 137°C slowly, while whisking on full speed.

4 Reduce speed, add the glacé cherries cut into quarters, chopped pistachio nuts, and the nibbed and flaked almonds.

5 Turn out on to a lightly oiled tray or rice paper and mark into pieces while still warm.

6 When cold cut into pieces and place into paper cases to serve.

590 Marshmallows

Makes approx. 50 pieces

granulated or cube sugar	600 g
egg whites	3
leaf gelatine, soaked in cold water	35 g

1 Place sugar in a suitable saucepan with 125 ml water and boil to soft ball stage, 140°C.

2 When sugar is nearly ready whisk the egg whites to a firm peak.

3 Pour in boiling water and continue to whisk.

4 Squeeze the water from the gelatine and add.

5 Add colour and flavour if desired.

6 Turn out on to a tray dusted with cornflour and dust with more cornflour.

7 Cut into sections and roll in a mixture of icing sugar and cornflour.

591 Chocolate fudge

Makes approx. 60–70 pieces

granulated sugar		200 g
glucose	syrup	75 g
water		60 ml
evaporated milk		25 g
fondant		200 g
butter, melted		30 g
plain chocolate, melted		250 g
natural vanilla essence		

1 Place the granulated sugar, glucose and water into a thick-bottomed pan, place on the stove and cook to 115°C.

2 Add the evaporated milk and again cook to 115°C.

3 Place into a machine bowl the fondant, melted butter and melted chocolate. Add a few drops of vanilla essence and mix for 1 minute at low speed.

4 Add the sugar syrup at 115°C and mix well.

5 Place on to a suitable lightly oiled tray and allow to set.

6 When set, cut into pieces and place into paper cases.

592 Turkish delight

Makes approx. 60–70 pieces

granulated or cube sugar	600 g
glucose	200 g
lemon, zest and juice	4
water	750 ml
sherry *or* rose water (optional)	
cornflour	150 g
leaf gelatine (soaked)	50 g

1 Boil together the sugar, glucose, lemon zest and juice with 625 ml water in a suitable saucepan.

2 Flavour with sherry or rose water.

3 Thicken with the cornflour diluted with 250 ml water. Add the soaked gelatine and stir well.

4 Pour into shallow trays and allow to set, then cut into sections and roll in cornflour.

593 Sponge fingers

Makes approx. 32 pieces

eggs, separated	4
caster sugar	100 g
flour	100 g

1 Cream the egg yolks and sugar in a bowl until creamy and almost white.

2 Whip the egg whites stiffly.

3 Add a little of the whites to the mixture and cut in.

4 Gradually add the sieved flour and remainder of the whites alternately, mixing as lightly as possible.

5 Place in a piping bag with 1 cm plain tube and pipe in 8 cm lengths on to baking sheets lined with greaseproof or silicone paper.

6 Sprinkle liberally with icing sugar. Rest for 15 minutes.

7 Bake in a moderately hot oven (approximately 200–220°C) for about 10 minutes.

8 Remove from the oven, lift the paper on which the biscuits are piped and place upside down on the table.

9 Sprinkle liberally with water. This will assist the removal of the biscuits from the paper. (No water is needed if using silicone paper.)

594 Cornets

Makes approx. 10–12 pieces

icing sugar	150 g
butter	100 g
natural vanilla essence	
egg whites	4
soft flour	100 g

1 Lightly cream the sugar and butter, add 3–4 drops of vanilla.

2 Add the egg whites one by one, mixing continuously, taking care not to allow the mixture to curdle.

3 Gently fold in the sifted flour and mix lightly.

4 Using a 3 mm plain tube, pipe out the mixture on to a lightly greased baking sheet into rounds approximately 2½ cm in diameter.

5 Bake in a hot oven (approximately 230–250°C) until the edges turn brown and the centre remains uncoloured.

6 Remove the tray from the oven.

7 Work quickly while the cornets are hot and twist them into a cornet shape using the point of a cream horn mould. (For a tight cornet shape it will be found best to set the pieces tightly inside the cream horn moulds and to leave them until set.)

Spreading a biscuit mixture on a Silpat mat, as a sheet or in a mould, to form a flat biscuit

595 Brandy snaps

Makes approx. 10 pieces

margarine or butter	75 g
caster sugar	200 g
golden syrup	200 g
plain flour	100 g
ground ginger	6 g

1 Cream the margarine and sugar until light and fluffy.

2 Add the golden syrup and cream well.

3 Gradually fold in the sieved flour and ground ginger.

4 Place mixture into a piping bag with a ½ cm plain tube.

5 Pipe on to a silicone-lined baking sheet into 1 cm diameter rounds.

6 Bake in a hot oven (approximately 220°C) for approximately 5 minutes until golden brown on the edges.

7 Allow to cool until slightly firm. Roll round a suitable wooden rod and allow to cool until crisp.

8 Remove from rod and use as required.

Uses

Brandy snaps can be offered as sweetmeats and pastries. The mixture can be shaped as required, e.g. tartlets, barquettes, and can be used as containers for sweets, e.g. filled with lemon syllabub, raspberries and cream.

SUGAR

Further information on pastillage, marzipan, chocolate and sugar products is also available in *Complete Confectionery Techniques* by Ildo Nicolello and Rowland Foote (John Wiley & Sons, 1995).

Boiled sugar

Sugar is boiled for a number of purposes – in pastry work, bakery and sweet-making. Loaf (lump) sugar is generally used, placed in a copper saucepan or sugar boiler and moistened with sufficient cold water to melt the sugar (approximately 125 ml per 250 g) and allowed to boil steadily without being stirred. Any scum on the surface should be carefully removed, otherwise the sugar is liable to granulate. Once the water has evaporated the sugar begins to cook and it will be noticed that the bubbling in the pan will get slower. It is now necessary to keep the sides of the pan free from crystallised sugar; this can be done either with the fingers or a piece of damp linen. In either case the fingers or linen should be dipped in ice water or cold water, rubbed round the inside of the pan and then quickly dipped back into the water.

The cooking of the sugar then passes through several stages, which may be tested with a special sugar thermometer or by the fingers (dip the fingers into ice water, then into the sugar and quickly back into the ice water).

Note: To prevent the granulation of sugar a tablespoon of glucose or a few drops of lemon juice per 400 g may be added before boiling. If using cream of tartar it is advisable to add this to the sugar three-quarters of the way through the cooking.

Degrees of cooking sugar

- **Small thread (104°C).** When a drop of sugar held between thumb and forefinger forms small threads when the finger and thumb are drawn apart. Used for stock syrup.
- **Large thread (110°C).** When proceeding as for small thread the threads are more numerous and stronger. Used for crystallising fruits.
- **Soft ball (116°C).** Proceeding as above, the sugar rolls into a soft ball. Used for making fondant.
- **Hard ball (121°C).** As for soft ball, but the sugar rolls into a firmer ball. Used for making sweets.
- **Small crack (140°C).** The sugar lying on the finger peels off in the form of a thin pliable film, which sticks to the teeth when chewed. Used for meringue.
- **Large crack (153°C).** The sugar taken from the end of the fingers when chewed breaks clean in between the teeth, like glass. Used for dipping fruits.
- **Caramel (176°C).** Cooking is continued until the sugar is a golden-brown colour. Used for cream caramels.
- **Black-jack.** Cooking is continued until the sugar is deeply coloured and almost black. Water is then added and the black sugar is allowed to dissolve over a gentle heat. Used for colouring.

Points to note

1 Never attempt to cook sugar in a damp atmosphere, when the humidity is high. The sugar will absorb water from the air and this will render it impossible to handle.
2 Never work in a draught as this will prevent the sugar from becoming elastic and it will be difficult to mould.

3 Work in clean conditions as any dirt or grease can adversely affect the sugar.

4 The choice of equipment is also important – copper sugar boilers are ideal as these conduct heat rapidly.

5 Never use wooden implements for working with or stirring the sugar. Wood absorbs grease, which can in turn ruin the sugar.

6 The amount of glucose you add to the sugar and water will vary depending on the effect you wish to achieve. You may add 10–20 per cent more glucose for blown sugar – this will make it more elastic and, in doing so, increase the cooking temperature by 1–2°C.

7 The precise cooking temperature varies according to the weight of the sugar being cooked.

8 If you are colouring the sugar, it is advisable to use powdered food colourings as these tend to be brighter. Before using, dilute with a few drops of 90 per cent-proof alcohol. Add the colourings to the boiling sugar when the sugar reaches 140°C. For poured sugar, if you want a transparent effect, add the colour while the sugar is cooking.

9 Once the sugar is poured on to marble and it becomes pliable, it should be transferred to a special, very thick and heat-resistant plastic sheet.

10 To keep the sugar pliable, it should be kept under infra-red or radiant heat lamps.

11 For a good result with poured sugar, use a small gas jet to eliminate any air bubbles while you pour it.

12 Ten per cent calcium carbonate (chalk) may be added to sugar for pouring to give an opaque effect and to improve its shelf life. This should be added as a slurry at 140°C.

13 To keep completed sugar work, place in airtight containers, the bottom of which should be lined with a dehydrating compound, such as silica gel, carbide or quicklime.

14 If you are using a weak acid, such as cream of tartar, to prevent crystal formation, it is advisable to add the small amount of acid towards the end of the cooking. Too much acid will over-invert the sugar, producing a sticky, unworkable product.

Sugar boiling: pulled, blown, poured

There are now available on the market a range of commercial products that greatly assist the pastry chef in the production of specialised sugar work. One such product is known as Isomatic. This product is *not* hyprosopic, enabling finished goods to be stored relatively easily. It can be used several times over and has a long shelf life. These commercial products are simple to use, quick and labour saving.

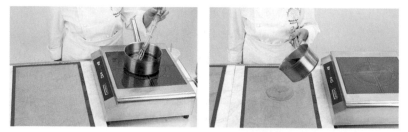

Boiling sugar

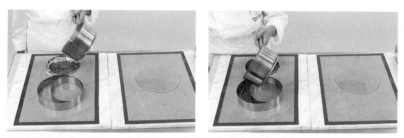

Pouring and moulding sugar

596 Poured sugar **v**

sugar cubes	1 kg
water	400 ml
glucose	250 g
peanut oil *or*	
pure vaseline for greasing	

1 Prepare templates from cardboard or metal.

2 Roll out plasticine to a thickness of 5–7 mm. The larger the model, the thicker the plasticine.

3 Using the template, cut out the shape.

4 Place the plasticine with the model cut out on to aluminium foil.

5 Grease the inside of the shape.

6 Boil the sugar and water. When it forms into a slurry, skim off any white foam.

7 Add the glucose, cook to 140°C, add any colouring or calcium carbonate.

8 Cook to 136°C, take off the heat.

9 Stand for 2 minutes, allow any air bubbles to escape.

10 Pour the sugar carefully in a continuous stream into the plasticine template until it reaches the surface.

11 Gently blow any air bubbles away with a gas jet or prick them with the point of a knife.

12 Leave to cool for approximately 20 minutes until it hardens.

13 Lift off the plasticine, leave to cool for 3–4 hours. Peel off the foil. Attach the model to a sugar base made from poured sugar.

14 Dip the base of the model in hard crack sugar, immediately stick it to the base.

15 Using a small paper cone, pipe a fine line of hard crack sugar around the perimeter of the base.

16 For transparent models, spray a thin film of clear varnish over the models when they are cold. Confectioners' varnish will protect them from damp, dust and fingerprints and act as a preservative.

Note: The sugar can be poured on to Silpat mats as shown above.

597 Spun sugar v

Spun sugar is used for decoration.

water	180 ml
cube sugar	500 g
glucose	125 g
pure peanut oil *or*	
vaseline for greasing	

1 Place the water into a pan, add the sugar, stir gently with a metal spoon.

2 Place over a gentle heat, stir until the sugar begins to boil.

3 Once the sugar starts to foam, skim off the white foam.

4 Clean around the inside of the pan with a clean brush dipped in clean water. This will help to prevent crystallisation.

5 Add the glucose, cook over a high heat.

6 When the sugar reaches 152°C, take off the heat and allow to cool for 2–5 minutes.

7 The sugar will not spin if it is too hot.

8 Dip the prongs of a fork or whisk into the sugar and flick the fork or whisk rapidly backwards and forwards over an oiled wooden rod or rods. The sugar will run down and form fine threads. Continue until a web or mesh of sugar is formed.

9 Carefully collect the spun sugar, place on a tray of silicone paper.

10 Use as required.

Note: Spun sugar very easily picks up moisture from the atmosphere and will soften.

Spun sugar is also used to make the stamens of sugar flowers. Gently roll a handful into an oblong shape approximately 2 cm diameter and with a heated knife cut off about 3–4 cm, taking care that the other end remains open. Dip the opened end into crystallised sugar tinted with colour.

598 Rock sugar v

As the name implies this gives a rocky effect and is used to decorate cakes and centrepieces.

water	200 ml
sugar cubes	500 g
royal icing	25–50 g

1 Preheat an oven to 120°C. Line a suitable bowl with foil.

2 Place water into a suitable pan, add sugar, stir with a metal spoon.

3 Gently heat the pan, stir until the sugar has dissolved completely and begins to boil.

4 When the white foam appears skim it off.

5 Clean the inside of the pan with a pastry brush dipped in cold water.

6 Cook the sugar over a high heat.

7 Add colouring at 120°C.

8 Cook until 138°C, remove from heat.

9 With a suitable metal spoon, stir in the royal icing quickly.

10 The sugar should rise and double in volume.

11 Pour quickly on to the prepared dish, where it will finish rising.

12 Place in a pre-heated oven for 10 minutes, it will then harden.

13 Store in a cool, dry place for 12 hours.

14 Turn the sugar out and remove the foil.

15 Use as required.

Note: The sugar may be sprayed with colour to give a number of different effects. Assemble pieces with royal icing.

Pulling sugar   Blowing sugar   Assembling

599 Blown sugar v

water	400 ml
sugar cubes	1 kg
glucose	250 g
peanut oil *or*	
pure vaseline for greasing	

1 Pour the water into a suitable pan, add the sugar.

2 Proceed as for poured sugar (see recipe 597).

3 Cook until it reaches 150°C. Allow to stand for 30 seconds.

4 During the cooking process (up to 140°C), the sugar will take on a yellowish tint – this is sometimes used as a base colour for painting models.

5 Pour the cooked sugar on to a marble slab, work with a palette knife.

6 Pull 5–6 times.

7 When the sugar is cool enough to handle, place one hand on one end of the mass and pull it out. Then fold it back on itself. Do this 20–30 times, alternating the direction each time, until the sugar becomes glassy and smooth.

8 Place the sugar on a Silpat or Tefal sheet under a lamp.

9 Cut off a ball large enough to make your desired shape.

10 The ball must be elastic and uniform in temperature.

11 Dig your thumbs into the centre to make a cavity. Heat the end of the aluminium tube of the nozzle of a sugar pump, so that the sugar will stick to it, then insert it halfway into the cavity. With your fingertips firmly press the edges of the sugar around the end of the tube so that it sticks.

12 Blow in air gently and regularly so that the sugar ball swells. Make sure that the thickness remains constant and even throughout the operation.

13 Use your hands to manipulate and control the bubble as it enlarges and begins to form the desired shape.

14 To maintain the air pressure inside the sugar ball, blow constantly while you shape.

15 When you have achieved your desired shape, mark it as you wish with a knife, grater or hard brush.

16 Place the finished object in a cold place.

17 Remove the sugar cord between the model and the tube with a hot knife or hot scissors.

Note: The finished objects may be painted with food colour.

Once the sugar has been sanitised (cooked and cooled) it may be kept in airtight tins with quicklime, carbide or silica gel, covered with foil. When required reheat under a lamp.

Lacquer may be used to give a high-gloss finish to models.

600 Pulled sugar v

cube sugar	1 kg
water	500 ml
cream of tartar	1.5 kg
peanut oil *or*	
pure vaseline for greasing	

1 Cook the sugar as in previous recipes, removing the white foam when it appears.

2 Add colouring when the temperature reaches 140°C.

3 When the temperature reaches 156°C, remove from heat and allow to stand for 30 seconds.

4 Pour sugar on to a clean, lightly greased marble slab or on to a Tefal or Silpat sheet.

5 Using a lightly oiled palette knife or metal scraper, fold the edges back on themselves for 3 to 4 minutes until the sugar almost stops spreading.

6 Fold the mass of sugar back on to itself, with your fingertips or using a palette knife. Pull 5–6 times.

7 With your hands, pull the sugar in and out using a folding action. Do this approximately 35–40 times. The sugar will begin to shine and will become quite smooth. If it starts to crack, it is ready for moulding.

8 Place the sugar in a plastic sheet under a lamp.

9 Cut off the amount you require and mould the sugar into a shape.

Note: Once the sugar has become a mass and is sanitised, any left-over pieces may be stored in airtight tins, lined with silica gel, carbide or quicklime covered with aluminium foil. When required, the sugar is reheated under infra-red or radiant lamp.

MARZIPAN

Most marzipan that is used today for culinary purposes is produced by large manufacturers. Much of this is of high quality, made from sweet and bitter almonds.

There are two distinct types of almond: hard or soft shelled. The hard-shelled types are grown in Italy, Sicily, Spain, Majorca and other European countries. Their kernels are more sweet and tender than those of the soft-shelled type, which are grown in California.

Sugar and water is added to the almonds and this is refined to a smooth paste through granite rollers and then roasted. The paste is then cooled before packing ready for use. Almond pastes are made from this marzipan by the addition of sugar and glucose.

Hard granulated sugar and white of egg is added to the almond paste to produce commercial macaroon paste.

601 Marzipan wafers

Makes approx. 24

marzipan	400 g
egg white	125–150 g
icing sugar	200 g
cornflour	50 g
milk	50 g
vanilla essence	

(Before using this recipe read page 135 on *Salmonella* bacteria.)

1 Work down the marzipan with half the egg white until pliable and smooth.

2 Add icing sugar, cornflour, milk, vanilla essence and the remaining whites.

3 Allow the mixture to stand for 24 hours, covered well. This is an essential maturing process, which will add to the plasticity of the marzipan when it comes to rolling up the hot shapes.

4 The baking sheet must be heavy duty and is best lined with silicone or 100 per cent fat, then dusted with flour.

5 Use stencils to acquire the desired shapes.

6 Bake at 210°C for approximately 5–8 minutes.

602 Almond drops and fingers

Makes approx. 24

marzipan	400 g
egg white	150 g
caster sugar	400 g

1 Break the marzipan down with a little egg white in a suitable mixing bowl.

2 When the mixture is smooth, add the remaining egg white and the caster sugar. The mixture must be smooth and free from lumps.

3 Pipe the mixture into a baking sheet lined with silicone paper with various shapes. Bake at 180°C for approximately 8–10 minutes.

4 The mixture may be piped into small fingers, rounds and ovals.

5 To finish, the biscuits may be sandwiched together with chocolate, apricot jam, buttercream or nougat and, if desired, partially dipped in chocolate.

603 English rout biscuits

Makes approx. 24

marzipan	800 g
egg whites	3
icing sugar	200 g
flavourings, as desired	
decorations, as desired	
gum arabic, to glaze	

1 Work down the marzipan with the egg white to a smooth, pliable paste.

2 Divide into 6 pieces. Leaving 1 plain, colour and flavour each piece with raspberry, orange, pistachio, lemon and chocolate.

3 Cut into small pieces and make into various shapes (using icing sugar for dusting).

4 Place on silicone-lined baking sheets, decorate as desired with almonds, glacé cherries and allow to stand for 24 hours.

5 Brush with eggwash, flash in a very hot oven (220°C) for approximately 2–5 minutes.

6 Finally, glaze with a solution of hot gum arabic.

604 Marzipan shortcake fingers

Makes approx. 36

butter or margarine	400 g
caster sugar	200 g
marzipan	600 g
milk	125 g
flour	500 g

1 Cream the butter and sugar together.

2 Work the marzipan down with 100 g of the milk to a smooth, pliable dough. Carefully add this to the butter and sugar.

3 Stir in the flour and milk.

4 Pipe on to silicone-lined baking sheets with a star tube, 9 mm. Bake at 190°C for approximately 8–10 minutes.

5 After baking, dip the ends in melted chocolate.

Note: Fingers may also be sandwiched together with apricot jam, buttercream or chocolate. The mixture may also be flavoured with the zest of lemon, lime or orange or, alternatively, vanilla.

If you require cups, cornets or baskets, shape while still warm.

CHOCOLATE

Chocolate must be treated with great care. If chocolate is over-heated it will taste strong and burnt. Water will change the characteristics of chocolate, causing it to thicken, and affecting the texture, taste and appearance.

Preparing and using chocolate

Equipment and types of chocolate

- thermometer
- double boiler or porringer
- dipping fork and ring
- moulds, preferably plastic
- paint brushes

Cooking chocolate is very often a chocolate substitute and is unsuitable for moulding and for luxury chocolate work.

Real chocolate is produced from cocoa beans, roasted and ground to produce a cocoa mass. Cocoa butter and chocolate liquor form the basis of all chocolate products; the higher the percentage of cocoa solids contained in the chocolate, the richer the chocolate.

Couverture is very high in cocoa butter and requires careful handling.

Dipping chocolate is sold by specialist suppliers – it gives a crisp, hard coat.

Chocolate is available in bars, buttons or drops. Buttons and drops have the advantage that they melt quickly and easily.

The melting process

Break the chocolate into small pieces and melt slowly in a bowl standing in hot water. If the chocolate is allowed to become too hot, the fats will not combine, the chocolate will lose stability, and its flavour and texture will be spoilt. Stir the chocolate gently until smooth; the temperature should never go above 50–55°C. Workable consistency is around 40–45°C.

Microwave melting

Break the chocolate into small pieces and place into a non-metallic bowl. Put the microwave on full power for about 30 seconds. After each 30 seconds, stir the chocolate. Do not allow too long before stirring, otherwise hot-spots develop in the bowl, resulting in burnt chocolate.

Tempering (see also page 375)

It is essential that a thermometer is used for this process. Tempering is necessary because of the high proportion of cocoa butter and other fats in the chocolate. This stabilises the fats in the chocolate to give a crisp, glossy finish when dry.

Ingredient additions to chocolate

- **Butter.** Always use unsalted butter as salt can affect the taste and therefore produce an inferior product.
- **Sugar.** Generally caster and icing sugars are used.
- **Milk.** Use whole milk rather than skimmed or semi-skimmed, as this gives more body to finished sweets.
- **Glucose.** Liquid glucose is easier to measure if you warm the syrup. Use warm spoons and knives to measure and scrape with.

Moulding

Many different types of mould are available for use in making confectionery. Moulds must always be scrupulously clean. Several days before you intend to use the moulds, they should be washed thoroughly, rinsed well and dried. Keep in a dry place. Immediately before use, polish the inside with cotton wool. Do not touch the inside with your fingers as this may tend to leave a mark on the finished item.

Even the smallest amount of oil from the skin may cause problems when removing the chocolate from the mould. It is not necessary to wash the mould after each use, but you must not touch the inside of the mould between fillings.

Protect finished goods from damp and humidity. It is advisable when decorating moulded items to wear cotton gloves to avoid marking the surface.

Moulded baskets

Baskets and bowls can be filled with chocolate or other sweets or marzipan fruits. They may also be served with fresh fruit and cream or ice cream to offer as a sweet. After having moulded the basket, make a handle from moulding chocolate. Attach the handle with a little melted chocolate.

605 Chocolate for hand moulding

plain chocolate	125 g
liquid glucose	90 ml

1 Melt the chocolate in a bowl over a pan of hot water.
2 Add the liquid glucose and stir the mixture well.

3 Form into a bowl and wrap in clingfilm. Allow to rest for 3 hours in the refrigerator.
4 When ready to use, uncover, allow to come to room temperature but do not allow it to become too soft, otherwise it will be difficult to handle. It should be solid but pliable, slightly oily and tacky.

Dipping chocolates

In order to dip centres in chocolate successfully it is important that sufficient chocolate is melted to cover them completely when dipped. It is easier to dip chocolates if you have a set of dipping forks. As you become proficient at dipping centres, you will soon develop the skills to make and decorate finished chocolate with the dipping tools.

Dipping hard centres

1 Drop the sweet into the chocolate and turn it over using a fork. When completely covered, lift out of the chocolate with the fork.
2 Tap the fork on the side of the bowl so that the excess chocolate falls away, then draw the bottom of the fork across the lip of the bowl to remove any accumulation underneath the sweet.
3 Place the dipped chocolate on to a sheet of parchment paper to dry. If the chocolate is difficult to remove, gently ease it off using a flat-bladed knife.
4 For round sweets, use a dipping ring. This metal ring is usually thicker than the prongs of the dipping fork and will not so readily penetrate the sweet as you proceed to dip.
5 Leave the dipped chocolates in a cool, dry place for several hours to set completely.

Finishes

As in all forms of food preparation the finishing of chocolates and truffles is very important. The finish can sometimes help to identify the flavour or content of the chocolate. They may be finished by piping designs on each chocolate or dipping in a different type of chocolate to the filling using a contrast of flavours and finishes (i.e. white, dark or milk). Chocolates may also be personalised, particularly if they are intended as a gift. Tiny chocolate or sugar flowers may be used. Crystallised or glacé fruits may be used alongside marzipan flowers and fruits. Rose and crystallised violet petals are sometimes used.

Using chocolate

Chocolate can also be used for finishing other foods. Chocolate coats are used for decorating cakes and gâteaux. Chocolate shapes cut with specialised cutters add impressive finishing touches to sweet dishes.

Chocolate leaves

The leaves from any non-poisonous plant may be used. Leaf moulds can be purchased.

When using fresh leaves, such as bay leaves, wash and dry thoroughly. Paint the underside of each leaf with melted chocolate, taking care to go to the edge. Allow to cool until set. When dry, carefully remove the leaf. If the chocolate is too thin and starts to break, paint another thin coat over the first and again allow to dry. It is not advisable to set them in the refrigerator as the cold temperature makes the leaves brittle and so they will not peel from the chocolate.

Chocolate marbling

Using tempered chocolate and white chocolate a marbled or combed effect may be created by spreading the chocolate on to acetate or polythene sheets. The flexibility of the acetate or polythene allows you to 'shape' the chocolate as it sets.

---

606 Truffles

Makes approx. 30

couverture	225 g
single cream	125 ml
rum to taste	

1 Break the couverture into small pieces. Bring the cream to the boil, then remove from the heat and stir in the couverture.

2 Flavour with rum and allow to set in a refrigerator.

3 Turn out on to a tray and dust with icing sugar.

4 Form into rolls, 1½ cm in diameter and cut into sections.

5 Roll on to a mixture of icing sugar and cocoa powder, or grated couverture, and place into paper cases.

---

607 White chocolate truffles

Makes approx. 20–25

white chocolate	200 g
unsalted butter	50 g
single cream	3 tbsp

1 Break the chocolate into small pieces and melt gently in a suitable double pan.

2 Stir the chocolate away from the heat.

3 Add the softened butter, then slowly add the cream.

4 Cover the mixture, allow to cool until it is firm enough to handle.

5 Mould the mixture into small balls.

6 Roll the truffles in desiccated coconut to cover completely.

Variations

Add:

- brandy   4 tbsp
- sloe gin   6 tbsp
- Malibu   4 tbsp
- Cointreau   4 tbsp
- whisky   4 tbsp.

608 Champagne truffles

Makes 35–40

milk chocolate	300 g
unsalted butter, softened	100 g
champagne	150 ml
white chocolate to coat	100 g

1 Break the milk chocolate into small pieces and melt in a double pan. Stir gently until the chocolate is melted.

2 Remove the top saucepan, leave the chocolate to cool.

3 Stir the chocolate thoroughly. Gradually add the butter; the mixture must be thick and creamy and slightly grainy in appearance.

4 Slowly add the champagne, stirring gently. Cover and leave to set.

5 Mould into small balls, chill down until firm.

6 Dip in melted white chocolate.

Champagne is very difficult to transfer from the bottle into chocolates. The addition of champagne or sparkling wine will produce a light and delicate texture to the truffle. The liquid must be added gradually. If the mixture starts to separate or curdle, do not add any more liquid. Allow to cool until set and stir gently. Leave the mixture to set completely before further handling.

PASTILLAGE

609 Gum paste (pastillage)

gelatine leaves	2
lemon, juice of	½
icing sugar	500 g
cornflour	100 g
egg whites *or*	2
gum tragacanth	
royal icing, no acid or glycerine added	800 g
gum tragacanth added to 500 g icing sugar	12 g

1 Soak the leaf gelatine in water and drain. Melt with lemon juice. Sieve the icing sugar and cornflour. Mix the egg whites in carefully, then carefully pour in the melted gelatine, which must not exceed a temperature of 48°C. Mix well, knead until a smooth dough is obtained.

2 Using gum tragacanth gives a better pastillage. Disperse the gum tragacanth in the icing sugar. Gradually add to the royal icing on slow speed. Cover with a damp cloth, allow to rest for 20 minutes. Remove from the mixing bowl, work to a smooth dough with additional icing sugar if required.

Note: Pastillage should be allowed to relax for 24 hours covered with polythene or a plastic bag to prevent crusting – this allows the paste to roll out better and prevents excess shrinkage during the drying process.

Pastillage is used for modelling centrepieces and caskets with the aid of templates.

Always use a mixture of icing sugar and cornflour for dusting. Allow cut pieces to dry on glass, although wooden trays may be used; turn once in the drying process. Drying may also be carried out by laying the pieces on silicone or good-quality wax paper.

The sugar pieces are assembled with royal icing, which should not contain glycerine.

GLOSSARY

A blanc To keep white, without colour

A brun To colour brown

Agar-agar Gelatine substitute, obtained from dried seaweed

Aiguillettes Small strips of cooked meat, poultry or fish

Akee A Caribbean fruit

Al dente Pasta or vegetables slightly underdone so that there is some resistance to the bite

Attereaux Cooked small pieces of food (meat, fish or vegetables) coated with a thick sauce, crumbed and deep-fried

Ballotine Boned stuffed leg of poultry

Bamboo shoots The inner shoots of the bamboo plant, used extensively in Chinese cooking

Barding To cover breasts of birds with slices of fat or bacon

Beurre blanc Sauce of finely chopped shallots, white wine and melted butter, emulsified

Bitok A type of hamburger

Blanc de volaille White flesh of poultry, breast or wing (or suprême)

Borscht Russian or Polish duck and beetroot-flavoured soup

Bouillabaisse A fish stew

Bourbon An American whiskey

Brioche Yeast dough, enriched with eggs

Calvados Apple brandy from Normandy

Carapace The shell of, for example, crabs and lobsters

Cartouche A buttered paper for covering foods

Cassolettes Individual dishes, ramekins in which foods are cooked or served

Ceps Edible mushrooms

Ceviche Fish marinaded in lime and lemon juice, of Spanish-Peruvian origin

Chanterelle Small yellow mushroom with a frilly edge

Chantilly cream Whipped cream, flavoured with vanilla and sweetened

Chapati Crisp wholemeal pancake

Chiffonade Shredded

Chowder Unpassed shellfish or sweetcorn soup from the USA

Clafoutis Fruit (e.g. cherries) baked in batter

Clam A type of shellfish

Cointreau A brand of orange-flavoured liqueur

Colcannon Irish dish containing cabbage and potato

Coulibiac Russian fish pie

Coulis (Fr) or Cullis (Eng) A purée in liquid form (e.g. tomato, raspberry) used as a sauce

Couscous Arabic dish made using a fine type of semolina

Couverture Covering chocolate

Craquelins Small, filled pancakes, crumbed and deep-fried

Crepinette Thin pig's caul (membrane)

Croustade Baked pastry cases in or on which cooked foods are served

Cru Raw, not cooked, or from the raw state

Crudités Raw vegetables (e.g. celery, carrot) cut in bite-size pieces

Curaçao Liqueur made from bitter oranges, originally from the West Indies

Dahl Indian dish using lentils

Demi-glace Refined brown sauce

Dipping Immersing into, for example, chocolate

Dock Pierce pastry with numerous small holes

Drambuie Whisky-based liqueur flavoured with honey and herbs

Dulse Edible red seaweed

Duxelle Chopped shallot and chopped mushrooms cooked together

Emulsify To mix oil and liquid together

En-croûte Wrapped in pastry (e.g. beef fillet)

En papillote Oiled greaseproof paper or foil in which raw food is cooked in the oven

Enrobing Coating with, for example, chocolate

Eviscerating Removing the innards or guts

Filo paste Very thin paste of Greek origin, usually purchased ready prepared

Fleurons Small, crescent-shaped pieces of puff pastry

Fraiser The action of scraping sweet paste to make it smooth and to mix before use

Fricadelles Chopped raw or cooked veal or beef steaks like hamburgers

Fricassée A white stew in which the main ingredient is cooked in the sauce (e.g. veal, chicken)

Fritots Savoury fritters of meat, fish or vegetables, battered and deep-fried

Forcemeat Savoury stuffings of meat or poultry

Fromage frais Fat-free, skimmed milk fresh cheese

Fruits de mer Seafoods: shellfish, crustaceans and molluscs

Fumet Concentrated essence of fish, meat or poultry

Fusion cookery The blending of ethnic ingredients and styles of cookery with other national methods of cookery (e.g. using Oriental and/or Asian herbs, spices, vegetables in European cookery)

Galette Small flat cake (e.g. of sweetcorn, potato)

Ganache Rich chocolate cream filling for gâteaux or petits fours

Garam masala A mixture of spices

Gazpacho Spanish cold soup of cucumber, tomato and garlic

Ghee Clarified butter, used in Indian cooking

Gosling Baby goose

Gravlax Swedish dish of raw salmon, marinated with dill

Grenadins Small, thick, larded slices of veal, which are usually pot roasted

Guacamole An avocado and chilli sauce used with meat, as a filling for tortillas or as a dip

Gum arabic A type of edible gum

Gum paste A type of dough used for modelling

Haunch For example, of venison, the leg and rump (hip, buttock and thigh)

Hummus Paste of chickpeas and sesame seeds

Ignite To light (to flame, e.g. brandy)

Infuse To extract flavour and aroma by covering an ingredient with liquid and allowing it to stand

Jus Meat juice lightly thickened by reduction

Jus-lié Thickened gravy made from veal stock

Kemangi Sweet basil leaves

Kirsch Distilled white spirit made from wild cherries, mainly from France and Switzerland

Larding Inserting strips of fat bacon into meat

Lea & Perrins Worcester sauce brand (a commercial product)

Lemon grass A grass classified as a herb: lemon flavour

Lesser galangal A spice similar to ginger used in Southeast Asian dishes

Liaison A thickening of yolks and cream used to finish certain soups and sauces

Macerating Steeping to soften or to absorb, e.g. fruit in a liqueur

Maigret Type of duck; menu term to describe breast of certain duck

Mangetout Type of pea (sugar pea), the pod of which is also eaten

Marinating Steeping in a marinade to tenderise, e.g. venison

Mascarpone An Italian cream cheese

Maw seeds Type of seeds similar to poppy seeds

Monosodium glutamate A flavour enhancer

Monté au beurre The adding of small pieces of butter to thicken a reduced cooking liquid to make a sauce

Morels Type of edible fungi, brown, irregular and cone shaped

Mozzarella Cheese originally made from the milk of water buffalo

Nam pla A Thai fish sauce

Noilly Prat A brand of dry vermouth

Oakleaf A type of lettuce

Okra Type of vegetable, also known as gumbo and ladies' fingers

Oyster mushrooms Ear-shaped, grey or greenish-brown wild mushrooms

Pacific Rim A style of cooking developed in Australasia and the Far East, which embraces the styles and ingredients of both areas

Panada or **panade** Thick base mixture, e.g. choux paste before eggs are added

Pastillage Gum paste for modelling

Paupiette Stuffed, rolled strip of fish or meat

Paw-paw Tropical fruit

Pecorino Ewes' milk cheese with peppercorns

Perdrix Older pheasant suitable for braising

Physalis Cape gooseberry used for petits fours

Pimentos Green-, red- or yellow-coloured vegetables, also known as peppers

Pitta bread Type of Middle Eastern unleavened bread

Plain russe Mixture of milk, egg yolks and sugar, set with gelatine and cornflour

Plantains A type of large banana

Pluche Small sprig, e.g. of chervil, used as a garnish

Polyunsaturated fat A healthier product than saturated fat as it produces less cholesterol

Porringer A double saucepan used in chocolate work

Praline Sugar and nuts cooked to hard-boil stage, crushed and used for gâteaux and ice cream

Prosciutto A type of cured ham, Italian

Quenelles 'Dumplings' of fish, poultry or game, made by finely mincing the flesh, beating in egg white and cream, and poaching

Quark Salt-free soft cheese, made from semi-skimmed milk

Râble Saddle, e.g. of hare (râble de lièvre)

Rack of lamb Best end of lamb

Radicchio A red-leaved type of lettuce, bitter in taste

Ramekins Small dishes for serving individual portions of food

Ricotta Cheese made from the discarded whey of other cheeses, Italian

Saccharometer An instrument used to measure sugar density

Saffron Stamens from a species of crocus used for flavour and yellow colouring

Sake Japanese wine made from rice

Salmis A brown stew of game

Salsa A sauce

Sauternes Sweet white wine from the Bordeaux region of France

Scorzonera Type of vegetable, also known as oyster plant

Sear To very quickly seal the outside of food

Sec Dry, not sweet

Serrano ham A cured ham, Spanish

Shiso A herb of basil-like flavour

Shitake A type of mushroom

Silicone paper Paper to which foods do not stick

Silpat tray A baking sheet used for jaconde mixture

Smetana A low-fat product – a cross between sour cream and yoghurt

Smoke box Equipment used to smoke food items

Smoking The use of smoke to cook or partially cook meat, fish or game

Socle A base of rice, wax or ice on which to place cold buffet items

Sorrel A bright-green leaf with a sharp taste

Subric A basic sweet or savoury shallow-fried, (e.g. spinach)

Sweet potato Potato with a chestnut flavour

Tahini Paste of sesame seed

Tandoor Indian clay oven

Tempering A process in chocolate work

Tian a) A type of gratin dish, which gives its name to food cooked in it

b) Round, moulded preparation, usually of vegetables, served hot or cold

Tiramisu An Italian trifle-like dessert

Tofu Soya bean curd

Torten A type of gâteau

Tortillas Type of unleavened bread, usually served with Mexican dishes

Tranche A slice

Tresse Plaited, e.g. sole

Vesiga The marrow of the spinal column of the sturgeon

Ve-tsin Chinese flavouring with a monosodium glutamate base

Water chestnuts A white, crunchy, sweet root vegetable, about the size of a walnut

Yam Type of vegetable

Yoghurt An easily digested fermented milk product

Italic page numbers indicate illustrations.

accident records 10
agar-agar 52–3, 378
aioli 189–90
allergies 25–8, 37–8
almonds
    carrot and coriander salad 61
    and chocolate mousse 399
    Danish pastry filling 395
    drops and fingers 436
    and prune tart 416
alu-chloe 292
anchovies
    potatoes in white wine 312
    sticks 86
animal food families 28
anna potatoes 318
apples
    and chestnut forcemeat 247
    and fig chutney 58, 58
    herring and potato salad 66
    soup 131
    strudel 413, 414
    Swiss tart 415
    tatin 415
artichokes
    with spinach and cheese sauce 325
    spinach and ricotta filo bake 346–7
    stuffed 333
asparagus
    and dressed crab 71
    and salmon salad 64, 64
    sauce 359
    tian of green and white 61–2, 62
aspic jelly 73–4
aubergines
    baigan ka chokha 291
    baked babagnough charlotte 356
    caviar 291, 321
    galette with tomatoes and mozzarella
        345–6
    raita 340
    soufflé 326
    stir-fry, Japanese style 343
    stuffed 333
avocados
    and celery sauce 110
    and fennel sauce 110
    mousse 63
    sauce 110
    smoked salmon and walnut salad 59, 59
    tropical salad 59
ayam kicap baah asam 297

babagnough, and aubergine charlotte 356

bacalhau trás-os-montes 300
bacon
    French beans and hazelnut salad 60, 60
    and hazelnut vinaigrette 57
    and red lentil soup 124
bacteria 37, 38–41
baigan ka chokha 291
ballotines 78, 246
    chicken leg with lentils and tarragon 255
    duck leg with black pudding and apple 261
balsamic dressing 57
balsamic jelly 217–18
bamboo shoots 326
    spring rolls 87
banana cake 389
barding 268
barley, with shitake mushrooms 341
barquettes 73
basil pesto 111, 153
batters
    crêpes 382
    tempura 381
bavarois, vanilla 400
bean sprouts 327
    stir-fried 327
beans
    bourguignonne 342
    vegetable and saffron risotto 347
béarnaise sauce 105
beef
    bò xào magi 305
    boeuf bourguignonne 224
    and bok choy with black bean sauce 305
    braised short rib with horseradish
        couscous 225
    bresaola 226
    cured silverside 226
    curry 294
    cuts 204–5
    daging masak meruh 296
    larding a fillet 220
    lasagne 362
    with mango and black pepper 287
    pickled ox tongue 229
    piononos 285
    in red sauce 296
    rendang 294
    roast wing rib with Yorkshire pudding
        228
    slow-cooked fillet with onion ravioli 220–1
    slow-cooked sirloin 223
    soup with chives 303
    spiced minced, with plantains 285
    tournedos Rossini 221–3, 222

INDEX

traditional braised oxtail with garlic mash 227
beetroot
    and orange salad 60
    sauce 110
    and treacle cured salmon 68, *68*
    and watercress soup 125, *125*
bergamot truffles 426
beurre fondu/emulsion 104
beurre noisette 103–4
biscuit Viennoise 412
biscuits 381 *see also* cookies
    almond drops and fingers 436
    English rout 436
    marzipan shortcake fingers 436
    strawberry cream 381, *381*
    Viennese 425
bitoks, lamb, peach and cashew nut 87
black bean sauce 287–8, 305
black pudding
    ballotines of duck leg with apple 261
    homemade with apple and onion salad *238,* 238–9
blinis 393
    potato 313, *313*
    smoked salmon with caviar 93–4
bò xào magi 305
boeuf bourguignonne 224
boning
    chicken *77*
    fish *146*
    game *246*
    veal *230*
borani 299
borscht 118
bouchées 72–3
bouillabaisse 175
Bramley apple sauce 236
brandy snaps 429
breads 389–93
    croissants 393
    healthy eating 25
    hot cross buns 392
    olive sour 392
    pickled walnut and raisin 391
    potato and yoghurt bread 391
    pumpkin seed and onion bloomer 392
bresaola 226
brill, poached with wild crayfish gnocchi 160
brioches 86, 389, *394*
broad beans, with tomato and coriander 327
broccoli sauce 111
bubble and squeak 322, *322–3*
buffets
    cold 68–72, *69*
        meats *69,* 74–5
        preparation 68–72
        shellfish *69*
        smoked fish *69, 71*
        smoked salmon *71*
        sushi *69, 71*

sweets *69*
    ease of service 68
    hot *69*
        hors d'oeuvres *70*
    hygiene 68, 70, 72
    light 72
    presentation 68
    savouries 73
bulgar wheat *see* cracked wheat
burgomeister rolls 397
burgomeistermasse 397
butter 369–70
    beurre fondu/emulsion 104
    beurre noisette 103–4
    butter sauce 104
    butter thickened (monter au beurre) 104
    clarified butter 103
    healthy eating 2, 3
buttercream 384
    praline flavour 386

cá xót ngot 306
cabbage
    bubble and squeak 322, *322–3*
    colcannon 330
    stuffed 334
cabbage, red
    braised 323, *323*
    braised with apples, red wine and juniper 324
cakes
    banana 389
    carrot 422
    chocolate fudge 421
    gingerbread 420
    Madeira 388
    muffins 388
    pound 388
    sponge 379, 384–9
calories 30–1, 36
calves' kidneys
    riñones al jerez 301–2
    sautéed with sherry sauce 301–2
    with shallot sauce 230–1
calves' liver with raspberry vinegar 234
canapés 90–5
canja 301
caramel
    e'spuma 410
    mousse 400
    sauce 404
    truffles 426
cardoons 328
    fritters 328
    with onions and cheese 328
carob gum 378
carrageen 378
carrots
    cake 422
    coriander and almond salad 61

and orange soup 126
cassis pâté de fruit 423
cauliflower
    risotto 217–18
    soubise 109
celeriac
    purée 110
    remoulade 60
celery and cheese soup, cream of 127
ceps
    stuffed 334
    and truffle jelly dice 53
    and truffle relish 360
cereals 25
cervelas de poisson 178
champagne
    sorbet 402
    truffles 440
chancho adobado 298
changezie champen *290, 290–1*
char-sui turnip cakes in spring roll pastry *70*, 88
chayotte *see* christophenes
cheese *see also* goats' cheese; mozzarella; Parmesan cheese
    and celery soup 127
    cream, and smoked eel 94
    filo pastry filled with tabbouleh and feta 348
    healthy eating 2
    omelette with potatoes and Gruyère 138
    spinach and cheese sticks 87
    storage 7
chemical hazards 37
cherries
    clafoutis 421–2
    rolls 424, *424*
    soup 132
chestnut and apple forcemeat 247
chicory, braised 321
chicken
    ayam kicap baah asam 297
    ballotines 78
        with black pudding and apple 255
        with lentils and tarragon 255
    boning *77, 246*
    canja 301
    confit leg with leeks and artichokes 256
    dajaj mahshi 299
    escalopes
        grilled with asparagus and balsamic vinegar 252
        with lemon, capers and wilted greens 255
        preparation 254
    forcemeat or farce 248
    galantine 78–9, *79*
    Kiev 254
    lemon and ginger 286
    mousse 248
    mousseline 248
    with peppers and black bean sauce 287–8
    with poached eggs, tomato and cream sauces 141
    quenelles 248
    roast
        with rice and pine kernel stuffing 299
        traditional 252–3
    sauté
        chasseur 251
        with mushrooms 251–2
        preparation 250
    selecting 241
    serving cold roast 74
    soufflé 249
        with creamed mushrooms 249
    soup
        with lemon and mint 301
        with mushrooms and tongue 127
    spiced fried and plum sauce 297
    stock 98
    suprêmes
        in a cream sauce 107
        Kiev 254
        preparation 250
    terrine of free-range chicken and foie gras *84,* 84–5
chicken livers
    eggs on the dish with mushroom and Madeira sauce 139
    omelette with mushrooms 137
chilled food 40–1
chilli sauce, sweet 306
Chinese cabbage 329
    spicy stir-fry 329
chive, potato and cucumber soup with cream 131
chocolate 373–5
    and almond mousse 399
    baked tart 412
    brandy mousse 399
    caramels 424, *424*
    champagne truffles 440
    chip cookies 421
    cold e'spuma 410
    décor paste 413
    dipping 438
    flourless sponge 385
    fudge 428
    fudge cake 421
    and fudge sauce 404
    hot e'spuma 409
    ice cream 401
    leaves 439
    marbling 439
    marquise 411
    melting 437
    moulding 437–9
    mousse 399
    and orange mousse 399
    rum mousse 399
    sauce 403
    sorbet 401
    spraying 423
    tempering 374–5, 437
    truffle torte 412
    truffles 439

types 437
    white truffles 439
choron sauce 105
choux paste 418
choux pastry
    choux buns *417,* 417–18
    gâteau St Honoré 352
    vegetarian terrine 352
chow-chow *see* christophenes
Christmas pudding 419
christophenes 329
    baked with onion and cheese filling 286
chutneys
    fig and apple 58, *58*
    tomato 191
clafoutis
    cherries 421–2
    griottines 421–2
clams
    chowder 122
    chowder and roast salt cod 166–7, *167*
    preparation 196
clarified butter 103
cleaning, working areas 40
cockles 180
    chowder 195
    preparation 194
cocoa 373–4, 437 *see also* chocolate
coconut
    dressing 90
    sauce 295
    and spinach soup 294
cod *see also* salt cod
    bacalhau trás-os-montes 300
    baked with ham, tomato and black olives 300
    oven-baked marinated with bok choi 168
    pla nergn 303
coffee jaconde sponge 384
colcannon 330
confits
    chicken leg with leeks and artichokes 256
    duck leg rillette 261
    of duck leg with red cabbage and green beans 258, *258*
    onions *323,* 324
    rabbit 123, *123*
    red onion 56
conflicts, managing 16
consommés
    borscht 118
    lightly jellied tomato and tea 91, *91*
    mussel soup 119
    shellfish with crayfish and Parmesan gnocchi 118–19, *119*
    tomato and garlic 120
    wild duck and beetroot 117
contamination 37–9
control, system of 4–8
cookies *see also* biscuits
    chocolate chip 421
    peanut butter 422

Copenhagenmusse 395
cornets 429, *429*
Cornish crab salad 65, *65*
coulibiac 178–9
coulis 55, 110–11
courgettes
    blossoms in tempura *70,* 90
    cooked with tomatoes 348–9
    Parmesan fried with pesto 322
crab 181, 185
    asparagus and dressed crab *71*
    cakes with rocket salad and lemon dressing 187, *187*
    dressed 186
    and ginger jelly discs 53
    malabar 289, *289*
    salad with lime, pimentos and grilled scallops 65, *65*
    salad with pink grapefruit 186–7
cracked wheat
    filo pastry filled with tabbouleh and feta cheese 348
    with honey-roasted vegetables 346
    and mint salad 345
    vegetable shashliks served on tabbouleh 350
cranberries
    spinach, ricotta and artichoke filo bake 346–7
crawfish 181, 193
crayfish 181
    consommé of shellfish with crayfish 118–19, *119*
    coulis sauce 102
cream 2, 7, 373
cream cheese and smoked eel 94
crème brulée 383
crème chantilly 384
crêpes 382
    vegetable olives 355
croissants 393, *394*
croquante 397
crostinis 88
    goats' cheese 89, *89*
    tomato and aubergine 88
cucumbers
    chive and potato soup 131
    raita 93
    stuffed 334
    and yoghurt dressing 56
cullis *see* coulis
Cumberland sauce 55
cured belly of pork 75, *75*
cured meats *71*
curries
    alu-chloe 292
    beef 294
    rendang 294
    rendang kambang kot baru 295
    Thai-style potato 341
    vegetarian 292
custard filling, for Danish pastries 396
customer relations 16

daging masak meruh 296

dairy products
    healthy eating 2, 25
    storage 7
dajaj mahshi 299
Danish pastries
    with almond fruit fillings 395–6
    with custard filling 396–7
    dough 394, *394*
dartois 86
dill and mustard sauce 56
dips *70*
diversity 15–16
dom yam nua 303
dressings
    bacon and hazelnut vinaigrette 57
    balsamic 57
    coconut 90
    herb oil 58
    honey-lime 197
    lime yoghurt 83
    rose petal 64
    smoked oil 57, *57*
    tofu salad 56
    truffle 57
    vinaigrette 56
    yoghurt and cucumber 56
Dublin Bay prawns 181
duck
    ballotine of leg with black pudding and apple 261
    confit leg rillette 261
    confit of leg with red cabbage and green beans 258, *258*
    garbure 259, *259*
    pan-fried breast with vanilla and lime *259*, 259–60
    Peking 288
    roast Gressingham with jasmine tea and fruit sauce 257–8
    serving cold roast 74
    wild *see* wild duck

eels
    fried with spring onion and mustard sauce 172
    preparing 171
    smoked
        smoked fish platter 66
    with white wine, horseradish and parsley 172
egg-based sauces 104–6
eggs 368–9
    Benedict *135*, 135–6
    on the dish
        with chicken livers and mushroom 139
        with grilled lamb's kidneys 140
        with sliced onion, bacon and potato 139
    en cocotte with shrimps, cream and cheese 138
    Fabergé 142
    food value 134
    poached
        with chicken and tomato and cream sauces 141
        with prawns, sherry and French mustard 141
    production 134
    raw 135

safe use 41
science of 133
snow 408
soft-boiled with mushroom duxelle and cheese sauce 140
storage 135
energy balance 30–1
English trifle 420
e'spurnas 408–10
    caramel 410
    cold chocolate 410
    hot chocolate 409
    mandarin 410
    thyme and ginger 410

fats and oils 24, 34, 36, 370–1
fermente 390
feta cheese, filo pastry filled with 348
fibre 25
figs
    and apple chutney *58*
    and port reduction 58
    tart 416
filo pastry
    filled with tabbouleh and feta cheese 348
    spinach, ricotta and filo bake with cranberries 346–7
fire-fighting equipment 9
first-aid equipment 9
fish *see also* types by name
    boning *146, 150*
    bouillabaisse 175
    en papillote 151
    filleting *149*
    fish stock 99
    forcemeat 177
    frozen 148
    gutting *149*
    healthy eating 24
    mousse 67, 177
    mousseline 177
    origins 143
    quenelle 177
    Russian fish pie 178–9
    sausages 178
    scaling *149*
    seasonality 148
    selecting 146
    shallow fried fillets with artichokes and potatoes 176
    and shellfish soufflé 179
    smoked *71*
    smoked fish platter 66
    smoking 147
    soufflés 179
    steamed Thai style 303
    stir-fried 176
    stock 151
    storage 147
    stuffed round fish 64
    with sweet chilli sauce 306
    trimming *150*

flaky pastry 382
flan paste, savoury 380
flans see also tarts
    tofu and vegetable with walnut sauce 353–4
florentines 424
flour 366–7
flying starter 391
foams see e'spumas
foie gras
    kromesky 94
    and prune stuffing 247
fondant potatoes 316
food allergies 25–8, 37–8
food safety 37–45
    legislation 42–3
forcemeat 246
    chestnut and apple 247
    chicken 248
    pork, sage and onion 247
    prune and foie gras stuffing 247
    quail 274
foyot sauce 105
frangipane 387
French beans, bacon and hazelnut salad 60, 60
French meringue 405
fritters
    cardoon 328
    salsify 333
fruit see also types by name
    coulis 403
    healthy eating 25
    mousse 398
    soups 131–2
    terrine 418–19, 419
fudge
    chocolate 428
    chocolate cake 421
    chocolate sauce 404
fungi see also mushrooms
    jamur kuping 294
    stock 340
    wood 294

galantines 78–9, 79
game see also types by name
    ballotine preparation 246
    boning 246
    buying 267
    cooking 244, 246
    farce 268
    feathered 267–8
    game pies 79
    hanging 243–4, 268
    preparation 245–6, 245–6, 267
    seasonality 244–5
    selecting 243
    serving cold roast 74
    storage 244
    stuffing 246

garlic
    mash 227
    mayonnaise 55
    red onion and ginger oil 113
    soubise 109
garnishes, for soup 115, 248
gâteaux
    japonaise 386, 386
    St Honoré 416, 416–17
gazpacho 130
gelatine 54, 378
Genoese sponge cake
    chocolate 386
    plain 385
ginger
    and crab jelly discs 53
    garlic and red onion oil 113
    and lemon chicken 284
    pickled and mirin-glazed tuna 92
    and thyme e'spuma 410
gingerbread 420
glazes 103–4
glucose 371
gnocchi
    Parmesan 130, 160
    potato 314
goats' cheese
    crostini 89, 89
    and plum tomato 95
    and red pepper tart 349
goose
    preparation 262
    roast with citrus fruits 262, 262
    serving cold roast 74
gooseberry sauce 111
Grand Marnier soufflé 407
gratins
    Dauphinoise 316
    lobster tail 190
    mussels with white wine sauce 194
    of nuts with a tomato and wine sauce 353
gravlax 63
green peppercorn and paprika sauce 352
grey mullet, policha meen 290, 290
griottines clafoutis 421–2
grouse 269
    roast 273–4
guar gum 378
guinea fowl
    en papillote with aromatic vegetables and herbs 257
    fricassée of, with wild mushrooms 253, 253–4
    poached with muscat grapes and salsify 256
    suprême 250
gum paste 440
gumbo soup 129

HACCP (hazard analysis critical control points) 42–5
hake, poached with cockles and prawns 166
halal butchery 22, 199

halibut
 kukus ikan sebalah madura 296
 malt-poached with chicken hearts and skin 165
 smoked fish platter 66
ham
 bacalhau trás-os-montes 300
 baked cod, tomato and black olives 300
 Parma ham and tarragon tart 94
 and pea soup 124
 and veal pie 85
hares
 game pie 79
 hanging 267, 279
 jugged 279
 selecting 267, 279
hash browns 315
hazard analysis critical control points (HACCP) 42–5
hazards 37–8
hazelnuts
 and bacon vinaigrette 57
 custards 397
 French beans, and bacon salad 60, 60
 nougat Montelimar 427
 praline 427
health and safety policies 9–12
healthy eating 2–3
 food allergies 25–8
 healthy food 24–5
 nutrition 29–36
herb oil 58
herb sauce 355
herring, smoked
 apple and potato salad 66
 smoking 147
hollandaise sauce 105
honey 372
hors d'oeuvres, hot 70
horseradish
 couscous 225
 eel with white wine and parsley 172
 foam 156
 and potato sauce 154
hot cross buns 392
hot holding 41
hot smoked mackerel 67
hot water paste 82
huachinango vercruzano 298
hygiene 9–10, 37–43, 68, 70, 72, 76

ice cream 375–7
 base 400
 chocolate 401
 storage 7
 vanilla 401
ikan bahan dengan kunyit celi padi 297
incident books 10
isomalt 372
Italian meringue 405

jamur kuping 294
jugged hare 279
jus
 lamb 100
 sherry 237

kencur 294
kidney beans, bean bourguignonne 342
kidneys
 lambs'
  eggs on the dish with Madeira sauce 140
  with juniper and wild mushrooms 218
 veal
  sautéed with shallot sauce 230–1
Kiev, chicken 254
kiwi fruit
 fruit terrine 418
 tropical salad 59
kohlrabi 330
kosher food 22, 199
kukus ikan sebalah madura 296

lamb
 braised-roast belly with cauliflower risotto and balsamic jelly 217–18
 chops, changezie champen 290, 290–1
 cuts 205
 with French beans 300
 jus 100
 kidneys
  eggs on the dish and Madeira sauce 140
  with juniper and wild mushrooms 218
 liver, flavoured with lavender and sage 219
 lubya khadra billahma 300
 palak 291
 peach and cashew nut bitoks 87
 pot roast chump with root vegetables 213–14
 rendang kambang kot baru 295
 roast leg with minted couscous and buttered peas 214–15
 roast rump and flageolets purée and balsamic dressing 212–13
 roast shoulder with potatoes boulangère 215, 215–16
 saddle
  preparation 209
  slow-cooked with braised cabbage and chocolate 210, 210
  stuffed with apricot farce 211–12
 samosas 293
 slow-cooked best end with lentils 216, 216–17
 in spicy coconut sauce 295
langoustines
 cleaning 190
 and mussel soup 188, 188–9
 poached with aioli dip 189–90
lard 2, 3, 370
lasagne 362
leaves, chocolate 439
leeks
 colcannon 330

and potato soup 126, *126,* 342
  roulade with ricotta and sweetcorn 349–50
  vichyssoise 130, *130*
lemon sole
  cá xót ngot 306
  fish with sweet chilli sauce 306
  fried, Thai style 304
  pla cian 304
lemons
  curd 383
  oil 159
  posset 383
  sauce 351–2
  sorbet 401
  tart 411
lentils
  and mushroom soup 121, *121*
  red and bacon soup 124
lesser galangal 294
lettuce, stuffed 334
limes
  sherbet 402
  yoghurt dressing 83
liver
  calves' with raspberry vinegar 234
  lambs' flavoured with lavender and sage 219
lobsters 181
  beignets with tomato chutney 191, *191*
  lobster sauce 103
  mornay 192
  Newburg 193
  tails au gratin 190–1
  thermidor 192
lubya khadra billahma 300
Lucerne fruit and pastry cream 386
Lyonnaise potatoes 317

mackerel
  baked stuffed 157
  smoked
    fish platter 66
    hot smoked 67
    storage 147
Madeira cake 388
madeleines 425, *425*
Maillard reaction 202
maltaise sauce 105
mandarin e'spuma 410
mangoes
  beef and black pepper 287
  mousse 398
  and passion fruit jelly 425
  and snapper salad 90
margarine 370
marinades 92, 351
marmalade, red onion 56
marquise 411
marshmallows 427
marzipan

almond drops and fingers 436
  English rout biscuits 436
  shortcake fingers 436
  wafers 435
mast va khiar 299
maxim potatoes 315
mayonnaise 112
  garlic-flavoured 55
  mustard and dill 56
  rouille 175
meat *see also* types by name
  bones 201
  carving 204
  cold 74–5
  cooking 200–3
  cured *71*
  cuts 204–7
  flavour 199–200
  healthy eating 24
  origin 199
  preparation *208*
  selecting 199–200
melons, tropical salad 59
menu development 18–24
meringues
  French 405
  Italian 405
  snow eggs 408
  Swiss 405
Merlot sauce 281
milk 372
  healthy eating 2, 25
  storage 7
mint
  canja 301
  and cracked wheat salad 345
  cucumber raita 93
  minted couscous 214
  new potatoes and mustard 61
  paloise sauce 105
monkfish, with bacon and bean cassoulet *164,* 164–5
monter au beurre 104
mooli 330
mousseline sauce 105
mousselines 177, 248
mousses 62
  avocado 63
  basic fruit 398
  caramel 400
  chicken 248
  chocolate 399
  chocolate and almond 399
  chocolate and orange 399
  chocolate brandy 399
  chocolate rum 399
  fish 67
  mango 398
  pear 398
  salmon 67

tomato 63
mozzarella
    galette of aubergines with tomatoes 345–6
    and penne with olive oil 60
    vegetable olives 355
muffins 388
mulligatawny soup 129
mushrooms
    cep and truffle jelly dice 53
    cep and truffle relish 360
    duxelle 140
    eggs on the dish with chicken livers 139
    and lentil soup 121, *121*
    nage 101
    omelette with chicken livers 137
    ragôut of 249
    shitake
        barley with 341
    stock 340
    stuffed 334
    wild 334–5
mussels *71*
    gratin with white wine 194
    and langoustine soup *188,* 188–9
    preparation 193
    soup 119
    in white wine sauce 194
mustard
    and cream sauce 233
    and dill sauce 56
    and spring onion sauce 172

nages 101–3, 163
norimaki, soba noodle 92, *92*
nougat Montelimar 427
nutrition 29–36
nutritional information boxes 35–6
nuts
    bacon and hazelnut vinaigrette 57
    carrot, coriander and almond salad 61
    chestnut and apple forcemeat 247
    French beans, bacon and hazelnut salad 60, *60*
    gratin with tomato and red wine sauce 353
    lamb, peach and cashew bitoks 87
    smoked salmon, avocado and walnut salad 59, *59*
    walnut sauce 354

obesity 29
oil/fat chart 3
oils
    garlic, red onion and ginger oil 113
    herb oil 58
    lemon 159
    roasted pepper oil 113
    smoked oil 57
okra 331
    soup 129
    stewed 331
olive sour bread 392

omelettes
    creamed smoked haddock and cheese 137, *137*
    light fluffy 138
    mushrooms and chicken livers 137
    potatoes and Gruyère cheese 138
    tortilla 136, *136*
onions
    bhajias 292
    confit 324
    potatoes and tomatoes 319
    ravioli 220–1
    soubise 108
onions, red
    garlic and ginger oil 113
    onion confit/marmalade 56
oranges
    beetroot and orange salad 60
    carrot and orange soup 126
    and tomato soup 128
osso bucco 231
Othello sponge 385
ox tongue, pickled 229
oxtail, braised with garlic mash 227
oysters 181, 184
    fricassée 185
    in shells 184

palak lamb 291
palm hearts 331
    stewed 331–2
paloise sauce 105
pancakes 382 *see also* blinis; crêpes
parfait 402
    raspberry 403
Parma ham and tarragon tart 94
Parmesan cheese
    basil pesto 153
    fried courgettes with pesto 322
    gnocchi *130,* 160
    tuiles 94
parsnips
    purée 109
    and vanilla purée 324
partridge 243, 267–8, 269
    braised with cabbage 273
    roast 272
passion fruit and mango jelly 425
pasta 356–7, *358 see also* ravioli; tagliatelle
    aubergine bake 344
    lasagne 362
    penne with mozzarella and olive oil 60
    sauces 359–60
    tortellini 357, *358*
pastillage 440
pastry *see also* choux pastry; Danish pastries; filo pastry
    flaky 382
    ingredients 366–80
    modern techniques and equipment 363
    oven temperatures 363

pie 82
   puff 379–80, 382
   sablé paste 380
   savoury flan paste 380
   sweeteners 371–2
pâté de fruit
   cassis 423
   pumpkin 423, *423*
pâtés 75, 80, *80, 81* see also terrines
peaches, fruit terrine 418
peanut butter cookies 422
pears
   and caramel truffles 426
   mousse 398
peas
   and ham soup 124
   and pancetta sauce 359
pectin 378
Peking duck 288
peppers
   goats' cheese and red pepper tart 349
   roasted pepper oil 113
   stuffed 334
pest control 39–40
pesto sauce 111, 153
petits fours 423–9
phat priu wan 303
pheasant 269
   roast breast with vanilla and pear *271,* 271–2
   roasted crown with chestnuts and cabbage 270
pickled walnut and raisin bread 391
pies
   pastry 82
   raised pork pie 82
   Russian fish 178
   veal and ham 85
pigeons
   pot au feu 266
   roast with red chard, celeriac and treacle 265, *265*
   salad with rocket, Parmesan and beetroot 266–7
pimentos, stuffed 334
pineapple soup 131
piononos 285
pla cian 304
pla nergn 303
plaice
   cá xót ngot 306
   fish with sweet chilli sauce 306
   fried, Thai style 304
   pla cian 304
   pla nergn 303
plant families 27
plantains, piononos 285
plum sauce 289
policha meen 290, *290*
Polish starter 391
porcini, cep and truffle relish 360
porco con ameijuas a alentejaru 302
pork

black pudding with apple and onion salad *238,* 238–9
chancho adobado 298
cured belly of 75, *75*
cured-confited belly with sauerkraut and sherry jus 237
cuts 206
fried with noodles and peanuts 304
lasagne 362
marinated with clams, tomatoes and coriander 302
in orange and lemon sauce with sweet potatoes 298
phat priu wan 303
porco con ameijuas a alentejaru 302
raised pie 82
roast shoulder with crackling and apple 236
roast stuffed suckling pig 239–40
and sage and onion forcemeat 247
slow-cooked loin with white beans 234–5
spring rolls 87
sweet and sour with snow peas 303
thit n'òng mi dâu phong 304
potatoes 310–11 see also sweet potatoes
   anna 318
   blinis 313, *313*
   boulangère 215–16
   cakes with chives 319
   chive and cucumber soup with cream 131
   colcannon 330
   cooked with button onions and tomatoes 319
   crispy olive 311
   deep-fried hash browns 315
   fondant 316
   gnocchi 314
   gratin Dauphinoise 316
   and Gruyère cheese omelette 138
   healthy eating 25
   herring and apple salad 66
   hot salad 313
   and leek soup 126, *126,* 342
   Lyonnaise 317
   mashed 317
   maxim 315
   mini baked créme fraîche *70,* 93
   new, mustard and mint salad 61
   rösti 312
   samosas 293
   Thai-style curry 341
   tortilla 136, *136*
   vichyssoise 130, *130*
   in white wine with anchovies 312, *312*
   and yoghurt bread 391
poultry see also types by name
   cooking 241
   selecting 241
   storage 242
   stuffings 247
pound cake 388
praline truffles 427
prawns 147, 176, 181
   bisque 121

Dublin Bay 190
with poached eggs, sherry and French mustard 141
poached hake with cockles 166
shellfish nage 102
protein sources, vegetarian 338
prunes
and almond tart 416
and foie gras stuffing 247
turkey escalopes and bacon 264
puff pastry 379–80, 382
pulses
bean bourguignonne 342
lentil and mushroom soup 121, *121*
red lentil and bacon soup 124
safe handling 41
pumpkin seed and onion bloomer 392
pumpkins
pâté de fruit 423, *423*
soup with confit rabbit 123, *123*
spicy soup 343

quails 267, 274
forcemeat 274
with pomegranate and blood orange 275
pot-roasted with roast carrots and mashed potato 275–6
quails' eggs 135
Fabergé 142
grilled salmon with pea soup 155, *155*
quenelles 177, 248

rabbits
braised baron with olive and tomatoes 277–8
casserole forestière 278
preparation 276
pumpkin soup with confit rabbit 123, *123*
saddle stuffed with own livers *276*, 276–7
radishes, white *see* mooli
raised pork pie 82
raita
aubergine 340
cucumber 93
raspberries
cream biscuits 381
parfait 403
ravioli *358*
onion 220–1
salmon and girolles with shellfish sauce 156–7, *157*
spinach and cumin with lemon sauce 351–2
receipt of goods 6
recipe development 18–24
red cabbage
braised 323, *323*
braised with apples, red wine and juniper 324
red lentil and bacon soup 124
red mullet
ceviche with organic leaves 162–3, *163*
nage with baby leeks 163
pan-fried with artichokes and Swiss chard 162
scaling, gutting and boning *149–50*

stuffed 64
with tomatoes, garlic and saffron 66
red onions
confit/marmalade 56
garlic and ginger oil 113
red snapper
baked with tomato and garlic fondue 153
huachinango vercruzano 298
and mango salad 90, *90*
stuffed 297
with tomato sauce, olives and potatoes 298
reheating 41
rendang 294
kambang kot baru 295
saus 295
resource management 4–5
rettiche *see* mooli
rice *see also* risotto
fried 286
safe handling 41
ricotta
and leek roulade with sweetcorn 349–50
spinach and artichoke filo bake with cranberries 346–7
riñones al jerez 301–2
risk assessment 11–12
risotto
cauliflower 217–18
with coconut milk and wilted baby spinach 350
vegetable, bean and saffron 347
roasted pepper oil 113
rock lobster 193
rolls
burgomeister 397
cherry 424
croquante 396
raisin 395
spring 87
rose petals
dressing 64
syrup 404
rösti 312
rouille 175
Russian fish pie 178–9

sabayon sauce 106
with olive oil 106
sablé paste 380
safety and security procedures 9–12
salads
beetroot and orange 60
carrot, coriander and almond 61
celeriac remoulade 60
crab with lime, pimentos and grilled scallops 65, *65*
cracked wheat and mint 345
French beans, bacon and hazelnut 60, *60*
herring, apple and potato 66
hot potato 313
new potato, mustard and mint 61
salmon and asparagus salad 64, *64*

smoked salmon, avocado and walnut 59, *59*
spinach and yoghurt 299
tropical 59
yoghurt, vegetable and herb 299
salambos *417*, 417–18
salmon
   and asparagus salad 64, *64*
   beetroot and treacle cured 68, *68*
   crispy seared with horseradish foam and caviar 156
   Eastern spiced tartare 91, *91*
   and girolles ravioli with shellfish sauce 156–7, *157*
   gravlax 353
   grilled with pea soup and quails' eggs 155, *155*
   marinated in dill 63
   mousse 67
   organic 'mi cuit' with buttered greens 154, *154*
   tartare 94
   terrine layered with scallops 83
Salmonella 135
salsify
   braised-roast 320–1
   fritters 333
   with onion, tomato and garlic 332
salt 24, 35, 38, 369
salt cod
   and akee 285
   roast and clam chowder 166–7, *167*
salt fish and akee 285
samosas 292
   lamb 293
   potato 293
   vegetable *70*, 89
sardines, baked stuffed 157
sauces *see also* coulis; dressings; mayonnaise
   apple 236
   asparagus 359
   avocado 110
      and celery 110
      and fennel 110
   béarnaise 105
   beetroot 110
   black bean 287–8, 305
   broccoli 111
   butter 104
   caramel 404
   cauliflower soubise 109
   celeriac purée 110
   chocolate 403
      and fudge 404
   choron 105
   crayfish coulis 102
   cream 107
   cream-thickened 106–8
   Cumberland 55
   egg-based 104–6
   fig and port reduction 58
   foyot 105
   fruit coulis 403
   garlic, red onion and ginger oil 113

garlic soubise 109
gooseberry 111
green or herb 55
green peppercorn and paprika 352
herb 355
hollandaise 105
horseradish and potato 154
lemon 351–2
lobster 103
maltaise 105
Merlot 281
mousseline 105
mustard 172
oil-based 112–13
onion soubise 108
paloise 105
parsnip purée 109
for pasta 359
pea and pancetta 359
pesto 111, 153
plum 289
roasted pepper oil 113
rose petal syrup 404
sabayon 106
   with olive oil 106
saus rendang 295
smitaine 107
soubises *108*, 108–9
spicy coconut 295
suprême 106
sweet chilli 306
tomato
   coulis (raw) 55
   fresh (cooked) 111
   and red wine flavoured with basil 353
valois 105
walnut 354
yoghurt/fromage frais thickened 108
sauerkraut 237
saus rendang 295
sausagemeat, pork, sage and onion forcemeat 247
savouries 73
scallops
   with caramelised cauliflower 196–7, *197*
   ceviche with organic leaves 198
   consommé of shellfish with crayfish 118–19, *119*
   crab salad with lime and pimentos 65, *65*
   history 196
   salad with honey-lime dressing 197
   Scotch salmon terrine layered 83
scampi 181
scorzonera 332
sea bass
   filleting and trimming *149, 150*
   policha meen 290
   roast fillet with vanilla and fennel 169, *169*
   steamed with asparagus and capers 170
   stuffed 64
      baked 171

shallots, purée 325
shellfish *see also* types by name
    consommé with crayfish 118–19, *119*
    crayfish coulis sauce 102
    and fish soufflé 179
    nage 102
    platter 66
    preparing *183*
    safe handling 41
    selecting 180
    stock 99, 182
    storage 180
    types 180–1
sherbet, lime 402
shrimps 181
    eggs en cocotte with cream and cheese 138
    potted 188
    spring rolls 87
skate
    with mustard and lemon on spinach 174
    pan-fried with capers and buerre noisette 174
smitaine sauce 107
smoked eel and cream cheese 94
smoked fish *71*
    platter 66
smoked haddock, omelette with cheese 137, *137*
smoked halibut, smoked fish platter 66
smoked herring, apple and potato salad 66
smoked oil 57, *57*
smoked salmon *71*
    avocado and walnut salad 59, *59*
    with blinis and caviar 93–4
snapper and mango salad 90, *90*
snipe 269
snow eggs 408
soba noodle norimaki 92, *92*
sole
    fried, Thai style 304
    pan-fried fillets with rocket and broad beans 158
    pla nergn 303
    whole grilled with traditional accompaniments 157
    whole, pla cian 304
sop bobor 294
sorbets 377–8
    champagne 402
    chocolate 401
    lemon 401
    syrup 401
    vanilla 402
    yoghurt 402
soubises *108,* 108–9
soufflés
    aubergine 326
    base 406
    chicken 249
        with creamed mushrooms 249
    fish 179
        and shellfish 179
    Grand Marnier 407

vanilla 406–7
soups *see also* consommés
    accompaniments 116
    beef with chives 303
    bouillabaisse 175
    canja 301
    carrot and orange 126
    chicken
        with lemon and mint 301
        with mushrooms and tongue 127
    chilled 130–2
    chive, potato and cucumber with cream 131
    clam chowder 122
    cockle chowder 195
    combination 115
    cream
        celery and cheese 127
        tomato and orange 128
    dom yam nua 303
    finishes 116
    fruit 131–2
    garnishes 116
    gazpacho 130
    gumbo 129
    healthy eating 115
    langoustine and mussel *188,* 188–9
    lentil and mushroom 121, *121*
    mulligatawny 129
    okra 129
    pea and ham 124
    potato and leek 126, *126,* 342
    prawn bisque 121
    pumpkin with confit rabbit 123, *123*
    red lentil and bacon 124
    red mullet with baby leeks 163
    roasted plum tomato and olive 128
    sop bobor 294
    spicy pumpkin 343
    spicy squash 343
    spinach and coconut 294
    stocks 98–100, 116
    vegetable broth 120
    vichyssoise 130, *130*
    watercress and beetroot 125, *125*
Spanish omelette (tortilla) 136, *136*
special diets
    cultural 22
    health reasons 22
    religious 22
    vegetarian 23–4
spinach
    and cheese sticks 87
    and coconut soup 294
    with pine nuts and garlic 325
    ravioli and cumin with lemon sauce 351–2
    ricotta and artichoke filo bake with cranberries 346–7
    risotto with coconut milk 350
    and yoghurt salad 299
sponge cakes 379, 384–9

sponge fingers 428
spring rolls 87
squash 333
    spicy soup 343
squid
    preparing 173
    stuffed 174
    tagliatelle with pesto and squid 361
    with white wine, garlic and chilli 173
stabilisers 378
steaks, tournedos Rossini 221–3, 222
stir-fried fish 176
stock control 6–8
stock-reduced base sauce 100
stocks
    brown vegetable 340
    fish 99, 151
    fungi 340
    shellfish 99, 182
    white
        chicken 98
        vegetable 340
storage 6–7
strawberries
    cream biscuits 381, 381
    fruit terrine 418
strudel, apple 413, 414
stuffings
    chestnut and apple forcemeat 247
    chicken 248
    game 246
    game farce 268
    pork, sage and onion forcemeat 247
    prune and foie gras 247
suckling pig, roast stuffed 239–40
suet 370
sugar 24, 38, 371
    blown 434, 434
    boiled 430–1, 432
    foods containing 26
    poured 432, 432
    pulled 434, 435
    rock 433, 434
    spun 433
    syrups 377
suprême sauce 106
sushi 69, 71
swedes, bubble and squeak 322, 322–3
sweet and sour pork with snow peas 303
sweet potatoes 318
    candied 318
    kofta 70, 93
sweetbreads, hay-baked with braised cabbage 232,
    232
sweetcorn, baby 326
sweeteners 371–2
Swiss apple tart 415
Swiss chard 333
Swiss meringue 405

tabbouleh see cracked wheat
tagliatelle 358
    Arrabiata 360–1
    aubergine pasta bake 344
    with pesto and squid 361
tartlets 73
    Parma ham and tarragon tart 94
    poached eggs with chicken and tomato and cream sauces
        141
    soft-boiled eggs with mushroom duxelle and cheese sauce
        140
tarts
    baked chocolate 412
    chocolate truffle 412
    fig 416
    lemon 411
    prune and almond 416
    tatin of apple 415
taste 46–7
teal 269
team management 14–15
teamwork 13–16
tempering 374–5, 437
tempura 381
terrines 75–8, 80, 81
    free-range chicken and foie gras 84, 84–5
    fruit 418–19, 419
    Scotch salmon layered with scallops 83
    vegetarian 352
Thai-style potato curry 341
thit n'òng mi dâu phong 304
thyme and ginger e'spumas 410
tian 349
    courgettes with tomatoes 348–9
    green and white asparagus 61–2, 62
tofu
    salad dressing 56
    and vegetable flan with walnut sauce 353–4
tomatoes
    and broad beans with coriander 327
    chutney 191
    galette of aubergine with mozzarella 345–6
    and goats' cheese 94
    lightly jellied tea consommé 91, 91
    mousse 63
    potatoes cooked with button onions 319
    and red wine sauce flavoured with basil 353
    sauces
        cooked 111
        raw 55
    soups
        and garlic consommé 120
        gazpacho 130
        and olive soup 128
        and orange soup 128
tongue
    chicken soup with mushrooms 127
    pickled ox 229
    sense of taste 46–7

tortellini 357, *358*
tortilla 136, *136*
tournedos Rossini 221–3, *222*
trifle, English 420
tropical salad 59
trout
    marinated and baked with red wine and herbs 301
    smoked fish platter 66
    truchas a'la navarra 301
truffles
    bergamot 426
    caramel 426
    cep and truffle relish 360
    champagne 440
    chocolate 439
    dressing 57
    pears and caramel 426
    praline 427
tuna
    braised Italian style 152
    mirin-glazed tuna and pickled ginger 92
    niçoise 151–2
turbot
    pan-fried with Alsace cabbage 161
    pan-fried with braised oxtail and lemon oil 158–9, *159*
turkey
    escalopes 263
        pan-fried with prunes and smoked bacon 264
    preparation 263
    roast
        serving cold 74
        traditional 263–4
    stuffed leg 263
Turkish delight 428
turnips
    char-sui turnip cakes *70*
    stuffed 334

umami 46, 47

valois sauce 105
vanilla
    bavarois 400
    ice cream 401
    sorbet 402
    soufflé 406–7
veal
    boning *230*
    chops with cream and mustard sauce 233
    cuts 206
    escalopes with cream sauce 107
    and ham pie 85
    hay-baked sweetbreads with braised cabbage 232, *232*
    kidneys
        with mustard and cream sauce 233
        riñones al jerez 301–2

    with shallot sauce 230–1
    liver with raspberry vinegar 234
    osso bucco 231
    preparing escalopes *229*
vegans 2, 23, 24, 337–9
vegetable pear *see* christophenes
vegetables 307–8
    à la Grecque 320
    and bean and saffron risotto 347
    broth 120
    brown stock 340
    deep-fried in tempura batter 336
    grilled 336
    healthy eating 25
    honey-roasted with cracked wheat 346
    nage 101
    olives 355
    oriental kebabs with herb sauce 354–5
    purées *108,* 110–11
    samosas *70,* 89
    shashliks served on tabbouleh 350–1
    stuffed 333–4
    and tofu flan with walnut sauce 353–4
    white stock 340
vegetarian curry 292
vegetarians 23–4, 337–9
venison
    medallions with red wine, walnuts and chocolate 282, *282*
    pot roast rack with greens and Merlot sauce *280,* 280–1
    preparation 280
vesiga 178–9
vichyssoise 130, *130*
Viennese biscuits 425
vinaigrettes 56, 112
vinegars 112

walnut sauce 354
watercress and beetroot soup 125, *125*
white radish *see* mooli
wild duck 269
    and beetroot consommé 117
wild mushrooms 334–5
wood fungus 294
woodcock 269
working relationships 13–16

yams 335
    fried cakes 335
yeast 26, 367
yeast products 389–97
yoghurt
    and cucumber dressing 56
    sorbet 402
    thickened sauces 108
    vegetable and herb salad 299
Yorkshire pudding 228